The Bṛhadāraṇyaka Upaniṣad

Volume 3 : Khila Kāṇḍa

Other English Books
By Nitya Chaitanya Yati

The Saundaryalaharī of Śankarācārya

The Psychology of *Darśana Mālā*

The *Bhagavad Gīta* (Commentary)

Neither This Nor That But...*AUM*

Love and Devotion

The Haunting Echoes of Spring

A Bouquet of Verses in Praise of the Supreme Mother

Experiencing the *Īśāvāsya Upaniṣad*

Śree Narayana Guru

Daiva Daśakam (Translation and Commentary)

Psychology: An Eastern Perspective

Bhakti

Vināyakāṣṭakam (Translation and Commentary)

God: Reality or Illusion?

Prāṇāyāma

Arivu - Epistemology of Gnosis

An Intelligent Man's Guide to the Hindu Religion

Rediscovering Indian Literary Classics, no. 5

The Bṛhadāraṇyaka Upaniṣad

With original text in Roman transliteration, English translation and appendices

Commentary by
Nitya Chaitanya Yati

Volume 3 : Khila Kāṇḍa

D.K. Printworld (P) Ltd.
NEW DELHI-110015

Cataloging in Publication Data -- DK

Nitya Chaitanya, Yati, 1924-
The Bṛhadāraṇyaka Upaniṣad.
(Rediscovering Indian literary classics; 2, 4, 5).
Includes index.

1.Upanishads. Bṛhadāraṇyakopaniṣad — Commentaries. 1. Upanishads. — Bṛhad-āraṇyakopaniṣad. English & Sanskrit. II. Title. III. Series : Rediscovering Indian literary classics; 2, 4, 5.

ISBN 81-246-0065-1 (vol. 3)
ISBN 81-246-0008-2 (set)

First Published in India in 1996

Published in India by:
D.K. Printworld (P) Ltd.
Regd. office : '*Sri Kunj*' F-52, Bali Nagar
New Delhi-110015
Phone : (011) 546-6019; *Fax* : (011) 546-5926

Typeset :
East-West University Press,
Bainbridge Island, Washington, U.S.A.

Printed at : Rainbow Processors and Printers, New Delhi-110028 (*Ph.* 5467547)

Contents

FOREWORD

We human beings are busy creatures, often narrowly focused on our activities of the day. Too often we forget that our lives are but tiny fragments of a grand drama that has been unfolding from time immemorial. Immersing ourselves in the pleasures and concerns of the moment, we often ignore and even deny our relationship to the universal. And yet there is always the need to understand the context within which our daily lives unfold. Each of us searches for ways to connect with what is real and enduring, to know the timeless essence of what we are about. This book by Guru Nitya Chaitanya Yati presents the distilled wisdom of thousands of years of Eastern thought in answer to our questions.

This is the first commentary of the *Bṛhadāraṇyaka Upaniṣad* which has undertaken the momentous task of digging into the hoary past in which the *Upaniṣad* was conceived, firmly taking hold of the invaluable treasures lying buried there and clearing away the dirt and debris of centuries of neglect and superstition. It reveals the wisdom of the ancient seer in a way that not only withstands critical scrutiny in the light of present-day understanding, but also sparkles with insights which help us to solve the riddles of our lives. Guru Nitya employs his comprehensive understanding of human nature, Eastern and Western philosophy, science, art and literature, to reveal the meaning of the mythical symbols and mystical dialogues in the *Upaniṣad* and their value in guiding both our everyday lives and our search for that wisdom which can carry us from untruth to truth, darkness to light and death to immortality.

This study of the *Bṛhadāraṇyaka Upaniṣad* is like the painting of a great master, spread over a vast canvas, yet rich with intricate detail. Before we look at the painting itself, let us take a moment to become familiar with the frame in which it is set. In ancient India, over a period roughly estimated to stretch from 1500 B.C. to 500 B.C., the hearts of the people of that time lifted up hymns of praise to the divine which they conceived of in the form of deities like the goddesses of the dawn and water and the gods of sun, wind and fire. Sensitive to the beauties of nature and filled with a sense of awe, they gave voice to their praises and supplications in poetry which has a beauty and dynamism with a timeless appeal. Over time, these poems were written down and arranged according to meter, tone and topic. The earliest collected verses came to be called the *Ṛg Veda* (*ṛg* literally means hymn or praise and *veda* means knowledge. It was followed by the *Sāma Veda*. *Sāma* means song and the *Sāma Veda* is the words of the *Ṛg Veda* set to music.

The *Yajur Veda* was written down later in history and includes some material from the *Ṛg Veda*. A *yajus* is a prayer or formula and *Yajur Veda* is a literary rendition of formulas guiding the specific performance of different types of sacrifices. It was written at a time when the priestly class in society was promoting the sacred importance of their role in the correct performance of sacrifices as the vital core of the Vedic religion and the most valuable aspect of social life. The *Atharva Veda*, although often listed as the last *Veda*, or sometimes not even accorded the status of a *Veda*, actually has its roots in India's pre-historic contemplative culture. As such, it provided a basis for the Vedāntic revaluation of religion and philosophy. On one hand, it carried ritual to an absurd extreme with many charms and spells that were used to invoke blessings not only for every type of activity or endeavor in daily life, but also on each phase of the already very elaborate ritual sacrifices. Unlike the injunctions governing the exact performance of the rituals, however, the charms and spells were known and employed by people at all stratas of society. The *Atharva Veda* also includes passages which represent clear advancements in the development of the non-anthropomorphic concept of the Absolute *(brahman)* which includes both being and non-being.

As time passed, religious observances became ever more complex. Each of the *Vedas* sprouted prose appendices which gave more detailed explanations of the Vedic rituals and their performance. These texts were known as *Brāhmaṇas*. Although much of their content is boring minutiae, they also include parts which illustrate the meaning of the ritual practices with myths and legends whose vitality has inspired writers and poets throughout the centuries. The foremost among the *Brāhmaṇas* is the *Śathapatha*, which means having a hundred paths or chapters. It was attached to the *Yajur Veda*. The last six chapters of the *Śathapatha Brāhmaṇa* are what is known as the *Bṛhad-āraṇyaka Upaniṣad*.

Another group of texts called *Āraṇyakas* were also appended to the *Vedas*. They de-emphasized the performance of the rituals and focused on the essential principals expressed by the different aspects of the rituals and ancient myths. As the centuries had passed, Indian society had become more complex and, largely at the prompting of the priestly group, more segmented. Divisions in society had hardened into castes with different social standing and functions. The priests were central in the courts of the many kingdoms and the rituals they performed were intrinsic to every aspect of life. The sense of sacredness with which life itself had been imbued in the times of the composition of the early Vedic hymns became restricted to the province of the rituals and those who performed them. The social ramifications of the caste system were often cruel and unjust, especially to those who ranked lowest in social respect and economic well-being. Many wisdom seekers and teachers decided to disengage themselves from society altogether and went to live in remote forest and wilderness areas. It is very likely that the move to revalue the religious practices of the time to a more universal perspective came from these forest dwellers, taking shape as the *Āraṇyakas*, books of the forest. *Āranya* means a forest, a wilderness or a foreign or distant land.

Bṛhad means to be great in magnitude, with the more specific connotations of having many parts and of being ever-increasing. The *Bṛhad-Āraṇyaka* is made up of six *adhyāyas* (chapters). This volume contains the commentary on the first two chapters, consisting of 145 mantras or verses. These two chapters alone present an archetypal sacrifice, two creation myths, legends which elaborate the creation myths and which address the problem of evil and how to overcome it, two wisdom dialogues between human students and teachers and a mythical wisdom dialogue between deities. This work can be understood as an *Āraṇyaka* both in the sense of being one of the "books of the forest" which treat of the symbolic meaning of rituals and in the sense of itself being like a fecund rain-forest, full of many wondrous forms of life.

For our journey through the forest, Guru Nitya is not only an able and trustworthy guide who is very familiar with the territory, having a comprehensive knowledge of the whole spectrum of Indian philosophical texts and their placement in the broader context of both Eastern and Western philosophical inquiry. He is also a poet who can tune our ears to the music of the ancient bard, a mystic who can lead us to the peaks from which we can catch a glimpse of the ancient seer's breathtaking visions of reality, an artist and psychologist who can reveal the meaning of the ancient symbols in terms we can understand and apply.

In addition to representing the Vedic tradition, partaking of some of the attributes of both the *Brāhmaṇa* and *Āraṇyaka* type texts, this work is also an *Upaniṣad.* Collectively the *Upaniṣads* follow the *Vedas, Brāhmaṇas* and *Āraṇyakas* both in historical time and in the progression of human philosophical understanding. The teachings in the *Upaniṣads* return the sense of the sacred to all of life and declare the pursuit of wisdom to be a pathway open to all. This *Upaniṣad,* perhaps more than any of the others, explicitly removes some of the traditional barriers which attributed sacredness and wisdom only to males of the highest placed *(brahmin)* caste. The opening dialogue of the second chapter is one in which the purported wisdom teacher, a *brahmin,* ends up petitioning his far wiser student, a king (of the *kṣatriya* caste), to teach him true wisdom. The next dialogue is one in which the wisdom teacher Yājñavalkya's most attentive and uncompromising student is his wife, Maitreyī.

The wisdom dialogues of the second chapter exemplify the meaning of the word *Upaniṣad* which literally means to sit down near to another to learn truth, to listen to the word of wisdom. The dialogues between the king Ajātaśatru and the *brahmin* Gārgya or between rishi Yājñavalkya and Maitreyī are examples of a student sitting together with a teacher and questioning and listening intently to the teacher's answers. The record of their dialogues and of the myths of the first chapter is also an *Upaniṣad;* the book itself is a means by which one can come close to a revealer of truth and see the intimate secrets of reality unveiled.

This wonderful treasure has been virtually inaccessible for centuries, obscured by language barriers – it was composed in the ancient and subtle language of Sanskrit – and the even more impenetrable wall of translations and commentaries afflicted by narrow religious ideologies and archaic philosophical hair-splitting. After completing an experiential commentary on the *Īśāvāsya Upaniṣad*, Guru Nitya decided to devote himself to exploring and unlocking the secrets of the *Bṛhadāraṇyaka*. He brings the poetry, myths and symbols of the *Upaniṣad* alive, helping us to deepen our understanding of our own nature, human intercourse and the cosmos. But what is even more valuable about this commentary is that Guru Nitya applies his wisdom and compassion to point to the mysterious reality which underlies all appearance, again and again leading us away from the myriad distractions and confusions to which we are subject to the side of our Self, which is the truth, light and immortality which we seek.

Nancy Yeilding

GUIDE TO SANSKRIT PRONUNCIATION

The sounds indicated in the examples are approximations of the original Sanskrit sounds. Only the consonants which are significantly different from English pronunciation have been included.

Vowels

a	like the u in "but"
ā	like the a in "far"
i	like the e in "me"
ī	like the ee in "beet"
u	like the o in "to"
ū	like the oo in "pool"
ṛ	like th ri in "rig"
e	like the a in "gate"
ai	like the i in "high"
o	like the o in "note"
au	like the ou in "loud"

Consonants

ṅ	like the ng in "sing"
ñ	like the n in Spanish "Señor"
c	like ch in "eschew"
ch	like ch in "much"
gh	like gh in "loghouse"
jh	like geh in "hedgehog"
th	like th in "Othello"
dh	like dh in "adhere"
ph	like ph in "haphazard"
bh	like bh in "abhor"
ś	like the sh in "shove"
ṣ	like the sh in "fish"
ḥ	echos the vowel which immediately precedes it

GENERAL INTRODUCTION

This commentary has been written with a much-needed missionary zeal to open up every secret of India's most logical and yet highly mystical and devotional insight to any person living anywhere in the world without any discrimination whatsoever. In order to prevent any part of wisdom from slipping into the dark dungeons of religious scruples or esotericism of any kind, it vigorously breaks down all traditional pretensions. It relies essentially on the soundness of logic (mathematical and semantic). Every statement in this book is substantiated by first-hand intuitive intimations of truth gained through incessant meditation.

The question of when the Vedic hymns came to be chanted by the Indian people is highly controversial. We have before us only shrewd guesses. Max Muller supposed the date to be 1200 B.C., Haug 2400 B.C., and Bāl Gangādhar Tilak 4000 B.C. Surendranāṭh Dāsgupta rightly notes that "The ancient Hindus seldom kept any historical record of their literary, religious or political achievements." [1] All that we know is that the *Vedas* were handed down from mouth to mouth from a period of unknown antiquity and the Hindus generally believed that the *a priori* truth of supreme wisdom did not dawn in the intellectual prowess of any individuated person.

The word *veda* is derived from *vid* which means knowledge. Knowledge comes to the cognitive faculty of a knower. Without a knower there is no one to know knowledge. The question arises: "From where does knowledge come to the recipient of knowledge?" Every idea or descriptive revelation of name, form and meaning has in it an intrinsic ability to reveal a fact that was never known before its perception or conception. Hence, it can be maintained that, independent of the human cognitive faculty, there is a source from which all shades of truth come to be registered in the recipient intelligence of the individual. Out of sleep, we wake up into the all-filling, all-embracing light of awareness. That awareness being with knowledge, knowledge is prior to the knower, *a priori*. Considered in that sense, everything is *veda*, and thus not a monitored proposition of truth deliberated by any person *(apauruṣeya)*.

However, both the Indian people and the scholars who have taken an interest in studying and interpreting the *Vedas* have recognized four recorded documents: *Ṛg Veda, Sāma Veda, Yajur Veda* and *Aṭharva Veda*. There has been no adequate critical study of the historical intrigues that have cast doubt over whether the *Aṭharva Veda* should be considered as part of the traditional sacred texts or whether they are rightly known as *Triveda (Three Vedas)*. The confusion generated by such smoke screens in the study of early Indian philosophy and mystical literature prevented a proper demarcation from being made between *śruti* and *smṛti*. *Smṛti* expresses conditional truth. *Śruti* indicates what is purely heard from the mouth of a wisdom teacher. It is a statement that has the distinct quality of being a universal pronouncement of truth not conditioned by time, the location and circumstance in which it is being announced, nor the personalities involved in its pronouncement and audition.

We should be very grateful to India's greatest masters who have sifted the ritualistic aspectsof the *Vedas* from the wisdom texts. One is Jaimini who propounded the systematized aphorisms of rituals known as *Dharma Mīmāmsa, Pūrva Mīmāmsa* or *Karma Mīmāmsa*. This section of the *Veda* stands apart as a closed chapter of esoteric revelations which guided the home life of the priestly class of people. As all the injunctions given in these *Samhitās* are mainly to be acted upon and experienced, the bulk of the *Yajur Veda* is to be considered *a posteriori* and thus of lesser merit than the *a priori* wisdom texts which appear as poetic gleanings in the *Ṛg Veda* and consequently as rhapsodies of the *Sāma Veda*. It is to Bādarāyana's credit that he wrote the Vedāntic aphorisms which clearly put the mandate of *śruti* on the *Upaniṣads*. Śankara is probably the only philosopher who clearly cognized the ingenuity of Bādarāyana. Following the wisdom vision of the great *sūtrakāra*, Śankara took upon himself the almost impossible task of eliciting from the Upaniṣadic mantras a meaningful structure that gives logically feasible correlations between the cosmic anatomy of truth and the psychological manifestation of that truth in one's empirical life on the one hand and metaphysical visions on the other. We stand firm with Śankara on this assumption and therefore do not give any exaggerated glory to the earlier mythological conception of Vedic symbols such as Agni,

Indra, Varuṇa, Mitra, etc. Only Sri Aurobindo was bold enough to sweep away all inflated credits given to the *Veda* in a language that is clear although it sounds drastic. He begins his great study, *The Secret of the Veda*, with the problem of the *Veda* and its solution:

> Is there at all or is there still a secret of the Veda? According to current conceptions the heart of that ancient mystery has been plucked out and revealed to the gaze of all, or rather no real secret ever existed. The hymns of the Veda are the sacrificial compositions of a primitive and still barbarous race written around a system of ceremonial and propitiatory rites, addressed to personified Powers of Nature and replete with a confused mass of half-formed myth and crude astronomical allegories yet in the making. Only in the later hymns do we perceive the first appearance of deeper psychological and moral ideas, - borrowed, some think, from the hostile Dravidians, the "robbers" and "Veda-haters" freely cursed in the hymns themselves, - and, however acquired, the first seed of the later Vedantic speculations. This modern theory is in accord with the received idea of a rapid human evolution from the quite recent savage; it is supported by an imposing apparatus of critical research and upheld by a number of Sciences, unhappily still young and still largely conjectural in their methods and shifting in their results, - Comparative Philology, Comparative Mythology and the Science of Comparative Religion. [2]

These words of Sri Aurobindo embolden us to uphold the vision of Yājñavalkya, the main hero of the *Bṛhadāraṇyaka Upaniṣad*, who was equally drastic in making a clean break with the plethora of ritualistic exaggerations in the *Kṛṣṇa Yajur Veda*. He consequently became the artificer of the *Śukla Yajur Veda*, a philosophically revalued version of the *Yajur Veda*. We have sufficient reason to maintain the pristine purity of the Upaniṣadic concepts of the creation myth, *prajāpati* and *hiraṇyagarbha*. We stand glaringly apart from all religious speculations about the origin of the world, the installation of life in it and the occurrence of consciousness. The uncompromising boldness of our conviction makes this commentary vary greatly from all traditional studies which have been guided more by pretentious devotion than critical scrutiny.

We honor Sureśvara Acārya as a fearless leader who has made a path for critical inquiry into the *Upaniṣads* and Śankara's *Bhāṣyas*. The works attributed to Sureśvara are the *Naiskarmyasiddhi*, the *Mānasollasa*, the *Pancīkaranavārtika*, the *Taittirīyopaniṣadbhāsyavārtika*, the *Bṛhadāraṇyakopaniṣadbhāsyavārtika* and the *Sambandhavārtika*. As Sureśvara was an eminent Mīmāmsaka before being defeated by Śankara in a debate, he was not allowed to write a commentary on the *Brahma Sūtra Bhāṣya* of Śankara. This is sad. However, he faithfully carried out his role as a continuator of Śankara by writing *Vārtikas* on *Aśvamedha Brāhmaṇa*, *Udgītha Brāhmaṇa*, *Maḍhu Brāhmaṇa* and the Yājñavalkya Maitreyī dialogue. "A *vārtika* means a work wherein there is the consideration of what is *ukta* (said), *anukta* (what is not said) and *durukta* (what is improperly said) by an author whose work is under the comment of the author of the Vārtika." [3] Needless to say that as Sureśvara's *Vārtika* was on Śankara's *Bhāṣyas*, the *ukta*, *anukta* and *durukta* in Śankara's commentary are sympathetically corrected by Sureśvara.

Sureśvara was a contemporary of Śankara who lived between 720 and 770 A.D. Narayana Guru, who came in our own century, 1854-1928, considered himself a sympathetic continuator of Śankara like Sureśvara. He restated *Advaita Vedānta* in his matchless classics, *Ātmopadeśa Śataka*, *Darśana Māla*, *Advaita Dīpika*, *Brahmavidyā Pancakam* and *Arivu* so that all criticisms brought against Śankara's *Advaita Siddhānta* and *Māyā Vāda* can be adequately contained in his revaluation in spite of the glaring deviations between Śankara's philosophy and the other major schools of *Vedānta* such as those of Rāmānuja and Madhva. To appreciate that any philosopher who puts forward a vision of truth cannot be totally wrong and that he has a point of view to justify his philosophy, one needs a unitive vision with an overall epistemology, methodology and axiology. Each school of philosophy can be brought to the appropriate niche to which it belongs in such a scheme of correlation. This was accomplished by Narayana Guru in his presentation of ten complementary visions of truth which in their totality provide us with a comprehensive epistemological unity. This work has been commented on by this author as the *Psychology of Darśana Māla*, and more elaborately by Narayana Guru's direct disciple, Nataraja Guru, under the title,

An Integrated Science of the Absolute in three volumes.

At this stage we do not want to go into the details of the very many intrigues to which the philosophy of the *Upanişads* was subjected to after the monumental works of Śankara: his commentary the ten *Upanişads*, *Gīta Bhāşya* and *Brahma Sūtra Bhāşya*. One hundred and eight well-known *Upanişads* are listed in the *Muktika Upanişad* and classified under the different *Vedas*. The *Ṛg Veda* has ten *Upanişads* connected with it, the principal ones being: *Aitareya and Kausitaki*.

Yajur Veda was split into *Kṛşṇa Yajur Veda* and *Śukla Yajur Veda*. *Kṛşṇa Yajur Veda* preceded *Śukla Yajur Veda*. There are thirty-two *Upanişads* associated with *Kṛşṇa Yajur Veda* of which the main ones are *Kaṭha, Taittirīya and Śvetāśvatara*. Of the nineteen *Upanişads* connected with the *Śukla Yajur Veda* the most significant are: *Īśāvāsya and Bṛhadāraṇyaka*.

There are sixteen *Upanişads* associated with the *Sama Veda*. The most important are *Kena and Chāndogya*.

Atharva Veda, which is often treated as a heretical *Veda*, not respectable enough to be counted along with the other three *Vedas*, has appended to it the cream of the *Upanişads*, which give the substance of *Advaita Vedānta*. They are thirty-one in number. the most significant are: *Praśna, Muṇḍaka* and *Māṇdūkya*. [4] In the *Maḍhu Brāhmaṇa* of the *Bṛhadāraṇyaka Upanişad* itself, there is an attempt to cover up the identity of Aṭharvan to whom the *Atharva Veda* is attributed. We have brought to light any such sleights of hand given in the *Upanişad* by later intruders.

The first volume of this commentary contains the full text of all the mantras given in the first two chapters *(adhyāyas)* of the *Upanişad* which are known collectively as the *Maḍhu Kāṇḍa*. They include the *Aśvamedha Brāhmaṇa, Udgītha Brāhmaṇa, Maḍhu Brāhmaṇa* and the dialogue between Yājñavalkya and Maitreyī. In this section, *śravana*, (listening to the wisdom narration of the first principles of truth) is most important. The *Maḍhu Kāṇḍa* stands apart as a comprehensive philosophy of the main *Upanişads* and Vedānta in general without any attempt being made to create a peg on which to hang anyone's private speculative systematization. That is why, even after Śankara's penetrating exposition of some of the most complicated mantras, Rāmānuja and Madhva felt they had enough room to elaborate their theories, copiously quoting from the same *Upanişad* Śankara used to establish his non-dual philosophy, *Advaita Vedānta.*

In Sri Aurobindo's estimate of the *Bṛhadāraṇyaka Upaniṣad* and Śankara's commentary on it, he says:

> The Brihad Aranyaka Upanishad, at once the most obscure and the profoundest of the Upanishads, offers peculiar difficulties to the modern mind. If its ideas are remote from us, its language is still more remote. Profound, subtle, extraordinarily rich in rare philosophical suggestions and delicate psychology, it has preferred to couch its ideas in a highly figurative and symbolical language, which to its contemporaries, accustomed to this suggestive dialect, must have seemed a noble frame for its riches, but meets us rather as an obscuring veil. To draw aside this curtain, to translate the old Vedic language and figures into the form contemporary thought prefers to give to its ideas is the sole object of this commentary. The task is necessarily a little hazardous. It would have been easy merely to reproduce the thoughts and interpretations of Shankara in the modern tongue; if there were an error, one could afford to err with so supreme an authority. But it seems to me that both the demands of truth and the spiritual need of mankind in this age call for a restoration of old Vedantic truth rather than for the prolonged dominion of that single side of it systematized by the mediaeval thinker. The great Shankaracharya needs no modern praise and can be hurt by no modern disagreement. Easily the first of metaphysical thinkers, the greatest genius in the history of philosophy, his commentary has also done an incalculable service to our race by bridging the intellectual gulf between the sages of the Upanishads and ourselves." [5]

After giving Śankara his due praise, Sri Aurobindo makes a very pithy remark: "Nevertheless, it remains true that Shankara's commentary is interesting not so much for the light it sheds on the Upanishad as for its digressions into his own philosophy." [6] It is exactly for this reason candidly given by Sri Aurobindo that we have taken the freedom to stand closer to the mantras of the *Upaniṣad* rather than going into any tangent to fortify a particular school of thought.

Our second volume, which contains the philosophical visions and summations of traditional knowledge so brilliantly declared by Yājñavalkya, has the solid foundation of reason. Even the most modern of books discussing the grammar and politics of truth cannot excel Yājñavalkya in the analysis of any given theme, however mythical, legendary, mystical or symbolic. Yājñavalkya has an honest way of confronting the numerous paradoxes and enigmas that are copiously presented before him. In fact, *Yājñavalkīya* is the heart of the *Bṛhadāraṇyaka Upaniṣad.*

In the third chapter Yājñavalkya is grilled by all who are aspiring to get the *dakṣiṇa* of a thousand cows decorated with gold. They stand up and ask questions of Yājñavalkya in the following order:

1. Aśvala, the court priest of Janaka, is the first to confront Yājñavalkya. He begins with a question about what philosophical vision *(darśana)* can save a sacrificer from death. Yājñavalkya meets all the questions of Aśvala by enumerating the instances of the sacrificing priest substituting for the sacrificer. In each, the priest plays a different role of identification with the transcendent factors which give an absolutist identity to the sacrificer.

2. Ārtabhaga, who belonged to the clan of Jaratkāru, initiated a long and elaborate discussion with Yājñavalkya about the bondage ensuing from the empiricism of the phenomenal world as *graha* and *atigraha*, and the release from these respectively as *mukti* and *atimukti*. In this dialogue we also come to know about the death of death.

3. Bhujyu, the Lāhyāyani, is the next contestor. He begins with the narration of an incident which can throw light on the extremely complicated life situations which can so totally transform a person that his or her faculties can be lamentably changed into pathological derangement. Bhujyu's questions take us to the most confusing subtleties of philosophical speculation. Yājñavalkya discusses threadbare the distinction between the manifested world and the unmanifested.

4. Uṣasta, the son of Cakra, then confronts Yājñavalkya. His questions are about the innermost Self and its identity with the Absolute *(brahman)*. Yājñavalkya gives several examples showing all shades of concepts in which the Self can be related with the Absolute.

5. Kahola, the son of Kuṣitaka, asks Yājñavalkya the secret of the Self that is envisioned directly by one's intuition. Yājña-

valkya suggests that this is possible only by transcending the horrors of this world such as hunger and thirst, sorrow and desire, disease and death.

6. The next questioner is none other than the most illustrious woman who was revered by all seers, Gārgī, the daughter of Vācaknau. She begins questioning Yājñavalkya about the foundation of the cosmic order, beginning with water. Yājñavalkya explains how the discursive is immanent in the unitive. She is satisfied for the time being.

7. Uddālaka, the son of Aruṇa, is the next to question Yājñavalkya. Like Bhujyu, Uddālaka also narrates the incident of a *gandharva* who possessed the wife of Patañcala Kāpya. To answer him, Yājñavalkya goes into the subtleties of the golden thread of *sūtrātma* running through every item of cognition and points out the immortal indweller *(antaryāmī)*, to the satisfaction of Uddālaka.

8. Once again Gārgī gets up to ask Yājñavalkya two formidable questions to clearly discern the warp and woof of the manifested world. Yājñavalkya goes into all the details of the paradoxes that lurk in the heart of the Absolute. He also introduces her to the secret of the imperishable word, *akṣara*.

9. The last questioner in this fascinating philosophical discussion with Yājñavalkya is Śakala's son Vidagdha. He asks about the number of gods. Yājñavalkya reduces the *devas* from three thousand and three to one. He also explains what the Vasus, Rudras and Ādityas are.

This third *adhyāya* closes with the tables turned in the conference hall. Yājñavalkya now questions all his rivals. This he does admirably by quoting traditionally known verses. This section gives us a full insight into the application of dialectical methodology in sorting out all the subtle philosophical questions.

The fourth *adhyāya* gives a deep insight into the multifarious functions, concepts and value-dynamics of the Absolute through a series of dialogues between Yājñavalkya and King Janaka of Videha. Yajnavalkya's questions to Janaka about his understanding of various points serve to clarify all aspects of the Self, the individuated person and the world of manifestation with all its cosmic and psychological details. It is not that Janaka was unaware of what Yājñavalkya was teaching. Their dialogue is a literary device to insure that no question relating to the search and realization of the Self is left unexamined. Janaka tells Yājñavalkya about his several teacher/informants and what each one had conveyed to him:

1. Jitvan, the son of Śilina, told Janaka that the organ of speech is the Absolute. As a correction of that, Yājñavalkya tells Janaka that the organ of speech is the body of the Absolute, space *(ākāśa)* is its foundation, and it should be meditated upon as *prajña.*

2. Next Janaka mentions Udaṅka, the son of Śulba, who taught him that the vital breath *(prāṇa)* is the Absolute. This instruction seems partial and inadequate to Yājñavalkya. So he says that the organ of smell is the body of the Absolute, space *(ākāśa)* is its foundation, and it should be meditated upon as what is dear. He elaborates on the idea of *prāṇa* and how it is dear.

3. Next Janaka tells Yājñavalkya that Barku, the son of Vṛṣṇa, told him that the Absolute is the organ of visual perception. Yājñavalkya reminds Janaka of those who have no faculty of visual perception. As before, he says that the faculty of visual perception is the body of the Absolute, space *(ākāśa)* is its foundation, and it should be meditated upon as truth.

4. Next comes Gardabhīvipīta, a descendent of Bharadvāja. He taught Janaka that the faculty of hearing is the Absolute. As before, Yājñavalkya says that the faculty of hearing is the body of the Absolute, space *(ākāśa)* is its foundation, and it should be meditated upon as infinite.

5. Then Janaka speaks of Satyakāma, the son of Jābāla, who taught him that the mind is the Absolute. After proving that instruction to be inadequate, Yājñavalkya tells Janaka that the mind is the body of the Absolute, space *(ākāśa)* is its foundation, and it should be meditated upon as *ānanda.*

6. Finally, Janaka tells Yājñavalkya that Vidagḍha, the son of Śakala, taught him that the Absolute is the heart *(hṛdaya).* This also, Yājñavalkya considers inadequate. So he says that the *hṛdaya* is the body of the Absolute, space *(ākāśa)* is its foundation, and it should be meditated upon as existence. With this, the first *brāhmaṇa* of the fourth chapter comes to a close.

In the second *brāhmaṇa,* Janaka adopts the position of a model disciple and asks Yājñavalkya to instruct him, even though he is a fully realized person. Yājñavalkya asks Janaka, "When you leave this body, do you know where you will go?" To this, Janaka replies "No," thus providing Yājñavalkya with the opportunity to fully explicatė his wisdom as a *śāsana* (authentic instruction) for posterity. Yājñavalkya tells Janaka that the *puruṣa* in the right eye is named Indha (from which Indra is derived) and the *puruṣa* in the left eye is named Virāj. They are seen as spouses who consummate their love in the heart. Then Yājñavalkya describes the heart, blood vessels and nervous system. Then he talks about the seer who is identified with *prajña* (the state of the Self in deep sleep).

The third *brāhmaṇa* presents another encounter between Yājñavalkya and Janaka. The king asks Yājñavalkya to describe the effulgence of the *puruṣa*. Yājñavalkya reveals it to be none other than the radiance of the sun. When Janaka asks further what serves as the source of brilliance when the sun has set, Yājñavalkya answers that it is the sheen of the moon. He continues with the statement that when the sun and moon are not shining, the radiance of the *puruṣa* is fire *(agni)*. When Janaka further questions him, he says that when the sun, moon and fire are not present, the light of awareness comes from the word and, finally, that when there is no sun, moon, fire or word, the Self shines by its own light. At this point, Janaka asks what the Self is and Yājñavalkya answers that *atma* is that light which has comprehensive cognition by its own light in the senses, mind and intellect.

In the eighth mantra of the third *brāhmaṇa*, Yājñavalkya gives the unusual revelation that when the individuated person *(puruṣa)* assumes a body, it is conjoined with evil and, at the time of death, all such accumulated evil is discarded. In the ninth mantra Yājñavalkya describes the several worlds in which we are destined to live – this world, the one beyond and the world of dreams. Then he elaborates a theory of dreams which has been incorporated into the studies of dreams done by modern psychologists. The third *brāhmaṇa* also includes a detailed discussion of the state of deep sleep.

In the fourth *brāhmaṇa* a descriptive psycho-physical and psycho-physiological explanation of death is given as a reversal of the process of individuation that happens at the time of birth. In its final culmination, the Self is fully identified with the Absolute. Yājñavalkya takes this opportunity to describe the ascending path of no return and the descending path of recurrence. In the fifth *brāhmaṇa* we return to the dialogue between Yājñavalkya and Maitreyī which is a repetition of what was given in the second *brāhmaṇa* of the second *adhyāya*. It serves as a review and additional emphasis on the instruction given in the *Maḍhu Kāṇḍa*.

The final volume of the *Bṛhadāraṇyaka Upaniṣad*, consisting of the fifth and sixth *adhyāyas*, is called *Khila Kāṇḍa*, the supplementary appendix. *Khila* literally means a wasteland. It is to be understood as the all-encompassing reality of which due cognizance has not been taken. In this case it is to be regarded as a comprehensive compendium which gives detailed attention to the basic notions of Vedānta philosophy. *Maḍhu Kāṇḍa* is mainly to listen to; *Muni Kāṇḍa* to ponder over with intensive critical awareness and sympathetic apperception; and *Khila Kāṇḍa* to experience whatever has been discovered and contemplated upon in the previous two *Kaṇḍas*. It thus comprehends the overall essence of Vedānta. The fifth *adhyāya* includes fifteen *brāhmaṇas* and the sixth chapter five *brāhmaṇas*. The sixth *adhyāya* concludes with a guru-disciple hierarchy. The lineage given at the end of the second *adhyāya* refers to the father of each guru while the one given at the end of the sixth *adhyāya* refers to their mothers. Each enumeration involves certain intricacies which we discuss.

The Peace Invocation with which the *Upaniṣad* begins is repeated at the beginning of the fifth chapter:

AUM pūrṇamadaḥ pūrṇamidam
pūrṇatpūrṇamudacyate
pūrṇasya pūrṇamādāya
pūrṇamevavaśissyate

AUM sāntiḥ sāntiḥ sāntiḥ

This serves the purpose of showing that the *Khila Kāṇḍa* is a recapitulation of the first two *kāṇḍas*. The rishi's own interpretation of the mantra is also given. *AUM* is specifically mentioned as the *ākāśa* identified with the Absolute. In the third verse of his *Ātmopadeśa Śatakam*, Narayana Guru adopts the Upaniṣadic rishi's teaching which identifies the unmanifested *ākāśa* with the Absolute that can be both causal and consequential:

Seemingly outside and yet immanent in the Absolute
as specific modes, seen here as the five elements, like sky,
when contemplated, should become like waves

> rising in rows from the treasury of the watery deep,
> without any separate reality whatsoever.

The archetypal model of the first manifestation of life, *prajāpati*, which was presented in the second *brāhmaṇa* of the first chapter, is remembered in the second *brāhmaṇa* of the fifth chapter. It shows a more active and continuous intimacy of *prajāpati* with the shining ones, human beings and the dark ones. The present age is considered to be the fag end of a cosmic cycle and the *modus operandi* of the contemplation that suits this age is given in the subsequent *brāhmaṇas* up to the thirteenth. The full implication of the *gāyatri* chant is given in the fourteenth *brāhmaṇa*. The *Īśāvāsya Upaniṣad*, which is also part of the *Śukla Yajur Veda*, is accepted as an epitomization of the *Bṛhadāraṇyaka*. The fifteenth *brāhmaṇa* gives four of the essential mantras of the *Īśāvāsya*.

In the *Yoga Vāsiṣṭha Rāmāyana* and the *Bhagavad Gīta* there is a descending dialectics in which the fully informed seer of realization is ultimately brought back to the here and now to live as a *pūrṇa prajña* to set an example to his contemporaries. The sixth *adhyāya* of the *Bṛhadāraṇyaka* is essentially used to complete the arch of the ascending and descending scheme of dialectics.

The author, being a direct disciple of Natāraja Guru and a grand-disciple of Narayana Guru, has taken all the guidelines they have given to write this fairly exhaustive commentary: firstly, to make the wisdom of the rishis available to all who care to know and live the word-wisdom of the *Upaniṣads;* and secondly, to give *Advaita Vedānta* its rightful place in the systems of Indian philosophy. Narayana Guru took upon himself the great task of steering the unitive philosophy of India past the confusion and sectarian exaggerations that have periodically arrested the progress of the Indian vision of truth. In this connection, we think it is appropriate to summarize his life and teachings as retold by Swami Ranganāṭhānanda of the Sri Ramakrishna Mission:

> Sri Narayana Guru came of a section of India's population which possessed no rights and privileges and which consequently received the name of depressed classes in modern times. Totally neglected and often oppressed and suppressed for a thousand years by the

higher classes, the seventy million depressed classes of India, as of other parts of the world, constituted the basis of economic prosperity and social well-being of the country, as they formed the entire labour front. Continued slavery for generations had produced in these classes, as it is bound to produce in any class of men, an oppressive sense of its own littleness and helplessness - a sense of despair. Slavery is bad enough; but a situation in which the slave begins to accept his position as part of a natural social order - a position in which there is dictated duty without any inherent right and privilege - is something which reduces man to the level of cattle and robs him of his human prerogatives. This was precisely the condition of the Indian masses at the beginning of the nineteenth century when India was thrown open to the play of world forces. The mingling of the age-old idealism of India with the thought-forms and forces of the modern world has ushered in a new epoch in Indian history...[which] does not exhaust itself in a mere political upheaval but assumes more enduring forms of a religious awakening and social transformation....

Social progress in India has always been on the lines of sharing the benefits of culture and of higher Hindu thought by larger and larger sections of the population. Democratization of knowledge and opportunity meant also elevation of the people. The best genius of Hinduism lay in this direction in a special sense. If there had been stagnation due to the dead weight of meaningless custom and oppressive tradition, it meant only that society had forgotten the larger plan and purpose of the ancient leaders. Society is then in need of a new dynamism. In India this urge to progress has always come from great saints and sages and not from mere political thinkers. A new passion for *dharma* has supplied the necessary revolutionary urge....

But the awakening of the conscience of the privileged is only one act in the drama of enfranchisement. The other equally, if not more, important part is the process of self-discovery on the part of the oppressed themselves. This period of awakening of the masses to a sense of their own worth and importance is a critical period in the history of a people. It may be either explosive and destructive or gentle and constructive, but the effect is revolutionary in both cases. The most serious criticism against a violent revolution is that it rarely achieves its original purpose. The second type is more permanent and far-reaching in its effects.

That these recent changes in Hindu society are of a peaceful and constructive character is as much due to the good sense of the Indian masses as to the soundness of Hindu social philosophy and ideals. The movement of reform associated with Sri Narayana Guru is unique in one important respect: it is entirely constructive and devoid of any bitterness against the higher classes....This is the meaning and significance of the Indian conception of *dharma* - a conception which seeks the unity of social endeavour through harmony and co-operation. It is to the eternal glory of Sri Narayana Guru to have inaugurated a movement which embodies in itself this unique genius of Hinduism and to have released the forces of the Spirit for the solution of the many pressing problems of even the mundane life of his people....In this, he takes rank with saints and reformers of earlier centuries and, more especially, with Guru Nanak, the founder of the Sikh fraternity. Except in one respect, there is striking similarity between the life and work of these two masters who are separated by about five centuries. Nanak belonged to the higher classes but fraternized with and reformed the lowly and the lost in Hindu society. Narayana Guru was born with the social stigma of an untouchable among those with whom he worked and whose life he transformed. The so-called lowness of his birth could in no way hide or smother the richness of his native endowment. It is this wealth of native genius that enabled him to raise himself and his people above the depressing circumstances of an unjust social order. He imparted life to the almost dead bones and muscles of his people and made them conscious of their human worth and dignity. Rightly is he called the *Guru* whose breath is hope and whose touch is life....

World events are compelling us to the view that the best legislative authority in the world is character. The

> *ṛṣi* or sage has always been recognized as the law-giver in India. His knowledge and his detachment constitute valid sanctions for the equity of his legislation. In Sri Narayana Guru the people found such a law-giver. Himself a monk and a man of God, in virtue of which he rose above all social conventions and obligations, he yet descended to the level of his fellow-men in an attitude of compassion, and lent his loving hand to drag them out of their misery. And he had the supreme satisfaction to witness, even in his own lifetime, the ample reward of his labours in the improved tone of the moral and material well-being of his people....
>
> *In all that he was and in all that he did, Sri Narayana Guru stands as the supreme symbol of hope and redemption to the depressed classes of India.*[7]

As this commentary is being written in both English and Malayalam, and each mantra is given time for insightful spiritual experience, it is a time-consuming work. The commentator is given only very little freedom by the Upaniṣadic rishi. As each mantra is commented upon after deep meditation, the heaviness of the work load is mitigated by the great joy of listening to the golden whispering of the rishi. It fills the mind of the commentator and his associates, the disciples and students of Narayana Gurukula, Fernhill, with so much joy that the work can be called a *tapasya* in *sānanda samādhi*. It is our hope that our readers will be equally benefited by the freshness of the ideas and the categorical certitude that each word brings to the listener and the reader.

Before undertaking this commentary, the commentator prepared himself with forty years of discipline and study. It is therefore almost a spontaneous recording of the three *kāṇḍas* consisting of six *adhyāyas* that is being made over the course of three years. I take this opportunity to express my gratitude to all the rishis of the past, the gurus and *ācaryas* both of the East and the West, among whom I should mention by name Śri Śankarācarya, Narayana Guru and Nataraja Guru, for having showered their grace on me all through this work. I am beholden to four other pilgrims on the path of the *Upaniṣad*, Swami Mādhavānanda, Swami Nikhilānanda and Swami Mridānanada, all of the Sri Ramakrishna Mission, and my most beloved comrade in learning, Dr. T.N.N. Bhattathiripad.

Before the commentary comes to the reader, many processes, both of the editorial mind and the technicalities of the computer, must harmonize. In editing and preparing the English manuscript of all three volumes, Nancy Yeilding, disciple, friend, and Registrar of the East-West University of Brahmavidyā, acted as a devoted friend in need. She also carried out the word processing both in India and the United States. In India, she was aided by M.D. Sanal, Ramakrishnan K.P. and Peter Moras, and, at the Western Headquarters of the East-West University in the United States, by Śraddha Durand and Swami Vyasa Prasad. Another friend who was a great aid in the US was Robert Tyson.

Finally, I feel very grateful to our publishers, D.K. Printworld, (P) Ltd., and I should especially mention K. Rai Mittal who has been enthusiastic from the very beginning to make this a book of aesthetic excellence. The drawing for the cover of this volume was made by the Gurukula's youngest disciple and artist, Sapna Balakrishnan. To all our associates and to the reader, I wish undiminishing happiness.

Nitya Chaitanya Yati

Notes:

1. Surendranath Dasgupta, *A History of Indian Philosophy*, Motilal Banarsidass, Delhi, 1975, p. 10.
2. Sri Aurobindo, *The Secret of the Veda*, Sri Aurobindo Ashram Trust, Pondicherry, 1971, p. 1.
3. Shoun Hino, *Sureśvara's Vartika on Yājñavalkya Maitreyī Dialogue*, Motilal Banarsidass, Delhi, 1982, p. 8.
4. *The Cultural Heritage of India*, *Vol. I*, The Ramakrishna Mission, Calcutta, 1937, p. 347.
5. Sri Aurobindo, *The Upanishads*, Sri Aurobindo Ashram Trust, Pondicherry, 1971, p. 397.
6. Ibid., p. 398.
7. Swami Ranganathananda, *Eternal Values for A Changing Society, Vol. II*, Bharatiya Vidya Bhavan, Bombay, 1985, p. 190-195.

INVOCATION

AUM pūrṇamadaḥ pūrṇamidam
pūrṇātpūrṇamudacyate;
pūrṇasya pūrṇamādāya
pūrṇamevāvaśiṣyate

AUM śantiḥ, śantiḥ, śantiḥ

Word Meanings

AUM - *AUM* (the all); *adaḥ* - that; *pūrṇam* - is complete; *idam* - this; *pūrṇam* - is complete; *pūrṇāt* - from the complete; *pūrṇam* - the complete; *udacyate* - is derived (emanated); *pūrṇam ādāya* - (when) the complete is deducted; *pūrṇam* - (from) the complete; *eva* - it is as if; *pūrṇam avaśiṣyate* - the complete remains

AUM. That is complete; this is complete. The complete is derived from the complete. When the complete is deducted from the complete, it is as if the complete remains.

This invocation is an exemplary mantra. Day after day, all through our lives we can dwell upon it for a continuous probe into truth without ever exhausting it. The invocation begins with the *praṇava, AUM*. *AUM* is a statement which stands by itself. It is a monomark which gives us a key to decipher the mystery of each mantra given here. Śankara quotes *Chāndogya Upaniṣad* I.1.1-9 as an elucidation of the importance of *AUM*:

AUM! One should reverence the *udgītha* (loud chant) as this syllable, for one sings the loud chant (*ud*+ *gī*)[beginning] with '*AUM*'.

The further explanation thereof [is as follows]-
The essence of things here is the earth.
The essence of the earth is water.
The essence of water is plants.
The essence of plants is a person (*puruṣa*).
The essence of a person is speech.
The essence of speech is the *ṛk* ('hymn').
The essence of the *ṛk* is the *sāman* ('chant').
The essence of the *sāman* is the *udgītha* ('loud singing').

This is the quintessence of the essences, the highest, the supreme, the eighth - namely the *udgītha*.

'Which one is the *ṛk*? Which one is the *sāman*? Which one is the *udgītha*?" - Thus has there been a discussion.

The *ṛk* is speech. The *sāman* is breath (*prāṇa*). The *udgītha* is the syllable '*AUM*'.

Verily, this is a pair - namely speech and breath, and also the *ṛk* and the *sāman*.

This pair is joined together in this syllable 'AUM'.

Verily, when a pair come together, verily, the two procure each the other's desire.

A procurer of desires, verily, indeed, becomes he who, knowing this thus, reverences the *udgītha* as this syllable.

Verily, this syllable is assent; for whenever one assents to anything he says simply '*AUM*'. This, indeed, is fulfillment - is, assent is.

A fulfiller of desires, verily, indeed, becomes he who, knowing this thus, reverences the *udgītha* as this syllable.

This threefold knowledge proceeds with it: saying 'AUM,' one calls forth; saying 'AUM' one recites; saying 'AUM,' one sings aloud, to the honor of that syllable, with its greatness, with its essence. [1]

These mantras represent a methodologic course for students

to go step by step in contemplative pondering on the essence to which our attention is summoned. *AUM* has a three-fold secret laid on the basis of what is called 'the fourth'. To articulate the three we have to bring our mouth to three different formations. Before we articulate, the mouth is closed. The upper lip and lower lip are in contact, and the in and out flow of breath clearly avoids the mouth. To pronounce '*A*', one opens the mouth. It is normal for outside air to enter into a closed area if it is opened. It is equally true that whatever is contained in a closed system will flow out into the open when an exit is allowed. The jaw bones and the lips are so structured that the door for the incoming substance is the exit for the outgoing substance. This itself is indicative of a character of the Absolute - it has a lurking paradox at its core. The opening of the mouth is preceded by a silence. The closing of the mouth is also followed by a silence. Silence is the ground, or frame of reference, in which two opposite motions are happening.

Opening can be indicative of an initiative, a design to create, and an intention to express. To pronounce '*U*' the mouth is kept half-opened and half-closed. The lips are rounded and the jaw bones are kept apart. That brings the activity of articulation to a homeostasis. This is indicative of sustaining what has been created. '*M*' is indicative of the closing down or conclusion of what is generated. The gestalt is closed with the articulation of '*M*'. This clearly marks a unit.

As we live in time, the sequences of creation, maintenance, and dissolution are considered contiguous. We start on another unit only after a pause between one unit and another. In *AUM* there is a recognition, conceptualization, and a recording for the future. When we pause, we go into the same silence which preceded the articulation of *praṇava*. That silence is continuous with the earlier silence. Yet the two silences have a qualitative difference such as between an unknown silence and a known silence. We have to think of the unnamed fourth, or the silence, as a frame of reference in which there is a transformation of the inertial into the kinetic and the kinetic back to the inertial. The second inertial state is not totally negative. It has in it a sublime impression. This is the scheme of articulation, this is the scheme of individuation, this is the scheme of creation, and this is the scheme of the universe. From *AUM* we derive a key to solve the mystery of the invocation mantra which to an ordinary reader will sound like a conundrum.

The first part of the mantra says, *AUM pūrṇam adaḥ* 'that is complete'. It is followed by *pūrṇam idam:* 'this is complete'. *Adam* (that) and *idam* (this) have both temporal and spatial implications. The distinction between 'that' and 'this' causes a semiotic movement within our consciousness. There is no specific reference to either 'that' or 'this'. We have to exercise our mentation to conceive or formulate the inner content of both words. Temporally 'that' can be far away in time, and 'this' can be close enough to be the central locus of the present moment. Similarly, when we say 'this' there is spatial closeness as well. The tangibility of 'that' is vague and general, whereas the tangibility of 'this' is clear and more certain. Whenever there is a distance between 'before' and 'after', we psychologically relate to the 'before' as having a causal status. 'This' in such a case can be the cause transformed into an effect.

In the transformation of an egg into a chick over a temporal interlude of twenty-one days, a mystery is implied. In the effect we see many features that were not in the cause. For a chick there is no need for a protective shell; there is no need to preserve the yolk which was previously the duty assigned to the shell. The central nucleus of the egg itself was constantly disturbed to be affected by a thermal chaos, and the result was the emergence of a new being. The latent has become actual, the parent bird or being from which the egg issued now seems to be renewed in the chick with a one-to-one correspondence between the chick and the parent. The transformation was not merely temporal, but material also.

Then we are told more explicitly, *pūrṇāt pūrṇam udacyate*. This is a more complete statement relating the first *pūrṇam* to the second *pūrṇam*. In both cases the same term *pūrṇam* is used and both have the same supportive sustenance, otherwise called *dharma*. The potent sustenance in the egg is also the actualized sustenance in the chick. Hence there is a justification in saying, *pūrṇāt pūrṇam udacyate: pūrṇam* has arisen from the *pūrṇam*. The English terms, complete, infinite, full, perfect or plenum, can only approximate the meaning of *pūrṇam*. The Sanskrit word *pūrṇam* itself is in a state of evolutionary process: the listener has to exercise his or her consciousness to begin from nowhere as it were, which is to be first given a location. From the location an emanating principle of existence has to fill in an area to be homogeneously completed. The process can be the filling of an egg;

it can be the filling of the globe; it can be the filling of the solar system; it can be the filling of the galactic system; it can be the filling of the universe; it can be the filling of pure consciousness. Thus the word *pūrṇam* is only a monomark. All major philosophical statements in sciences are established on people agreeing to each other's concepts. By common consent we decide what the *dharma* of each articulated sound is.

The next phrase in the mantra is *pūrṇasya pūrṇam ādāya*, the *pūrṇam* is taken away from the *pūrṇam*. This is reminiscent of the beautiful haiku by Basho:

> By the road, a beautiful flower.
> Oh!
> My horse ate it.

The emergence of the flower and its vanishing both happen in the context of a surprise: 'Oh!' What happens to the flower after it is swallowed by the horse? It continues in memory. It has not gone anywhere. What happened to our grandparent's grandparents? Or to our grandparents who have left their bodies? What happens when our parents are away (away can mean in the other room)? They are still with us. What happens to the little child in us even when we have grown to the age of sixty, seventy or eighty? We started saying 'I' at the age of one or two, and even when we are eighty or ninety we say 'I'. When something is given in the form of a Sanskrit mantra, it looks very venerable, sacred and mysterious. After all, it is only a simple statement. Life is also like that. It is simple, but we complicate it by filling the simple egg with a highly complex chick who is going to be the cause of millions of generations of chicks. Every fertilized egg is a continuator of the past into the future, in and through the present moment.

In India a word is traditionally interpreted by looking at the root from which it is derived. A word can have a nominal significance. Every word also has an operational dynamic which pertains to the transformation of the consciousness which receives the articulated sound of the word. Consciousness becomes identified with the operational energy of the word. Pāṇini, the great grammarian of India, identified one of the fundamental semiotic functions of a word as *sphoṭa*. When the sound that is articulated falls on the ear drum, consciousness can instantaneously assume an identity with the gestalt that is roused by that particular sound.

The meaning of every sound is generated in the listener as a consequence of listening to the word. So if a term is not understood as a process, it will remain as a dead fossil in the mind. *Pūrṇa* is etymologically related to the English term 'pouring'. We can pour a liquid into a vessel until it comes to the brim. *Pūrṇam* means filled to the brim. If there is enough liquid to fill a vessel, then we say that the liquid was adequate and the vessel was also adequate to hold that much liquid. Wherever *pūrṇam* manifests there is a reciprocity between the potential and the actual which it is adequate to accomplish.

When we say that *pūrṇam* is the material cause for the accomplishment of this *pūrṇam*, it means that the potential adequacy has become the actual adequacy. There are enough potentials in earth to bring forth any number of flowers of any color, with any fragrance and calyxes filled with honey. The potential which exists prior to the manifestation of the flower is referred to as *pūrṇam adam*. Each time a flower opens up, dances in the breeze, reveals to us its color and fragrance, and attracts bees with its sweet honey, it is *pūrṇam idam*. The flower is only one item. There are millions and millions of *idams*. What is happening through all these manifold manifestations is in conformity with the single principle of fulfillment.

The flower that looks so beautiful, bright and full of fragrance, which enchants and bewitches the bee, droops and falls the next day. This is referred to here as *pūrṇasya pūrṇamādāya*, the manifested that is taken away from the source of the potential. But that does not put an end to the principle of adequacy, or the principle of future fulfillment, hence it is said *pūrṇam eva avaśiṣyate*.

In his commentary on this invocation, Śankara emphasizes that *pūrṇam adam* is not a transformed state. It is self-founded and complete in itself. In another sense, it means it does not allow us to think of a space or time or mass to be filled by it. It is like the total immanence of total transcendence. The term *adam* is to be taken as the pronoun 'that' which stands for *brahman*. 'That' indicates it is complete in itself. It has within it no break; it has no conditional relationship with anything. It provides for conditions and for the interdependence of names and forms which provide for all transactions. It is as if the supreme Self allows itself to be a myriad of names and forms.

The one without a second by itself presents varied specificities as if transactional entities are arising out of transcendental unity. This kind of view is possible only with the postulation of a causal whole presenting various consequential effects by conditional projection. The primordial reality designated as 'that' becomes the multitude of specific 'thises'. The original non-dual unity is maintained within the substance of being in spite of its projection of varied conditionings. The implied transformation from 'that' to 'this' actually happens without any restructuring or remanifestation. 'That' is to be known as 'this', that's all. In either case, whether understood as 'that' or conceived as 'this', substantially nothing is produced in the effect which is not eternally in the original cause. Existence and essence here remain undifferentiated.

For the convenience of epistemological contemplation, the mantra states the principle of eternal law, then the actualization of the potential which essentially appears as beginning, expansion and evolution. In principle, that can be identical with the cosmos, having the possibility of all variegations, changes and transformations. The unchanging, eternal law which is beyond the possibility of perception is called 'that'. When the possibility moves towards probability and beginning to be actualized, that initiates the perceptibility of manifestation, here referred to as 'this'. Both the potential and the actualized are described as complete in themselves.

For the sake of clarity, we shall take an analogy of a pure principle becoming actual. The law that governs a mathematical point is universally the same for any point anywhere in space at anytime. This governing law tallies with the principle of a point. That which qualifies a line to exist is also similarly universal. A triangle, however small or immense the area it occupies, obeys, in principle, the laws of triangularity. When the laws of geometrical principles are applied in the specific context of time and space, they become perceptually manifested. For the perceptual manifestation, the general law is not to be changed even a wee bit. Yet, there is a distinction between the imperceptible original cause and the perceptual actualization of the same.

Actualization is also understood as manifestation of 'being' into 'thingness'. It is this epistemological consideration of the potential, in contrast to the manifested, which accounts for Indian philosophers' claim that Truth is divisionless, homogeneous and always whole. Until manifestation comes into the portals of actualization, perception is inoperative. The beginning of things arises only when perception is operative. The beginning of things does not contradict the principle of being which is beginningless and endless. Philosophy in Sanskrit is *tattvajñāna*, the knowledge of 'thatness' and 'thisness'. 'That' *(tat)* is the imperceptible which is beyond the possibility of being visualized. 'This' (*tvam*) is the context where you and I stand face to face and there is the possibility of encounter between subject and object. Subject-object duality brings another great change in the causal factor, transforming it into the manifoldness of millions of names and forms. The forms have the basis of being a thing and everything is describable with its specific qualifying properties of perceptibility. In the word *tattvajñāna*, two major implications of knowledge become unified. The reality of 'being' is transfused into the reality of 'thingness' and *vice versa*. 'Thingness' becomes fully supported by the eternity of 'being'.

Śankara, in his epistemological estimation of this mantra, goes to considerable length to define every philosophical term that he uses. He takes care to point out that the specific things of actualization never sublate the validity of the eternity of truth when it is conceived of as 'being'. This is a very subtle point in the philosophy of Vedanta which has been glaringly misunderstood by even the best minds who have tried to uphold the philosophy of Śankara. Consequently, the great unity of monism has been compromised by the admission of many theistic considerations which are alien to Śankara's philosophy. Those who have come after Śankara sadly compromised themselves by trying to make their systems more acceptable to the requirements of various sentiments, especially religious sentiments. Consequently, Śankara has become misunderstood, unjustly criticized and to some extent, ridiculed. We consider it our duty to restate and reevaluate the salient points of Śankara's arguments which comprise an estimation of the truth that governs pure 'being' and 'thisness' as a unified field of total philosophy which is contemplatively holistic and unitively reasonable.

This peace invocation (*śantiḥ pada*) requires us to meditate on our own prenatal state and formation in the womb, birth, development, formation of our ideas, the programming of our life and how we are led to a termination in the future. When we consider the death and decay of all those who have come before us and gone into oblivion, we can very easily understand that our participation in the universal cycle of being, becoming and dissolution makes no difference in the perennial scheme of manifestation.

After meditating on the 'being' as the eternal basis of becoming, let us call to our minds the triple phases of consciousness that manifest in our individuated life: wakeful consciousness with the duality of subject and object, subjective consciousness which has a unity of its own irrespective of the manifold variegations of the dream; and the fading of all wakeful and dream experiences to naught without our deliberation from which we can wake again without our prompting.

Such a meditation will help us to know we are not the same as we usually think of ourselves. There is a little known truth about us that transcends the socio-psycho-biology of all personal aberrations. From the wisdom texts and our preceptors, we come to know that this ever-present being in us, although little known, passes through the gates of death and birth to bring another cycle of the same program of being conceived in a womb, growing into a fetus, developing faculties and transforming into a child. The embodied program continues. These thoughts can give us a sense of permanence and our belongingness to reality. With them, we gather our scattered consciousness to the core of our hearts and prepare ourselves for the *upāsanā* to which the *Khila Kāṇḍa* is leading us.

We were told from the very beginning of the study of this *Upaniṣad* that mantras are to be heard, meditated upon and lived in the light of the final teaching of each lesson. The *Madhu Kāṇḍa* was an exercise of composition by which the manifoldness could be pieced together to become a universal basis to account for the fleeting transience of all occurrences in time and space such as of our encounters with names, forms and actions. In that kind of universalizing of ideas, most people are sure to stumble on the dead weight of the mass of the body in which the spark of consciousness is imprisoned. Even that spark is not free of the characteristics of the five-fold elements that are anatomically used to house the conscious-unconscious entity of a person. It is also subjected to the changing alternations of the triple modalities of nature, occasionally mirroring clear images and at other times, the psycho-physical and psycho-chemical dimensions of images can curtail all our ideological assumptions to sensory piece-meal clichés.

The *Khila Kāṇḍa* takes into consideration the plight of the aspirant who lives in a body, has many biologic needs to attend to and the ways in which he or she is subjected to psychological eddies and whirlpools, going round and round in self-wrought confusion, and, after many years of such plights, facing the throes of death with a sense of dissatisfaction, feeling unworthy and unwanted. The compassionate seers of the *Khila Kāṇḍa* bring us out of our idealistic dreams to sit firm in our earthly home and sort out the facts of life with an acute sense of finding the real under our own feet. They guide us in taking the threads of life into the nimble fingers of our own hands to spin and weave our own fabric of life with a sense of collaboration with the first and continuing universal cause. This act of showing reverence to our given being with a body, resplendent with many a promising possibility, should make us more responsible than ever.

INTRODUCTION

Salutations to all the wisdom teachers of the world. I am whatever this world is. This world is whatever this Self is. This Self is the origin, the manifested middle and also the ultimate.

This eye is the alpha point. It is identical with all the configurations of perception. Consciousness is the conceptual interpretation given to every form that is given an appellation reflecting its special signification. A name is given to each item so that it can be registered and recalled. A certain value is visualized in every concept. Thereafter it can be considered the meaning of the name or word posited in one's faculty of memory. Consequently, the simplest pulsation of cognition is an act of becoming aware of being, knowing and then being affected by the situational significance of the Self and the world from moment to moment.

The *Bṛhadāraṇyaka Upaniṣad* is one of the world's largest compendiums of the registry of several wise people who have given elaborate conceptualizations of what they thought the Self was. In India's ancient lore we have two forms of recording. They are called the 'heard' *(śruti)* and the 'remembered' *(smṛti)*. *śruti* is revered as a valid pronouncement of truth that is absolutely infallible and to be perennially respected. *Smṛti*, on the other hand, has a situational value of relativistic merit which needs to be revalued and restated again and again. This *Upaniṣad* enjoys the status of a *śruti*, a documentation of infallible perennial truth.

The most accredited way to record truth is by defining the basics that are always recognized to be true. For the sake of clarity, each definition should be illustrated with an example. No example can explicate a definition. Hence every wisdom statement is to be subjected to an intense, critical, contemplative perusal to ascertain its veracity. In the first two volumes of the *Upaniṣad*, such contemplative perusal of wisdom conclusions came from the discussions of a number of anterior critics and posterior evaluators. As the *Khila Kāṇḍa* is the concluding section of this wisdom text, its emphasis is more on actualizing whatever we have already become familiar with as *Upaniṣad dharma.*

Khila indicates the breaking of new ground. It literally means a land of virgin soil which has never been exposed to cultivation of any kind. The basic reference here is to the seeker of truth who has not achieved any substantial degree of cultivation of his or her personal self with proper discipline and comprehensive knowledge to be the recipient of higher wisdom. Like the raw materials of natural resources which can be transformed into valuable aids by various processes, we can engage in creative efforts by which we can arrive at the finale of being and receiving the gift of the ultimate of the material world and the spirit that dominates in the manifestation of all corporeal beings.

In the history of the world, we see many situations in which something belonging to an earlier age was subsequently converted into a more finished product. In pre-historic India, living beings of all sorts lived as inhabitants of a common nature. We can speak of that age as the *Khila.* Out of that came hunters and cultivators making roofs over their heads and living huddled together in small communities. From the early brutes, human beings evolved and passed through the ages of primitive communism, feudalism, monarchies and democratic systems of government. Society has been tamed by religious beliefs and ideals and discoveries of natural laws followed by inventions. Slowly we have developed into the present consumer society with elaborate devices and strategies of management.

In the course of evolution we have learned how to make teams to collectively produce food, houses, clothes and most of our other requirements. Every item of production gave us both the general layout and specific requirements that can be accepted as a production science. Each activity of production naturally holds before its executives a goal to achieve. Goals are value-oriented. Therefore, along with the production science, a value science is also necessary. All value sciences converge to a central value, the value of values. That prime value is the happiness that spells total liberation from all obligatory needs. While Indian seers call it *mokṣa,* Christians call it salvation.

Like other well-conceived activities, perfecting oneself to attain the highest goal of life is also a business which can be called *sad dharma.* When a value is visualized, there is the need to apply the right methodology to relate one's physical, moral or spiritual effort to the goal aspired for. In the event of wanting to actualize a physical goal, the methodology is that of the system science of production. If the goal visualized is moral excellence, it is to be followed by a well-conceived method of structuring one's behavioral pattern and undergoing a purificatory process guided by contemplation. If final emancipation is the goal, one should move towards beatitude.

Every management process involves a theoretical scheme and a practical application. Theory refers to the general anatomy of one's epistemological vision and a methodological suggestion that is helpful to carry out the theory. Once a valid theory is before us, it is possible to apply it. The *Khila Kāṇḍa* shows us how to culture our psycho-physical *persona.* This processing in Sanskrit is called *samskāra.*

In the *Madhu Kāṇḍa* we learned where this world has come from, how it came and into what elaborations it has evolved. The *Muni Kāṇḍa* undertook the task of revaluing the world that our forefathers fashioned for us, so that our revised goal can be easily arrived at. In the present volume we are going further to have a critical review of whatever has been achieved so far. Such a review can give us a new vista and vision of life which can enormously improve our goal-orientation. With a revised value-orientation we can economize time, space, material and energy resources as well as greatly reduce the misery generated by our clumsy handling of things. Although the *Khila Kāṇḍa* of the *Upaniṣad* was presented to the world in the wake of the first millennium B.C., we are restating it to suit the spiritual experiencing and actualization of the Upaniṣadic ideals of *dharma* in modern life.

Every great book has a revised and revalued supplement which marks the *Khila Kāṇḍa* of that particular thesis or scripture. The *Bhagavad Gītā* is the *Khila Kāṇḍa* of Vedantic philosophy. The *Japji Saheb* is the *Khila Kāṇḍa* of the *Guru Granth Saheb.* The new findings in physics, pioneered by Rutherford, Planck, Einstein, De'Broglie, Heisenberg, Schrodinger, Eddington, Jeans, and, in our own day, Stephen Hawking, are the *Khila Kāṇḍa* of modern science.

Every country also has a *Khila Kāṇḍa.* Periodically there are fresh visions and the remaking of civilizations. The India which came through the visions of a new humanity heralded by Indian seers and thinker like Ram Mohan Roy, Dayananda Saraswati, Śri Ṛamakrishna, Vivekananda, Śri Narayana Guru, Śri Aurobindo and Mahatma Gandhi is a *Khila Kāṇḍa* which it is our responsibility to redesign. We are now at a time when both India and the world at large have to emerge with a new solidarity and a spiritual vision that can enhance the dignity of humankind.

ADHYĀYA V

Brāhmaṇa 1

Mantra 1

AUM kham brahma; kham purāṇam; vāyuram khamiti ha smāha kauravyāyaṇīputraḥ; vedo'yam brāhmaṇā viduḥ; vedainena yadveditavyam.

Word Meanings

AUM kham brahma - *AUM* (is) the *ākāśa brahman; purāṇam* - (it is) the timeless, beginningless; *kham* - incomprehensible *ākāśa; kauravyāyaṇīputraḥ* - the son of Kauravyāyaṇī; *āha sma ha* - said; *vāyuram kham* - it is the *ākāśa* containing air; *brāhmaṇāḥ* - the knowers of *brahman; viduḥ* - have known; *ayam* - that; *yat* - which; *veda* - (is) the means of knowing *(veda)*; *enena* - (for) through it; *veda* - (one) knows (that); *veditavyam* - (which is) to be known

AUM is the *ākāśa brahman*. It is the timeless, incomprehensible *ākāśa*. The son of Kauravyāyaṇī said: "It is the *ākāśa* containing air." The knowers of *brahman* have known that which is the means of knowing *(veda)*, for through it one knows that which is to be known.

This mantra is an explication of the term *brahman* as the ground of the universe or the manifested world. Starting with the unmanifested indicates that the *Khila Kāṇḍa* is a study which starts from scratch. Although *brahman* is translated into English as 'the Absolute', there is no word in any other language which is an exact synonym for it. In the *Amārakośa*, *brahman* is defined as 'that which increases progeny'. The root of the word *brahman* comes from *bṛhi*, 'that which increases by itself', and *bṛhati*, which means expanding or proliferating. According to Monier Williams, *brahman* is a noun form which means growth, expansion, evolution, development and swelling of the spirit. There is an implied dynamic of the growth of an unknown latency of projection.

In the Invocation, we have treated *AUM* as a mantra which stands by itself. We have already seen that the *praṇava*, *AUM*, refers to the schematic division of the transactional, wakeful consciousness (*jāgrat*), selective subjectivity such as of dreams or assumptions (*svapna*), prime cause (*suṣupti*) and transcendence (*turīya*). Apart from this, nothing is experienced by anyone. Hence *praṇava* itself indicates the All (*sarvam*). However, Śankara says that here *AUM* is to be read together with *kham brahma*. Even though Śankara qualifies *AUM kham brahma* as a mantra, it is not used as such in any other *Upaniṣad*. In the *Aitareya Upaniṣad* (3.5.1-3) we read:

> Who is this one?
> We worship that one as the Self (*ātman*).
> Which one is the Self?
>
> That whereby one sees, or whereby one hears, or whereby one smells odors, or whereby one articulates speech, or whereby one discriminates the sweet and the sour; that which is heart and mind - that is, consciousness, perception, discrimination, intelligence, wisdom, insight, steadfastness, thought, thoughtfulness, impulse, memory, conception, purpose, life, desire, will. All these, indeed, are appellations of intelligence.
>
> That is Brahma; that is Indra; that is Prajāpati; that is all these gods; and these five gross elements, namely earth, wind, space, water, light; these things and those which are mingled of the fine as it were; origins of one sort and another...horses, cows, persons, elephants; whatever breathing thing there is here - whether moving or flying, and what is stationary.

All this is guided by intelligence, is based on intelligence. The world is guided by intelligence. The basis is intelligence. *Brahman* is intelligence *(prajñānam brahma)*.[2]

Verse three closes with one of the four great Upaniṣadic dicta *(mahāvakya): prajñānam brahma. Tat tvam asi* (that thou art) is the great dictum of instruction given by a *guru* to a disciple. The disciple meditates on the purport of it with two other great dicta, *prajñānam brahma* (intelligence is the Absolute) and *ayam ātma brahma* (this Self is the Absolute). There is a subtle but important difference between these two dicta. From the description of intelligence *(prajñānam)* given in the *Aitareya*, we see how everything in this world is recognized by the connotation of the name given to each item of cognition. All things having name, form, meaning and potential action are accepted as objects of experience. The experiencing device is *prajñānam*. Thus *brahman* in the sense of *prajñānam* is not a noun but the qualifying and modifying aspects of noun and verb.

A misunderstanding can arise that the Absolute is a general term that is not applicable to relativistic items of experience. But this is corrected by the *Kena Upaniṣad* (4.29-31) which says that *brahman* is to be understood as it occurs in both cosmic and individuated phenomena:

> Of It there is this teaching.--
>
> That in the lightning which flashes forth, which makes one blink, and say 'Ah!'--that 'Ah!' refers to the Absolute.
>
> Now with regard to oneself.--
>
> That which comes, as it were, to the mind, by which one repeatedly remembers--that conception is It. [3]

We recognize It as *tadvana*, the desire which is prompting us to cognize and connote. On hearing this, the disciple asks to be told the mystic doctrine *(upaniṣad)*. The *guru* replies:

> The mystic doctrine has been declared to you. Verily, we have told you the mystic doctrine of *Brahma (brāhmī upaniṣad)*.
>
> Austerity *(tapas)*, restraint *(dama)*, and work *(kar-*

man) are the foundation of it. The Vedas are all its limbs. Truth is its abode. [4]

These references indicate that we are always in *brahman* and in the knowledge of *brahman*, imperientially as wonder (Ah!) and experientially as desire. Yet as individuated persons we experience a certain opacity of comprehension. This is also recognized in other scriptures like the Bible and the Qur'an where we read: "One has eyes to see but does not see, ears to hear but does not hear; and a mind to think but does not comprehend." That is why *brahman* is called secret and the *upaniṣad* is called a mystic doctrine or secret knowledge.

When *prajñānam brahma* is contrasted with the other *mahāvakya* of meditation, *ayam ātma brahma* (this Self is the Absolute), we can see a contradiction like that between 'not this, not this' and 'the truth of truth', although the order is reversed. In *prajñānam brahma*, we examine the experiential aspect of the cosmic and individuated presentation in order to understand that the only foundation is the mirroring *prajñānam*. Then, through an introspective contemplation, what mirrors in the *prajñānam* and what is deeply felt as the self-luminous light is then recognized as the Self in *ayam ātma brahma*.

Śankara says that he presents *AUṂ kham brahma* as a mantra to show that the indication in the *Khila Kāṇḍa* is for those who are giving their love and devotion to the Absolute as *upāsanā* which he terms *dhyāna karma*. Although *upāsanā* (ritualistic worship) and *dhyāna* (contemplation) are usually distinguished as two disciplines, Śankara says that such a duality need not be dragged into this mantra. He says that *AUM kham brahma* is the verbal presentation of the non-verbal truth. In both cases the reference is to *AUM*, as *śabda vācya* and *śabda svarūpa*. He maintains that the principle of homogeneity *(kham or ākāśa)* gives unity to *AUM* and *brahman*. The dialectics of the one and the many can be resolved by identifying *AUM* with its four limbs and *ākāśa* which has no specific direction yet is thought of as having four directions, North, East, South and West. There is a temporal and spatial union of terrestrial space.

The *Īśāvāsya Upaniṣad*, which belongs to the ritualistic *mantra bhāga* of the *Śukla Yajur Veda*, is treated as an *Upaniṣad* (*Vedānta*) even though it truly belongs to *Veda*. Similarly, although *upāsanā* belongs to the Vedic context, its purport is to be experienced as *sādhanā*. Vedāntins make a dichotomy of *para* and *apara*. They attribute *param*, the transcendental, causal aspect, to *dhyāna*, whereas *apara*, the world of relativistic details, is attributed to *upāsanā*. To get over this unwarranted duality between *para* and *apara*, Śankara advises us to read *Katha Upaniṣad* (1.16-17):

That is AUM!
That syllable, truly, indeed, is Brahma!
That syllable indeed is the supreme!
Knowing that syllable, truly, indeed,
Whatever one desires is his!

That is the best support.
That is the supreme support.
Knowing that support,
One becomes happy in the Brahma-world. [5]

This is further supported by the *Māha Narayana Upaniṣad* (75.17-18):

O Supreme, Thou art the giver of the wealth of supreme knowledge to us. Thou hast become all. Thou unitest the individual Souls in the *Sūtrātman*. Thou pervadest the universe. Thou art the giver of the lustre to fire. Thou art the giver of light and heat to the sun. Thou art the bestower of the riches of light to the moon. thou art taken in the *upayama* vessel as *soma* juice for oblation. We worship Thee the Supreme who art such for the manifestation of Light.

(The *sannyāsin* having meditated upon the Supreme) should concentrate his thoughts on Him uttering the syllable *AUM*. This, the syllable *AUM*, verily is the substance of many great Upaniṣads and a secret guarded by the gods without imparting to the unfit. He who practices meditation on the Supreme thus with the aid of *praṇava* after *sannyāsa* attains to the unlimited greatness of the Supreme. By that he attains to the greatness of Brahman. Thus the secret knowledge has been imparted. [6]

Śankara takes so much trouble with the details of this short mantra, *AUM kham brahma*, because it contends with the universal problem of appearance and reality. Both in the East and the West, philosophers stand divided among themselves, some supporting the purity of 'being' while others see manifold forms of 'becoming' in the 'being'. The acceptance of one perspective or the other in the countries of the world has even influenced the national character of their people. In Taoism, the Tao is a mystery that cannot be comprehended yet it is symbolized by a continuously transforming pattern of *yin* and *yang* in which one aspect of becoming cancels out the other. In India there are masses of temple-goers who can see the Absolute in the symbol of an idol, a picture or a word, and a few who consider the Absolute the imperishable immortal indweller *(akṣara amṛta antaryāmī)*. In more structured religions like Judaism, Christianity and Islam, the dichotomy is between God and the devil. So there is a great relevancy in attempting to resolve the epistemological duality that shrouds the religious concepts of almost everyone in the world. The *Khila Kāṇḍa* does not want to make any concession to accommodate ignorance under any pretext.

In the phrase *AUM kham brahma*, the identity of the operational meaning of space *(kham* or *ākāśa)* is compared to the operational significance of *brahman*. The root meaning of *kham* is 'that which cannot be comprehended by the intellect'. The intellect cannot comprehend it because it is formless. It also means 'that which brings a presentation of something manifested; i.e. space'. The definition of *ākāśa* is *avākāśa dātur ākāśa*, offering space for any object to exist. *Avākāśa* means the claim to be; *avākāśa dātur* means that which allows the claim of a thing to be. So *ākāśa* is that which permits to exist or the sanction of the claim to be. In other words, it can be considered as the void within which both being and becoming are accommodated. The mystery implied in such a concept enabled Indian *rishis* to equate *ākāśa* with *brahman*.

Thus the phrase *AUM kham brahma* also conveys the idea that the Absolute is incomparable. All world religions share this conviction and have devised ways to maintain the uniqueness of the Absolute. The Jewish tradition uses symbols like Yahweh to refer to the unnamable Absolute. The Christian faith has conceived of the Trinity as a way to ponder the inconceivable. Islam uses the term Allah which actually means 'that which is not'. Allah is not anything which can be perceived or named. In Islam, *haq* serves the same purpose as the Trinity in Christianity – providing a conceivable word suggestion. In the *Upaniṣad, brahman* is described as 'not this, not this' and then complemented as 'the truth of truth'. *Ākāśa* also means pervading brilliance. If we add the qualities of *kham* and *ākāśa* to *brahman,* it comes to mean that the potential which actualizes everything is self-luminous. It does not have to borrow light from anything else to shine forth.

The *Madhu Kāṇḍa* and *Muni Kāṇḍa* have familiarized us with the epistemology, methodology, and axiology of the *Bṛhadāraṇyaka Upaniṣad.* The epistemology is to know what is to be known; the axiology is to realize the Self; the methodology is going from the known to the unknown, step by step, building up the general structure of the philosophical vision and filling it systematically with whatever is relevant, applying reasoning which implies dialectical engineering of opposites, fixing conceptual meanings with the aid of symbols and allegories; and arriving at an axiologic conclusion through an act of self-purification, in which one becomes imperientially identified with intuitive visions which can be the proper foundations of wisdom.

In this mantra this perfected approach of arriving at ennobling conclusions was first started with the postulation of a field. With the phrases *kham purāṇam* and *vāyuram kham*, the first correlates are presented. In the Indian concept of consciousness there are three tiers of knowledge: the unknown, which is also the unconscious, that which is presenting as a nucleus of knowledge which emerges from the unconscious to the preconscious, and finally the peripheral knowledge where objectivity is pronounced. These references are only anticipatory and not actualized. Any manifestation has to be bracketed with correlatives. *Kham* is qualified as *purāṇam.* In the word *purāṇam* there is an indication of flowing in. Space is an abstraction which enables us to understand the in-between of objects. All objects are relative in their existence, such as close or far, above or below, right or left. Space accommodates all such notions as long as the law of the impenetrability of matter is not tampered with. *Purāṇam* means 'previously' or 'thus always', so *kham purāṇam* means 'space was always so'.

In a general sense, *purāṇam* indicates the source of myth. Myth is a device of visualizing archetypes. An archetypal symbol is not generated by anyone; it is the latent potential of the collective unconscious. What has filled in and become past is *purāṇa*. In ancient days, when a chronicler wrote a registry of events, the history thus maintained was called a *purāṇa*. *Purāṇa* is interpreted in the *Amarakośa* as that which brings knowledge of the beyond never received before. An epic is also called *purāṇa*. An epic should have five characteristics: 1) being divided into chapters; 2) having subheadings; 3) giving the chronology of dynasties; 4) having reference to what happened in which period of time; 5) considering whether the reference belongs to the material world (*ādhibhautika*) to the mental world (*ādhyātmika*) or to the Divine (*ādhidaivika*).

The Indian concept of the past is not fully accounted for by a memory that can be recalled. The two great Indian epics, the *Rāmāyaṇa* and the *Mahābhārata*, along with the eighteen mythical chronicles called the *Purāṇas* refer to many cycles of the origin of the world from deluge and going back to deluge. All the subtleties that we speak of as being conceived of in the 64 codes of the genetic map are an example of the past inscribed into the present.

The next phrase, *vāyuram kham*, indicates that space is not a mere void. At least in our common-sense experience, we know that the possibility of life on earth is perpetuated by the atmosphere whose main content is moisture-filled air (*vāyu*). But *vāyu* is not just air. It has an intimate aspect - the vital breath (*prāṇa*) which is imperative for the commencement of individual life and its sustenance at the most ontological level. It also includes the metaphysical postulation that the vital breath has the assignment of differentiating the functions of the organism sustained by breath.

Ākāśa is the first of the five elements. It is the pure pre-causal postulation in which the first possibility arises which is indicative of vibrations. From the primeval potential, whatever became probable, such as light and sound, has the quality of pervasiveness, filling more and more space. Passing from the causal to the subtle, the first body emerges. The first identifying characteristic (*lakṣaṇa*) of a body is that it is tangible. It can touch and be touched. Air molecules touch each other. Where there is contact, there can be friction. Where there is friction, matter becomes thermally charged. Matter is thus slowly concretized through the elements of air, fire, water and earth. The universe in the process of being manifested begins with the undifferentiated cause and becomes more and more complex. As we move from *ākāśa* to *vāyu* the non-formulated becomes formulated, the non-configured becomes configured. That implies the time/space continuum which is basic for any manifestation.

This statement, *vāyuram kham iti*, is attributed to the son of Kauravyāyaṇī which is a reference to the Kuru dynasty from Viṣṇu to Śamtanu. Bhīṣma was born to Śamtanu by Ganga. Śamtanu's second wife was Satyavatī in whom Vyāsa was born by Parāśara. Vyāsa had two sons, Dhṛtarāṣṭra and Pandu, by Ambikā and Ambālikā respectively. Thus *kauravyāyaṇīputraḥ* refers to Vyāsa as the ancient *guru* who revealed this truth. When the mantra refers to the knowers of *brahman*, we have to think of *brāhmaṇas* like Vyāsa and Yājñavalkya who know the secret of *brahman.*

The mantra says that "the knowers of *brahman* have known that which is the means of knowing *(veda)*, for through it one knows that which is to be known." In this mantra *veda* is used as the basic monad of our understanding. Whenever we use a traditionally known term such as *veda* which has been prejudicially conceived and maliciously used, we need to revalue it. In the *Amarakośa*, *veda* is defined as 'that which is the factor which enables one to discern the right and wrong foundations of everything presented to cognition'. *Veda* is also synonymous with *śruti*, meaning 'that which is heard or is to be directly listened to'; *amnāya*, 'that which instructs the distinction between *dharma* and *adharma*'; *trayī*, the three scriptures (*Ṛg*, *Yajur* and *Sāma*); and *dharmaḥ*, 'injunctions given in sacrificial rituals'. It is further identified with *AUM.*

The identification of *brahman* with *veda* in some sense contradicts the non-dualistic philosopher's concept of *brahman.* In the first and second *Kāṇḍas*, the *Bṛhadāraṇyaka* was maintaining the *Upaniṣads* claim for *brahmavidyā. Veda*, if taken as the anterior explication of what is to be known, naturally relates to the relativistic world and is hence to be treated as *dharma. Brahman* is that which transcends *dharma.* In a general sense *Veda* is considered as a mandate of authority because each *Veda* has a posterior part called *Vedānta* which is identified with the *Upaniṣads.* Jaimini's interpretation of the Vedic scriptures was mainly as injunctions to perform rituals, *dharma mīmāmsā* As such, they are considered to be opposed to the philosophical vision of *uttara mīmāmsā* or *brahmavidyā.* When mantra V.1.1 says the knowers of *brahman* know that which is the means of knowing, it raises the question of what is to be known. In Jaimini's *Dharma Sūtra*, *dharma* is defined as that which is characteristically of the nature of seeking or putting questions. In contrast to the *dharma jijñāsa* of Jaimini, Bādarāyaṇa (Vyāsa) speaks of *brahma jijñāsa*. These riddles can only be resolved by resorting to the position of *Vedānta* rather than that of the *Veda*.

This implication is evident from the evaluation of *Veda* given in the *Bhagavad Gītā* where Kṛṣṇa speaks of *Veda* as dear to people who indulge in pedantic speech of decorative words. In Chapter Two, verses forty-two to forty-four, the *Vedic* discipline is disparagingly narrated:

> Such flowery speech as uttered by the foolish adhering to the doctrine of the Veda negating any other (transcendental) verity, the self of which is nothing but desire-made, holding heaven for highest goal, offering only birth as the result of works abounding in many special observances which aim at enjoyment and domination: in the case of those whose minds are under the sway of such teachings, who are attached to enjoyment and domination, a well-founded reason does not come under the sway of the peace of contemplation (*samādhi*).[7]

In verse forty-five, the *Veda* is blatantly discredited:

> The *Veda* treats of matters related to the three *guṇas* (modalities of nature); you should be free from these three modalities O Arjuna; free from (relative) pairs of opposites, established ever in pure being, without any yoga (discipline) or well-being (as dual factors but remain) one (unitively) Self-possessed (*ātmavan*).

Therefore, Śankara gives an elaborate commentary to defend his position in interpreting this mantra as identifying *brahman*-knowledge with *Veda*. In his book, *Aparokṣa Anubhūti*, he distinguishes piecemeal external experiences from the holistic total immersion in truth. He says that *brahman*-knowledge cannot be categorized as perceptual knowledge (*pratyakṣa*) or knowledge coming from hear-say (*parokṣa*). His *guru* was Govinda whose *guru* was Gaudapāda, who commented on the *Māṇḍūkya Upa-*

niṣad. In his commentary, Gaudapāda says that three experiences are implied in the *praṇava*, i.e., the wakeful, transactional experience, the subtle subjective experiencing of dream, and the state of oblivion that one remembers after waking up from deep sleep.

To honor *brahman* in its purest aspect, the *Māṇḍūkya* brings in the concept of the fourth, *turīya*. *Turīya* is not mentioned in any other *Upaniṣad*. Hence Śankara has to explain or, rather, explain away the presentation of the world consciousness which is in intimate relationship with *prājña*, the intelligence that remains in the state of deep sleep, described in mantra five of the *Māṇḍūkya Upaniṣad:*

> The deep-sleep state *(suṣupta sthāna)*, unified *(ekī bhūta)*, just a cognition mass *(prajñāna ghana)*, consisting of bliss *(ānanda māyā)*, enjoying bliss *(ānanda bhuj)*, whose mouth is thought, *(cetas)*, this is the cognitional *(prājña)*. [8]

Mantras six and seven are to be meditated upon to get the deep significance of what Gaudapāda and Śankara want to stress about the transcendental state of unitive wisdom *(turīya):*

> This is the lord of all *(sarveśvara)*. This is the all-knowing *(sarva jña)*. This is the inner controller *(antar yāmin)*. This is the source *(yoni)* of all, for this is the origin and the end *(prabhavāpyayau)* of beings.

> Not inwardly cognitive *(antaḥ prājña)*, not outwardly cognitive *(bahiḥ prājña)*, not both-wise cognitive *(ubhay-ataḥ prājña)*, not non-cognitive *(aprajña)*, unseen *(adṛṣṭa)*, with which there can be no dealing *(avyavahārya)*, ungraspable *(agrāhya)*, having no distinctive mark *(alakṣaṇa)*, non-thinkable *(acintaya)*, that cannot be designated *(avyapadeśya)*, the essence of the assurance of which is being one with the Self *(ekātmya pratyaya sāra)*, the cessation of development *(prapañcopaśama)*, tranquil *(śānta)*, benign *(śiva)*, without a second *(advaita)* -- such they think is the fourth. He is the Self *(ātman)*. He should be discerned. [9]

This mantra refers to the omniscience of the Absolute which regulates everything that is involved in the process of manifestation. In the potential are all the uncharted possibilities; out of possibilities, the probabilities can start surfacing; out of the probable comes the feasibility of actualization. Evolution from the causal to the subtle and the subtle to the gross is the basic process of instrumentation. To manifest means to reveal the intrinsic quality of that which is manifesting. Hence Chattampi Swāmigal, a rishi of modern days says, "The *veda* is not a book; it is this world." Everything in this world, the blue sky, the motion of the wind, the sounds that are pronounced and carried through the vibrations in air, the light that illuminates, the fire that burns, the cloud that rains, the river that flows, are all revelations. Even a blade of grass which nobody will mistake for anything other than a blade of grass is as much a *veda* as anything else. So here *veda* is not the Hindu religious scriptures, but the implied principle of the invisible becoming visible and the potential becoming real.

By applying the essential teachings of these mantras, we can imperientially live the revelation of the *Upaniṣads*. The central piece of this mantra is *kham*. To be is to exist. To exist means physically to be placed in time and space with a ponderable substance that has a mark of its own which can be distinguished from other manifestations that occupy other spaces and times.

To begin our *upāsanā*, we should turn to the being of which we are fully conscious in the location where our personal dimensions are in close intimacy both with space and time. So, to begin with, each of us can say "I am this, a corporeal being in the here and now, which is to be marked, so far as I am concerned, as the central point, core or nucleus of my world. There may be other beings like me who also think of this world with their central core marking the centerpiece of their universe. But when I say 'I am' I am the world. However distant the stars of the heavens may seem, so far as I am concerned, the reality of each such luminary rests entirely on the matrix of consciousness from which I am evolving from time to time. I am the *ākāśa*, (*kham*). Even when I sit in absolute darkness, I don't need any light other than the light of my own Self to know I am. I am the space that is spatializing and the time that is temporizing.

It is fascinating to be in this *ākāśa* and watch the triple modes of time that alter the presentation of images day by day, cyclically and periodically. I am the central hub from which all the spokes of the spatio-temporal events of my life-program radiate. The core of my being is like an ever-rotating axle. The axle is symbolic of the path that I traverse from the day of conception to the moment of cremation. Transactions, subjective ideas and withdrawal into silence are symbolically expressed in *'A'*, *'U'*, *'M'*. However, my being as the axle of the vehicle of my personalized existence is not expressive.

The sun is real to me when I see it; otherwise it is an imagination. The air is real to me when I breathe. Here, I shake off all hear-says and imaginations and directly relate to that part of my being recognized as sight, hearing, touching, tasting and smelling. It is a wonder that I lend reality to and animate all that I see, hear, taste, smell and come into contact with in my daily life. From childhood to this day, I treated them all as separate entities. For example, when light reflects from a body to strike against my cognitive attention and carry my consciousness back to the source of illumination, I get stranded either in the subject or the object. To do the *upāsanā* of this mantra, I should admire and appreciate every quanta of energy that comes to me as a photon, sound wave or other provocation, simultaneously at its source and where I undergo transformation. This is the real reverence I should show to the scheme to which I am subjected.

'I am the seer; I am the seen; I am the seeing'. In this conviction I become the creator, the created and the all-permeating value of all that is created. Such participation will help me to feel the worthwhileness of the world I generate from moment to moment. What I encounter is *ānanda*. The act of encountering is *ānanda* and the impact it has on me is also *ānanda*. It is not a flimsy image because this *ākāśa* which I fill is the very essence of life which I am breathing in and breathing out. It is an act of continuous creation which is not bound in time or space because time and space are co-created with me. Hence it is called *purāṇa*.

All these days, it was a mistake for me to think that I am alien to that which is to be known and I was to seek knowledge elsewhere. What I need to ponder is 'I am the known and I am the knower', not as a single entity but as everything that fills the consciousness of my world. Just as every leaf of the tree is as real as the tree, the seemingly passing phenomena of my being is happily real in all its details." Such is the joy of a *brahman*-knower.

Brāhmaṇa 2

Introduction

In this *brāhmaṇa* there are three mantras. They have a sequential relevancy. The *Madhu Kāṇḍa* commenced with the *aśva* and the *aśvamedha brāhmaṇa*. That was followed by the *virāj* and a description of the process by which the unmanifested potential became the manifest. From the beginning, the *Bṛhadāraṇyaka Upaniṣad* has explicated the fundamental principle of the cause spreading itself into sequential effects. Whatever is potent or latent in the cause is unfolded when the cause is elaborated into its effect. The mainstay of the *Upaniṣad* is an unbroken stream of cause and effect which is like a thread going into the future, stringing on it all effects that issue forth from the cause. This method naturally justifies the normal types of reasoning with which the human cognitive system is familiar. The *Upaniṣad* avoids dogmas and theories of belief. Every presentation has to be reasonable and logical in its content, structure and operational elaboration.

The first *Adhyāya* presented the highest need with which every living being is confronted: hunger. Hunger naturally results from the principle of expending. In the unmanifested as well as the manifested there is one homogeneous truth which is the truth of being. If any specificity springs forth from that being, it is sure to imply an operational dynamic by which the being will appear to produce a specific form of becoming out of itself .

In one sense, anything that becomes claims a space in which to be and a time factor sequentially arranged for the beginning and establishment of manifestation. Therefore, each manifestation is exposed to space as well as time. If it is possible for one thing to extend itself in space, it is possible for another thing to also extend itself. The simultaneity of becoming brings contact and conflict. The process of becoming naturally brings forth a fresh release of energy to elaborate it. For the same reason, the action propensity will cause the expenditure of energy. This is called hunger.

Expenditure in another sense is burning away. Thus wherever there is hunger there is also the fire of burning. The creative process always has to find fuel for the power of combustion. The potential in this case is the omnipotent. Omnipotent means potency that is available for the elaboration of all spaces and the potency that can continuously convert itself from the possible to the probable, and the probable to the actual. The first cause is elaborated as the ever-growing or ever-expanding *brahman*.

The main style of *Vedic* literature is to employ anthropomorphic symbols. This is a pre-Vedāntic style developed by the ancient poets of India. To them, every occurrence in heaven, in midair, on earth, and in the uncharted depth was to be treated as a spirit of inconceivable potentials that could elaborate itself through the sheer power of imagination. In our work-a-day world we have before us the tangible object of which an image is formed in our mind which we retain as a memory. But in the *Vedic* postulation, it is the image that sculpts forms and orchestrates the music of life. The cast is made in the mold of the image. Thus in the *Vedic* epistemology, one can generate only what one can imagine. Poetry is a neat arrangement of images. Hence the Indians call their seers the poets of imagination. Truth is also an image, an image which ensues from one's Self. Therefore the Self is considered to be the womb that begets images. Just as no machine can make itself, the Self cannot be imagined. We can only give analogies which will never approximate the real Self. Henri Bergson puts it in another way: the being or the Self is the gold coin which can never be equaled by all the copper coins which are considered to be the small tender of a sovereign.

The first two terms we have to reckon with are cause and effect. At the same time, cause cannot be imagined as an entity because a cause comes only if there is an effect. The effect retrospectively points to a cause, and the cause prospectively points to the effect. This is a dialectical situation in which the counterparts are dependent on each other. The cause is as much a dependent factor as the effect and *vice versa*. Even where it is not permissible to formulate a cause and deduce an effect, *brahman* is considered to be the source and the world is considered to be a resultant effect. This is not a linear conception of a cause and effect where one cause results in one effect.

To begin with, the cause is one, and the effect comes in the plural. The relationship between the cause and the effect is of the one and the many. The many effects that come from a single cause can have a cumulative effect to generate a new situation of want and a new situation of possibilities vying for the probable to produce an actual. The many effects transform themselves into a new cause. Now we have a dialectical formula of the many leading to the one which is the reverse order of the relationship between the first cause and subsequent effects.

This is somewhat similar to the growth of a snowball. The unity of one is always maintained even when it grows into an unimaginable elaboration. The first effect which we saw coming to satisfy the need of cosmic hunger was the *prajāpati* issuing forth from the vexed mind. This is a process which is going on even now. The principle of finding the means for life is to become parasitic. The *prajāpati* is a parasite which was generated by the parent body of the need or hunger. The hunger in turn became a parasite which feeds on the *prajāpati*. The entire structure of the world is parasitic. When we speak of parasite, it is not only the parasites we see among living beings. We read in Guy Murchie:

> This sort of drastic interdependence of microbes evidently achieves its ultimate complexity in parasitism, which, as I mentioned in Chapter I, has evolved natural chains or hierarchies, such as viruses that are parasites of bacteria that are parasites of certain very small mites that are parasites of lice that are parasites of egrets that are parasites of cattle that are parasites of man who is a parasite of Earth which is a parasite of the sun which is a parasite of the Milky Way which is a parasite of the Virgo Supergalaxy...with each host bigger than its parasite like a next of Chinese boxes all the way (if enough were known) from the heart of the atom to the horizon of the universe. [10]

The food we eat is broken up into bits by our digestive fluids and in turn the digestive organs receive nourishment from the newly generated energy to continue the process of elaborating the biological organism. The husband is a parasite of the wife; the wife is a parasite living on the resources of the husband. Children are born as parasites. The same children satisfy several needs of the parents such as fulfillment of many urges. The child itself is born out of the sexual exploitation of the male by the female, and the female by the male.

For convenience the first *prajāpati* is numbered as one. But its replicas are many. In the *Bṛhadāraṇyaka Upaniṣad* itself, we have seen how *prajāpati* split one homogenous body into two, generating the heterogeneity of the male and the female throughout the hierarchy of beings. At the lowest levels there is no need for a separate male and female. Within one gene there can be the mutually exploiting, the mutually irritating and the united aspects of the plus and minus. Like the interaction of *yin* and *yang*, the plus has in it a potential minus, and the minus has in it a potential plus.

There is a dependability of need and supply which cannot be fixed in any one set of symbols. This process is afterwards beautifully laid out in the magical cycle of creation and dissolution. For one moment there is something valid, the next moment it is invalid. Hence the question, *yā mā:* "What is this magic?" The answer is, *sā māyā:* "This is verily magic." The evolution of *prajāpati* into countless trillions of different patterns and designs, with multi-purpose complexes of need and supply, is said to have two complementary dynamics. One hides the source, the other generates from the source something which looks fabulously different. The hiding part is called *āvaraṇa;* the projection from it is called *vikṣepa*. *Āvaraṇa* means veiling; *vikṣepa* literally means depositing specificity. Each one of us is a *prajāpati*. But there are also innumerable *prajāpatis* within each of us because each cell is an entity that is self-generated, self-maintained and self-regulated.

Prajāpati incorporates three variations: One represents the pure-clear (*sattva*) which is contrasted by dark opacity (*tamas*). The link between the two is a graded sharing of the pure-clear and the dark which includes all the pure elements, colored elements, and conditioned elaborations of the two polarized ends (*rajas*). These three formations are in the matrix of creation. In the poetic elaboration in this *brāhmaṇa*, these three are expressed by the images of the shining ones (*devas*), the human beings (*manuṣyā*), and the dark ones (*asura*).

Human beings are earthlings. We are destined to live on earth for around a hundred years. So we cannot afford to be vulnerable like will-o-the wisps. The earth is called *dhara* in Sanskrit, 'that which supports'. We need to have a material, anatomical frame in which all the delicate instruments can be safely carried around. That is why the human body, like other living organisms, is considered to have two basic components, earth and water, animated by fire and air, placed in the environment of time and space.

Other living beings also very much belong to earth, particularly those of the vegetative world. The roots of trees and plants go deep into the dark regions of earth while their leaves and flowers are exposed to the shining luminaries of sun, moon and stars. Similarly, human beings also have an unconscious depth within and a mind often illuminated with the stimuli received through ears, eyes, tongue, nose and the all-pervading sense of touch in the skin with which we are covered. Thus we are modeled with the dark and the hard on one side and the light and the subtle on the other.

The three mantras which follow present the shining ones and the demons as the offspring of *prajāpati*. Both the bright and the dark are in us as necessary occupants out of which we have to make a blend to walk on this earth for our allotted time.

Mantra 1

trayāḥ prājāpatyāḥ prajāpatau pitari brahmacaryamūṣuḥ – devā manuṣya asurāḥ; uṣitvā brahmacaryam devā ūcuḥ, bravītu no bhavāniti; tebhyo hatadakṣaramuvāca da iti; vyajñāsiṣṭā iti; vyajñāsiṣmeti hocuḥ, dāmyateti na ātheti; aumiti hovāca, vyajñāsiṣṭeti.

Word Meanings

prājāpatyāḥ - *prajāpati* brought forth; *trayāḥ* - three (kinds of) offspring or children; *devāḥ* - the gods; *manuṣyaḥ* - humans; *asurāḥ* - (and) demons; *pitari prajāpatau* - with the original *prajāpati*; *ūṣuḥ* - they lived; *brahmacaryam* - a life of truthfulness; *brahmacaryam uṣitvā* - after finishing their term; *devāḥ* - the gods; *ūcuḥ* - said; *bhavān bravītu iti* - please teach; *naḥ* - us; *tebhyaḥ* - to them; *uvāca ha iti* - (the *prajāpati*) said; *etat* - the; *akṣaram* - syllable; *da* - *da* (and asked); *vyajñāsiṣṭā iti* -

have you understood; *ūcuḥ* - they said; *vyajñāsiṣma iti* - (we) have understood; *ātha iti* - (you) said; *naḥ* - to us; *dāmyata* - control (yourselves); *iti* - this; *uvāca ha* - *(prajāpati)* said; *aum iti* - yes; *vyajñāsiṣṭa iti* - (you) have understood

Prajāpati brought forth three kinds of offspring: gods, humans and demons. With the original *prajāpati* they lived a life of truthfulness. After finishing their term, the gods said, "Please teach us." To them the *prajāpati* uttered the syllable "*Da*" and asked, "Have you understood?" They said, "We have understood. You said to us: 'Control yourselves (*dāmyata*)'." *Prajāpati* said, "Yes you have understood."

The first part of the mantra says that the *prajāpati* brought forth three kinds of offspring. Under many circumstances, life assumes a unitary position in an embodied state. It can be an algae, a plant, or a tree; it can be an insect, a reptile hatched out of an egg, or an animal nurtured in the womb of a mother. The act of coming out of the hidden source into the open is called *prajananam*. That which is thus born is a *praja*. The protective power that supervises the inception, embodiment and coming into the external world as a separate being is called *prajāpati*. Thus the *prajāpati* of each one of us is always present as a supervising light and general controller of our life. The *prajāpati* is the witness in all the forms of life which the embodied being goes through. Ultimately, it merges back into the Absolute when all the cycles of *karma* have been lived. The witness does not induce an individuated being to do any *karma* or to desist from *karma*, but gives company through all the trials and tribulations of the individual.

Each embodied being has a three-fold principle rolled into one: that aspect of consciousness in which both spirit and matter are mirrored truthfully, or mirrored with translucent colorations and conditionings or reflected in dark silhouetted nature. These are respectively aided by the triple *guṇas* of *prakṛti*: *sattva*, which is honest in its replication; *rajas*, which has several grades of possible exaggeration and distortion; and *tamas*, which gives a dark impression tending to become more morbid and crystallized.

The first is called divine, the second human, and the third demonic. All three aspects are given a period of nurturing in their intrinsic quality which enables them to maintain their respective roles. This initial period is called *brahmacarya*.

Brahmacarya is a term much misunderstood in the world influenced by the Sanskrit language and Vedic and Vedāntic literature. Everything conforms to the pattern of life which is to be lived not only by the embodied being, but by all that has name and form. In fact, form is the basis of embodiment and name is the connotative aspect which identifies the general nature of an embodied being or substance. The form is unique for every identifiable body. Even an outline sketch is enough to distinguish one thing from another. The formal identities of all living beings, whether vegetables, lower animals or higher animals, have been scientifically classified and categorized as distinct morphologic patterns. As biology insists on a use value for any formation of body parts, morphology is not a mere external semblance. The formal aspect has its basis in the universal existentiality of the Absolute.

The nominal has its basis in the universal cognitive aspect of the operational dynamic of a thing. Hence it pertains to the triple aspects of consciousness: consciousness through and through which has a veiled nature; consciousness that assumes images received retrospectively, actually and prospectively; and the light of consciousness which allows itself to be the luminosity by which things are illuminated. In our individuated life these three represent the unconscious, the individuated consciousness, and the collective consciousness. They are held together by three universal principles: truthful existence, interpretive word power and the conditioning by which individuation can be maintained.

The first aspect is represented by the shining ones; the second aspect is mainly lived by human beings with graded varieties of impressions and expressions; and the third aspect is represented by the dark ones. Indian philosophers have a prejudicial apathy towards the dark (*tamas*), but as a nature modality, it is the binding and stabilizing memory tool to retain the past and the present as a useful mode for all future development, transformation or categorization.

All three are governed by intrinsic laws. There is a *dharma* of the *deva*, a *dharma* of the *manuṣyā*; and a *dharma* of the *asura*. Instituting each one in their respective nature and maintaining their own *dharma* is what is termed here as the *brahmacarya* of each. Unfortunately many people take *brahmacarya* in the narrow sense of abstaining from erotic passion. This is only an incidental meaning or connotation. Any truthful function is *brahmacarya.*

Indian philosophy speaks of four stages of human life: *brahmacarya, gārhasthya, vanaprastha* and *sannyāsa.* The studenthood of a person is specifically called *brahmacarya.* Even after a person has lived a quarter of life in wisdom discipline and then takes to the family life of a householder (*gārhasthya*), he or she continues as a *brahmacārī.* One is expected to continue to be morally and spiritually honest in living one's married life. During *vanaprastha,* the period of preparing to leave the desires and passions of this world and reach out to a higher appreciation of the supreme values of life, *brahmacarya* is also to be maintained. That is a time when one is expected to be absolutely truthful to oneself and one's ideals. In the final stage called *sannyāsa, brahmacarya* is to be maintained, not as an individuated *brahmacarya,* but as a complete dedication to the laws governing the totality of life.

Human life also has four goals (*puruṣārthas*). The first relates to one's understanding (*dharma*),the second to the acquisition of means (*artha*) and the third to the intense volition coupled with one's efforts (*kāma*). When these four aspects culminate in the perfection of one's ultimate fulfillment, the individuation in each life comes to its natural termination (*mokṣa*). These four goals and four periods of life can be clearly seen in human life.

It is expected that through a long process of evolution beings become more perfected to assume a higher nature. The Indian people are not worried about time at all. They have a concept of a *kalpa* being made up of four *yugas*, each of which is made up of the time span of many, many generations. This concept of the Indian people takes the sharp edge of anxiety away from death. Each death is only one death an individuated being undergoes. Before that and after that, many deaths are probable. All through this, if honesty is maintained, *brahmacaryā* continues.

We should note that the mantra depicts the *devas* as asking for guidance from the *prajāpati* who is the ever-protecting, ever-witnessing spirit in which the *deva* dwells. They are not going to another place or to a new instructor in search of wisdom. The concept of *prajāpati* comes close to what the Semitic religions call the creator, universal father or eternal benefactor. We read in the

Bhagavad Gītā that the lower self is to be elevated by the higher Self. The person who lives in this world is the lower self (*prajā*). It has in it the consciousness that percolates into the mind, animates the sense organs and in return becomes influenced by energy in the form of sensations that come from the external world into the mind/body complex. This is presided over by one's ego (*aham*). This lower self, which usually identifies with the I-consciousness and me-consciousness, raises itself to the higher consciousness through meditation on the Self (*ātman*). The true Upaniṣadic way does not lie in the disciplines of prayer, supplication or elaborate invocations, but in contemplative pondering which is often called *dhyāna*, based on *dhāraṇā*.

There is an intimate relationship between the divine or shining principle and the nature to which it is often exposed through the psycho-physical frame in which the higher Self lives. Because nature (*prakṛti*) can influence the higher Self through constant exposure, the passion to be happy can become a binding factor on the *devas*. So when the *devas* made a supplication to the *prajāpati* for instruction, the *prajāpati* articulated the sound *'da'* meaning restraint (*dama*).

Our heart and other organs have built-in devices for control. In the heart the flow of blood is made unidirectional through a control system of valves. But our consciousness is subject to the danger of becoming polluted by malevolent ideas. That is why it is said that when the passion for happiness overrides, it is necessary to exercise restraint.

The *Upaniṣad* relates this episode as a means for our instruction. From our early days with our parents, teachers, and wise preceptors of spiritual institutions, we have been hearing great dictums of understanding and instructions for spiritual discipline. We should meditate on the mantra each day, taking stock to make sure that our exposure to this world has not in any way vitiated our desires or disturbed the virginity of our life and its spiritual content. Again and again we have to correct any deviations in our paths. To deviate is called *vyabhicarya*. Prostitution is also *vyabhicarya*. Instead of taking the evil of prostitution literally, Jesus Christ wanted us to look into our hearts to see whether we have deviated from our moral discipline. Similarly, the *dharma* of the *deva* is not only to be maintained in principle, but also in practice as a high degree of spiritual honesty. Then alone we are truly *brahmacārīs* exercising restraint.

Mantra 2

atha hainam manuṣyā ūcuḥ bravītu no bhavāniti; tebhyo haitadevākṣaramuvāca da iti; vyajñāsiṣṭā iti; vyajñāsiṣmeti hocuḥ, datteti na āttheti; aumiti hovāca, vyajñāsiṣṭeti.

Word Meanings

ātha ha - then; *manuṣyāḥ* - the humans; *ūcuḥ* - said; *bhavān bravītu iti* - please teach; *naḥ* - us; *tebhyaḥ* - to them; *uvāca ha iti* - (the *prajāpati*) said; *etat eva* - the same; *akṣaram* - syllable; *da* - *da* (and asked); *vyajñāsiṣṭā iti* - have you understood; *ūcuḥ* - they said; *vyajñāsiṣma iti* - (we) have understood; *ātha iti* - (you) said; *naḥ* - to us; *datta* - be charitable; *iti* - this; *uvāca ha* - (*prajāpati*) said; *aum iti* - yes; *vyajñāsiṣṭa iti* - (you) have understood

After finishing their term, the humans said, "Please teach us." To them the *prajāpati* uttered the syllable "*da*" and asked, "Have you understood?" They said, "We have understood. You said to us: 'Be charitable (*datta*)'." *Prajāpati* said, "Yes you have understood."

Mantra 3

atha hainamasurā ūcuḥ bravītu no bhavāniti; tebhyo haitadevākṣaramuvāca da iti; vyajñāsiṣṭā iti; vyajñāsiṣmeti hocuḥ, dayadhvamiti na āttheti; aumiti hovāca, vyajñāsiṣṭeti; tadetadevaiṣā daivī vāganuvadati stanayitnurda da da iti - dāmyat datta dayadhvamiti; tadetattrayam śikṣet - damam dānam dayāmiti.

Word Meanings

atha ha - then; *asurāḥ* - demons; *ūcuḥ* - said; *bhavān bravītu iti* - please teach; *naḥ* - us; *tebhyaḥ* - to them;

uvāca ha iti - (the *prajāpati*) said; *etat eva* - the same; *akśaram* - syllable; *da* - *da* (and asked); *vyajñāsiṣṭā iti* - have you understood; *ūcuḥ* - they said; *vyajñāsiṣma iti* - (we) have understood; *ātha iti* - (you) said; *naḥ* - to us; *dayadhvam* - be merciful; *iti* - this; *uvāca ha* - (*prajāpati*) said; *aum iti* - yes; *vyajñāsiṣṭā iti* - (you) have understood; *tat etat eva* - that very (instruction); *anuvadati* - is repeated; *eṣā* - by the; *daivi* - heavenly; *vāk* - voice; *stanayitnuḥ* - in the thunder-cloud; *da da da iti* - as *da da da; dāmyata* - control yourselves; *datta* - be charitable; *dayadhvam iti* - be merciful; *tat* - therefore; *śikṣet iti* - (one) should learn; *etat* - these; *trayam* - three; *damam* - self-control; *dānam* - charity; *dayām* - (and) mercy

After finishing their term, the demons said, "Please teach us." To them the *prajāpati* uttered the same syllable "*da*" and asked, "Have you understood?" They said, "We have understood. You said to us: 'Be merciful (*dayadhvam*)'." *prajāpati* said, "Yes you have understood."
That very instruction the heavenly voice in the form of the thunder-cloud repeats as *'da da da'*: 'Control yourselves', 'Be charitable', 'Be merciful'. Therefore one should learn these three – self-control, charity and mercy.

The second and third mantras present the human and demonic aspect of our personas. There is a wholesale confusion which is common to all types of theological speculations. Unfortunately, improperly conceived views have percolated into the religious, moral and spiritual concepts of all major faiths. Therefore these mantras require a close examination to sort out the misconceptions that have come into even the most illustrious teachings of humanity. As a preliminary step we should confine ourselves to the epistemological frame of reference within which we have to remain in this *Upaniṣad.*

At the very outset of the book we were given a binary method of reducing the entire universe to the structural compactness of a single organism such as a horse, and expanding it into all its elaborations to accommodate all the details of the universe. The horse was chosen as an archetypal symbol because it is a carrier.

In the study of genetics great importance is given to the carriers of the genes, the chromosomes. In the study of an organism, similar emphasis is put on the body that carries its energy or animation, its faculties of functional instrumentation, its senses and sensory system, its meticulous system of energy production, distribution and consumption, and its awareness of surface clarity and different levels of depth. Hence a detailed study of the body (*śarīra*) as a carrier of the individuated persona is required.

There are many conveyances for the transfer of food via the digestive system and air via the respiratory system. These intakes are complemented by the outgoing and circulating principles such as of blood, oxygen, rare and important biochemicals, sensations, and commands for motor operation. Hence the container and the contained are to be studied together. The vehicle and the operator of the vehicle are to be studied holistically. The carrier or conveyer in the case of living beings is like a horse which senses the intentions of the rider. Our sensory system brings messages from outside and our commanding energy directs the motor system to meet external confrontation. They are like a managerial system where the will of the general manager is represented by various message-giving centers of the body.

To make our study comprehensive and without confusion, the whole system is to be delimited to a single unit called *loka*. Although literally the word *loka* means 'the world', when it is closely examined, it is reduced to a precise point of view. Vision comes into the eye and the interpretation of it comes from the intelligence (*prajñānam*) which is always vigilant in the inner *ākāśa* of the organism which governs the perceiving eye (*dṛk*). The fabrication of the world, however enormous it looks, is through cohesive aggregates of several points of view. Instead of looking into the plurality of points of view, we should apply the method of reduction to the essential. By accepting this methodology for our study of the Self, then we simplify the task of knowing ourselves by examining thoroughly one unity which is put in the center of our focus of study. *Prajāpati* is a single functional system producing within it the essentials that are required to be, to grow, to change, to elaborate, to visualize values and to function for the actualization of values.

Within the *prajāpati* we see its essence which is a tribasic system. The first is the sublime which is closer to the idealized spirit in which many approximations of the divine can be traced.

The origin of the *prajāpati* as a satisfactory answer to the eternal need of life can be epitomized in the idea of the divine. Without going into the details of the operational commencement of the light of awareness that is required for all subsequent system-building, we go to the creative aspect of generating images. The world in which we live is, so to say, built stone by stone, with a foundation, superstructure, and roof - an infrastructure which provides for the actualization of several values which are sublime and profound, necessary and aesthetic, utilitarian and mundane. The third aspect is a depth from which crude energies can be received for sublimation and into which waste can be conveniently disposed. This darkness is absolutely necessary and it acts beneficially as a foundation. Thus the divine, the human, and the demonic are all to be seen sitting juxtaposed within a single person. They are complementary, although when they are undisciplined there can be conflict. The harmonies of coexistence and the contingencies of conflict bring pleasure which can be maximized as ecstasy of the highest order, and pain which can be compared to hellfire.

Our personas are not built by stones, but by ideas (*kalpana*), small units of images which are fed from the unconscious to the preconscious and brought to their final finish in the light of the luminosity of the Self. However, this does not happen smoothly. Imagination (*kalpana*), when favored by *sattva*, becomes *sankalpa*, leading to positive results. But it can also be afflicted by *tamas* and manifest as *vikalpa*, which is governed by dark urges and leads to negativity. The substance of what we have said so far is that for each one of us there is only one world. That is what we each call "myself". That world is an actualization of the total creative energy of one's manifestation, i.e., the *prajāpati*. In that, one cluster of attitudes makes one divine, another set of attitudes makes one a human, and a third set of primitive urges makes one a demon. However ugly those urges are, out of them the most sublime aesthetic sensibility and spiritual wisdom are to be evolved. Looked upon this way, there is no hell outside, no heaven outside, no world outside. All pluralities organically belong to the unity of one's being.

Now we can see how the false fabrication of heaven and its denizens, the earth with its socio-political histories, and hell with its wildest screams of fear causes millions of people everywhere to undergo excruciating pain, shame, and misery. All these are man-made hypotheses which have become the most deplorable concepts of theology, religion, science, sociology, political economy, and every kind of belligerency. To clear the board of all such misconceptions we should make a valiant attempt to go through the entire maze of conceptualized beliefs.

A deep psychological analysis is to be made to understand the images we generate inside, the emotional energy source that generates imaginations that can foster sustaining faith in us, the energizing value which is fed into images and the shifting values that intrinsically belong to the inner dynamism of personality formation. In Sanskrit these basic terms are given as *bhāva* (attitude), *bhāvana* (imagination), *āśakti* (mercurial fluctuation of pain/pleasure), and *rasa* (the basic modes within each person's personality conceived to be kaleidoscopically functioning.

In an ultimate sense, if you ask "What is *brahman?*" your answer is "This"; if you ask "What is *ātman?*" your answer is "This"; if you are asked "Who is *prajāpati?*" your answer is "This". "This" can also be interpreted as "I am." So you can say, "I am *brahman,*" "I am *ātman,*" "I am *prajāpati,*" "I am this world." If these questions have the same answer, we can ask one more question, "Are you always the same?" The answer is, "No." If we continue and ask, "What is always the same in you?" the answer is, "My intrinsic form (*svarūpa*)." And if we ask, "What is changing in you?" the answer is, "My attitude or nature (*svabhāva*) and my innate potential (*svadharma*)."

"How do you explain your *svarūpa?*" The answer is rather complicated. "In certain respects I resemble my father or some person in the family tree of my father from whom the gene which decides my morphology has come. I also resemble my mother or somebody in the family of my mother from whom I have genetically inherited certain other of my morphological specialties. It is only natural that when two metals are made into an alloy they make a third metal which is not like either of them. It is much more complex than this in living beings. Before entering into this body, I came from another father and mother and their family tree, and before that my genetic inheritance came from the common seed of two other family trees. Thus it goes back *ad infinitum.*

So there is a third factor in me which belongs neither to my paternal seed nor to my maternal egg. It comes from my true being. This is the *manuṣyā* in me. Thus I am the product of an alchemy of my paternal and maternal genes plus a continuing *puruṣa* in me."

Now we ask another question, "If the *puruṣa* in you is the same, why do your *svabhāva* and *svadharma* sometimes vary?" The answer to this is also complicated. My attitude *(bhāva)* is influenced by the divine in me, the human in me and the demon in me. The divine refers to the element *ākāśa* and its benevolent quality of generating the vibrations of melody, harmony, contemplation and sublimity. For instance, if my mind is raised by an elevated contemplative pondering, I feel one with the whole world. Then I am a being without frontiers, very much like the sky. The most subtle and sublime poesy of the highest form of transcendental aesthetics can easily absorb me into its serenity. Then what shines in me is the quality of the divine. Then my *bhāva* also becomes blissful, meditative, devotional and loving without frontiers. That is the *īśvara bhāva* in me. There is nothing to obstruct or bind me, and I am one without a second, yet not having any body identity.

This *īśvara bhāva* cannot be maintained all through. I am exposed to several gradations of the *rajasic* quality of nature. They can make me take the several roles humans can play such as of a teacher, a husbandman, a father, a brother, a mother, a sister, a therapist, a musician, an artist, a person of creative responsibility, a servant, a trader - anything that brings me to an altered phase of attitude within the structured life of a human. Then I have *manuṣyā bhāva*. If it is influenced by my *īśvara bhāva*, then I have the quality of a contemplative seer, a *rishi*. If my *rajas* becomes intensified as a possessor of gratifying values, my *bhāva* can change into that of a jealous husband or an infatuated wife. I can feel very attached to a son or daughter or I may cling to my wealth as if that is my sole treasure. Then I will be far from the attitude of the divine.

Every living being is given some device for personal defense. The birds are given sharp beaks and steel-like claws. Even such small beings as wasps, scorpions, or centipedes have their protective devices. The demonic character is shared by all living beings. When it comes to the worst of the worst, I can also be cruel, ugly, aggressive, brutish, or remorseless. Then my *bhāva* is that of an *asura*. Evidently I am neither a god nor a demon, but these are two polarized extremities of my self into which I can conveniently shift the main thrust of my being.

What is said of one's *bhāva* is also applicable to one's *dharma*.

Dharma is the innate law which decides what is to be unfolded from the potential or latency of anything. First of all, *dharma* is the opposite of *brahman*. If *brahman* suggests the generality of universal being, *dharma* implies the specificity of individuation. Each individual being has a governing intrinsic law which makes it what it is. Some people think that *dharma* is righteousness but that is a narrow definition. It is not righteous for a *brāhmaṇa* to smite another person. But it is the perfect *dharma* of a cobra to charge at its enemy and to bite and kill with its deadly venom. So righteousness and the lack of righteousness do not conform to the normative notion of human sociology. It is perfectly right for a wasp to sting if its hive is attacked. So I do not have to be ashamed if I am sometimes called to have a demonic *svabhāva* or *svadharma*. Even in the legal codes of civilized countries, sanction is given to take extreme measures if you are convinced that your life is in danger at the hands of another.

Life is situational, circumstantial. We are not omniscient beings to know all the pros and cons of every situation. Our conclusions can be erroneous, hasty, and to that extent unjustifiable. It is to this realm of uncertainty and vagueness the occurrence of fate is attributed. Actually there is no fate. Fate is a name for a situation in which the innumerable hidden causes that lead to the occurrence of a tragedy cannot be easily traced and the cause and effect are comprehensively correlated. In spite of this the *devas* were advised to exercise control, the demons were advised to be compassionate and humans were advised to give and share.

Now another question, "Why is the divine asked to control?" The divine behavior pattern of control is to be exercised by each of us. Within each of us is a sympathetic divinity which is mirrored in the *sattva* quality of the person in whom nature provides for a whole-hearted appreciation of the sublime, the harmonious, and the beautiful. But as there is a human element involved, *rajas* will act upon *sattva*. Consequently the person will be infatuated to return to a situation where joy can be precipitated and perpetuated. The nature modality of *sattva* can bring the bondage of pleasure-seeking. So where there is pleasure, control is to be exercised so that horizontalization will not come in a person's life to deflect him or her from the norm of righteousness.

The demonic represents the *tamasic* modality of nature which is the very foundation of the world of empirical existence (*loka*).

Society is based on the foundation of static principles such as mores and conventions. Husbands and wives universally know that they do not belong to each other, but they profess this lie for the preservation of society. There is an old saying that it is certain who the mother is, but it is a belief who the father is. When Joseph was told by Mary that she had had a visitation from God who had impregnated her, he nobly did not want to make her a public example and have her stoned to death. So he agreed to take upon himself the foster fatherhood of Jesus. That is the great guarantee of *tamas*. Some things are agreeable to society only if they can be covered up. It is demonic, but in such cases the demon wins. If we consider the rulers of the world who are publicly acclaimed as the saviors of humanity, how many heads have they chopped in the history of mankind to preserve their seats of honor as heads of governments? How many people can speak the truth and the whole truth all the time in life if they are part of a family, a clan, a society, a government? The very system itself necessarily makes a person demonic to preserve all the diabolic secrets of the family, the home and the clan. *Tamas* is thus publicly denounced and privately adored.

The importance of the obstructing role of the demonic is supported by modern physiology which postulates the existence of a blood-brain barrier. Even though blood is the most rejuvenating liquid that should flow in to make every faculty work, experiments have shown that when acid dyes such as trypan blue were injected into living animals, all the tissues were stained except most of the brain and spinal cord. It has been established that "bile salts and catecholamines do not enter the adult brain in more than minute amounts. Proteins cross the barrier to a very limited extent, and it is because they are bound to protein that acidic dyes fail to stain neural tissue." [11] Even God requires a barrier so his innovations will not fall apart.

We should come to study the nature of *manuṣyā*, the human, with a well-scrutinized and well-measured understanding of norms. The human being is relativism incarnated with a capital R. So the norm for the human is moderation: to be moderately truthful, to be moderately moral, and consequently to be moderately simple also. The major sin of the human is avarice. A man always wants to put aside something for the fast approaching winter, not only for himself, but also for his wife and progeny, even at the cost of pushing his neighbor into the winter snow.

That is why *prajāpati* said, "Share." The admonition given by Jesus to his contemporaries in the Sermon on the Mount was this great theme of sharing. If you go back to the Ten Commandments of Moses and the dictates of the *Holy Qur'an*, you will find the echoes of the same teaching which *prajāpati* gave to the person who includes both the divine and the demonic as true aspects.

Why should the divine tolerate the demonic? According to the Biblical story of Genesis, God's dearest angel was Lucifer who became God's eternal enemy. However maligned Satan or the demons are, they have a vital role to play. Satan was allowed to survive along with God. Didn't God allow Job to be tested by Satan with only the slim condition that his life should not be taken away? Considering such stories which are abundant in the scriptures of all the major religions, the thundering voice saying, *"da, da, da,"* is relevant at all times and for the entire human race, which is at once divine and demonic.

In Genesis, the Bible says that God made man in his own image. It also says that out of the dust of the ground he formed an image and breathed his spirit into it. Here we see two elements in the composition of the man created by God: that which gives form - dirt, clay or dust - and that which gives animation - the spirit of God. This is a clear presentation of the *deva* and the *asura* in the human. Together they generate in a physical body a resemblance to the one who aspired to create something in his own image.

All religions present this same theory in one way or the other. The *Upaniṣads* say that the creator who was the spirit had no body, so it aspired to have a second one to give it company. That aspiration brought physicality as a companion. Whether we begin with matter fashioned into the human being and animated with the spirit of God, or with the original being assuming a physical form to fulfill a need for company, the duality of spirit and matter is always there. Sri Aurobindo takes the example of the coarse matter which is fashioned to be a chalice to hold the spirit of life. Matter is needed to give cognizability and it is filled with spirit so that everything about it becomes perfect.

We have a need to remake ourselves, since our origin is the dirt that has come from several human beings. The most smelly parts of a person's body are where one's excretions are made. All the excretions of a person are dirt: blood, saliva, urine, feces, tears, sweat, semen, the lubricant in the female organ. We come from exactly where the most smelly dirt is excreted. The beautiful lotus flower also is born in dirt. Brahma, the creator, is said to be born of a lotus which is born from the genital of Viṣṇu, the sustainer. Here genital is to be understood as the flowering aspect of a person. Like the lotus, our roots are in the mud, but we have the possibility of putting forth a beautiful blossom.

My mother is different from your mother; your father is different from another's father. But they all have erotics in common. We have all come from the compulsive urge of male and female to unite, to copulate. The most unrestrained act of a man is the emitting of his semen: he feels helpless about it and cannot do anything to stop it. As a result of the compulsion of the father, a sperm is emitted into the womb of the mother. In that dirty place it joins with an egg to make a small being that starts clinging like a leech to the wall of the womb, drawing out the vitality of the mother like a parasite. And from this beginning the image of God is produced. All the aspects of birth are archetypal: the passion between man and woman, the compulsion to unite, the thrusting of the male organ into the female, the compunction of the sperm shooting out of the man into the woman, the clinging to the mother, the duplication and proliferation of one cell into many.

In your own personal birth you can see the sum and substance of all of the archetypal behavior of human beings. You have been growing with all those instincts up till now, twenty, thirty, forty or fifty years. You have brought a lot of darkness with you: passion, aggressiveness, ego. And now you are being instructed how to transform that into a model human being who is a combination of the divine *(puruṣa)* and the natural *(prakṛti)*. It is here that the *Upaniṣad* says: "You are the god, you are the demon. But you can see neither the god nor the demon in you." When you love, you know you are god-like. When you hate, you know you are demon-like. You alternate between loving and hating. So the challenge before you is what Nataraja Guru called normalization and renormalization.

As an animal you are subnormal and as a human you have become abnormal. Your subnormality is to be raised to normalcy and your abnormality is to be brought down to normalcy. When the *Upaniṣad* tells us that we should listen to the mantra, make *manana* and then live it, we should understand that "live it" means to live the normalization. If you go out of your room and walk, the first thing that you experience is the air that you breathe which is continuously flowing to you from far-off time and space. It comes free to all of us and waits to be breathed in by us. This is the first benevolence a person experiences in this world. If you are not cognizant of that factor, something in you is dead, benumbed. You should see how the air that you breathe brings life-giving energy to every cell, how it fills your lungs. Your respiratory system is like a tree with millions of branches on it. When breath comes, it is like when the wind blows: every tree sways in the wind which flutters every leaf. The same happens in our respiratory system where the innumerable little leaf-like things that make up our respiratory tree all tremor with life. When you are aware of that, you are not a dead person; you are not in the dark; you have a sensibility to know the breath around and within you.

Then you see the sunlight coming and fondling every leaf, every blade of grass. It fills the atmosphere with a very special texture. When you notice such things, the demon in you is raised to a state of compassion. The world is always passionately hugging you. You become com-passionate to the world when you recognize the beauty of it.

This morning we saw the wonderful changes in the eastern sky - how the color was changing, how brightness was coming into the dark and finally how the sun made its appearance behind a cloud. This evening we saw the same sun behind clouds in the western sky, making the same kind of picture with the illumination of the clouds. You need to cultivate your sensibility to notice that the whole world is helping you to make yourself beautiful, to feel beautiful, to see beauty, and to resonate with the spirit that is embracing the whole world.

When we stand on the green lawn, some of us do not even notice that there is grass under our feet. If somebody stands on our toes, it hurts, but this tenacious grass is such that even when we stand on it, it is as if nothing is happening to the very gentle leaves. They continue to be fresh and green. It's a wonder. But to see it, you should have a heart which is mellowed with your humanity. More spirit needs to be put into the darkened aspect of your cognition. Every cognition is followed by a connation and then affection. If you are not affected by what you see, what you touch, what you feel, what you notice, what is the difference between you and a stone?

Reading a book and enjoying it is good, but reading yourself is more important. The language used to write a book has a grammar and a logic which govern how the words should be arranged to make meaningful sentences. Similarly, when you look at life to discover its grammar and logic, then alone are you participating in the remaking of your being.

A four year old child is automatically attracted to you and he comes toward you. He knows that you have love for him in your heart. You also feel the love which he recognizes. You automatically put your hand on his head. You can feel in the touch a vibration of human love. This is how you transform - not just by walking callously, not minding the huge trees that stand on either side of the road. The trees are older than you, bigger than you, yet they look so humble. They don't beat or bite you. It is as if they have all listened to the *prajāpati* not to hurt but to be compassionate. The *Upaniṣad* is not the only book which teaches you how to restructure your spirit. The whole world is teaching us how to restructure our being. There is a creeper waving in the breeze. Each flower holds itself out to us. It is only natural for us to bless the flowers, to touch, to look at each one of them. It is like holding the hand of a dear one.

When we see one spirit in all and extend cordiality to it, we allow ourselves to be bound by everyone around. But this should not be done with hypocritical pretense. People in the world around us may be going from organic to plastic, but we should be different. We should take it seriously that, although we are born out of dirt, we are growing into beauty that can be more than that of a flower. We should remember that "a thing of beauty can be a joy forever." We can be the essence of the beauty of humanity, the essence of the beauty of poetry, art, music, meditation. Such should be our attitude. Then alone will we be able to transform ourselves, restructure ourselves.

Brāhmaṇa 3

Mantra 1

eṣā prajāpatiryadhṛdayam; etad brahma, etat sarvam;

tadetat trayakṣaram – hṛdayamiti; hṛ ityekamakṣaram; abhiharantyasmai svāścānye ca ya evam veda; da ityekamakṣaram; dadatyasmai svāścānye ca ya evam veda; yamityekamakṣaram; eti svargam lokam ya evam veda.

Word Meanings

eṣaḥ - this; *prajāpatiḥ* - (is) *prajāpati; tat yat* - that which; *hṛdayam* - (is) heart (intellect); *etat* - it; *brahma* - (is) *brahman; etat* - it; *sarvam* - (is) all; *tat etat* - this; *hṛdayam* - (name); *hṛdaya* - *hṛdaya; trayakṣaram iti* - consists of three syllables; *hr* - (is); *ekam* - one; *akśaram* - syllable; *asmai* - to one; *yaḥ* - who; *veda* - knows; *evam* - thus; *svāḥ ca* - relatives and; *anye ca* - others; *abhiharanti* - bring (presents); *da* - *da; iti* - is; *ekam* - another; *akṣaram* - syllable; *asmai* - to one; *yaḥ* - who; *veda* - knows; *evam* - thus; *svāḥ ca* -relatives and; *anye ca* - others; *dadati* - give (their powers); *yam* - *ya; iti* - is; *ekam* - another; *akśaram* - syllable; *yaḥ* - one who; *veda* - knows; *evam* - thus; *eti* - goes to; *svargam lokam* - the world of heaven

This is *prajāpati* - that which is the *hṛdaya* (intellect). It is *brahman;* it is all. This name *hṛdaya* consists of three syllables. *Hṛ* is one syllable. To one who knows thus, relatives and others bring presents. *Da* is another syllable. To one who knows thus, relatives and others give (their powers). *Ya* is another syllable. One who knows thus goes to the world of heaven.

In the previous two *brāhmaṇās* we saw three progeny of *prajāpati,* respectively known as the shining one (*deva*), the human (*manuṣyā*) and the obstructor or shielder of light (*asura*). Further we have seen that the *prajāpati* is like a universal father who is interested in the welfare of all and keeps his progeny under his personal care. When Jesus was about to be crucified, he told his disciples that he would go to God his Father and send in his place the Holy Spirit to be in each person's heart to give them his guidance, benediction and support (St. John 15:26). Similarly, we should understand the one *prajāpati* as having become all embodied beings within which there is a spark of illumination, a spark of mentation, and a proportionate degree of veiling or brutish character. *Prajāpati* as the caretaker of each being's welfare sits in the heart like the Holy Spirit.

Dama or restraint is to be applied in interpersonal relationship. That fosters a sublime awareness in us and we come to a state of at-one-ment. When restraint is applied in intrapersonal relationship it is called *sama,* tranquillity. All living beings have fear which is the most dominant of all instincts. The first fear is of death. Even microbial beings take precaution not to be destroyed, and the fear of death is very much in the preconscious and unconscious minds of human beings. Modern people who are very sophisticated experience varieties of fear pangs, but they are obliged to hide most of them. This causes the agony of repressed fear. Maintaining the outward facade of calmness creates such a conflict that most people have a built-in schizophrenia.

Human beings not only hide their fear. They also take precautions to safeguard their security by hoarding food, clothing, and other amenities of life, land and as much money as possible in all forms like bank deposits, hidden cash, gold and precious stones. From the drive for self-preservation, a counter instinct that supports fear waxes in the human mind in the form of greed. If happiness breeds desire, greed builds up avarice, hoarding tendencies, and anxiety about threats to one's security symbols. The repressions of the shining ones and the human go to the very grassroots of life where the demons lie dormant in a person. Therefore, the catharsis of rage comes when the most gentle person will flare up and become an assassin if rubbed the wrong way.

Where do all these seeds of discord as well as concord lie? They are in the heart. Both the demonic spirit and the holy spirit have their co-existence in the heart. Thus a person is fated to always have a tormented mind, torn between piety and cruelty. In the seat of the spirit, *deva, manuṣyā* and *asura* all live hushed in a single unit. The *prajāpati* or the all-seeing spirit is in one's very heart and no person can hide any thoughts, words or deeds from it. Therefore the heart is called the spirit-witness *(manasākṣi).* In the heart the sense of guilt accumulates and one starts feeling sinful. So one has to seek in one's own heart the redeemer from sins and befriend the divine which dwells in the heart.

This theme is very prevalent in the religions of Judaism, Christianity and Islam. Vaiśnavism, Śaivism, and Śāktaism also think of the divine dwelling in the devotee's heart. The Vaiśnava people think of Viṣṇu as the indwelling immortal enshrined in the heart of each person. The followers of Śiva think that a spark of Śiva has been lent by him to be the soul of every living being. Another group in India thinks of the divinity enshrined in everything as the Mother. The Buddhists, especially of the *Mahāyāna* sect, have developed so many concepts of arranging the most weird as well as the most sublime into a symbolic language where the word itself indicates that the prime requisite is the heart.

Traditionally, *hṛdaya* has been translated as intellect in these mantras. In the *Amarakośa,* the entire subject of the relationships between mind, intelligence and the central value system of consciousness are all given in the chapter titled *dhīvargaḥ*. It is very interesting to see the order in which the synonyms are given in the *Amarakośa*. It begins with *citta,* taken from the root defined as *cittī samjñāne. Samjña* refers to the mark of recognition. Recognition has within it cognition and recognition. Whatever we cognize goes to our faculty of memory from where it can be recalled. Thinking needs a feeding in of primary notions and a reconsideration of those through recognition. *Citta* is the faculty of remembrance as a key idea, what is called the noem. All the other words are noematics derived from the noem, *citta.* which is related to an aspect of *cit* consciousness unalloyed and pure. This consciousness is said to have its origin in the self-luminous light of the soul or Self. As everything is pervaded by the light of pure consciousness or the Self, it is called *cinmaya.* When the light of the Self animates a psycho-physical body, the light of the Self shining through the organism is called *caitanya.* When the animation is a singled out instance of the luminosity of the Self, it is called *cetas.*

The syllable *hṛ* in the word *hṛdaya* is related to sounds like *hara, hari, haraṇa.* It refers to the dynamics of attraction. Śiva is called Hara, and Viṣṇu is called Hari. The art of thieving is called *haraṇa,* that is, appropriating a value which belongs to another. The heart is considered to have all these qualities. Each person's heart is a cupid to another's heart. The heart sucks into it anything enjoyable. As the highest value of all is God, God is considered to be enshrined in the heart. When a thing is seen or heard, the heart takes it to its deepest core to ponder over its significance, its depth, and its sublimity. This act of pondering is called *manana.* Hence heart can also be called *mānasa.* The term *mana* on the one hand indicates a functional aspect of memory and recognition and hence it is *manascitte,* belonging to *citta.* But it is also the intellectual function of cognition and hence is called *manīṣāyām.* As the intellect is like a spotlight which focuses on what it wants to know precisely, it is called *buddhi.* As consciousness is always on the move, the flow of consciousness is given as *manīṣa (manasaḥ īśa). Īśa* also means plowing into. The mind plows into the hidden truth. As intelligence gives people expertise, the term *dhiṣaṇā* is derived. It is called *prajñā,* because everything that comes to our conscious mind is supposed to remain latent in an inner space. The inner space is called *cidākāśa,* and the latency is called *avyākṛta.* The inner sky with the potentials of revealing the world is *prajñā* which is seen in one's deep sleep. *Prajñā* is otherwise called *śraddha. Śraddha* is bringing consciousness to a one-pointed attention. From all these derivations and synonyms we can see that even the language has mainly developed from the qualities of the heart and the powers of manifestation.

In this mantra we read that presents are brought to the one who understands the syllable *hṛ. Hṛ* is the attracting power of the heart. In a dead person, the heart is no longer pulsating. No feeling is there. So people want to dispose of that body as fast as they can. A corpse is sometimes preserved for a few days or embalmed only because that body once contained a heart. Love is considered to be the most precious gift of the heart. God is even called a stealer of hearts, *hṛdayacora* or *hṛdayahara.*

The next syllable after *hṛ* is *da. Da* means that which enables you to share, give gifts, or give yourself to another. *Ya* indicates the difficulty to discern. Nobody can really know how valuable the heart is, and what it preserves. Only the person who owns the heart knows the full value of it, and what it holds. Heaven is in one's heart. With whatever one preserves in one's heart, even when the body is given up, one can live in the heart of others. A person's love, kindness, compassion, beauty, wisdom and service are remembered by others until they die. So one can live on in one's reputation *(kīrti).* Thus a eulogy is paid to the concept of heart.

In the previous *adhyāya* (III.5.24-28), a dialogue between Yājñavalkya and Śākalya established that the highest wisdom of the Absolute is known only to the wise person who can fully establish the greatness and meaning of the heart. Here *prajāpati* is identified with *hṛdaya*. When we study the physiology of a living body, the heart is the most central faculty which is in full governorship of the organism. It not only gathers into it all the elements that are required to generate and circulate the vital sap of the body, but also distributes the most vital elements required for our origin, growth and development. The blood is vital not only to the body, but also to the mind, especially in generating emotive energies and controlling them. Our bodily function itself is a highly complicated biophysical, biochemical system which is intrinsically connected with the release and control of various chemical energies as well as electrical energies. Just as we began life as a fertilized egg, every little organ in us came pushing through from its latent aspect to its actualization. Every cell of our bodies, every physiological organ also has its *prajanana*, birth or projection. We can take the heart as the source from which the birth of every other part of our body has come. So it is very appropriate to say that the *prajāpati* is the heart.

In the *Vedas* as well as the *Upaniṣads* certain words are indiscriminately used as having the same meaning. For instance, the two terms *brahman* and *ātman* are exchangeable in their connotation in accordance with the context where the word is used. The Self (soul) and the body are both called *ātman* in the *Upaniṣads*. In most places *ātman* means the animated body and not the soul or Self. Similarly, *prajāpati* is indiscriminately identified with *hiraṇyagarbha* and *virāj*. *Virāj* is the first concept in the *Veda* which integrates the highest into one single formation described in the tenth *maṇḍala* of the *Ṛg Veda* as the Cosmic Person (*virāṭ puruṣa*). This concept of transactional identification comes between the first cause and its universal effect. *Brahman* is sometimes referred to as *kāraṇa brahman*, absolute cause, and *kārya brahman*, the unbounded manifestation of the universe. Although in principle *Vedānta* is supportive of the idea of the One without a second, in our daily life, we always encounter the notion of the many. Therefore there has to be a continuous exercise of the mind to again and again find similitude between the seemingly diverse forms, names, and functions. There is a central focal point to which all the pluralities are to be centripetally referred, to give full orientation of our understanding of *brahman*. This central focus is found in the heart. That is why *prajāpati* is identified with the heart.

The heart is the physical terminus of life in this organism. At the same time, the most sublime of our thoughts such as love, devotion, reverence to truth, fidelity, sense of justice, compassion and willingness to share, are all direct consequences of the state of the heart. Heart is also to be seen as the origin of life. For all these purposes any spiritual quality that is to be attained is to be ultimately experienced or imperientially reckoned with in the heart. In the light of this important role which the heart plays, we should see how the divine in us originates in the heart and finds its evolution and nurturing through the heart's condition. Although our physical heart looks rather sensitive and made of soft material, it is one of the toughest functional parts of the body. Even when all the other parts of the body get their opportunity to relax and cease active functioning for a little while, no such privilege is given to the heart muscles. They have to be active right through, insuring that everything happening to a person will be brought to a homeostasis in spite of the continual fluctuations that happen from moment to moment.

Genetically and culturally, the person within our person is always alive to the purpose of our life. Freud gave it a title of the super ego, but he did not adequately explain how the super ego is like a watch dog keeping the external activities in tune with the social mores and laws as well as aligning the outward hypersensitiveness of socio-cultural life with the innermost vision of the purposiveness of individuation. If *deva* or the shining one is identified with the super ego, it also has to function as the heart. The grassroots of the ego have to be in the psycho-biologic sources of life as well as the sociobiology of exterior situations. It is the interior situations which bring all the pathological control and chaos of psycho-neurosis. Even before a certain desire is hatched out in the secret core of the mind, it is to be corrected by *sama*. The counterpart of that is the external arouser of emotive dynamics. The *Upaniṣad* is now speaking of the regulator of the environmental arouser, but that is also to be seen as the internal counterbalancing principle which fosters habitual conformity to the right form of behavior.

What *prajāpati* wanted the shining one (*deva*) to do was not the brute control of passion. There are many restrictive structural arrangements within the body to checkmate inner passions. External vigilance is to be understood as being in the makeup of a personality which is mainly established on serenity, calmness, love, willingness to sacrifice and other such higher qualities. The shining one is not a separate person; it is a part and parcel of our personality. The cultural evolution of living a decent and dignified life among the members of one's society is thought to be the prime duty of the *deva*.

The instruction given to the extreme aspect of individuation, the dark one (*asura*), is to have compassion. The *prajāpati* asked the rigid inner defense principle to tame itself. That is called *daya*. One meaning of the word *daya* is 'yielding'. In traffic, if one lane is about to infringe on another, a sign is displayed which says 'Yield'. In a situation where you are asking the chief controller of your heart, "What should I do?", the answer is, *da*, "Give up your defenses, be compassionate." Give the benefit of the doubt to the other. That gives more emphasis to the person who holds both the transcendent and aesthetic aspects of life's sublime beauty within, while maintaining vigilance for the safety of the being by policing interpersonal relationships.

The human is considered to be rational and intuitive. The middle '*da*' directs us to part with our fortunes to the benefit of the other because in our higher understanding we will come to appreciate that the one who seems to be the other is none other than ourselves. There is an intriguing word in Sanskrit for that, *apara*. *Para* means the other person. *A* means not. So *apara* is one who is not another person but yourself. Seeing the other as yourself is *advaita*, non-dualism.

The main crux in asking human beings to give is that of cutting asunder our social inclinations. We give but we normally do it only when there is a favorable link between ourselves and another. One gives to his wife or children, or close relatives, and refuses to give when the relationship is not engraved in the depth of kinship. Only with a philosophical vision of seeing all in one can we share beautifully. That is why Christianity put forward the ideal of a common fatherhood which transcends the affinity of the biological father: from the fatherhood of God comes the brotherhood of man, sharing everything you have without any discrimination of caste, community, nationality or language.

This kind of arrangement is given in Freudian psychology also. Freud places the ego between the id and the super ego. The id is like the *asura*, the brute, a creature of needs and wants. In our social life the id is like an infant, a child, who is always obstinately desiring to fulfill its needs. Its weapon to make its parents yield is crying to make life intolerable for the parents. The parents always have to see if the child's action will find acceptance in the social circle. The social decree is identified with the mandate of the super-ego. The ego is like the human who is caught between love and authority. The adult is authoritarian; the child is irrational. The ego is an embodiment of both love and righteousness. There is always a tussle between these two. Thus a person is torn between the paradoxical tenacity of the brute, and the overall sympathy of the divine.

To show the oneness of all hearts, the *Upaniṣad* goes into a philological tangent, showing that the three syllables of *hṛdaya* are one, and making a supplication to the heart. This gives a mystical touch to the mantra. References to *hṛ*, *da* and *ya* can be found in several sources such as the *Chāndogya Upaniṣad, Katha Upaniṣad, Śvetāśvatara Upaniṣad, Maitri Upaniṣad, Mahānārayana Upaniṣad, Praśna Upaniṣad, Gauḍapāda Kārika*, and various *Yoga Upaniṣads*. [12]

Brāhmaṇa 4

Introduction

At the very commencement of the *Bṛhadāraṇyaka*, the symbol presented for contemplative meditation was the figure of a sacrificial horse. In the pre-Upaniṣadic period, sacrifice meant the annihilation of a victim to be burned in the sacrificial fire. The first injunction given to Moses in the Pentateuch was "Thou shalt not kill." The same is repeated in the teachings of Christ. The cardinal teachings of the *Upaniṣads* are stated as *ahimsa*, non-hurting, *satyam*, truthfulness, and *asteyam*, non-stealing. Thus we find a departure from killing to non-killing. According to the Old Testament, God wanted the patriarch Abraham to kill his dearest son, Isaac, as a sacrifice to Him. Abraham was willing, but at the very last moment, God showed his mercy and asked the sacrifice of Isaac to be substituted with the killing of a ram. Killing was not avoided but was transferred from the human to an animal.

In the genesis given in the *Bṛhadāraṇyaka Upaniṣad*, life was generated to appease the universal hunger of fire. When the first living organism came into being, hunger opened its mouth, wanting to devour the tiny wisp of life in the form of *prajāpati*. The very first articulation by the first of all beings was given as *bhān* which was in another sense asking death to spare the little being. Thus the first of all invocations recorded by the *Upaniṣad* was an invocation to show compassion.

The *udgītha*, which was meant to be a device to save one from mortality, came in the form of a hymn to be recited: *asatomā sat gamaya, tamaso mā jyotir gamaya, mṛtyor mā amṛtam gamaya*. In these three lines, there are three pairs of contradictory phenomena. In the first line, the unreal *(asat)* is matched against the real *(sat)*. In the second line, darkness (*tamas*) is to be destroyed by light *(jyotis)*. In the third line, mortality (*mṛtyu*) is to be transcended by immortality *(amṛtam)*. All three invocations stem from fear and a seeking of refuge in truth, light and immortality respectively .

The Greek mystics spoke of the primeval chaos which is like the disorderly mixing up of truth and untruth. The reconstruction of chaos into cosmos came second. The appeal is to love which can bring order into the darkness of life. Consequently, death is pushed away and its place is taken by the harmony of the cosmos. In most religions, the Supreme is invoked as the benevolent and the merciful. In Islam, at the opening of any endeavor, the mercy of Allah is remembered as characterized by *rahman*, the most gracious, and *rahim*, the benevolent. The three great descriptions of the Divine are the omnipresent (the existential basis of everything); the omniscient (the light of knowledge that kindles wisdom or right knowledge in the manifested) and the omnipotent (the possibility of transforming even death into immortality).

In every contemplative discipline, the excesses of two opposites are canceled out to arrive at a neutral normalization as the homeostasis of what originally appear to be uncompromising opposite characters. In the first *adhyāya*, mind itself was depicted as being first craved for as a means to transcend the enigma of the polemics of life and death. Mind is to effect the bipolarity of opposites. The possessor of the mind *(manas)* is the *manuṣyā*. Etymologically, the Indian term '*manu*', the first possessor of the mind, is identical with the English term 'man'. The secret indication in the term man or *man* is that of transcending mortality and living in a name. In the *Upaniṣad* it is said that the only thing that remains after death is the name. The first part of speech, noun, is also the indicator of name.

Light and darkness are the dialectical counterparts of everything that has assumed a form and a name. Before a formation comes, the being remains midway between the real and the unreal. The sperm is not real until it makes its way into an ovum. The ovum will deteriorate and be washed away if not fertilized. Thus it is from an opening incident of a 50-50 probability of being and non-being that birth comes. Until birth, the form is not released. Once it is revealed, it is ready to be named. In the *Upaniṣad* it is said "the name is the *ṛk*." *Ṛk* gives the status of having nomenclature. What is private, unknown, secret and personal becomes a public knowledge to which the attention of the world is turned. With name, every form is introduced to the perceiver. From the darkness, identity is raised to an eternal position. Jesus says, 'the candle is not to be lit and kept hidden under a bushel. It should be put on a candle stand in a prominent place where all can see it." The invocation of the *udgītha*, bringing us from darkness to light, is a supplication that is answered by giving a name to that which has come into the status of the real. Once the real is emphasized it goes into universal memory. Appearance will fade out but the essence remains.

Such are some of the indications we have when we go from the first chapter of the *Bṛhadāraṇyaka Upaniṣad* to the last chapter where the same truth-seeking being who craves for knowledge comes to the portals of death. Death has to favor that being with the secret of the essence of life. We have an *Upaniṣad* entirely dedicated for this purpose where a truth-loving youngster, Nachiketas, seeks out death to know from death's own mouth what life is. It is to that death, sought out in the netherland, that the invocation is made to show compassion.

In the universal myth of the world of death presented in the Greek stories, we read of Orpheus going into the dark world to claim his love, Eurydice. The king of death agreed to give her back provided Orpheus would not turn back and look at his beloved while she was following him back to life. But his compassion was so much that he turned to see her and the story goes that they were both confined to darkness forever. In Indian mythology, the god of death claims the life of Satyavan and takes him away to oblivion. But his wife Savitri follows her ill-fated husband and brings him back to the miracle of life. What is mythically given and metaphysically explained in such stories is presented here as a riddle. No such riddle can be solved without effacing one's ego and merging with the neutral zero where the paradox manifests. These indications provide us with guidance to the interpretation of this *brāhmaṇa*.

Mantra 1

tadvai tadetadeva tadāsa--satyameva; sa yo haitam mahadyakṣam prathamajam veda satyam brahmeti, jayatīmāṁllokān; jita innvasāvasat, ya evametam mahadyakṣam prathamajam veda satyam brahmeti; satyam hyeva brahma.

Word Meanings

tat vai tat- that (*brahman*); *āsa* - was; *eva* - verily; *etat* - this; *satyam* - *satya; eva* - only; *saḥ yaḥ* - whosoever; *veda* - knows; *etam ha* - this; *mahat* - great; *yakṣam* - adorable; *prathamajam* - first-born one; *iti* - as; *satyam brahma* - *satya-brahman; jayati* - wins; *imān* - these; *lokān* - worlds; *it nu* - thus; *asau* - the (enemy); *yaḥ* - (of one) who; *veda* - knows; *etam ha* - this; *mahat* - great; *yakṣam* - adorable; *prathamajam* - first-born one; *iti* - as; *satyam brahma* - *satya-brahman*; *jitaḥ* - (is) vanquished; *asat* - (and becomes) a nonentity; *hi* - for; *satyam* - *satya; eva* - verily; *brahma* - (is) *brahman*

That *(brahman)* was verily this - *satya* only. Whosoever knows this great adorable, first-born one as the *satya-brahman* wins these worlds. Thus the enemy of one who knows this vast, adorable first-born being as the *satya-brahman* is vanquished and becomes a nonentity. For *satya* is verily *brahman*.

This *brāhmaṇa* is an epitomized elucidation and propitiation of truth. Truth is a small word that has somehow become the most revered among all spoken or written words. Even people who have a hesitation about believing in God or paying homage to God think of truth as paramount. One reason for this reverence for truth is its non-anthropomorphic distinction. It implies a categorical stress that anything other than truth will be disputed and ultimately disregarded. For this reason all philosophers give arguments and counter-arguments to establish the truthful foundation on which their systems are established. Liturgies, psalms, anecdotes, miraculous episodes, poetic effusions, proverbs and compendiums of the teachings of masters all have the intention of claiming truth as the hallmark of their respective religion. No other word, thought, spoken or written, can give supremacy over the glory of truth.

We come to the fifth *adhyāya* after discussing threadbare even the most minute item that attracts people in their various daily experiences. We have had occasion to consider untruth and half truths, or what Yājñavalkya called one-footed truths. Now we reach the inevitable conclusion about truth to which we should come to close the gestalt started from the first mantra of the first *brāhmaṇa* of the first *adhyāya*. We initiated the fifth *adhyāya* with a promise to chart the previously unobserved and unscrutinized aspects of the possibilities of life that can benefit humanity at large. The conclusion stated here is a commencement of a new adventure of the spirit in its search for hitherto unknown truth. It makes the *Khila Kāṇḍa* thrice more important and even adorable.

We began with an invocation of *AUM* which includes the four-fold scheme of the Supreme comprised of the three altering states of consciousness which have for their ground the unaltering constant which is also inexpressible. After that, the first mantra of the first *adhyāya* was *AUM kham brahma* which presented the pure space of consciousness (*ākāśa*) as an analogy for the idea of *brahman*. We saw *ākāśa* as the unmanifested pure space of all potentials. It was complemented with the possibility of being chronologically filled to accommodate all the evolutionary aspects of creative forces. Thereafter we came to space being filled with the invigorating vitality of air as *prāṇa*. Then we went into a detailed analysis of the tribasic aspect of individuation. Suggestions were made of how the raw energies of the divine, the human and the demon can be brought to their superior end-goals with a program of transmuting them with restraint, the love of sharing and compassion.

Now we want to consider this word truth from all possible angles of word analysis. In English, another word which sometimes substitutes for truth is the real or reality. To understand the distinction between truth and the real we should go to their parallels in Sanskrit. In Sanskrit, the ultimate truth is called *paramārtha* and the real is called *yathārtha*. *Param* means the transcendental, *parama* means the ultimate.

When physicists consider the truth of this world, the very first thing they do is discredit what is being presented as the data of sensory perception. They go beyond what is seen. Although scientists make a big fuss about the objectivity of the truth they establish, they have come to a clearer understanding that what they seek is a universal conviction which belongs to an indefinable faculty which is continuously giving a foundation to the normative notion of being. Like us, physicists also see the earth, water, mountains, individual trees, iron ore, and refined iron or steel. But their interests lie elsewhere. They always wonder how the phenomenal world can be reduced to mathematically calculable entities where measuring proves a consistency that enables them to declare universal truth. They pin their faith to the constancy of the speed of light being emitted from the sun which comes to our earth every day. This calculable certitude of light is more truthful to them than the fact of seeing things in sunlight. The characteristic radiation of energy which can be explained by quantum mechanics is more meaningful to them than the utility of energy. The truth the scientists want to declare is that which is uniform, universal and predictable, which can be shared with all other people who have a disciplined intelligence.

The term *satya* is more a question than a noun. The question is "What is this?" *Sa* stands for whatever is, and *ya* expresses one's wonder at the indiscernablity of the existential factor. *Ta* stands for a veiling of the eternal being, which offers constant and continuous challenge to the inquiring mind. *Ta* suggests *tamas*, meaning the dark. That is why in the *Chāndogya Upaniṣad* it is said *sa* is real, *ya* is real and *ta* is a lie. Nataraja Guru, in his *An Integrated Science of the Absolute*, says that there is a lurking paradox in the heart of the Absolute. The same can be said of truth and God. Even the best of human minds suspects at least for a split second the validity of what is heard for the first time. That is why the votaries of science have to kowtow before proof. Ever since man was struck with the wonder of lightning coming from the sky, he was postulating someone mightier than him up there producing the lightning, but to this day man doubts the postulation of God as an outside being. The same skepticism is held against truth also. But we need a normative notion to measure everything before we pin our faith to it. We want to go beyond, transcend the given, the presented.

To explain this paradox, Einstein says the world is a mystery like a closed watch. The frame of the watch is so made that it cannot be opened to look into the function of the inner structure. All that we see is the uniform movement of the hands of the watch and the ticking of time from within it. It is mostly the need for truth which makes truth unavoidable. The Vedāntins coined a word *prama,* which means certitude. Truth should be that which brings certitude. For a long time, mathematicians thought that they had overcome the problem of certitude by postulating the axiom, which they defined as that which is self-evident, thus needing no proof. It is this faith of the mathematician in the axiom that tempted Rene Descartes to establish a mathematical foundation for philosophy. He doubted God and the infallibility of scripture, and finally came to an axiom, 'I think therefore I am' (*cogito ergo sum*). But when physics changed, mathematics also changed. Modern philosophers, scientists and mathematicians have become skeptical of axiomatic truth.

Instead of basing the certitude of an axiom on the similarity of the subject and the predicate, Vedāntins use a term very similar to axiom. They call it *svātmanicchayam,* the irrefutability of a thing which is experienced in the heart or the Self. David Hume tried to bring clarity in what we call the irrefutability of truth. In his attempt, he spoke of the difference between logical truth and psychological truth. To avoid the confusion caused by psychological truth, Indians required three testimonies of truth: *anadhigatam* (not known before), *apūrvam* (not having existed before, incomparable) and *abādhitam* (an accepted truth cannot remain if it is sublated by a counter-statement of truth). The truth derived from experience is inferential and not perceptual. When you speak of truth being sublated by something which you already know, that is also a prejudicial influence. In spite of all the hallucinative effects which can stem from our visual or auditory faculties, we have no other windows for our souls to look at the presented world than our senses. Thus we are torn between our ideal of certitude and our means for arriving at truth. Mathematical rationality is not the same as empirical rationality. That is why philosophers of science like Bertrand Russell put forward the idea of logical positivism. He found it necessary to support the empirical evidence of utility without which scientific theories can be very misleading.

In Vedānta we find a similar stand of consistent denial of every particular experience as untruthful, "not this, not this" (*neti neti*) Yet the Vedāntins also say that the ultimate is the truth of truth (*satyasa satyam*). When they are squarely met and asked, "What is the truth?" their answer is surprising: "This, what you see." What is denied is the appearance empirically established by the special function of the five senses which mainly refer to the morphology presented in the vision and the conventional interpretation given to such data based on the memory registered in the *citta*. The true seer transcends the *citta* and goes to the *cit*, pure consciousness, which is the nature of the Self.

It is like a break-through of intelligence commissioned by the Self to see the universal truth of the Self itself through which the empirically established appearance is consciously recognized as a semblance for transactional purposes. Thus, even when the appearance is cognized along with the foundation, it is treated only as a phenomena which should not rouse any affectivity that can disturb the ego. This is like when a knowledgeable person automatically corrects a visual illusion such as refraction by applying the refraction index. Such a person knows that the bending does not belong to the object but only to the mechanism of the eye and the optic engineering implied in the illuminating light that reflects from objects.

When you take what you see as it is, that is what we call *yathārtha*, accepting a thing as it is. Apart from inductive or deductive logic, there is an intuitive assurance which comes from what Bergson and others call entering into a thing and being it. This can be quite confusing if people use their usual testimonies of truth such as perception, inference, analogy, residual truth and contradiction. This mechanical way of thinking and knowing is transcended by the wise person with the acceptance of an intuitive flash of truth. It is from that the word *para* is taken in *paramārtha*, which we here consider as equivalent to absolute truth.

The word 'real' (*yathārtha*) is used for the conformity of an accepted truth again and again in the same or similar circumstances. Here one caution is to be given: truth is not an entity and, even so, the real is also not an entity. Truth is the comprehensiveness of total understanding and the real is the unitary summation of whatever is individually encountered. We humans vouch for both the truth as well as the real, *yathārtha* as well as *paramārtha*. That is why Indians have accepted two frames of reference just as Emmanuel Kant was obliged to make a *Critique of Pure Reason* to complement the *Critique of Practical Reason*.

The emphasis that ensues from this mantra is that those who aspire for a thoroughgoing critical envisioning of the phenomenal world and its ground should necessarily go through a discipline which will cleanse their faculty of cognition and connation, leaving no residual memory to influence them or prejudice them as they make a case to case evaluation of the merit of life.

The Christian mystics have developed, in their faith in the adorable, a reciprocal profundity which makes 'that there' and 'this here' come to a state of at-one-ment. Although it is an anathema in Islam for a person to claim that he is God, Mansoor Hallaj, several hundreds of years after he was martyred for professing his intuitive oneness with truth, is still adored because of his innocence and honesty, which brought him to the uncompromising point of saying *an al haq*: "I am the truth."

This mystical point of view is also developed by the Taoists in the complementarity of *yin* and *yang* which occurs for just a split second because *yin* and *yang* are always on the move and always in a contradictory reciprocation. The same is developed by Zen masters who come to *satori* when contradiction pushes them to a neutral zero between the right and the wrong, the left and the right, the plus and the minus. It is in the spirit of that neutrality that Zen becomes accomplished. Thus this mantra is to be faced with a mystical fervor. Such a case was reported in the life of St. Francis of Assisi, who went into ecstasy on seeing the smile of Jesus in a blooming violet. You cannot enter into the spirit of these mantras without imbibing the poetic intuition of a mystical bard.

In the *Chāndogya Upaniṣad* when Uddālaka Āruni teaches the secret of *brahman* and gives the dictum *tat tvam asi* to Śvetaketu, he gives many examples to demonstrate the one existential truth which covers many presentations that one can see or know with the sense organs and the mind. Then he identifies *tat* with *tvam*. In this mantra we are told *tat vai tat*, "that *(brahman)* is verily this": the first principle *(tat)*, the universal being, is the *tat* which is seen individually also. It is further qualified as: (*satyam eva)* that alone is truth (*satya)*. When we say "this is a pot," we are referring to a gross manifestation which can be perceived with our visual faculty. When we say "this pot is clay", the clay aspect is the underlying principle out of which the potness is brought by the potter. The knowledge of clay comes to us only when we transcend the formal aspect of the pot and go to the substantiality of it. The existential verity of the pot is to be transferred into another mode of knowing the pot. Potness is subsisting in the material cause from which it is drawn, which is the clay. We can take it further to: "This is the pot I wanted to have because its dimensions and capacity to hold a certain quantity of water or cooked rice is just right." Here the reference is to the value aspect which takes us to a further degree of transcendence of the pot as well as the clay. It is possible to get stuck at the existential level, the subsistential level, or the value level. So philosophy is a necessity, not the joy of a verbal play with words.

The three aspects under consideration are *mahādyakṣam (*the existential*)*, the first born son of truth (the subsistential), and the heart where the manifestation of truth is felt even in ordinary folks (value aspects). As we are closest to our hearts the correct methodology to comprehend the meaning of the mantra is by going from our hearts where truth is experienced. There is a simple test of whether a person is speaking truth. If you unexpectedly ask someone to speak out a truth of which they are apprehensive, they will not be able to speak spontaneously. They have to pause before opening their mouth to speak. That pause indicates an inborn fear of letting out the truth. This physiological and physical reaction of the heart is what a lie detector registers. A person who knows the whole truth is the most successful in distorting it to the most efficient level of lying, because such a one can visualize truth from inside and go on modifying it bit by bit, falsifying everything. As human beings are much assailed by both rational and irrational fear, we are always on the defense. Untruth is used as a defense. But this mantra says that however much you fashion truth into untruth the truth will ultimately come out. "The enemy of one who knows truth is vanquished" - this is another way of saying, "Truth alone will shine forth and not untruth."

Infant babies and children of two or three years experience many eidetic illusions. But a sensible parent will not punish a baby for saying what it sees. If the child says, "Mummy, look at this golden wolf," the mother will only say, "Yes my darling, what a beautiful golden wolf." At the level of a child's comprehension that is how the child sees - like a dream vision. But if her husband says to the same woman, "Here is a golden wolf," she will protest and call in the psychiatrist. That means we have two versions of truth in our interpretation of life. One is a simple comprehension of the whole truth. The other is a compromised version of it to suit social circumstances. That is why the *Upaniṣad* gives us two solemn instructions: *satyam vaca*, 'speak the truth', and *dharmam cara*, 'live in *dharma*'. We are not asked to live truth; we are asked to speak truth. That means truth is a universal idea and not a specific manifestation.

The highest truth has a radical note; it is devoid of compromise. However, in social life, truth is watered down to many degrees of acceptance. In this context we are making a distinction between the all-inclusive truth which is felt in the heart, and truth that is compromised when the heart is moved by favoritism or personal affection. That is why in law, favoritism is considered as the worst enemy of justice. Justice in India is described as *ṛtam* and *dhruvam*, both of which imply uprightness from the root *ṛju* which implies an inner dynamic which upholds itself. The central meaning of this mantra is also reflected in presenting absolute truth as immediately experienced in one's heart. That is termed here as the *satya* of the heart, which is identified with *mahadyakṣam*.

Śankara brought in the theory of *māyā* to account for two kinds of universal errors. One is the specific error to which individuals are exposed because of several different kinds of weakness: physical, intellectual, moral and spiritual weakness. All these specific possibilities of error are termed *avidyā*. Hence from childhood intense training is needed to enable one to sort out appearance from reality. *Satya*, truth, is enveloped by *mithya*, deluding appearance. Discriminating between them is not to be just an intellectual exercise. Even animals know by instinct where there is love and where there is pretentious love. It is not the intellect which discerns here, but the heart. Between spouses, when the slightest aberration comes in the mind of one, the other instinctively feels a separation setting in. In our daily life, this discrimination of truth and untruth is to be exercised in almost all contexts. A lion or tiger or cobra never pretends. It is absolutely truthful in presenting its attitude to the offender. As man knows how to fashion truth he is the worst of all pretenders. We are cautioned that the scanning of truth should be meticulous, uncompromising and radical.

Out of compassion even great *gurus* sometimes condescend to accept certain gradations of compromise. Rāmānuja speaks of *svarūpa tāratamya*, which means a comparative degree of difference in the comprehension of truth about oneself. In this matter Śankara is uncompromising. He holds to the principle of total acceptance of truth and total rejection of untruth. A similar uncompromising attitude is held in the *Holy Qur'an* in which one hundred percent trust without the slightest compromise is insisted upon. These are certain principles of verity we have to hold in our mind to understand this mantra.

Brāhmaṇa 5

Mantra 1

āpa evedamagra āsuḥ, tā āpaḥ satyamasṛjanta, satyam brahma, brahma prajāpatim, prajāpatirdevān; te devāḥ satyamevopāsate; tadetattryakṣaram satyamiti; sa itye-kamakṣaram, tītyekamakṣaram, yamityekamakṣaram; prathamottame akṣare satyam, madhyato'nṛtam; tadeta-danṛtamubhayataḥ satyena parigṛhītam, satyabhūyam eva bhavati; naivam vidvāmsamanṛtam hinasti.

Word Meanings

idam - this (universe); *āsuḥ* - was; *eva* - only; *āpaḥ* - water; *agre* - in the beginning; *taḥ* - that; *āpaḥ* - water; *asṛjanta* - revealed; *satyam* - *satya; satyam* - *satya; brahma* - is *brahman; brahma* - *brahman; prajāpatim* - (revealed) *prajāpati; prajāpatiḥ* - *prajāpati* (revealed); *devān* - the shining ones; *te* - the; *devāḥ* - shining ones; *upāsate* - meditate upon; *satyam* - *satya; eva* - alone; *tat etat* - this; *satyam* - (name) *satya; iti tryakṣaram* - (consists) of three syllables; *sa* - *sa; iti* - (is); *ekam* - one; *akṣaram* - syllable; *ta* - *ta; iti* - (is); *ekam* - another; *akṣaram* - syllable; *yam* - *ya; iti* - is; *ekam* - another; *akṣaram* - syllable; *prathama uttame* - the first and last; *akṣare* - syllables; *satyam* - (are) truth; *madhyataḥ* - (the one) in the middle; *anṛtam* - (is) untruth; *tat etat* - this; *anṛtam* - untruth; *parigṛhītam* - (being) enclosed; *ubhayataḥ* - on both sides; *satyena* - by truth; *satyabhūyam bhavati* - has a predominance of truth; *eva* - alone; *anṛtam* - untruth; *na* - not; *hinasti* - hurt; *vidvāṃsam* - one who knows; *evam* - thus

This universe was only water in the beginning. That water revealed *satya*. *Satya* is *brahman*. *Brahman* revealed *prajāpati*, and *prajāpati* revealed the shining ones. The shining ones meditate upon *satya* alone. This name *satya* consists of three syllables: *sa* is one syllable; *ta* is another syllable; and *ya* is the third syllable. The first and last syllables are the truth. The one in the middle is untruth. This untruth, being enclosed on both sides by truth, has a predominance of truth alone. Untruth does not hurt one who knows thus.

Our empirical experience can be generally divided into knowledge and the known. There is a one-to-one correspondence between subjective knowledge and what is objectivized. We presume that what we infer, interpret, or comprehend on the basis of our perceptions is in exact correspondence with the objects of perception. This is the foundation of what we call our certitude of existence. In an experience, the agency that knows and the object that is known come into an intimate proximity. The knowledge arrived at through the organs of perception and the interpretation arrived at by the mind become so identified with the object that we cannot separate our knowledge from the known.

Through an overall awareness, we know that the knower is in us and that it is the knower who knows. The knower and the knowledge turn out to be a unified confection of the same phenomena viewed from two points of reference. This gives a hope that however big or small the known is and whatever its properties are, whether far or near, bright or dark, singular or plural, the truth of it can be comprehended by the self-luminous quality of awareness. Thus from our claim of irrefutable existence we come to the conclusion that existence is substantiated by knowledge.

Here a new identity emerges. What is existent is known; what is known has existence. If existence is termed *sat* in Sanskrit, subsistence is termed *cit*. Thus existence is of what is known, and subsistence is founded on the ground of existence. Normally such empirical experience comes from the five senses, and also from a psychological as well as logical coordination of the various sensory data affected by the cognitive process. Apart from the five senses and the objects comprehended by the senses, there is a reference which makes every percept fascinating. The excitement or fascination which truth brings to the central focus of a human being is in the heart which is considered to be the source of one's emotive life. It is not exposed to the presence of the outer world, and it does not function as a conceptual phenomena, but its impact on the total person is holistic, instant, very arresting and compelling.

That is why in the previous mantra *brahman* is identified with the heart. *Brahmavidyā* is the cream of mystical profundity. What certain mystics call the *mysterium tremendum* is to be attributed to the heart. There the absolutist version of existence *(sat)* and the substantiality of it *(cit)* are brought to the mystery of highest value, *ānanda*. We human beings experience the existential verity of a thing as a compelling acceptance of the irrefutable presence of something to our senses. That is called *asti*, which literally means, "this is." Hence in this mantra it is said, "What is recognized as this is that" meaning the absolute truth. Although the Absolute transcends time and clime, it can be individually referred to every point in space and every point in time and every formation which is named. We experience what is "out there" as truth. We testify to it by what is felt within as an irrefutable acceptance of truth.

In the hierarchy of individuation it is postulated that the supreme basis of truth is the Absolute (*brahman*). Its intense or intimate quality is luminosity, or, what is more precise, its numinous character. When the numenon is reflected in the physiologic medium of a person, its first-rate genuine quality is interfered with by the crudeness of the physical medium through which the numenon comes to mentation; this secondary experience of the numenon is called phenomena. In Sanskrit, especially in Vedānta, the intimate ground of absolute truth is pure awareness through and through, called *cit*. When *cit* horizontalizes and becomes *caitanya*, it percolates through the physiological medium, the biochemistry of the brain, the physical apparatus of vision, audition, and such sensory mechanisms. We get only a faint reflection or refraction of it which provides us with the data for piecing it together into a gestalt. Thus the gestaltation of the original is like an image of the image.

It is very intriguing that all knowledge we speak of is reported to us by organisms which are similar to our own, all made of the same coarse material which, when deprived of animation, becomes a corpse. The corpse continues to have all the physical features of a living person. But it is treated differently - either mummified, embalmed, entombed or burnt to ashes. The physical remains of a dead person speak no story, but while animation is there every person has some experience to relate. Living individual persons gather their information by listening to each other and comparing notes. But that which follows the actual imperiential impact of truth on the senses and mind, in which a person excitedly participates, is a secondary story. Anecdotal hearsay about the refracted secondary images of intimate expressions are pieced together as the common knowledge of humanity.

The meaning which is conventionally assigned to existence is misleading. We have to understand the whole process of the idea of existence that is so engineered to be the stable foundation of objectivized notions. This requires us to go into the very basics of the Vedāntic vision of truth. What is, is the Self alone. That means, what is can only be affirmed and it does not permit any denial. The affirmation, "is," as in "this is," is neither "is" nor "this." It is the self-luminous light which proclaims itself as "is" which, while being "is," is also affirming that it is. There is no separation between the concept of existence and the contents of it as a revealed truth. It is not anything else that is revealing one's being to oneself. It is the Self alone.

When we say, "this is truth," because of the peculiar requirements of verbalizing an idea and the application of parts of speech, an artificial language structure is made which seems to break the one and the same into a subject which is predicated with the intrinsic quality of the subject. The necessity of having language to communicate the self-revelation of being causes the concoction of one duality after another. Each time, because of the relativistic nature of concepts, knowledge always remains as if incomplete when clothed with words. True knowledge is only when knowledge, the known and the knower are undifferentiated. There are no separate items called existence, subsistence and value. So each time we use the word existence, we should know that, apart from our being, there is no existence. Our knowledge of being and our knowledge are not two things. Similarly, when knowledge is referred to, that is also to be understood as the knower and the known. In the same way, value is not to be understood as anything other than itself. Unless this is made crystal clear, the student will only be beating around the bush.

It is said here that the term *satya* has three factors in it: *sa*, that which is presented; *ya*, that which is mysteriously formulated within our heart which gives us a compulsion to accept it as a truth corresponding to what is being experienced; and in between, stands *ta*, this meager little creature of a person, which is none other than a perishable body with its anatomy and morphology and various kinds of bio-chemical metabolisms packed with filth, which is ever tending to decay and ultimately will be lost. That is why in the *Upaniṣad* it is said *sa* is truth, *ya* is truth, but *ta* is a dark spot *(tamas)*. There is a lurking darkness, an island of ignorance, in the very heart of truth. This is not to be known merely intellectually, but through contemplation.

Three factors are to be recognized to contemplate on *sa*. First, *sa* refers to the totality while the individual is looking at it from a fragmentary point of view. We insert ourselves into the total by our own conceptual ability which is rather meager. Only the divine or shining principle in us, that is, the numinosity of the Self, is capable of meditating on the Self. That is the only channel by which the individual gets even a meager idea of truth. Secondly, the Absolute (*brahman*) is a tremendous mystery, *mahādyakṣa*. What is so magnificent or tremendous is like the gold coin that can never be fully paid with our copper change. We should know this limitation to begin with. Thirdly, as there is a shadow cast by the light of the Supreme, truth is again and again interfered with by untruth. But one who knows the whole, including the limiting adjuncts, will be able to transcend that which seems to blindfold the individual seeker from time to time. It is not throug sensuous perception or mentation the seer becomes a seer of truth, but only by exercising a contemplative transcendence.

Mantra 2

tadyattatsatyamasau sa ādityaḥ, ya eṣa etasminmaṇḍale puruṣaḥ, yaścāyam dakṣiṇe'kṣanpuruṣaḥ; tāvetāvanyonyasmin pratiṣṭhitau; raśmibhireṣo'sminpratiṣṭhitaḥ, prāṇairayamamuṣmin; sā yadotkramiṣyanbhavati śuddham evaitanmaṇḍalam paśyati; nainamete raśmayaḥ pratyāyanti.

Word Meanings

tat - that; *yat* - which (is); *tat* - that; *satyam* - *satya; saḥ* - (is); *eṣaḥ* - the; *ādityaḥ* - sun; *puruṣaḥ* - the being; *asau* - that; *yaḥ* - who (is); *etasmin maṇḍale* - in the orb; *ca* - and; *ayam* - the; *puruṣaḥ* - being; *yaḥ* - who (is); *dakṣiṇe akṣan* - in the right eye; *tau* - these; *etau* - two; *pratiṣṭhitau* - rest; *anyonyasmin* - on each other; *eṣaḥ* - this (being in the sun); *pratiṣṭhitaḥ* - rests; *asmin* - on the (being in the eye); *raśmibhiḥ* - through (its) rays; *ayam* - this (being in the eye rests); *amuṣmin* - on the (being in the sun); *prāṇaiḥ* - (through its) organs; *yadā* - when; *saḥ* - it (the individual self); *bhavati* - is; *utkramiṣyan* - about to depart; *paśyati* - (it) sees; *etat* - the; *maṇḍalam* - (solar) orb; *śuddham eva* - clearly (without rays); *ete* - those; *raśmayaḥ* - rays; *na* - no longer; *pratyāyanti* - come to; *enam* - it

That which is that *satya* is the sun – the being who is in the orb and the being who is in the right eye. These two rest on each other. The being in the sun rests on the being in the right eye through its rays, and the being in the right eye rests on the solar being through its organs. When the individual self is about to depart from the body, it sees the solar orb clearly without rays. Those rays no longer come to it.

In the previous *adhyāya,* we spoke of the right eye as *indra,* otherwise called *indha,* and we spoke of the left eye as what is seen as this phenomenal world. The phenomenal world is none other than the world of forms and the names given to each to denote the unique individuality of each item of perception. In fact, the phenomenal world and the world illuminated by sunlight are the same. In principle what is seen in the sun and what is seen on the earth as fire are similar. The sun is luminous: even so is the fire. The sun has thermal energy, as does the fire.

There are many latent forms of the same thermal principle such as in the cloud, the vital breath and vegetation. The fire in the cloud is electrical and it reveals itself as lightning and thunder. The fire in the vegetative world shows its affinity to the heavenly fire, because vegetation grows upwards as if the life in the plants and trees wants to reach the sun. The fire in the word is probably the subtlest of all fires. It tests the truth of existence, and of what is spoken and written. If a person speaks truth and nothing but truth, all pretentious falsification will be scorched and burnt to ashes. Words which contain the fire of verification will not spare anything other than the whole truth.

In this mantra, the orb in the outer firmament, which we call the sun, can be totally meaningless if there is no eye to see what wonders the light of the sun and its thermal energy are causing in this world. The very first wonder of the sun's light is that it paints the entire universe into a colorful panorama without using any pigment or brush and without having any artist to execute this grand job. Every blade of grass turns emerald green when sunlight falls on it. The sky becomes blue. The ocean prefers to have one degree more blue than the sky, and sometimes, for a change, it gains a green shade.

Every flower is given its preference to shine forth into the sunlight. The hibiscus prefers to be blood red in color, while the sunflower loves to show its yellow petals, the jasmine is white, and the lotus is either reddish with a slight shade of violet or pure white like a lily. Sunlight splits into seven colors. The seven parent colors can be the source of seven million shades of colors. Each color is a concealed dance of atomic particles. We do not see the dance, but we see the choreography of that dance.

Sunlight has another great magical device. It casts a shadow in proportion to the brightness of the light which the sun focuses on an object. There can be graying white turning into more translucent darkness until it assumes an opacity of absolute negation of light. The phenomenal world assumes dimensions with these contrasting shades. When we say we see objects in sunlight, that is not true. We see objects when light is contrasted with shades of darkness. These are only momentary incidents so far as the sun is concerned. It is not so for the humans who capture and immortalize them in paintings, photography, sculpture, poetry, music, dreams, and remembered images.

Although we know that the earth goes around the sun, for all practical purposes, it is as if the sun is going around our globe, bringing sunrise sequentially to one place after another, so that every point on the entire globe witnesses its own sunrise and sunset. The rising sun and the setting sun are two poetic visions which human beings are never tired of seeing. At midnoon the sun is white-hot and glittering like molten silver. This is the phenomenal sun. Thank God that we never get closer to the sun to have a good look at it. While the unreality of the sun is so beautiful and so beneficial, the reality could be devastating. This gives us a lesson - do not try to probe too deep into any phenomena. The most beautiful one, the wisest person, the most poetic mind, the gifted voice of the musician – all are outside manifestations which add to the charm of our phenomenal experience.

To know the sun inside us, we don't open our eyes. Rather, we close our eyes and look into the deepest core of our soul. There the sun is not a blazing light. It is a certitude of being. The conviction that the being belongs neither to any place nor time, has no form or name, yet leaves no doubt of existence is the same as your total awareness. That is how existence becomes a by-word for subsistence. All the items that please us in the phenomenal world become pale when compared to the overwhelming ecstasy of knowing that we are that imperishable being. The eye requires the illuminating sun outside and the I-consciousness needs the inner being, the numenon.

We live our lives of phenomenal existence transacting our business in the light of the external sun where we value the colors that gladden us, and the light and shade that help us to play hide and seek. With that model design given to us by the grand architect of the phenomenal world, we enter into our world of dreams. In the darkest crevices of the folds of our brains we generate the vastness of space which can be equaled only by the infinitude of the sky and sea which we crowd with any number of people with different features, comically wearing all kinds of raiment, walking, motoring, flying. If that is not our preference, we can walk alone in wilderness to see the most wonderful sights which dreams permit or be confronted by the ghosts and devils of nightmares. We do not even suspect that the good sun shining in the sky gave us a hint for all of it.

Then deep sleep takes us over. Like Alice in Wonderland falling through the rabbit hole, we go into the deep of our own being. Then we have no form, no name; there is no color and no sound. Such is the magic show of the sun. It is *satya*, because we learned to have forms through the intervention of the sun.

The forms of perception give us the ability to figure out the specialty of each unique feature. Out of the unforgettable features of each item, say a lady bug, a little violet, a toddler, or a toad, we come to conceive images. Then we are clever to assign names to the concepts. The name is a replica of the image. Hence in Sanskrit it is called *pratibha (prati* - counter, *bha* - light). Truth which begets the truth-seers in us gives us the status of the shining ones (*devas*).

Do not mistake the *deva* for any fanciful angel in some paradise of comic book stories. It is just you - your ability to see, think, formulate words, structure sentences, give to every sentence a logical relevancy and, at the other end, to give each thing or concept a use, a value, a meaning. Such is the function of the *deva* in you. You adore what you conceive and you adore when someone passes to you an image they have perceived or a description of what they have conceived.

This begins from the very first day of your opening your eyes in this world and recognizing item after item. Each day you are given an intermission to withdraw from the external physicality to the green room of your processing of images into ideas. Then the great day comes for you to stare into the face of the brilliant sun and know it is going to be your last glimpse of the counterpart of your eyes in the sky. When the sun gathers all its radiant rays into its own truth and your own eyes as the very being of the sun, you know the time has come to say good-bye. Your eyes will never see the sun again and they will not rest again on any object illuminated by the sun. That is how the departure comes.

Mantra 3

ya eṣa etasminmaṇḍale puruṣastasya bhūriti śiraḥ; ekam śiraḥ, ekametadakṣaram; bhuva iti bāhū, dvau bāhū, dve ete akṣare; svariti pratiṣṭhā; dve pratiṣṭhe, dve ete akṣare; tasyopaniṣadahariti; hanti pāpmānam jahāti ca ya evam veda.

Word Meanings

eṣaḥ - (of) this; *puruṣaḥ* - being; *yaḥ* - who (is); *etasmin maṇḍale* - in the (solar) orb; *bhūḥ* - *bhur; tasya* - the; *iti śiraḥ* - (is) head; *ekam* - (for there is) one; *śiraḥ* - head; *etat* - (and there is) this; *ekam* - one; *akṣaram* - syllable; *bhuvaḥ* - *bhuvar; iti bāhū* - (is) the arms; *dve* - (for there are) two; *bāhū* - arms; *svaḥ* - *suvar; iti pratiṣṭhā* - (is) the feet; *dve* - (for there are) two; *pratiṣṭhe* - feet; *ete* - these; *akṣare* - syllables; *dve* - (are) two; *tasya* - the; *upaniṣat* - secret name; *ahaḥ iti* - (is) *ahar; yaḥ* - (one) who; *evam* - thus; *veda* - knows; *hanti* - destroys; *ca* - and; *jahāti* - shuns; *pāpmānam* - evil

Of this being who is in the solar orb, *bhur* is the head, for there is one head and there is this one syllable. *Bhuvar* is the arms, for there are two arms, and there are these two syllables. *Suvar* is the feet, for there are two feet, and there are these two syllables. Its secret name is *ahar*. One who knows thus destroys and shuns evil.

This mantra is significantly symbolic. A symbol in the Sanskrit language is *vigraha*. We have seen in the third *adhyāya* of the *Muni Kāṇḍa* that there are eight *grahas*, graspers, and eight *atigrahas*, counter-graspers. Phenomenal occurrences like sound waves passing by the organ of hearing or lights flashing to the organ of sight are short-lived. They have only a certain quantum of energy which is presented as a mere sound or a mere flash of light. However momentary they are, the transient presentation of sound and light are grabbed by the faculties of hearing and seeing respectively. In that split second the meaning that is presented by the sound or the form that is presented by the light are an instantly registered in memory. Even when the sound and the light are no longer interacting with us, what has been ingrained as the memory of the sound or the figure continues to grow in us so that its hidden message or connotation can be drawn to its maximum elaboration. Thereafter, the mind holds on to it to the very end of life. Thus there is a magical device in us that transforms the transient into a comparatively lasting impression. What is true of hearing and seeing is true of all five senses.

The structure of each of our sensory faculties has a peripheral aspect in which many afferent receiving devices are embedded. In these receiving stations there is a precise time orientation. They come together into a central focus of attention. The messages from the receptors go to their respective depth centers in the brain. They are screened through the cortex and coordinated through several devices of liaison. Then more serious processing takes place in each center in association with the stimuli received in other faculties.

It can take time to complete the processing. An impression can continue to haunt the cognitive faculty until an acceptable explanation is given by the interpretive devices in each of the sensory faculties. Sometimes a correct picture will be projected only after decades. Thus we are caught between two systems, one for immediate registry and the other for long-term internal research and processing, which is documented by the reorganization of the biochemistry of the brain cells, first electrically and then chemically. Each of our faculties initiates and carries on millions of such operations day after day. All this happens in our heads.

Each sense organ has a wide area which is its feeding ground. For instance, the ear is fed by every vibration of the monads of air in the space which is the ear's frame of reference. Air, while being a catalytic agent within empty space (*ākāśa*) has a more tactual stimulating power. Air conducts not only sound but also the heat and cold variations of the atmosphere. Air is also in resonance with fire, water and earth. The tactual sensory system is in immediate contact with the exterior of the body and the interior of the body. Here the *Upaniṣad* focuses on the area of the human body where allsignificant knowledge originates: the head. A serious meditation on one's being begins with acknowledging the importance of the head by saying *bhur*.

Among ancient scholars, there is some dispute about what *bhur* refers to. Some say the reference to the origin and process of knowledge is only of spiritual significance, while others hold the view that *bhur* is indicative of the source and origin of all knowledge, both of the numenon and the phenomenon. What is important here is that the entire gamut of knowledge is brought to one center which is indisputably in the brain. In the pursuit of knowledge, we first analyze knowledge before going into the action implications which arise. We are essentially homo sapiens - knowledge comes first.

In spite of all the reverence we give to knowledge, to gain it and make it meaningful, knowledge is to be accompanied by several forms of action. When we read a book or listen to a word, our central interest is in the message conveyed by the word that is read or spoken. This is to be preceded by many initial preparations such as going to a person who is wise, looking for an opportunity to sit at the feet of the wise person, bringing the whole body to a state of attention, and then listening or reading. Many preliminary actions go along with receiving a word. So, after the head, reference is made to the organs of action.

There is only one organ of action in the head, the organ of speech. It is in the head because that is the most convenient place for information gathered by the five sense faculties to be passed on to the speaker in us who can efficiently advocate the cause of each faculty. Further, speech deals with and dispenses with all values of relationship. The sensory faculties are not only action-oriented (verb), but they are also concerned with the connected qualifications of the subjects of study (noun). Nouns are often to be understood in terms of adjectives. All actions are to be looked upon as verbs which in each circumstance have their own modifying factors (adverbs). Structuring a sentence is in itself creating a miniature world. Most people think by talking to themselves. Thus the origin of action in the head, the tongue, is in perfect liaison with the faculties of cognition as well as connation, and ultimately with the affection of the person.

After *bhur* comes *bhuvar* which refers to the organs of action in general, and particularly to the two hands. There are many situations where both hands come together symmetrically from two sides to clasp or grip. They also often carry out different but complementary functions. A violinist has to use one hand for maneuvering the bow while the other hand is busy with the stress and release of the strings. A pianist has to have two sets of memories in his mind, one for the right hand fingers and the other for the left hand fingers. An artist holds the palette with the pigments on it in one hand and paints with the brush in the other. Even though both hands are disciplined for efficient action, they mostly have to use the designs of alteration or reciprocity and sometimes of contradictory movements. The person who is supported by knowledge and action is a whole being whose mobility is very important. The sensory system is to be complemented by the motor system. The two legs represent the power to move. They also support the body. Only if the legs move can the various systems within the system facilitate each other.

The total person is referred to here as *suvar*. The word *suvar* is derived from *svarṇa* which means gold and refers to the golden flames of fire. *Bhur* refers to the earth and *bhuvar* to the water that nourishes the earth to grow many things. Thus *bhur* and *bhuvar* indicate the complementary aspects of the ground as the seed bed and the field of nurturing. So the three essential components of life, earth, water, and fire, all go into the formation of the person. Thus the *Upaniṣad* gives us a scheme by which we can reduce the whole world into miniature symbols and then elaborate each one through a series of correlates. The entire design which is implied shows that creativity is nothing but making a central symbol and then elaborating it into many programs for execution.

Going from one mantra to another has a holistic effect on our psyches as we become informed of our own resources. The inspiration we can draw from this process is boundless. Here the person is conceived as *ahar*. Many secret implications are in the term *ahar*. Yesterday the sun was here. It rose, moved to the zenith of the sky, reached the west and disappeared. Today at just the same time it reappeared. It will do so tomorrow also. Life is a continuous process. The words which we have once understood, the actions that we once made ourselves familiar with, the friends we once knew, the enemies we have encountered, the food we have eaten, will all be repeated. *Ahar* means that which never leaves. It has a cyclic or rotational quality. If we make a mistake, we will go back to it again and again till that mistake is rectified. If we see a need to be met, we take it as a theme for our repeated labor until it is accomplished. Thus *ahar* indicates that we are instructed to go on and on from one meaningful project to another.

Two things happen through these repetitions: error is corrected and functional verity is re-established. Thus wrongdoing is rectified and virtue is enriched. The term *ahar* thus gives us fresh inspiration.

Mantra 4

yo'ayam dakṣiṇe'kṣanpuruṣastasya bhūriti śiraḥ; ekam śiraḥ; ekametadakṣaram; bhuva iti bāhu; dvau bāhu, dve ete akṣare; svariti pratiṣṭhā; dve pratiṣṭhe, dve ete akṣare; tasyopaniṣadahamiti; hanti pāpmānam jahāti ca ya evam veda.

Word Meanings

eṣaḥ - (of) this; *puruṣaḥ* - being; *yaḥ* - who (is); *dakṣiṇe akṣan* - in the right eye; *bhūḥ* - *bhur; tasya* - the; *iti śiraḥ* - (is) head; *ekam* - (for there is) one; *śiraḥ* - head; *etat* - (and there is) this; *ekam* - one; *akṣaram* - syllable; *bhuvaḥ* - *bhuvar; iti bāhū* - (is) the arms; *dve* - (for there are) two; *bāhū* - arms; *svaḥ* - *suvar; iti pratiṣṭhā* - (is) the feet; *dve* - (for there are) two; *pratiṣṭhe* - feet; *ete* - these; *akṣare* - syllables; *dve* - (are) two; *tasya* - the; *upaniṣat* - secret name; *aham iti* - (is) *aham; yaḥ* - (one) who; *evam* -thus; *veda* - knows; *hanti* - destroys; *ca* - and; *jahāti* - shuns; *pāpmānam* - evil

Of this being who is in the right eye, *bhur* is the head, for there is one head and there is this one syllable. *Bhuvar* is the arms, for there are two arms, and there are these two syllables. *Suvar* is the feet, for there are two feet, and there are these two syllables. Its secret name is *aham.* One who knows thus destroys and shuns evil.

The third and fourth mantras are almost identical in their purport except that in the third mantra the name of the person is given as *ahar*, and in the fourth mantra it is given as *aham*. There is a subtle difference between *ahar* and *aham*. When we look at the world with our empirical sense organs and become conscious of it, its objectivity is more pronounced than the subjective person who comprehends it. On the other hand, when the world is perceived from the point of view of the self, the subject becomes more pronounced and what is seen outside becomes phenomenological.

There is a vast difference between empiricism and phenomenality. In the empirical world, forms are formulated from the perceptual images which come as stimuli from the physical world which is externally structured around our physical being. In the wakeful world of empirical transaction, objects can be enumerated and physically described in terms of dimensions, shapes, colors and functional properties. With that we have formulated a system which is identified as actual objects which are interpolated into our biophysical, biochemical and sociobiological construct to get the whole world. In that particular study related to *ahar*, the wakeful experience of daytime is the specific field in which transactions are examined. In the structuring of the external world, we have developed scientific, socio-economic and political standards with relative levels of good and evil .

Three faculties are specially taken into consideration in the world pertaining to *aham*: the faculty of reasoning, the faculty of feeling, and the faculty of willing. Our volitional world decides our interpersonal relationship. In our relations with the external world, a social science of values has been codified and kept as part of our mores, traditions, civil and criminal laws, social attitudes and behavior patterns, economic dealings, and political ideologies. They all give direction in how to live harmoniously as a citizen or member of society with reverence to one's fellow beings according to spiritual, moral and ethical norms. All these come under the purview of right volition.

There is a hierarchy of values going from bare necessity to the approved ideals of the community. Usually they are graded as need or want, desire, wish, will and act. At every step of this graded hierarchy, we are taught to discriminate between good and evil. There is policing to make sure that members of the society give full conformity to the requirements of right behavior. There are courts of law which are also graded hierarchically from the lower courts to the supreme court. Thus we are confronted by the requirement of law all through life.

The second great domain in which we have to nurture ourselves is the world of aesthetic and cultural refinement. Feeling is the main consideration in this field. We have innate urges which come from the unconscious and present themselves as desires and ideas that we are obliged to express in words or deeds. Although there are certain higher values which have an archetypal similarity, there are also many personal manifestations of individual feelings which are dissimilar from person to person. In this also there is interaction between external standards of aesthetic requirements and a subjective area of incubation where the fountain source of the sense of beauty or goodness is always in the process of developing our personal style in whatever we do.

The primal energy which comes from a child can be an annoying and even terrible noise. Parents try to pacify their screaming child. Slowly it comes to understand that its gurgling laughter is more appreciated than shrieking, sobbing or crying. Words are gradually put in the child's mind. Almost every word in every language has the great power to tame the mind of the child by giving it conceptual figures in the words it is taught to articulate. Through nursery rhymes, ballads, songs and poetry, the growing child comes to appreciate the beauty of audition. Human beings have developed such varieties of musical expressions that each historical stage of development has contributed a special musical mode to the world. In this field also there are many rights and wrongs. Although a sweet melody is very thrilling, one single note of dissonance can upset us. Thus great care is taken to make music a harmonious orchestration; melody is brought under the requirement of harmony.

The configurations of sounds are expressed in the various visual arts in which humans are engaged. From a peasant's hut to the extravagance of a palace or the temples, cathedrals, mosques and other centers of worship, we can see that one center is vying with another to create an impressive decorative art in which utility is matched by aesthetic excellence. Each person takes care that their form is right in others' eyes. Men and women adopt different costumes and styles. Color and shape are brought together, sometimes in symmetry and sometimes in deliberate asymmetry. As world clothing fashion changes from day to day, the most spectacular demonstration of art comes in the clothes of children, women, and gentlemen. Modern culture also requires every person to make sure all aspects of their home, living room, dining room, kitchen and even toilets are properly outfitted and kept.

What we have said about the visible aspect of life and the audible aspect of life is only a small part of human aesthetic considerations when compared to our sense of touch, our easily tickled sensitivity to odor, the varieties of cuisine cooked and served. All have a stamp of cultural patronage. In all these, to be appreciated as a cultured person, one has to maintain a high standard of conformity. In interpersonal relationship, aesthetics takes one to the innermost core of one's life. Music, poetry, and visual arts can even become the contours of one's soul. A beautiful work of art, poem, piece of music or theatrical presentation can achieve a landmark in history for the person who puts the special signature of his style in it. We well remember Bach, Mozart, Haydn, Beethoven, Tchaikovsky, Debussey, Schubert. Their names have become so familiar to us it is as if they are our contemporaries. Indian people speak with great pride of Valmīki, Vyāsa, Kālidāsa and other great literary figures like Bhāsa, Daṇḍin and Bhāmaha, as if they meet them everyday. All such great figures try to set norms of aesthetics for humanity.

The huge cultural development of humanity is overshadowed by the advances made by people of reason. They believe that truth is the main foundation of all knowledge. The truth they speak of has to be the truth that decides both the external as well as the internal. Today the world is functioning as a great reality of a factual network because of the findings of the great philosophers, scientists, and theologians who have shown the anatomy of truth through their reasoning. We have a great impatience to correct untruth and to establish truth at all costs. Thus in every person there is one who gives great care to the requirements of truth that is presented in the empirical world of the solar light represented by *ahar*. There is also one *(aham)* that has to conform to the requirements of truth, beauty and justice which are upheld in the light of one's spirit by one's cosmic inner consciousness Between the empirical and the phenomenal, we live our lives. In the empirical world the conformity has to come between the presentative world and the representative world, and in the phenomenal world the conformity is between the ideas of transcendence and the facts of immanence.

We are programmed. When a program is on, we become

tense. The tension mounts as we go deep into the actualization of the program. When the program is consummated, our energy package is depleted. For a while, our tension is gone. We are at ease with ourselves and the station where we are placed. As we sit or lie down, ruminating with a sense of ease, the next program summons us to get up and equip ourselves with the right instruments to carry out another assignment. If the assignment is given to a pianist, he moves to his piano. If the assignment is given to a surgeon, he goes to the operating theater and examines the sterilized instruments and starts briefing his assistants and nurses about the procedure to correct a fellow being's malady. If the assignment is to teach children, the environment is different and the teacher's instruments are not of a plumber, chef or chauffeur. In this world there are many assignments for which many are deputed.

In our body/mind/spirit complex presided over by the I-consciousness, all the designers and executors of different schemes, the programmers and the program are within ourselves. There are three special centers from which coordination has to come to correlate everything involved in this grand scheme called personal life. One center is that of cognition for which we have the very elaborate system of our brain and its extensive neurologic network. Another center is in the heart from where life energy is to be circulated to carry out every assignment. The third center is in the genital which insures a purposeful life by bringing the individual into collaboration with other individuals. These triple stations of life have many sub-divisions with separate executives and associates under the manager who is in charge of the plan called human life.

Each person is only one unit of which he or she is the sole performer. At the same time, he or she has to wait upon the supreme manager of a million units which constitute the various aspects of the universe with different kinds of instrumentation and programs of maneuvering and bringing each day's work to a satisfactory production goal. It is by placing ourselves in our appropriate stations of life that we come to know what our command is and what the commands of others are. We cannot study all other units and the commands given to all. So what the *Khila Kāṇḍa* requires of each of us is that we delimit ourselves to our own assignment and listen to our own commands.

We have a set of instruments which are permanently fitted to function without the need for individual operation, such as the respiratory system, the pulmonary system, the digestive system and other such vital functions. They are all in the hands of very strong, tenacious mechanisms which the grand designer of life has installed. The longevity of a person and his or her ultimate achievements rest in these autonomous areas which are compared to a demon of enormous strength. It has to function in the manner of steady-state facilitations given to electronic devices which have a large quanta of energy flowing through them. So the supreme programmer gives them only one advice - to be kind to themselves and to all the other instruments they handle. The parent machine always hears the command of its master: "Go slow. Haste makes waste." When our conscious programs come under the spell of the unconscious, we may become overwhelmed. In our wild enthusiasm we make our machine explode. Hence the demon is asked to control its energy flow.

We have a world above us, a world below us and a world in between: the earth's crust, the biosphere and the stratosphere. The volcano comes from the crust; drought or flood happen in the biosphere and the stratosphere can even be pierced by meteors coming from beyond it. We have to be vigilant to understand the messages coming from the earth, the atmosphere and the sky. Every brain is a broadcasting as well as receiving station. Five of our major offices are stationed in the head itself to receive messages and give commands. They have to be ever-responsible. The only light we have is the light of our cognitive, connative and intuitive functions of our intelligence. That is the *deva* in us, ever-watchful, who is able to give us our share of all entertainment. It is asked not to indulge or misuse the boundless amenities given into its care. So it is told to keep its cool. Like the military marks certain zones as "Out of Bounds," our eyes, ears, and senses of touch, smell and taste are all to be kept within permitted bounds. That is another lesson we have to learn from the *Khila Kāṇḍa.*

But all these have to report the meaning and gravity of the situation to the presiding officer called the Self, seated in the heart, placed between the voluntary and autonomous systems, between the celestial heavens above and the subterranean regions of earth below. It is in charge of all the logarithms of life. It is a mathematician who balances assets and liabilities with appropriate numerators and denominators. That is the *manuṣyā* in you and me and countless millions of others. Yet my assignments cannot be carried out by you because in this management game there are no proxies and the chief executive in each unit is not granted any holiday. This is the lesson we have to draw from this *brāhmaṇa.*

Brāhmaṇa 6

Mantra 1

manomayo'ya puruṣo bhāḥsatyastasminnantarhṛdaye, yathā vrīhirvā yavo vā; sa eṣa sarvasyeśānaḥ, sarva-syādhipatiḥ, sarvamidam praśāsti yadidam kiñca.

Word Meanings

ayam - this; *puruṣaḥ* - being; *manomayaḥ* - reflected in the mind; *bhāḥ satyaḥ* - radiant by nature; *tasmin antaḥ hṛdaye* - (is realized) in the interior of the heart; *yathā* - like; *vrīhiḥ vā* - a grain of rice or; *yavaḥ vā* - a grain of barley; *saḥ eṣaḥ* - it (is); *īśānaḥ* - the lord; *sarvasya* - of all; *adhipatiḥ* - the ruler; *sarvasya* - of all; *praśāsti* - governs; *sarvam* - all; *idam* - this; *yat idam kim ca* - whatever there is

This being reflected in the mind, radiant by nature, is realized in the interior of the heart, like a grain of rice or barley. It is the lord of all, the ruler of all and it governs all this - whatever there is.

In this mantra we are given a yogi's vision of the Absolute. In the sixth chapter of the *Chāndogya Upaniṣad* a similar vision of the Absolute is presented. Uddālaka teaches his son Śvetaketu the quintessence of that which envelops all and that which is enshrined in all. This teaching is built up slowly. First of all Śvetaketu is asked to forget the plurality of modifications that can come to the most subtle of essences which make each thing what it is. The very earth on which we stand is so big that we cannot visualize the whole of it from a single point of view. It has in it mountain ranges, valleys, agricultural lands, cities and villages, deserts, high plateaus, lowlands, but the whole of this is made up of the same earth which is under our feet. We can grab a handful of that mud and look at it. What is in it is in the huge mountains and a little of it is what is fashioned by the potter into pots, jars, vases, cups and saucers. Then each item is different, not only in its form, but also in its name and its utility.

All these great palaces, cities, mud huts, roads, and pots are made of the same earth. We find that earth is made up of particles which can be cohesive when wet. It is this cohesiveness of sticky mud called clay that gives us the ability to fashion earth into countless useful forms. The pebble is different from the rock, the rock from sand, and sand from clay. Each one not only reveals a specific characteristic but it also stops us from identifying one item with another item. Therefore, what an aspiring yogi should learn is that the Absolute has within it countless millions of relative aspects and each one brings separation within unity. But earth as such is of one unitive thing-in-itself, *mātra*. (*Mātra* is that which is measured only by itself.) This gives us one example of employing the method of reduction to come to the essence of an otherwise complex totality of being. Similarly, we can see many utensils made out of copper which can all be reduced to a single element of copper. This is also possible with iron or gold. In Narayana Guru's *Ātmopadeśa Śatakam* we read two verses which clarify this point (73 and 74):

In one substance there are many,
and in many things there is one meaning; reasoning thus,
everything becomes inseparably inclusive in knowledge;
not all know this great secret.

Innumerable particles of dust inhere in earth,
and there is no difference in the earth
that constitutes the particles;
just as inert matter exists in consciousness,
consciousness finds its expression

here in the body; therefore, when contemplated, this is one.

This is exactly what the physicist has done – irrespective of the plurality of characteristics, he reduces everything that is measurable, countable, perceptual, audible and tangible into a single entity called matter. The word matter is derived from a Latin term *mater* meaning mother. A mother may have several children, but she is the single cause of all of them. Similarly, the plurality of things comes from the parent matter. In the world of chaos we come to order by reducing the plural into a single entity. The manifold beings are held together by a principle of homogeneity (*samāna adhikaraṇa*).

After giving these few examples of the reduction of the plural into one essential unity, we have to look for a key in our own mind which we use as an instrument for reduction and unification. Suppose we ask the question, "What was there before all these manifold names, forms, bodies, motions, activities, space and time, came into being?" We can only say, "Nothing." Now we look close at this word, "nothing." We are negating everything known; and we are asserting the fact that there was nothing. This assertion we make has in it a certitude because we are saying there *was* nothing. Was is the past tense of is. Thus nothing gains an affirmation of being. So the first proposition before us is that everything came from the being of nothing. In Jean Paul Sartre's voluminous book, *Being and Nothingness*, he asserts that being is the mother of nothing. Certainly we were not like we are now a year before our birth. In fact, there was nothing like us. But each one of us is now a solid entity sitting here, claiming our being. We will protest with a loud scream if somebody says we are nothing. Thus there is a magical transformation of being into nothing, nothing into something, something into everything, and everything which disappears and reappears Although we try to trace the essential being of the self-revealing truth, numenon, we stumble on something and we can grasp only the phenomenon.

When we spoke of clay, we stumbled on the cohesiveness of particles. Something other than the particle is needed to hold them together. That something is none other than water. So the magic of formation happens in water. Water can be vaporous or remains in separate gas forms like oxygen and hydrogen. Or think of the oceans in which we navigate and in which food is growing in the form of water animals. Think of the slipperiness of water which allows all kinds of vessels to navigate and the billowy waves that continuously fashion the shorelines of the land. Or think of the grand distribution of moisture which is lifted out of the bosom of the oceans and lakes to form clouds which can float into higher and higher regions until it is snowed or rained on high mountains. This is nature's engineering device to take water all over the globe without pumping stations and pipelines. Thus the nothing becomes being and the being assumes a plurality of forms. There is growth and change from moment to moment which has the highest utility for our pretty world. When you think of this amazing cosmic picture of earth and water playing games between the sky and earth, it is marvelous to see how many adjuncts the one totality has. We can refer to that single principle as "that". "That" is the mountain peak; "that" is the clouds; "that" is the river which runs from one end of the continent to the other. Everything is included in the small little reference "that" (*tat*). This is the grandest of all methodological reductions.

After Uddālaka leads Śvetaketu to understand how everything can be reduced to "that," he shows him the methodological way of understanding how being is transformed. Our most common experience is that when we are famished and fatigued, and have no energy to sit up, talk, or lift our heads, we wish that we had some food which could make us a little stronger, give us a little energy. If we eat at that time, our food becomes divided into three parts. The grossest ingredients transform into feces, the middle ingredients change into flesh, and the subtlest ingredients become mind. Similarly, when thirst makes us drink water, water is divided into three parts. The grossest ingredients become urine, the middle ingredients become blood, and the subtle ingredients become vital breath (*prāṇa*). Fatty foods are called fire. When they are eaten the grossest ingredients become bone, the middle ingredients become marrow and the subtle ingredients become speech.

Śvetaketu is further instructed that mind is made up of food, *prāṇa* is made up of water, speech is made up of fire. Uddālaka teaches him that of the curd that is being churned, the subtlest part rises upward and becomes clarified butter. Similarly, of the food that is eaten, that which is the subtlest part rises upwards and becomes mind. Of the water that is drunk, the subtlest part rises and becomes *prāṇa*. Of the fire that is eaten, the subtlest part rises upwards and becomes speech.

Then Śvetaketu is given an experiment. He is told that a person consists of sixteen parts. His father tells him not to eat for fifteen days, but to drink as much water as he likes. *Prāṇa* is made up of water, and the *prāṇa* of one who drinks water is not cut off. After not eating for fifteen days, Śvetaketu approaches his father who asks him to chant the *Ṛg*, *Yajur*, and *Sāma Vedas*. But the boy finds that they will not rise in his mind. So his father points out to him that because of his fasting only a spark of life is left in him and with that he cannot perceive the *Vedas*. After Śvetaketu eats, he can readily remember everything he had learned before. From a microbial being to the whale or elephant, all can function only because of the food that is eaten. This is another way of teaching how you can apply the method of reduction to come to the most essential nucleus from which everything gets elaborated and branches off. After disciplining Śvetaketu, his teacher gives the following example in *Khaṇḍa* 10 of *Adhyāya* 6:

> These eastern rivers, dear boy, flow along to the east and the western ones to the west. They rise from the ocean and merge in the ocean, and become that ocean itself. And as these rivers do not know from where they have come and where they have gone, even so, dear boy, all these creatures, having come from Being, do not know, "We have come from Being."

From that he concludes,

> That Being which is this subtle essence, even That all this world has for its self. That is the true. That is the *ātman*. That thou art, O Śvetaketu. [13]

This mantra brings us to the same nucleic essence. It is here described as being as minute as a grain of rice or barley, but it is that nucleus which transforms into all of us, into this world and into the cosmos. It is the inner ruler which maneuvers and manifests in many different ways. This mantra is given to correct our false notion of *brahman* as a solid piece, a single entity, immaculate, and uniform. *Brahman* is one which is countlessly many and, in the magnitude of its complexity, it is maintaining the simple principle of being. This is how we have to meditate on this mantra.

Brāhmaṇa 7

Mantra 1

vidyudbrahmetyahuḥ; vidānādvidyut; vidyatyenam pāpmano ya evam veda vidyudbrahmeti; vidyuddhyeva brahma.

Word Meanings

iti āhuḥ - (they) say; *vidyut* - lightning; *brahma* - is *brahman; vidyut* - (it is called) lightning; *vidānāt* - because it dispels (darkness); *yaḥ* - (one) who; *iti veda* - knows; *evam* - this; *vidyut* - (that) lightning; *brahma* - (is) *brahman; vidyati* - dispels; *pāpmanaḥ* - evils; *enam* - (ranged against) him; *hi* - for; *vidyut* - lightning; *brahma* - (is) *brahman; eva* - indeed

They say lightning is *brahman*. It is called lightning *(vidyut)* because it dispels darkness. One who knows this - that lightning is *brahman* - dispels evils ranged against him, for lightning is indeed *brahman*.

The reference to lightning given in this mantra is a basic quality of truth. In the *Udgītha Brāhmaṇa* we read the liberating mantra: "From untruth may we be delivered to truth; from darkness may we be delivered to light; from death may we be delivered to immortality." These three requests are aimed at an electrical function which is like a flash. The pure, clear light (*sattva*) in our psycho-physical organisms becomes smothered by many refractions and its energy content is split into fragments (*rajas*). Consequently, even a person's consciousness becomes fragmented.

Thereafter each bit of the broken fragments are drowned in inertial darkness *(tamas)*. *Sattva, rajas* and *tamas* are the modalities of nature *(prakṛti)* to which the spirit or *puruṣa* is conjoined by proximity. We get only very minor glimpses of that which comes from the spirit in us. But even while we are going through the labyrinths of nature, the spirit keeps its vigil. It is ever on the lookout to bring absolute release to the imprisoned splendor in every living body. However, people of good spirit and good cheer who are energetic can be affected by a worldly situation in which their transparency is adversely acted upon by a growing translucency or even drowned in a swamp of darkness.

If a person goes to a house where someone has died, the dead person lies there as a corpse unable to recognize even a very dear visitor. All the people of the home look gloomy, tearful, as if they have all changed. Nobody smiles, nobody says a cheerful word. Even if the visitor is young and healthy, mentally alert and full of reasons to be jovial, he also feels that as a man of etiquette he should imitate the sorrow-stricken people of that home. Like this psychic turbulence that comes from the impact of external inertia and fragmentation, when a person contracts a disease, he loses his quietude. He becomes restless. and in his body it is as if each cell is revolting. The body gets heated, his temperature rises, inner communication becomes clogged, his heart rhythm changes. But when the same person is in a healthy condition, he has natural respiration with a rhythmic expansion and contraction of his lungs, the circulatory flow of blood is kept normal, body metabolism is regular and the outside heat and cold of the atmosphere are well responded to by the metabolic balance of the body. All the faculties that control and regulate life function normally.

When we look into the origin of life, we are surprised by the strange behavior of the atomic particles from which life begins. The positive and negative aspects of the basic particles in an atom generate a magnetic field in which the component parts are brought together for the structuring of a body. At the same time there are many devices by which protoplasm is separated from its external environment which is the liquid in which the protoplasm is formed. Even the barrier between the external and the internal is made up of the basic material of life, of which electricity is a major component. Because of electrical charges that happen between the component parts of the protoplasm, an alchemy is generated. In one sense we can say it is the electrical which is abundantly functioning in the electromagnetic field by which every person is generated and kept continuously alive. Any heat of any sensation that occurs in the genesis of life is treated by the *Upaniṣad* as *vidyut*. There are a number of references to the electrical content, mode, and behavior of the basic stuff of life given in the various *Upaniṣads*.

We can see the dominance of the electrical function at all levels of life. For instance, the climate and the environmental forces which are always on the move in a random fashion are sometimes favorable to a living organism and sometimes fatal. All living beings are properly covered by a sensitive outer layer. Even the thick shells of turtles and tortoises have a sensitive film over them to keep them in touch with the environment. The sensitivity of our skin is a continuous electrical function which safeguards our life. As we learn more and more about how the vibrating waves of sound are received in the lobes of our ears and transmitted, that can even be a model for the latest audio devices. Everything for our enjoyment as well as for personal safety is classified and transmitted as messages to alert the motor system. It is the same skin that is electrically stimulated in all of the sensory faculties. The chemistry of the body is such that the basic chemicals we hold in our system are like reservoirs of inertial energy. When they are brought into a fusion or fission, impulses can be released. The very automation of our physical life is controlled and maneuvered by this basic electrical function.

There are higher functions where electro-psychology becomes complementary to electro-biology. The vibrations of a sound produced by a person can mean volumes to a fellow human who listens and interprets the sound. Sights and sounds are almost interchangeable phenomena so far as life is concerned. It is as if you can see music and hear painting. There is a spectrum of one-to-one correspondence between the seven modes in light and the seven modes in sound. Everything from little sensations to a magnificent vision of the totality of truth can come to a person. It is generally believed that the mysteries that are lying as latent powers in human brain cells are only sparingly used. The world has always marveled at the mathematical possibilities revealed by a brain such as Einstein's and in our own contemporary world we do not understand how a totally paralyzed person like Stephen Hawkings, with a little electronic aid from outside, can envision a highly complicated mass of electronic potentiality in the world of mathematics. The Indian rishis were probably the first among human beings to postulate, with sufficient reason, that this splash of lightning within is the sure voice of God, when they said that *vidyut* is *brahman*.

The most recent studies in physiology and psychobiology indicate that the mind is not just a stimulation of the neurophysiological system. The revised concepts about the mind are tending to prove that there is an overall purposive observer and regulator present wherever life manifests. According to the ancient rishis, the supreme Self is to be taken as the originator of life. Even though it is poetic to say that the world comes from the Self, the anthropomorphic picturization of the situation is to be excused, because no other example is so handy to explain a cosmic phenomena of mind. In the western world, a pioneer in the postulations of mind/body relationship was Sir Charles Sherrington. Even 40 years after his unique observations he is still honored as an authority in such matters. He wrote:

> The physical basis of mind encroaches more and more upon the study of mind, but there remain mental events which seem to lie beyond any physiology of the brain. When I turn my gaze skyward I see the flattened dome of the sky and the sun's brilliant disc and a hundred visible things underneath it. What are the steps which bring this about? A pencil of light from the sun enters the eye and is focused there on the retina. It gives rise to a change which in turn travels to the nerve-layer at the top of the brain. The whole chain of these events, from the sun to the top of my brain, is physical. Each step is an electrical reaction. But now there succeeds a change wholly unlike any which led up to it, and wholly inexplicable by us. A visual scene presents itself to the mind; I see the dome of sky and the sun in it, and a hundred other visual things beside. In fact, I perceive a picture of the world around me. When this visual scene appears I ought, I suppose, to feel startled; but I am too accustomed to feel even surprised.

The field of neuroanatomy refers to the physical basis of mind. The human brain is the most complex structure in the known universe. It consists of approximately ten to twelve billion neurons and even more glia (nonneural brain cells). The number of possible interconnections among the neurons in a single human brain is greater than the number of atomic particles that constitute the entire universe. Every part of the brain has in some sense a complex structure which cannot be easily studied. However, there is a roof bearing the cerebral cortex which is a supremely distinctive organ of the human species. It has a hemispheric allocation of functions. The first clues that certain regions of the cerebral cortex are specialized for complex abilities and aspects of consciousness came from medical studies of patients suffering various types of brain damage. The function is called complex because the right and left hemispheres do not function alike. Damage to a part of the left hemisphere of the cerebral cortex in a right-handed person essentially abolishes the ability to understand or speak language intelligently. Damage to the corresponding part of the right hemisphere has no such effect. However, a right-handed person with right hemisphere damage has great difficulty in performing spatial tasks: he may lose his way, forget a well-traveled route, and have difficulty understanding complex diagrams and pictures. Although we are here looking at the pathological aspect of the electrical function of the brain, that shows us how these minute parts in the human brain, not of one single person, but of the countless millions living in the past, the present and the future, are all ordained with acute accuracy. So it is no wonder that the rishis praised the electrical function in life as a major role of *brahman*.

We should think of the cerebral cortex not merely in terms of jelly-like cells, but as a fully oriented device to play the highest game of life in every field of our understanding. The worlds of art, literature and drama all present an insider's view of the complex activities of the cerebral cortex. When we are intrigued by the music of masters and the staggering architectural power to model the most complicated edifices of palatial buildings, all these are first sketched in the cerebral cortex. This small bit of the human brain is what we use to interpret this mantra and understand how such details are worked out in the entire universe where electrical and magnetic energies are not sent through any visible conducting materials. Our idea of electricity being conducted from one point to another point by a live wire is to be given up to understand its cosmic significance.

The inner arrangement of the electrical power stations within our body and the allotment of their tasks can never be fully studied. If we take the sympathetic system, for example, there is a division of work between the brain and the spine. The eye, the salivary gland, the heart, the liver, the stomach, the small intestine, the pancreas, the adrenal medulla, the bladder, the large intestine, the rectum and the genital are all furnished with the right amount of electrical energy at the proper time. The rishi assigns to the head, the heart, and the genital a master plan of the entire living world. We see it presented and explained differently, but on parallel grounds, in modern books of psychobiology. To open windows to the magic of the electrical firing of the brain molecules we now have many devices to scan the functions of the brain. Here is another very beautiful quote from Sir Charles Sherrington: "The brain is an enchanted loom where millions of flashing shuttles (nerve impulses) weave a dissolving pattern, always a meaningful pattern though never an abiding one; a shifting harmony of sub patterns."

The mantra is referring to how the doors of our awareness can be opened and closed to promptings coming from desirable and undesirable forces. We get a full detail of this when we come to the study of the synaptic transmission of stimuli. Just as there are openings, there are also inhibitory paths. The learning process itself is a great study in how right discrimination can be accomplished. What is studied today in modern science both complements and supplements the moral science developed by the great scriptures of the world. It is with such a view that we should integrate modern science with spiritual postulations so that we can make spiritual studies more efficient while enabling scientific studies to keep before them laudable goals for the well-being of humanity in particular and the world at large.

Brāhmaṇa 8

Mantra 1

vācam dhenumupāsita; tasyaścatvāraḥ stanāḥ – svāhā-

karo vaṣatkāro hantakāraḥ svadhākāraḥ; tasyai dvau stanau devā upajīvanti svāhākāram ca vaṣaṭkāram ca, hantakāram manuṣyāḥ, svadhākāram pitaraḥ; tasyāḥ prāṇa ṛṣabhaḥ, mano vatsaḥ.

Word Meanings

upāsīta - (one) should meditate; *vācam* - upon speech (the *Vedas*); *dhenum* - as a cow; *tasyāḥ* - her; *catvāraḥ* - four; *stanāḥ* - teats; *svāhākāraḥ* - (are) the sound *svāhā; vaṣaṭkāraḥ* - the sound *vaṣaṭ; hantakāraḥ* - the sound *hanta; svadhākāraḥ* - (and) the sound *svadhā; devāḥ* - the shining ones, the gods; *upajīvanti* - live on; *dvau* - two; *tasyai* - (of) her; *stanau* - teats; *svāhākāram ca* - the sound *svāhā; vaṣaṭkāram* - the sound *vaṣaṭ; ca* - and; *manuṣyāḥ* - humans; *hantakāram* - on the sound *hanta; pitaraḥ* - departed ones, manes; *svadhākāram* - on the sound *svadhā; prāṇaḥ* - the vital breath (is); *tasyāḥ* - her; *ṛṣabhaḥ* - bull; *manaḥ* - (and) the mind; *vatsaḥ* - (her) calf

One should meditate upon speech (the *Vedas*) as a cow. Her four teats are the sounds *svāhā, vaṣaṭ, hanta* and *svadhā.* The shining ones live on two of her teats - the sounds *svāhā* and *vaṣaṭ,* humans on the sound *hanta,* and the departed ones on the sound *svadhā.* The vital breath is her bull, and the mind her calf.

In a general sense we can say *brahman* is the main theme of the *Upaniṣad.* When we settle down to study about *brahman,* the references to *brahman* become less prominent and its place is given to *ātman.* The total being cannot be charted or enclosed in any figurative scheme. Yet for the convenience of description, suppose we draw an infinite circle such as the horizon seen from where we stand on any part of the world. Then the central locus of that circle is where the observer stands. To be more precise, the center of the total he or she experiences is in his or her heart. Suppose innumerable radii are drawn from that central locus. If the radii are like beams of light encircling the globe, then all that is included in the horizon can be called *brahman* and the central locus from where every point on the circumference is reached (which can be theoretically extended to infinity) is *ātman*. The fact that countless millions are participating in such a vision provides for the circumference of the Absolute to be everywhere while its center can be anybody and everybody. The plurality of envisioners does not alter either the unity or the extension of being. That unity is ensured by the one being that allows itself to be in the central core of everyone, whether man or beast, bird or sea animal, flowers or seeds, or microbes which appear and disappear in a million ways. In spite of the vastness of the quantitative variation that is teeming within this unimaginable figure, it has only one quality, "thisness," identified with knowledge through and through. Thus *ātmavidyā* and *brahmavidyā* become identical.

The most authoritative text for the study of *brahmavidyā* is the *śruti*. *Veda*, meaning knowledge, can be understood as the *a priori* text of *brahmavidyā*, the science of the Absolute. *A priori* here means the primeval testimony which gives a seeker the mandate to enter into the secrets of the *śruti*. *Veda* implies several psychological aspects of knowing such as the act of knowing (*vid*), the principle of knowledge (*veda*) and the function of making known (*veditam*). What is complementary to knowledge is actualization of knowledge. In actualization there occurs the word 'act'. When an action propensity is latent and can be actualized, it is a fact of knowledge. Only what is factual can be actualized. The subject matter of the *veda* is knowledge of the Self. The method enjoined to know the Self is by pondering over the revelation of a testimony that throws light on the nature of the Self. Hence the primary method to know is to listen to the word of self-knowledge.

Even when primacy is given to knowledge, the three *Vedas* are grouped in such a way that a methodical approach is made to get initiated into the proper search for knowledge. As seeking or searching is of the nature of exerting oneself, the preface to the *Veda* is learning the various methodical approaches to the right kind of acquisition of knowledge. The first part of the *Veda* is significant for the nomenclature by which both the profound and the profane are known. The *Ṛg Veda* is essentially nominalistic. In a way, this prepares the mind to give primacy to the word before commencing to act upon the suggestion of a word. One sacred formula is adopted to stand as a representative expression of all words. That is called the *praṇava* or *AUM*. The entire wisdom of *brahmavidyā* can be cryptically epitomized in the term *AUM* which is elaborated as the four *Vedas*, the major *Upaniṣads*, the two main epics, and the eighteen legendary myths, *Purāṇas*. The action that goes in unison with *AUM*, the all-filling knowledge *(pūrṇam)*, treats all the vital functions of life as an act of sacrifice. Thus the *Ṛg Veda* is complemented by *Yajur Veda*. The final conclusion or unitive axiologic outcome of the Vedic lore is to express the ultimate joy of all by singing the *Sāma*. There are three aspects: to know, to do, and to sing. These three aspects refer to an analytical form of group life.

In the synthetic or holistic evaluation of life there is a spiritual synthesis which goes beyond word, deed and action to the silence of transcendence. The fourth *Veda*, *Atharva*, has a mystical dimension which is represented by the finest example of perfected beings *(sthitaprajñā)*; those of unitive knowledge *(jñānī)*; those who are perfected in unitive action *(karma yogī)*; those who are inseparable from the Absolute *(brāhmī sthiti)*; those who transcend nature *(guṇātita)*; and those who are in the mystical union of love *(bhakta)*. Thus the four *Vedas* play four important roles in leading a person from relativistic existence to pure existence, relativistic knowledge to perfected wisdom and from the duality of pain and pleasure to the equipoise of transcendence.

This unitive way of putting the four *Vedas* together is given as the central theme of the present mantra, that is, to meditate on speech as if it were a cow. To begin with, there is only silence. When one opens one's mouth to speak, that is symbolized by *'A'*. Then one has to breathe out and breathe in and interspace the spoken word with unarticulated silence. That is symbolized by the expression of *'U'* with the half-closed mouth. Then one withdraws. That is indicated by *'M'*. It is followed by a profound meaningful silence that bears upon it the stamp of the expression of subject/object duality, the experience of subjectivity and the transcendence of subject/object duality. This variation comes between words and silence. The unspoken word is the most perfect, and the spoken word is the imperfect one. This is beautifully put in the *Tao Te Ching* of Lao Tzu where it says the *Tao* has no name, and yet it is described by ten thousand names. The most dynamic looks still and non-expressive.

If the unitive figure of knowledge is like a cow it is animated by the breath. Nothing can be articulated without breathing. So the breath is called the bull which is the counterpart of speech. A very elaborate study of nourishing food is given in the *Upaniṣad.* Food is essentially that which sustains. The first sustenance comes in the form of granting space for both being and becoming. Space (*ākāśa*), which gives no hindrance either to being or becoming, is as if it were our primeval food. Food is like *brahman:* it spreads, it pervades, it brings the joy of sharing the spirit of life. This quality is what we see in the vital breath. If there is a cow mating with a bull, naturally one can expect a calf. If speech is the cow and breath is the bull, then what ensues from that union is the mind. Thus the mind is considered as a child of the *Vedas.*

Veda, as we have seen, first initiates its votaries to a series of programs of action because that is the sure way to gain the experience of knowledge. We learn by hurting ourselves. If a cell has to preserve itself from not being destroyed by its own horizontalized life expansion, it has to divide itself, cut itself into two. That is an act of the one cell sacrificing itself to become two cells. In the entire theme of life we can see one thing being sacrificed to become another thing – to become more. It is by sacrificing the seed one obtains the sprout, roots and the trunk of a tree. Sacrifice is a very central theme in the actualization of knowledge.

The theme of the world is immortality and hence we begin with the immortal in us (*devas*), who derive their being from the word and knowledge. The immortal is to be followed by the mortal. Mortal is the *manuṣyā,* the human who stands close to the immortal and becomes immortal by perfecting one's discipline. The grand scheme of turning the mortal into the immortal is through a continuous program of recycling. The recycling is represented by those persons who lived here as mortals and were absorbed into death to return again. In the interim period they are called the *pitrus* (departed ones). The sacrifice is being done by *manuṣyā* to whom *prajāpati* gave the advice *dāna,* to share through sacrifice. Indian culture begins with the burnt sacrifice in the homestead. Retrospectively people gratefully look towards their parents and forerunners for their efforts which have provided a heritage of knowledge, health and wealth for the present occupants of the world.

The cow that is speech is said to have four teats. The first two teats are called *svāhā* and *vaṣaṭ.* These are for the receivers of the sacrifice, as the twain are considered the dual aspect of *Veda* and

Vedānta. The third is a nourishment given to humans according to their need and in proportion to their ability to receive it. So when the sacrifice is directed to the presiding deity, the sacrificer says *svāhā.* Along with the sacrifice there is the chanting of liturgy made by specially appointed priests and what they say is *vaṣaṭ.*

Human beings are in various stages of evolution. In one lifetime itself we have infancy, childhood, adolescence, youth, middle age, old age and dying. We are at several levels of needs. So each one is to be asked, "What do you want and how much do you need?" This aspect of nourishing humanity with the milk of knowledge is termed here as *hanta.* A part of the nourishment is to be given to our forerunners from whom we have inherited our bodies, our wealth and our cultures. To them we say, *svadhā.* This mantra gives us a comprehensive picture of a person gathering knowledge, imbibing the spirit of knowledge, living a life of sacrifice and relating to the past, present and future.

Brāhmaṇa 9

Mantra 1

ayamagnirvaiśvānaro yo'yamantaḥ puruṣe, yenedamannam pacyate yadidamadyate; tasyaiṣa ghoṣo bhavati yametatkarṇāvapidhāya śṛṇoti; sa yadotkramiṣyanbhavati nainam ghoṣam śṛṇoti.

Word Meanings

ayam - this; *agniḥ* - fire; *yaḥ* - which; *antaḥ puruṣe* - (is) within a person; *yena* - (and) which; *pacyate* - digests; *idam* - the; *annam* - food; *yat idam* - that; *adyate* - is eaten; *vaiśvānaraḥ* - (is) *vaiśvānara; tasya* - its; *ghoṣaḥ* - sound; *bhavati* - is; *yam* - that; *etat* - which; *śṛṇoti* - (one) hears; *apidhāya* - by closing; *karṇau* - the ears; *yadā* - when; *saḥ* - it (the individual self); *bhavati* - is; *utkramiṣyan* - about to leave the body; *śṛṇoti* - (it) hears; *na* - not; *enam* - this; *ghoṣam* - sound

This fire which is within a person and which digests the food that is eaten is *vaiśvānara*. Its sound is that which one hears by closing the ears. When the individual self is about to leave the body it does not hear this sound.

The life in the human body is the warmth of the soul. The special feature of warmbloodedness is shared by many members of the animal world. We have seen in previous mantras that a clue word is given for the reduction of the many into one central entity. The present mantra refers to the digestive fire which receives nourishment from the fuel of nature. The fire that transmutes inertial fuel into the dynamics of life is called *vaiśvānara*. Human beings share that transformative inner benevolence with everything which is hatched out of an egg or transformed from a seed or a gene. It is easy to see our kinship with the animal world, the vegetable world, the gaseous world, the mineral world, and the atmosphere in which all beings live their one life.

To formulate a science the scientist has to hitch upon a holistic principle which finds its proliferation, propagation and elaboration into many systems which are both autonomous and controlled by a single law which underlies that particular science. Here our reference is to biology. Just as the physicist claims that there is only one matter, and the chemist thinks of one principle by which all organic and inorganic compounds are compounded, the biologist thinks that there is only one life. Pioneers in biology like Leeuwenhoek, Linnaeus, Darwin, Lamarck and Mendel in the West gave a systematized elaboration of the biotic principle. The Greeks, the Indians, the Chinese and the Japanese have all taken for granted that a single principle of nature (*prakṛti*) can be specialized in structure and function, maintaining a spiritual homogeneity along with the inertial as well as the dynamic.

Here the rishi made this reference very precise, simple and easy to grasp. It is simply mentioned as the fire within a person which digests food. This is not a temporary service expected of fire within us. The fire in a hearth can be a good example to see how the fire is built in a living organism. The organism as such is almost filled to the brim with water and watery substances. Inside it is all wet. If we observe any part of nature, nature is so resourceful that it is always generative. If a seed is to develop, from the seed comes the sprout and the root, and from the sprout come the main trunk and branches. From the branching off parts come the sprouts of leaves. Nature is so economical that it makes any self-generated being also self-dependent to its maximum possibility. The roots are sent downward into the resourceful earth where gases, acidic chemicals, alkaline salts, and minerals can all be sucked into the generative system of the plant. From the seemingly tender, soft and clean hands of the roots, they are immediately brought to the newly developing leaves which interact with the sunlight to produce food. Activity goes on between leaves, roots and shoots, and the tree grows, finally flowering and producing several seeds like the one from which the plant originally came. Outside is the solar fire, inside is the digestive fire. How it is in the vegetative world, so it is in the animal world also. This process came into vogue even when the first protoplasm came into being. Its finalized form is the fire in the digestive system of a person.

This fire is also like God. It is not visible, but its effect is visible, audible, tangible, fragrant, or tasty. Certain things are self-luminous, like a firefly, a lamp that is burning, or radium, but certain others reveal themselves with the magnitude of their self-expansion. If you watch the unfurling of the flowers in your garden, you will be stupefied to see that a magical illumination is given to each flower with such pure tints that we cannot even dream of manufacturing. It is not just a fire that burns, it burns to transform the gross into the subtle and to regenerate from the subtle things which are factual as well as regally beautiful. When it is in transformation such as the first sprouting of a bud, a bud in formation, a bud that has come to maturity, the splitting of the calyx and the unfurling of the petal – it is all in the process of filling (*puran*). The process continues even after the accomplishment of the flower such as in the wafting of its fragrance and the display of the pollen. Every stage has a beauty of its own and a perfection that cannot be rivaled. The dandelion and our own globe of earth fluttering in space vary only in their quantitative mass. Otherwise, both are generated and put into the vortex of time by the same fire *(vaiśvānara)*.

The intake of a living organism is transformed through digestion. Then outside factors become an inner reality both for the purpose of life and for the propagation and recycling of those materials as another splendid display of spirit. The *vaiśvānara* fire does not work alone – it wants the earth to lend the necessary materials. Although fire is opposed to water, fire hides in the evenly mixed molecules of water. When these components leave water, one part becomes a blazing hydrogen fire and the other a catalyzing oxygen that makes the burning dynamic and perfect. Two main features when fire burns are the light it emits and the heat it conducts. What can we do without our light and without our heat? So fire is our *īśvara*. *Īśvara* means the lord that oversees, regulates, maneuvers, sustains and puts into each thing the law of its identity (*dharma*).

When the fire is camouflaged in another form we do not recognize it. There is fire in the vital breath. There the stress is on the flow of energy. It is vehicular in its purport and intention. The one *prāṇa* changes into five different kinds of *prāṇas*. Our digestive system is so elaborate that it has its sub-offices in every cell of the body. When we take our breakfast, lunch or dinner, we only think of the other people sitting with us at the same table as our co-diners. But inside us a great feast is going on. When we eat and drink, all our faculties separately enjoy the goodies given to them. There is big singing and dancing going on within us when food goes into the system.

The ear consumes its food only as sound. In the sound itself, there are sounds for recognition such as names, sounds for the performance of action such as verbs, and sounds for beautifying or qualifying, like adjectives and adverbs. When a name is incomplete it is given a prefix, and to bring it to its termination a suffix is given. There are shrieks, cries and exclamations. In the world of hearing there are elated listeners like the musicians and connoisseurs of music. Going into the world of sound is like slowly penetrating into the innermost shrine of St. Theresa's *Interior Castle*. It is as if God is seated in the august throne of his sanctum and all the spheres are singing and playing on bugles and horns and beating drums. Then there are private sessions where the elite meet to discuss the nature of truth. There are decorators of truth who arrange values. The fire there is not a scorching fire or a burning fire – it is flying around like a cherub.

Fire does not always like to be noisy like an opera house. It gets into the thinnest layer of our outer covering, our skin. No other part of the body is so sensitive to heat and cold. Life is sensitivity and the more refined life is sensibility. The skin looks so innocent, but the fire of the skin whispers to its counter-fire in another's skin all erotic romances that are communicated between lovers. Poets tell us that the most burning fire is felt in the skin by exposing it to love as well as by separating it from love. In Indian poetics the highly sensitive poet looks for words which can allude to every shade and every degree of warmth which love can display through its fire. These enormous areas of fire as fuel for the spirit and the temple of love are subdued aspects of fire.

The whole glory of fire comes when it arranges its banquet for the visual faculty. It makes us fickle, we cannot choose between our love for red and yellow, green and violet, blue and maroon. When we go to a fabric shop to buy a yard of linen we spend two to three hours going through the specimens of not seven but seventy thousand colors, not knowing that it is *vaiśvānara*, the great trickster, programming the visual faculty to keep on getting excited not only by color but also by form and style. The skin as a great cousin comes back into the arena of light and whispers into the admirer's ears not to forget the texture of whatever color it is. It has a preference for firmness. Unfortunately, this cannot be kept for long because what is firm today is saggy tomorrow.

So far it was all talk, but when you walk into the eating parlor a big hush comes. Then the real business of smelling and tasting, invites the other three cousins also, the eye to see, the skin to touch and the ear to listen. There is no good eating place in this world without the finest music put as a backdrop. People eat and get energy. Instead of going back home and sleeping, they are assigned the great duty of bringing forth more people. The central fire is the sexual fire in which the male and the female are blended to assume new forms who can in turn develop new personalities, new tastes, and new excitements. Such is the world of *vaiśvānara.*

Well-digested food is an assurance of a lot of energy, but if *vaiśvānara* gets over-excited, it may turn around and burn you to ashes. Indian mythology speaks of a great sacrifice arranged by Dakṣa. Dakṣa, the son of the Creator, offered the richest libations into the leaping flames of the sacrificial pit. He was showing off this extravagance only to spite the divinity of Śiva. Śiva kept away from the scene as a true ascetic. His wife was the sacrificer's own daughter, Dakṣāyinī. When she saw her father was heaping sin upon sin upon himself, she gave herself as a sacrament in the fire of *dakṣayaga.* This was too much for Śiva to bear, so he burnt off the sacrificer's head. Moved to pity, Śiva gave Dakṣa the head of a goat. This story is used by the medical men of India to emphasize that overindulgence in food is dangerous and you will pay for it with your own head.

Death comes to our physical bodies when the *vaiśvānara* becomes more and more morbid and less inclined to support the life in us. Slowly we are turned back into the dust from which we have come. This earth is considered to be the repository of the fragrance of all our past lives. There is not one living being which came to be born on this earth which was not reclaimed by earth to become its fodder for tomorrow. Those who have come and gone are more than the living. They are part and parcel of the sod of our planet. They continue with us as the flavor of all previous creations. In Sanskrit smell is called *vāsana* or *gandha.* Earth is extolled in the *Bhagavad Gītā* as the retainer of sacred fragrance. The *gandha,* smell, when wafted into the air, is taken around as the music of the celestials by the demiurges called *gandharvas.*

When the *vaiśvānara* is in the body, *gandharvas* sit behind the ears and continuously play on the *tamburu.* That is the celestial melody which all humans have as their companion all through life, the *anāhata.* If you have never heard the *anāhata,* close your eyes, put your two fingers in your ears, and hold your breath – then you will start hearing it. Both the tragedies and the comedies of fire have the *tamburu* of the *anāhata* for their background music.

Brāhmaṇa 10

Mantra 1

yadā vai puruṣo'smāllokātpraiti sa vāyumāgacchati; tasmai sa tatra vijihīte yathā rathacakrasya kham, tena sa ūrdhva ākramate; sa ādityamāgacchati, tasmai sa tatra vijihīte yathā lambarasya kham, tena sa ūrdhva ākramate; sa candramasamāgacchati, tasmai sa tatra vijihīte yathā dundubheḥ kham, tena sa ūrdhva ākramate; sa lokamāgacchatyaśokamahimam, tasminvasati śāśvatīḥ samāḥ.

Word Meanings

yadā vai - when; *puruṣaḥ* - a person; *praiti* - departs; *asmāt lokāt* - from this world; *saḥ* - he; *āgacchati* - reaches; *vāyum* - the air; *vijihīte* - (which) makes an opening; *tatra* - there; *tasmai* - for him; *yathā* - like; *kham* - the hole; *rathacakrasya* - of a chariot wheel; *saḥ* - he; *ākramate* - goes; *ūrdhvaḥ* - upward; *tena* - through that; *saḥ* - he; *āgacchati* - (and) reaches; *ādityam* - the sun; *vijihīte* - (which) makes an opening; *yathā* - like; *kham* - the hole; *lambarasya* - of a tabor; *saḥ* - he; *ākramate* - goes; *ūrdhvaḥ* - upward; *tena* - through that; *āgacchati* - (and) reaches; *candramasam* - the moon; *vijihīte* - (which) makes an opening; *tatra* - there; *tasmai* - for him; *yathā* - like; *kham* - the hole; *dundubheḥ* - of a drum; *saḥ* - he; *ākramate* - goes; *ūrdhvaḥ* - upward; *tena* - through that; *saḥ* - he; *āgacchati* - (and) reaches; *lokam* - a world; *aśokam* - free from grief; *ahimam* - (and) free from cold; *vasati* - (he) lives; *tasmin* - there; *śāśvatīḥ* - everlasting; *samāḥ* - years

When a person departs from this world, he reaches the air, which makes an opening there for him like the hole of a chariot-wheel. He goes upward through that and reaches the sun, which makes an opening there for him like the hole of a tabor. He goes upward through that and reaches the moon, which makes an opening there for him like the hole of a drum. He goes upward through that and reaches a world free from grief and from cold. He lives there for everlasting years.

One question which most people ask when a dear person dies is, "Where has he or she gone?" If we go to visit someone and find that they are not at home, we miss them. We know that they must be somewhere, but we do not have enough knowledge about their whereabouts. A similar situation arises when someone dies, leading us to ask where they have gone. We ask this even when we stand by them as they die and watch how their last breath is given, and see a change of morbidity come to their face. In a few minutes it is confirmed by a knowledgeable person that the person concerned has died. There is a contradiction in saying that the departed person is gone when their visible physical remains are still seen lying close by. The tangibility of the person is still there, but he or she does not respond to any provocation.

What can be legitimately considered as having left the body? We know that the breath has stopped in a person who had been breathing from their first day on earth to that last day. So we think that their breath has gone. The idea of going comes from the breath leaving the body. But where has the breath gone? If air is identified with the living principle, we can pump air into a person's nose. But that will not revive them. There must be a difference between the air that we breathe and the *prāṇa* that sustains our life. That difference is great, but we have not enough data to establish what that difference is. There are persons who foresee that their breath is going to stop and they may even say farewell to the people around and leave in grace. Still the mystery remains, "Who has left and where has the departed gone?" When the last breath leaves a person, we do not know where to locate a number of things which we associate with that breath.

The rishi always likes to teach with imaginable possibilities or rather with images. There are death images in all civilizations. The Greeks thought that dead souls crossed over the river Styx to arrive at Hades, the land of the departed. In the *Divine Comedy* of Dante there is a full imaginary description of all the details of the departed in the Inferno, Purgatory and Paradise. That may look very fanciful to modern minds. Only the essence of mythical images or symbols is relevant. So here we should not take sun, moon, and such phenomenal luminaries of the sky literally. People who are familiar with astronomy may even accuse the rishi of not having enough knowledge of astronomy to correctly understand the positions of the sun and moon. But here we are not studying astronomy or astrophysics – we are studying meditation.

A human life begins with eight or nine months in the womb of a mother who is affected by the altering phases of the sun and moon. The incumbent child is influenced by the mother's reaction to the sun which makes day and night. During these nine months, the fetus is not breathing the external air. The processed *prāṇa* of the mother circulates through the fetus. Every moment is a living moment where the *prāṇa* is carrying not only nourishment, but also genetic elaboration so that all the organs within the child assume their complete shape and function before the birth of the child. The main engineering devices are the *prāṇa* of the mother which she mainly draws from the physical air outside and the purposiveness indicated by the genetic code of the child to be. We can say that the child is living in a sea of *prāṇa*. Every cell in the body of the child is kept alive with the *prāṇa* given to the baby by the mother.

Once the umbilical cord is cut the mother and child are two separate entities and the child breathes to maintain its body as an existential functioning device in this world. The child and then the adult experience the altering phases of the work-a-day world *(vyavahāra)* and the dream phenomena *(svapna)*, like a big fish which travels in a stream, going sometimes to the left bank and sometimes to the right bank. The living person has to actively participate with the exterior world, drawing information through the five senses which are all fed by *prāṇa*. *Prāṇa* becomes more specialized as the incoming, the outgoing, the circulating, the distributive, and that which is maneuvering all these functions. Living means being kept alive and active by *prāṇa*. That is why, when it comes to a point where the lungs stop functioning, the throb of the heart stops with a command from the brain.

There are many vital points in us where life can be tied into knots. In some people these knots are not easily undone. Then the patient shows anguish - the agony of extricating the self from the body. This is described in the previous *adhyāya* with the image of a man loading an old cart with all his household utensils and furniture, taking the cart up a hill and, with great difficulty, mounting to the summit. At every point, the cart makes cracking sounds as if it cannot hold everything together. This kind of anguish is explained by the function of the *prāṇa*. Then suddenly everything stops. There is no more pain, no agony, no struggle. A look of peace comes. This is not just peace for a little while; you know there is no return from this peace. If the breath has gone, where could it have gone? Naturally, into the surrounding air.

That is why it is said that when a person departs, the *prāṇa* becomes diffused in the air.

But when the *prāṇa* was functioning within the body it was not the air that was maneuvering it, guiding it, programming it. That was all done by the sun. Sun means that light which is like an awareness by which phenomena can be discerned and the inner knower of that phenomena reacts to it with various motivations. We live in this motivational world by the programming of the day on one side and by the programming of the dream on the other. But both are finished when the final breath is gone. *Prāṇa* has to take light from the sun to generate names and forms, time and space, and a four dimensional world. If the *prāṇa* is going away, the source from which the phenomenality has come is naturally dissolved. That source is light and its shadow. So first we leave the impression of the empirical world. To describe how the memories of the empirical world laid in us are diffused, the rishi says a path is made through the sun.

Then it is said we go further, into the moon. The moon is a symbol of our dreams, the subtle aspects of phenomenality, the shadows. Moonlight itself is somewhat like a shadow of a shadow. Shadows are suggestions. When they also diffuse we go into the origin from which we have come. We enter the world of possibilities symbolized by the golden egg *(hiraṇyagarbha)*. That is like getting into an unhindered world where we are freed from two things: the physicality of the world and the grip of the psyche. Physical deliverance is spoken of here as redemption from cold. Transcendence from the psycho-physical world into something like causal consciousness is spoken of as being free of the grievances of the mind. So first is physical death and physical deliverance from phenomenality. Second is the deliverance of the psyche which frees the imprisoned splendor in us to fly wherever it belongs. So this mantra describes the kinds of semi-morbidity through which we go back to the world of hope.

All three phenomena – the break from the airy world, the break from the world of phenomenal light, and the break from the psyche – bring degrees of relief. We are told that our redemption comes when we leave the world of our imagery also. That brings a final release from the mortal psycho-physical organism. This *adhyāya* is essentially for living philosophical truths. So one should take time to ponder over each image and see what is in us, what problem it offers, and how we can get over it.

Brāhmaṇa 11

Mantra 1

etadvai paramam tapo yadvyāhitastapyate, paramam haiva lokam jayati ya evam veda; etadvai paramam tapo yam pretamaraṇyam haranti; paramam haiva lokam jayati ya evam veda; etadvai paramam tapo yam pretam-agnāvabhyādadhati, paramam haiva lokam jayati ya evam veda.

Word Meanings

etat - this; *vai* - indeed; *paramam* - (is) excellent; *tapaḥ* - austerity; *yat* - that; *tapyate* - a person suffers; *vyāhitaḥ* - (when one is) ill; *yaḥ* - (one) who; *veda* - knows; *evam* - this; *jayati* - wins; *paramam* - excellent; *lokam* - world; *ha eva* - indeed; *etat* -this; *vai* - indeed; *paramam* (is) excellent; *tapaḥ* - austerity; *yam* - whom; *pretam* - (when) dead; *haranti* - (they) carry; *araṇyam* - to the forest; *yaḥ* - (one) who; *veda* - knows; *evam* - this; *jayati* - wins; *paramam* - excellent; *lokam* - world; *etat* -this; *vai* - indeed; *paramam* (is) excellent; *tapaḥ* - austerity; *yam* - whom; *pretam* - (when) dead; *abhyādadhati* - (they) lay; *agnau* - on the fire; *yaḥ* - (one) who; *veda* - knows; *evam* - this; *jayati* - wins; *paramam* - excellent; *lokam* - world

This indeed is excellent austerity that a person suffers when one is ill. One who knows this wins an excellent world. This indeed is excellent austerity that a dead person is carried to the forest. One who knows this wins an excellent world. This indeed is excellent austerity that a dead person is placed in the fire. One who knows this wins an excellent world.

The life of each person is like a promotion from one transit camp to another. Two biological paths run in parallel to carry life. One comes from the father's genetic stream to his testes and the other comes from the mother's genetic stream to her ovary. The incumbent new individual genetically waits in his or her respective camps until the union of the sperm and the ovum is effected and they become one cell. The first transfer is from two separate individuals into the womb of the mother to begin a new series of transfers. It is a mystery how a person who previously lived in a body, dies and becomes united again in a single body taken from the biological constituents drawn from two separate individuals.

The significance of that which arrives in the fertilized egg is only partially genetic. There are three continuing factors in the individuation of a person. One comes from the genetic sources of the father, the other from the genetic sources of the mother, and the third is a psycho-spiritual entity which takes and leaves bodies. The genetic providence is only a vehicle for one lifetime. The passenger in the vehicle is the reborn individual entering into the situation in which there are two aspects. One is the *sūtrātma*, the continuing thread of the Self. The other is the main characteristics of the previous individual who died and is now being reborn which are strung on that thread. That is the *liṅga śarīra*, also called the *kāraṇa śarīra*.

After a period of waiting in the womb for a single cell to gather to itself enough physical accessories to function as an embodied person, that is, maturing as a child within the mother's womb, the first physical transfer comes from inside the mother into the lap of mother nature. From that moment the journey of the fully manifested individual person with a body/spirit complex comes into being. The newly born person has a spiritual belongingness to the spirit of the universe. The extension goes from *brahman* (God in certain religions) to the Self, from the Self to the pure light of awareness (*cinmaya jyoti*). From the pure light there arises the individuation which relates itself to a body system. The link between the spiritual side and psychobiologic side is *prāṇa*. *Prāṇa* has a gross aspect which is the atmospheric air, and a spiritual aspect which is a purposiveness that becomes the innate dynamics of consciousness.

The dynamics of consciousness have certain qualitative features which conform to the general features of the species into which individuation came. In a human being four general characters come in the functional aspect of vital breath. These are called *antakaraṇas* or inner organs. The first is called mind (*manas*) which cogitates and registers the impression in the subtle body. The second (*buddhi*) is to discern what is appropriate and the third (*citta*) is to make the registry binding for future time. There is a kinship between *citta* and *buddhi*. *Citta* is the grasping and reviving memory and *buddhi* is the faculty of judging. All these are encased in an ego factor called *ahaṃkāra*. These inner organs are linked with the external world by the five organs of perception through which all the reflections from outside come into the individual being. For reacting to the situation there are five organs of action. Between the sense organs and organs of action there is a liaison in which volition happens. That accounts for the fully individuated person.

The physiological body is like a neatly executed specimen of biological engineering which has for its main functional fuel certain biochemical constituents and a network for electrical facilitation. When a person is transferred into a family for parents to take care of, for five years the child is under the personal care and protection of the mother. Then comes the transference from maternal protection to paternal care and the period of instruction under educational tutors. In ancient India at the age of twelve the child was removed to the *gurukula* for study until graduation. The initial time for preparation to live was considered to be the first twenty years of life.

Then comes the next transfer in life. After boyhood or girlhood, a person is assigned the responsibility of rearing a family. In ancient days this stage went on till the age of fifty or sixty. At that time, one left one's householder role to be continued by one's grownup children and entered into a spiritual search. This was called *vanaprastha*. Then there was another transference, this time from home into the homeless life of freedom in the spirit, *sannyāsa*. In the present *brāhmaṇa* one lives through this final stage and comes to the doors of extinction. That comes differently according to the physical and mental health of the person concerned. By living in a body for seventy to a hundred years a man or woman comes to love the body home and does not want to leave it, even when old age brings disease, debility and disintegration.

The main feature of such an occasion is falling ill which makes most people panicky. They look for a therapist, a clinic, a hospital.

But one who has been properly self-disciplined during the long period of life on earth rejoices. The knowledge that this sickness is the final call to the next possibility prepares one to accept illness. He or she thinks of the last illness as the arrival of the best friend who can now take one into a world without obligations, a world without conflict, a world without pain, a world which is not cluttered with relativistic arrangements. He or she starts dreaming of the great expanse into which he or she is going unbound, limitless, where there is no need to carry the heavy burden of a body like a shell of a tortoise. He or she rejoices in the deliverance which is coming. The final disease which brings extinction in the body is considered a great blessing. There is no need to fight disease. It gives a sense of ease about what is beyond death. He or she is approaching the final friend who can redeem him or her from all the ills of this world. That friend is none other than death. When one befriends death, death comes with ease and one rejoices. At this level all the sense organs are unhooked from the stimuli of the world in which one lives in a body. Every faculty is closed down. Then there is no longer anything to hear, to touch, to see, to taste or to smell – peace comes.

Then all that remains is this home which was one's habitat for a whole lifetime. When priests and relations carry one's dead body on a bier to the cremation field, there is no consciousness, but one can anticipate that event before it happens. One can rejoice how the home is left behind and bridges are burnt. No more any father, mother, wife, child, neighbor, friend or foe, no sins, and no debts, no authority to be heeded – what freedom! One who entertains such a thought before leaving his or her senses is surely a blessed person. It is not a horrifying death that such a person is meeting. There is union with the infinite, the nameless, the non-hurting. There is a great acceptance of one into infinity.

Then only one thing remains to end the story of life on earth. That is to place the body on the pyre of cremation. The body which one cared for from babyhood to the last breath served as one's best friend, one's best vehicle. But now it is of no use anymore. One can imagine how the cremation flames are like the flames of *vaiśvānara* leaping upwards, licking every bit of the body. Whatever one has received as fragrance is taken away into the atmosphere by the infinite wind which omes from all sides. What little water is left in the body goes from its liquid form to its gaseous form. The head cannot be distinguished from the feet; there are no separate hands and legs; no eyes that see; no ears that hear. There are only very soft gray ashes. The earth will soon absorb them. The story is over. One who understands all these possibilities is a blessed person, who can leave everything in peace, with no anxieties, no concerns. This is the glorious death given for meditation in this mantra.

Brāhmaṇa 12

Mantra 1

annam brahmetyeka āhuḥ, tanna tathā, pūyati vā annamṛte prāṇāt; prāṇo brahmetyeka āhuḥ; tanna tathā, śuṣyati vai prāṇa ṛte'nnāt; ete ha tveva devate ekadhābhūyam bhūtvā paramatām gacchataḥ; taddha smāha prātṛdaḥ pitaram, kim svidevaivam viduṣe sādhu kuryām, kimevāsmā asādhu kuryāmiti; sa ha smāha pāṇinā, mā prātṛda, kastvenayorekatābhūyam bhūtvā paramatām gacchatīti; tasmā u haitaduvāca viti; annam vai vi, anne hīmāni sarvāṇi bhūtāni viṣṭāni; ramiti; prāṇo vai ram, prāṇe hīmāni sarvāṇi bhūtāni ramante; sarvāṇi ha vā asminbhūtāni viśanti, sarvāṇi bhūtāni ramante, ya evam veda.

Word Meaning

eke - some; *āhuḥ* - say; *annam* - food; *brahma iti* - (is) *brahman; tat* - it (is); *na* - not; *tathā* - so; *vai* - for; *annam* - food; *pūyati* - decays; *prāṇāt ṛte* - without the vital breath; *eke* - some; *āhuḥ* - say; *prāṇaḥ* - the vital breath; *brahma iti* - is *brahman; tat* - that (is); *na* - not; *tathā* - so; *vai* - for; *prāṇaḥ* - the vital breath; *śuṣyati* - dries up; *annāt ṛte* - without food; *tu* - but; *ete* - these two; *devete*

- deities; *ha eva* - themselves; *ekadhābhūyam bhūtvā* - being united; *gacchataḥ* - attain; *paramatām* - perfection; *tat* - so; *prātṛdaḥ* - Prātṛda; *pitaram* - (to) his father; *āha sma* - said; *kim* - what; *sādhu* - good; *svit eva* - indeed; *kuryām* - can (I) do; *viduṣe* - to one who knows; *evam* - like this; *kim* - what; *asādhu* - evil offense; *eva* - indeed; *kuryām iti* - can (I) do either; *asmai* - to him; *saḥ ha* - the father; *pāṇinā* - (silencing him) with the hand; *āha sma* - said; *mā-* oh no; *prātṛda* - Prātṛda; *kaḥ tu* - (for) who; *gacchati iti* - would attain; *paramatām* - perfection; *ekadhābhūyam bhūtvā* - by being identified; *anyoḥ* - with them; *u ha* - then; *uvāca* - (the father) said; *etat* - this; *tasmai* - to him; *vi iti* - (it is) *vi*; *annam* - food; *vai vi* - (is) *vi*; *hi* - for; *sarvāṇi* - all; *imāni* - these; *bhūtāni* - beings; *viṣṭāṇi* - rest; *anne* - on food; *ram iti* - (it is) *ram*; *prāṇaḥ* - the vital breath; *ram* - (is) *ram*; *hi* - for; *sarvāṇi* - all; *imāni* - these; *bhūtāni* - beings; *ramante* - delight; *prāṇe* - if there is the vital breath; *sarvāṇi* - all; *bhūtāni* - beings; *viśanti* - rest; *yaḥ* - (on one) who; *veda* - knows; *evam* - this; *asmin ha vai* - (and) in such a one; *sarvāṇi* - all; *bhūtāni* - beings; *ramante* - delight

Some say that food is *brahman*. It is not so, for food decays without the vital breath. Others say that the vital breath is *brahman*. It is not so, for the vital breath dries up without food. But these two deities, being united, attain perfection. So Prātṛda said to his father, "What good indeed can I do to one who knows like this, and what evil indeed can I do to him either?" The father, silencing him with a gesture of the hand, said, "Oh no, Prātṛda, for who would attain his highest by being identified with them?" Then he said this to him: "It is '*vi*'. Food is '*vi*', for all these beings rest on food. It is '*ram*'. The vital breath is '*ram*', for all these beings delight if there is the vital breath." All beings rest on one who knows this, and in such a one all beings delight.

A consistent question that comes to the human mind, moment after moment, is, "What next?" There are people who answer this spontaneous innate question satisfactorily to themselves. But most people wait for someone to tell them "what next," meaning what they should do. A person who cannot ask this pertinent question and answer to his or her own satisfaction is obliged to carry out the wish of another. Naturally there are a few who recognize the importance of freedom. Those who do not have the temperament to be free, but only an attitude of obeying and carrying out errands or commands, become submissive. They become alienated from the freedom which is their birthright. When one submits to another and caters to his wishes, even if he also gives orders to others, always has in mind an idea of what will make the boss happy. In the case of the few who live to be free and who answer their own question, "What next?" they visualize at least a glimpse of the meaning of their life. There are two paths: one is the path of the self-employed and the other is the path of being employed by someone else. The self-employed has the light of freedom to decide what next. One who is employed by another has before him or her an aggressive compelling call of necessity, Necessity with a capital N.

In the *Bhagavad Gītā* we read of the two kinds of roots which human life has. One is the root above which brings the light of pure existence (*sat*); the light of pure awareness (*cit*); and the eternal nourishment for the fulfillment of the happiness of one's own Self (*ānanda*). This tree of life is described in the fifteenth chapter of the *Bhagavad Gītā* which speaks of the tree whose branches are hanging down in all directions. Those branches have thick clusters of foliage and each leaf represents a spoken word. Where a number of people gather together and engage in endless conversation, their words are more disturbing than consoling. They are inadequate expressions of requests to oblige. This down-to-earth life is characterized by binding verbiage called *samsāra*. These hanging branches which fill the world with the dual forces of pain and pleasure, produce prop roots which reach the *terra firma*. Roots of one get entwined with the roots of another. Familial relationships, social relationships and institutional relationships become a bondage of the highest magnitude.

Although our origin is in freedom and immortality, what could be a growing awareness of the most sublime kind, that could be nourishing forever, is truncated at the lower level. Then we lose our path into the dark dungeons of necessity. Each day we are reminded by the gnawing hunger of our appetite and the thirst of our parched throats that it is necessary for us to eat and drink. Food and drink give a little relief and fill us with certain physical energy and mental confidence. The question comes, "What next?" When this question is first asked in the dawn of the day, the answer is, "Breakfast." After satisfying oneself with breakfast, when the same question is repeated, the answer is "How to get lunch?" After lunch, maybe the need is to have a siesta because the digestive system into which fuel is put blunts the intellect while the body is processing the food that is consumed and channeling it as energy through the vital breath to all parts of the body. When one comes back to a wakeful state after a siesta, the question again comes, "What next?" The answer is "Find your dinner."

When the sun leaves and the body is less energetic, the need climbs up from the belly to the dreaming mind. Now there is the hunger for companionship, the need to get close to one's spouse. The compulsion of sex seems to each person more demanding than the need for food or drink. This necessity is suggested not by another person, but by nature. Nature wants this game in which the vertical roots from above are horizontalized into the social matrix and continued with fresh prop roots of new generations which can get bound to each other and keep the world going. In spite of this, a part of it is ever-rotting, ever-degenerating and being turned into filth and meaninglessness. Thus human beings have a master in their neighbors and another severe master in their body in the form of nature. This is the pathetic state of human life.

Our eyes are so constructed that we can look at only one thing at a time with full focal attention. Our ears can listen only to one word at a time to interpret its meaning. Our skin identifies one sensation at a time which is painful or pleasurable. The taste of what we put into our mouths is distinguished by this tastebud or that tastebud. Our noses are so created that the identification of smell comes only when there is a direct impact of particles on the olfactory nodules. The stream of consciousness comes as if from nowhere, it makes situational sense and then flows away into the folds of memory. Thus we have a characteristic inadequacy to have a holistic experience. Experience becomes fragmented in our psycho-physical world. Therefore what one person experiences at a given time need not necessarily be the awareness prevailing in another mind. This brings a confusion which is recognized in the Bible as the Babel of voices. Each one is asking the other, "How are you?" "What should I do?"

In this mantra it is said that somebody answers, "Eat food, you will be all right." Then the person who was advised to eat thinks of what he ate day after day and what result it brought to him. There was appeasement of hunger and thirst for a little while. Costly food made palatable with several ingredients, cooked with talent and served in beautiful dishes was certainly enjoyable for a few minutes. But once it went beyond the throat it had no taste. The whole enjoyment of the food was only within the range of two cubic inches. How it was split into protein, carbohydrate, amino acids, phosphorus, sugar and iron are all the secrets of nature, which are foreign to the person who eats. Then every input came out not as the delicious enjoyable thing that he received into his mouth but as dirt that the eater himself did not dare to look at. It was so stinky that he wanted to discard the output, bury it forever, forget it. One half of his body enjoyed it, the other half of the body was in a feverish haste to get rid of it. So in this mantra we are told that food is not the Absolute. It is a dependent factor for a little while. Then it becomes abominable.

Then the mantra suggests an alternative. All the things which have gone into the belly through the alimentary canal are supplied with the necessary bacteria, acids, alkalis and other secretions to be digested. This service is rendered to food by the vital breath. Without the vital breath the faculties do not function. The heart and the brain are dependent on the pulsating supply of *prāṇa* coming from the lungs; the lungs cannot work if the heart does not give them blood; the heart cannot function if the brain stops. No faculty is free to be fully autonomous. If the vital breath is transforming food to give energy to all the faculties, then of course, the vital breath is more important than food. This is a great paradox. If food does not give its energy to the lungs, to the heart, and to the brain, then the pulsation of life comes to a standstill. It is inevitable to have food to keep the pulse of life beating. It is inevitable for the circulatory system of the vital breath, the circulation of blood, to keep the neural matrix functioning meticulously. So we cannot say that *prāṇa* is everything; we also cannot say that food is everything.

Here we have been describing more of the body functions and metabolism than the person for whom all these facilities are given. In the depth of the whole system there is something very different from the gross body and the subtle body. There is a will to live.

If we make ourselves familiar with the volition of the employer as well as the volition of the employed, that will is geared by the great need to avoid pain and to put in its place the exhilarating joy of life. Thus we come to the very foundation called *ānanda*. When we are in this temporary arrangement, having a psychosomatic organism to conduct ourselves from the moment of inception till we are consumed by the flames of the funeral pyre, there is a possibility of pain invading our lives, crippling our systems, and making any further journey of life impossible. This is the great necessity of life.

When its demands are met from the opposite side, as it were, a sense of fulfillment comes. Both the slave and the master are familiar with aspects of this fulfillment: a moment of relief, a moment of joy, a moment of satisfaction. Then one can think of the vastness of the sky, the continuous blowing of the winds, the rain from above, the water veins beneath one's feet, the lush vegetation, nourishing food and drink, the atmosphere filled with the songs of birds and the laughter of fellow human beings. The eye that sees even a flicker of light rejoices. The ear that receives a note of melody rejoices. The gentle arm that goes around you in a cuddle and the lips that meet yours give an assurance that life is beautiful. All these are occasions for rejoicing.

The *Upaniṣad* calls it *ram*. *Ram* is derived from the root *ramayanti*, 'that which pleases you'. It is the joy of life which sustains everything. Even in the slave there is a joy when he is relieved from his master or from the burden of his task. The masters, who are few, also rejoice when they can forget the necessity of life for a little while. The one universal value shared by all, from the brute to the philosopher, from the bug to the monarch, is the happiness that one can touch at least momentarily in one's heart, in one's thought, in one's aesthetic feelings and even in the bonds of life where every member of the family of the world becomes a source of fulfillment of a glorious life. Such is the message of this mantra.

The *Taittirīya Upaniṣad* and an earlier *adhyāya* of this *Upaniṣad* teach that food (*annam*) is *brahma* on the basis that everything is born of food, everything is sustained by food and everything turns into food for another. Thus food has the well-known mark of the Absolute. The Absolute is prior to any manifestation and it is from 'that' 'this' is manifested. Even when this manifestation is annulled, the Absolute continues as the all-filling. The invocation at the beginning of this *adhyāya* familiarized us with two possibilities of the Absolute. *Brahman* does not merely mean that which is big, it means 'the filling' *(pūrṇam)*. When a seed is bursting out into life, the sprout that comes and the first root that appears are perfect. Even though it shows only two cotyledons, the nucleus of the tree and the root which penetrates into the earth are the indications of the principle of projection. Ultimately, when leaf after leaf comes and branch after branch spreads out, the tree blossoms and is covered with fruit which is filled with seeds of the same species of tree. There is no stage where what is designed is imperfect. It begins with the seed and comes back to the seed. There is a unity and homogeneity between the primary seed and the ultimate seed. We were given the lesson at the very outset that *brahman* is that which is the origin of things, functional expression of things, and final reduction to the thing in itself.

But we human beings come to this world, hunger after food, consume food, relish food, and think of it as the primary source of pleasure. All this preoccupation with food takes us to a relativistic aspect of food which generates various kinds of attachment (*raga*) in us. *Raga* is of such nature that it causes other ramifications that go into different aspects of *karma*. That is why in this mantra, when somebody says that food is *brahman*, a correction is given. In the sense in which food is thought of by *samsāris*, it is not the Absolute. So what is said here does not sublate the earlier teaching . When *annam* is to be taken as the principle of *pūrṇam*, we can say *annam brahmeti*, food is the Absolute. Then the origin, sustenance, and dissolution can all be seen as the Absolute and the occasion for it is by properly meditating on food. In his commentary Śankara elaborates on this.

Just as we were told earlier that food is *brahman*, we were also told that *prāṇa* is *brahman, prāṇo brahmeti*. The process of the unmanifest becoming manifest, and the manifest being reduced to a subsequent potential can be seen in the process of food which is gross changing into energy which is subtle. The gross and subtle interlace the form and its meaning and once again become the formless. The psychophysical significance is reduced to a causal entity that transcends both time and space. Our first hypothesis when the *Upaniṣad* commenced was that every cause is to be followed by its consequences. The *Upaniṣad* did not present the first cause as *brahman*, but as a negation of existence. This is so not only in the *Bṛhadāraṇyaka*, but also the *Taittirīya Upaniṣad*.

When it is said, *āsīd agre'satevedam*, a pun is given. The phrase can be read as *āsīd agre* asat *eva idam:* "In the beginning there was non-existence only." By making the article '*a*' unexpressed, the same is read as *āsīd agre* sat *eva idam:* "In the beginning there was only the potential of existence." Śankara saw the mark of *māyā* in the mystery of *sat* and *asat* coming together. So he defined *māyā* as *sadasat vilakṣaṇa*. Narayana Guru brings the beauty of *asat* and *sat* into the context of dream, not the dream of an individual, but the dream that ensues from the will of the Supreme. A parallel of this can be seen in the philosophy of Bishop Berkeley. Berkeley's explanation of existence was "that which is perceived:" *esse est percipi*. Things exist because they are perceived. When an objector put the question "What happens when everybody is asleep and nobody perceives?" Berkeley answered, "God perceives." What is significant in the phrase *āsīt agre'sadevedam* is the word *eva*, meaning "as if" – "as if non-existence," as well as "as if existence." The world does not exist for a person prior to one's experiencing of it. Therefore we can say "as if non-existence." Experience itself is an effect and no effect can proceed except from a cause. Since there must have been a causal factor to produce the effect, we can say "as if existence."

In still water the wave is as if it does not exist. Then we find that a wave rolls up. The previously unseen and unexpected wave is then a matter of fact. In the next moment, that wave disappears into still waters. Only this much is behind the entire panorama of creation or manifestation. Whether the wave is or the wave is not, what exists is water. But water by itself does not create a wave. There has to be pressure put on it by air. We cannot extricate the wave either from the water or from the air that has caused it. Such is the relation between *annam* and *prāṇa* in the world of cosmic projection as well as cosmic dissolution.

The main difference that is shown here is the relativistic understanding of the fragmentary aspect of the universe on the part of the *samsārī*. Such knowledge is treated as conditioned knowledge (*sopādhikajñāna*). The *Upaniṣad* is only helping us to move away from conditioned knowledge to unconditioned knowledge (*nirupādhikajñāna*). In the *Jñāna Darśana* of Narayana Guru's *Darśana Mālā*, he presents these two distinct aspects, *sopādhika* and *nirupādhika*. The same can also be put in another way. When *annam* and *prāṇa* are understood as *brahman*, it is a revelation of how in the absolute sense *annam* is *brahman*, and *prāṇa* is *brahman*. Ultimately, there is no *annam*, there is only *brahman*; there is no *prāṇa*, there is only *brahman*. But as realities of the empirical world, *annam* as the food we eat is *yathārtha* - it is empirically real and valid. The same can be said of *prāṇa* also. Nobody breathes before the first living cell pulsates; nobody breathes after the organism is dismantled. The breath has a *yathārtha* aspect, it is empirically valid. But from an absolutist point of view it is transitory.

When we are asked to do *manana* on the present mantra, apart from intellectually knowing the significance of food or vital breath, we should go into the discipline of phenomenological transcendence. That is to be exercised in terms of the phenomena that is seeming to be the occasion of one's experience. It is to be simultaneously carried out with phenomenological transcendence of ego. It is not really a canceling out of the seer and the seen, but an identification of the seen and the seer, so nothing is rejected and nothing is added. The process of attaining non-differentiation is termed *samādhi*. In the path of yogis, transcending the ego comes in a gradation. First is identifying with the object (*savitarka samādhi*). Then that is reversed. Objectivization is transcended by identifying with the seer (*sasmita samādhi*). Then *sat* and *cit* are reduced into *ānanda* pure and simple (*sānanda samādhi*). When there is no trace of any form of awareness which pertains to the organism there is a transition from *savikalpa* to *nirvikalpa*. When in *nirvikalpa* all dualities fuse into a single unity, that is the state which can be described as *brahmevabhavati*.

Brāhmaṇa 13

Mantra 1

uktham; prāṇo vā uktham, prāṇo hīdam sarvamutthāpayati; uddhāsmādukthavidvīrastiṣṭhati, ukthasya sāyujyam salokatām jayati, ya evam veda.

Word Meanings

> *uktham* - (one should meditate on the vital breath as) the *uktha* (a hymn of praise); *prāṇaḥ* - the vital breath (is); *vai* - indeed; *uktham* - the *uktha; hi* - for; *prāṇaḥ* - the vital breath; *utthāpayati* - upholds; *sarvam* - all; *idam* - this; *asmāt* - from one; *yaḥ* - who; *veda* - knows; *evam* - this; *uttiṣṭhati ha* - is raised, is born; *vīraḥ* - a son; *ukthavit* - who is a knower of *uktha* (the vital breath); *jayati* - (and) he achieves; *sāyujyam* - union with; *salokatām* - (and) abode in the same world; *ukthasya* - as the *uktha*

> (One should meditate upon the vital breath as) the *uktha* (a hymn of praise). The vital breath is the *uktha*, for it upholds all this. From one who knows this is raised a son who is a knower of the vital breath, and he achieves union with and abode in the same world as the *uktha*.

Uktha comes in the *mahāvrata* ritual given in Śabaraswami's commentary on the *Jaiminīya Sūtras*, which represent the *karma kāṇḍa* or action-oriented aspects of the Vedic tradition. The *mahāvrata* ritual was used to propitiate the *devas* connected with granting food and other necessities of life. Both women and priests took part in the ritual. The women would play music on percussion and string instruments to accompany the litany which was sung by the priests. The *mahāvrata* ritual joined priestly ingenuity to theological concerns in that it was connected with popular festivals performed at the time of the winter solstice to encourage the sun to regain its strength to nurture the growth of crops planted in the earth.

In Vedānta, the archetypal Vedic symbols are reevaluated. In the *Khila Kāṇḍa* each mantra is given to meditate upon. A meditation yields its result only when the subject of meditation and the object of meditation are united in the unification of the body, senses, mind, intellect and the Self. This is a process by which the inertial lifeless material with which the body is composed becomes animated. When it is animated, the rigidity of matter is transformed into the flexibility of life. When such a status is given to the instrumentation of life, the personal self (*jīvātma*) gets a grip on the ten sense organs and the mind. The whole living organism gains the status of *cittendriya ātma.*

Our organs of action are adequate for our normal psycho-physical functions. Where there is an inadequacy of the body, it is complemented with an instrument. If we want to cover long distances, we use vehicles of transportation. To peel a banana and eat it, we do not need a knife or a chisel. But if we want to fashion a log of wood into a piece of furniture, then the hand needs to be equipped with hammer and chisel and other carpenter's tools. We have developed our technology to such a vast extent that we can now handle things which are out of reach of our hands such as sending a space craft to Mars to dig into its surface and bring a little of the crust back to earth. Thus instrumentation is necessary for the organs of action.

The organs of action themselves are instruments of the inner organ which gives the command to react in all action situations. If the organs of action are gross, the organs of perception are subtle. They are all instruments of the Self. Even for a robot to be automated, a living person has to feed it with his or her intelligence. Thus ultimately, we come to the center or dynamic of function which is the Self. The Self has its means to organize, stimulate and program purposive action. The dynamic of function belongs to *prāṇa. Prāṇa* is like the energy that goes into an automobile or an airplane or spacecraft. But behind that there is an operator. The operator is the Self.

If you schematically look at any function, the very first action is the releasing of energy into the equipment to animate the system. There is a constant dialogue between the equipment and its driver or operator. The operator gives a command. If the command is right, the equipment answers with a smooth function. Modern electronic devices can even speak back. If the command is wrong, the machine will not function, but for courtesy it will say, "Bad command." When energy is at the lowest ebb, the machine suspends its work. In our case we lie down and sleep. If our autonomic functions are short of energy, we may go into a coma. If there is no spark of energy, we die. This intrapersonal dialogue between the Self and the body and the response of the body conveyed back to the Self is taken as a model of the individuated person relating with the cosmic whole to which we belong.

Our placement in the cosmos is on the planet earth. Wherever we are, above us we have the unbounded space of the heavens from where we receive the provisions supplied by innumerable luminaries. With gravitation we are held tight to the ground beneath. There is a dialogue going on between heaven and earth which we experience in time as day and night and in space as the earth orbiting around the sun. The orbiting is the basis of our animation. Even before knowing all this scientifically, the Indian rishis knew that we receive two graces, one from above and one from below. We are a joint product of both. The early people woke from sleep to stand on their feet, look towards the heavens, and say, "Glory to you, O benefactors." The benefactors above were the sun (*savitā*), the source of rain (*varuṇa*), and the air which gives the nourishment of *prāṇa* (*mārut*). They gave equal veneration to the earth which is like a mother. The first praises they gave were raised to the sky with their spoken words. The vehicle or carrier for every spoken word is the *prāṇa*. Something manifests in an otherwise inert body and rises towards the self-luminous sun.

If we make a parameter from earth to heaven, human beings are at the lowest pole of the vertical axis and the sun is at the highest pole of the same axis. Our aspiration goes from the alpha to the omega, and from the omega, grace comes to the alpha. There is a constant exchange of aspiration and benevolent grace. The voice of aspiration going up from earth to heaven is called *uktha*. There are two intentional pointers of meaning in the term *uktha*. One is of speaking and the other is of raising. This later became recognized as the word that is uttered as a praise known as the *ṛk*. In an indirect way we are told that our first spiritual direction is where the *ṛk* is. *Ṛk* is the primary and prime source of knowledge. To know is to relate with. A child first comes to know its mother and that knowledge is to relate with the mother. The child cries for milk, the mother benevolently gives her breast milk. The hungry child's cry for milk is the first *ṛk* and that is heeded to by mother earth. It is through language, word, that one's aspiration is expressed and grace comes in return. Even a little seed buried in the soil, when given the right environment, breaks the hard shell of the seed and comes out pointing its sprout towards the sun and its root down into the earth. Not only human beings, but also the very first forms of life have an aspiration to fulfill and a grace to receive.

We give here two praises given in the *Ṛg Veda*. The first is to Uṣas, the dawn (VII, 79):

Arousing the lands where dwell the five peoples,
Dawn has made visible the pathways of Men.
The beautiful dawn clouds convey her radiance.
The light of the Sun has disclosed earth and heaven.

The Dawns advance like clans arrayed for battle,
their bright rays tingeing the sky's distant bounds.
The Sun extends his arms;
the rose-colored dawn clouds,
imprisoning the darkness, beam forth their luster.

Goddess Dawn has arisen, endowed with great wealth,
eliciting homage - our welfare is assured!
Noblest of the noble, this Daughter of Heaven
grants to her worshipers varied treasures.

Give to us, Dawn, that copious bounty
with which you have rewarded
those who sang your praises!
Loudly they acclaimed you,
like the strong bulls that bellowed
as you unbarred the doors of the firm-set mountain.

Prevail on each God to give us his bounty!
Now at your appearing impart to us the charm
of pleasant voices and thoughts for our uplift.
Preserve us evermore, O Gods, with your blessings! [14]

Ṛg Veda (X,127) gives praise to *Rātrī*, the immortal night:

Here comes the night; with her twinkling eyes
the Goddess has lit many places,
adorned once again with all her beauty.

The immortal Goddess enwraps the world,
its valleys and lofty peaks.
By the shining of her light she repels all darkness.

Advancing quietly the Goddess has restored
once again her sister the Dawn.

The shadows will now also steal away.

Be gracious this night! At your approach
we now repair to our homes,
like birds seeking their roosting places.

The villagers likewise and all that walks
or flies have gone to their rest.
Even the hungry hawks are still.

Ward off wild beasts, the wolf and his mate
or the robber, O night undulating.
May your passage bring us safely to the other side!

The shades of night enfold me now,
arrayed in black apparel.
Banish them, Dawn, like haunting debts!

O Daughter of Heaven, to you I direct
my hymn like a precious offering.
Accept it, O Night, as a paean of praise. [15]

The donor of life is perfect. That which aspires to live is inadequate. Between these there has to be a link. That link is the vital breath. When we wish to be benefited by providence, we put our wishes into words. The wishes we articulate can be symbolically transferred to libation which is poured into a sacrificial fire. The fire goes up. There is a limit to which the flame can go, but its light (*jyotis*) can go beyond. And the fragrance of the things burnt in the fire can waft into the air. So supplication has a vertical range as well as a horizontal range. This can be fully understood by looking at a model ritualistic prayer. A person is linked with his home by the hearth where his food is prepared. He makes a sacrificial pit with bricks like a hearth. In that he arranges pieces of firewood with which fire can be generated. He and his dear ones sit around that fire with whatever they have received from mother earth, such as wheat, rice, corn, gram, and other such edibles, clarified butter, a vessel containing water, and a burning lamp to witness. When the flames come, the Supreme, the All-inclusive, the One without a second, is remembered and addressed, *AUM tat*. The sun above and the fire below are in principle the same. So after building the fire, the sacrificer says, *AUM agne tava yat tejas tat brāhmam:* "O fire, this light of yours belongs to that Supreme light of *brahman.*"

What is below and what is above, what is locally understood and what is universally known are to be mentally united. This is the proper foundation for any meditation. What is felt in the heart and what goes beyond the horizon and even beyond the sun and moon – these two are to be coordinated. In recognition of that coordination, we say "O fire, this luminosity of yours belongs to the eternally luminous One." We have to establish an intimacy of perfect understanding with that. What we see in the palm of our hand is a symbol of certitude because it is visible and tangible. We see the light and feel the warmth of the fire on earth. The Supreme or *brahman* has unity with it because of the principle of homogeneity. What is cosmologically visualized is psychologically experienced in one's own body and the sacrificer says, *atastvam pratyakṣam brahmāsi:* "This way we have to become certain of our being."

Then he further says, *tvadīyā indriyāṇi manobuddhiriti saptajihvāḥ:* "A similar light is in this person which is like a fire." The fire in the sacrificial pit is described as having seven tongues: *kāli, karāli, manojavā, sulohitā, sudhūmravarṇa, sphuliṅgini,* and *viśvaruci* for its tongues. *Kāli* is the fire with dark smoke, *karāli* is the fire with leaping flames, *manojavā* is the fire that sends its rays with the speed like that of mind. *Sulohitā* is the fire with a flame that combines in it the red and blue color. *Sudhūmravarṇa* is the fire with several designs of smoke. *Sphuliṅgini* is the fire that scatters sparks. *Viśvaruci* is the fire that tastes, enjoys, everything in the world. A person also has a fire within with seven tongues. The fire in a person is represented by the five sense organs, the mind and the intellect. The fire is seen as an appropriate link between the psychological and the cosmological.

The offerings, i.e., the grains moistened with clarified butter and sprinkled with water *(samit),* are put into the fire with these words, *tvayi viṣayā iti samidho juhomi:* "We are sacrificing in you the objects of our nourishment." After the body is given for consumption, the inner organ represented by the ego is offered in the form of clarified butter with the words, *aham ityājyam juhomi:* "I am offering this libation of clarified butter as a sacrificial symbol of giving myself to you." Then it is taken for granted that the deity representing the Supreme at the omega is pleased with the sacrificer who is at the alpha. This is accompanied by the words, *tvam naḥ prasīda prasīda:* "May you be pleased."

Then the request is made, *śreyaśca, preyaśca, prayaccha svāhā:* "Let this bring *śreyas* and *preyas.*" Offerings are always accompanied by the sound *svāhā.* Although the sacrifice is an act of self-denial, and everything is burnt to ashes, the sacrificer gains what he or she has never experienced before. In the Vedic sacrifice, the benefit that comes from sacrifice is called *apūrva,* what has never been experienced before. This stands in contrast to the joy of receiving; here it is the joy of giving. The ritual is closed by saying: *aum śānti, śānti, śānti.*

The accruing result is one becoming a perfected child of one's own being. When a man impregnates his wife, it can be seen as he himself incarnating in his wife's womb as his son. Son is called *tāta* which is the same as saying, "I am that I am." The reference to a son here can be taken literally in the case of people who aspire for their own extension in progeny. As for the contemplative, each meditation renews one to be one's own perfected offspring. The person who goes into meditation on this mantra is going into a purificatory process which burns off all imperfections. He or she comes out as a reoriented person, wise and disciplined.

Mantra 2

> *yajuḥ; prāṇo vai yajuḥ, prāṇe hīmāni sarvāṇi bhūtāni yujyante; yujyante hāsmai sarvāṇi bhūtāni śraiṣṭhyāya, yajuṣaḥ sāyujyam salokatām jayati, ya evam veda.*

Word Meanings

> *yajuḥ* - (one should meditate on the vital breath as) the *yajus; prāṇaḥ* - the vital breath (is); *vai* - indeed; *yajuḥ* - *yajus; hi* - for; *sarvāṇi* - all; *imāni* - these; *bhūtāni* - beings; *yujyante* - are united; *prāṇe* - (if there is) the vital breath; *sarvāṇi* - all; *bhūtāni* - beings; *yujyante* - are united; *śraiṣṭhyāya* - to give eminence; *asmai* - to one; *ya* - who; *veda* - knows; *evam* - this; *jayati* - (and) he achieves; *sāyujyam* - union with; *salokatām* - (and) abode in the same world; *yajuṣaḥ* - with the *yajus*

(One should meditate upon the vital breath as) the *yajus*. The vital breath is indeed the *yajus*, for all these beings are united if there is the vital breath. All beings are united to give eminence to one who knows this, and he achieves union with and abode in the same world as the *yajus*.

Veda, knowledge, is to reveal the world in its general sense and its specific details. A thing is known through a revelation of its form. The form is identified as a unique mark by assigning a name to it. Thus the first phase of knowledge is nominal. Name is primarily used to indicate, to recognize, to mark off. When a name and form are put together, a unit of knowledge is presented for further familiarization. Familiarization is a method by which we come to descriptive knowledge. Within a system there are many correlative coordinates and special structures meant for different functions. Calling one's attention to each such specific part and indicating the structural arrangement and functional propensity are all functions of revelations which come through spoken words.

To determine the exact meaning of every word used in a sentence, grammar is employed. Thus the first stress in language is the correct syntactical structuring of words to make a meaningful sentence. All revelations are purposive. Purposes sometimes occur as causal factors and sometimes as effects. The mind has to move from the past to the present, and from the present to the future. This role of inquiry assigned to the mind is known as *codana*. Knowledge becomes exact when what is presented is approached with several appropriate questions. Each answer to a question is a revelation. Considering the purposiveness of connected sentences in the presentation of an argument shows the postulations to be examined. The verity of a position is to be ascertained through experience. From individual observations, a general statement is made. Holding the general statement as a definition, a formula, or a theorem, the relevancy is established.

After the syntactical study, logistics becomes important. The main justification of logic is the ensuing result that can be predicated or prophesied. Part of the proof comes from the very structure of knowledge itself. Every form of existence is to be presented in awareness as knowledge and every knowledge and its existence should be shown to contribute to an infallible meaning. Meaning implies value and its relevancy, and the inevitability of a certain result ensuing from a certain cause or a certain configuration of coordinates which can contribute to an achievement of a certain purpose. All purposes are intended to lift a person from distress and establish one in comfort, satisfaction, fulfillment and perfect harmony. All these are covered by the word *ānanda*.

The awareness of any existence can stand the transience of time and space only by establishing the validity of the result of promises. Knowledge has to release the latent to manifest in full magnitude. What is latent is a potential energy which can actualize or be sublimated. According to Heidegger, after a package of energy gathers momentum and finally explodes into the desired event of actualization, it is depleted and the energy itself assumes a phase in existence. The whole process of stimulating the call for energy, propelling it to maximum momentum, and bringing it to its ultimate transformation involves actions of various kinds. Thus the final aspect of any revelation is to actualize the desired result. Syntactics and logistics are followed by pragmatics. Pragmatics is that which can bring about the desired fruition or result. The nominal aspect of the *Ṛg Veda* is helpful to provide all the accessories and equipment to enter into the dynamics of full-fledged function. The *Ṛg Veda* is essentially theoretical. To move from theoretical knowledge to its application, it is to be complemented by *Yajur Veda*. In other words the *Ṛg* is the answer to the question, "What is this?" and the *Yajus* is the answer to the question, "Now what is to be done?"

Dharma is a package of energy. The package of energy in a hen's egg is to bring forth a chicken; the package of energy in a seed is to bring forth a special plant: the mango seed a mango tree, the coconut seed a coconut tree. In nature two correlatives are kept ready for a fusion at an appropriate moment. For instance, sodium and potassium are kept side by side so that they can come together through a liaison to develop an electrical impulse. Every individual thing in this world has its innate *dharma*, its propensity to unfold, to actualize, to serve a purpose. Therefore, *dharma* always implies action.

The epistemology of Indian philosophy is provided by the *Samkhya Darśana* of Kapila which presents the binary principles of *puruṣa* and *prakṛti*. *Puruṣa* is similar to magnetic forces and *prakṛti* to electrical forces. Although *puruṣa* is singular, the many activities of nature happen due to its sheer presence. There is no end to the possibilities of functions arising from the combination of the two principles of *prakṛti* and *puruṣa*. While *dharma* is unique and specific, it contributes to becoming more and more general and universal. The heterogeneous principle is placed in the homogeneous principle. Action is limited to the heterogeneous device, while the intention of the action is devised from the general homogeneity. This is the basic plan. In the presentation of the *Veda*, the syntactics, the logistics, and the pragmatics are expanded and laid out as the *Ṛg*, *Yajus* and *Sāma*.

In the present mantra, we are asked to meditate on *prāṇa* as *yajus*. We have already meditated on it as the spoken word *(uktha)*. The philosopher is in the wrong when he separates the *ṛk* from the *yajus* and the *yajus* from the *sāma*. Also no such division is allowed between *sat* and *cit*, and *cit* and *ānanda*; existence and subsistence, subsistence and value. In all this a holistic vision is necessary. For each function a very apt model is given. If praise or eulogy is the model for *ṛk*, sacrifice is the model for *yajus*. When we carry out the *vidhi* and the *niṣedha* in the ritualistic function of *Yajur Veda* we come to the arena of work *(karma)*. There is no *dharma* which can be separated from *karma*. *Dharma* is the seed and *karma* is its germinating process.

The first goal presented in the earlier Vedic lore was seeking pleasures of an immortal. That is going to heaven. Hence the first definition of a *brāhmaṇa* was one who performs *yajña* to go to heaven (*svarga*). This tendency of the *Veda* was later corrected by *Vedānta*. The main revaluation came through the ten major *Upaniṣads*. The meaning of the actualization of *dharma* changed from precipitating happiness to being unified with the total basis of *dharma* which is none other than *brahman*. In all scriptures which promise the release from *karma*, the method used by earlier Vedic rituals of sacrifice is employed with a revised pragmatics. The earlier vision that the purpose of a *jīva* is to become immortal was revised. The ultimate motivation came to be knowing what one truly is. In true knowledge there is no becoming; there is only the re-cognition of being.

A bunch of threads put together will automatically get entangled. Only by untying all the knots can you bring the threads to their original non-tangled state. Similarly, when an eddy is generated in the unlimited and omnipresent knowledge, a notion of the "this" and the "here and now" become entangled. The entangling comes because energy functions in a certain mode. The same energy is used for disentangling. *Prāṇa* is the cause of bondage and *prāṇa* is also the means of gaining release from bondage.

The *Bṛhadāraṇyaka Upaniṣad* is both a *śāstra* for *brahmavidyā* and a *śāstra* for ultimate union. Just as it is said that the horse cannot change direction in midstream, you cannot disentangle yourself from your *karma* without knowing the binding and unbinding tendencies of *karma*. The *karma* that we are asked to meditate on as *prāṇa* in this mantra is to be understood like a sacrifice. Books like the *Bhagavad Gītā* assure us that all *karmas* leading to bondage can be burnt away with the flames of knowledge *(vidyā)*. Thus meditating on the same as the *yajus* is a process by which all conditionings which came into this body/mind matrix are to be deconditioned by careful scrutiny. Everything colored is to be decolored. That which has become complicated is to be reduced to its simple basis.

The *Bhagavad Gītā* recommends dexterity in action as a means to be established in yoga: *yogaḥ karmasu kauśalam* (II:50). Having *kauśala* in *karma* is to have a clear notion of the functional reality of the manifested world (*idam*), which has come from the unmanifested *(adaḥ)*, and of transcending from *idam* to the *pūrṇam* to which all this belongs. *Pūrṇam* means the perfection of the Ultimate. These three are suggestive of the three states: the wakeful, in which one engages in *karma;* the dream, which mirrors or reflects the *samskāras* accumulated in the wakeful; and the *suṣupti*, in which the same Self can withdraw from being a participant in the games of the phenomenal. One goes beyond *suṣupti* if one knows what one was performing and has a deciphering method by which the prompting for action can be continued, not in pursuit of hedonistic pleasures, but to return to one's origin. It is a total transcendence of the scheme which is called *turīya*.

The actual performances of ritualistic sacrifices such as the horse sacrifice, which had a political intention, a social maneuvering, a psychological significance, and a detailed working out in the physical world, are to be reversed. Instead of the propitiation of icons, the implied symbols are to be reflected on. Instead of the ego having three distinct roles of the knower *(jñātā)*, the doer *(kartā)* and the enjoyer *(bhoktā)*, action becomes complementary to knowledge through unitive discipline. All through the text we are advised that we should achieve the Absolute by making true action complementary to true knowledge. The *Khila Kāṇḍa* is to give us a practical orientation in the discipline of union for integral life.

Just as we have noticed how the *Bṛhadāraṇyaka* makes an expansion of the scenario by lifting the *Upaniṣad* out of the context of time and clime, the entire *Upaniṣad* is worked out as an elaborate science of the Absolute which can be accepted without any dogma by anyone, anywhere in the world. Consequently, the sacrifice referred to here is not a local fixed ritual, done by any specific person. Already we have seen in the *Madhu Kāṇḍa* that even physical elements are considered to be sacrificing themselves for all beings and accepting from all beings benefits which on either side can be compared to invaluable honey. To interpret the present mantra, we do not have to go to any specific form of ritual, such as the moon sacrifice, *soma* sacrifices, or the horse sacrifice. Instead we sacrifice our microcosmic interests in the macrocosm and accept the macrocosm to get into fusion with the microcosmic polarity. Each person's life is considered to be a sacrifice.

In a sacrificial ritual, the symbol of a cosmic fire is accepted which is the recipient of whatever is offered in the sacrifice. In the present context, there is no duality between the sacrifice, the sacrificial fire and the sacrificer. This is clearly explicated in the *Bhagavad Gītā* (IV:24): "The act of offering is *brahman*, what is offered is *brahman*, the offering is made in the fire of *brahman;* the doer of the sacrifice is also *brahman;* the concentration in *karma* is also *brahman;* the result of this action is also *brahman;* everything is *brahman*."

This is an apt mantra to examine how, from the crown of our heads to the toes of our feet, every part of our bodies contributes to a sacrifice. We are giving to enhance the well-being of the entire universe. We are a honey to all and all are a honey to us. In this there can be a peripheral contemplation of the participation of our sensory faculties in making our life a ritualistic sacrifice. First of all we are told that what we hear should be auspicious. This induces us to be selective in our enjoyments of all auditory experiences. Our criterion should not be to get hedonistic pleasure from hearing. We come to know the highest form of wisdom by hearing. Even people outside the Vedic context, such as the Buddhists, concede to this suggestion. The Buddhists chant daily, *mūsāvādaveramaṇī śikhāpadam samādhiyāmi*: "I take the pledge not to indulge in any gossip or vain speech. Every word that I hear should be spiritually inspiring and every word that I speak should be beneficial to the whole world."

In a way, all hedonistic pleasures come from tactual pleasures. The peak pleasure is called *śṛṅgarasa*. *Śṛṅga* is the peak, and *rasa* is pleasure. This is the synonym for erotic pleasure, from which the seeker of highest truth abstains. Hearing the voice of the beloved is a joyous experience; touching is a joyous experience; seeing is a joyous experience; kissing is joyous; copulating is joyous. Withdrawing from all this is a sacrifice for the totality of beings. Sacrifice essentially means giving up what you love most for the benefit of others. Burning yourself in the fire of these pleasures is also a sacrifice, but one with a selfish end. There are sacrifices of omission and sacrifices of commission. All benevolent sacrifices are of omission. For that there has to be the giving up of self-centered pleasures.

In the example of a candle, it has three component factors: the cotton wick, the fat that is used as fuel, and the burning flame. Into the burning flame both the fat and the wick are giving themselves up. Consequently, the flame becomes radiant and its rays are going in all directions. Many are benefited by the light of the burning candle, but the candle burns away into nothingness. After complete burning, nothing of the wick is left nor of the fat, and finally the flame also extinguishes. Individually we are all like burning candles. If we are also altruistic like the candle or lamp, we can burn our physical energy, intellectual energy and emotional energy, all the resources we have, for the benefit of the whole world.

In all such sacrifices it is the *prāṇa* that is being burnt. The same *prāṇa* is helping us for all our transformations, from the zygote to the child, the child to the adult, and the adult to the dying person. It is with such a holistic vision that we are advised to promote the universal sacrifice for which the *Upaniṣad* stands. Just as every part of your body contributes to the sacrifice of life, every member of society can contribute with his or her sacrificial self-denial to the welfare of all. The cardinal teaching of the *Madhu Kāṇḍa* was that we should look upon the entire universe as a benevolent fraternity where everything is a honey to every other thing. In the present mantra we are asked to look upon truth itself as a continuous process of sacrifice.

Fire has a position among the five elements as the central

entity that holds its balance between space (*ākāśa*) and air (*vāyu*), on the one hand, and earth (*pṛthvī*) and water (*ap*), on the other. It is as if the fire is in charge of all the engineering of composition and decomposition which is the central theme of producing, maintaining, recycling, dissolving, and continuing for all eternity, the appearance and disappearance of the phenomena. Vaguely or certainly, everybody knows the central secret of the creation of this world. Emily Dickinson gives us the following very beautiful lines which open up a great secret to us. She begins with an invocation to the muses:

Awake ye muses nine, sing me a strain divine,
Unwind the solemn twine, and tie my Valentine!

Oh the Earth was *made* for lovers, for damsel,
and hopeless swain,
For sighing, and gentle whispering, and *unity* made of *twain*.
All things do go a courting, in earth, or sea, or air,
God hath made nothing single but *thee* in His world so fair!
The *bride* and then the *bridegroom*, the *two*,
and then the *one*,
Adam, and Eve, his consort, the moon, and then the sun;
The life doth prove the precept, who obey shall happy be,
Who will not serve the sovereign, be hanged on fatal tree.
The high do seek the lowly, the great do seek the small,
None cannot find who *seeketh*, on this terrestrial ball;
The bee doth court the flower, the flower his suit receives,
And they make merry wedding,
whose guests are hundred leaves;
The wind doth woo the branches, the branches they are won,

And the father fond demandeth the maiden for his son.
The storm doth walk the seashore
humming a mournful tune,
The wave with eye so pensive, looketh to see the moon,
Their spirits meet together, they make them solemn vows,
No more he singeth mournful, her sadness she doth lose.
The *worm* doth woo the *mortal*, death claims a living bride,
Night unto day is married, morn unto eventide;
Earth is a merry damsel, and *heaven* a knight so true,
And Earth is quite coquettish,

and beseemeth in vain to sue.[16]

Emily Dickinson is not a rishi of ancient India. She was an American woman of the last century. But she clearly sees how everything in this world is so poised and polarized that one thing complements another, or contradicts only to reciprocate, and, even when they cancel out each other, it is only to come to a neutral zero of all-pervading love. It is no wonder that the rishi, who is far more sensible than any poet, has seen in the fabric of life the warp and woof of belongingness where one thing lends its inner strength to the other and gains from the other the magnificence of beauty.

On hearing the word 'sacrifice' those who are familiar with old texts will think of tragic pictures of innocent animals butchered and burned in the leaping flames of a sacrificial pit. We have to forget the ancient connotation of sacrifice and revalue it as the continuous process of making and remaking this universe so that all shades of its imperfections are corrected and new possibilities proclaimed. There are two ways of knowing this world. One is going out in time and space, picking up a pebble, breaking it to pieces, pulverizing it, then looking at every tiny bit of it like a culprit who is hiding the truth of the world. The seeker, in that case a physicist, has to break through the atom to arrive at something which is at once identified with a particle as well as a wave of energy. It is this paradox which is in the heart of truth everywhere: duality which on further examination by a contemplative mind will reveal to us non-duality.

A sacrificial fire is an instrument to bring about transformation. The fire is too crude an agent to handle the subtleties of life. So the rishi asks us to see fire as a less tangible, less gross, and highly poetic intentional creativity hiding in everything which we can locate in our own person as our breath. We are asked to meditate on that breath as *yajus*. We have seen that of the three Vedas, *Ṛg*, *Yajur*, and *Sāma*, *Ṛg* is the indicative, and *Yajur* is the instruction to act, and *Sāma* is to rejoice at the outcome.

Here the rishi asks us not to go out, but to seek the same principle within us. The wisdom of the ancient people assures us that what is above is the same as what is below. That being so, the macrocosm is best understood by looking into the microcosm. If you know yourself, you know the world. In another *Upaniṣad* we are told that to know water all that is needed is a cup of water; one does not have to empty the contents of the seven seas to familiarize oneself with the principle of water. To know the nature of iron, you only need to study a pair of scissors, you do not have to examine all the iron ore of the world. A ring of gold can tell you all about gold. Even so, by looking at the function of your breath, you will also know how the cosmos is created and maintained.

In a sugar factory, raw sugar cane is fed into a receiving vault and, at the other end of the factory, sugar cubes or fine crystals properly packed and labeled come out. Only the workers inside the factory know how many processes are to be arranged in a series to convert sugar cane into sugar cubes. In the same way, we see iron and steel and aluminum all going into an automobile manufacturing plant and streamlined motorcars being driven off of the assembly line. We have studied the strategies of cosmic manifestation and copied them into our own technological devices. It is this area to which the rishi points his finger and says that everything in this world is to promote the welfare of everything else.

Space has to sacrifice areas for bodies to occupy. From a subatomic particle to the galaxy, space is the donor for all gross and subtle bodies to come into being. Space lends itself to be broken up and cluttered with impenetrable bodies through an act of sacrifice. The second element, air, is also like a willing sacrificer. It fills the entire biologic sphere and gladly waits around every living being to find a passage into the organism to replenish it with vital energy. Nobody goes out in search of air to breathe; air spontaneously, lovingly, enters our nostrils. Once having entered, it gets into the labyrinths in our bodies. All that we know is that our lungs have something to do with it. But what is that "something?"

We can go into it step by step. Let us first take into account a magnificent task done by the air that we breathe - that of supplying to every cell of our bodies the essence of what we put into our mouths as morsels of food or sips of liquid. Fortunately, we have far advanced in this understanding in the present century thanks to the researchers in the fields of molecular biology. They have unraveled the mystery of life by telling us how a living cell is formed and maintained. Physiology gives us many unforgettable illustrations of sacrifice going on all the time in all of us. We read here a summary given in the *Molecular Biology of the Cell*, a textbook for medical students:

> Living cells are highly ordered and must create order within themselves to grow and survive. This is thermodynamically possible only because of a continual input of energy, part of which is released from the cells to their environment as heat.
>
> [Give special notice to this word heat. Wherever there is heat, it symbolizes the cosmic significance of sacrifice. There is no need for a sacrificial pit with other priests sitting around it to carry out a sacrifice, because all this began at least ten million years before any living being made strategies for the upkeep of life on earth.]
>
> The energy comes ultimately from the electromagnetic radiation of the sun, which drives the formation of organic molecules in photosynthetic organisms such as green plants.
>
> [The mighty sun is blazing forth millions of miles away, and the little blade of grass holds itself forth with a prayer to receive the benediction of the sun. Only in that way does the blade of grass becomes green.]
>
> Animals obtain their energy by taking up these organic molecules and oxidizing them in a series of enzyme-catalyzed reactions that are coupled to the formation of ATP (adenosine triphosphate). ATP is a common currency of energy in all cells and its hydrolysis is coupled to other reactions to drive a variety of energetically unfavorable processes that create order. [17]

It is here we look into the function of the air we breathe. The green plant prepares its nourishment in a leaf and carries it to the rest of the plant from its roots up to the new sprout that is coming at the tip of the branches. The same sacrificial order and coordinations can be seen in our own digestive system. In the same book we get a description of food and the derivation of cellular energy: "The proteins, lipids, and polysaccharides that make up the major part of the food we eat must be broken down into smaller molecules before our cells can use them. The enzymatic breakdown, or catabolism, of these molecules may be regarded as proceeding in three stages." [18] For a detailed study, please refer to the book under reference which also includes a simplified diagram of the three stages of catabolism that lead from food to waste products. This series of reactions produces ATP, which is then used to drive bio-synthetic reactions and other energy-requiring processes in the cell. So there is a unit of sacrificial operation going on in any organism where the nourishment from food is to be derived.

Although air is willingly waiting in front of our nostrils to be breathed in, on most occasions we are not even aware that we are breathing in life-giving air. If we make ourselves a little more conscious, such as the *prāṇāyāmis* do, we can feel air passing through our nostrils. Without any special activity on our part, it goes through the wind pipe to the lungs. Of course, we know the lungs expand and contract. Why do they do it rhythmically? We do not know. The lungs are in collusion with the heart, which also pulsates. The lungs function like the bellows of a blacksmith. The blacksmith's bellow is only made out of sheep skin, while our lungs can be compared to a forest of trees with a few trunks and branches and millions of leaf-like structures called alveoli. There are about 300 million alveoli in the two lungs, each having an average diameter of about 0.25 mm. The alveolar walls are extremely thin, and within them is an almost solid network of interconnecting capillaries which facilitate the flow of blood in the alveolar walls, and it has been described as a "sheet" of flowing blood. Thus it is obvious that the alveolar gases are in close proximity to the blood of the capillaries. A study of this will resolve one of the paradoxes which confronts anyone who thinks of the relationship between gases, matter and water. Blood is like water and the air we breathe is gaseous. The one is introduced into the other to make water the carrier of gas to every part of our body. Every cell is animated by this vitality. In this way we have to see the suggestion of the rishi that everything lives for the other.

We have cited these examples from modern textbooks of medicine only to caution the reader not to take the sacrificial ritual alluded to in the present mantra as *yajus* in a crude and narrow sense of the term, but with a holistic outlook so that our understanding can be shared by humanity everywhere.

The teaching of the *Upaniṣad* needs to be re-translated into the language of the newly educated so that these mantras won't look like the lisping of a baby. If we look into the history of Indian civilization in Will Durant's monumental work, *The Story of Civilization*, he praises the Indian for his sagacity, wisdom and love, but sees the *Upaniṣads* as 'baby talk'. There was no one to tell Will Durant how to go deep into the archaic language of the *Upaniṣad*. Even in modern days those who have translated and commented on the *Upaniṣads* have been sticking to an ancient tongue and outmoded ways of commenting on them. Even though they have made great efforts at publishing the *Upaniṣads*, they made them look as useless as old fables. However, the fables at least have some fascination because of their poetic flavor, while most Upaniṣadic commentaries are as dry as the bones of a dead cow discarded by the eagles. So we solicit the favor of the reader to cooperate with us in our effort to correlate the ancient in the scriptures with the modern positive sciences.

Mantra 3

> *sāma; prāṇo vai sāma, prāṇe hīmāni sarvāṇi bhūtāni samyañci; samyañci hāsmai sarvāṇi bhūtāni śraiṣṭhyāya, kalpante sāmnaḥ sāyujyam salokatām jayati, ya evam veda.*

Word Meanings

sāma - (one should meditate on the vital breath as) the *sāman; prāṇaḥ* - the vital breath (is); *vai* - indeed; *sāma* - the *sāman; hi* - for; *sarvāṇi* - all; *imāni* - these; *bhūtāni* - beings; *samyañci* - are united; *prāṇe* - (if there is) the vital breath; *asmai* - for one; *ya* - who; *veda* - knows; *evam* - this; *sarvāṇi* - all; *bhūtāni* - beings; *samyañci* - are united; *kalpante* - (and) they succeed; *śraiṣṭhyāya* - in giving him eminence; *jayati* - (and) he achieves; *sāyujyam* - union with; *salokatām* - (and) abode in the same world; *sāmnaḥ* - as the *sāman*

(One should meditate upon the vital breath as) the *sāman*. The vital breath is indeed the *sāman*, for all these beings are united if there is the vital breath. For one who knows this, all beings are united, and they succeed in giving him eminence, and he achieves union with and abode in the same world as the *sāman*.

We each came to this world with an individual consciousness. At that time, consciousness had no sense of the other and was like a passive witness which John Locke described as a *tabula rasa*, a clean slate. Then one by one our faculties of perception brought stimulus after stimulus. Even if an infant does not ask anything, we take it for granted that it is to be informed about the world around it. Those who are concerned about enlightening the baby first familiarize it with a number of names. Every item is distinguished by a specific name (*ṛk*).

Once a perception is processed, cognition is prompted to recognition. Recognition is based on the figure or form of an object, and that perception is registered in the consciousness of the perceiver in seed form as a concept. The concept is affixed to a name which has to last in place of the object. The name is used as a memory tag to recall the form and content of the characteristic of the percept. These are all brought into a confection, so to say. Every concept is a confection of the form, name and functional properties of what is seen. That is why we said *ṛk* is a familiarization not for one instance, but to be retained in our memory for the rest of our life. It is the verbal indication of a permanent mark of uniqueness.

The child is told, "This is your mother, this is your father, this is your brother, and this is your sister." This is only the beginning of a series. At least for the first twenty years every person is fed with name after name, and each name belongs to a class of its own. These are the primary bricks with which a person's world is built. Then comes a series of recognitions of relationships. Every name indicates a certain relationship. Even one relationship can branch off into many relationships, such as, "This is my mother. That is my mother's husband. Therefore he is my father." Or: "This is my mother's son. Therefore he is my brother. That is my mother's daughter. Therefore she is my sister." Or: "That person is my neighbor. Therefore his wife and children are all my neighbors. I belong to this country, and my country has innumerable people. They are all my countrymen." In all these instances, relationships are enumerated and recognized. From each relationship there arises the specificity of a certain value: "My mother is dear to me, so I am her darling. She gladdens my heart; I gladden her heart." Not only is this a fact, this is a relationship to be established forever. "She should not hurt me, and I should not hurt her. She cares for me. I should care for her." At first we were familiarizing ourselves with names. Now we are familiarizing ourselves with relationships.

This automatically takes us to the consideration of innumerable values. A value is not only indicative of the presence of an object, it also elicits from us several shades of emotions. In the word emotion there is a suggestion of something that is going to move you in some direction. After establishing an emotional relationship, no person is static in relation to the thing, person or idea which evokes emotion. A motive is actualized only with an action. From the sphere of knowledge we come to the sphere of action. All values have dynamics of action potentialities. It is here the *ṛk* summons the *yajus*.

In India it is a prerequisite for everyone to know the integral law of life called *dharma*. Even within a person, the eye is for seeing, the ear for hearing, the finger for touching, the tongue for tasting, and the nose for smelling. Corresponding to these there are other laws such as, light to illuminate, air to bring sensation. The world of activities that arises from the obligatory relationship of values in a very large world increases day by day. An individual's main preoccupation becomes never-ending adjustments in interpersonal relationships as well as intrapersonal relationships. Life itself is to attend to the various activities and become the center of all possible relationships with everything and everyone around us. We need orientation to know what is on which side, and how to reach out each and every moment to fulfill our obligations, duties and responsibilities.

We are now brought to a comprehensive vision of life in spite of all the individual differences of everything we come across. Every person we relate with, every word we speak, every action we do, is likely to bring disharmony, separateness and a negative attitude. With a little care we can change this gloomy aspect of life and make everybody happy and in turn share the happiness of all. There is a single principle of truth in all of us. In all life forms there is the same life. In every formulated being there is a chemistry of unification. We start seeing not just persons with names, relations with values, but the joy of recognizing unity. *Sāma* means equal. When your knowledge, passions, and propensities to act have all equalized you are in a state of equipoise.

When the day breaks, members of the family get up and each one goes to his or her assigned duties. In the night all return to sit by the family altar to sing and pray together. All sit around the same table to dine and all sleep under the same roof. Where a Vedic ritual is done, all the participants gather together at the end of the ritual, jubilant with satisfaction. In gratitude they want to sing in praise of the grace that blesses all with union. This is called the *sāma*.

Here we are lifted out of such singled out rituals and told that we are one with the velvety grass of our lawn, the flowering plants of our garden, the trees that sway in the wind, the birds that sing, the floating clouds, and the sky which awaits the stars. We can spread ourselves out into the cosmos filling all space and all time and establishing joyous relationships with everything. A friend visiting with us and a breeze that wafts into our leisurely moment are both welcome. Everything is friendly. Nothing and no one is to be rejected. If each day we add to our festivity of life and our camaraderie, *sāma* is on the increase.

There is a dialectical interplay between the many and the one. In the *Bhagavad Gītā* we are given a chance to see the one Absolute in all relative factors. To relate yourself with Kṛṣṇa you need not look for a dark person decorated with the peacock feather, enticing you with his flute. In the *Gītā*, Kṛṣṇa helps us to train our mind to recognize the eternal presence of the Absolute in everything, "as unborn and beginningless, as the great lord of the world." What is before us and what is held away from us is the same adorable truth.

When you are reasonable, you are with the Absolute. Then your mark is wisdom. If you are not deluded, you are one with the Absolute. Your patience is experiencing the divine. The certitude that comes naturally to you, your calmness, your ability to live with pleasure and pain, becoming and non-becoming, security as well as insecurity, all assure you that you are one with the Absolute. As there is nothing alien to you, naturally you become non-hurting, well-balanced; your contentment shows how there is nothing extraneous to you. Like a candle burning with an unflickering flame, you can burn for others, because you are benevolence. You are not elated when fame comes and you are not depressed if you are exposed to shame. All the great ones, the law givers, are so close to you, they are all eternally present in your loving mind. You act like the Absolute when you are led by the fundamental principles of life.

In the *Gīta* Kṛṣṇa says to Arjuna, "I am in you when you balance yourself with everything, through non-wavering contemplation, and when you are not assailed by death." The Absolute which Kṛṣṇa identifies himself with speaks in the first person in Chapter Ten, verse eight: "I am the source of all; from Me everything moves outwards; understanding thus, the wise adore Me, endowed with the intuition of pure becoming."

If you ask how you can meditate on *sāma*, Kṛṣṇa says (IX:34):

> Gather yourself in me. Let all your life tendencies permeate with the harmony of my eternal song. When you meet your friend and you are not tired of speaking to him or her of your love for Me, and tirelessly when you listen to your friend, with what fond affection your friend is holding Me, then I am the link between you and your friend. You are like a drunk person, one lost in an eternal embrace, always in a state of affectionate adoration. The slightest sight of anyone in pain is enough to make your eyes brim in tears and for your heart to miss a beat. Your sensibility embraces everything.

These words of Kṛṣṇa affect Arjuna and he starts seeing everything in him, and himself as the one unifying truth of truth, love of love. Coming to such a state of ecstasy, Arjuna asks Kṛṣṇa (X:17-18):

> How shall I, constantly meditating on You, know You, O Mystic (yogi); in what particular expressions, O blessed One, are You to be cognized by Me? Tell me, again in detail, O Janardana (Kṛṣṇa), of your balanced perfections and specific expressions, for I am never satiated by hearing your words of ambrosial immortality.

Pleased with Arjuna's words, Kṛṣṇa says (X:19-20):

> Ah! I shall recount to you the (bright) glorious values that pertain to Myself, (graded) according to their importance, O Best of the Kurus (Arjuna), for there is no end to the elaboration of items pertaining to Me.
>
> I am the soul, O Gudākeśa (Arjuna), seated in the heart of all beings; and I am the beginning, and the middle and even the end of beings.

Each one of us can develop our own ever-abiding harmony with all and make ourselves into a bouquet of fresh flowers gathered from the past, present, and future. Such is the suggestion of this mantra: to give yourself a feast of peace and serenity, beauty and comradeship, with everything in this world. Then you have experienced the *sāma*, the song of equity, the song of union.

Mantra 4

kṣattram; prāṇo vai kṣattram, prāṇo hi vai kṣattram, trāyate hainam prāṇaḥ kṣaṇitoḥ; pra kṣattramatram-āpnoti, kṣattrasya sāyujyam salokatām jayati, ya evam veda.

Word Meanings

kṣattram - (one should meditate on the vital breath as) the *kṣattra* (literally 'which saves from wounds'); *prāṇaḥ* - the vital breath (is); *kṣattram* - the *kṣattra; hi* - for; *prāṇaḥ* - the vital breath (is); *vai* - indeed; *kṣattram* - the *kṣattra; prāṇaḥ* - the vital breath; *trāyate ha* - protects; *enam* - the (body); *kṣaṇitoḥ* - from wounds; *yaḥ* - (one) who; *veda* - knows; *evam* - this; *prāpnoti* - attains; *kṣattram* - this *kṣattra; atram* - which needs no other protector; *jayati* - (and) achieves; *sāyujyam* - union with; *salokatām* - (and) abode in the same world; *kṣattrasya* - as the *kṣattra*

(One should meditate upon the vital breath as) the *kṣattra*. The vital breath is the *kṣattra*, for it is indeed the *kṣattra:* the vital breath protects the body from wounds. One who knows this attains this *kṣattra* which needs no other protector, and achieves union with and abode in the same world as the *kṣattra*.

The name itself of the Indian medical science, *Ayurveda*, reveals that it is a scripture concerning the life-span of a person (*ayus* = life span). The presence of life is indicated in a being by the signs of animation in the organism. Some of the features of animation are pulsating, breathing, moving, and variously functioning. All these can happen only when there is a rhythmic continuation of the process of breathing. There is the outgoing breath and the ingoing breath. The ingoing breath is *śvāsa* and outgoing is *ucchvāsa*. Thus respiration is *śvāsocchvāsa*. The respiratory system needs protection of various kinds. First of all, it is placed in the thorax, well fortified with muscles and kept upright with the spinal column. Injury is warded off with an encasement of ribs.

The passage into the lungs is protected with several guards. The hairs in the nostrils are the first column of defense provided to us. The air that we breathe in may be moist or dry, hot or cool. The ingenious device of passing the breath through a thick brush of hairs makes wet air comparatively dry and dry air moderately wet. If dust particles or other molecules escape the vigilance of the hairs in the nose, a more efficient screening is done in the throat where sticky mucous is generated. The defense system uses mucus like a flypaper screen to prevent pollutants from entering the respiratory system. Another defense device in the nose is the instantaneous sneeze that drives the polluted air back into the external environment. These reactions do not come from our conscious behavior. They are regulated by the autonomous system.

The nose itself can act as a defense guard at the time of the intake of food. If food with a suspicious odor is brought to the mouth, its pollution is detected by the nose which is even clever enough to bring a reaction of nausea. If one eats and drinks despite the prevention made by nausea, there is every likelihood of throwing up. From the very outset of life, the *prāṇa* is helping us to relate and shake off relations.

The respiration on which our life depends from moment to moment has to be safeguarded if a person is to live for a considerable length of time to carry out his or her assignment on earth. People who assume the responsibility of not only taking care of themselves but also working for the welfare of the entire community have programs which are never easily terminated. One may have to live with one's duties to the very end of one's life. The rishis think that it is only normal to expect to live for a hundred years. So we have to see how breath protects itself and removes the likelihood of death as far as possible into a distant date in the future. Although the artificer of the universe is giving every care to protect every item for its normal function, in its allotted period, the individual in every organism should also participate in the scheme of the universal deviser. This being a subject of vast dimension we have to approach it from several angles. We will take them one by one. First the physical, then the psychological, then the social and finally the moral and spiritual.

Whether you call the first cause of this Universe *brahman, ātman, akṣara, praṇava,* God or Allah, these concepts belong to some language or another. Each concept is a word conceived by the mind. We are continuously impressed by our external and internal environment. The state of consciousness, awareness or even sensation is the nucleus of what can be termed mind. The reaction or reciprocation to an impression is the basis of the word or the words that go into the fabrication of the languages of science and philosophy of erudite humans. The world is that which impresses. The mind is that which is impressed. The impression is as it were a revelation.

Hence everything that looms into sensation or awareness is technically *veda,* that which makes itself known. Whatever the basic mind-stuff of lower beings, the human mind is the actualization of the stream of consciousness manifesting in words. Words can be instrumental for the human to preserve peace and avoid distress which can bring the discordance of war. Hence the *Arthava Veda* offers the following prayer:

> *AUM.* May we, O Gods, hear with our ears what is auspicious. May we, efficient to worship, see with our eyes what is auspicious. May we, who sing your praise, live our allotted span of life in perfect health and strength.
>
> May Indra, the Lord extolled in the ancient scriptures, Pūṣan, the nourisher, Tārkṣya, the designer, and Bṛhaspati, the master of words, who enhances our clarity of expression, vouchsafe us prosperity in our study of the scriptures and the practice of the truths that are proclaimed in them.

We need words to think, to meditate, to speak, to proclaim truth, to instruct, to explicate, to illustrate, to pray or to exhort. A seer needs to employs words in the attempt to relate human beings to God and to establish God in the human mind. We need words to caution, to prohibit, to ban, to command and to judge merit. That is what a ruler of people does. We need words to bargain, to impress and influence others and create interest in communicable values. That is how a trader employs words. The executive who is weighed down by duties uses words to learn the needs of all in order to carry out the daily chores. He uses words to appeal, supplicate and even to lament his grievances.

We constantly need to help to overcome three great recurring contingencies: falsehood, ignorance and impending death. These universal anomalies are met with the saving power of words. Hence this universal prayer:

asato mā sat gamaya
tamaso mā jyotir gamaya
mṛtyor mā amrtam gamaya.

From untruth may we be delivered to truth,
From darkness may we be delivered to the light of wisdom,
From death may we be delivered to immortality.

By chanting *(udgītha)* we invoke grace and say what protection we need against untruth, ignorance, and death. From monosyllables, sounds can weave words, sentences, paragraphs, and books of voluminous size like the *Mahābhārata* containing one hundred and twenty-five thousand verses. The minutest elements of spoken language are microtones and pauses of silence. Whichever language is spoken anywhere in the world, it needs the structuring sounds that have secured the common consent of those who speak that language. The fact that one spoken or written language can be translated into the words of another language shows that there is a conceptual unity in the universal mind.

Brahman is *kṣattra.* Everything in this universe is purposively correlated. The purpose of everything, from an iota to the solar system, is to relate to one or several items to enrich, enhance, and protect another item that is progressing towards its fulfillment of a purpose. When an item achieves its absolute purpose it is to be annulled to give space, time and opportunity to another to continue the universe afresh with its eternal purpose of proliferation. This is true in the physical world, chemical world, biological world, physiological world, psychological world, sociobiological world and politico-economic world of civilizations.

In the physical world, we can see a careful pairing of opposites 1) to complement, 2) to reciprocate, 3) to contradict, and 4) to cancel out each other. In all these we can see vividly the eternal and perennial scheme of affirming the origin of existential designs, their elaborations called growth, improved replications, evolution, disintegration of the non-productive and extinction. In that continuing process there has to be a fortress of protection and an umbrella of defense to meet every contingency that can spell disaster or blockage to the harmonious fulfillment of a mooted purpose.

To understand this seemingly infinite range of possibilities in the closest knitting of the cosmos with known and unknown finite systems of overall purposes and partial justification of purpose, let us begin with the minute atom. An atom is a basic structural unit of matter, being the smallest particle of an element that can enter into chemical combination. It is this provision of the atom that requires careful maneuvering to preserve its uniqueness and to guide its destiny with purposiveness as it relates with other atoms.

Each atom has its characteristic physical and chemical properties. These characteristics are determined by the number of constituent particles - protons, neutrons, and electrons - of which it is composed. In this structuring what is most important is the number 'Z' of protons in the nucleus of each atom. To be electrically neutral the number of electrons in an atom must also be 'Z'. The arrangement of these electrons in the internal structure of an atom determines its chemical properties. All atoms having the same atomic number (Z) have the same chemical properties, but differ in greater or lesser degree from atoms having any other value of Z. That means - *brahman* is not a crude god of theistic fabrication. *Brahman* is the essential calculus of all possible coordinations and correlatives.

A chemical element may be defined as a collection of atoms of one type which cannot be decomposed into any simpler units by any chemical transformation, but which may spontaneously change into another unit by radioactive processes. A chemical element is a substance that is made up of but one kind of atom. Of the over one hundred chemical elements known, only ninety are found in nature. The remaining elements have been produced in nuclear reactors and particle accelerators. What is most interesting is that almost all living bodies are fashioned out of the versatility of carbon. The term organic, which means pertaining to plant or animal organisms, was introduced into chemical terminology as a convenient classification of substances derived from plant or animal sources. The modern definition of organic chemistry has been changed to mean the chemistry of carbon compounds. Specialized families of compounds like carbohydrates are the body-building materials of living organisms including humans. They include hydrates, terpens, alkaloids, steroids, lipids, proteins, enzymes, vitamins, etc. When we study these basic factors of life on earth we will not fail to notice the meticulous care taken in all details of organic compounds for the defense of the one purpose for which all manifestations come into being.

Today biochemistry concerns itself with the chemistry of molecules found in and associated with living systems, especially the chemistry of the interaction of these molecules. Most biochemists operate in a particular philosophical framework. Biochemistry in a large measure is a reductionist science. The usually unspoken assumption is that the activities of cells, for all their complexity, must be susceptible to explanation as chemical and physical phenomena as they perform the various requirements of keeping the organism functioning in its oxygenation, nourishment, physical activity, mating and reproduction, etc. All animals and plants are made up of cells. Some lower forms of life, such as bacteria, may be nothing more than a single cell. Larger plants and animals are built up by the gluing together of many of these cells into a larger mass. The human body itself begins as a single cell. This cell divides to form two cells and these divide in turn to form four, etc. The plan of division and enlargement is not to make cancerous growth, but a well-defined, well-structured organism that can bring an all-round improvement to its species and its environment. Each cell may be thought of as having a life of its own. The cell has capabilities beyond those of its sub-systems. Its abilities are to release and control all available faculties to meet its assigned purpose. After a human being dies, it may require hours, even days before all the cells are dead. There is perfect care and defense given to the whole organism and such protection and care are also given to each cell that constitutes a body.

In the evolution of the cell we can study small molecules, energy and biosynthesis and how they are put together to make macromolecules which can be structured into shapes. Information is passed on to give each molecule a definitive role to play in association with other cells. The best study one can make of defense in the biological world is to have a detailed and clear notion of the maintenance of tissues for which there is such an elaborate immune system.

We are not the only living beings in our residential areas. There are bacteria (both benevolent and malevolent), viruses, fungus, and parasites of all kinds. The immensity of our immune system is equally impressive. There are two broad classes of immune responses: the first is humoral antibody responses which involve the production of antibodies that circulate in the blood system and bind specifically to the foreign antigen that induced them. The binding of antibody to the antigen makes it easier for phagocytic cells to ingest the antigens and often activates a system of blood proteins, collectively called complement. That helps to destroy the antigen.

There is also a cellular basis of immunity. The immune system is composed of billions of lymphocytes. This is the most important defense system in the organism to checkmate diseases and for the recovery of the tissues. Lymphocytes are white blood cells. They are found in large numbers in the blood and the lymph. When we think of all these defense devices, from the atom to a full-fledged human, we are overwhelmed. This is only a minute fragment of the loving care implied in the creation (projection) of the universe. That is why in the *Gītā*, Kṛṣṇa says (X:41-42):

> Whatever entity is unique in perfected value, in grace or in radical strength, understand that to have manifested itself from a mere fractional spark of my brilliance.
>
> But what use is there for you Arjuna, in this pluralistic knowledge? Supporting this whole world by a single fraction (of myself), I remain still as ever.

That is the best analogy we can give to *brahman* as *kṣattra*. From the cell to the Self, it is like a sovereign state with a benevolent governorship by a philosopher king. The cell is autonomous, self-born, self-governing. So is a person as well as the cosmic universe. The same is also true of the omniscient, indweller, immortal, *akṣara-brahman*. Each has a device (*yantra*), a means to impress as well as express (*mantra*), and a self-maneuvering, a *modus vivendi* and a *modus operandi (tantra)*. A philosopher king symbolizes the true *kṣattra*. With his loving care and generosity, the king conceives, generates, nurtures, nourishes, educates, shelters, disciplines, controls and makes happy.

We have now seen that each of us amidst our countless fellow creatures is given a well-equipped body with immeasurable resources, a goal to reach and a path well laid out and considerably illuminated. To understand the governing principle of life, we have looked at its physical basis, its atomic, molecular, and cellular constituents, the magical alchemy provided by nature's abundance of earth, water, fire and air. Now let us see what role we have to play in the scheme of *kṣattra*. We are provided with a body which is like a miniature city well-equipped with internal furniture, provisions, security devices, and communication lines. We have the most sophisticated office equipment, observatory, and laboratory. We have assigned chores and errands.

Each member of human society is a person with a mind which expresses with words and we are each governed by the laws of grammar, logic, ethics and aesthetics. The mouse can squeak, the cat can mew, the dog can bark, the donkey can bray, the pig can grunt, the lion can roar, the little birdie can sing and we have the most elaborate of languages to communicate with. On one side we are expected to choose from the abundance of vocabulary the most appropriate words in a well-structured manner. On the other hand, we have to think about logistics. Logic is the main truth. With logic we get a criterion of verifiability. While a sentence may be emotionally or poetically significant to the speaker, it should be literally significant to the listener. Secondly, an expression in speech should be practically verifiable more than being merely theoretically verifiable. A proposition is said to be verifiable in the strong sense of the term, if and only if its truth can be conclusively established in experience.

Communication between two people is like establishing diplomatic conventions between two sovereign nations. This involves home affairs as well as foreign policy. Cognitive observation, recall of memory, the counsel of internal ministers – our inner organ uses these to prepare a message. This preparation implies the team work of brain activity, automation, the individual's habitual behavior, and the influence of the unconscious propensities which Indian psychologists term *vāsana*.

Just as the cells of our body reciprocally participate in a corporation without giving up their autonomy or sovereignty, individuals are also members of the human corporation. Our mutuality of complementarity and reciprocation implies our belongingness to a general good. A person cannot find his or her individual identity and supreme value in the *summum bonum* of another. We live in bodies which have mass, extension and theoretical impenetrability. So each person's spatial beingness is lived in his or her allotted temporal life situation and one has to fill the natural niche to which he or she belongs. Finding one's natural niche is the same as finding one's *svadharma*.

On the psychophysical side there are several kinds of belongingness which are of a binding nature (*graha* and *atigraha*) which cause both bondage and the pleasure/pain duality of *samsāra*. Spiritual belongingness is only to the Absolute. The sense of *svadharma* can come in both interpersonal and intrapersonal relationship. The *svadharma* that comes in intrapersonal relationship can give one a sense of fulfillment and spiritual enlightenment. This will often be thwarted by interpersonal relationships of social or familial moorings. This can be our major challenge - to extricate ourselves from bondage. Worldly sentiments can ambush an individual with the display of many tacit contracts which demand loyalty. Thus, *brahmavidyā*, the science of living in absolute freedom, is often defeated by *dharma śāstra*. That is why Kṛṣṇa says in the *Gītā* (XVIII:66), *sarvadharmān parityajya mām ekam śaraṇam vraja aham tvā sarvapāpebhyo mokṣayiṣyāmi mā śucaḥ:* "Abandoning all duties, come to me, the one, for refuge; I shall absolve you from all sins; do not despair."

There is a catch in deciding how our actions are to be chosen. Narayana Guru presents the problem of unitive action in five verses (21-25) of his *Ātmopadeśa Śatakam*. Reproduced here are the translations and commentaries of two of these verses given by his direct disciple, Nataraja Guru:

> A certain kind is dear, that is dear to me;
> what is one's own desire
> And what is to another, so variously thus
> puzzlement prevails
> Round each object of desire: what to oneself is dear
> That verily know to be another's desire also.

Life expresses itself through attractions and repulsions, likes or dislikes, preferences or rejections, strong or weak. When we come to examine the different kinds of interests or value-appreciations that human beings generally are capable of having, we can think of them in four different kinds of combinations. There is (1) the self that relates itself to outside object, or (2) to a certain specific quality outside itself, as when we say, "I like a rose", or "I like beauty". (3) When we say "this is my preference," we have a personal and subjectively directed movement of interest. As against this self-directed kind of interest there are (4) interests which have their accent on the opposite pole of the non-self. In all four cases we have the field or seeds of confusion, puzzlement, or discontent. In fact all mental troubles may be said to have their origin in such possible confusions.

The verse ends with a generalized axiomatic statement which could be said to enunciate the basis for all ethics of right or morally correct conduct. How morality stems out of philosophical considerations is a question that has often puzzled thinkers and writers. In such a context one often hears of a voice within called conscience or the will of God. The categorical imperative of the philosopher Kant corresponds to the same moral or ethical principle innately present in man. In the context of the *Bhagavad Gītā* we have the notion of the *sameness (sāmya)* that the yogi should see with all beings because of their being analogous with the Self that is within each of us. Modern phenomenology, axiology (the science of values), and eudiamonology (*eu* = happiness or well-being, *diamon* = spirit; the science of well-being) adopt the same method of putting together subjective and objective value factors to harmonize inner and outer life. Equating somehow the Self with the non-Self so as to arrive at unitive or non-conflicting interests, is the method that underlies this way of solving the question of morals.

After having systematically laid the foundations required epistemologically (i.e., in the science of the ways of knowing) and methodology (i.e., in the science of means and disciplines) for a discussion of ethical values, the Guru here devotes the next few verses to the basic considerations of a morality that he intends to be broad-based on a proper philosophy.

This work is not meant to be a code of ethics and is to be kept free from degenerating into a mere *dharma śāstra* (text-book on right conduct) or *smṛti* (remembered application of heard wisdom) which would belong more to the side of action rather than to understanding. The present work is devoted mainly to Self-realization and should be free from the social and obligatory aspects of morality. Therefore the author contents himself with broad generalizations which have more of a wisdom interest than one of obligatory social action.

The axiomatic conclusion of the verse, "what to oneself is dear, etc.," merely draws attention to the philosophical verity that there is no fundamental difference as between the desires, appetites or aspirations of one man and another. All persons need food, sleep, waking activities or companionship involving many individual items of interests. Whether it be man, woman or child, a civilized or a primitive human's needs have basic uniformity of character. Although, considered in detail, tastes might differ, basic satisfactions depend on items that are alike. A wheat-eater and a rice-eater are both consumers of cereals. Looked at in this way, the basic axiom of good conduct reduces itself to one law: namely, one is right when one's own taste accords with what is truly human, or conversely, to choose what one should rightfully prefer in life, one should be guided by what would be conducive to the happiness of humanity in general.

The next verse is as follows:

> The other man's interest, that is even mine;
> what to oneself
> Is beneficial is so for the other man also;
> such is the course of
> Discrete conduct; all acts aiming
> each man's Self-happiness
> Must spell at once the happiness
> of the other fellow-man.

As we have said, this verse completes and resolves the

complication referred to in the previous verse. The Guru takes particular pleasure in playing on the strings of the same note or melody. By this he only wishes to underline the law of human relations and conduct which is here enunciated in keeping with the correct dialectical approach.

Desires can come into conflict when treated unilaterally and horizontally, but are resolved into the harmony of unity when both the counterparts of the relational situation are brought together through correct Self-knowledge.

This way of confronting the problem of evil which otherwise puzzles theologians and philosophers equally, is the prerogative of the dialectical, as against the merely rational approach. Steeped in scientific or unilateral rationalism, modern philosophers in the West have forfeited their more ancient heritage of wisdom. In what has been called the Nicomachean ethics of Aristotle (named after Nichomachus, the father of that classical philosophers of Greece), the West had the beginnings of this way of looking at moral problems. Rationalism as with Voltaire found no explanation for evil, and suggested no remedy that took man beyond good and evil. Theologies retained a God who could punish and excuse sin and thus help man to transcend evil, but the roots of theology in the reasoning faculty of man were overcovered by myth or by pseudo-science. The identification of one's own best interest with that of one's neighbor, who, in principle, represents one's own dialectical counterpart among human beings whom one comes into daily relationship, is the secret and time-honored way of peace on earth and good-will to all mankind, which is the philosophical basis of human ethics as directly derived from wisdom through Self-realization. The fatherhood of God and the brotherhood of Man contains the same ethical law.

The equation of the Self and the non-Self which is the essence of dialectical wisdom, implicit in the ethics presented in this and in the previous verse, has its philosophical echo in the *Bhagavad Gītā*, Chapter VI, verses 5 and 6:

By the Self the Self must be upheld; the Self should not be let down; the Self indeed is (its own) dear relative; the Self indeed is the enemy of the Self.

The Self is dear to one (possessed) of Self, by whom even the Self by the Self has been won, for one not (possessed) of Self, the Self would be in conflict with the very Self, as if an enemy.

The ambivalent aspects of the same Self can be conceived unitively or dualistically, the former resolving conflict and the latter accentuating it.

The foundation of the ethics on which the Guru's idea of human relations are based is in the latter half of the verse, "All acts aiming each man's self-happiness, must spell at once the happiness of the other fellow-man." The law of all morality is stated here in unequivocal terms. This law is conceived strictly according to the Science of the Absolute whose method is dialectical, and not merely rational. It should be noticed here that the ends and means of morality and the subjective and objective aspects of it are brought together in a way which is in keeping with the Science of the Absolute. The personal and moral factors or elements involved have to be submitted to a dialectically valid operation to yield correct results.

The use of dialectics is for double affirmation as double negation cancels each negation by its positive and unitive import of a highly imaginary order. When we say for example, "darkness has no existence apart from light" the double negation of darkness involved in its denial in absolute terms, which brings into being an absolute notion of light in a double sense. This verity is implied already in grammar and in mathematics where dialectics is tacitly recognized. The good of man must be understood as belonging to the context of the Absolute, and what is good for humanity and what is good for the individual both subjectively and objectively understood, must all point to the Absolute Human Value representing the good of Each and All at once. No act can be considered ethically valid if it is only of partial application.

> It is often thought that religion and ethics depend on the person concerned and are therefore relative to the individual. This is not the way to look at truth. It has to be from both its aspects of self and non-self. Correctly speaking, morality though personal cannot afford to connive at error in the furthermost corner of the world. Each man is his brother's keeper. One man unjustly treated anywhere in the world calls for retribution from the whole of humanity with one voice. It is in this sense that slavery is immoral, and a mere mechanical equality is not desirable either. The dialectics of the one and the many involved here has to be kept in mind if the full implication of this law enunciated here is to be understood in the spirit it is intended by the author. [19]

We have already seen that the main functional secrets of all manifestations are based on the dialectical polarization of two opposites. The relationships between the constituent members of a family show a variation between them according to the space each occupies in the psychophysical and materio-spiritual configuration of the family. To this is also added the significance of the time-sequence of the arrival of each into the family circle. Nobody can predict whether the first born in a family will be a son or a daughter. It is so with the second child and the third child. For this reason, the hexagrams of the great Chinese book *I Ching*, the *Book of Changes*, include representations of the Father, the Mother, the elder son or elder daughter, the second son or second daughter, and the third son or third daughter. Eight trigrams are derived from the various combinations of family members which represent certain processes in nature.

According to the *Book of Changes*, the eight trigrams are images that are constantly undergoing change. Attention centers not on things in their state of being – as is chiefly the case in the West – but upon their movements. The eight trigrams therefore are not representations of things as such but of their changing transitional states. Because of this natural flux of life, it is almost impossible for one to behave in such a way that all members of one's family will always be pleased with what one does. In Oriental countries, especially India, a family unit will have many satellite families clinging to it with several shades of loyalty. It is like the vast spreading tree "with ramified roots which bind to action in the world of men." If a person's action or life-interest is not in tune with the interests of their parents or brothers or sisters, there will be a torrential flow of tears. Being tied to each one of them with familial loyalty, the person can be pushed to his or her wit's end. One may become obliged to swallow his or her bitter disappointment while conceding to the irrational sentiment of a father or mother or brother or sister. It is in this context *brahman* is to be looked upon as a saving factor, *kṣattra*, which can come and redeem the victim of *samsāra*.

In addition to the two verses and commentaries given above, Narayana Guru gives three more verses in his *Ātmopadeśa Śatakam* to give a complete picture of the tragi-comic situation that can happen to a person in the socio-familial context:

> For the sake of fellow-man, unceasing day and night
> Unstinting strives the kindly man;
> The niggard lying prone,
>   what frustration's toil undertakes,
> That is for his own sake alone.

After laying down the subtle dialectical law of ethics in which the counterparts of interest as between oneself and a fellow-human who is "no other" than himself, judged by the common human interest that binds them both, in the two verses preceding the present one, the Guru here passes on to point out how static self-centered striving, ego-centrically carried on, finishes up in vain frustrations, eliminating in the process, both general good and good for oneself.

These last two aspects of taking and giving, when correctly viewed in the light of dialectical ethics, hang together. Closed ethics ends in the desert sands of exclusive isolation; while the open and inclusive way, which rises from the particular to the universal in a dynamism implied in all things that develop and grow, gives life more abundance, and makes life generally better for oneself and for all others. Moreover, selfish toil involves a great deal of energy which defeats its own purpose, paradoxically. Niggardliness means lack of the open and bold generosity which widens the circle of man's opportunities. the ungenerous man closes the bars against himself.

Here the Guru clearly enunciates the basis of ethical conduct, not in terms of a categorical imperative or an inner compulsion, nor merely in the name of the specifically human element in man, but based on a dialectical formula as between oneself and one's own counterpart in the world of human relations. Many of the ordinary theories of unilaterally conceived ethics are here bypassed by the Guru in favor of an approach more in keeping with the non-duality which is the basis of the whole philosophy of self-knowledge as understood in this composition.

This verse teaches the same principle as the dictum "love thy neighbor as thyself"; only the dialectical bipolarity is more explicit and the unworkability of one-sided interest in the Self more categorically denounced.

What here we view as this man or that
Reflection reveals to be the Self's prime form;
That conduct adopted for one's Self-happiness
Another's happiness must also secure at once.

The principle viewed above from the social and ethical standpoint is here restated in terms of Self-knowledge. The duality that is apparent between the interests of two individuals can be viewed unitively as referring to the self-same central or neutral Self conceived in the context of the Absolute. The *Bhagavad Gīta* (VI.32) alludes to this way of establishing "sameness" *(sāmam)* between the Self and the Cosmos.

It is not according to the ordinary laws of thought, which admit of contradiction and an excluded middle that this kind of unitive vision of the Self, which is all-embracing, is to be established. The equation of the Self and the non-Self, has implicit in it the dialectical method known to ancient wisdom the world over, but overcovered and lost in later philosophies. Remnants of it are to be found in different degrees of rationalized versions in Kant, Hegel and Fichte. Modern phenomenology has this way of thing implied in it.

Looking at the verse in a commonsense way, we could derive the simpler principle of human quality from it.

When the poet Burns writes, "A man's a man for a' that" the principle of equality which is at the basis of Western civilization and variously named democracy, socialism or communism is implicit, in spite of the closed interpretations or forms that interested political bodies might have given to it. Perhaps exponential or degree differences of intensity only, might distinguish them. Treating thy neighbor as thyself implies the equation of the Self with the non-Self.

> What spells benefit to one,
> while to another distress brings,
> Such conduct is one that violates the Self; beware!
> That spark of pain intense to another given
> Into inferno's ocean it falls, there to burn its flames.

Further implications of the same subtle reciprocity of the Self and the non-Self are here unitively developed from the negative side. Like the quality of mercy, kindness has to be conceived as a double blessing and its absence as a double disaster. The non-dual way is the only escape when conflicting interests develop in a given situation due to unilateral action. Favoritism is a form of duality to whichever the side the favoritism might be applied. What is evil is the duality implicit in the unilateral interest that is taken.

Ethics is not to be conceived as depending on the conduct of a good man taken by himself; it is to be understood as a double-edged situation cutting both ways. It has to be conceived not as a lame or one-sided affair, but as a process in which donor and beneficiary belong to a unitive and universal context. Violation of the unitive Self-hood on the one side is equated here with its dialectical counterpart of a general fire of inferno for which the spark of pain given to a single individual could be the partial stimulus to create a wholesale reaction. Just as intense pain in the tip of one's toe would suffice to upset the balance of the whole person in suffering, so the subtle reciprocity implied here, when the slightest discrimination is made between favorites or enemies, brings unforeseen quantitative or qualitative effects. Consequences flare up into a general conflagration. The sum total of human suffering consists of small sparks of partiality shown by men somewhere or other at one time or another. The general cause of war should be thought of in this way. Like one spark setting fire to the neighboring faggot, the continuity of the process of evil effects is to be imagined as operating ceaselessly in the world of human relations. Clashes of clan with clan, time-old feuds, racial, national or other rivalries, and preferential pacts, all work together to keep the flames of inferno constantly fed with fuel and burning incessantly.

When the dualistic attitude has once been abolished and generosity spreads evenly like sunlight without distinction, on all human beings, even on the publican and the sinner, that kind of generosity belongs to the context of the absolutist way of life and is one that, in the context of Self-realization is very important to keep in mind. The Self can itself become the worst enemy of the Self. This has been brought out with the full force of delicate dialectics in the *Bhagavad Gītā* (VI.6). [20]

Brāhmaṇa 14

Mantra 1

bhūmirantarikṣam dyaurityaṣṭāvakṣarāṇi; aṣṭākṣaram ha vā ekam gāyatryai padam, etadu haivāsyā etat; sa yāvadeṣu triṣu lokeṣu tāvaddha jayati yo'syā etadevam padam veda.

Word Meanings

bhūmiḥ - *bhūmi* (earth); *antarikṣam* - *antarikṣa* (sky); *dyauḥ* - (and) *dyaus* (heaven); *iti* - these (make); *aṣṭau* - eight; *akṣarāṇi* - syllables; *ekam* - one (the first); *padam* - foot; *gāyatryai* - of the *gāyatrī*; *aṣṭa akṣaram* - (also has) eight syllables; *ha vai* - verily; *u ha eva* - hence; *etat* - this (foot); *asyāḥ* - of the (*gāyatrī*); *etat* - (consists of) these (three worlds); *saḥ yaḥ* - one who; *etat evam* - thus; *veda* - knows; *asyāḥ* - the (first); *padam* - foot; *jayati* - wins; *yāvat tāvat ha* - whatever there is; *eṣu* - (in) these; *triṣu* - three; *lokeṣu* - worlds

Bhūmi (earth), *antarikṣa* (sky) and *dyaus* (heaven) - these make eight syllables. The first foot of the *gāyatrī* also has verily eight syllables. Hence this foot of the *gāyatrī* consists of these three worlds. One who thus knows the first foot wins whatever there is in the three worlds.

The *gāyatrī* mantra is addressed to the sun (*sāvitrī*) as follows:

AUM bhuḥ, bhuvaḥ, svaḥ,
tat savitur vareṇyam
bhargo devasya dhīmahi
dhīyoyo naḥ pracodayāt.

The first invocational mantras are *bhuḥ, bhuvaḥ, svaḥ. Bhuḥ* is an invocation of earth, the *terra firma,* where we live and on which the life of all earthly beings is based. It is the firm foundation of life. The *Amarakośa* lists many other attributes of *bhu,* such as: the immovable, the governor of the universe, steady, that which supports the world, that which has the quality of sound, the habitat of living beings, where everything transforms, the all-bearing, the treasury of wealth, that which veils the underworld, that which produces vegetables which sustain living beings, that which is wide, that which accepts without revolt, the savior, the spacious, that which has caves, that which nurtures everything like a mother, that which has the ocean as its girdle, that which allows to be fashioned, that which allows foundations to be made, that into which everything enters, the home of all. The second invocation *bhuvaḥ* is given to the atmosphere which envelops earth, which *Amarakośa* names as the source of everything. The third invocation, *svaḥ,* indicates *svarga,* the heaven which is shining like gold.

In the *gāyatrī* mantra, *AUM* is to be taken in the sense of indicating the Absolute, that is, the three changing phases of consciousness – wakeful, dream, deep sleep – and transcendence. That which is the sustaining principle is here termed as *tat* in all four states. *Tat* is that which embraces everything, the all inclusive. *Tat* is the answer which comes to the question *yat* – "What is?" *Tat* means "That is." *Sāvita* literally means that which causes comprehensive knowledge. It also means that which rouses those who are sleeping. It is a synonym for the Self, or for the pure consciousness which is the nature of the Self. Some of the other Sanskrit synonyms of the sun are: *sūrya* (that which travels in the sky); *aryamā* (that which is of the nature of moving always); *āditya* (the son of Aditi); *dvādaśātmā* (that which has twelve forms); *divākaraḥ* (that which makes the day); *bhāskaraḥ* (that which shines); *ahaskaraḥ* (whose presence is called the day); *bradhnaḥ* (that which removes darkness); *prabhākaraḥ* (that which brings brilliance); *vibhākaraḥ* (that which gives specific brilliance); *bhāsvān* (the resplendent); *vivasvān* (that which has rays); *saptāśvaḥ* (drawn by seven horses); *haridaśvaḥ* (whose horses are of green color); *uṣṇaraśmiḥ* (one who gives warm rays); *arkaḥ* (one who is worshipped); *mārtaṇḍaḥ* (that which resurrects); *mihiraḥ* (one who causes rain); *pūṣā* (one who nourishes); *dyumaṇiḥ* (one who is like a precious jewel in the sky); *taraṇiḥ* (one who takes people across the ocean of phenomenality); *mitraḥ* (one who is friendly); *citrabhānuḥ* (one who has many colors); *virocanaḥ* (one who shines in a special way); *vibhāvasuḥ* (one whose wealth is his light); *tapanaḥ* (the giver of warmth or heat); *raviḥ* (the adored); *chāyānāthaḥ* (the lord of the shadow); *karmaśākṣī* (one who witnesses all actions); *amśumāli* (one who is garlanded by the beams); *lokabāndavaḥ* (one who is a friend of the world); and *bhargaḥ* (the brilliant).

Vareṇyam means 'worthy of being invoked for blessings'. In the present mantra *sāvita* and *bharga* are similar in meaning. *Bharga* is that which removes darkness, disease or anything malignant. It is the remover of obstructions. Another meaning of *bharga* is that which roasts things in its fiery flames. *Bhargo* is an appeal to the brilliance of the sun to illumine our senses. It also means purifying the senses by scorching away all the dross. *Deva* is that which shines, the sense organs. There are considered to be three hundred and thirty million shining principles. *Dhī* is the faculty for meditation, identified with the cognitive intelligence. *Mahim* is that which is worthy of being worshipped. *Dhīmahi* means we meditate. *Yaḥ* means one who; *naḥ* means our or mine; *pracodayāt* means inciting, urging on, or illuminating. *Pracoda* is also connected with *cuda* and *codana* (*cuda* means spread out; *codana* means examining, testing, and inspiring; *pracodaya* means to inspire properly).

The *gāyatrī* is variously translated. One meaning of the *gāyatrī* mantra is: "We meditate on the adorable light of the divine sun who stimulates our spiritual faculties." Another translation is: "We meditate on that adorable blissful form of thine which is in our heart. Mayest thou illumine our spiritual faculties." Another translation is: "We meditate on the most resplendent and adorable light of the self-luminous spirit in our heart as its inner ruler which manifests as the physical, emotional, mental, spiritual, essential, creative and eternal spheres, or alternatively manifests successively on all the stages of the path. May it guide our thoughts and action along the right path." Another translation is:

> *AUM* that which embraces the whole of the deep unconscious and the subjective consciousness from which all imagery surges up, the transactional consciousness which makes a dichotomy of subject and object to facilitate interaction between the knowing subject and the object of knowledge and the all transcending which is the beyond!
>
> That which embraces both the transcendent truth and the substantiating immanence of all, the self-luminous and all-illuminating source of all knowledge, the Self, the most adorable resplendence, which cleanses our senses and mind, O divine light, inspire our cognitive intelligence to become the supremely adorable.

Gāyatrī is used in India as a meter for writing poetry, as a personal goddess representing the feminine aspect of Sāvitrī and as a *japa mantra*. The feminine sense is also called *sāvitrī*. The poet seeks *gāyatrī* as a highly venerated meter for composing poems in Sanskrit. The worshippers of the Supreme as the creatress Mother use *gāyatrī* to offer the blossoms of their contemplative mind in a continuous act of worship of the divine. All over India the mantra is often used to observe what is called *sandhya*.

The three *sandhyas* are dawn, i.e., the conjunction between night and day, noon, and dusk, i.e., when the day merges into night. Some people treat midnight also as a *sandhya* because it marks the juncture between one day and another. For the practice of *japa*, *gāyatrī* is divided into three and each division is taken as a line *(pāda)* within the meter called *gāyatrī*. The meditator rehearses the three movements by chanting the *praṇava* backward and forward three times. Then it is optional whether to limit the mantra to the invocation of earth, water, and sky, by saying *bhuḥ, bhuvaḥ svaḥ*, or to chant *bhuḥ, bhuvaḥ, svaḥ, mahaḥ, janaḥ, tapaḥ, satyam*, and then come to the *gāyatrī* mantra.

After the *gāyatrī* mantra is given it is concluded with the *sāvitrī* mantra:

AUM pūrṇam adaḥ, pūrṇam idam
pūrṇāt pūrṇam udacyate
pūrṇasya pūrṇam ādāya
pūrṇam eva avaśiṣyate
AUM śāntiḥ, śāntiḥ, śāntiḥ.

The yogi aspirant sees in *gāyatrī* a very helpful theme of meditation to raise himself or herself to the supreme consciousness which is identical with *ātman* or *brahman*. We have a body and our bodily response to the spirit is by activating an appropriate sense organ or faculty to initiate our contemplative search, so *gāyatrī* is recommended as a mantra to ponder on. When a disciple receives a mantra from a *guru* it is like offering oneself to be the beacon carrier of ancient wisdom to posterity. Several mantras are given to novices by experienced spiritual masters of which some are for chanting out loud. One begins with an open mouth and then comes to the silence of stillness. The foremost of such mantras is the *praṇava, AUM*.

The geometrical design of the sacred mantra *AUM* is like that of a funnel in which the three articulated sounds enable the mantra to be taken from a fully opened mouth to half-opened and then to the closing together of lips. Then the tapering of the *prāṇa* goes into a deep silence. As part of it can be heard, the *praṇava* is categorized under *udgītha*. It is called *udgītha* because the breath to chant it originates from the *mūlādhāra* and passes through *svādhiṣṭhāna, maṇipura* and *anāhata*, to come to *viśuddhi*. Then the sound *'A'* is articulated, which represents the all-embracing full consciousness. Then the open mouth comes to a rounded half-closed position, *'U'*. The lips are flattened and the mouth is closed, *'M'*. This tapering of the mantra funnels the concentration of the meditator to the core of the heart from where *anāhata* is lifted to the level of the ear. The *ājña* is between the two eyebrows where the syllable *'A'* is brought to a centralized position. The sound is then brought between the two external ears, and between the nostrils and the lower lip to give the emphasis on *'U'*. Even when the lips are closed, the sound is still between the eye and the mouth. As we proceed from *'A'* to *'U'* to *'M'*, the sound that is heard by oneself diminishes. After closing the mouth, the muffled sound of *'M'* becomes a reverberation between the heart and the crown of the head.

Yogis practice the chanting of *AUM* so that it reverberates in the entire cranium. Then it changes character from a mere articulation. It vibrates in the ears, the cheeks, the eyes, the nostrils and the throat. With a gush which is more of energy than of air, it brings all the synergic centers of the body *(ādhāra cakras)* into a vibratory participation. The monotonous rote repetition of *japa* is given up for a thrilling, dynamic alertness or awareness, where the tapering of the vibration of *'MM'* goes beyond audible sound like the quality of transcendence of *anāhata* which is heard in the middle of the brain. *AUM* also takes us from the most expressive mundane sound to the dream world of memory and ultimately to a state of transcendence in which both the conscious and unconscious blend.

Before we go further into the psychodynamics of the spiritual significance of *gāyatrī*, we wish to share a general appreciation of the *gāyatrī* mantra which is very beautifully given in *The Vedic Experience – Mantramañjarī*, by Raimundo Panikkar, which begins with a quote from Manu:

> "There is nothing more exalted than the *Gāyatrī*." It is the most renowned mantra of the Vedas. It is addressed to the life-giver as supreme God, symbolized in Savitṛ, the Sun. For this reason this prayer is also called Sāvitrī. It is recited daily at sunrise and at sunset. This mantra derives its name from the meter in which it is written, the *gāyatrī* being a Vedic poetic meter of twenty-four syllables, of which the author according to tradition was the sage Viśvamitra. . . .The Bṛhadāraṇyaka Upaniṣad explains

how the world came into being by the union of Mind (*manas*) with Word (*vāc*). The mantra is neither a mere sound nor sheer magic. Words have not only a sound but also a meaning, which is not apparent to all those who simply hear the sound. Living words have, furthermore, a power that transcends the purely mental plane. To acquire this energy of the word one has to grasp not only its meaning but also its message, or its vibrations, as they are sometimes called in order to stress the link with the sound itself. Faith, understanding, and physical utterance, as well as physical continuity (the mantra has to be handed down by a master), are essential requisites for an authentic mantra. Every word links us up with the source of all words. The ultimate character of the word, *śabdabrahman*, is a fundamental concept in Indian spirituality.

Several hymns of the Atharva Veda allude to the privileged position occupied by the Gāyatrī mantra. When the poet is attempting to define the First Principle, the Absolute, and to locate the "Unborn," he says, in order to give us a notion of his inaccessibility, that he is:

> Loftier even than the lofty Gāyatrī,
> beyond the Immortal he strode forth.
> Where was the Unborn then? This even
> the knowers of Vedic lore cannot tell.

In another hymn, composed in honor of Rohita, the Sun, which also extols the grandeur of an earthly king, the poet describes the king's subjects assembled at dawn for the offering of the sacrifice; he depicts them awaiting the appearance of the rising Sun, called in this passage the "tawny Calf," and his "mother" the Dawn, here identified with the Gāyatrī:

> Your people, the offspring of sacred Fervor,
> have come in the wake of the Calf and the Gāyatrī.
> May they enter your presence
> with intentions of peace,
> preceded by the tawny Calf and his mother!

In similar fashion another verse calls the Gāyatrī "Mother of the Vedas" (*Atharva Veda* XIX:71:1). [21]

In the first line of the *gāyatrī: AUM tat savitur vareṇyam, tat* is identified with *savitur* or *savita*. The most clear exposition of *tat* is given in the *Chāndogya Upaniṣad* 6.9.4 to 6.16.3. There is a conventional way of knowing Vedāntic terms which is of little use to anyone. The symbol *AUM*, either written in calligraphy or pronounced by a teacher, has been so eulogized and exaggerated that most people are carried away by the imagined significance of the visual or auditory expression of the *praṇava*. This practice in India is nothing short of idolatry. When a teacher tries to explain the all-embracing truth, he uses the word *satya*. To give a comprehensive idea of the all-inclusiveness of truth it is termed *tat*. Not knowing the specific psychological function of a certain pronounced sound which acts on our hearing faculty, many people think that the term *tat* or *sat* gives them a total insight into *brahman* or truth.

In the *Upaniṣads* like *Chāndogya* the *praṇava* is glorified as the true name of *brahman*. This can be factually very misleading. For instance, when you hear the term 'cow' there may not be any cow around you but the sound itself can elicit from your memory a mental image of a cow. The conceptual cow is a phenomenological reduction made by you to have a correlation between the sound 'cow' and the mental image of a cow. This is far from actually experiencing a cow as a visible tangible animal which you can milk. This is often illustrated as the need to differentiate the map from the territory. That is why Uddālaka takes pain to give so many examples to Śvetaketu like the clear exposition in 6.9.4: "That being which is this subtle essence even that all this world has for its Self. That is the true; that is the *ātman*, That thou art Śvetaketu." It means you have to the depth of the meaning of the terms *tat* and *sat*. In his *Darśana Mālā* Narayana Guru works out a clear notion of *tat* by making the student go through a series of five *Darśanas: Adhyāropa, Apavāda, Asatya, Māyā* and *Bhāna*. Only at the end of the *Bhāna Darśana* does he establish *tat eva sat:* That alone is real *(satya)*. And what is 'That'? When a term is pronounced or written, the mind demands the purport of what is heard or what is seen. To satisfy the mind, a mental image associated with a particular sound is recalled from memory *(citta)*. Then the individuated consciousness becomes identified with that specific memory. This is called *bhāna vṛtti*. With that process a certain image is superimposed in consciousness. It is only a process of rationalization. That is why Narayana Guru started with *Adhyāropa Darśana* (Vision of Superimposition). Then he wanted us to know that what comes as a mental image is only a mentally fabricated replica which is presented to the mind that approximates the basis of the illumination (*bhānāśraya*). The modulation in consciousness that is happening at that time is *adhyāsa*. The process is called *bhāna vṛtti* and the result of it is the image.

Every time we meditate with a particular term, our conditioned mind brings up a memory recall. We do not go anywhere beyond the presented image evoked by a word. That is how the empirical world prevents us from knowing truth. It is clearly said in Patañjali's *Yoga Sūtras* that the first stumbling block in the path of realization is our criterion for what is empirically valid. When we are satisfied by superimposing an empirically valid conceptual image of the presentative image in perception, we take for granted that we have known the truth. What we have known is not truth; it is only a representative image of truth, at best a sign or symbol. That is why Narayana Guru suggests that it is to be given up. The Sanskrit term for this is *apavāda*, philosophical rejection. Philosophical rejection can come only when we clearly see that what is presented to the senses is unreal (*asatya*). Then alone can we seek what is real. It is only by *asatya nirṇaya*, determination of what is untrue, that one comes to truth.

Our bodies are animated by breath and the nourishment of food. We are so in tune with the demands of our body identity that we cannot get out of it to look for the one truth which is everywhere. We need to transcend both generic and specific ignorance. So when we sit to meditate on *AUM tat savitur vareṇyam*, we should not call to mind the image of the sun in the sky, or anything that has a name or a form. Anything which is presented to the mind formally or nominally is an *adhyāsa*. Only when all *adhyāsas* are transcended can one come to the pure essence which is *satya*. It is not through any drill or exercise of repeated chanting that we can get over the hurdles placed before us by the conceptualizing of the mind. So in one sense, all religious rituals are deceptive in their dynamics.

The *gāyatrī* mantra makes a special appeal: *bhargo devasya dhīmahi*. The shining aspects of our physical reality are the senses called the *devas*. The conceptual dross that has gone into them is to be burnt away. *Bharga* has two meanings. One meaning is the all-filling transparency of vision which transcends space, time, mass and motion. The other is the total burning away of the irrelevant. Only when all the aspects of the *antakaraṇa*, that is, the interrogative mind, memory recall, rationalizing intellect, and the affective ego, are gotten over, do we receive the senses in their most pure forms. Thereafter they are not sense organs at all - we are one with the Self. Meditation commences only from there.

To guide us in getting over nescience, Narayana Guru examines eight different modalities of *māyā* in *Darśana Mālā*. In the first verse of the *Adhyāropa Darśana*, he pairs the Supreme *(para)* with the imagination of the creator *(apara)*. The second verse contains one's own power to project or postulate (*vidyā*), and the accomplished postulation by which phenomena are presented (*avidyā*). The third verse gives the example of seed and tree. The seed as such is only the essence which has in it the dynamics to proliferate and preserve the empirical validity of the projected phenomena for a long time. This comes under *prakṛti* and *pradhāna*. An accomplished tree does not evaporate away like the rainbow. It sustains itself as a relatively permanent record *(tamas)*. The fourth verse gives the example of seeing the snake in the rope *(māyā)*, which is circumstantial. If there is no darkness, it is not likely one will see a snake in a rope.

In Vedanta these initial studies are recommended as preparation for the actual entry into the contemplative promotion that one gives to oneself to arrive at what is termed in the *gāyatrī* as *tat*. In India, an aspirant student goes to a *guru* who is known to be a fully realized master and remains in the presence of the *guru* for twelve years so that all the dross of ignorance *(avidyā)* can be removed from one. Then he or she is given certain exercises so that when the mind habitually tries to wander from one mental fixation to another, it is prevented from doing so. Several terms are called to mind again and again to bring the aspirant to a single notion. Thus many modulations are chosen which will in effect bring unity.

For example, a person devoted to Viṣṇu is given a thousand names of Viṣṇu to meditate on or a devotee of Devi is given a thousand names of the Devi. Unfortunately, many people get stuck in such exercises which are given to them only to help them find the central focus of their meditative experience. As the thousand names are taken from Indian mythology, such as the

Viṣṇu Purāṇa or *Devi Purāṇa*, the names stimulate elaborate studies of mythology and people become story addicts. Religion itself has become the greatest snare to stop a person from the vertical ascent of spiritual pursuit.

The *Yoga Vāsiṣṭha* says that the most vociferous teacher of Vedānta is at best only a person who has memorized verses from a Vedānta text and uses that knowledge as a means to feed and clothe himself. For such a person, even the finest attempt to be on the true path ultimately becomes career seeking. A professional teacher can never be a real teacher. In Chapter Twenty-one, verses three and four of the *Nirvāṇa Prakaraṇa* of the *Yoga Vāsiṣṭha* we read,

> He who reads the *śāstras*, and practices his learning as a practitioner for earning his livelihood, without endeavoring to investigate into the principles of his knowledge, is called a friend to learning.
>
> Whose learning is seen to be employed in busy life only, without showing its true effect in the improvement of the understanding; such learning being but an art or means of getting a livelihood, its possessor is called a fellow of learning; and no doctor in it. [22]

The entire chapter *Nirvāṇa Prakaraṇa* of *Yoga Vāsiṣṭha* is given to help us determine whether we are true seekers or ones who have made our search a conventional form of getting recognition from society. It instructs us that, for a lay person, this world is as one sees it. The world does not drop off or melt away or get dissolved on realizing *brahman*. It will continue like our shadow follows us when we walk in the sun. But one can come to know how to discern the shadow from the Self. Then one sees the totality of truth in this very here and now. That clarity is referred to in the second part of the *gāyatrī: bhargo devasya dhīmahi*. As long as one is still in the body, there is a possibility for the compelling aspect of previous conditioning to make the intellect a tool in the hands of the ego and one again becomes a victim of *avidyā*. That is why the final prayer is made, *dhīyo yo naḥ pracodayāt:* "Help us to rectify our intelligence of all the dross it has accumulated by associating with the body, senses, and the mind." We need to have such a thoroughgoing meditation on *gāyatrī* for it to be helpful to us.

We have seen that *gāyatrī* is also a poetic meter. The other two poetic meters which are relevant here are the *triṣṭubh* and *jagatī*. The colorations of the psyche in India can be understood in terms of the poetic excellence of a person. We see a gradation of sensibility in human beings. Human evolution brings each person to a stabilization of one's values. Those who are in the transactional world meet with various contingencies in life. They have to use their bodies, senses, and manipulating minds to solve the problems of the empirical world. For the continuation of socialized life on earth they have to generate one life situation after another so that they can justify their position in this world. These people who are down to earth, calculative, conscious of profit and loss, and who generate interaction with others, are friendly, without ever sacrificing their vested interest. They are called *vaiśya*.

This is not a caste, it is the attainment of a certain state of mind. Unfortunately this secret has been lost and people think it is a class name in accordance with one's occupation. Even the highly elevated person may have to adopt a gross attitude for a little while every day to adjust with the external world. The *Upaniṣad* suggests that they are psychologically reborn in the poetic meter *jagatī* which mainly deals with the gross world.

When people glorify themselves as capable of the overlordship and protection of their fellow beings, they prepare themselves for the highest sacrifice. This attitude has a taint of romantic idealism. When such a person becomes pathologically afflicted, it is likely that he will become a megalomaniac. If his ideal is pure, altruistic, and fully established in his humane nature, then he can even excel as a philosopher-king. If one comes to a highly elevated inner identification as a loving, caring, father of the community, that psychological coloration is that of *kṣatriya*. To maintain the purity of the *kṣatriya* attitude in life one has to be prepared for any sacrifice. For this reason he is honored by his fellow beings and he is said to be born psychologically a second time in accordance with the meter *triṣṭubh*.

There are those people who can go beyond the empirical world and its transformation into the philosophical subtleties of the origin of everything and who comprehend the highest principles of life as neither gross nor subtle, but causal, leading to transcendence. Nobody is outside their compassion. The plurality of this world never afflicts them. Then their psychic coloration is of a *brāhmaṇa*. This is not a state one attains by being born as the progeny of a *brāhmaṇa* family. '*Brāhmaṇa* family' itself is a misnomer - there is no such thing. One who can envision the whole world as a fragmentary spark of the supreme *brahman* is a *brāhmaṇa* . Such a person is said to be reborn in his or her psychic personality from the poetic meter of *gāyatrī*.

Before chanting *gāyatrī*, the aspirant invokes *bhuḥ, bhuvaḥ*, and *svaḥ*. Here the word *svaḥ* is not used in the common ritualistic fashion of *svaḥ*. It refers to the golden hue of the highest state of mind. The invocation of *bhuḥ, bhuvaḥ* and *svaḥ* refers to a methodology of reduction of the three configurations of the human person. Every person has a physical body with the physiological fittings of the five senses and the five organs of action. By relating our sensory system and motor system with the gross external world we get into all our empirical experiences. When we invoke that physicality of ours with the term *bhuḥ*, we conceive of the origin of the dual principles of the body/mind complex. Whatever comes into being is covered by the term *bhuḥ*. It specifically refers to the earth. But that is to be taken only as a symbolic reference.

This body of ours has two environments. One is the external environment of earth, water and fire which also means the sun, stars and outer skies. We are in continuous interaction with the external environment from the moment of our birth until our last breath leaves us. Internally there is another environment. That is the faculty in us of hearing, touching, seeing, tasting, smelling and integrating consciousness in which all sensory occurrences are coordinated, correlated and synthesized as the awareness of the world within.

Atmosphere means the atmosphere outside and the atmosphere inside. All our inside faculties are coordinated by the liquids of the body which can easily conduct chemical as well as electrical configurations. In the external atmosphere also the air that we breathe has moisture in it. The luminaries in the sky are responsible for evaporating physical water to produce a living condition in the atmosphere. And this all-enveloping eco-system is what we call the *antarikṣa* or atmosphere invoked here with the mantra *AUM bhuvaḥ*.

Then we come to *svaḥ*. All occurrences of being and maintenance are made possible by an ascending and descending fire of golden hue. This is a poetic conception. We are often drawn to the future with an ever-growing hope. In the otherwise dark sky of eventuality this hope gives a gilded edge to clouds that have to rain in future. The hopeful potentials in life are often symbolized by the golden egg, *hiraṇyagarbha*. *Hiraṇya* means golden, *garbha* means the incumbent good fortune that is furnished by the divine. When we say *svaḥ* we invoke That sustenance of hope without which life becomes morbid and meaningless. When we go from *bhuḥ* to *bhuvaḥ* to *svaḥ* we spiritually ascend from the gross to the subtle and from the subtle to the causal. The causal becomes identified with the transcendental. These are some of the implications which one should bear in mind when one takes to *gāyatrī*.

In the previous mantra we had an occasion to know how the whole world is conceived as a system of defense In the term *kṣattra* there are two aspects, *kṣata* and *trānana*. *Kṣata* means bruise, disintegration, degeneration, etc. *Trānana* means protecting or resurrecting. What cures the bruise, reorganizes the organism and rejuvenates it are all suggested in the term *kṣattra*. The root of *trānana* is also in the two terms, *gāyatrī* and *mantra*. *Gāyatrī* is that which saves you by singing it; *mantra* is that which saves you by meditating on it. Here the emphasis is that progress or evolution in life is to be attained by tempering our physicality with our mentation and making our minds grow in higher sensibility through poetic imagination.

The physical world of which we are a fragment is a colony of umpteen constituents where plurality is our basic nature. In that world, coordinations are brought, many correlatives are designed and a great organizing of parts into wholes is accomplished. The plurality changes into a multifaceted unified truth, if, from the unified achievement of the psychophysical, we transcend to the higher state of becoming One without a second.

All religions put their emphasis on that One. The Jewish people speak of the unnamable, all-sustaining reality which they symbolically call *Yahweh*. The *Vedas* describe it as the one alone, *ekam eva*, without a second, *advatīyam*. In Islam the Supreme is defined as *la illaha illa'llah*. In the *Guru Granth Sāhib* the reference is to *ek aumkār*. This mantra is to be meditated upon as a very beautifully conceived spiritual scheme of emancipation which leads us from from the multifarious plurality to the unified whole and then to the One without a second.

Mantra 2

ṛco yajūṃṣi sāmānītyaṣṭāvakṣarāṇi; aṣṭākṣaram ha vā ekam gāyatryai padam; etadu haivāsyā etat; sa yāvatīyam trayī vidyā tāvaddha jayati yo'syā etadevam padam veda.

Word Meanings

ṛcaḥ - *ṛcaḥ (Ṛg)*; *yajūṃṣi* - *yajūṃṣi (Yajus)*; *sāmāni* - (and) *sāmāni (Sāma)*; *iti* - these (make); *aṣṭau* - eight; *akṣarāṇi* - syllables; *ekam* - one (the second); *padam* - foot; *gāyatryai* - of the *gāyatrī*; *aṣṭa akṣaram* - (also has) eight syllables; *ha vai* - verily; *u ha eva* - hence; *etat* - this (foot); *asyāḥ* - of the (*gāyatrī*); *etat* - (consists of) these (three *Vedas*); *saḥ yaḥ* - one who; *etat evam* - thus; *veda* - knows; *asyāḥ* - the (second); *padam* - foot; *jayati* - wins; *yāvati tāvat ha* - as much as; *vidyā* - knowledge; *iyam trayī* - the three *Vedas* represent

Ṛcaḥ (Ṛg), *yajūṃṣi (Yajus)* and *sāmāni (Sāma)* - these make eight syllables. The second foot of the *gāyatrī* also has verily eight syllables. Hence this foot of *gāyatrī* consists of those three *Vedas*. One who thus knows the second foot wins as much knowledge as the three *Vedas* represent.

The word *veda* is very sacred to the Indian people. They are proud that they inherit the spiritual foundation given in the *Vedas*. *Vid* means to know; *veda* is to make anything known. Life commences from the experience of knowing the simplest sensations such as heat and cold and pain and pleasure. There are several grades of knowledge. When knowledge takes possession of our consciousness, our consciousness automatically assumes an identity with what is made known.

There are several levels at which knowledge is impressed on us or registered in the consciousness. The lowest is the reflexes which have their origin in our autonomous system. From the autonomous system the inducement of a certain effect flashes like lightning into our voluntary system and the unknown makes a previously hidden fact known to us. This has the quality of a revelation. Elaborate measures are taken by the Supreme to give us maximum defense in all situations. If a very tiny dust particle falls in one of our eyes, we immediately feel its sting. Our eyelids automatically close and blink in quick succession. Along with the pain, the tear glands become alerted and tears come profusely. The successive opening and closing of the eyelids creates an eddy of tears to flush the dust away. The reflex behavior of the eye protects it from damage. If we inadvertently step on a thorn, the prick is felt as such an unbearable pain that we withdraw our foot and immediately give our attention to removing the thorn.

We can see *veda* beginning to function in this supreme care that is taken to maintain the structural and functional well-being of all living creatures. What comes from *veda* is *vedanam*, a message of sensation. All five types of stimulation of the sense organs are called *samvedana*. When a sensation comes it is immediately recognized as painful or pleasurable and our memory never fails to register the stimulation as something either to be desired again and again or as something to be avoided at all cost. This we understand as attraction and repulsion.

The great poet Valmiki made a theme out of this basic differentiation of pleasure and pain by dramatically presenting them as the hero and villain respectively of the great epic *Rāmāyaṇa*. The word *rāma* means that which makes you rejoice and the word *rāvaṇa* means that which makes you cry. Thus the epic heroes Rāma and Rāvaṇa are allegorical representations of pleasure and pain. There is always a hide and seek game going on between attraction and repulsion. Pleasures come to our lives like grace, and pain comes to our lives like fate. These very basic secrets of life are presented in a very telling manner in the Indian literature of the *Vedas*, *Vedānta*, the epics, *Purāṇas* and the systems of Indian Philosophy.

All these elaborations need sounds to convey the meaning of the sensations that are experienced, the ideas that are conceived, the reasons that are proffered, the arguments that are established and the ultimate guidance to which we are exposed. We can reduce the whole theme of communication to using the word as a tool for self-expression and dynamic reaction. A child is very intrigued if it cannot identify an object which comes into its life for the first time. The child asks the parent, "What is this?" and the parent names the object. Thus the first thing that comes to a child's mind is the noun – the name. Human consciousness has a binary function. As soon as a person comes to know what is presented to him or her, the next immediate response is to relate with that which is named. Relating oneself actively makes the knower change into a doer. The child is advised what to do and action is joined with knowledge. When they are put together these two counterparts of human life precipitate the third element called experiencing. Experience means receiving the consequence of knowing and doing either as a pleasurable input of harmonious sensation or a painful input which is causing agitation to wriggle out of the situation. In either case one has to put up with the *samvedana*. *Samvedana* makes a person a sufferer as well as an enjoyer.

Every day countless million of beings enter into the path of the knower, the path of the doer, and the path of the enjoyer. From this common experience of living beings, what has been generalized for the welfare of humanity has been recorded in all the major scriptures of the world. In India the first recording of such generalities was in the *Ṛg Veda* which is intended to make a person a knower. Then it was followed by *Yajur Veda* which advises what is to be done. The conclusive aspect is put in the *Sāma Veda*. These three have special references to the group life of people. Wherever there is a grouping of three we will always find a fourth which is put outside the bracketing of the three. The *Ṛg*, *Yajur* and *Sāman* are within the bracket called the *triveda* and outside we find the *Atharva Veda*, the fourth.

Similarly, three states of consciousness are bracketed as *bhāvatraya* (the wakeful, the dream and deep sleep) and the purest aspect is given as the fourth called the *turīya* or transcendence. This transcending awareness is pure consciousness which is the foundation of the three changing states. It is in the wakeful, the dream, and the unconscious. In its true nature it never becomes modulated - there is only an appearance of modulation.

Sri Aurobindo made an elaborate study of the poetic expressions of psychic affinity which the early people of India felt for the world. He called it *The Secret of the Veda*. The first part of the book covers traditional Vedic theory, various modern theories, the foundations of the psychological theory, the philological method of the *Veda*, and the basic symbols and allegorical references. In the second part, he quotes selected hymns of the *Vedas* and the *Upaniṣads*.

The most beautiful aspect of the *Veda* is its rich poetic visualization. In *The Hymn to the Dawn* we get an elevated feeling of transcendence:

> O Dawn, come with all thy splendours of heaven, awaken us today to the great felicity, even as one thou awakenedst us, – in the sonhood of the birth of knowledge, in the inspired hearing of the Truth.
>
> O, thy birth is complete! O, truth is in the tramp of thy steeds!
>
> Thou who breakest forth into dawning, O daughter of heaven, in him who has the perfect leading of the flaming chariot of light, so break forth today, – O greater still in thy force, in the sunhood of the birth of knowledge, in the inspired hearing of the Truth.
>
> O, thy birth is complete! O, truth is in the tramp of thy steeds!
>
> Break forth into light a bearer of treasures, O daughter of heaven, as once thou brokest forth, - O greater still in thy force, in the sonhood of the birth of knowledge, in the inspired hearing of the Truth.
>
> O, thy birth is complete! O, truth is in the tramp of thy steeds!
>
> There are bearers of the sacrifice who bring thee out in their speech, by their hymns they manifest thee, O wide and lustrous Dawn; they are glorious with thy plenty, O queen, their gifts are lavish, their boons are full.
>
> O, thy birth is complete! O, truth is in the tramp of thy steeds!
>
> When these companies of thy godheads seek to pleasure thee in hope of thy plentitudes, they set their desires all around, they lavish thy undeviating felicity.
>
> O, thy birth is complete! O, truth is in the tramp of thy steeds!
>
> These are thy seers; O Dawn, queen of plenty, set in them the splendour of thy heroic powers; lords of thy plenty, they shall lavish on us thy undeviating riches.
>
> O, thy birth is complete! O truth is in the tramp of thy steeds!

O Dawn, our lady of plenty, bring to them thy illumination, a vast glory; they shall give us enjoyment of the felicity of thy steeds and the felicity of thy herds.

O, thy birth is complete! O, truth is in the tramp of thy steeds!

Bring to us too, O daughter of heaven, powers of impulse full of the troopings of thy light; let them come campanioned with the rays of thy Sun, linked with the purity of his bright and burning light-givings.

O, thy birth is complete! O, truth is in the tramp of thy steeds!

Break forth into light, O daughter of heaven! And spin not out too long the work. For thee thy sun afflicts not with his burning ray as he afflicts the foe and the thief.

O, thy birth is complete! O, truth is in the tramp of thy steeds!

So much thou shouldst give or more than this; for to thy adorers thou breakest forth into the full wideness of thy glories and thou art not limited in thy dawning.

O, thy birth is complete! O, truth is in the tramp of thy steeds!

Hymn To the Dawn (V.80)

Dawn of the luminous journey, Dawn queen of truth, large with the Truth, how wide is the gleam from her rosy limbs, -- Dawn Divine who brings with her the heaven of light! Her the seers adore with their thoughts.

This is she who has the vision and she awakens man and makes his paths easy to travel and walks in his front. How large is her chariot, how vast and all-pervading the goddess, how she brings Light in the front of the days!

This is she who yolks her cows of rosy light; her journey does not fail and such is the treasure she makes that it passes not away. She hews out our paths to happiness; divine is she, far-shining her glory, many the hymns that rise to her, she brings with her every boon.

Behold her in her biune energy of earth and heaven, how she comes into being in her whiteness and discloses her body in our front. She follows perfectly the paths of Truth, as one who is wise and knows, and she hedges not in our regions.

Lo, how brilliant is her body when she is found and known! How she stands on high as if bathing in light that we may have vision! Driving away all enemies and all darknesses Dawn, the daughter of Heaven, has come with the Light.

Lo, the daughter of Heaven like a woman full of happiness moves to meet the gods and her form travels ever nearer to them. Unveiling all blessings for the giver of sacrifice the goddess young for ever has created the Light once more even as in the beginning. [23]

This mantra makes a pointed reference to the three *Vedas: Ṛg, Yajus* and *Sāman*. It says that one who understands the second foot of the *gāyatrī* is making a wholehearted appeal to the shining principles to take full possession of the faculty of knowledge and fill it with the great vigor of light and knowledge. Consequently, one will become a recipient of all that is taught in the three *Vedas*. Unfortunately, people make a fetish of the *Vedas* and of propitiating the symbolic figures of the deities eulogized in the *Veda* such as *Agni, Varuṇa, Mitra, Aśvini, Indra, Viśvadeva, Sarasvatī, Uṣas*, the Cow. Usually very little care is given to understand what these names suggest. It goes to the credit of the rishi Aurobindo in our own days that attention has been focused on deciphering the symbols represented by these names in the *Vedas*. The entire theme of the *Veda* is ciphering and deciphering. Many ciphers that have been given to us still remain closed books.

That necessitated this section of the *Upaniṣad* called *Khila Kāṇḍa* which makes an appeal to all intelligent and responsible people of the world to revise and restate their heritage of cultural and spiritual wisdom. *Khila* means the barren, untouched and uncharted world of possibility. Thus any person who turns to the *Khila Kāṇḍa* of the *Bṛhadāraṇyaka Upaniṣad* is assigned a duty which will benefit all blessed people who are endowed with pure intelligence to decipher the paradoxes and enigmas of life, and at the same time, to be deeply devoted to the cause beyond causes. The message of this mantra is that the Supreme is in love with every part of itself, and every part has to reciprocate that love by furthering the message of the *Vedas* which can bring one to the silence of wonder that washes away the bitterness of the phenomenal which is superimposed on the numenon.

Mantra 3

prāṇo'pāno vyāna ityaṣṭāvakṣarāṇi; aṣṭākṣaram ha vā ekam gāyatryai padam; etadu haivāsyā etat; sa yāvadidam prāṇi tāvaddha jayati yo'syā etadevam padam veda; athāsyā etadeva turīyam darśatam padam parorajā ya eṣa tapati; yadvai caturtham tatturīyam; darśatam padamiti dadṛśa iva hyeṣaḥ; parorajā iti sarvamu hyevaiṣa raja uparyupari tapati; evam haiva śriyā yaśasā tapati yo'syā etadevam padam veda.

Word Meanings

prāṇaḥ - *prāṇa; apānaḥ* - *apāna; vyānaḥ* - *vyāna; iti* - these (make); *aṣṭau* - eight; *akṣarāṇi* - syllables; *ekam* - one (the third); *padam* - foot; *gāyatryai* - of the *gāyatrī; aṣṭa akṣaram* - (also has) eight syllables; *ha vai* - verily; *u ha eva* - hence; *etat* - this (foot); *asyāḥ* - of the *(gāyatrī); etat* - (consists of) these (three forms of the vital breath); *saḥ yaḥ* - one who; *etat evam* - thus; *veda* - knows; *asyāḥ* - the (third); *padam* - foot; *jayati* - wins; *yāvat tāvat ha* - all the; *idam prāṇi* - living beings; *atha* - now; *asyāḥ* - its; *turīyam* - fourth; *darśatam* - (seemingly) visible; *parorajāḥ* - (and) above the world; *padam* - foot; *etat eva* - is indeed; *yaḥ eṣa* - this (the sun); *yat* - that; *tapati* - shines; *turīyam caturtham* - *turīyam* (means) the fourth; *eṣaḥ vai* - it is; *tat darśatam* - (seemingly) visible; *padam iti* - foot; *hi* - because; *dadṛse* - it is seen; *iva* - as it were; *eṣaḥ* - it is; *parorajāḥ iti* - above the world; *hi* - because; *eva* - it alone; *tapati* - shines; *sarvam* - (on) the whole; *rajah* - universe; *upari upari* - from on high; *saḥ yaḥ* - one who; *etat evam* - thus; *veda* - knows; *asyāḥ* - the (fourth); *padam* - foot; *tapati* - shines; *śriyā* - with splendor; *yaśasā* - (and) glory

Prāṇa, apāna, and *vyāna* - these make eight syllables. The third foot of the *gāyatrī* also has verily eight syllables.

> Hence this foot of the *gāyatrī* consists of these three forms of the vital breath. One who thus knows the third foot wins all the living beings.
> Now its fourth, seemingly visible and above the world foot is indeed this - the sun that shines. *Turīya* means the fourth. It is 'seemingly visible' because it is seen, as it were. It is 'above the world' because it alone shines on the whole universe from on high. One who thus knows the fourth foot shines with splendor and glory.

The third *pāda* of the *gāyatrī* is *dhīyo yo naḥ pracodayāt*. This foot is divided into three parts which are said to correspond to *prāṇa, apāna*, and *vyāna*. This is a simplified way of looking at the relationship between what is said and what is practiced. The reason given here for equating the third *pāda* of the *gāyatrī* with *prāṇa, apāna* and *vyāna* is the correspondence between their syllables. To a modern mind this kind of an explanation can look too simple to be recognized as fitting into the context of such an important work like the *Bṛhadāraṇyaka Upaniṣad*. When we look at the function of *prāṇa, apāna*, and *vyāna*, we get a more laudable key to interpret the correspondence between them and the third *pāda* of *gāyatrī*. We have already seen that *bhuḥ* indicates the existential foundation of everything and *bhuvaḥ* is pure existence being transformed into the impressions that are generated in the world of consciousness. *Svaḥ* points to the omega of one's search and represents the axiology of the search where one comes to the final result of a sacrifice.

If we watch our own *prāṇa*, we see three functional levels. The first is the transformation of cosmic air into the vital energy of a living organism *(prāṇa)*. The second is the energy of the macrocosm canceling out several pairs of opposites such as *prāṇa* sublating *apāna*, and *apāna* in its turn sublating *prāṇa*. The third is a synthesis which transmutes the physical or physiological into the mental and spiritual aspects of an evolutionary growth within the organism *(vyāna)*. The same scheme is presented by the three *Vedas*. The *Ṛg Veda* invokes all the deities that are relevant in human life, the *Yajur Veda* propitiates all those deities with appropriate sacrifices, and every sacrifice is concluded with the chanting of the *Sāma*. Elaborate symbolic correspondences are given in almost all the *Upaniṣads*, particularly the *Bṛhad-*

āraṇyaka and *Chāndogya*.

Although the *Bṛhadāraṇyaka* teaches its votaries to transcend all fruition of one's *karma*, the Vedic tradition is also continued in the *Upaniṣad* which mentions what one gains after the performance of a certain action or after acquiring knowledge of a certain kind. When we look into all the forms of sacrifice which are given to a particular presiding deity, there is an expectation that every *karma* should bear fruit. The propitiation of the deity is followed by requests or prayers. And there is an expectation that the deity who is propitiated will reciprocate with blessings. Thus there is a contract model implied in all Vedic rituals. Even when we go on from *Veda* to *Vedānta*, a ghost of the contract can still be seen.

In the *gāyatrī* there is an invocation and a purificatory sacrifice which is followed by a prayer, a request for a result. The third *pāda* of the *gāyatrī* is the final phase in which one wants to be fully inspired. The word inspired is important. Breathing in is inspiring. It naturally brings about the process of respiration in which there is inspiration and expiration. The consequence is the renewing of cells of a mortal person. From the formation of the first cell to the death of the adult in old age, the expenditure of energy is to be replenished, and one has to revitalize oneself to continue the game of life. There is a subtle interplay presented in the *Upaniṣad* with regard to the general ground of the three states of consciousness, wakeful, dream and deep sleep. The general ground in its purest form is inconceivable. It is known simply as *turīya*, the fourth.

The word *turīya* rarely occurs in the Indian philosophical texts outside of the *Māṇḍūkya Upaniṣad* and *Gaudapāda's Karika*, the *Yoga Upaniṣads*, the *Maitri Upaniṣad* (VII:11) and in this *brāhmaṇa* in mantras three, four, six and seven. In all other *Upaniṣads* no differentiation is made between *suṣupti* and *turīya*. The highest form of *ānanda* described elsewhere is the transcendental quality of *suṣupti* in which a person goes beyond all triads such as the knower, the known and knowledge, or the doer, the motivation of the doer, and what is achieved as a result of action. But there is an impression of nescience or ignorance implied in the *suṣupti*, also called causal consciousness *(kāraṇa)*. When a seed germinates, it grows into a tree and bears fruit and again culminates in a seed. All the activities of the tree are annulled. Yet there is a potential in the seed which can bring back the tree with all its details. A person's various activities in the wakeful and all the good and evil dreams that subsequently come seem to be absolved of all dross in the state of deep sleep. Then one has no name, form or body requirements. But they are all waiting when one returns from deep sleep to the dream world or the wakeful world. The ignorance that accounts for the rounds of birth and death remains. When a person is in deep sleep (*suṣupti*), we cannot decide whether he or she is going to wake up or perish in the unconscious itself. Mostly people do wake up and come back to their normal chores. This is the picture we have of the ordinary world.

But our aspiration is not to wake up again. Our highest aim is to get lost, to submerge, in the Absolute which brings a final exit from the rounds of birth and death. This is not vouchsafed in deep sleep. This creates a very serious question for Vedantins to answer: "How, out of the millions of beings that are reborn, can one finally reawaken in the Absolute, and be free?" In *turīya*, one does not return from deep sleep back into dream or wakefulness, but instead passes on to the Absolute. Thus far the *Bṛhadāraṇyaka* has given us a full description of life on earth, our aspirations to free ourselves, disciplines to follow and the ultimate release. This mantra presents the problem of how to make *suṣupti* as effective as the *turīya*. For this, our attention is called to the sun which is mainly responsible for bringing the world of phenomenality to us. This is accepted as a effective meditation in Narayana Guru's *Ātmopadeśa Śataka:*

> The inner organs, the senses, the body,
> the many worlds known by direct perception,
> Everything when contemplated is the glorious
> embodiment of the sun which shines beyond.
> This should be known through relentless search.

After seeing a world with ten thousand names and ten thousand forms and ten thousand special functions of each, one turns one's mind to the source of this magic. It lies in the homogeneity of the outer light, which creates the phantom of visual images outside, and the inner light of the Self which, in response to the outer magic, creates the countermagic of superimposing on itself the world identity. The phenomenality of the world is effaced by a general exercise of identifying the sun beyond and the sun that shines as one's own consciousness. Narayana Guru points to the outer sky where the sun shines and to an inner sky of consciousness where the Self is continuously transforming itself into everything visible, everything audible, and everything functional. Reclaiming one's unitive vision from the plethora of pluralism is the challenge which every student of *Vedānta* has to face.

Mantra 4

saiṣā gāyatryetasmiṃsturīye darśate pade parorajasi pratiṣṭhita; tadvai tatsatye pratiṣṭhitam; cakṣurvai satyam, cakṣurhi vai satyam; tasmādyadidānīm dvau vivadamānāveyātām, ahamadarśam, ahamaśrauṣamiti, ya evambrūyādahamadarśamiti, tasmā eva śraddhyām; tadvai tatsatyam bale pratiṣṭhitam; prāṇo vai balam, tatprāṇe pratiṣṭhitam; tasmādāhurbalam satyādogīya iti; evam vaiṣā gāyatryadhyātmam pratiṣṭhitā; sā haiṣa gayāṃstatre; prāṇā vai gayāḥ, tatprāṇāṃstatre; tadyadgayāṃstatre tasmādgāyatrī nāma; sa yāmevāmūm sāvitrīmanvāḥ, eṣaiva sā; sa yasmā anvāḥ tasya prāṇāṃstrāyate.

Word Meanings

sā eṣā - that; *gāyatrī* - *gāyatrī*; *pratiṣṭhitā* - rests; *etasmin* - on this; *turīye* - fourth; *darśate* - (seemingly) visible; *parorajasi* - above the world; *pade* - foot; *tat vai tat* - that ; *pratiṣṭhitam* - rests; *satye* - on truth; *cakṣuḥ vai* - the eye; *satyam* - (is) truth; *hi* - for; *cakṣuḥ* - the eye; *vai* - indeed; *satyam* - (is) truth; *tasmāt* - therefore; *yat* - if; *idānīm* - even today; *dvau* - two (persons); *vivadamānau* - are disputing; *eyātām* - one (saying); *aham* - I; *adarśam* - saw it; *aham* - (and another) I; *aśrauṣam iti* - heard it; *śraddhyāma* - (we) believe; *tasmai eva* - the one; *yaḥ* - who; *evam brūyāt* - says; *aham* - I; *adarśam iti* - saw it; *tat vai tat* - that; *satyam* - truth; *pratiṣṭhitam* - rests; *bale* - on strength; *prāṇaḥ* - the vital breath; *vai* - verily; *balam* - (is) strength; *tat* - hence; *pratiṣṭhitam* - (truth) rests; *prāṇe* - on the vital breath; *tasmāt* - therefore; *āhuḥ* - (they) say; *balam* - strength; *ogīyaḥ iti* - (is) more powerful;

satyāt - than truth; *evam u* - thus; *eṣā* - the; *gāyatrī* - *gāyatrī*; *pratiṣṭhita* - rests; *adhyātmam* - (on the vital breath) within the body; *sā ha eṣā* - that (*gāyatrī*); *tatre* - saved; *gayān* - the *gayas*; *prāṇaḥ* - the organs; *vai* - indeed; *gayāḥ* - (are) the *gayas*; *tat* - so; *tatre* - (it) saved; *prāṇān* - the organs; *tat yat* - because; *tatre* - it saved; *gayān* - the *gayas*; *tasmāt* - therefore; *gāyatrī nāma* - (it is) called *gāyatrī*; *amūm* - the; *sāvitrīm* - *sāvitrī*; *yam eva* - that; *saḥ* - he (the teacher); *anvāha* - imparts; *sā eṣā eva* - is none other than this; *trāyate* - (it) saves; *prāṇān* - the organs; *tasya* - of one; *saḥ yasmai* - to whom; *anvāḥ* - it is communicated

That *gāyatrī* rests on this fourth, seemingly visible, above the world foot. That rests on truth. The eye is truth, for the eye is indeed truth. Therefore if even today two persons are disputing, one saying, "I saw it," and another, "I heard it," we believe the one who says, "I saw it." That truth rests on strength. The vital breath is strength. Hence truth rests on the vital breath. Therefore they say strength is more powerful than truth. Thus the *gāyatrī* rests on the vital breath within the body. That *gāyatrī* saved the *gayas*. The organs indeed are the *gayas*; so it saved the organs. Because it saved the organs, therefore it is called the *gāyatrī*. The *sāvitrī* that the teacher imparts is none other than this. It saves the organs of one to whom it is communicated.

In this mantra we get an ingenious way of epitomizing the epistemology, methodology and axiology of *Vedānta* in a very poetic and allegoric manner. If it is properly elaborated, it will cover all that the student of *Vedānta* has to know from the start to the solemn day of his or her realization. In spite of the revaluation which *Upaniṣads* like the *Bṛhadāraṇyaka*, *Chāndogya*, *Īśāvāsya*, *Muṇḍaka* and *Māṇḍūkya* give, the fountain source of these *Upaniṣads* is in the *Ṛg Veda*. When the first form of life was organized as the presiding deity of the very formation of life, that first being was still in danger of disintegration and death. The mind which the first-born was endowed with was a very primitive and crude desire-generating mind.

The first-born *prajāpati* came to be modeled after *hiraṇya-garbha* which symbolizes the island of hope to which we come in the ocean of desolation. Everything is dark and in the middle of that darkness there is a spark of light. That spark, however meager, is more meaningful than the infinitude of the blindness caused by darkness and chaos. Hence it is to be treated as the little pearl of priceless worth. Its light beckons to the hopeless to become hopeful. The ideas of God, the savior, the grace-giving fountain-source of life and all such epithets came from the envisioning of a spark of hope.

When a child is born, he or she is in darkness. The child does not know from where it came, why and who is responsible for its birth. It has no food and it does not know how to accept food from outside. It has no breath because the respiratory system has not started functioning. Light is of no use to it because it cannot discern whatever is illuminated by light. The words it hears mean nothing to it. In this terrible context the child instinctively cries for help. The SOS of the child comes as a plea to be saved. As the primal scream is so forceful, the lungs open into the wind pipe and the wind pipe into the organ of speech. From the mouth the child's utterance comes. The child gains its breath and is successful in announcing the arrival of a person. Naturally the mother's breast is given to the child at that point. Thus, the hunger that can lead to death and the breathlessness that can lead to death are all solved with the primal scream. From this it is deduced that nothing can be achieved without speaking aloud. Speaking aloud is calling for help. This is called *udgāna*. The primal scream was the first *udgāna*.

Seeing how it was helpful, life implored each faculty to sing *udgāna* aloud. The only efficient outpouring of the will to live came from the vital breath in the mouth. We have seen in the first *adhyāya* that the chief breath which sits in the mouth was the savior of life with loud chanting. With its help every faculty becomes functionally efficient. The first *udgāna* is recorded in this *Upaniṣad* as, *asato ma sat gamaya*, "deliver us from non-existence to the existent;" *tamaso ma jyotir gamaya*, "deliver us from darkness to light;" *mṛtyor mā amṛtam gamaya*, "deliver us from death to immortality." Thus the call to light as the nourisher-savior is given in the *Ṛg Veda* V.81:

Men illumined, yoke their mind and they yoke their thoughts to him who is illumination and largeness and clear perceiving. Knowing all phenomena he orders, sole, the Energies of the sacrifice. Vast is the affirmation in all things of Sāvitrī, the Divine Creator.

All forms he takes unto himself, the Seer and he creates from them good for the twofold existence and the fourfold. The Creator, the supreme Good, manifests Heaven, wholly and his light pervades all as he follows the march of the dawn.

In the wake of his march the other gods also reach by his force to the greatness of the Divinity. He has mapped out the realms of earthly light by his mightiness, - the brilliant one, the divine Creator.

And thou reachest, O Sāvitrī, to the three luminous heavens; and thou art utterly expressed by the rays of the Sun; and thou encompassest the Night upon either side, and thou becomest by the law of thy actions the lord of Love, O God.

And thou art powerful for every creation; and thou becomest the Increaser, O God, by the movings: and thou illuminest utterly all this world of becomings, *shyavashwa*, has attained to the affirmation of thee, O Sāvitrī. [24]

In this mantra the organs are called *gayas*, which also means cows. A cow is docile. It has no intelligence of its own unless it is stimulated to act in a certain way. If the cow is led to a pasture, without any further thought she will eat the green grass until she is put back in her pen. A cow does not know that she is a channel to bring solar energy to other living beings on earth. The universal deposit of energy is in a green blade of grass. The cow eats the grass and in return she gives back dung and urine which revitalize the earth with organic manure. The essence of the grass changes into the cow's blood stream and then comes to its udder as milk. When the same cow is stimulated by her calf knocking against her udder, she gives elixir-like milk. What the cow does is also done by the goat, the deer, the elephant and the rabbit. The milk nourishes the body of the calf with its protein and fat. Until the last day of its life on earth a cow is renewing the vitality of the earth as well as enabling other living beings to flourish. So it is no wonder that the Indians think of the cow as the mother of all beings.

Breath saved the organs (*gaya*) and hence it is called *gāyatrī* (*gaya* means the organ; *tri* means the savior). But the nourishment that comes from the *gaya* (cow) is supplied by the sun. Hence the prayer is made to the sun as *sāvitrī (savita* - one who saves). Thus *gāyatrī-sāvitrī* combines in it the most original sources of life - milk and sun. The sun is the indicator, the illuminator, and an incarnation of light. It is with light that the world is brought to our knowledge. That which reveals knowledge is the *veda*. Hence the sun is the *veda* of *vedas*.

Even when the sun shines forth and illuminates everything in the world, all the effort of the sun is in vain without a pair of eyes. There has to be the counterpart of the sun on the face of a living being, whether it is a worm, snake, tiger, monkey, brute, scientist or philosopher. In the dialectical pairing of the sun and the eye, the sun shows the truth and the eye recognizes the truth. Seeing is truth. What the eye sees is complemented by what the ear hears, hand touches, tongue tastes, and nose smells. All these physical organs have a high sensitivity with the quality of the spirit (*cetana*). The essence of the five senses is gathered by a synthesizing organ called mind (*manas*). *Manas* is the first to manifest for the whole world to be brought to an order of corporeal organization. The nourisher is the nourisher of the physical organism as well as the knowing mind.

The image of the cow is constantly associated in the *Veda* with the dawn and the sun. We are heliotropic beings who experience energetic wakefulness when the sun comes to the eastern horizon. Then we become like heroes, movers of things. We are the offspring of each night. We become radiant with the golden hue of our spirit. *Savita* or the sun can reach anything anywhere in the world with its beams. The touch of that beam is enough to make anything radiant and come to the visibility of the world. The sun is also called *bhāskara* because not only does an image fall on the retina of our eyes, it impresses us with a replica of it in our very soul so that we can remember it for the rest of our lives and cherish it by correlating it with other images. Hence *bhāskara* contributes to the *bhāna vṛtti*, the mentation of living beings.

Between the macrocosmic sun and the microcosmic eye the world is generated. Between them they produce form after form and every form is described by a new name, a unique name. It is this uniqueness of the names that are presented as the *ṛk*. When that vision of life, vision of being, vision of form, stimulates you, you become overjoyed and you sing your praise. A *ṛk* that is sung is the *sāma*. Such are the beautiful indications in this mantra.

Mantra 5

tām haitāmeke sāvitrīmanuṣṭubhamanvāhuḥ; vāg-anuṣṭup, etadvācamanubrūma iti; na tathā kuryāt; gāyatrīmeva sāvitrīmanubrūyāt; yadi ha vā apyevamvid-bahviva pratigṛhṇāti, na haiva tadgāyatrayā ekañcana padam prati.

Word Meanings

eke - some; *anvāhuḥ* - impart; *tām ha* - that; *sāvitrīm* - *sāvitrī* (hymn to the sun); *etam* - which (is); *anuṣṭubham* - in the *anuṣṭubh* meter; *vāk* - saying; *etat vācam* - speech; *anussṭup* - is *anuṣṭubh; anubrūmaḥ iti* - (we) shall impart; *vācam* - speech; *kuryāt* - (one) should do; *na* - not; *tathā* - like that; *anubrūyāt* - (one) should communicate; *eva* - only; *sāvitrīm* - (that) *sāvitrī; gāyatrīm* - (which is) *gāyatrī; yadi ha vai api* - even if; *evamvit* - one who knows this; *pratigṛhṇāti* - accepts (as a gift); *tat* - it; *bahu* - too much; *iva* - as it were; *na ha eva* - it is not (enough); *prati* - for; *ekañcana* - even one; *padam* - foot; *gāyatrayāḥ* - of the *gāyatrī*

Some impart that *sāvitrī* which is in the *anuṣṭubh* meter (saying), "Speech is *anuṣṭubh;* we shall impart speech." One should not do like that. One should communicate that *sāvitrī* which is *gāyatrī*. Even if one who knows this accepts too much as gift, as it were, it is not (enough) for even one foot of the *gāyatrī*.

Mantra 6

sa ya imāṁstrīmllokānpūrṇānpratigṛhṇīyāt, so'syā etat

prathamam padamāpnuyāt; atha yāvatīyam trayī vidyā yastāvatpratigṛhṇīyāt, so'syā etaddvitīyam padam-āpnuyāt; atha yāvadidam prāṇi yastāvatpratigṛhṇīyāt, so'syā etattṛtīyam padamāpnuyāt; athāsyā etadeva turīyam darśatam padam parorajā ya eṣa tapati, naiva kenacanāpyam; kuta u etāvatpratigṛhṇīyāt.

Word Meanings

saḥ - one ; *yaḥ* - who; *pratigṛhṇīyāt* - accepts; *imān* - these; *trīn* - three; *lokān* - worlds (earth, sky and heaven); *pūrṇān* - full (of wealth); *saḥ āpnuyāt* - will be receiving; *asyāḥ etat* - only its; *prathamam* - first; *padam* - foot (i.e., the results of knowing it); *atha* - now; *saḥ* - one; *yaḥ* - who; *pratigṛhṇīyāt* - accepts; *yāvatī tāvat ha* - as much as; *vidyā* - knowledge; *iyam trayī* - the three *Vedas* represent; *saḥ āpnuyāt* - will be receiving; *asyāḥ etat* - only its; *dvitīyam* - second; *padam* - foot (i.e., the results of knowing it); *atha* - now; *saḥ* - one ; *yaḥ* - who; *pratigṛhṇīyāt* - accepts; *yāvatī tāvat ha* - as much as; *idam prāṇi* - (all) the living beings; *saḥ āpnuyāt* - will be receiving; *asyāḥ etat* - only its; *tṛtīyam* - third; *padam* - foot (i.e., the results of knowing it); *atha* - while; *asyāḥ* - its; *turīyam eva* - fourth; *darśatam* - (seemingly) visible; *parorajāḥ* - above the world; *padam* - foot; *yaḥ eṣa* - that; *tapati* - shines; *āpyam* - can be secured; *na* - not; *kenacana eva* - by any (gift); *kutaḥ* - how; *u* - indeed; *pratigṛhṇīyāt* - could (one) receive (as a gift); *etāvat* - so much

One who accepts these three worlds full (of wealth), will be receiving the results of knowing only the first foot of the *gāyatrī*. One who accepts as much knowledge as the *Vedas* represent will be receiving only the results of knowing its second foot. One who accepts as much as all living beings, will receive only the results of knowing its third foot. While its fourth, seemingly visible, above the world foot that shines cannot be secured by anything. Indeed how could anyone receive so much as a gift?

There is a controversial reference in this mantra. Although nothing is said explicitly about rivals who are trying to mislead the students of *gāyatrī*, the *Yajur Veda* represented by Vaiśampāyana was revised and restated by Yājñavalkya as the *Śukla Yajur Veda*. Therefore we can naturally see in the *Bṛhadāraṇyaka Upaniṣad* a certain disagreement with anterior critics. The internal evidence in this mantra is so scanty that we cannot say who is being corrected. All that we should note here is the mantra's conformity with the methodological requirement of the epistemology of *Vedānta* in which *brahman* is to be understood as having four *pādas*. In the *Māṇḍūkya Upaniṣad* we read of the four *pādas* in the *praṇava*. The first three *pādas*, *akāra*, *ukāra* and *makāra*, represent the wakeful, the dream and the deep sleep. Here the fourth *pāda* is referred to as equivalent to *turīya* and identified with the sun that illuminates the whole world.

This can create a doubt because the sun is a visible luminary in the sky which can be seen with our eyes. There is a duality between the eye that sees and the sun that is seen. Eyesight depends entirely on the illumination of the world by the sun. This duality can be resolved by bracketing the sun and the eye. We have already explained that the sun is not presenting the phenomena nor does the Self project the phenomena. The phenomena is an aspect of interrelation in which the sun contributes the illuminating light and the Self contributes the interpretation of the psycho-chemical link between the Self that animates the faculty of vision and the sun that animates the visible world. Thus we find the link between the psychic and the physical is phenomenal whereas the true sun is identical with the true *dṛk*, seer. It is through the unifying identity we arrive at the *turīya* state of the sun as well as the transcendence of the triads of *bhuḥ*, *bhuvaḥ*, *svaḥ*, *ṛk*, *yajur* and *sāman*, wakeful, dream and deep sleep. It is in this way the *catuṣpāda* is completed.

The altering states of consciousness are interpreted in terms of awareness. Awareness of subject and object with a one-to-one correspondence is the wakeful. Awareness of the subject phenomenologically becoming many objects in the dream is a state of awareness which has no validity either in the empirical world of transaction or in the world of causal consciousness *(suṣupti)*. In the *turīya* there is no awareness at all. It is *cit* through and through. We have given elsewhere how *cit* apparently loses its purity when it is illuminating the world of the *jīva*. In the nondual state of the unconscious in the deep sleep there is no subject or object and no conditioned awareness. This is closest to the pure state of *cit*. When one passes from *suṣupti* into dream, the dream phenomena is experienced with *caitanya*, the first horizontalization of *cit*. In *Vedānta* this is specially called *taijasa*. In the wakeful, the subject and object are completely bifurcated and the subject is identified as entirely apart from the object.

In spite of the similarity between the causal consciousness of the third state *(suṣupti)* and the fourth, *turīya* is not a state but the only truth and foundation on which the other three states are manifesting. We pass on from causal consciousness to transcendence which is not consciousness or awareness, but the ultimate basis of all. As one has to make a breakthrough of the empirically conditioned state, psychologically conditioned state, and biologically conditioned state, normally a person does not recognize transcendence. Only in the phenomenology explained by Husserl, Heidegger and Jaspers, is this problem properly met by seeing the unity of transcendence in immanence, and immanence in transcendence.

A tree which is illuminated by the sun is seen as external to the person who sees it. It is considered to be empirically valid because everyone can share that experience. At the same time, each person who sees the tree has a tree image in his or her visual faculty which is a processed picture in which the psycho-chemical operations of the brain and the organ of vision are all implied. That causes the *bhāsya*. Whereas the *bhānāśraya* is the same for all people, the *bhāsya* is a unique presentation only to the mind of the person or persons placed in the same wakeful transactional circumstance. But to retain the image of the tree in the mind, the eye has to go again and again to observe the tree outside and the I-consciousness has to revive the idea of the tree presented as a mental image within oneself. There is a continuous oscillation of an interest between the subjective and objective. It gathers all the special characteristics of the object and corrects the mental image to be more at par with the external image. This constant correction is called *bhānavṛtti*. The result is the registry of the modulation of an experience deep in one's *citta vṛtti*, the faculty of grasping and memorizing. The memory of the tree image can be recalled.

When we pass on from this transactional wakeful situation to a dream experience, it is inside and not outside, yet the dream looks like the wakeful. There is an apparent space element to frame every dream. There is also a time sequence in every dream, but the space in the dream is no space, the time in the dream is no time. On an illusory ground of time and space, memories are reconstructed to make dreams. The stuff out of which every dream figure is created is *taijasa*. The subject becomes both the subject and the object. So one cannot share a dream with another, even with his bedfellow, when the process of the dream is going on. In deep sleep, *taijasa* itself is rid of all fluctuations. The *sattva* element of nature is reflecting the pure state of the Self. That is not the Self; it is only the reflection of the Self in the *sattva* aspect of nature.

The true Self is unapprehensible and thus it is not an object to be inquired into. Similarly, the sun that we see is not the real sun. It is a phenomenological image of the sun. The sky we see is not the real sky, but a phenomenological sky in which we see a phenomenological sun. There is a common element in transcendence and immanence. The homogeneity of that which gives the ability to make existence subsistential, and remove the plurality of subsistential existence is *ānanda*. Both the sun that illuminates and the Self that witnesses the illumined are to be reduced to *ānanda* to understand the fourth *pāda*. The *catuṣpāda* is identical with *brahman* in its two-fold aspects, *kārya brahman* and *kāraṇa brahman*. We have to use the indications given in this mantra to help us to get across the duality of *kāraṇa* and *kārya*, cause and effect, and establish ourselves or lose ourselves in the truth of unity which is called realization.

Mantra 7

tasyā upasthānam gāyatryasyekapadī dvipadī tripadī catuṣpadyapadasi, na hi padyase; namaste turīyāya darśatāya padāya parorajase; asāvado mā prāpaditi; yam dviṣyāt, asāvasmai kāmo mā samṛddhīti vā; nā haivāsmai sa kāmaḥ samṛddhyate yasmā evamupatiṣṭhate, ahamadaḥ prāpamiti vā.

Word Meanings

tasyāḥ - its; *upasthānam* - salutation; *gāyatrī* - O *gāyatrī*;

> *asi* - you are; *ekapadī* - one-footed; *dvipadī* - two-footed; *tripadī* - three-footed; *catuṣpadī* - four-footed; *apat* - (and) without foot; *hi* - for; *na* - not; *padyase* - (you) are attainable; *namaḥ* - salutations; *te* - to you; *turīyāya* - the fourth; *darśatāya* - (seemingly) visible; *parorajase* - above the world; *padāya* - foot; *prāpat iti* - may attain; *mā* - not; *asau* - the (enemy); *adaḥ* - that (his object); *dviṣyāt* - (should the knower of the *gāyatrī*) bear hatred; *yam* - to anyone; *iti vā* - either (he should say); *asau* - so and so; *asmai kāmaḥ* - his desired object; *mā* - never; *samṛddhi* - flourish; *evam* - then; *saḥ* - that; *kāmaḥ* - desired object; *asmai* - for him; *yasmai* - against whom; *upatiṣṭhate* - (he) salutes the *gāyatrī*; *ha eva* - never; *samṛddhate* - flourishes; *iti vā* - or (he may say); *prāpam* - may attain; *aham* - I; *adaḥ* - that (object)

> Its salutation: "O *gāyatrī*, you are one-footed, two-footed, three-footed and four-footed, and you are without any feet, for you are unattainable. Salutations to you, the fourth, apparently visible, above the world foot! May the enemy never attain his object!" Should the knower of the *gāyatrī* bear hatred to anyone, he should either say: "So and so - may his desired object never flourish!" Then that object of the person against whom he salutes the *gāyatrī*, never flourishes – or he may say, "May I attain that object!"

The first line of the *gāyatrī* is an invocation to the sun that shines in splendor in yonder sky. "Oh Great Splendor, we invoke your grace, because you are the most gracious Being to be invoked for a boon." The person who gives the invocation is an earthling born of this planet, sustained here and ultimately returned to it. All this is illuminated by the sun. In these opening words we see three regions of the universe coming in a vertical line: the human on earth, the atmosphere which gives the blessings of life and holds all living beings in the compassionate care of vital sustenance, and the beyond from which comes the showering light and life of the sun. Hence, it is appropriate that the *Upaniṣad* equates earth, atmosphere and sky with the first three words of *gāyatrī*.

Our habitat is this firm earth. It supports the immovable as well as the moveable. The gross stability of the soil on which we stand is not anything which can be purchased. We did not pay anything for this priceless foundation of our earthly life. Every bit of earth has a value of its own. It includes within it the finest clays and rugged rock formations. With clay we can make pots and many other articles for our use. With gravel we build our houses, and pave our roads. Out of rock we can cut large blocks to make pillars and foundations for buildings. All the organic food with which we sustain our life also comes from good earth. All these are given free to us. Without earth there is no possibility of the actual occurrence of life.

Our great planet is girdled by the ocean and there are watery veins everywhere on earth. The ocean that evaporates, rises into the sky and comes down as rain provides us with the moisture that maintains all life forms from little blades of grass to the mighty oak, the tiny bug to the human being. The rain forms puddles and ponds on earth which can hold water for some time. In these bodies of water the particles flying in the sky and the particles floating in the water are drawn to a meaningful center where the pulsation of life begins. The sun is like a creative eye which benignly looks at the particles gathering in earth's puddles. Like magic it generates the electrolysis which commences life.

There is no wealth greater than this earth, atmosphere and sun - interlaced together to give us our life. Hence, it is most appropriate to begin the *gāyatrī* with the three mantras which call attention to creative energy: *AUM bhuḥ* (earth), *AUM bhuvaḥ* (atmosphere, watery substance), and *AUM suvaḥ* (the golden world). *Bhuḥ*, the earth, has no light by itself; *suvaḥ*, like heaven, is all light. Forms evolve where there is a coming together of light and darkness. What comes from earth are sprouts of life that aspire to rise to the sky. The river receives the rain of the clouds and the abundant benevolence of the atmosphere. The sun is like a benign father continuously bestowing blessings on earthlings. The golden sheen of the heavens prompts living beings to grow tall in the verticalization of life. The light that generates life also stimulates us to think high and make our thoughts soar to the heights of sublimity.

The earth is wrapped with air full of life-giving oxygen. Air comes close to our nostrils and, without any persuasion, passes through the orifices of our nose. The air finds easy passage through the respiratory system to reach every cell of the body. It returns to our nostrils and mingles again with the atmospheric air. If the earth nourishes life, the atmosphere invigorates it These are the two basics, earth and atmosphere, that invite solar energy to generate life. The sky has no limit. It is extensive on all sides. The breath in us allows our awareness to magically spread out into the infinitude of the sky, and our small, twinkling eyes can establish a comradeship with the twinkling stars of the far off heavens. The light of the heavens helps us to maintain a universe built on ideas which guide us. The scheme of integration suggested in the first line of *gāyatrī* is a symbolically and scientifically conceived formula, poetically uttered.

The second line of the *gāyatrī* mantra is a call for a purificatory service. Our prayer is to remove from this self-produced, self-manipulated, self-sustaining life, all dross, all darkness and all evil, by cleansing our faculties with discriminating knowledge. The *Upaniṣad* compares the three parts of the second line to the three *Vedas, Ṛg, Yajus* and *Sāma.* When a child is born, he or she comes to this world with sense organs ready to perceive. Without any prompting the ears listen, the skin touches, the eyes see, the tongue tastes and the nose smells. Thus, the entire outside world is classified into the audible, the tactile, the visible, the gustatory and the olfactory. In spite of the continuity of sound vibrating in space, the contiguous spreading out of energy which can be felt in all directions, and the unbroken character of light which is all-pervading, the central focus of human consciousness needs delimitation of all its sensory apprehensions. For that purpose, a name is given to everything, without which there cannot be any classification or categorization.

The symbol of identity is the name. Even the most transient particle is assigned a name. Assigning name is the function of the *Ṛg.* With such a device we move from the world of things to the world of knowledge. Knowledge is inferred from millions of memory tags. To know is to do. Hence, the *Ṛg Veda* is complemented by the ability of *Yajur Veda* to perform. The second part of the second line of *gāyatrī* is indicative of program fixation and the carrying out of programs. The third part of the second line refers to the *Sāma Veda* and recognizes that every work is a consummation that gives fulfillment and joy. Joy unifies everybody. Nothing gives fulfillment to hearts more than the all-pervading joy of togetherness.

The third line of *gāyatrī* enables us to enter into our own Being. We have an unbroken activity not initiated by our ego or accompanied by our knowledge. This is the activity of the life-giving energy, *prāṇa*. There is not much space in our little bodies to hold on to everything that comes into them. So the *prāṇa* that is drawn in needs to be expelled. The air that goes out of the body is renamed *apāna*. These are the two polarized aspects of life, to breathe in (*prāṇa*) and to breathe out (*apāna*). They each have to go to every cell and operate under synaptic control. The third line refers to this inner working dynamic of our vital energy. It is in this context that the solar energy given by the visible sun in the firmament is also spiritually redesignated as the ever-caring Spirit of life.

Beyond the light of the sun, is the light of the self-luminous presidency of the Self, *ātman*. Here the mind goes backward and forward, inward and outward. Outwardly it goes to the sun, and inwardly it holds on to the thread of names, conceptualizations and the memories of everything perceived. In this integration of the form and the name, things are substantiated with psycho-physical contents and natural properties consciously remembered by names. Such an integration brings *gāyatrī* to be identified with *sāvitrī*.

It is a paradox that the self-luminous, self-produced, self-maintained inner light can illuminate all without any physical radiation, yet cannot see itself. This *turīya* is the all-seeing basis of knowledge, the known and the knower. All that we seek to gain in the world is brought to consciousness by the illumination of the sun. With this extrapolation of the world and our ritualistic actions, we seek the hedonistic pleasures of life. That brings the vulgarization of knowledge. This is the theme given in the fifth and sixth mantras.

When we think of our outgoing consciousness and the sublime consciousness that is being absorbed into the Self, each one has different kinds of freedom. One is the freedom to go by one's own will into the electromagnetic field of being, subjected to the continuous push and pull of psychosomatic urges. By our own free will, we barter our freedom forever. The other is losing our identity in the freedom of pure Being. In spite of the polemics between the outer and the inner, both are necessary and complementary to arrive at the final step of transcendence of the outwardly conditioned world and the inwardly conditioned states of mind. That takes us to the rest of this *brāhmaṇa*.

In this seventh mantra, we get an intimate familiarization with the structure and form of *gāyatrī* and an instruction on how to offer *gāyatrī* as a *udgāna* so that it can result in the highest welfare of those who take refuge in it. All through the chanting and deep pondering *(manana)* of the *gāyatrī*, the meditator should not forget that it is not a simple ritualistic function that is being performed. It has an ascending range. It begins with the world of becoming, *bhuḥ*. The Supreme or the Ultimate has its counterpart which is of the nature of becoming. Becoming is most evident in the here and now where we see offspring coming from spouses, seeds coming from fruits, and one form transforming into another. Our knowledge goes from small pieces of information into elaborate and encyclopedic knowledge. Everything is coming into specific formation. Just as the blade of grass comes, human beings also come. Everything in between is also proliferating. As such no one is an alien to us.

When a baby is introduced to its mother, in spite of her having another body, she is adored and her friendship is cherished. The mother introduces the child to the father who has donated his seed to be nurtured in her womb. She reveals to the child who else has come from the same womb. They become the child's dear brothers and sisters. As the child grows, their relationships grow – it has cousins, aunts, uncles, in-laws, who in turn have their brothers and sisters, parents and grandparents. We love our cow, bull, and baby calf, we love our garden and its flowering bushes, we love the fruit-bearing trees of our orchard. Our intimacy has no limit – it pervades. This is all part of the first *pāda* of *gāyatrī*. What we said so far is only about the physical world where we live. Immeasurable is the elaboration to which the mind can be taken by such pondering.

That world has a past, it has a present and it has a future. The becoming that is happening in our present world is a fragment of human experience through which the continuous stream of becoming has been flowing through millennia. Before we scan the present, the present becomes the past, and the future is already ushered in as the present. Our world is enveloped by its environment, an environment that is conducive to generating life on earth. It has moisture, gases, particles flying in the air and sunlight that seeps through it. The atmosphere is like father and mother put together. Without the atmosphere we cannot live even for a minute. We refer to that as *bhuvaḥ*.

When we chant *bhuḥ*, our attention and homage should go to the *terra firma*, the hard ground on which we can trustfully sit, walk and lie down. When we say *bhuvaḥ*, we should feel the life-sap in us filling our whole body from the crown to the toe. And all over our bodies where our sensitive skin is, we feel the gentle sensation that is brought by the atmospheric air, its heat and cold. By simply knowing the warmth of the air, we are relating ourselves with the solar energy and we are realizing how friendly the universal wafting of the wind is. Through that wind and water the earth is sending us its fragrance and sapidity.

Thus even when we are not doing anything we are enjoying our atmosphere. We are smelling it, we are tasting it, we are seeing the manifold manifestions that are brought about in our environment by our atmosphere. But we are not confined to the earth and its atmosphere. Our eyes can go far into the sky, beyond the beyond, and witness a twinkling star. Although it gives an illusion that we are seeing the immediate radiation of the star, it could have started millions of light years ago to reach us. Such is the magic of the heavens beyond.

The first *pāda* of the *gāyatrī* encompasses all that is included in the earth, the atmosphere and the heavens. If we meditate on *bhuḥ*, *bhuvaḥ* and *svaḥ*, we cannot be selfish again, we cannot be conceited, we cannot be thinking only of ourselves. The I-consciousness *(aham)*, in us melts and dissolves in the totality of being. It goes everywhere, it meets with all contingencies and it savors its freedom.

Only after that comes the prayer invoking the very source of blessedness, *AUM tat savitur vareṇyam*, *Vareṇyam* indicates that the *savita* or *savitur* is the source of all blessedness and that is identified with *tat*. *Tat* is a sound symbol which can include everything that exists. Here existence is not to be looked upon as a fragmentary foundation of that which impresses itself on our senses and mind. The reference is to the basis of bases, the truth of truth. Of course truth has many faces. Everything has a nomenclature. That is the *ṛk*.

It also has a dynamic functional reality. Even when we see a body of a person and name it, the person is not sitting there as a block. He or she is breathing, cerebrating, digesting food and sending the essence of it to every part of the body. These are ritualistic. Day after day, one wakes up, spends one's energy through work, and has to replenish the energy expended during the day. This functional aspect is elaborated and ritualistically symbolized as *yajus*. Every action is sure to come to its culmination. We function to rejoice *(sāma)*. The rejoicing of our function is a confirmation of our truth. Hence the three *Vedas, Ṛg, Yajus* and *Sāma*, constitute the second foot of the *gāyatrī*.

All through, like the stream of consciousness, there is a continuous replenishing of energy with the *prāṇa, apāna* and *vyāna*. This is not merely an individual function. All living beings, despite variations in their bodily structures and assignments, have to breathe in energy and breathe out what has been soiled in the body. The air is not just to be taken in. It has to meet its opposite *(apāna)*. With the commingling of the *prāṇa* and *apāna*, the function of the *vyāna* makes the *prāṇa* and *apāna* available to every cell of the body – in us, in our neighbors and in our domestic animals, plants and micro-beings. That is another aspect of the *gāyatrī*.

Mere chanting of a verse does no justice to this inbuilt structure of *gāyatrī*. Ultimately blessings are sought from what is above the world. What shines over our heads as a truth of the beyond is the sun. The sun makes sense to us because it is so close, close to the retina of the eye. The sun does not stop there – it stimulates the rods and cones. By generating an electrical impulse, the sun enters into us and travels to the deepest core of our visual experience. Then we start interpreting form after form of whatever is illuminated by the external sun which we have directly seen and heard about through the accounts given to us by our parents, teachers and neighbors.

We have before us vast recordings of what blessings the sun (*gāyatrī*) was giving for millennia. There is no country without hundreds of libraries displaying thousands of volumes of what our fathers and grandfathers have heard and even what message is sent to each gene from the origin of life to this day. Such is the description given to us of the body of *gāyatrī* with three *pādas*.

Ultimately the fourth *pāda* is given which is no *pāda* at all. From the previous mantras we learned that the sun out there in the firmament and the sun as the cognitive faculty within us together make the foundation for all figures to emerge from the ground, be sustained on that ground, and be transformed for the future. Hence we are told in the present mantra: "O *gāyatrī*, you are one-footed, two-footed, three-footed and four-footed, and you are without any feet, for you are unattainable. Salutations to you, the fourth, apparently visible, above the world foot!" It is this visible sun which is the key to the invisible seer in us. There is only one seer who sees for everyone. This is very well presented in the *Kena Upaniṣad* as the hearer of all sounds; the toucher of all touches; the seer of all sights; the taster of all tastes; the smeller of all smells and the mind of all minds. It is to that *savitur* a prayer is made.

In this mantra there is a reference to the enemy. In the prayers of all religions, we hear supplications asking the Supreme to keep the petitioners away from the path of sinners. Sin is the caving-in of the walls of the mind which smothers the Self. Sin is being self-centered and self-conceited. The more we look at the nature of sin, the more we will be convinced that we fashion sin out of our own petty darkness. In his *Gītāñjali*, Tagore presents the paradox of man weaving sin around him and crying out for help. In *Gītāñjali* 29 we read:

> He whom I enclose with my name, is weeping in this dungeon. I am very busy building this wall all around; and as this wall goes up into the sky day by day, I lose sight of my true being in its dark shadow.
>
> I take pride in this great wall and I plaster it with dust and sand lest a least hole should be left in this name; and for all the care I take, I lose sight of my true being. [25]

In certain other scriptures the references to the enemy have a social coloration. There the enemy is actual people outside who are held in hatred and contempt. Such a concept is inconceivable to those who understand and appreciate *gāyatrī*. As the *Gītā* says, "You are your best friend and you are your worst enemy." The plea here is that we should not become our own enemy. If we aspire for something which is going to hinder our spiritual welfare, let that not be granted. It should not be understood as a prayer to take away from some other person the fruits of his or her labor. Rather, the petition is that we not be granted our prayers if our prayers are born out of ignorance, avarice, greed or revenge. Such is this noble prayer.

Mantra 8

etaddha vai tajjanako vaideho buḍilamāśvatarāśvimuvāca, yannu ho tadgāyatrīvidabrūthā atha katham hastībhūto vahasīti; mukham hyasyāḥ samrāṇna vidāñcakāreti hovāca, tasyā agnireva mukham, yadi ha vā api bahvivāgnāvabhyādadhati, sarvam eva tatsandahati; evam haivaivamvidyadyapi bahviva pāpam kurute, sarvameva tatsampsāya śuddhaḥ pūto'jaro'mṛtaḥ sambhavati.

Word Meanings

tat etat ha vai - on this (subject): *janakaḥ* - Janaka; *vaidehaḥ* - Emperor of Videha; *uvāca* - said; *buḍilam* - to Buḍila; *āśvatarāśvim* - the son of Āśvatarāśva; *tat yat nu* - well; *abrūthāḥ* - (you) called (yourself); *gāyatrīvit* - a knower of *gāyatrī; atha* - then; *katham* - why; *ho* - alas; *hastībhūtaḥ* - have (you) come to be an elephant; *vahasi iti* - and are carrying (me); *uvāca* - he replied, *hi* - because; *na* - not; *vidāñcakāra iti* - (I) did know; *asyāḥ* - its; *mukham* - mouth; *samrāṭ* - O Emperor; *agniḥ* - fire; *eva* - (is) indeed; *tasyāḥ* - its; *mukham* - mouth; *yadi ha vai api* - even if; *bahu iva* - a large quantity (of fuel); *abhyādadhati* - is put; *agnau* - into the fire; *tat* - it; *sarvam* - all; *eva sandahati* - is burnt up; *evam ha eva* - similarly; *yadi api* - even if; *evamvit* - one who knows this; *kurute* - commits; *bahu iva* - a great many; *pāpam* - sins; *sampsāya* - (he) burns up; *tat* - them; *sarvam eva* - all; *sambhavati* - (and) becomes; *pūtaḥ* - pure; *śuddhaḥ* - cleansed; *ajaraḥ* - undecaying; *amṛtaḥ* - (and) immortal

On this subject Janaka, Emperor of Videha, said to Buḍila, the son of Āśvatarāśva, "Well, you called yourself a knower of the *gāyatrī;* then why, alas, have you come to be an elephant and are carrying me?" He replied, "Because I did not know its mouth, O Emperor." "Fire is indeed its mouth. Even if a large quantity of fuel is put into the fire, it is all burnt up. Similarly, even if one who knows this commits a great many sins, he burns them all up and becomes pure, cleansed, undecaying and immortal."

In this *brāhmaṇa* we have been given the three *pādas* of *gāyatrī* which are known to people and the fourth *pāda* which is not obvious. Here one more factor is added which refers to the very beginning of this *adhyāya* where the hierarchy of beings is graded as *devas* (shining ones), the humans who are embodied and placed in the transactional world of empirical reality, and the *asuras* (demonic ones) who are only known from the effects of the darkness in which they are given their assignments. Actually speaking, these three are not three separate beings. They are all born of *prajāpati*. In the *Bṛhadāraṇyaka Upaniṣad* everything is self-manifested. Therefore there is no separate Creator or *īśvara*. *Īśvara* is a function in the totality, by its intrinsic nature of benevolence.

In the opening story there was a mention that the *devas*, *manuṣyas* and *asuras* turned to the *prajāpati*, seeking advice for their spiritual perfection. In the manifestation of the world, the spirit presents itself in the materiality of beings as the matrix of nature. Nature is said to be of three modalities, *sattva*, *rajas* and *tamas*. The shining ones are supposed to have a large affinity to the *sattva* aspect of nature. *Sattva's* quality is to reflect whatever is in nature in pure and clear terms without distortions. Therefore the *devas* are well placed to appreciate the hierarchy of values. So they clearly see the manifestation of truth, beauty, goodness and justice.

Because of this clear apprehension of values, those who have the intrinsic quality of *sattva* are attracted to that which is beautiful. Beauty has the qualities of being bright, affective of heart, and of the pure impression of the senses. Beauty is also a source of temptation. The shining ones are truthful, benevolent and just. But they have one weakness. They are easily carried away by the temptations of the heart - and they know it. The *pāpam* (sin) that can come to a person of *sattvic* quality is to become spiritually blinded when he or she is exposed to infatuation. So the *devas* understood their instruction from the *prajāpati* to be: "We are asked to restrain, to have *dama*."

The *prajāpati* then turned to the humans and asked what they understood by *'da'*. They knew that their weakest point was to hoard, to grab what belongs to other people. In the *Īśāvāsya Up-*

aniṣad this tendency is highlighted and it is said, *mā gṛdhaḥ kasyasviddhanam*, "Whose is wealth? Do not covet it." In human society one is considered a success if one can possess means of power, means of sustenance, means of domination. In the Bible we read how Jesus was irate with the high priests and accused them of being people who want to have the place of honor in feasts and who are so inconsiderate as to grab the wealth of widows. He turns to his own disciples and asks them what they are anxious about. Then he himself points out the anxiety they share with all humanity about what they will eat the next day, and with what they will clothe themselves. In the world of economics Jesus gave his fundamental teachings of loving one's neighbor as oneself and trusting in the benevolent grace of God. The peace invocation with which *gurus* and disciples start the day is the pronouncement of a contract between them that they should together be protected and nourished, so that they may together become energetic and beam forth in their excellence.

At least eighty percent of the complaints in civil and criminal courts are about people who rob and grab their neighbor's property. Thus the human sin is mainly that of losing one's sense of propriety and becoming self-centered. Sharing what you have with your neighbor is considered to be righteous behavior. This is also made the central theme of the *Īśāvāsya Upaniṣad:* "How can one who sees his Self in all, and all in his own Self, ever hate another or have wrong desires?" The sin to which a person is easily led is to lose the largeness of his mind, the infinitude of his mind's horizon.

When it came to the turn of the demons, they knew they had no mercy. Their nature is that of the brutes of the jungle. Hardly a lion, leopard or wolf thinks of the cruelty involved in preying upon the gentle animals of the forest. So when they were asked what they understood by *'da'*, they said, "We are advised to show compassion to others, *dayā*."

There are three types of sin. The first belongs to the category of *sattva*, the second belongs to the category of *rajas* and the third belongs to the category of *tamas*. In the Semitic religions all these are put into one - disobedience to God. There is no religious book in the world that does not warn against sin. In I.5.20 we were told that the essential nature of a human being is to be in unison with all and hence exemplary in virtue. From that we can also deduce what is vicious. The mantra says:

> The divine vital force from water and the moon pervades one. That is the divine vital force which, moving or not moving, neither suffers nor perishes. One who knows thus becomes the Self of all beings. As is this deity, so is one. As all beings worship this deity, so do they worship one who knows thus. Whatever grief these beings suffer from is indeed joined to them. But only good result goes to such a one. Evil result never goes to the gods. [26]

Here the one referred to is the sage. In verses such as the following from the *Tao Te Ching* of Lao Tzu, we hear the exemplary character of the sage which is the normative notion of the Absolute, the high-water mark of virtue:

> Heaven and earth last forever.
> Why do heaven and earth last forever?
> They are unborn,
> So ever living.
> The sage stays behind, thus he is ahead.
> He is detached, thus at one with all.
> Through selfless action, he attains fulfillment. [27]

In the *Praśna Upaniṣad* we read about a psychophysical aspect of the main functional instrument of life, the *prāṇa*. It says that out of the hundred nerves which go from the heart to the *ājña* between the two eyes, the *udāna* goes upward and becomes radiant in the brain. This *udāna* is like one who is keeping vigil over the behavioral pattern of a person. Nobody can sin without adversely affecting their heart. In a person's heart there is a reckoning of all actions. This is evident from the fact that a person is likely to feel a sense of guilt when he or she is about to tell a lie or hurt another. In the *Taittirīya Upaniṣad* a virtuous person par-excellence is described as one who keeps his mind always in the Absolute. Regardless of what incidentally happens by the provision of nature, he does not know whether he is exposed to right or wrong, to virtue or viciousness. Because of equanimity of vision, such a person does not see the social complexity of human behavior. In *Taittirīya Upaniṣad* (II.9) we read,

> Wherefrom words turn back,
> Together with the mind, not having attained –

> The bliss of *Brahma*, he who knows,
> Fears not from anything at all.
>
> Such a one, verily, the thought does not torment: 'Why have I not done the good *(sādhu)*? Why have I done the evil *(pāpa)*?' He who knows this, delivers *(spṛṇute)* himself *(ātmānam)* from these two *[thoughts]*. For truly, from both of these he delivers himself - he who knows this!
>
> Such is this mystic doctrine *(upaniṣad)*! [28]

Again we read in the *Chāndogya Upaniṣad* (I.2.7-8):

> Then they meditated on the *Prāṇa* in the mouth as *Udgītha*. The demons came in clash with it and were destroyed, just as a lump of clay is destroyed, striking against a hard rock.
>
> Thus it is that the *Prāṇa* in the mouth has not been destroyed and is pure. Even as a lump of clay striking against a hard rock is destroyed, so will he be destroyed who wishes to do evil to one who knows this (the purity of *Prāṇa*) or who actually) injures that knower, for he is like a hard rock. [29]

Again we read in VIII.13.1 of the *Chāndogya Upaniṣad*,

> From the dark I attain to the variegated, from the variegated I attain to the dark. Shaking off evil as a horse his hairs, shaking off the body as the moon frees itself from the mouth of *Rāhu*, I, having fulfilled all ends, obtain the eternal *Brahman*-world yea, I obtain it. [30]

From all these examples given in the *Upaniṣads* we can easily see that *pāpam* is intrinsically related with one's understanding that gives the motivation for any action, one performs. If the motivation is wrong, the action becomes evil and hence in the *Bhagavad Gītā, karma yoga* is recommended as a way to avoid wrong motivation. Instead of thinking that you are the doer, if you understand yourself as an instrument of God and your performance always aims for the universal welfare, then no sin is incurred.

In the mantra under discussion Janaka reveals to Buḍila, the son of Āśvatarāśva, that the mouth of *gāyatrī* is fire *(agni)*. The *pādas* (feet or lines) of *gāyatrī* have to be supplemented with the mouth of *gāyatrī*. We have already pointed out that in both the terms *mantra* and *gāyatrī* there is reference to the saving factor. Who is to be saved? The Christian religion implicitly and explicitly says that humanity is in need of being saved from sin and Jesus is presented as the savior. For that, he had to sacrifice his whole being by surrendering himself to those who crucified him. The example given by Janaka is *agni*, the power that burns away all dross leaving nothing but ashes. The Buddhist concept of *nirvana* is 'burning out'. The Indian concept of *tapas* is also that of burning away one's sins. Thus a universal concept is taken here for discussion and clarification.

Brāhmaṇa 15

Mantra 1

hiraṇmayena pātreṇa satyasyāpihitam mukham; tat tvam pūṣannapāvṛṇu satyadharmāya dṛṣṭaye; pūṣannekarṣe yam sūrya prājāpatya vyūha raśmīn; samūha tejaḥ yatte rūpam kalyāṇatamam tatte paśyāmi; yosāvasau puruṣaḥ so'hamasmi; vāyuranilamamṛtamathedam bhasmāntam śarīram; aum krato smara kṛtam smara krato smara kṛtam smara; agne naya supathā rāye asmān viśvāni deva vayunāni vidvān; yuyodhyasmajjuhurāṇamenaḥ bhūyiṣṭhām te namauktim vidhema.

Word Meanings

mukham - the face; *satyasya* - of truth; *apihitam* - is covered; *hiraṇmayena* - golden; *pātreṇa* - with a disk; *tvam* - you; *pūṣan* - O nourisher (sun); *apāvṛṇu* - remove; *tat* - it; *dṛṣṭaye* - (so that I) may behold it; *satyadharmāya* - whose reality is truth; *pūṣan* - O nourisher; *ekarṣe* - O lone wanderer; *yama* - O controller; *sūrya* - O sun; *prājāpatya* - O offspring of *prajāpati*; *vyūha* - restrain; *rasmīn* - (your) rays; *samūha* - curb; *tejaḥ* - your brightness; *paśyāmi* - (I wish) to behold; *te tat* - that; *rūpam* - form; *te* - of yours; *yat* - which is; *kalyāṇatamam* - most auspicious; *aham* - I; *saḥ asau asmi* - am; *yaḥ asau* - that; *puruṣaḥ* - person; *vāyuḥ* - (may my) vital breath; *anilam* - (return) to the cosmic vital breath; *amrtam* - immortal; *atha* - and; *idam* - this; *śarīram* - body; *bhasmāntam* - reduced to ashes (go to earth); *AUM* - *AUM*; *krato* - O deity of resolutions; *smara* - recollect; *kṛtam* - all that I have done; *smara* - recollect; *krato* - O deity of resolutions; *smara* - recollect; *kṛtam* - all that I have done; *smara* - recollect; *agne* - O fire; *naya* - lead; *asmān* - us; *supathā* - along the bright path; *rāye* - to prosperity; *deva* - O shining one; *vidvān* - (who) knows; *viśvāni* - all; *vayunāni* - mental states; *yuyodhi* - remove; *juhurāṇam* - treacherous; *enaḥ* - evil; *asmat* - from us; *vidhema* - (we) offer; *bhūyiṣṭhām* - repeated; *namaḥ uktim* - salutations; *te* - to you

The face of truth *(satya)* is covered with a golden disk. You, O nourisher (sun), remove it, so that I, whose reality is truth, may behold it.
O nourisher, O lone wanderer, O controller, O sun, O offspring of *prajāpati*, restrain your rays, curb your brightness. I wish to behold that form of yours which is most auspicious. I am that person.
May my vital breath return to the immortal cosmic vital breath, and this body, reduced to ashes, go to the earth! *AUM*, O deity of resolutions, recollect, recollect all that I have done.
O fire, lead us along the bright path to prosperity. O shining one who knows all mental states; remove the treacherous evil from us. We offer repeated salutations to you.

This *brāhmaṇa* of the *Bṛhadāraṇyaka Upaniṣad* has adopted mantras fifteen to eighteen of the *Īśāvāsya Upaniṣad* to end the fifth *adhyāya*. Emmanual Kant described our world as a training ground for the soul to come to perfection. Narayana Guru divides his *Darśana Mālā* into ten chapters. The first five elucidate the specific and generic errors to which human consciousness is subjected. The first is *adhyāropa*, the superimposition of a construed erroneous idea on the Self with varying patterns. Each pattern refers to the classical errors of humanity. Yet in each modulation of the false there is something fascinating. The first common error is the inability to distinguish between a dream and a wakeful experience. In the dream there is a magical presentation of totally non-existent scenarios decked with all kinds of subjective stimulation that cater to the pleasures or pains of the five sense organs. There is a basic division between dreams that are enjoyable and dreams that are frightening or miserable. In states of misery, both believers and unbelievers think of God. Believers think that pleasurable experiences are a gift of God and painful experiences are God putting the faithful to various crucial tests to decide their fidelity to the Lord. They praise God for the pleasurable, and they try to do penance to please God so that they may be redeemed of pain. Unbelievers, even though they have no faith in God, think God is cruel to make a world of distress and pain only to please his sadistic enjoyment of ignoble cruelty.

The second model that Narayana Guru gives is to think in terms of the continuation of life from seeds or genes which have come from a family tree. People are happy when they have innate talents and are able to live a successful life in society. Many mourn that they came from seeds of inferior quality. They want to think that they are lost people who have been crippled even from the level of genes. They are not thinking of God; they are thinking of fate, a crazy superpower planning a destiny for all, and fashioning beings to go through predetermined paths of little joy and much misery. They think that once life is initiated in a body/mind complex there is no return and the destined path is to be tread. This gives the impression that life on earth is an imprisonment arranged by the caprice of an unknown overseer.

Next Guru postulates an enjoyable scene when everything is favorable and life looks like a beautiful painting that has come from the colorful brush of a master painter who puts the right pigments in the right way to bring total harmony of color and perceptual perfection. This picture is counterbalanced by the mind of one who goes to the center of his being and alienates the outer world and the social companionship with which he is provided. Instead he sees only his self-centered life. His lot is miserable because the terrible picture he sees of the world around him is of ghosts and goblins. Every night to him is a frightening nightmare. Some others think of the world undergoing evolution and that they are on a long waiting list to be ultimately chosen for the final rehearsal of a successful life. These are all the petty ideas of people of poor imagination. Most of us live with such beliefs. Amidst millions of such human beings, a few struggle to find out reality.

The cave allegory in Plato's *Republic* gives us a general picture of an archetypal seeker who is lost in the company of the blind. He meets with what he considers the most wonderful gift of reason. With this pearl of priceless worth, which gives light to his thoughts and deeds, he thinks that he can weave a variety of arguments at the end of which he may comprehend the most secret truth of life. Then the faculties with which reason is to be correctly applied bring frustration to him. His ear can turn to the sound of music or of fury. He can touch the soft and warm object of erotics, or he can take to the path of the rugged and rough. He can look at beautiful forms or ugly ones. He can taste sweetness or bitterness, saltiness or sourness. He can smell the gentle fragrance of the jasmine or the stench of putrefied flesh. He has some control over all his senses, but the grand interpreter, moderator and monitor of all senses is the mind. Where is the mind? To this day we have not discovered where the mind is and how it operates. Consequently we come to the most confounded confusion. Thus the pearl of priceless worth, the pearl of reason we handle, often slips away from us and we have to sit struggling for days and nights.

Here is the most baffling of all games: what we see as truth for one moment turns out to be a frightening falsehood the next moment. Narayana Guru defines eight altering modes of the real-unreal paradox. The two comrades who get involved in this stage play of life are the sun in the firmament and the reasoning faculty in the folds of our own brains. The external light represented by the sun and the internal salesmanship that comes from the subjective world generate an orchestration of values ranging from the blaring noises of disturbances to the subtle nuances of heavenly music. The sun above us is *bhānuman*, the conjurer of visions, and the mind that takes the aid of the sun to shift from one vision of life to another is chiseled out of millions of memories.

We have to choose between the duality of appearance and reality. In the second five chapters of the *Darśana Mālā* the Guru gives guidance to the struggling soul that is in a feverish state to find peace. One identifies oneself with the world of facts and figures and feels that there is no time to rest because the world is at odds with him or her. As the earth moves around the sun, it passes through at least four seasonal phases. The rains from above give us great hope that our fields will be irrigated, so we sow the seeds of security for the future. But the rain is erratic. Sometimes it never stops; it brings floods. We have to be vigilant so that a flooding river may not swell and carry away our homes and the people who live there. Our cattle may drown in the water; crops can be submerged. So we are put into terrible situations.

When spring comes it makes spouses amorous. Pregnancy comes to women. The parents become anxious about what is in store for the family. What kind of a child is coming - still born, handicapped, mentally retarded or a son or daughter with great promise? Even if the child who comes is blessed with good intelligence and sound body, who knows what diseases might strike? Parents always have to be on their toes to support themselves and their children.

A wrong word slipping from a man's mouth or an erratic action can bring the hands of the law to him. The police can apprehend him. If he has not earned enough the tax collector may pester him. A whole country can be caught in the wrath of a belligerent neighbor or its own national chief. This is the world of action (*karma*). *Karma* is hydra-headed. Humanity tries to beat it theologically, psychologically, scientifically. People find partial success, but no peace of mind. So they burn out in the heat of their *karma*.

Some people turn away from unreasonableness, illogicality and ineffective logistics. Their minds are diverted from action programs to managerial science and their search for truth becomes intense. Then they find the deception of appearance throwing before them millions of masquerading counterfeits. They are caught in the trap. They can even be betrayed by their best friends. So they have to be cautious from moment to moment. Then they find that there is a pattern of truth which suits a majority of people with whom they live. They call it objective truth: they believe what they see. Humanity has coined certain rules of thinking and fact-finding methods such as perception, inference, analogy, and learning truth through bitter experience. Even with such thoughtful reasoning, the ocean of *saṃsāra* is not easily navigated. There are invisible and hidden rocks in the sea against which ships can collide.

In such a state a person starts distrusting the one device that has taken him or her all the way from childhood, adolescence, and middle age to the maturity of old age. The world is too complicated for reason to steer past all the unknown tragedies of life. At that moment one realizes that the conditioned modulations of truth with which one has been so familiar are only a fragment of the real truth. A person comes to that point and throws up his or her hands and says, "I am deceived by you, sun, who is out there, and by my reason in here. The face of truth is covered with a golden disk. That, O nourisher, may you remove so that I see the truthful performance of duties." To the very last, even a dishonest person wants to believe that there is a core of honesty within and if he or she failed to bring out that truth it is because of the niggardly provision of a step-motherly-like nature.

Here the sun referred to is no longer merely the sun seen in the sky. It is the counterpart of one's ability to see. Why are we kept outside this grand scheme of the perceiving eye honestly interacting with the illuminations of perception? We feel we have a right to be admitted into the scheme of the world order. The person who sees is as much serving the purpose of God as the sun which shines in the firmament and keeps the world going through its alternation of day and night, rest and work. The psychological factor of the ego is intrinsically connected with the cosmological function of the sun which presides over the solar system. Just as the sun leads all the planets in their respective orbits, the eye leads all human beings on their paths.

Sun is a nourisher. Without the sun there would not have been life on earth. We see no other wanderer meticulously traversing over our heads for twelve hours a day, day after day, year after year. So the sun is called the lone wanderer (*ekarṣi*). What would we do if the sun did not keep its face away from earth for at least twelve hours out of every twenty-four? That is the time when we give rest to our bodies and minds and refuel them for the next day's flight. Even when the sun is outside our vision, our earth orbits around it because of its magnetic power. But why is it that the very light which is meant to reveal truth creates instead a world of light and shadow, the phenomenality which hides total truth? It is true that the sun nourishes us and carries us along with it. Yet it and our reasoning faculty within always mislead us from appearance to appearance. Hence the prayer is given in mantra sixteen of the *Īśāvāsya Upaniṣad:*

> O nourisher of this world, lone wanderer, who gives a meaningful pause between events, the supreme magnetic center of the heavens, born of the primal father of all beings, restrain thy beams. Gather this brilliant effulgence. Let me see that, your most auspicious form. That Person *(puruṣa)* who shines in the sun, let me assure myself that I am that.

For the whole world the sun is the *prajāpati* which commissions us to conduct ourselves as self-luminous lights on earth. The sun is both the origin of life and its echoing reflections. This can be understood as the review of a person in old age who had a daily encounter with the sun who witnessed all his or her actions. A person who desired to live a hundred years doing his or her duties has now come to the fag end of the performance. He or she is lovingly laid to rest with legs stretched, hands folded, and eyelids heavy with the call of time to retire. The old man or woman slowly opens his or her imploring eyes to have a last look at the most trusted friend and caretaker of a whole life-time and makes the following supplication:

> O venerable protector, my eyes are too weak to look at your dazzling beams. Please restrain them for a moment. Your form is auspicious to see. Let me have your caressing look and consoling glance for the last time in my life. I want to get from you one last assurance. That is why I want to look full into your eyes. All through my life, in the morning when I offered my oblations to you, I addressed you as *sūrya nārāyaṇa* because the ever-present illumination in you comes from the Absolute on whom you and I depend as *nārāyaṇa.* And every time I saw you, I gratefully paid my homage to that One which lends its light to me. You are a cosmic reality; my status is of the psychologic microcosm. In fact, you and I and the Supreme are one and the same (*so'ham*).

A person's life on earth closes with the release of the vital breath that had been like a bolt holding all the limbs of the living organism together. This is given in mantra seventeen:

> Breath enters into the atmospheric wind. This body will end in ashes. *AUM*, remember the purpose of my doing actions, remember what I have done.

The departing soul has none of the faculties of the individual. We are told that all of the impressions created by a person's deeds are nullified. But the essence of a person's intentions goes with them because death is only a pause. A door closes to this life and a door opens to the next. The intentions become the causal consciousness which reenters a new body to continue the purposes which were being worked out by the person who was on earth. The last two lines of this mantra are attributed to the departing soul envisioned as lingering in the cremation ground to bid a final farewell to the world of memory. When a body dies, the ego dies and takes with it the mind and the power of judgment. But memory remains both in the soul of the dead person and in the world at large. Hence the repetition of the soul's last reminder, *AUM, krato smara, kṛtam smara krato smara, kṛtam smara.*

The last mantra of the *Īśāvāsya Upaniṣad* which is given as the last mantra of this *brāhmaṇa* is a general prayer of all who have witnessed how their forerunners lived a full measure of life and ultimately passed away:

> O fire, by a bright path lead us to prosperity, shining one who knowest all the ways. Keep far from us the sin that accrues as action. Most ample expression of adoration to you we render.

When we pray we expect that there is a benevolence in the Absolute which will respond to our prayer. The common belief in India is that there are two paths. One path leads into the southern way called the *pitṛyāna*, or smoky path. It will bring us back once again to live in this world to correct our mistakes so that we become noble and virtuous to enter into the northern way, the path of no return. The Absolute is the plenum which is always perfect and needs nothing. Each one of us is a gift unto ourselves by the Absolute. So all that we are capable of is folding our hands in reverence and adoration and saying, "Obeisance to That, Obeisance!"

ADHYĀYA VI

Brāhmaṇa 1

Mantra 1

AUM; yo ha vai jyeṣṭham ca śreṣṭham ca veda jyeṣṭhaśca śreṣṭhaśca svānām bhavati; prāṇo vai jyeṣṭhaśca śreṣṭhaśca; jyeṣṭhaśca śreṣṭhaśca svānām bhavati, api ca yeṣām bubhūṣati, ya evam veda.

Word Meaning

AUM - AUM; *yaḥ* - one who; *veda* - knows; *ha vai* - that which; *jyeṣṭham ca* - the oldest; *ca* - and; *śreṣṭham* - the greatest; *bhavati* - becomes; *jyeṣṭhaḥ ca* - the oldest; *ca* - and; *śreṣṭhaḥ* - the greatest; *svānām* - among (his) relatives; *prāṇaḥ* - the vital breath; *vai* - (is) indeed; *jyeṣṭhaḥ* - the oldest; *ca* - and; *śreṣṭhaḥ* - the greatest; *ca* - and; *yaḥ* - one who; *veda* - knows; *evam* - thus; *bhavati* - becomes; *jyeṣṭhaḥ ca* - the oldest; *ca* - and; *śreṣṭhaḥ* - the greatest; *svānām* - among (his) relatives; *svānām ca api* - as well as; *yeṣām* - among those of whom; *bubhūṣati* - (he) wishes to be (such)

AUM. One who knows that which is the oldest and greatest becomes the oldest and greatest among his relatives. The vital breath is indeed the oldest and greatest. One who knows this becomes the oldest and greatest among his relatives as well as among those of whom he wishes to be such.

Guy Murchie, the author of *The Seven Mysteries of Life*, became inspired to lift himself to be an observer of earth from outer space and to invite us to join him in his adventure of the spirit. He writes in the prelude of his book:

> Behold the body of Earth floating in living reality a thousand miles below us. See it, big as day, basking upon the black night of nothing, bedizened with stars - its mammose rotundity all fluted and furled in softest shades of bluish gray streaked with white.
>
> Sometimes, looking at it out of the space station I imagine I'm in, I get the definite but indescribable feeling that this my maternal planet is somehow actually breathing - faintly sighing in her sleep - ever so slowly winking and wimpling in the benign light of the sun, while her musclelike clouds writhe on their own meteoric tempo as veritable tissues of a thing alive.
>
> I was not brought up to think of the earth as a being. Such an impression has come to me only in this new outer perspective of space, which so provokes the thought that I cannot but wonder upon it. Could it? Just could the earth be alive?
>
> Of course no one who lives down there would likely expect the terrestrial organism to be breathing with literal lungs. But, reflecting on it, lungs are far from essential to life. Insects and lesser creatures breathe easily without lungs. And obviously any being of planetary size, to live at all, must live in a very different way from the minuscule parasites that inhabit it, as do I in turn live so differently from my germs. Yet those germs - who are presumed never to have heard of me - remain as vital symbols and symptoms of my living. [31]

The rishi of the *Bṛhadāraṇyaka Upaniṣad* believes that the vital breath was in this world even before the first gene came into being. It was not a caprice of the wind that the dust particles whirled to make the first formation of a smoke-like nebula to initiate the creation of the universe. Whatever these particles were, there had to be a moving force, a vehicular conveyance with a definite purpose to arrange the microscopic foundation as much in a star as in a living cell. The wind in Sanskrit is called *vāyu*.

The definition of *vāyu* is that which moves and makes other things move. This is a little different from the Aristotelian concept of God as the Unmoved Mover. What is unmoving in the wind is not the molecules of the air, but its eternal law of vitalizing everything. As such we have to think of the motion of the vital breath from the very start, the first cause.

We are handicapped by the narrowness of our spatial and temporal vision of the ever-growing and the ever-changing. A cause in our mind is infinitely small to begin with. When it unfurls, a sequence of effects are projected, not into space or into time. Space and time are also part of the effects which arise from the cause. Our scientific search has not been able to go to the distant past where time was sleeping and space was not discovered. It is the prerogative of the poet, the seer, the mystic to go beyond the world of hurdles and impossibilities to the vast expanse of possibilities. Further, we think of effect as a material reduction from conceptual matter. That need not be. Ideas can replicate and can take on ever-increasing dimensions of new shapes and forms.

It is easy to learn this by looking into the science of geometry. The first cause in geometry is not the configuration of any model. It begins with a mathematical point which has no dimension. It is handy to locate the beginning of beginning. If the ideal point is duplicated as an actual point, it immediately requires a space in which to be located, a time in which to begin. This simple event is followed by points interrelating to become lines which then deviate to cause triangles. How many geometrical figures are in this universe? Nobody can enumerate them all. Geometry is aided by arithmetic on one side and algebra on the other. If arithmetic leads us to the prosaic mechanical enumeration of things, algebra infuses poetry in our envisioning of mathematical possibilities. We cannot mark a time or space to say from here commenced the science of the calculus or the science of logarithms. The rishi takes us to the mysterious beginning of motion and the expansion of our awareness of creative elaboration when he speaks of the vital breath as the cause of causes.

Commenting on this Guy Murchie says,

> While this bubble of life is materially concentrated in the fifteen mile-thick earth skin of sea, soil and densest air, it is fueled and fed from energy in the planet's core and

> mantle and from the sun and stars. And it is bound together not only by gravitational, electromagnetic and nuclear cohesion but also by a kind of surface tension of interdependence, of chemical and psychological needs and intellectual accelerations interlaced with mystic, sometimes explosive, spiritual forces.
>
> From a chemical standpoint alone, animal life without plants to eat would starve quicker but no more surely than most plants would die without animals. Even minerals would be drastically disturbed without both these higher kingdoms. It has been calculated that photosynthesis in present terrestrial vegetation would literally consume all the carbon dioxide out of the atmosphere within a year or two if it were not replenished by smoke from fires, engine fumes and the exhalations of animals and other consumers or decomposers. [32]

It is heartening to find a plethora of evidence presented to us with the expansion of the frontiers of physics, chemistry and biology and the linking of these positive physical sciences with the elusive function of consciousness which is a direct offspring of the vital breath. It is remarkable that the rishi thought of the vital breath as the oldest and the greatest. In a number of cases we turn to our positive values by relating to our negative notions. What we see everywhere is the death of the manifested. By negating death conceptually we arrive at the idea of immortality. There are several ways of relating even a dust particle to other dust particles in the world. The ingenuity with which a power relationship is established makes a thing benevolent or malevolent. We are born of breath *(prāṇa)* and we die with the counterpart of breathing in, which is breathing out *(apāna)*.

When we think of our breath, the conception of our own being in the history of life, we are looking near. When a male and female become linked with faith in the other as loving and lovable, their breath quickens and passion arises, of which the immediate evidence is the thumping of their hearts, the blushing of the woman, the man failing to pronounce his first word. A total frenzy is caused in the organism by the breath losing its harmony and tranquillity. Every organ in both the male and female becomes frantic. To win the heart of the other, the breath makes many maneuvering tactics. Even the upheaval in the couple can be made charming by bringing beauty into thoughts, poetry into words and gentleness into touch. When finally they interlock, both the man and the woman think of the possibility of an off-spring coming from them. All that happens between mating couples is not known to their conscious minds. When the seminal fluid is released from the testes, what carries the sperm to the ovum? What is waiting in the doors of the ovum to decide the winner, and honor it by giving entry into the ovum? Although *prāṇa* is the passenger in the sperm, the throwing out of the sperm from the male body is conducted successfully by *apāna*, and the reception at the other end is arranged by the *prāṇa* which keeps the door open for friendly visitors. From there on *prāṇa* nurtures the fertilized egg to become a fetus and then a child. *Prāṇa* plays a very vital role in this orchestral function. These details were in the mind of the rishi when he presented this mantra. And even Śankara, who was probably innocent of the theories of modern science, could see these possibilities with his poetic eye:

> The pupil tempted by this mention of the result, is eager to put his question, when the teacher says to him: *The vital force is indeed the oldest and the greatest.* But how is one to know that it is such, since at conception all the organs (of the embryo) are equally connected with the formative elements contributed by the parents? The answer is that nevertheless the seed, if lifeless, will not develop; which means that the vital force begins to function earlier than the eye and other organs; hence it is oldest in age. Besides, the vital force goes on fostering the embryo from the moment of conception, and it is only after it (the vital force) has begun to function that the eye and other organs begin their work. Hence the vital force is legitimately the oldest of the organs. [33]

One may further wonder how the vital breath becomes the greatest. If one is dependent on another in a relationship, and that dependence is crucial for the existence of the dependent, the source of dependence is greater than the means it provides. Remember that we have taken the origin of vitality back beyond what is conventionally looked upon as living organisms to something which can be as mean as dirt and includes basic elements. Thus it gains the protective parenthood of everything.

In this *adhyāya* we begin with the vital breath as such because its various evolutes have already been explained such as the word *(uktha)*; the creative urge *(yajus)*; the exaltation of results *(sāman)* and the protective power *(kṣattra)*. These are like the offspring of the vital breath (*prāṇa*).

Mantra 2

yo ha vai vasiṣṭhām veda vasiṣṭhaḥ svānām bhavati; vāgvai vasiṣṭhā; vasiṣṭhaḥ svānām bhavati, api ca yeṣām bubhūṣati, ya evam veda.

Word Meanings

yaḥ - one who; *veda* - knows; *vasiṣṭhām* - what is the most excellent (*vasiṣṭhā*); *bhavati* - becomes; *vasiṣṭhaḥ* - the most excellent; *svānām* - among (his) relatives; *vāk* - the organ of speech; *vai* - (is) indeed; *vasiṣṭhaḥ* - most excellent; *yaḥ* - one who; *veda* - knows; *evam* - this; *bhavati* - becomes; *vasiṣṭhaḥ* - most excellent; *svānām* - among (his) relatives; *svānām ca api* - as well as; *yeṣām* - among those of whom; *bubhūṣati* - (he) wishes to be (such)

One who knows what is the most excellent (*vasiṣṭhā*) becomes the most excellent among his relatives. The organ of speech is indeed the most excellent. One who knows this becomes the most excellent among his relatives as well as among those of whom he wishes to be such.

Vas means to be the indweller; *iṣṭha* means that which pleases. Poets listen to the music of nature. The gentlest of voices is what is not heard. Its quality is a pregnant silence. When the words we hear tire us, they are not dear to us. They may be frightening or boring. Even the best of musicians who gives his whole life to the pleasing sounds of music sometimes needs to withdraw from articulated or created sound so that he can go into the several layers of consciousness ranging from the preconscious to the deep unconscious. Although the universe is occupied by millions of bodies which affect the space around them, the starry heavens do not disturb our peace. The sun and moon might not be very pleasant if we were to be physically near them, but otherwise they are silent friends, alternately visiting us in the day and night. The sun speaks to us by revealing the exquisitely beautiful forms of nature such as the far off sky, the mountain peaks, the still waters of the lakes, blossoms that bloom in the morning, the green lawn under our feet and the changing forms of innumerable animals, specifically the human.

The sun never identifies any of its presentations with nomenclature. But we need to go closer and deeper into every form we visualize, so we have given names to everything. On one side we have an absolutely silent world of bewitching visual beauty and, on the other, the world of innumerable nouns. We are special beings who want to know what we can do with every noun. Consequently we predict possibilities. When a subject is predicated it brings verbs. Thus we have invented a whole structure of verbal devices using different parts of speech.

Just as we oscillate between wakeful activity and deep sleep, we also oscillate between action programs and the enveloping silence that resides in us. Either we go into pondering (*manana*), reasoning (*vicāra*) and vexation (*cinta*) or into states of unison with nature, such as having *dhāraṇa*, stabilized concepts which will enable us to go deeper into the essence of meaning called *dhyāna*. When we find our *summum bonum* in the depth of silence, we are in *samādhi*. Thus we have a whole range of the world of sound and silence to traverse. It is entirely up to us when to be in the world of clamor and when to avoid it and go into silence. Our own soul or *ātman* is the most silent of all realities. This indwelling silence haunts us and we rejoice in sitting alone, walking alone, and meditating alone.

Of the five elements, that which has the most silent language is the evanescent sky. The language of the sky is called *nāda*, the most basic vibration of this universe. As it fills everything it is also called *nāda brahman*. The music of the ancient world was a worship of the heart offered to the all-embracing core of adoration. Music here does not mean sounds that break (*āhata*), but unbroken sound (*anāhata*). Every particle of our body sings and there is an interim fusion of the tones of the particles. They are micro-micro-tones. This is a continuous music in us and hence the *anāhata* is to be treated as the richest heritage of a living person.

When we come to this world, fragmentation happens in everything. Existence is fragmented into totally existing, partially existing, apparently existing and states of withering away and dying. Speculation arises regarding each part that is separately presented to the senses. Consequently our questions about these parts are never exhausted. When our interpretation of the phenomena of existence is fragmented, it is also endless. When the innate harmony is fragmented, several shades of disharmony come as well as harmonies that enrapture us. Samsāra is characterized by the phenomenality of pain and pleasure, birth and death, loving each other and fighting each other. In this fragmentation the one music is replaced by a babble of voices.

By nature human beings are always afraid of insecurity. Security comes through assurances. The first language a child loves to hear is the voice coming from its mother. Indian philosophers think of the mother as a repository of wine, milk and honey. Her words are like honey which pleases the child. Hence to every child its *vasiṣṭhā* lives in the voice of its mother. When the child is tired, the mother puts him or her in a cradle, gently rocks it and sings a lullaby. That is one way of enriching the quality of a child's equipoise. The gentle tone of the mother's lullaby has nothing parallel to it in the world. We can say that the mother who enjoys singing a song that puts her listener to sleep is a great wealth.

When we look at the organs of action, the highest is the tongue and the lowest are the feet. Feet are for mobility. Without feet a person cannot move freely, walk, run or jump. A person needs his or her two feet to go from where they are to another place, or to return. A similar need is fulfilled by the organ of speech. We each want to inform others of our likes and dislikes. We report a dislike in order to move to a situation which we can like. In a human being both the need to move and the need to communicate are very strong. Behind both these needs there is motivation. The language which we speak is an external aid, an instrument to carry out our motivation. Each motivation adds to one's wealth of attainment (*siddhi*).

Trees and plants cannot articulate. They have devised a language of richness which is exposed for everyone to see: colorful and fragrant honey-filled flowers and good-tasting and sustaining fruits. When one grain of the humblest of weeds like rice or wheat is put in the mud or filth, it brings forth hundreds of such grains. The grains which we consume, whether rice, barley, corn, oats or wheat, are called *dhānya*. One who has an annual crop of an abundant harvest of grains becomes the nourisher of the whole world. His language is silent, but he understands the needs of people. Every hungry person looks towards a person with full granaries. Such a person is called *dhanī* or *dhanavān*, the possessor or provider of grains. His greatest joy is when all join to eat.

Eating is made into a social function at the homestead. Everyone from the smallest child to the oldest great grandfather or grandmother comes to sit around a lunch or dinner table. They celebrate the ecstasy of eating with a backdrop of music. The sense of fulfillment which is seen in each face while they eat fills the provider with satisfaction beyond measure. The cook is pleased. They slow down their eating to speak to their friends and loved ones. They speak of everything - of far-off lands, the mysteries of the world. This richness is not of one person's possession, but each one sharing their joy with every other heart.

Small children will put their father's or mother's shoes on and walk clumsily around in them, wanting to grow up soon. Children pick up the books of the grownups and turn the pages even though they cannot read a word. Children also want to run to far-off places and to communicate with the most enjoyable subjects of the world. Knowing this need, parents arrange schools, teachers, tutors of all kinds. The child is made familiar with the language the society has adopted and thus enrichment begins with words of instruction, words of information, words of correction, words of purification, words which can bring out all the hidden talents. Words can nourish each talent to grow as new ideas, new designs, new aspirations, new goals.

The word not only makes an individual rich, but a whole community rich, a country rich, humanity rich. Like a farmer gathering his grains and storing them in granaries for tomorrow, there are farmers of words. They sow words and make each one attractive, sensible, logically useful and relevant. Words are required in every branch of life. There are historians who never allow time to whither away. They bring the past into the present and show how the people of the present can make a future by knowing the history of humanity. There are geographers who make surveys and put a whole world onto a globe even smaller than a balloon. They can silently give the orientation of where a person is, whether another place is near or far; and how one can reach each such place.

Some people reveal the ability of words to suggest higher truths of life; they become poets. They develop a language of metaphors and allegories. All words need not be technically true. They can be so assembled that a person can relive life's adventures in spirit a thousand times over or find the highest truth by reading a well-written epic like *Rāmāyaṇa* or *Mahābhārata* or *Iliad* or *Odyssey*. How can we ever fully describe the richness we have gained from the pursuit of religious prophets, the systematic discoveries of the scientists?

Words have the power to take the sharp teeth out of anger. Every country needs its diplomats to go to all the neighboring countries to make goodwill. Hence the description here of the organ of speech as the richest entrepreneur is a new light shed by the *Upaniṣad*. It is also a suggestion that we should mind what we speak. Let our words be truly nourishing kernels and not the chaff that can be thrown away. Meaningless words dissolve more easily in the atmosphere than anything else. Words of wisdom will ever lie cherished in the heart of all. The knower of the word and the speaker of the word - they both know that this world is made of words.

Mantra 3

> *yo ha vai pratiṣṭhām veda pratitiṣṭhati same, pratitiṣṭhati durge; cakṣurvai pratiṣṭhā, cakṣuṣā hi same ca durge ca pratitiṣṭhati; pratitiṣṭhati same, pratitiṣṭhati durge ya evam veda.*

Word Meanings

yaḥ - one who; *veda* - knows; *pratiṣṭhām* - that which steadies (*pratiṣṭhā*); *pratitiṣṭhati* - remains steady; *durge* - in rough (places and times); *svānām ca api* - as well as; *same* - in smooth (places and times); *cakṣuḥ* - the eye; *pratitiṣṭhati ha vai* - indeed (is); *pratiṣṭhām* - that which steadies (*pratiṣṭhā*): *cakṣuṣā* - with the help of the eye;

pratitiṣṭhati - remains steady; *durge* - in rough (places and times); *svānām ca api* - as well as; *same* - in smooth (places and times); *yaḥ* - one who; *veda* - knows; *evam* - this; *pratitiṣṭhati* - remains steady; *durge* - in rough (places and times); *svānām ca api* - as well as; *same* - in smooth (places and times)

One who knows that which steadies (*pratiṣṭhā*) remains steady in rough as well as smooth places and times. The eye indeed is that which steadies, for with the help of the eye one remains steady in rough as well as smooth places and times. One who knows it as such lives steadily in rough as well as smooth places and times.

Earlier in the *Upaniṣad* we learned that if instruction is given on the many facets of the Supreme, the teacher should also tell the student what is the abode (*āyatanam*) and foundation (*pratiṣṭhā*) of what is raised to the status of the Absolute. We have just heard about the word that nourishes and enriches our life in so many ways. What we say with our words is either about what we have seen or what someone else has seen. It can be classified as immediate perception, mediate or partial perception, perception by another, mental perception; moral perception, hallucinative perception and spiritual visions.

Sound comes from a direction. We cannot see a sound but we can make out from which direction it comes. Even if there is nothing there to see, the eye searchingly looks in that direction. From this it is evident that we look for the source of that which calls our attention. We also want to know whether we are invited to understand something of lasting value or only of ephemeral interest. We see birds flying in the sky or hear waves rumbling in the sea. Such transient occurrences, even though they are not of lasting value, give us the knowledge that there are many things happening in this world which are peculiar to a place or to a time. Thus a general idea of the transient also makes a permanent mark in the registry of our memory. But there are other perennial values of great importance which are to be recalled again and again to the very last days of our lives.

In daily life we move from one situation to another. Each situation is spatially localized, and temporally programmed or charted. We recognize things by their form. The presentation of a form comes as a direct perception. As we are social beings, others who are present in various situations will amplify our perceptions by giving names to what is seen. This enables every percept to be properly put in a niche which can be categorized with similar percepts. There is a one-to-one correspondence between the processed percept and its corresponding concept. Once the foundation of a concept is properly laid, one can recall the perceptual memory which was duly appellated.

The process commences with actual seeing. But as a form becomes inseparable from its established name, by seeing the form we also remember the name. As this experience intensifies, when we hear the name we also get a mental image of the concept that goes with the name. The mental image will have the latest impression of that form coming to the mind as a gestaltation. In most languages one and the same form is given many names, which in the course of our life we recognize as synonyms with various degrees of emphasis. As our childhood and adolescent days mainly bring us objects and persons not seen before, and names are given for the first time, there is an intense coordination of percepts and concepts in the first quarter of life. In the course of time a concept that can be recalled with a word image is as good as seeing the percept with our naked eyes.

In the course of history human beings learned that the main amenities of life which have more or less permanent use values can be bartered for getting other amenities. The idea of trade came and use value became symbolized in token values. The first universal token value was gold. Then it became printed promissory notes of governments which were said to have gold reserves to back them. Similarly, we do most of our transactions with verbal tokens for things which first came as percepts. We have derived a new foundation for perception in the word images of things. Many new classifications of images have come to human life.

An image can vouch for a certain event which happened in the past which can be significant in the present and which will hold good in imagining the future. One such is the image of our mothers and fathers whom we perceive at the very outset of our lives. Then the social significance of nouns like father, mother, brother, sister or home are stamped as permanent fixtures of great importance in our lives. The foundations of these social positions are also laid when the representations are seen once by the eye and then afterwards duplicated by mental images called to our attention with the appellations given by those people or entities. Even the most common man has within him the storage of a large number of verbal foundations originally testified to by his perceptual experience. Later the functional activities of those foundations are shifted to one's conceptual mind.

What we have directly seen and established corresponding images of is very meager compared to our visually established foundation of knowledge. By and large we have borrowed from other people what they have seen more than we have laid the foundation of concepts by direct perception. Knowledge comes to us more as printed names in books of history, geography, science and the detailed accounts given in the vast variety of books of knowledge which are increasing by geometric proportion every day. It is not absolutely necessary to see everything in person, but there is an absolutist certitude in what we personally see.

In Henri Bergson's *Introduction to Metaphysics* he says there are two ways of seeing: one is going around a thing and seeing several details of it; the other is entering into a thing and identifying with it. He gives the example of a man going to a famous church such as the Cathedral of Notre Dame, and taking several hundreds of pictures from all vantage points of the Cathedral, both from inside and outside, and finally presenting all those pictures to another person. Even so, the person who looks at the photographs will have only a relative vision. To gain an absolute experience one has not only to enter the Cathedral but has also to soak himself into the interaction between the church and the believer in it. Another example given by Bergson is of a poem written in a certain language and translated into another language. Several translations can be attempted, but none of them will ever match the original poetic vision of the poet. These examples are given to support the idea that the foundation spoken of here is not a mere impression gained from a peripheral or superficial look at things.

Most people come to this world like travelers and leave after accumulating many impressions. Just as we have two physical eyes which can look at forms and mental eyes which can seek and find their significance, there is also an eye of the spirit that is looking into itself. It is said many times in various *Upaniṣads* that the eye cannot see itself, the ear cannot hear itself, the mind cannot think itself. There is a greater foundation on which all the sense organs and the mind are established. That is the eye of the eye called *ātman*. The perception of the *ātman* is not immediate perception, nor is it mediate perception. Knowledge arising from absolute perception cannot be categorized as inference or comparison or even word testimony. It is an unparalleled experience where the seer, the seen and seeing lose all distinctive marks of tribasic transaction. It is the imperiential (identified with inner truth) certitude of gaining at-one-ment.

The mantra specially states that it is the certitude or reliability of the foundation that serves good in easy and difficult places and times. When we see a thing outside, that place is easy to locate. When we look for certitude inside, that place is not apart from us but it is difficult to locate. Whether the time is of the past, present or future, there are many documentations which can aid us. But that which transcends past, present and future is a difficult time. Thus this mantra, however short, gives us the warp and woof of wisdom established in the knower of the Absolute *(brahmavit)*.

Mantra 4

yo ha vai sampadam veda sam hāsmai padyate yam kāmam kāmayate; śrotram vai sampat, śrotre hime sarve vedā abhisampannāḥ; sam hāsmai padyate yam kāmam kāmayate ya evam veda.

Word Meanings

yaḥ asmai - one who; *veda* - knows; *sampadam* - prosperity; *ha vai* - surely; *sampadyate* - attains; *yam* - whatever; *kāmam kāmayate* - is desirable; *śrotram* - the ear; *vai* - indeed; *sampat* - (is) prosperity; *hi* - for; *sarve* - all; *ime* - these; *vedāḥ* - Vedas; *abhisampannāḥ* - (are) acquired; *śrotre* - when the ear is intact; *yaḥ asmai* - one who; *veda* - knows; *evam* - it; *sampadyate* - attains; *yam* - whatever; *kāmam kāmayate* - is desirable

One who knows prosperity (*saṁpad*) surely attains whatever is desirable. The ear is indeed prosperity, for all these *vedas* are acquired when the ear is intact. One who knows it to be such attains whatever is desirable.

We have two kinds of wealth *(dhana)* - inherited and acquired. Our motivation comes mostly from our inheritance. The father donates his seed to forge out of it a person; the mother receives the seed from the father and nurtures it first in her ovum and then for its full growth in her womb. Therefore our parents are our first inherited grace. In the course of our growth in the mother's womb from a single cell to a fetus and then into a child, our dimension increased. Space donated enough room for us to grow and when we emerged from our mother's wombs, space gave us the entire surface of the earth to continue to grow in. Thus space is a great *dhana*. Time enables a living being to grow. If the time is not favorable, the being will perish. So, time, the donor of our longevity, is another *dhana*. Our atmosphere is enriched with all the necessary constituents for an organism to manifest, grow and multiply. That is another inherited *dhana*. Our organism has been provided with all the faculties that we need and nothing more is to be added to live a full span of one hundred years on earth. That is a very benevolent *dhana*.

Our genetic basis structured out of our father's sperm and mother's ovum is the foundation of our individuation. It is called *adhiṣṭhānam* in the *Bhagavad Gītā* (18:14). We are also equipped with mental and physical instruments which we have brought with us. These instruments are the four-fold inner organ of consciousness *(antakaraṇa)*, the five-fold vital breath *(prāṇas), the* five organs of perception *(jñāna indriyas)*; the five organs of action *(karma indriyas)* and internal devices which find nourishment and replenish us again and again with the energy that we expend from moment to moment. Within us we carry seeds which are programmed for our future acquisition and growth. These are the basics out of which we are expected to enrich ourselves. We are provided with an infinite range of possibilities to meet all the needs of the body, senses, mind, urges to act, and faculties that can appreciate every shade of value. In other words, God has given everything from his (or her) side.

The beginning of acquisition *(sampat)*, starts much before we are aware of it. It is through the act of listening. Our mother is the first announcer of the *veda*. *Veda* means that which reveals to us the secret of things which were never known to us explicitly. Once we have chosen with interest to know what is passed on to us by the word, it clicks with our motivation. Motivation is the ground engineering of our mind which maneuvers, manipulates, envisions and provides us with innumerable devices to make the possible into the probable. Each day we will be exposed to hundreds of possibilities. Out of them even if we actualize only ten probabilities, it is a good beginning investment.

We are able to relate with everything for which we have a name. So the first path to prosperity is to become familiar with names and then to be informed about the hidden possibilities behind each name. When the discovery of a law of this mysterious world can be verbalized, it is no longer a private possession. It is like lighting a lamp and putting it on a high pedestal so that everybody may see it. From the very beginning of human life we learned to share by giving names. In the *Qur'an* it is said that when Allah had completed the manifestation of the universe, he called the first man and familiarized him with everything to be classified, categorized and individually named. Then he called an assembly of his angels and asked them to give the names of things. They failed. He then turned to Adam and asked him to reveal the name of everything, which he did.

Anyone who wants to prosper should begin with the knowledge of names. A name is only a verbal sign or symbol which can be elaborated. When a thing which is sitting outside is named, it no longer remains outside. Of course, it has its unique form in space and time, but a replica of it is imprinted in your mind which accepts the qualitative uniqueness of that thing to be permanently stored. Thereafter it is a part of you. You have become wealthy by integrating it into the folds of your experience. A rose which you have seen is an impression that can delight you for the rest of your life, even though the flower that imprinted that joy in you physically perishes. Prosperity is a great art of preservation and conservation of everything in this world which you have translated into your acquisition of images. On a single day you acquire a million impressions, some into the very core of your focus of attention, some around it, making satellite impressions, and some only at the fringes of your attention. The faculties of perception are to be enhanced with your keen power of attention. The more attentive you are, the deeper you go into the unfathomed possibilities of even a dust particle. Thus a word or name is a gateway to enter into the secret of truth.

Many people complain of boredom and an absolute lack of concentration on what they hear, what they study, and the work they perform. Most people are below average in raising their motivation to a red-hot quality. But it can be brought to the white heat of attention. You begin with hesitation, forcing yourself into a situation. But when you make yourself suffer to look for potentials, you will be amply rewarded. You will be dragged into the secret hideout where you can find new fortunes of interest.

The Indian people have chosen one element out of the constituents of this world as a great transformer of a person as well as the external world. If the *Ṛg Veda* is famous for the familiarization it brings through names and adoration, the *Atharva Veda* provides us with a spiritual laboratory where we are invited to discover the possibility of alchemy. In a hidden way, alchemy is everywhere. When two totally strange young people, man and woman, look into each other's eyes, alchemy begins. They are stirred inside and they long for nearness. They get together and the eyes are never tired of looking at each other. They are eager to listen to every word of this most wonderful being they have come across. For long they stand in silence, then slowly, words begin to germinate in them. Tagore says that when lovers meet and become dumbfounded, the poet comes in between them and gives them words to communicate with. It is the word that initiates the alchemy. From simple familiarity they come to total dedication and make pledges to live together for the rest of their lives, sharing pain and pleasure.

Every theme of life has a central alchemy in which the seer and the seen, the observer and the observed, the lover and the beloved are all melted, fused and transformed into a single unity. When two things are put together their value doubles. When man and woman, with all their differences, are exposed to the libidinal fire, they multiply. They build a home over their heads, they make a hearth to bake their bread. They divide their services: if man is hunting in the forest, the woman is in the kitchen to roast the meat he brings home. If he is sowing corn, his helpmate is there to harvest the corn, pulverize it, and make bread out of it in the hot hearth which she keeps alive in the kitchen. The cities we have devised, the machinery we have made, the water on which we navigate or the air through which we fly are all products of alchemy. Alchemy puts together physics and chemistry, biology and the ephemeral notations of sounds which are forms of names with which we become familiar.

This is in general how the *vedas* enrich us. One who gains a mantra from a preceptor goes into *tapas*, which is heating oneself into the ultimate ashes out of which one rises again into a new life with fresh ideas. The person who got *mantra dīkṣa* (initiation) becomes a *mantra dṛṣṭa* (seer) – one with enough light, enough vision of truth, to make another *mantra*. Thus a whole hierarchy of *mantra dṛṣṭas* comes. This is how the prosperity of the world has increased in every field of knowledge. General textbooks of physics, chemistry, botany, biology, arithmetic, geometry and algebra, astrophysics and astronomy, medicine and theories of psychology, instructions in teaching and chronicles kept of the past are all *vedas* which have made humanity very prosperous.

Even in the modern computer age, we do not know how programs are put into microchips, but if we give our ear to one who is an expert, tomorrow we will become a greater expert than our teacher. Once we credited our rishis to have superhuman powers, but now, as Sri Aurobindo says, it is as if there has been a supramental descent into even coarse materials like iron, steel, and other allied minerals. The secret of *cit* and *jada* made us superior beings who can stand bewildered before our own creations which can speak back to us and give us more memories than we can store in our own craniums. Such is the prosperity of which we speak here.

Our inherited wealth, *dhana*, was a necessity to gather *sampat*. *Sampat* is what each person individually gathers to make an ensemble of beauty, usefulness and provisions for helping the world. There are truly prosperous people whose prosperity is not counted by the figures of their bank balance, but in the astounding display of what they have acquired for the whole world with their ingenuity, wisdom, visions of truth, and great sensibility of discerning true beauty.

We have to recognize three things here. One is our foundation, the second is our instruments, and the third is our motivation. These three become united in our individuation and that gives our true personality. A person begins from a little drop of mucus which is the treasury of the potentials for tomorrow's prosperous world which can be shared by all. Satellites in space not only bring the events of the world to every individual who listens to a radio, but have made the human mind a single unit which can get into most useful dialogues with the entire cosmos. Such is the beautiful contribution of the listening ear that is spoken of in the Upaniṣadic mantra.

Mantra 5

> *yo ha vā āyatanam vedāyatanam svānām bhavati, āyatanam janānām; mano vā āyatanam; āyatanam svānām bhavati, āyatanam janānām, ya evam veda.*

Word Meanings

> *yaḥ* - one who; *veda* - knows; *āyatanam* - the abode; *bhavati* - becomes; *āyatanam* - the abode; *svānām* - of (his) relatives; *svānām ca api* - as well as; *janānām* - of (other) people; *manaḥ* - the mind; *vai* - (is) indeed; *āyatanam* - the abode; *yaḥ* - one who; *veda* - knows; *evam* - this; *bhavati* - becomes; *āyatanam* - the abode; *svānām* - of (his) relatives; *svānām ca api* - as well as; *janānām* - of (other) people

> One who knows the abode (*āyatanam*) becomes the abode of his relatives as well as of other people. The mind (*manas*) indeed is the abode. One who knows this becomes the abode of his relatives as well as of other people.

In the previous mantra we spoke of word as a causal factor of interpersonal alchemy. The word is an instrument, an occasion, and an agent to relate one person with another. When one speaks with another and the other speaks back, neither of them thinks of themselves by their name. The proper noun is substituted by a pronoun. The speaker says "I" and the listener is addressed as "you." If a third person asks them, "What are you doing there?" the speaker as well as the listener will say, "We are having a dialogue." In this case, the first person and the second person are amalgamated into a common binding term of intimacy, "we." If a person goes to another country and if the people of the host country ask the visitor about his nativity, he might say, "In our country we are a peace-loving happy people." What gives one person the mandate to speak on behalf of all the people of his country? Each person of a country has a loving regard for that geographical part of the world. If the same person is asked, "How is your father?" he may say, "He is all right, but he is a little old now and cannot be very active." A person can directly relate himself to another who is very close to him as well as to all the people of his country. The alchemy of relationship is not a myth, not a mere idea; it can be the very meaning of your life.

When we spoke of the word as the home, we were only speaking of the possibility of communication between people. But the word belongs to each person to fully represent his or her consciousness, likes and dislikes, urges and appetites, pain and pleasure. In fact, we cannot fully analyze all the constituents of the dynamic expressive awareness of a person about himself or herself which has a latitudinal as well as a longitudinal reference. A man looks upon another as his father or another as his mother not simply because a sperm came from that man or because he was nurtured in the womb of that woman. He continues to be an evolution of that sperm and egg. Whatever happens to the physical person of the father, the son is the blood of his father's blood, flesh of his father's flesh, bones of his father's bones. It is so also with his mother. When his father and mother come to the fag end of life and are withering away on their death beds, the son, in spite of his many quarrels and fights with them, tempers those remembrances with memories of all the beautiful moments of life they shared. All such memories are frivolous compared to the strong magnetic relationship between parents and offspring. In this bond, even when you are in the white heat of anger, even in situations where it seems as if the last drop of your sympathy or love has been squeezed out of you because of the uncouth behavior of your parents or your children, you may say harsh words, you may even raise your hand against them. But in your heart of hearts you will hear the ring of a bell, soft, almost silent, which you feel in your soul like a clap of thunder.

Maxim Gorky portrays one such situation in his famous novel, *Mother*. The father in the story, who was a drunkard, lost all the dignity of a man. One day, after losing his mind with heavy drinking, he came home and took a big stick to beat his wife. His strong son held the father's hand and said, "Put that stick down and never touch my mother again!" The young man was angry, but restrained. He could have easily knocked down his father and mercilessly kicked him. But that is not what he did. He said, "Never touch my mother again!" It is poignant how human relationship is held intact even though there is a paradoxical crisis. The person who addresses his father and who cares for his mother has a home for both the father and the mother in his heart. The father, mother and son in his story were not in any way related to Maxim Gorky, but his sensitive soul was choked. We read in the next line that the father stood still, like a statue, dropped the stick and turned away, leaving the mother and son. The pathos created in the scene touches us deep in our hearts, tears collect in our eyes. Who are the imaginary characters of the novel to us? Who is the mother? Is she a particular mother in Russia? Is it a particular son or father? There is an archetypal father and archetypal mother in all of us. We ourselves become the archetypal son or daughter. From a single incident, even an imaginary incident, we can reach out to a situation of life where relationship lends itself to a synthesis, a confection, out of which comes something greater than one person - compassion, love. This is not love as in the maxim "God is Love." It is not the word written with the letters l-o-v-e that goes home to us. Gorky brings tears to our eyes and that is love. That is the home which the rishis point out.

The great saviors of humanity left their small hamlets, slums, cottages or mansions to build out of their own tears, care and toil a home where all could live. Today millions of people lay down their heads in peace and sleep in the home of Christ. Many others rest in the refuge they have made of the words of Buddha. We do not know the rishi who wrote this mantra, but to us his word is our succor.

As we go from one mantra to another, there is a golden thread of an inevitable penetration from a well-known reality to a lesser-known causal factor which on becoming familiar is no longer a secret to anyone.

Mantra 6

yo ha vai prajātim veda prajāyate ha prajayā paśubhiḥ; reto vai prajātiḥ; prajāyate ha prajayā paśubhirya evam veda.

Word Meanings

yaḥ - one who; *veda* - knows; *prajātim* - (*prajāti*) that which has the attribute of procreation; *prajāyate ha* - is enriched; *prajayā* - with children; *paśubhiḥ* - (and) animals; *retaḥ* - the seed; *vai* - indeed; *prajātiḥ* - has this attribute of procreation; *yaḥ* - one who; *veda* - knows; *evam* - this; *prajāyate ha* - is enriched; *prajayā* - with children; *paśubhiḥ* - (and) animals

One who knows *prajāti* (that which has the attribute of generation) is enriched with children and animals. The seed indeed has this attribute. One who knows it to be such is enriched with children and animals.

In this *brāhmaṇa*, we have been asked to meditate on speech as *prāṇa*, the eye as *prāṇa*, the ear as *prāṇa*, and the mind as *prāṇa*. Finally we are asked to meditate on procreation. The *Upaniṣads* are perhaps the only sacred books of spiritual import which ask their votaries to meditate on procreation. In all other religions the very idea of sex is a taboo and it is much linked with the concept of sin and guilt feelings. An eminent Indian who was even considered a philosopher-statesman once wrote that the Indian way of life was that of an idealist. Far from that, the *Upaniṣads* are squarely placed on realism, with one difference. It is realism tending to become absolutism which also necessarily permits the relativistic contingencies of life.

A soulful advocacy for renunciation comes in the *Upaniṣads* like *Bṛhadāraṇyaka*, *Īśāvāsya*, *Kena*, *Muṇḍaka*, *Māṇḍūkya*, *Praśna*, and *Katha*. These *Upaniṣads* glorify the fiery free life of the renunciate who has burnt all his bridges and soars high into the heaven of sublimity, not to enjoy paradise, but to stand face to face with truth and get totally lost in it. But such a steep ascent can be achieved by only very few seekers of the Self. Hence the rishis were willing to make concessions, taking into consideration that even the most ascetic of rishis have to breathe and accept at least a enough water and food and protection from heat and cold to sustain life. Considering the multitudes that are drawn to the world of the senses and the compelling force of nature in each embodied being, they decided not to tear themselves away from the entirety of nature. Even when they curb their passionate urges and decide not to run after the hedonistic pleasures of the world, they also retain their wit to amuse themselves with the shadow play of this world. They hold three jewels of life tightly to their bosom: compassion (*karuṇa*), cheerfulness (*mudita*), and wisdom-insight (*prājña*).

Nature infuses passions of all kinds into a person and it is up to the person to sublimate crude passions into many levels of sensibility. The rishis do not advise anyone to bleed themselves in order to extricate themselves from nature. In the *Īśāvāsya Upaniṣad* it is said that those who see everything in this world, including the minutest mote, as enveloped by God (*īśā*), may give up everything and take to the life of a renunciate. They should give up all obligations and live without grabbing whatever naturally belongs to another or is in another's possession.

Then immediately the rishi hurries to caution the students of the *Upaniṣads* that if they are not game to such a program, they can live a householder's life, giving due credence to every possible responsibility that one may have to discharge in one's life in the world. The rishi is one in a million, while others are multitudinous. They should be given a chance to be born in this world so that they can know there is a path of unitive action (*karma yoga*) and also one of unitive knowledge (*jñāna*).

Those who turn to *karma* are initiated into various rites. A householder is expected to keep the fire of sacrifice burning always in the sacrificial pit. The society that developed with that attitude thinks of many social processings which are necessary to make life in the world harmonious. Even after living a quarter of his life as a *brahmacāri*, a wayfarer in the path of *brahman*, one is allowed and sometimes advised to go into the more wide and accepted role of *dharma* and be a *dharmacāri*. For a *dharmacārin*, it is easy and convenient to have a soul mate, a companion to live with and with whom to be helpful to the world by begetting good children. For this one enters into a life-long contract with a spouse. A man takes a wife not to play games with her but to share *dharma* and to rear disciplined and well-informed children of the highest virtues. For this the *Upaniṣads* also teach the generative science, its philosophy and ethics. They are quite in tune with the two aspects of life: *brahmavidyā*, which leads us to the Absolute, and *dharma mīmāmsā*, which guides us to live a prosperous, noble and meaningful life in this world.

Mantra 7

te heme prāṇā ahamśreyase vivadamānā brahma jagmuḥ, taddhocuḥ; ko no vasiṣṭhā iti; taddhovāca, yasminva utkrānta idam śarīram pāpīyo manyate sa vo vasiṣṭhā iti.

Word Meanings

ha - once; *te ime* - these; *prāṇaḥ* - organs; *vivadamānaḥ* - disputing about; *aham śreyase* - who was superior; *jagmuḥ* - went to; *brahma* - Brahma, *ūcuḥ ha* - (and) asked; *tat* - him; *kaḥ* - which; *naḥ* - of us; *vasiṣṭhaḥ iti* - (is) the most excellent; *tat* - he; *uvāca ha* - said; *saḥ vaḥ* - that one among you; *vasiṣṭhaḥ iti* - (is) most excellent; *yasmin* - by whose; *utkrānte* - departure; *idam* - this; *śarīram* - body; *manyate* - is considered; *pāpīyaḥ* - to suffer most

Once these organs, disputing about who was superior, went to Brahma and asked him, "Which of us is the most excellent (*vasiṣṭhā*)? He said, "That one of you is the most excellent (*vasiṣṭhā*), by whose departure this body is considered to suffer most."

Vasiṣṭha, we have seen, is another term for abode. The home is an abode. As an abode it is both a citadel of protection and an island of freedom for each one to grow and express himself, herself or itself as required by the integral value structure of each. We have been seeing how the individual can relate with the whole as part and parcel of all. Now we are taught how to delimit each one's field of choices and understand the probabilities of correlation and coordination within a group.

The best corporation in the universe is a corporeal body. If you look at any body, you are impressed by its morphology which can be classified on the basis of formative likenesses. A form has many parts. From the form, when we go into the total content of the body, we can see a central framework on which the various organs and faculties of the body are fixed so that each organ can share in the general purpose of the corporation. Even when different medical sciences such as Indian, Chinese or Occidental differ in the classification of diseases, methods of nursing, and prescription of medicines, their observations of the parts of the body and the function of each organ have a uniformity. So any scientifically conceived textbook of physiology shows the anatomical structure.

The greatest social order which came into being in this world is the coordination that is effected between each cell in a multicellular living organism. There are cells in which functions are concentrated and there are cells which are supportive. Even when a monitor cell becomes defunct or defective, another cell can take over the monitoring. This interior management of a physiological organism is adopted to understand social sciences such as the study of balancing needs with supplies.

Every day, whether we are wakeful or sleeping, the main furnaces within this body provide a continuous supply of energy in different forms to the specially structured plants within the body. We can see such amazing harmony being maintained in this universe at several levels. At the cosmic level there is a macro-harmony that stars do not collide and planets keep their respective distances between each other.

In spite of all this, there are what we call freaks of nature. The cosmic harmony, natural harmony, biological harmony, physiological harmony and neurological harmony are all sometimes overlooked by psychological disharmony, because that is the one place where the ego is asked to preside. The ego is an individuation in consciousness. The awareness of autonomy is looked upon as a prerogative for wielding power and dominating. In a family, if somebody makes a mistake and it is loudly reported, the instinctive reaction of every person is to deny that it is their fault. Everybody wants to be a clean person, even when they are dirty to the brim.

All the same, we know that only one who is fully accommodative can contain all. When one person contains many persons within his interest, he represents the interest of all. That claim is called sovereignty. In any society disputes often arise about who the sovereign is.

In this *Upaniṣad* the hierarchy of teachers is given three times at the end of each *Kāṇḍa*. Each time the hierarchy is listed from the bottom to the top. The first names given are the most recent in the generations. Whichever one we take, from the source up to most recent, it is the principle of sovereignty which is important, and not individual persons. The first three listed in the hierarchy are *brahma, svayambhu and parameṣṭhi*. As these are not designations of persons, *brahma* and *prajāpati* are interchangeable. It is to this principle that the faculties mentioned in the present mantra turn for guidance.

The faculties are anthropomorphised very dramatically. The human faults of rivalry, jealousy, pride, ambition, backbiting and cunningness are all projected on to them. The faculties go to the creator and ask who among them is the most excellent (*vasiṣṭhā*). The two marks of the *vasiṣṭhā* given in mantra two were being the oldest and being the greatest. It is evident from this example that beings are all limited in their knowledge to arrive at a final decision, so an authority is to be consulted.

Here the authority is the patriarch of life, *brahma prajāpati*. Just as he once said '*da*' to the gods, human beings, and demons, meaning respectively, *dama, dāna,* and *dayā,* he now gives his ruling in this matter so that the faculties can find out for themselves who is the greatest and the oldest among them.

He says it is the one by whose departure this body is considered to suffer most. What is very striking in this remark is "to suffer most." That means the merits of the different faculties are of a relativistic order. What helps is also what handicaps. Help and handicap are dialectical. It is a great help to hear; it is a great handicap not to hear. It is a benevolence to speak and a handicap to become dumb. It is the same with other faculties also.

In this mantra we are given an opening to understand the relationships between various faculties. They are each of great advantages to us. But none of them can conduct our life in all its excellence by itself. In the coming mantras we will be told how the specialty of each is established and also projected to the rest.

Mantra 8

vāgghoccakrāma; sā samvatsaram proṣyāgatyovāca, kathamaśakata madṛte jīvitumiti; te hocuḥ, yathā kalā av-

adanto vācā, prāṇantaḥ prāṇena, paśyantaścakṣuṣā, śṛṇvantaḥ śrotreṇa, vidvāmso manasā, prajāyamāna retasā, evamajīviṣmeti; praviveśa ha vāk.

Word Meanings

vāk - the organ of speech; *uccakrāma ha* - departed; *proṣya* - being absent; *samvatsaram* - after a year; *sa* - it; *āgatya* - came back; *uvāca* - (and) said; *katham* - how; *aśakata iti* - did (you) manage; *jīvitum* - to live; *mat ṛte* - without me; *te* - they; *ūcuḥ ha* - said; *ajīviṣma iti* - (we) lived; *evam yathā* - just as; *kalāḥ* - the mute (live); *avadantaḥ* - without speaking; *vācā* - through the organ of speech; *prāṇantaḥ* - (but) living; *prāṇena* - through the vital breath; *paśyantaḥ* - seeing; *cakṣuṣā* - through the eye; *śṛṇvantaḥ* - hearing; *śrotreṇa* - through the ear; *vidvāmsaḥ* - knowing; *manasā* - through the mind; *prajāyamānāḥ* - having children; *retasā* - through the organ of generation; *vāk* - (so) the organ of speech; *praviveśa ha* - entered

The organ of speech departed. After being absent a year it came back and said, "How did you manage to live without me?" They said, "We lived just as the mute live, without speaking through the organ of speech, but living through the vital breath, seeing through the eye, hearing through the ear, knowing through the mind and having children through the organ of generation. So the organ of speech entered.

The main means of communication in our social life is the word with which interpersonal dialogues are conducted. Word makes the greatest link between individual members of the community. Those who want to live amidst others as leaders and be appreciated by all, educate themselves to enrich their vocabulary. They choose their words carefully to impress their listeners. Great orators can even have the power to carry their whole country with them. They are able to manipulate the minds of others by infusing their words with poetic allure, logical relevancy and the breath of truth.

But in the course of time, a social leader who has developed the oratorical abilities of a Mark Antony or a Seneca may develop the pathological traits of megalomania. If a person is adversely afflicted with pride and conceit, he will think that without his leadership the country cannot progress any further. In modern days any leader who aspires to become the head of the state or occupy other powerful positions employs people who have power over others through their undeniable rhetoric. Even to prepare oneself for a managerial position, one's word is to be made sophistically accentuated. In interpersonal relationships the need arises again and again to justify oneself or what one stands for with appropriate arguments.

In great conferences and gatherings there is a dialectical interplay between the one and the many. The one will be in possession of the sound system in the podium or pulpit and from such a position a great influence can be exerted over the many listeners. Successful speaking can put an audience into a spell of silence and even convert their religious beliefs, political convictions or economic visions. It can even confound their legal conscience. From the local court to the supreme court we can see how the attorneys of rival parties speak with force and parade exhibits to prove their point so the judge will see certain subtleties which others may not even notice.

Thus speech is powerful. But the ancients believed that silence is golden and that it has an edge over the eloquence of speech. The present mantra reminds us how the ability to speak can make one conceited, selfish and rebellious and how it can even become a self-alienating factor in personal life. It says that the faculty of speech left the organism for a full year, curious to know how the whole organism would fare without it.

In the folklore of India there is a pithy story which exposes the conceit of such an attitude. A village grandma had a rooster which religiously woke up at five in the morning and crowed seven times so loudly that no villager could possibly sleep after hearing its clarion call. Every day the old woman saw people getting up and beginning their active life after her rooster crowed. Unfortunately she became a megalomaniac and began to think that the entire activity of the village depended on it. She wanted to teach the village a lesson so she secretly took the rooster away to a far-off village where some relatives lived. Like speech returning to the person, the old hag came back to see what had happened to the village. She saw no appreciable change. When she asked the neighbors how they got up in the morning, she was told that the sun rouses everyone at dawn and her rooster was also roused only by the sun. The same wisdom taught by the folk story is here presented in a dignified mantra.

Mantra 9

cakṣurhoccakrāma; tatsamvatsaram proṣyāgatyovāca, kathamaśakata madṛte jīvitumiti; te hocuḥ, yathāndhā apaśyantaścakṣuṣā, prāṇantaḥ prāṇena, vadanto vaca, śṛṇvantaḥ śrotreṇa, vidvāmso manasā, prajāyamāna retasā, evamajīviṣmeti; praviveśa ha cakṣuḥ.

Word Meanings

cakṣuḥ - the eye; *uccakrāma ha* - departed; *proṣya* - being absent; *samvatsaram* - after a year; *sa* - it; *āgatya* - came back; *uvāca* - (and) said; *katham* - how; *aśakata iti* - did (you) manage; *jīvitum* - to live; *mat ṛte* - without me; *te* - they; *ūcuḥ ha* - said; *ajīviṣma iti* - (we) lived; *evam yathā* - just as; *andhāḥ* - the blind (live); *apaśyantaḥ* - without seeing; *cakṣuṣā* - through the eye; *prāṇantaḥ* - (but) living; *prāṇena* - through the vital breath; *vadantaḥ* - speaking; *vaca* - through the organ of speech; *śṛṇvantaḥ* - hearing; *śrotreṇa* - through the ear; *vidvāmsaḥ* - knowing; *manasā* - through the mind; *prajāyamānāḥ* - having children; *retasā* - through the organ of generation; *caksuh* - (so) the eye; *praviveśa ha* - entered

The eye departed. After being absent a year it came back and said, "How did you manage to live without me?" They said, "We lived just as the blind live, without seeing through the eye, but living through the vital breath, speaking through the organ of speech, hearing through the ear, knowing through the mind and having children through the organ of generation." So the eye entered.

Our main self-expression comes in the form of speaking out how we feel about an immediate encounter. What is termed here as immediate encounter is clearly seeing an object presented to us in the immediate present. It can be a person, thing or event which evokes questions in us about its nature which prompt us to recall similar experiences. The mind asks the mind itself to report to it on the spot how it is experiencing the encounter. Consequently we verbalize our first impression to ourselves or to someone nearby. This is like the police going to a crime site and making a first impressions report to the civil authorities. Even if there is no one to listen to us, we make statements in our mind.

The mind is characterized by doubting everything, so the need constantly arises to rethink and restate. Any first impression report is bound to be prejudicial. Rethinking is a criticism of what has already been stated. *Prima facie* we have only been seeing the object under question. In our revision we look more deeply into the same fact. Thus the eye has the double function of checking and rechecking, cognizing and recognizing, knowing and evaluating. We evaluate in order to know whether our first impression was justified or not. There is an intrinsic intimacy between the impression that comes to the eye and the word that describes it. On rethinking, if a new impression is formed which calls for a revised statement, the first impression will be discarded as false, untrue or illusory. Thus there is a close relationship between seeing untruth and speaking untruth, seeing half truth and speaking half truth, seeing truth and speaking truth.

The eye is called *locana*. *Locana* is our biological instrumentation to scan the world in which we live. The word *loka* (world) comes from the intrinsic relationship between the world and the eye (*locana*) that sees it. And if the passive sight of the world is found lacking, the eye (*locana*) returns to the world (*loka*), to make a thorough search. This is called *avalokana*, comprehensive observation. For this the eye gets a new dimension: intelligence becomes its associate to gain a comprehensive vision. That is *alōcana*, applying the eye in all its possible potentials so that every observation can be truly justified.

The eye leads all other organs in their function by giving the orientation of the place and time in which each organ is given its assignment. The eye sees a whole situation and the many factors which are involved in it. It can therefore dictate to the intellect how best it can function so that there will be less opposition to carrying out its decisions. Similarly, in society, one who is blessed with a correct vision of truth, who can carry out the affairs of life, enlisting the goodwill of all, is like an eye of the society. In spite of all these good things we can say about the eye, if the vision of a person is vitiated by the pride of the ego, the leadership can take a dubious turn which will bring only tragedy.

One beautiful thing to observe is that the world presented to us through our eyes is a specially structured holographic environment which suits all the limitations of our eyes. There is a dialectical polarity between the cosmic structure and the structure of the psyche. For instance, the sun is several times greater than the earth. But what we see in the orient sky when the sun rises is only a disk. Its distance from us is so great that we can look at it as well as its surrounding areas with our small eye. Further, the intensity of the solar rays can be shorn off as in censorship and the eye receives only the amount of light that suits its capacity. The sun's rays fall on the rods and cones which are assigned special functions. While one set of nerve ends, the rods, only measure the brightness of light to balance light and shade impressions, another set, the cones, stimulate the nerve energy to generate chemical color impressions. These two combined generate an image which comes to the mind by a strange interpretation. Although in our awareness we seem to see the image of what we look at, it is more like the digital signals that go from a computer to a printer to create a figure. In the actual brain there is no image; there are only electrical impulses. Thus the physical and psychic aspects make a mosaic of vision. In its formation there can be many defects, yet a million pairs of eyes can bring to their corresponding brains the same visual experience.

Even though Śankara was of the eighth century A.D. he was able to see how many possible slips can happen between the cup and the lip in the process of the visual manifestation of an impression. This is very beautifully narrated in his *Dṛk Dṛśya Viveka.* The Indian philosopher holds the view *yathā dṛk tathā sṛṣṭi* - how you see, so is your creation. Repeated practice makes a person more and more honest in observing and making pronouncements. When nobody can find a lacuna in the critical study of a person, he or she becomes an authority to speak truth.

The world depends on the statements of honest persons who have earned acceptance as reliable authorities. The word of such a person gains the testimony of *śabda* which is often equated with the word or logos. The propounder of truth is honored as a seer or rishi. A rishi is one whose mind attains a high degree of clarity which can reflect in it even the subtlest truths which belong to the Self. The rishi's statement of truth is not the mechanical description of a cold-blooded logician. It has the warmth of a poet's vision. Hence the rishi is called a poet and the universal Self or soul which has projected into this world is itself described as a self-expression like the exaltation of a poet. Hence it is no wonder that every thoughtful person wants to make his or her eyes as clear as the sun so they can see the deeper truth which naked eyes cannot see.

A seer has a greater claim for befriending the world than one who just speaks. Every science springs from the vision of a poetic genius. What is seen in physics, when looked at from another angle, will become the truth of chemistry, and from still another angle, one sees the wonder of the biologic foundation. These are the greater magnitudes of seeing. But one who does not go into these depths will swear by what he or she superficially sees only as a form imprinted in the brain through an electromagnetic process of the gray matter of the visual area. In that case the chance factor of coming across a fragment of truth can make a person conceited, forgetting that the laws of the world are ever operating and it took millions of years for the human mind to attain a certain transparency to mirror the knowledge by which life itself is carved out of the phenomenal world.

When we speak of the eye and vision, we are only looking into a partial functioning of the phenomenal. The *Upaniṣad* is interested in leading us into a holistic understanding of the relationship between the mind and the senses and how both are only products of the vital breath (*prāṇa*). When it operates one way it is called hearing, when it operates another way it is called speaking, still another way, seeing, and when it is thinking it is called mind. By the end of this *brāhmaṇa* we will see this lesson clearly. No faculty in the human body can function without interdependence with other faculties. This gives us an exercise in *manana* which takes us from the ludicrous surface data to the profound inner truth.

Mantra 10

śrotram hoccakrāma; tatsamvatsaram proṣyāgatyovāca, kathamaśakata madṛte jīvitumiti; te hocuḥ; yathā badhirā aśṛṇvantaḥ śrotreṇa, prāṇantaḥ prāṇena, vadanto vācā, paśyantaścakṣuṣā, vidvāmso manasā, prajāyamānā retasā, evamajīviṣmeti; praviveśa ha śrotram.

Word Meanings

śrotram - the ear; *uccakrāma ha* - departed; *proṣya* - being absent; *samvatsaram* - after a year; *sa* - it; *āgatya* - came back; *uvāca* - (and) said; *katham* - how; *aśakata iti* - did (you) manage; *jīvitum* - to live; *mat ṛte* - without me; *te* - they; *ūcuḥ ha* - said; *ajīviṣma iti* - (we) lived; *evam yathā* - just as; *badhiraḥ* - the deaf (live); *aśṛṇvantaḥ* - without hearing; *śrotreṇa* - through the ear; *prāṇantaḥ* - (but) living; *prāṇena* - through the vital breath; *vadantaḥ* - speaking; *vācā* - through the organ of speech; *paśyantaḥ* - seeing; *cakṣuṣā* - through the eye; *vidvāmsaḥ* - knowing; *manasā* - through the mind; *prajāyamānāḥ* - having children; *retasā* - through the organ of generation; *śrotram* - (so) the ear; *praviveśa ha* - entered

The ear departed. After being absent a year it came back and said, "How did you manage to live without me?" They said, "We lived just as the deaf live, without hearing through the ear, but living through the vital breath, speaking through the organ of speech, seeing through the eye, knowing through the mind and having children through the organ of generation." So the ear entered.

The ear is tuned to all directions. Directions are of special importance to know space (*ākāśa*). Space is understood in terms of the East, the North, the West and the South. In between there are Northeast, Southeast, Northwest and Southwest. Any number of divisions are possible because space is mainly conceived circularly. From a central locus, three hundred and sixty degrees can be marked on the circumference, and the radii within each quarter can point to a subdirection. We easily recognize our position with regard to the four directions of space by listening to the sounds that come from our front or back, left or right, below or above. The ears are put on the two sides of the head so they can give equal attention to the sound that comes from the front as well as the back. However, the main function of the ear is to receive names which help us to identify individual objects in this world. The ear does not function alone. As the name is a counterpart of the form, the eye and ear work together. Further, listening is also the stimulation to speak. Names are fed into the ear through speech or they are written and shown to us. Thus the ear is in intimate relation with the eye on one hand and the organ of speech on the other.

The mother's sweet lullaby is fed into the child's ear. From then on for at least twenty years, the ear is the most important faculty to listen with attention and formulate concepts to go with every word that is heard. All the major attainments in the world of communication depend very much on the ears that hear. The ear is also an instrument of defense. The faculty of hearing can be attuned to even the music of the spheres. In India, *nādayogis* attain at-onement by listening to microtones, especially of music. If a musician cannot hear, he considers it as a great punishment given to him. Only few like Beethoven have gotten over the barrier of deafness to make a breakthrough into the beauty of sound. Becoming deaf, even for a short while, can have a very tragic impact on a person's personality. If one cannot hear, that handicaps speech also, because there is an organic coordination between the faculty of hearing and the faculty of speaking. We have to look into all these details when we consider this mantra.

This mantra is specially given to us to learn the importance of bracketing associates to work on a cooperative basis. Although figuratively we are speaking of the faculties of a living organism, the reference belongs to human beings in general who are inattentive to the advantage given by hearing. The wisdom that is taught by great masters is often repeated to congregates, to students, and in public places. Yet words of wisdom fly over our heads, without our giving attention to them. We are hard of hearing not only physically, but also psychologically. That is why in the Vedānta philosophy, two great behavioral qualifications to walk in the path of truth are *śraddha* and *vairāgya*. *Śraddha* is listening with one hundred percent attention and *vairāgya* is not getting stuck or attached to anything that evokes sentiment. Living without hearing is not easy. We have already said that the attention of each sense organ is complemented by the attention of all of the sense organs. Personality is a holistic phenomena and not partial. We will gain more insight into this mantra when we go to the next mantra which speaks of the exit of the mind.

Mantra 11

mano hoccakāma; tatsamvatsaram proṣyāgatyovāca, kathamaśakata madṛte jīvitumiti; te hocuḥ, yathā mugdhā avidvāmso manasā, prāṇantaḥ prāṇena, vadanto vācā, paśyantaścakṣuṣā, śṛṇvantaḥ śrotreṇa, prajāyamānā retasā, evamajīviṣmeti; praviveśa ha manaḥ.

Word Meanings

manaḥ - the mind; *uccakrāma ha* - departed; *proṣya* - being absent; *samvatsaram* - after a year; *sa* - it; *āgatya* - came back; *uvāca* - (and) said; *katham* - how; *aśakata iti* - did (you) manage; *jīvitum* - to live; *mat ṛte* - without me; *te* - they; *ūcuḥ ha* - said; *ajīviṣma iti* - (we) lived; *evam yathā* - just as; *mugdhāḥ* - idiots (live); *avidvāmsaḥ* - without knowing; *manasā* - through the mind; *prāṇantaḥ* - (but) living; *prāṇena* - through the vital breath; *vadantaḥ* - speaking; *vācā* - through the organ of speech; *paśyantaḥ* - seeing; *cakṣuṣā* - through the eye; *śṛṇvantaḥ* - hearing; *śrotreṇa* - through the ear; *prajāyamānāḥ* - having children; *retasā* - through the organ of generation; *manaḥ* - (so) the mind; *praviveśa ha* - entered

The mind departed. After being absent a year it came back and said, "How did you manage to live without me?" They said, "We lived just as idiots live, without knowing through the mind, but living through the vital breath, speaking through the organ of speech, seeing through the eye, hearing through the ear and having children through the organ of generation." So the mind entered.

In the first mantra of this *brāhmaṇa*, the vital breath (*prāṇa*) was declared to be the oldest and greatest and it was equated to the abode of all (*vasiṣṭhā*). In the second mantra the organ of speech was identified with the expressive aspects of a person. We were reminded how speech can annex everything in this world to be housed in its scope through familiarity and the cultivation of friendship. Then there was a search for the foundation that brings all details of this world to speech. This foundation was recognized in the eye. For the retention of anything as a value there are two requirements. One is the nomenclature of every item that is annexed to a person through relationship. The other is discerning the value for retaining any such relationship in memory. They help a person to have the acquisition of intrinsic values called *sampat*. In the fifth mantra, mind (*manas*) was conceived of as the all-encompassing habitation of all the above-said faculties. In the sixth mantra, the device for the propagation of the species was established. From mantra seven to twelve, the faculties are anthropomorphized in something like a psycho-drama. The vital breath (*prāṇa*) plays a key role to expose the malevolence of the ego thrust. In the fourteenth mantra the sublimation of the ego is portrayed in a very beautiful manner.

This ingenious presentation of the faculties, as if their representative characters are equivalent to social malevolence, can be fully appreciated if we study this mantra in the light of medical pathology in both Indian and Western thought. Temporary aberrations, or to be more precise, dysfunctions of the faculties including the mind are what is pertinent here, since none of the faculties leave the organism forever. Only a partial non-functioning is what is under discussion.

In the ancient Indian medical study of *Āyurveda*, a living person is considered to be constituted of a governing and overseeing spirit or Self (*ātman*), well-coordinated with a body with a gross physiologic constitution. The body is conjoined to the Self by a subtle system of psychobiologic energies. It is equipped with organs of perception and organs of action which are governed by the managerial science of a mind. Suśruta, one of the foremost expounders of *Āyurveda*, looks upon a person as a *karma puruṣa*, a person of action. In the *karma puruṣa* there are three main factors: the Self *(ātman);* the mind that is coordinated with all sense organs and metabolic functions; and the organs of perception and action.

The material cause of the body comes from the basic elements (earth, water, fire, air and space). Corresponding to these elements are: the monad with the quality of odor (*ghrāṇa tanmātra*); the monad that gives taste (*rasa tanmātra*); the monad that shines as forms (*rūpa tanmātra*); the monad that gives tactual sensation (*sparśa tanmātra*); and the monad that enables sounds to go into extension as vibration in space using the medium of air (*śabda tanmātra*). This quintiplicated elemental complex is activated by the three modes of nature: *sattva, rajas* and *tamas*. The nature of *sattva* is to reflect the illumination of spirit with clarity. It can give an honest one-to-one correspondence of an illuminated object to the sensory system of a living being and formulate the image of it in a conscious mind. The nature of *tamas* is darkness or opacity. *Rajas*, which comes between *sattva* and *tamas*, has partial light and partial darkness. The proportional mixture of light and darkness varies from person to person. What is transparent to *sattva* becomes translucent to *rajas* and can be obliviated by *tamas*. Consequently, one person's normal vision can be abnormal or subnormal with regard to another's.

Hence Caraka, another expounder of *Āyurveda*, says that we each create a world which is in consonance with our mental makeup. How a person is, so is his world; to which world a person belongs, so is his mind. Thus, according to Caraka, each person is a world unto himself or herself. By knowing the world of a person we can understand the person who is the knower of such a world. By understanding a person, we can also presume what kind of a world he or she makes.

In this mantra what is under discussion is not just the mind, but how it becomes temporarily psychotic. The mind fluctuates in accordance with the changing facets of the material composition of the body and the varying ascendancy of the nature modalities that influence the psychophysical organism of which mind is an epiphenomena. Although we are very impressed by the mind, it is not the be-all or end-all. In the *Katha Upaniṣad* we read,

> Beyond the senses is the mind; beyond the mind is the highest created being; higher than that being is the Great Self; higher than the Great Self is the unmanifested.

In the *Aitareya Upaniṣad* we get a more detailed reference to the mind which is an instrument of the Self. To the question "Which one is the Self?" the answer is given as follows:

> He whereby one sees, or whereby one hears, or whereby one smells odors or whereby one articulates speech, or whereby one discriminates the pleasant and the unpleasant. This is also that which is heart *(hṛdaya)*, or mind *(manas)*, consciousness *(saṁjñāna)*, perception *(ājñāna)*, discrimination *(vijñāna)*, intelligence *(prajñāna)*, wisdom *(medhas)*, insight *(dṛṣṭi)*, steadfastness *(dhṛti)*, thought *(mati)*, thoughtfulness *(manīṣa)*, impulse *(juti)*, memory *(smṛti)*, conception *(saṅkalpa)*, purpose *(kratu)*, life *(asu)*, desire *(kāma)*, will *(vaśa)*.

Here a question comes, "If the mind is derived from the Self, why is it afflicted with base tendencies that distort the ego's motivations?" The physiobiologic basis of the mind is the brain and nervous system. Therefore, instead of *sattva* always prevailing in the mind's power to reflect, its purity and clarity can be adversely affected by the impact of *rajas* or *tamas*. The mind does not simply reflect what is outside. It contains motivational propensities, and representations of the innate qualities of the person concerned. Doubt arises in it. It can also have faith or lack of faith, memory as well as forgetfulness. Therefore, even if a person is affected in only one of the organs, the mind perceives it.

In *Āyurveda* mental diseases are studied in the light of the modalities of nature which have their separate characteristics. *Sattva* is radiant by nature. It has transparency to give honest reflection and it is pleasant. *Rajas* on the other hand, is characterized by its quality of fluctuation, restlessness, exaggeration. *Tamas* is inertial which can lead one to pathologic morbidity as in catatonia. Although *Āyurveda* mainly agrees with the *Sāṁkhya* philosophy, it also accepts the theory of rebirth maintained by the Vedāntins. The mind is subject to compulsive urges because of the impact of *rajas* which brings with it the dynamics of previously acquired traits. Hence, *Āyurveda* classifies varieties of mental aberrations.

One main heading is *unmada* which comes from *mada*. *Mada* is a state of intoxication such as when one drinks or uses psychedelic drugs. In a normal person, there are rational linkings of causes and effects, and motivations are related to reasonable actualizations of predictable results. In an intoxicated mind this neat system of perceiving a course of action breaks up into fragments. In the place of a well-coordinated memory there comes the mere association of ideas. If there is similarity in the sound of two words, the mind will jump from one urge of motivation to another, not knowing the actual implications of the word that has triggered the interest.

The intensity of *mada* comes as a consequence of chemical excesses in the blood stream or such extraneous things that can weaken the coordination between the motor system and the controlling volitional aspect of a sober brain. For example, when a person takes to alcohol or psychedelic drugs, his or her stream of consciousness becomes accelerated. From the normal flow of neural energy known as *kṣipta*, one goes into *vikṣipta*, the erratic shifting of interest which causes anxiety, anger or aggression. In such a state the person feels a sort of emptiness in the head and may hear whistling sounds in the middle ear. In such a person the breath becomes fast and the sense organs become either sharp or blunt.

Unmada is classified according to the dysfunction or malfunction of *vāta*, *pitta* or *kapha*. When a person's *vāta* (wind) is affected, that person gets *vātonmada*. Such a person becomes restless and will move around listlessly. The patient cries without reason and also laughs without any reason. Another kind of insanity comes from the malfunction of *pitta* which brings *pittonmada*, an abnormal function of bile. Such a patient gets easily annoyed, cannot tolerate anyone, shows symptoms of anxiety neurosis and can become violent. This patient gets uncontrollable thirst. When it is an aggravated case, the patient may strip naked and run around.

The third type is *kaphonmada*. This patient is affected with nausea, goes into a state of withdrawal and sits motionless like a statue. He or she has no control of saliva and wants to be alone. Inflammation comes on the face, and he or she sleeps too much immediately after a meal. These kinds of patients are very erotic. There is a fourth kind of insanity which comes from a mixture of all three, *sannipāta unmada*. These patients can easily go into a coma. However, all these forms of insanity are curable. When we read that the mind departed for one year and then returned we should not be under the impression that mind can withdraw without affecting the other faculties. This is only given as an example and metaphors are not to be pressed too far.

The *Upaniṣad* wants us to know that in absolute reality there is no fragmentation of any sort. All the same, the finite is a counterpart of the infinite. One drop of water is the same as the water of the ocean with regard to the reality of water. The drop has a time/space limitation. To clarify the relationship between the finite and the infinite, logicians postulate two errors in human thinking - one is called the error of division and the other is called the error of composition. If we think of the ocean as an infinite volume of water and think that it cannot be identified with the wateriness of a drop, it is an error in division. If we see the ocean as a composition of several drops of water and argue that we can therefore launch a steamer on a drop of water, it is an error of composition.

When *cit*, consciousness pure and simple, is considered to be the total reality of infinite values, it follows that existence is always one, it is presented by the subsistence of knowledge, and it gives us the entire foundation of value. Theoretically there is nothing wrong with this, but in actual practice, we see only circumlimited existence, such as of a pebble, a tree, a man, or a patch of land. When thus circumlimited, each is structurally and functionally different from another. The essential characteristic of mind and the Self is consciousness. But consciousness has conceptual variation, according to its expression. The empirical expression of consciousness is different from the ideational existence of consciousness.

This *Upaniṣadic* way of looking at the finite and infinite has a close resemblance to the homeopathic concept of the individual and the universe. Even when a homeopath has to consider the physical uneasiness of a person, the therapist does not begin with one symptom as in allopathic medicine. Instead the world is seen first. In the world, the possibilities of harmony and the very many dissonances that can happen are taken as the general backdrop of a disease in any person. Thus the world is seen, its nature is seen, its manifestation in an individual is looked into, and finally attention is given to the particular symptoms of which a patient complains. The homeopath knows that one symptom alone cannot be responsible for the ill-feeling of the patient. All other possible associated dissonances that constitute the general illness are located.

According to Homeopathy, there is a readily identifiable hierarchy in the construction of the human being. It is characterized by three levels: 1). Mental/Spiritual; 2). Emotional/Psychic; 3). Physical (Including sex, sleep, food, and five senses). In reality these levels are not separate and distinct. Rather there is a complete interaction between them. Nevertheless, the degree of health or disease of the individual can be evaluated from a survey of all levels. The highest and most important level through which the human being functions is the mental and spiritual. It can be generally defined as that which registers changes in understanding or consciousness. Whether these changes are initiated by internal or external stimuli, they are registered on this plane of existence. It is on the mental level that an individual thinks, criticizes, compares, calculates, classifies, creates, synthesizes, conjectures, visualizes, plans, describes, communicates, etc. Disturbances of these functions in turn constitute symptoms of mental illness.

The mental level is the most crucial level for the human being. It is the mental and spiritual content of a person which is the true essence of that person. If the inner tools of attaining a higher consciousness are disturbed, the central idea of the possibility of an evolution in consciousness is lost. Where then is the meaning of life? A person can continue to live, be happy, and be of creative service to others and to himself or herself despite a crippled body, the loss of limbs or even the loss of sight or hearing. But if there is a disturbance on the mental/spiritual plane, the person's very existence is threatened.

In the Western sphere, many radical changes have come in the notion of the animation of a living body in the last twenty years or so. After the advent of modern science, almost from the time of Francis Bacon, the thought of reducing biology to physics or chemistry was an anathema. But this hesitation is slowly disappearing and has resulted in the new advanced sciences of neurophysiology, and physiological psychology. Both the physical and mental sciences have been asking questions about whether physical and mental states exist, whether they interact and whether they are otherwise related. Today this is known as the body/mind problem or the psycho/physical problem.

One of the conceivable solutions is in interactionism, the theory that mental and physical states interact. This leads more precisely to a description of the body/mind problem as the brain/mind problem, since it is to be argued that the interaction is to be located in the brain. This has led some interactionists, notably John Eccles, to formulate the body/mind problem as the problem of describing in as much detail as possible the liaison between the brain and the mind. The old theory that the mind is an epiphenomenon, a byproduct of qualitative change coming through the quantitative configuration of physical entities is no longer tenable. After all these years of such a materialistic view, the scientists working in this field, i.e., the no man's land between mind and body, do not claim that they have come to a final understanding.

They remember how when the physicists tried to grapple with the interaction between light and matter, they got into a region of knowledge which left one of the greatest pioneers in this field, Neils Bohr, so baffled that he said he had to renounce the hope of understanding the subject of quantum theory. Previously the materialists thought only of one world, the world of matter in which all mechanical functions were only cumulative effects of more and more subtleties emerging out of the finer aspects of matter, working sometimes in an incomprehensible way. Nobody disputes that a book is a physical object. But the effect it has on one who reads its contents can bring about so many changes in a person that his or her meaning of life can be totally changed and his or her pursuit turned in an altogether different tangent.

A Shakespearean character like Hamlet comes to the stage undecided about whether to act and turns out to be the cause for a series of murders in which he becomes as much a victim as others, making the audience in a theater go into a grim silence, wiping their tears with inconsolable grief. This is not a self-arranged display of molecules. An idea that comes to one person's mind can alter his pulse rate or blood pressure, and, when he expresses it, all who associate with him may come to another attitude.

History speaks of the influence of Buddha, Jesus Christ, and the Prophet Mohammed, who all continue to haunt the imaginations of millions of people all over the world. If a scientist has to justify the several theories put forward to explain the behavioral patterns of individuals as well as masses, there has to be a postulation of something other than the physical that affects large sections of human beings. The new concept is returning to the most ancient concept of an unembodied reality interacting with subtle realities such as memories, thoughts, ideations, etc., and also the physical world of objects. Thus Western science is beginning to accept not a soul in the machine, but the universal influence that comes from the idea of the good, the beautiful and the just.

This is not a revival of ancient religious thought or the fad of people who call themselves spiritualists. We know that many oriental thoughts are now considered by scientists of repute who see the necessity of a more holistic philosophy of understanding this world and the consciousness that dominates most of the living beings, especially humankind. R.H.G. Siu in *The Tao of Science* makes the following observation:

> Even among hardened skeptics we find a lapsing usage of the terms: predisposition, insight, vision, hunch, instinct, penetrating mind, imagination, feel, and intuition. The Upanishads long ago admonished against the inadequacy of the intellect. St. Augustine states, "I believe in order that I may understand." Coleridge calls it a "willing suspension of disbelief." These are indications of the subconscious obeisance that everybody pays to a hazy extrarational source of inspiration. [34]

Even a thoroughgoing rationalist has no defense against habits, reflexes, prejudices, appetites, passions and emotions. As far as romanticism goes, nonrationality is even exalted and feeling is preferred to thinking. Pavlov's dogs know that they are salivating, but do not know the cause. By calling it a conditioned reflex we are only giving a label to an unaccountable experience of the dog. We know that so-called conditioned reflexes frequent us also on many occasions. It is understandable that after the tragic and dirty games played by religious adventurers, the world is wary of accepting the concept of an autocrat God. We have to make a breakthrough of all such accumulated prejudices of the mind to appreciate teleologic correlations such as that between sunlight and the eyes of earth-bound beings. Humans evolved a heliotropic habit which regulates not only their behavior but also their thoughts and hopeful strivings to make life better from moment to moment.

In recognition of such influences the previous attitudes of Western psychology have considerably changed from experimental psychology and existential psychology and even from the classical Freudian psychoanalysis to an appreciation of psychosynthesis along with psychoanalysis. The two are complementary. If in psychoanalysis the unconscious is the dominant factor, in psychosynthesis the Self monitors life, especially in human beings. C.G. Jung coined the term collective unconscious, while Robert Assagioli and others conceived of a universal Self.

Western medical schools are very obsessed with the therapeutic potentials of drugs. They are still trying to correct aberrations of the mind (not knowing what mind is) by administering drugs that can at best benumb the limbic system of the brain or make wholesale war on bacteria or tamper with hormones or enzymes. Although Freud, Jung, Adler and Rank made a good start of investigating the depth of the mind in order to help a patient to return to health by substituting diseased thoughts with healthy aspirations, the whole scope of therapeutic psychology has been thrown away in favor of medical psychiatry.

Now the main point regarding this mantra is to locate the reason for dysfunction in any faculty as a part of a self-defense against the anomalies of competitive life. This is given in a covert manner through the poetic device of personalizing the faculties in a psychodrama. The ultimate aim of the *Upaniṣad* is to teach that life is a holistic reality in which there is a central core which alone gives unity to all the general and special functions of the various faculties. These mantras are informing us of the situations in which we are placed and the facilities we have to reorganize our life to set our feet on the right track of Self-realization. The goal of the *Upaniṣad* was clearly stated in the fourth *adhyāya* when King Janaka was brought to a state of fearlessness and a knowledge of the Self as contributing to his being established in the Absolute *(brahman)*. The same is our goal also.

Mantra 12

reto hoccakrāma; tatsamvatsaram proṣyāgatyovāca, kathamaśakata madṛte jīvitumiti; te hocuḥ, yathā klībā aprajāyamānā retasā, prāṇantaḥ prāṇena, vadanto vācā, paśyantaścakṣuṣa, śṛṇvantaḥ śrotreṇa, vidvāṁso manasā, evamajīviṣmeti; praviveśa ha retaḥ.

Word Meanings

retaḥ; - the organ of generation; *uccakrāma ha* - departed; *proṣya* - being absent; *samvatsaram* - after a year; *sa* - it; *āgatya* - came back; *uvāca* - (and) said; *katham* - how; *aśakata iti* - did (you) manage; *jīvitum* - to live; *mat ṛte* - without me; *te* - they; *ūcuḥ ha* - said; *ajīviṣma iti* - (we) lived; *evam yathā* - just as; *klībāḥ* - the impotent (live); *aprajāyamānāḥ* - without having children; *retasā* - through the organ of generation; *prāṇantaḥ* - (but) living; *prāṇena* - through the vital breath; *vadantaḥ* - speaking; *vācā* - through the organ of speech; *paśyantaḥ* - seeing; *cakṣuṣā* - through the eye; *śṛṇvantaḥ* - hearing; *śrotreṇa* - through the ear; *vidvāmsaḥ* - knowing; *manasā* - through the mind; *retaḥ* - (so) the organ of generation; *praviveśa ha* - entered

The organ of generation departed. After being absent a year it came back and said, "How did you manage to live without me?" They said, "We lived just as the impotent live, without having children through the organ of generation, but living through the vital breath, speaking through the organ of speech, seeing through the eye, hearing through the ear and knowing through the mind." So the organ of generation entered.

In the primary forms of life, unicelled beings like viruses and bacteria, a single cell breaks and proliferates without needing the paraphernalia of male/female differences or the union of sexual counterparts. But for human beings the generative organs of the male and female are crucially important for the propagation of the species. Human beings have attributed the highest divinity to sexuality and also tabooed it as a faculty which belongs to the profanity of sinful life.

Here the *Upaniṣad* gives the generative organ its ultimate place in the scheme of things and points out that without it, successive generations would not be brought forth.

Mantra 13

atha ha prāṇa utkramiṣyanyathā mahāsuhayaḥ saindhavaḥ paḍvīśaśaṅkūnsamvṛhet, evam haivemānprāṇānsamvavarha; te hocuḥ, mā bhagava utkramīḥ; na vai śākṣyāmastvadṛte jīvitumiti; tasyo me balim kuruteti; tatheti.

Word Meanings

atha ha - then; *prāṇaḥ* - (as) the vital breath; *utkramiṣyan* - was about to depart; *samvavarha* - (it) uprooted; *imān* - the; *prāṇān* - organs; *evam eva ha* - just; *yathā* - as; *mahāsuhayaḥ* - a great noble horse; *saindhavaḥ* - from Sind; *samvṛhet* - pulls out; *paḍvīśa śaṅkūn* - (its) tether pegs; *te* - they; *ūcuḥ ha* - said; *bhagavaḥ* - please venerable sir; *mā* - do not; *utkramīḥ* - leave; *śakṣyāmaḥ iti* - (we) shall be able; *jīvitum* - to live; *na vai* - not; *tvat ṛte* - without you; *tasya u me* - then to me; *kuruta iti* - give; *balim* - tribute; *tathā iti* - very well

Then as the vital breath was about to depart, it uprooted the organs just as a great, noble horse from Sind pulls out its tether pegs. They said, "Please do not leave, venerable sir, we cannot live without you." "Then give me tribute." "Very well."

Mantra 14

sā ha vaguvāca, yadvā aham vasiṣṭhāsmi tvam tadvasiṣṭho'sīti; yadvā aham pratiṣṭhāsmi tvam tatpratiṣṭho'sīti cakṣuḥ; yadvā aham sampadasmi tvam tatsampadasīti śrotram; yadvā ahamāyatanamasmi tvam tadāyatanamasīti manaḥ; yadvā aham prajātirasmi tvam tatprajātirasīti retaḥ; tasyo me kimannam, kim vāsa iti; yadidam kiñcā śvabhya ā kṛmibhya ā kīṭapataṅgebhya-statte'nnam, āpo vāsa iti; na ha vā asyānannam jagdham bhavati, nānannam parigṛhītam, ya evametadanasyānnam veda;

tadvidvāṃsaḥ śrotriyā aśiṣyanta ācāmanti, aśitvācāmanti; etameva tadanamanagnam kurvanto manyante.

Word Meanings

sā - the; *vāk* - organ of speech; *uvāca ha* - said; *vasiṣṭha tat vasiṣṭhaḥ* - that attribute of being the most excellent; *yat* - which; *aham* - I; *asmi* - have; *asi iti* - is; *tvam* - yours; *cakṣuḥ* - the eye; *pratiṣṭhā tat pratiṣṭhaḥ* - that attribute of steadiness; *yat* - which; *aham* - I; *asmi* - have; *asi iti* - is; *tvam* - yours; *śrotram* - the ear; *sampat tat sampat* - that attribute of prosperity; *yat* - which; *aham* - I; *asmi* - have; *asi iti* - is; *tvam* - yours; *manaḥ* - the mind; *āyatanam tat āyatanam* - that attribute of abode; *yat* - which; *aham* - I; *asmi* - have; *asi iti* - is; *tvam* - yours; *retaḥ* - the organ of generation; *prajātiḥ tat prajātiḥ* - that attribute of procreation; *yat* - which; *aham* - I; *asmi* - have; *asi iti* - is; *tvam* - yours; *u* - then; *kim* - what; *annam* - (will be) food; *tasya me* - my; *kim* - what; *vāsaḥ iti* - (will be) my clothes; *yat idam kin ca* - whatever (food) there (is); *ā svabhyaḥ* - including (that of) dogs; *ā kṛmibhyaḥ* - worms; *ā kīṭapataṅgebyaḥ* - insects and moths; *tat* - that (will be); *te* - your; *annam* - food; *āpaḥ* - (and) water; *vāsaḥ iti* - (is) clothes; *yaḥ asya* - one who; *veda* - knows; *idam* - this; *etat* - about; *annam* - food; *anasya* - of the vital breath; *na ha vai* - never; *jagdham* - eats; *bhavati* - is; *anannam* - anything not food; *na* - nor; *ha vai* - indeed; *na parigṛhītam* - does not accept; *anannam* - anything that is not food; *tat* - therefore; *śrotriyāḥ vidvāṃsaḥ* - sages who are versed in the *Vedas*; *ācāmanti* - sip water; *aśiṣyantaḥ* - just before eating; *aśitvā* - after eating; *manyante* - (they) regard; *tat etam eva* - it as; *anagnam kurvantaḥ* - remove the nakedness; *anam* - vital breath

The organ of speech said, "That attribute of being most excellent which I have is yours." The eye: "That attribute of steadiness which I have is yours." The ear: "That attribute of prosperity which I have is yours." The mind:

> "That attribute of abode which I have is yours." The organ of generation: "That attribute of procreation which I have is yours."
> The vital breath said: "Then what will be my food and my clothes?" "Whatever food there is, including that of dogs, worms, insects and moths, that will be your food, and water your clothes."
> One who knows this about the food of the vital breath never eats anything that is not food, nor indeed accepts anything that is not food. Therefore sages who are versed in the *Vedas* sip a little water just before and after eating. They regard it as removing the nakedness of the vital breath.

This *brāhmaṇa* is brought to a close with these mantras which establish the primacy of the vital breath. Death is often described as the withdrawal of the perceiving light of the faculties of perception from the object to the respective organ, then the return of the organs to the mind, and finally the mind returns to *prāṇa*. In that process we see the function of the faculties diminishing little by little. Most dying people go into silence and remain in a semi-conscious state while the body is slowly released from the bonds of *prāṇa*. At that time, if a person is asked by relatives, "Do you recognize me?" the dying person does not respond, showing that the mind has lost memories which have been stored all through life. As there is no memory, the faculty of speech cannot find the necessary name to state whether any identification is established. When the eye sees a person, along with that goes their name. Every perceptual memory is tied up with the conceptual memory of the name that goes with the percept. Thus the silence of the mind is shared by silence of word, sight, hearing, etc. At this last moment, the dying person is not given any special drink. In India only drops of water are administered to moisten the lips and help the phlegm to be cleared so that the last breath can go out freely.

Here, when the *prāṇa* is withdrawing its support to the faculties like a premature death, the faculties realize that they have been functioning only because the *prāṇa* animated them. In response the organ of speech says: "That attribute of being the most excellent which I have is yours." The organ of speech gives dwelling or occupancy in the conceptual memory for every name with which a person is familiar. That is how the organ of speech came to have the status of *vasiṣṭha*, the home of all specialized entities in this world.

The individuality of things is maintained in the world with the help of the eye that has established the inseparable form of each thing. Thus the eye came to have the status of the foundation of things in consciousness (*pratiṣṭhā*). So the eye says to the vital breath, "That attribute of steadiness which I have is yours." We read that it is by hearing the attribute of a thing that we have acquired our prosperity (*sampat*). The ear was credited for that. Now the ear knows that it does not singularly merit that honor. Hence the ear says, "That attribute of prosperity which I have is yours." The mind is given the honor of the home (*āyatanam*) where all the five senses have their abode. Now the mind confesses, "That attribute of abode which I have is yours." There is a continuing significance which belongs to the organ of generation. And it also confesses, "That attribute of generation which I have is yours."

Then the breath asks, "If all your abilities to function come from me, how do you recompense me?" The faculties reply that the vital breath will be provided with its food and clothing. Everything edible is considered to be food for the vital breath, meaning that the breath digests everything. The material to be digested needs to be dissolved in water. We cannot eat stones or metals. Food is always that which can be easily turned into a paste or a liquid.

This mantra covers the entirety of the self-projection of the universe, its maintenance or sustenance and final dissolution, in which spirit and matter are equally accepted as the material cause, efficient cause, incidental cause and final cause. It is in one sense an elaboration of the invocation with which the *Bṛhadāraṇyaka Upaniṣad* commenced the epistemology of the science of the Absolute (*brahmavidyā*). It enunciates the methodology which implies the pulsating character of the universe seen as the dialectically opposing principles of expansion and contraction. Its axiology is to prove that in and through the phenomenal appearance of the universe is a secret which can be grasped by an all-comprehending meditation through which both the expansion as well as the contraction are understood without violation to the general and total epistemology of *brahmavidyā*.

Every event that happens in the time/space continuum is accommodated. The central postulation here is of the magical inclusiveness of air which has the ability to envelop and fill in wherever there is unoccupied space. At the same time it aids the alchemy of the properties of fire, water and earth, which are transformed and transfigured into all conceivable foundations from the massless to the massive principles of becoming.

Commenting on this mantra has certainly offered great difficulty to Indian scholars because their minds were conditioned by the observance of religious rituals which are almost as old as the *Upaniṣadic* mantras. But the *Bṛhadāraṇyaka* is not dealing with a subject matter which is relevant only for India or its people. It is in all truth a science that can be true everywhere for everyone who has a power to discern truth. That is why *prima facie* the *Upaniṣad* commenced with a eulogy of *AUM* and described it as *pūrṇam*, all-filling. It is all-filling potentially, existentially, as well as in transmutation and transcendence. It is as important to give our full attention to all four aspects of *praṇava* to understand the revelation of the deep secret given here.

The last two *adhyāyas*, five and six, are together called *Khila Kāṇḍa*. An area of knowledge which had never been studied properly and never critically investigated was brought to the consideration of wise people so they could enter it and transmute it. Its chaotic manifoldness had never been classified, systematized or well-organized. It was like a barren land untouched by a plow. The secret of its vast possibilities had been kept hidden under the ritualistic concepts of people who were pursuing hedonistic pleasures. They could not uncover the secret because of their social and psychological allegiance to the *Vedas*. Even people who have studied *Vedānta* all their life and tried to learn by heart the mantras of the major *Upaniṣads* have been handicapped because their study was an extension of their Vedic culture. As a result, Indian scholars have not been able to take full advantage of the treasury of immaculate wisdom which is deeply inset in the mantras of the *Upaniṣad*.

There is a long history of the human search for the origin of life, although for many years it was inhibited by the vested interest of Church theologians to feed people only with ignorance. There are two parallel instances in history of man deluding man. One is the custodians of the *Vedas* trying to blindfold their fellow humans by making the Vedic language a rhetoric of power. On the heels of the *Vedas* came the *Dharmaśāstras* which brought fetters and chains to the Indian people. Their adherents plugged the ears of the people so that they might not hear the scriptural texts and made women chattel to be used only for begetting progeny and doing the chores of the house. What these so-called *brahmavādins* did to India was done in Europe with crueler and darker intentions by the Schoolmen of Christianity, following the examples of the high priests of Judaism. Now it has come also to the institutional life of Islam. Religion has been used everywhere to enslave the human spirit. No wonder Colonel Ingersoll said, "The King and the Priest are two vultures hatched out of the same egg. One feeds upon the blood of people, and the other feeds on the soul of people. Both are tyrants, hypocrites and rascals." We can speak of the *brāhmaṇic* scholars and the Christian theologians as two vultures hatched out of the same egg of treachery.

Among the commentators of the *Upaniṣad*, the great teacher Śankara used his critical acumen well to unravel the esoterics of this mantra. He was the first to define *Upaniṣad* as 'secret wisdom'. Fortunately Śankara's grand-guru, Gaudapada, was not of the Vedic strata, being a follower of Lord Buddha. Gaudapada traced a close affinity between *nirvāṇa* and the conclusion of the *Bṛhadāraṇyaka* which proclaims *brahman* as *neti neti*, "Not this, not this." The same was also immediately complemented in the *Upaniṣad* as *satyasya satyam*, "Truth of truth." This enabled Gaudapada to see the same truth in *nirvāṇa* where it is *śūnyata* because it gives up name and form, structure and function. At the same time, he could also see the underlying truth of name and form and the transformation of mass. He derived the dynamics of becoming from the very being that itself validates existence, knowledge, and the value which came to be looked upon as the *summum bonum*.

It is time that we declare to the world that the hedonistic *Veda* and the contemplative *Vedānta* are not the same. Śankara boldly said that the ritualistic *karma* precipitated by Jaimini and further nourished by Yāska, Śabarasvami, Kumārila Bhaṭṭa, and Prabhākara, only serves as fetters of the human mind. *Veda* is to speak; *Vedānta* is to keep silent. That silence is like the Tao which has no name, but is described by ten thousand names. As a result of Vedic influence, this simple mantra has been given the most ludicrous commentary by India's best scholars who were unaware that what is referred to here is the secret of fission and fusion in the world of chemistry which maintain biologic possibilities. In the Western world, the studies of physics, chemistry and biology have widened to include the study of psychology and all the hinterland of understanding filled by anthropology, psychobiology and sociobiology. Physics itself became complemented by astrophysics and later by particle physics and the elaboration of quantum theory. But these *Upaniṣads* go further than all the discoveries so far made by the valiant scientists. What is discussed in this *brāhmaṇa* is the true secret of creation on which the entire bulwark rests - the element air which is habitated in space, transforming fire, water and physical matter to evolve bodies that can reason, plan, scheme and make programs to help themselves and the entire world.

The reference to eating and drinking in this mantra is one of the finest metaphors used by the *Upaniṣadic* rishis. Here eating is not to be conceived as a *brāhmaṇa* ritualistically eating his food. If concentrated sulfuric or nitric acid is put on a piece of flesh or carcass, it will eat it away. In *The Seven Mysteries of Life*, Guy Murchie graphically describes how every element has the power to eat. If you bury something under the earth and look for it later, you will find that the earth has eaten it. Leaves that break away from a tree and fall to the ground are eaten by the earth and recycled back into the same tree to reappear as fresh leaves. Water is a solvent of everything, including very strong iron blocks. It can rust them away. Fire is also a great transformer. Thus the reference to *prāṇa* here points to the vast arena of the chemical transformation and transmutation of solids, liquids and gases into ever-new forms.

In the mantra when the *prāṇa* asks, "Then what will be my food?" the reply is "Whatever food there is." When it says, "Including that of dogs, worms, insects and moths," it only means that there is nothing in this world which is not undergoing transformation. It is a pity that the proud scholars of India thought it was a discussion of dietetics. They misinterpreted food as what is served on a platter. The role which water plays is also interpreted ritualistically. But water is literally made into a garment for food that is prepared in any kitchen anywhere. Food is both the solid part and the gravy. The first thing that is served anywhere in the world is a glass of water. Even in ordinary restaurants the first thing that is served is water. A mosquito does not bite a person without first spitting on the body to make the skin soft enough for it to thrust in its blood-sucking needle. This universal phenomena is made very ridiculous by commentators who say that it is a *modus operandi* given to the *brāhmaṇa* to sip a little water before eating. The highest and best of teaching is insulted by that kind of commentary. That is why this section is called *Khila Kāṇḍa*, a field never critically examined before. This gives us every freedom to give wisdom its due honor by seeking truth in its truest light, without any facade.

Brāhmaṇa 2

Introduction

In his discussion of this *brāhmaṇa*, Śankara calls our attention to a methodological device which was indicated in the third *brāhmaṇa* of the first *adhyāya*. In one sense it traces the evolution of life from primeval beings to humans. It is followed by a consideration of death, the cause of death, and the probable attainment of immortality. From a single-celled organism like a protozoa to the human, all beings are assailed by hunger. Hunger will ultimately lead the embodied being to its death. Day to day survival is a fight against death, and in this even microbial beings instinctively use certain devices by which food can be somehow gained. The animals have no idea what they do and why they do what they do. They do not relate the effect to the cause.

Instinctive hunger causes all living beings to try to find means to appease their hunger. Human beings do not want to just lie down and die. They look into the causes of the physical disharmony which comes when the energy expended in a day's work is not replenished. Although human beings have consciously become seekers of food and drink, creating the roles of the breadwinner and the maintainer of an atmosphere conducive to living in harmony, most of them remain brutes who have not brought any managerial system in their life. They lack a sound philosophy of economizing their needs and finding means to supply their demands. Even the young of so-called lower animals like lions, wolves, mice and cats, know that part of saving themselves when they are in dire need is to continuously make piteous cries to get help. Humans also instinctively developed crying. This cry for help afterwards evolved into the sophisticated social function of praying to be saved from all kinds of distress.

For several millennia the animal world was conditioned by the correlation between hunger and food. Slowly human beings developed who saw the perennial presence of natural benevolence coming from the sun that shines every day, the wind that blows constantly and the fire that can be made a friend, both in the hearth and in the lamp which burns in the dark. Consequently, the idea of the perennial came to stay, always generating the yearning to become ever-recurring like the sun, the wind, or the fire.

Śankara calls our attention to one of the earliest futuristic concepts shared by human beings everywhere – to become one with the immortal which seems to be ruling over the destiny of the mortals. Further, the perishable is contrasted with the imperishable. The food and drink that one gets to appease one's hunger and quench one's thirst are only helpful for a few hours. Everything born and proliferating on earth which has spatio-temporal limitations came to be recognized as the mortal. On the other hand, the natural benevolence one enjoys such as the sun filling the entire sky with its brightness and illuminating all things in the world came to be recognized as the immortal. The inclination to move from the mortality of embodied beings to immortality became a fixed goal in the mind of contemplative people. This occurred in the mind of the same creatures who had been living for millennia in the sway of animal needs, the fulfillment of which never took them beyond death.

Even though each person identifies his or her own separate father, the unifying idea of a universal father came to stay in the mind of the people. That amounted to the recognition of the *prajāpati* as the father of all. In I.3.1 the descendants of *prajāpati* were said to be of two kinds, the shining ones *(devas)* and the dark ones *(asuras)*. It is only natural for earthlings to see the luminaries of the sky as being like tiny specks. So they decided that the shining ones are few. On the other hand, on earth they saw the death of the prey in a hunt, the withering of flowers, fish dying soon after being netted.

Right from the beginning the human personality has been

seen as having an identity which is divided between the bright ones and the dark ones. Brightness has always been recognized as a symbol of good and darkness as a symbol of evil. In the course of human history, darkness became identified with sin. Even now in Christianity we hear the evangelist threatening people by saying death is the price of sin. Thus in collective human life, the ritual developed a two-fold significance: the psalms and hymns that are sung at the performance of the ritual and the sharing of the leftovers of the burnt sacrifice by the participants. This is the archetypal beginning of the two aspects of ritualistic life. One is knowledge, and the other is acting in accordance with knowledge. The *Vedas* provided a description of the major luminaries to be propitiated in a ritualistic sacrifice. In the acts of sacrifice performed by archetypal social heroes, Śankara sees the first expressions of the latent desire of human beings to become immortal. He finds the immortal to be a worthy ideal to be meditated upon.

To be more critically factual, the presence of the shining ones was idealized not by looking into the sky or seeing the luminaries of the heavens such as sun or moon and planets. It came from a more personalized experience of the eye seeing the sun again and again, the ear hearing the voice again and again, the fingers touching and feeling, the taste that gives pleasure and the discrimination the nose makes between fragrance and stench. Thus the *devas* were not seen in the sky above, but in the body here and now. In the same body the dark ones were recognized as blindness as opposed to sight, deafness as opposed to hearing, dullness as opposed to touching, the unpalatable in contrast to the palatable, stench in contrast to good odor. There was a dominant feeling that the darkness in us was striving to do evil.

Immortalizing the shining ones became an obsession that was pursued through sacrifices intermingled with the recitation of psalms. The dark ones have an advantage over the shining ones because darkness is enmeshed in the body. The body being a part of nature, proliferation and growth are normal to it. The fecund power of the duplication of cells is not generated by wisdom or understanding. Even worms can multiply and become million-fold in a short time in the midst of darkness. Human beings are susceptible to the promptings of their public and private lives. In public life we are led by certain ideals and principles. In private life we can abandon all scruples. Just as a cell is self-centered, the ego is more in the dark than the surface phenomena of I-consciousness. These are some of the deep areas to be examined.

This brings us to a very fundamental principle of life - in all formations of production, whether creative or projective, there always has to be a combat between two opposite principles. The polemics between the shining ones and the dark ones are illustrative of the dialectical polarities of all forms of life. The first encounter between *asuras* and the *devas* is within a single body. In the third *brāhmaṇa* of the first *adhyāya*, each faculty in the body which showed an affinity with knowledge, such as smell, sight, hearing and the mind, was asked to give the *udgītha* for the sacrificial ritual. As quantity can overwhelm quality, the dark forces of the body were always pitted against the spark of the shining ones in the faculties. Smell became polluted with stench; sight became polluted by the uncouth and ugly; hearing became polluted by its susceptibility to illusions. Finally the vital breath came to save the individuation. *Prāṇa* was holding together both the bright and the dark. As it has no partiality and it is equally distributive of the energy of life, *prāṇa* is seen as a savior which lives to the extent that respiration goes on in a living body. Respiration also enabled the causal, subtle, and gross body/mind complex of the individual to be built up. The saving power of breath in the mouth of living beings is responsible for weaving the garment of life by putting together the warp and the woof of all the correlatives of a living body.

Mantra 1

śvetaketurha vā āruṇeyaḥ pāñcālānām pariṣadam-ājagāma; sa ājagāma jaivalim pravāhaṇam paricārayamāṇam; tamudīkṣyābhyuvāda, kumārā iti; sa bho iti pratiśuśrāva; anuśiṣṭo'nvasi pitreti; aumiti hovāca.

Word Meanings

śvetaketuḥ - Śvetaketu; *āruṇeyaḥ* - the grandson of Aruṇa; *ha vai* - verily; *ājagāma* - came; *pariṣadam* - to the assembly; *pāñcālānām* - of the Pañcālas; *saḥ* - he; *ājagāma* - approached; *pravāhaṇam* - Pravāhaṇa; *jaivalim* - the son of Jīvala; *paricārayamāṇam* - who was being attended on; *udīkṣya* - seeing; *tam* - him; *abhyuvāda* - (the king) addressed him; *kumārā iti* - boy; *saḥ* - he; *pratiśuśrāva* - replied; *bhoḥ iti* - yes; *nu asi iti* - have (you) been; *anuśiṣṭaḥ* - taught; *pitrā* - by (your) father; *uvāca ha* - (he) said, *aum iti* - yes

Śvetaketu, the grandson of Aruṇa, verily came to the assembly of the Pañcālas. He approached Pravāhaṇa, the son of Jīvala, who was being attended on. Seeing him the King addressed him, "Boy!" He replied, "Yes." "Have you been taught by your father?" He said, "Yes."

Mantra 2

vettha yathemāḥ prajāḥ prayatyo vipratipadyantā iti; neti hovāca; vettho yathemam lokam punarāpadyantā iti; neti haivovāca; vettho yathāsau loka evam bahubhiḥ punaḥ punaḥ prayadbhirna sampūryatā iti; neti haivovāca; vettho yatithyāmāhutyām hutāyāmāpaḥ puruṣavāco bhūtvā samutthāya vadantī iti; neti haivovāca; vettho devayānasya vā pathaḥ pratipadam, pitṛyāṇasya vā - yatkṛtvā devayānam vā panthānam pratipadyante, pitṛyāṇam vā; api hi na ṛṣervacaḥ śrutam -
dve sṛtī aśṛṇavam pitṛṇā -
maham devānāmuta martyānām;
tābhyāmidam viśvamejatsameti
yadantarā pitaram mātaram ca iti;
nāhamata ekañcana vedeti hovāca.

Word Meanings

vettha - do (you) know; *yathā* - how; *imāḥ prajāḥ* - people; *vipratipadyantā iti* - take different paths; *prayatya* - after death; *na iti* - no; *uvāca ha* - he replied; *vettha u* - do (you) know; *yathā* - how; *apadyanta iti* - (they) return; *imam* - to this; *lokam* - world; *punaḥ* - again; *na iti* - no; *uvāca ha eva* - he replied; *vettha u* - do you know; *yathā* - why; *asau*

- the other; *lokaḥ* - world; *na* - never; *sampuryatā iti* - is filled up by; *evam* - thus; *bahubhiḥ* - so many people; *prayadbhiḥ* - dying; *punaḥ punaḥ* - again and again; *na iti* - no; *uvāca ha* - said he; *vettha u* - do you know also; *yatithyām* - after how many; *āhutyām* - oblations; *hutāyām* - are offered; *āpaḥ* - water (the liquid offerings); *samutthāya* - rises up; *bhūtvā* - endowed with; *puruṣa vācaḥ* - a human voice; *vadantī iti* - speaks; *na iti* - no; *uvāca ha* - he replied; *vettha u* - do you know; *pratipadam* - the means of access; *devayānasya pathaḥ* - to the way of the gods; *vā* - or; *pitṛyāṇasya* - the way of the departed ones; *kṛtvā* - doing; *yat* - which; *pratipadyante* - people attain; *vā* - either; *devayānam panthānam* - the way of the gods; *vā* - or; *pitṛyāṇam* - the way of the departed ones; *naḥ* - we; *śrutam* - have heard; *vācaḥ* - the words; *ṛseḥ* - of the mantra; *aham* - I; *aśṛṇavam* - have heard of; *dve* - two; *sṛtī* - routes; *devānam* - the way of the gods; *pitṛnam* - the way of the departed ones; *ejat* - going; *tabhyam* - along them; *idam* - this; *viśvam* - universe; *sameti* - is united; *yat* - they (lie); *antara* - between; *pitaram* - the father (heaven); *ca* - and; *mātaram* - the mother (earth); *uvāca ha* - he said; *ahāmi*- I; *veda* - do know; *na* - not; *ekañcana* - even one; *ataḥ* - of them

"Do you know how people take different paths after death?" "No," he replied. "Do you know how they return to this world?" "No," he replied. "Do you know how the other world is never filled by so many people dying thus again and again?" "No," said he. "Do you know after how many oblations are offered, water (the liquid offerings) rises up endowed with a human voice and speaks?" "No," said he. "Do you know the means of access to the way of the gods, or that to the way of the departed ones – doing which people attain either the way of the gods or the way of the departed ones? We have heard the words of the mantra: 'I have heard of two routes, the way of the gods and the way of the departed ones. Going along them this universe is united. They lie between the father and the mother (heaven and earth)'." He said, "I do not know even one of them."

It is very significant that Śvetaketu was chosen to discuss the point of sin and its absolution. In his commentary, Śankara makes the following observation:

> *Śvetaketu, the grandson of Aruṇa,* after being taught by his father, *came to the assembly of the Pañcālas* to display his learning. The Pañcālas were famous (for their learning). With the proud idea of conquering first their assembly and then their royal court, *he approached Pravāhaṇa, the son of Jīvala,* and the King of Pañcāla, *who was being waited on* by his servants. The particle *'ha'* refers to a past incident, and *'vai'* indicates certainty. The King had already heard of his pride of learning, and wished to teach him a lesson. *Seeing him,* he *addressed him* as soon as he arrived, 'Boy!' Thus addressed *he replied, 'Yes, sir'.* [It was not customary in those days to answer a king in this manner, but Śvetaketu wanted to show his resentment to the King who addressed him as a boy.] The King said, *'Have you been taught by your father?'.* [35]

In the *Bṛhadāraṇyaka Upaniṣad,* Yājñavalkya is the chief sage and *guru.* Similarly, in the *Chāndogya Upaniṣad,* Uddālaka, the son of Aruṇa, is the sage and the *guru.* Śvetaketu is a classical example of a good son of the best of teachers going into a deviation of ignorance because of his conceited desire to enjoy the kind of honor which is considered supreme in society. In the *Īśāvāsya Upaniṣad,* the very first mantra speaks of the divine heritage of all and ends by saying, *ma gṛdhaḥ, kasya sviddhanam:* "Do not grab, whose is wealth?" Natural wealth, like the *prāṇa* which comes free to all of us, cannot be robbed or grabbed. But the secondary wealth that we make by using natural gifts is an evil. Hence the question *kasya sviddhanam,* "Whose is wealth?" and the warning *ma gṛdhaḥ,* "Do not grab!" The allurement of wealth comes differently: with form and without form. When temptation comes from physical sources it is called *rūparāga;* when there is no physical source of temptation and there are only imaginary values such as reputation, fame, power or acceptance, they are called *arūparāgas.* The *arūparāgas* creating desire in a person are of a higher degree of evil than the craving for anything physical.

We become rich by listening to the words of wise or knowledgeable people. The more we are exposed to the words of others, the more our vocabulary grows. Our speech organ can create in others a sense of a superior, well-versed person. In the second *adhyāya*, we saw how a person who has power over words can steal the hearts of people. Śvetaketu's great desire is to defeat others in rhetoric and logic. It is this subtle attraction which prevents him from becoming a sage of repute like his father. Pravāhaṇa, the wise king, intends to give him a super gift. But first the ego that is fascinated by false glory is to be destroyed. Sin is rectified only by sacrifice.

In this context we should know more about sin and sacrifice which are worked out in detail in all religions of the world, especially the Hindu, Jewish, Buddhist and Christian religions. The Islamic concept of *Ramadan* is a sacrificial purging of the bloating of the ego. Islam also adopted the habit of sharing what is naturally yours for the benefit of all, which they call *sakāt*. According to St. Thomas Aquinas, God's law is bound by Necessity. Whatever is necessary for a thing to be structured and function as it is, is meant to be, according to St. Thomas Aquinas. For him, carrying out God's will is having a clear insight into the necessary plan that is fulfilled by each thing or being. It is not to be taken in the sense of obedience to social commandments. This law of the necessary can be easily seen from the structural and functional arrangement of a blade of grass, a bug, a fly, or the complicated organism of a human being. As science advances its probes into the structural and functional complementarity of organs in the body, we can easily see that the discoveries of physics, chemistry, biology, physiology, and all such allied sciences of life are proving that that which is functionally appropriate as an integral part of being is necessarily good. When freaks occur in organizational ability, they result in dysfunction and malfunction which can incapacitate a being, a person, a tool, a society or a law. They are an evil in contrast to harmonious functioning.

We have been tracing the self-governing characteristics of the self-created universe and its innumerable adjuncts. Ethical norms and social contracts slowly came into vogue in group life. Humanity has passed through many historical phases where necessity was at the mercy of the brute. Only slowly did people come to see that the weakest among them also had the right to live in this world. This led to the concept of social good and evil. It became more and more clear that the good is to be maintained, protected, defended and upheld by humanity through the promulgation of laws which can be complementary to the laws of nature and to what is considered to be the law according to the sages of wisdom. It took millions of years for a certain good to evolve from the continuous making and remaking of living species.

Even in the history of humanity, we have the record of mythologies in which good and evil were always at loggerheads. The *devas* and *asuras* are presented as the balancing counterparts in the human personality. As human culture stemmed from the period of nomadic life and hunting, for several centuries human beings were blood-thirsty creatures. Consequently they imagined a God who resembled them. God was seen as superior, so God was to be served first with whatever people were pleased with. As a result, in all the evolving cultures of human society, everywhere in the world, what God supposedly liked most was the blood of his creatures. Sacrifice was honored almost from the dawn of human history for the expiation of evil and the restoration of the good.

The Anglo-Saxon term God was derived from the Indo-Iranian word *huta*. During the transformation of God from *hut*, he was also 'good'. In the Indian context, *huta* is the fire that receives sacrifices. Thus a strange culture of word affinity came between God, good, fire and sacrifice, which originally meant burnt sacrifice. In the *Old Testament* we read how the love-bird was burnt to please Jehovah, who liked its fragrance. Jehovah demanded that the best of all his devotees, the Patriarch Abraham, sacrifice his son Isaac. Abraham took him to a sacrificial altar on a mountain top to behead him. The narrator of that story felt a deep compunction in his heart so he let Isaac off by substituting him with a ram.

In the *Dictionary of Scriptures and Myths* evil is defined as:

> A condition of soul due to the partial and unbalanced development of the qualities, and to the ignorance in which the ego is immersed. It is a state of emptiness in its degree, and not of fullness; and as emptiness is no real thing, but the absence of the real, so an evil state of soul has no reality in itself, but needs the presence of the good and true, which are realities and endure for ever. The evil state is, therefore, relative, negative, and transitory, and implies the absence of completeness during a process of evolution of qualities and of knowledge. [36]

In the same book, Pseudo-Dionysius is quoted as saying: "The nature of evil is negative. If evil, as evil, positively subsisted, it would be evil to itself and would therefore, destroy itself." [37] Among Western philosophers, Meister Eckhart was considered the most balanced of thinkers who was highly sympathetic to his fellow humans:

> Eckhart like his predecessors, conceded to evil only the character of privation. As denoting a necessary stadium in the return of the soul to God, evil is part of the divine plan of the universe, as a calamity decreed by God.[38]

This idea of evil is also shared by St. Augustine and Thomas Aquinas even though they do not agree on many fundamentals. Another version is:

> Evil is the negation of God or good:- man's need of expansion and nutrition and consequent perception of this negation, of this evil within and around him, are the cause of his further vision of God or good. This further vision of God is born of effort which promotes all growth. Thus evil and the recognition of evil by man must be an inevitable step in his further consciousness of and progress towards God or good. Thus are sin and suffering embodied in the Divine Love which manifests itself through the *individuation* and *evolution*, from the chaos of formlessness, of the *Godhead of man*. [39]

From the *Gītā* we understand that the fear of sin comes out of irrational fear of a commitment in life about which one is not convinced. The idea of sin *(pāpa)* in the *Gītā* comes the first time not from Kṛṣṇa, but from the mouth of Arjuna who is in a dilemma about the ethics of warfare (I:36-39):

> Having killed the sons of Dhritārashtra, what delight can there be for us, O Janardana (Kṛṣṇa)? Only sin would come to us after killing this marauding rabble.
>
> And so we ought not to kill the sons of Dhritārashtra our relations; for how, indeed, can we be happy after killing our own people, O Madhava (Kṛṣṇa)?
>
> Even if they whose minds are overpowered by greed

> see no wrong in the destruction of family (and) no crime in treachery to friends,
>
> Yet why should we not learn to turn away from this sin, we who do see wrong in the destruction of family, O Janardana (Kṛṣṇa)?

The first Chapter of the *Gītā* comes to a close with Arjuna grieving over the tragic circumstances which bring him to do a great sin. In verse forty-five he says,

> Alas! a great sin are we engaged in committing in endeavoring to kill our own people through greed for the pleasures of kingdom!

Kṛṣṇa first speaks of sin in verse thirty-three of Chapter Two of the *Gītā*. There is a subtle rebuttal in Kṛṣṇa's words. Arjuna is not speaking as a lover of humanity or a man of wisdom. He is only speaking of the partial protection of his relations. So Kṛṣṇa responds in the spirit of Arjuna's own words (II:32-33):

> True warriors *(kṣatriyas)* have reason to be happy too, O Pārtha (Arjuna) to have the chance of such a war presenting itself unsought before them as an open door to heaven.
>
> If on the other hand, you will not take to this battle which conforms to the requirements of righteousness, then thwarting what is consistent with your own nature and your good repute you will become involved in evil.

We should take special notice of the word heaven. Heaven is the goal of a hedonistic pleasure seeker and not of a wise man. At the beginning of the second Chapter, Arjuna still belongs to the ritualists who sacrifice to go to heaven. In Chapter Three, *Karma Yoga*, there is an expiation of evil *(pāpa)*, for which sacrifice and expiation of sin are bracketed. Kṛṣṇa says (III:13):

> The good man who eats of the remnants of a sacrifice is absolved of all faults: they, however, eat of evil (itself) the sinners who cook with themselves (alone) for motive.

Here *pāpa* is equated with self-centered action of vested interest. Arjuna, obsessed with the fear of *pāpa*, returns to the subject in verse thirty-six of Chapter Three. He sees a compulsion in committing sin:

> Then impelled by what does man lead a life of sin even against his will, O Vārṣṇeya (Kṛṣṇa), as if forcibly enjoined?

Kṛṣṇa is in agreement with the Christian theologians that true knowledge and faith can make the negativity of sin a relative factor which can be washed off by one's higher knowledge. In verse thirty-six of the fourth chapter, Kṛṣṇa says,

> Even if you should happen to be among the evil-doers the most evil-doing man, by the very raft of wisdom you will be able to cross over sin.

The great redeeming principle given in the *Gītā* is the Absolute. The symbolic significance of sacrifice is surrendering all actions in the Absolute. In verse ten of Chapter Five we read,

> Placing all actions in the Absolute, having given up attachment, he who acts is not affected by sin, like a lotus leaf by water.

The marked difference between good and evil is placed outside the purview of the Absolute in the *Gītā*, whereas in the *Bible* and *Qur'an*, God is absolutely concerned with the good or evil in every person's action. In the *Gītā*, the question of good and evil is a person's own doing in which God is not interested. In verses V:14-15 we read,

> The Supreme does not generate either the idea of agency or activity in regard to the world, nor the union of action and benefit; the innate urge in beings, however, exerts itself.
>
> The all-pervading One takes cognizance neither of the sinful nor of the meritorious actions of anyone; wisdom is veiled by unwisdom; beings are deluded thereby.

Two great Christian theologians who gave their considered

opinions on good and evil are St. Augustine and St. Thomas Aquinas. St. Augustine speaks of three things: measure, form and order. According to him there is generic good in the things made by God. God is above every measure of the creatures, above every form and above every order. For evil he says,

> Whence is evil, it must first be enquired what is evil? Which is nothing else of corruption either of the measure, or order or form, which belong to nature. Nature that has been corrupted is evil. When incorrupt is God. But so far a uncorrupt so far it is nature, it is good. So far it is corrupted it is evil. [40]

Where St. Augustine speaks of nature, he is not speaking of the empirical world we see, but that which is part of God's nature. According to Thomas Aquinas, good or evil is to be placed in the circumstance of its occurrence and it should be seen if there is a tilting of the balance of the natural equilibrium in which a person is placed. He says: "The good of moral virtue lies in the poise of reason. The mean between excess and defect is an equality or conformity." [41] In his *Summa Theologica* (1031) we read,

> The form of goodness in moral virtue derives from the measure of reason; its subject-matter lies in what we do and feel. As regards the former, virtue holds the position of one extreme, namely conformity to reason, while both excess and defect lie at the other extreme of non-conformity. As regards its matter, however, it holds a midway position even-minded among the passions. Hence, Aristotle says that virtue is a mean in respect of its substance, but an extreme with regard to what is best and excellent. [42]

St. Thomas Aquinas makes a very good observation of virtue and evil. He says, "Extravagance and niggardliness, between which moral virtues mediate, must not be taken according to absolute quantities, but in relation to right reason." [43] In Jewish philosophy the reference to virtue and evil comes in accordance with the Commandments of Moses. Hesiod said that vice may be bad in abundance, without trouble, for the way is smooth and her dwelling place is near, but before virtue the gods have set toil. The

Jewish concept is a follow up of the *Genesis* of the *Old Testament.* For further references regarding the Christian concept of sin, we recommend *Summa Theologica* Vol. I.

In the light of what we have just said about evil or sin, we have to examine how sacrifice was introduced in socio-cultural life in all major religions and what sacrifice means in the Vedic and Vedāntic culture. The *Bṛhadāraṇyaka Upaniṣad* keeps a reasonable equilibrium between knowledge and action. A great tilt was made in the very beginning by presenting the *aśva* and *aśvamedha* as a major correction of the blood-thirsty sacrifices of the *Vedas.* We will see here also that sanity prevails.

According to the *Bṛhadāraṇyaka Upaniṣad,* the first model of life which manifested itself to meet hunger exerted itself to meet the contingency of the ever-awaiting death. The *Upaniṣad* says that he had nothing else to worship other than himself, so he moved about worshipping himself. The word sacrifice first appears in *Adhyāya* I, *brāhmaṇa* 2, mantra 6 which says: "Let me sacrifice again with the great sacrifice." When a single-celled living body grows to its maximum by swelling up, it is prone to die. The swelling is called *aśvat.* There is no way to save a single cell when it swells up; it is being sacrificed to make a multicellular being. This is the *aśvamedha,* the sacrifice of the first born to proliferate life on earth which happens universally in the duplication of cells. Thus death is the cause of life, and without life death cannot be prolonged. Therefore death becomes the Self *(ātman).*

In the course of time, sacrifice came to be recognized as an archetypal device to nourish a being and to bring it to perfection by relinquishing the lower desires in the soul in favor of higher qualities of goodness, love and truth. We read in *Laws of Manu* (v.39): "Svayambhu (the Self-existent) himself created animals for the sake of sacrifices; sacrifices have been instituted for the good of this whole world." [44] Manu considers that herbs, trees, birds, cattle and other living forms which perish in the sacrifice are reborn as improved and higher models of life and hence there is no violence to life implied in a sacrifice. He further maintains, "Sacrifice is the true type of progress. We sacrifice a lower life to cultivate and enjoy a higher. All improvement is a sacrifice in this sense." [45] To revitalize one cannot begin with inorganic rocks. The sap or blood of the living being is the catalyst to transform a lower grade into a higher grade. The highest of all sacrifices is the everlasting sacrifice of *dharma.* Our inferior or selfish feelings and passions are the true beasts which should be sacrificed and thereby transformed.

> To sacrifice is to stir up, actually to beget, two divinities, of the first rank, the two principles of life *par-excellence*, Agni and Soma. "Agni" is the force aspect of *ātma buddhi* and "*Soma*" is the Divine Life; these emerge in the soul as growth proceeds. In the *Taittirīya Brāhmaṇa* we read that "By sacrifices the gods obtained heaven." "The 'gods' are the Divine Sparks, who descend to rise", meaning that without the mortals' sustaining them, the gods in heaven would not survive. Therefore, sacrifice is a bond of mutuality between the mortals on earth and the immortals in heaven. For the Hindu the sacrifice is neither expiatory nor placatory; it is necessary for the food and support of the gods. "If there were no sacrifices the gods would starve to death." [46]

Gods are the shining one's within ourselves: the ear that can hear, the skin that can touch, the tongue that can taste, and the olfactory organ that can smell. If you starve them they will not function.

> The 'gods' (in Hindu literature) are the highest ideals, or highest qualities within the human soul. They always grow in strength and beauty as the lower desires and passions are overcome and abandoned. It is said, therefore, that 'sacrifices' are for the sustenance of the gods.[47]

The 'demons' signify underdeveloped erroneous conclusions which are swelled up by disciplined urges. They are also necessary for the *prajāpati's* evolution. "The main object of sacrificial performances generally is the reconstruction of [*prajāpati*]." [48] When we are in the mother's womb, there is no one to construct or organize our parts except ourselves. Hence everyone who was formulated in a mother's womb is to be looked upon as a separate *prajāpati*. "This re-formation of Divinity in humanity is effected by the offering up of the lower nature to the higher." [49] This idea is taken in the Christian faith as Jesus Christ offering himself for sacrifice to God the Father, for the reconstruction of the soul of humans.

According to the *Tāṇḍya-brāhmaṇa*, the Lord of creatures offers himself up as a sacrifice. Sacrifice *(yajña)* itself was sometimes personalized as a god. *Soma* undergoes sacrifice when he hides in the *soma* creeper. He is crushed and pressed to offer the essence of the *soma* plant as the *soma* juice for the sacrifice. The *soma* that emanates has a higher and lower aspect.

> "The higher Self (the most pleasing) remains inoperative and potential." The lower self limits itself in what is being sacrificed. That is to be absorbed to perfect the sacrifice. Thus the "Self, or the Archetypal Man, from One becomes many, he is born in each soul or quality during the period of evolution." [50]

According to the Greeks, everything was only chaos to begin with "out of which arises the first duality, spirit and matter, it is said that the primal differentiations (gods) delivered the soul (world) from chaos by sacrifice. This they did by becoming involved in matter, as the first qualities of Spirit. Man prevents the soul from lapsing back into unfruitfulness by the sacrifice of his lower nature, which implies the evolution of his higher," [51] and it manifests in his higher ideals.

What is termed by the Greeks as spirit is recognized in India as *puruṣa:*

> "the spirit involved in matter, that is, the introduction into the vibrations of atoms of all the energies and qualities afterwards to be evolved out of atomic vibrations is the Archetypal Man [the *prajāpati*] whose dismemberment, or division into many, constitutes the origin of the human race with its multitude of separate souls." The "sacrifice" is the involution and apparent death (latency) of the Divine qualities. . . . When the Absolute out breathed, the Second Logos was emanated to become the Divine Sacrifice, as Spirit involved in Matter, - *Maya*, Mother, the veil of matter (feminine) in which manifestation takes place."[52]

In the *Vedas* and *Upaniṣads* we come across numerous references to *yajña* as the main theme. Those who are interested may look into: *Kauṣītaki Upaniṣad* - I:1; *Chāndōgya Upaniṣad* -

I:10:7; II:23:1; II:24:16; III:16:1&2; IV-16:1,3&5; IV:17:4,8,9&10; VIII:5:1; *Bṛhadāraṇyaka Upaniṣad* - I:2:5&6; I:3:28; I:4:1; III:1:1; III:1:3; III:1:6; III:8:9; III:9:10; IV:1:2; IV:5:11; and *Katha Upaniṣad* - III:2.

The third chapter of the *Bhagavad Gītā* discusses sacrifice in verses eight through ten:

> Do engage yourself in action that is necessary; activity is indeed better than non-activity and even the bodily life of yours would not progress satisfactorily through non-action.
>
> Outside of activity with a sacrificial purpose, this world is bound by action. Even with such a purpose, do engage in work, O Kaunteya (Arjuna), freed of all attachments.
>
> In ancient times, having created the peoples with sacrifice as pertaining to them (necessarily), *prajāpati* (the Lord of the peoples) said, "By this shall you grow and multiply: let this be to you the milch cow of all desires.

The very basis of life is described in the *Gītā* as the actualization of a sacrifice. The dual principles implied in all creations can be seen in the mutuality of *prakṛti* and *puruṣa*. In verses 37 to 39 in answer to Arjuna's question as to why there is compulsive behavior that drags a person to compulsive actions, Kṛṣṇa says,

> Such is desire, such is anger, born out of the modality *(guṇa)* called active, affective *(rajas)*, all-devouring, all-vitiating; know this to be the enemy here.
>
> As smoke shrouds fire, as a mirror (is beclouded) by dirt, as the fetus is enclosed in the amnion, likewise by such is This surrounded.
>
> Wisdom is enveloped by this which is the eternal enemy of the wise, remaining in the form of desire, O Kaunteya (Arjuna), which is a fire too that is difficult to satiate.

The main references to look into for the study of sacrifice in the *Gītā* are Chapter IV:25, 30, 32; Chapter V:12, 25; Chapter 8:27; Chapter IX:15,16,17, 20, 23; Chapter XVI:1,17; Chapter XVII: 1, 4, 7, 11, 12, 13, 23, 24, 25; Chapter XVIII:3, 5.

In the *Īśāvāsya Upaniṣad* we read that those who have totally given themselves to action born out of desire are living in darkness. It further says those who indulge only in theoretical knowledge of speculation live in greater darkness. It also says that those who rejoice in non-action or non-accomplishment are in darkness and those who have excess of desire for achievement live in greater darkness. King Pravāhaṇa confronts Śvetaketu for his pride of scholarship which, of course, comes under what the *Īśāvāsya* calls "living in greater darkness." Moderation is to be brought both in the life of the activist and the contemplative. It is this moderation which is pointed to in this *adhyāya* which gives a final recapitulation of all that has come so far for a final contemplative pondering and the actualization of the teaching (*nididhyāsana*). The culminating conclusion of the *Upaniṣad* is that rote learning or parrot-like recitation of the *Vedas* and *Upaniṣads* will not lead us anywhere unless we live what we have understood. Thus the whole *Upaniṣad* is our *aśvamedha* - our sacrificing of all tendencies to exaggerate.

A student coming from the world of phenomenality has a need to normalize himself or herself. Those who have gone into the search for the transcendental have to be renormalized. Thus the *Upaniṣad* ultimately brings us to the golden mean or the middle path. Along with the teachings of asceticism, celibacy and sacrifice, the *Upaniṣad* also sees the mating of man and woman to conceive progeny as a sacrifice in which both the husband and wife are equal in their responsibility of sharing parenthood. This is similar to the *Yoga Vāśiṣṭha Rāmāyaṇa* in which there is an ascending scale of evolution which brings a person to absolute *brahma* consciousness. After realization a person is given a descent into the actualities of life. In the *Bhagavad Gītā* also we see an ascending dialectics which takes Arjuna to the highest point of identification with the Absolute in the last verse in the ninth chapter:

> Become one with Me; be devoted to Me; sacrifice to Me;
> unifying thus yourself, you shall surely come to Me,
> your supreme Goal none other than Me.

At the end of the *Gītā* Arjuna is ready to face his responsibilities. He says:

Gone is my delusion and Self-recognition has been gained by me through Your grace, O Acyuta (Kṛṣṇa); I am properly established with doubts gone; I shall carry out Your word.

The very Arjuna whom we saw in the first chapter throwing down his bow and arrow, making a pledge not to fight, now stands ready, fully determined to bring absolute justice. Keeping this scheme in mind will help us to understand this last *adhyāya* of the *Bṛhadāraṇyaka Upaniṣad.*

Most of us have brothers and sisters. We are born of the same mother; our sperm came from the same father. The mother nurtured us in her womb and brought us to the same world. We have breathed the same breath, we have been taken care of by the same parents. We speak the same language. When we came of age, we were given the same education and discipline. We have the common heritage of our country; we are part of the same history; we are exposed to the same culture. In spite of these circumstantial similarities we rarely find brothers and sisters acquiring the same talents or preparing themselves for the same career. They understand neither the external world nor the inner self in the same way.

Just like two branches which grow out of the same tree, yet stretch themselves in opposite directions, divergence comes to us in our lives. If one sibling turns out to be an introvert, the other becomes an extrovert. If one is forgiving, the other becomes revengeful. There are innumerable divergences between people which we can categorize. Both the Sindhu and Brahmaputra rivers originate from the snowy peaks of the Himalayas. The Sindhu flows towards the West and comes to the Arabian Sea; the Brahmaputra flows to the East and comes to the Bay of Bengal. What causes these divergences among brothers and sisters, in the branches of a tree and in the rivers? Many religions believe that human beings are of divine origin. According to the *Old Testament* there was only God and he created a man in his own image by molding him from the earth. Out of him was taken another person – a woman. If we take for granted the veracity of the Biblical story, humanity got divided into two categories: men and woman. Two persons who came from the same source had divergent roles to play - the father's role and the mother's role. Adam and Eve had two children, Cain and Abel. Cain was hateful, jealous, cruel and murderous, while Abel was dignified, sensible, industrious and devoted to God. Roused by the jealousy of God's recognition of Abel's clean life, Cain murdered his brother. These two brothers came from the same parents but the elder became a murderer and the younger became the murdered. Over time, humanity developed ethics which condemn the murderer to be thrown into the dungeon while the righteous person goes to God's ultimate company. Where does such divergence come from?

In the Indian concept of life, every person occupies a separate space. They have different bodies. Even though father and mother are common to children, each child is different. Why? In the great epic *Rāmāyaṇa*, Rāvaṇa is the mortal enemy of Rāma, but his brother Vibhīṣaṇa was an ardent devotee of Rāma. Why are there such differences in the attitudes of people? We have not yet heard how this question is answered by Pravāhaṇa. But it is a question which challenges us. We all belong to families and groups with many members but no two of them have the same finger prints. When there is difference in such a small thing as the pattern of the skin on our thumbs, how much more divergence is in the personality makeup of people?

We are told that each of us was born out of a single cell. The cell has proliferated into millions of cells. Some are the cells with which our faculty of hearing is constituted; some other cells have formulated our eyes; still others are the innumerable cells that are juxtaposed to make the skin of our bodies. In the tongue itself, there are taste buds with which we know bitterness and others with which we taste sweetness. Our olfactory organ can distinguish odors of all kinds. Why this divergence? Although all the cells originate from the primary cell, the quality of one group of cells is different from the quality of another. Our heart has two sets of vessels that carry blood, the arteries and the veins. The heart itself has four chambers: each one assigned a different function. We are very fascinated by the idea of one, but our bodies and mind are constituted of a plurality of features. We have two sets of organs: organs of perception and organs of action. The eye sees and the hand manipulates; the ear listens and the tongue speaks.

Sometimes heredity is opposed to environment and a person becomes a misfit. Sometimes environment is complementary to heredity and there the nurturing is excellent. In certain hilly tracts a river may divide itself and begin to flow in opposite directions. Then in the valley the two come together again. Here both the divergence and remergence are created by the contour of the land and the nature of water to flow because of the pull of gravity. Divergence becomes very prominent when we consider the paths tread by people instinctively, or under social compulsion, or through helplessness which drags one into a vocation not to one's liking. The multitudinousness and diversities of life create tragic compulsions which a person has little strength to oppose.

Different eventualities can bring hell-fire to one and the ambrosia of paradise to another. Is there any justice if they have a common creator? Or is it by chance that they grow differently? Is there something called predetermination? If everything is predetermined, why do we bother at all about disciplining ourselves? These are common questions asked. We see certain people who are again and again exposed to tragedy while before the eyes of these people there are those who are promoted to higher and higher positions. Then it is natural that one disbelieves either the omniscience of God, his omnipotence, or the quality of his love. Carl Gustav Jung portrays God as a ego-infatuated being thinking only of the merits of his craftsmanship and not about the welfare of his creatures. Is it justifiable for a great philosopher-psychologist like Jung to condemn Jehovah as a malicious being? We read in the *Old Testament* that God himself handed over his most devoted lover, Job, to be exposed to the most pernicious kinds of torture by Satan. Why? Jesus is considered to be the only begotten son of God, but when the governor Pontius Pilate gave an opportunity to people to choose one condemned to death to go free and the other to be crucified, people who were lovers of Jesus and had followed him almost to the very last moment cried out furiously that Jesus should be crucified and Barabbas released. Why? This question offers us one of the greatest enigmas of human nature. If we cannot answer it, our own personal lives will be a riddle to us; if we solve it, the greatest paradox which has always challenged humanity will be resolved.

To answer the question of Pravāhaṇa, we should know what a system is. Further we should know what functions are. Systems and functions are selective operations belonging to structure. A structure is intended for bringing about functions to produce certain effects. Every effect which is conceived of as bringing a goal of activity has within it a motivational dynamics and a production dynamics. Motivation refers to a series of productions in which one accomplished result is necessary for the next achievement. Each achievement has an implied value. What ultimately comes in the designing of something is the value system. A value system can be accomplished only when there is a production system. The production system caters to the demand for a certain supply which has an economic significance. Thus all production systems belong to economic systems. An economic system is feasible only when a managerial system is implemented.

The operational field of a managerial system ranges from the transformation of raw or non-processed material or mind to the ultimate actualization of perfecting the value implied in the entire motivational range. At the base, apart from an unprocessed entity, there has to be the material or moral or spiritual means for effecting all motivated transformations. Usually it is considered as a reserve energy, which can be natural substances or an equivalent money value with which raw substances can be purchased. Money or raw wealth by themselves have no dynamics of their own, so there has to be an action programmer. The programmer should be infused with a total value orientation so that a person can function as something like a flywheel to create a chain of actions in all the participants. Within one production unit it becomes necessary to make many complementary production units with various value systems and various *modus operandi*.

One of the most elaborate systems is this globe of earth. The earth is only one of the planets in the solar system. There are many solar systems in various galaxies. We are now concerned with the animated corporeal beings called humans. In their latitudinal life from moment to moment, hour to hour, morning to evening, from sunset to sunrise, and in their longitudinal life from birth to death, we observe two kinds of divergence in individual beings. One is the motivational dynamics in their temporal consciousness and the spatial extension to which their personal consciousness is attuned. The other is the span of life allotted to each individual for reasons beyond a person's control, such as their origin from the genes which come together from a father and mother at an intersection of time and space. It has within it a great starting point of both structuring and function. This happens in an area where neither a person's awareness nor the attention of other people connected with him or her is drawn. Therefore the natural cause of divergence is mostly obliviated – it happens in the dark. In any case, to understand this origin of divergence we have to look into the time/space continuum to which a person belongs. As the globe of earth is spherical, varying from North Pole to South Pole and has a moving time orientation from East to West, the simultaneity of occurrences such as the conception or birth of a child cannot be located easily. So we are actually not together to commence our journey or to end it. Even when we live together, there are divergences in the spatial, temporal and biologic corporeality to which we belong.

We are all subject to varying impacts which come from the cosmological system, terrestrial system, regional system and biological system to which we belong. There are also genetic, physiological and psychobiological factors that cause divergence, as well as the socio-cultural environment in which the individual is nurtured. The more important and very difficult probe is the eschatological mystery which causes a person to be born in a certain situation which is rich or impoverished. Another important probe is how the genetic factor intervenes in the growth of a person. In all production sciences, the ultimate value has a determining effect as a final cause in drawing from a person his best.

Most thoughtful people are convinced that we live in a universe and not a haphazard chaotic world. The main reason to think that we live in a universe is because of the regularity with which we are exposed to day and night every twenty-four hours, and the eternal passage of the sun and moon (seemingly) from the East to the West. We regulate our main programs to be carried out in daylight while in the night our nature is to go into restful sleep and wake up each morning with more energy. We can add to this list thousands of factors of everyday life which show the regularity of natural events. We can see several correlations and coordinations in this natural relationship which seem to be meticulously structured. There are certain freaks of nature in individual cases where the structuring is not perfect and, even in the case of perfectly structured organisms, hereditary malevolence or environmental incidents disrupt functioning so it is not entirely rhythmic to our full satisfaction.

Looking at this world two hypotheses are mooted, apart from the very many hunches of people who lived in the past and in the present. The first is that the entire universe is created by a single being who seems to be omniscient, omnipresent, and of infinite possibilities. This idea is eulogized into an ideal and sometimes even into a religious idol and many look upon that ideal or idol with great veneration, thinking of themselves as the faithful. Yet there are people in the very society of the faithful who disbelieve or doubt such a common origin for the whole world and the countless galaxies that constitute this universe. The other possibility is that the archaic formation came on its own and slowly evolved into various kinds of stratifications which became the repository of finer and subtler changes that successfully brought variations in elements. In the course of time life evolved from that basic raw matter. Each time transformation came, part of it fell off into oblivion and more and more adaptation came so that what we see now are evolutes of an unrefined beginning. These two postulates have been given many other sub-postulates riddled with many philosophical questions, new postulations and counter-criticisms. Now this ancient book prompts us to sharpen our intelligence and critically examine whatever findings human beings have made in order to restructure a world which can reasonably explain to us the meaning and purpose of an individual's life on this planet floating in an unknown extension of space.

One of the postulations made by Indian philosophers is that this world is probably a transforming entity which demonstrates individuated formations such as birth, growth and change from one form to another, with periodic leaps into new stratifications, also called evolution (*pariṇāma*). It also shows disintegration and extinction into oblivion, probably with the intention of being recycled and brought back to this world to continue as new formations. This is the Samkhyan concept put forward by Kapila, one of the earliest rational philosophers of India. Those who hold such a view see a one-to-one correspondence between the outer manifestation of the law of change and a mathematical compulsion which correlates certain functions which they call reason. In this thematic apperception of the world there are previously recorded postulations called *śruti*, or *a priori* concepts. That is the given word wisdom which should be questioned by an open mind of relentless critical acumen. If most or all the concepts yield satisfactory results, then each such result is to be tested by one's day to day experience (*anubhava*). If many have endorsed the teaching of the *a priori* postulation through observation and experiment over the centuries, that is considered a law.

Today many avenues have been pursued by innumerable thinkers all over the world for the single purpose of verifying and substantiating theories. Of late, a body of study called scientific search was made. In the time of Thales there was a search for unity, for all understanding to be correlated to a central principle. That yielded great results in two areas, one of science which stemmed from Thales himself. Between the time of Thales and Socrates or Plato there was a trend of generating postulations and rejecting them through criticism, leading to the emergence of new theories which were counter-criticized. So the progress of thought was like that of a pendulum or spiral from thesis to antithesis to a verticalizing synthesis. This trend which was first initiated by philosophers and then by scientists continues in European countries.

Among Vedāntins there are five trends. Śankara said that there is being which never undergoes any change and apparent becoming which he called the phenomenality of superimposition. After him came Rāmānuja, who was more a mystical lover of God. He explained everything in terms of a God of infinite powers who is ever expressing his care in the form of new and revised expressions of perfection *(vibhūti)*. After him came an outstanding stalwart of uncompromising logic in the person of Madhva who considered all occurrences, incidents or differentiating principles operating in this world as dependent factors. He called the foundation or independent reality, God.

In this mantra where we are asked to look into the question of Pravāhaṇa to Śvetaketu, the challenge is aimed at everyone in all ages - "What brings divergence in things?" Or "What is the difference between persons who have come to this world which causes them to behave differently, to postulate their views of life differently, to move in different paths of life, and, ultimately, to die differently, in graceful peace and serenity, or wretched, suffering intensely and finding no rhyme or reason in this world?" Both Śankara's *Vedānta* and the *Sāmkhyan* philosophers agreed to being, birth, growth, evolution, degeneration, and death. Even though Śankara gives a fresh meaning to evolution *(pariṇāma)*, he basically sees that there is change in life. A simple example is a fetus changing into a child, a child into an adolescent, an adolescent into a youth capable of producing progeny. Finally the person becomes incapacitated for all functions and dies. When scientists like Darwin and Lamarck speak of evolution, it is not exactly in this sense, yet they also see evidence of changes happening in the present which culminate in new beings in the future.

The following quote will give us an idea of the modern perspective on the history of evolution:

> **Geological Evidence of Evolution**
>
> *Paleontological observations prove beyond doubt that living organisms have been changing all the time,* with some degree of continuity in the transformation from one form to the other and in the generation of new forms that diverge from previous ones, sometimes supplanting them. The ages of fossilized organisms can be estimated by dating of the rocks in which they appear. The further back in time we look, the less frequently we see organisms that correspond closely to those that are alive now.
>
> The oldest rocks in which fossil organisms have been found (inevitably the simplest organisms: bacteria) are about three and a half billion years old. From the fossil record, it appears that only prokaryotes existed for the next two billion years. Simple multicellular animals date from only shortly before the beginning of the Cambrian period (600 million years ago); fossils of that age include softbodied jellyfishes, sessile echinoderms, and worm-like organisms. Shortly after, with the Cambrian period, there begins an explosive increase in the number of invertebrate, and they exhibit a great variety of types. Being provided with skeletons these organisms have been preserved more easily, but this factor is not enough to account for the explosion. There are many hypotheses--none totally satisfactory--regarding the Cambrian rise in numbers of species and of individuals. There is no question, however, that the Cambrian period is marked by a major increase in the diversity of living organisms.
>
> *Diversity has probably been increasing most of the time,* and this trend is generally expected in an evolutionary process, *but the increase is not regular and continuous.* In fact, there have been some periods of marked increase and others of critical decrease, and these phenomena are more noticeable in some groups of living organisms than in others. Major crises occurred in the Pemian period (225 million years ago) and in the Cretaceous period (62 million years ago). In the Permian period

> all continents coalesced into one, and there was a profound decrease in the number of marine invertebrates, especially from shallow waters. All trilobites, most ammonites, and many other groups disappeared. After the Permian period, the first flying vertebrates appeared. The other major crisis was the Cretaceous extinction, 62 million years ago. This event may have resulted from a decrease in temperature, caused by dust that was thrown up by the impact of a large meteorite and that reduced the solar energy reaching the ground. The chief victims were again marine invertebrates, but they also included the big terrestrial reptiles (the dinosaurs). [53]

Human genetics provide some important clues to the differences between people, even siblings:

> ...Genes can be mixed by the fusion of gametes from two different individuals. But genetic variation is not produced solely by this means. Unless they are identical twins, no two offspring of the same parents are quite alike. This is because long before the two gametes fuse, two different kinds of genetic reassortment have already occurred during meiosis.
>
> One kind of reassortment is a consequence of the random distribution of the different maternal and paternal homologs between the daughter cells at meiotic division I, as a result of which each gamete acquires a different mixture of maternal and paternal chromosomes. From this fact alone, the cells of any one individual could, in principle, give rise to 2n genetically different gametes, where *n* is the haploid number of chromosomes. In humans, for example, each individual can produce at least 223 = 8.4 x 106 genetically different gametes. But in actuality the number is very much greater than this because of **chromosomal crossing over,** a process that takes place during the long prophase of meiotic division I and in which part of homologous chromosomes are exchanged. On average, between two and three such crossover events occur on each pair of human chromosomes. This process scrambles the genetic constitution of each of the chromosomes in gametes.

> Chromosomal crossing over involves breaking the single maternal and paternal DNA double helices in each of two chromatids and rejoining them to each other in a reciprocal fashion by a process known as **genetic recombination.** Recombination takes place during prophase of meiotic division I, at a time when the two sister chromatids are so tightly packed together that their individuality cannot be distinguished. Much later in this extended prophase, the two separate chromatids of each chromosome become clearly visible. They are now seen to be connected at their centromeres, and each of the four chromatids in each bivalent can be identified as belonging to one homolog or the other. The two homologs remain attached to each other at points where a crossover between a paternal and a maternal chromatid has occurred. At each such point, called a **chiasma** (plural **chiasmata**), two of the four chromatids are seen to have crossed over between the homologs. Chiasmata are thus the morphological consequences of a prior, unobserved crossover event.
>
> At this stage of meiosis, each pair of homologs, or bivalent, is usually held together by at least one chiasma. Many bivalents contain more than one chiasma, reflecting the fact that multiple crossovers can occur between homologs. [54]

However, this data does not provide us with a complete answer to the question of what makes divergence. We still have to account for the purposiveness of such genetic variations. This we can see only from a commonsense point of view of the necessary constituents of any structural complex. For example, our two arms are symmetrically built. Each arm can be rotated three hundred and sixty degrees in either direction as well as reaching what is in front of the body and behind the body. When we straighten our arms, the rigidity of the elbow gives all-purpose strength but the rigidity is lessened at the wrists. Although it is easy to close our fists, we cannot open our fingers to the same extent that we can close them, for they also become rigid. This enables the two hands to clasp each other and manipulate hundreds of things. The divergence shown in the hands seems to be highly ingenious. The thumbs are separated from the palm with almost a ninety degree divergence from the index finger to the thumb, and the four fingers are uneven in their length. So the ingenious divergence of the five fingers is very necessary for all the manipulations which the hands are capable of. We can extrapolate this principle to all parts of our organism internally and externally. From this it is clear that our formation is not by chance. Every bit of it answers what Thomas Aquinas called Necessity. He spoke of God as a conscientious engineer who has never made any design which is unnecessary to maintain the body/mind/spirit complex called the human organism.

When we analyze the constituent operational functions of the mind, we see a liaison between the five organs of perception and the organs of action. The assumed mind is the main center for orientation and coordination. It is a correlative area that initiates intrapersonal reaction as well as interpersonal subject/object reaction and even transpersonal reaction. There is a lot of speculation about whether the mind is only an epiphenomena that is secreted by the biophysical and biochemical functions of the body or whether there is a spirit which takes possession of everything in the body as a part of its purposive instrumentation so that a person can be created out of the body constituents. Those who uphold this view relate human life to the biological principle that manifests as life forms which vary from a single bacteria, virus, or alga to a great scientist, philosopher or person of creative imagination. The artificer of life is attributed to an oversoul or overseeing spirit which is recognized in religion as God. There are thinkers who refuse to accept that the mind comes with innate ideas or a sense of purposiveness and who believe that they are only locally generated in each body because of exposure to environmental factors.

Genetics alone does not show the deeper roots of a person or personality which, according to *Vedānta*, come from a previously living person's spirit. It is the indweller that carries with it the purposiveness of individuation which is the basis of divergence from person to person. We have on one hand the selection of chromosomes that will adequately fulfill the needs of the soul for a lifetime. Each separate child is incubated in the womb of the mother. But the mother is not just an encasement; she is living as a member of a society. Every day she has to interact with other members of her community and with certain people with great intimacy, such as her husband, parents and her other children.

Just as the baby is a part of her own body, her mind also can be feeding into the incumbent mind of the child within.

From the moment the child comes into the open, all the major faculties are initiated. First is respiration and the primal scream which makes a child listen for the first time to its own voice. Then a sudden release of urine from its bladder, and, perhaps a little belatedly, the dirt accumulated in its colon. For all this, the child is interacted with by the nursing relatives around. Even though the child knows nothing of language, those who surround the child speak to the child as if it has a language and word system. The child passively hears all these sounds. Its basic receptive system transmutes all stimuli into the seedbed for sensory experiences. Amorphous processing is going on from the very first instance of its being exposed to the world. Psychologists and physiologists think that for a period all the basic interpersonal reactions are fed into the automation of psychophysical, psychochemical and even psychospiritual conditionings.

After the birth of a child, for at least a few moments, the child is not separated from the immediate attention of the mother or whoever is attending to it on behalf of the mother. Psychologists are of the opinion that this acute attention given to the child by the mother or mother-representative lays a foundation for the archetypal mother image in the depth of the growing consciousness of the child. C. G. Jung calls it the coming of the archetypal mother into the unconscious of the new-born. At first it is an acceptance necessitated by the immediate needs of the child, such as sucking the mother's breast, getting protection from the excesses of environmental conditions, getting enough sleep without interruption in a comfortable bed or cradle. To most children, even if there is father near by to fondle and mentally claim the child to be his, the father image does not go so deep as the mother image.

As different mothers give different attention to their newly born children, peculiarities of mothers generate variances in the mother images of children. That is the basis of divergence between children of one mother and children of another mother. Even for the same mother, maternal expectation and value assessment can vary between the birth of one child and another child. The mother's attitude towards a male child is different from her attitude to a female child. A male child psychically represents an epitomization of the father of the child, the husband of the mother, so she is erotically more inclined to the son than to a daughter. The attentive care that is given to a daughter by the mother has a lot of self-identification in it. The mother transfers her hopes, fears and emotional dynamics more to a daughter than to a son. This generates wide divergence between a brother and a sister.

In the biological world the externalities of the body formation are rather superficial and all living beings share certain common natural trends such as the loving care shown to their young by cows, dogs, cats and hens. That animal-like aspect of mothering persists alongside the aspects which become more refined through education and exposure to culture and sophistication. In India four kinds of female images are superimposed on the archetypal female: at the bottom she is Kāli, the dark, above that she is Durgā, the protective; above that is Lakṣmī, the ambitious; and at the peak isSarasvatī, the sublime. Within the psyche a four-fold imagery is made to account for the fluctuating aspects of the personality that come to the surface from time to time.

After the fulfillment of the basis for the psyche gives the necessary roots on which a person can be grafted, the father image becomes deeply ingrained in the psyche of the child as the voice of authority and correction. In the archetypal father image also there can be an admixture of the demonic, the human and the divine. At the peak is the magician who is the benevolent father who can sometimes go beyond the powers of a mortal in order to bestow upon the growing child higher forms of intuitive intelligence and qualities of the heart. At the base is the trickster who can again and again lead a growing person into disastrous situations. Ambitious calculations can cause one to be trapped into many masochistic or sadistic situations. When the divergence between the magician and the trickster is sharp, a pathological condition sets in which brings the disaster of a split personality. Thus the trend to become schizophrenic begins very early in the formation of personality.

These basic trends become more expressive in an outgoing mind which is tied up with the objects that confront the sensory system. That type is called the extrovert. When there is more of an inner search for meaning on the supposition that divinity lives in the heart of a person, the more spiritually inclined child or baby begins with a strong introversion. There are also combinations of introversion and extroversion, resulting in four major types: extrovert-extrovert; extrovert-introvert; introvert-introvert; introvert-extrovert.

Up to this stage the development of a person comes from the deepest roots of the psyche. Then comes divergence through the acquisition of culture, which begins with the ballads, rhymes, fairy tales and epics which are fed into the child. Thus, before a child becomes fully tied up with rational fixations, irrational and mythical imaginations are roused. In India, the great epic of psychic divergence is the *Mahābhārata*. Instead of the archetypes of Jung, it presents an archetypal study which is not based on anthropomorphic imagination. Rather, its basis is in the interplay of the four humors: *vāta, pitta, kapha and sannipāta;* the triad of the modalities of nature: *sattva, rajas* and *tamas;* the two-fold cultural heritage: the gods favoring *daivi sampatti*, and the demons favoring *āsurī sampatti;* and the four-fold psychic conditioning: the *brāhmaṇa, kṣatriya, vaiśya* and *śūdra*. There is also a super-*varṇa* class by itself which has developed the attitude of the renunciate.

This is the basis for the Indian concept of the structure of the psyche. In the general growth and culmination of a developed psyche, nine major moods are seen, ranging from erotics to serenity, which are complemented by forty-nine minor moods which manifest temporarily. Within erotics itself there can be a wide variety of amorous behavior which can range from the sublime to the malicious. Similar differences can be seen in the other eight moods called *bhāvas*. Every *bhāva* has its essence called *rasa*. This gives in general the Indian concept of the psychic formation of a person, whether male or female.

As in the Western study of the human mind, India has also developed a counterpart to the healthy mind. There is a wide classification of divergence in human behavior based on pathologic tendencies. That also has four divisions The first is the physical or chemical basis for malfunctioning of the mind, especially because of malnutrition or an unhygenic social set-up. Then comes the physical chemistry of life being wrongly handled by parents and members of the society who blindly interact with their kids with a view to pushing them to complete their own ambitious designs. Above that comes personality disturbance, emotional disturbance, and spiritual confusion. Two great books of India take up this study very seriously. The *Gītā* gives a classical example of a confused person. Arjuna comes to the battlefield with a resolution to fight and then loses his mind. He exhibits many physical symptoms such as eyes smarting, skin getting the feeling of burning, throat drying up, stuttering and stammering for words, physical energy becoming suspended, hands losing the power to hold his bow in the right position, legs shivering, head going dizzy. It is a good example of mental pathology being transferred to physical disturbance. The eighteen chapters of the *Gītā* are given as a psychotherapy to make Arjuna again stand firm and pick up his bow and quiver of arrows from the ground.

The other story is of Sri Rāmā who became confused about the meaning of life. He became very withdrawn even to the extent of going into catatonia. He was not bathing, not eating, not changing his clothes, not relating with anyone. Viśvamitra found him in that state of mind and wanted him to be taught by the family preceptor Vasiṣṭha. Out of their encounter came the greatest book on depth psychology, Vālmiki's *Yoga Vasiṣṭha Rāmāyaṇa.*

In addition to the general laws and principle differences in heredity and environmental factors which lead one person in one way and another person in another way, King Pravāhaṇa wants Śvetaketu to know the dynamic implied in divergence which ultimately leads a person on a path which passes beyond death. C. G. Jung, in his autobiographic narration called *Memories Dreams and Reflections*, feels inclined to express his gratitude to an unknown hand which led him through the labyrinths of life, bringing him to the right place and right time to be influenced by a certain event or to meet a certain person to turn his path into a certain track. Most people, especially believers in God, think of a hidden destiny which leads people to paths which are benevolent or malevolent. With the advent of institutional religions, groups of people were incorporated into communities of certain doctrines and dogmas. The main cause of a person following the Gospel of Christ or the Word of the *Qur'an* came as a result of historical consequences. People who underwent a change of faith or path did not have any inbuilt hereditary affinity to the religion they joined. It is through a chance factor that the path of a native Indian becomes deflected to the path of the Gospels or the teachings of Islam. Once this deflection is made, not only during that person's life, but for several generations to come, the descendants of the convert hold on to the dogma or creed of these religions which radically separate them from the lifestyles of their forefathers.

The *Upaniṣadic* conviction is that a man is not his ego but his

Self which is existence, subsistence and value dynamics. When such a person's course of life is taken to the path of Christian belief, he has to identify himself as a sinner not for any wrong thing he has done, but because in the articles of faith of the Christians, every person is a descendant of Adam and Eve who disobeyed God and were subjected to the wrath of God. That is considered the original sin. Thus without rhyme or reason, simply because a man was baptized at the time of birth in a church, he and many generations to follow have to believe ardently that they were, are and will be sinners. We should re-state King Pravāhaṇa's question: "What causes a person to lose his original faith that he came from divine origin and believe that he is a sinner?" Then, for the expiation of his sins, a man is not recommended to adhere to the dictates of God all twenty-four hours, but to pay penalties in a church. How money paid to a church can expatiate a man from sin is neither asked nor explained. At the same time, the same man's brother or cousin who has not converted will be keeping the original faith that his being is *sat-cit-ānanda* or *sat-cit-anantam*.

The *Bṛhadāraṇyaka Upaniṣad* teaches the great dictum, *abhaya vai brahma*, "fearlessness is the mark of Self-realization." But if a man embraces Islam, he has to live from that moment in the fear of God. One path advocates fearlessness and another path advocates fear. Hence it is necessary to know what leads a person to have an experience which is radically different from the experiencing of his brother human. We can easily say chance. But chance is not to be left unexamined.

We have to ask ourselves - "Where will I go after my death?" The Christian is assured that he will go to eternal life. The Hindu, on the other hand, believes that if he has not trained himself to bring his knowledge of the Self to regulate his action to absolve him from bondage, he will have to go through chains of rebirth or reincarnation. This possibility is totally denied by the Christian who is willing to wait for God's decree postulated to happen in an unknown future. We cannot examine the postulated theories or dogmas of salvation or *mokṣa* like chemical compounds. That is why in the *Bṛhadāraṇyaka Upaniṣad* there is a graded approach to examine and disprove false assumptions, one after another, until the votary of the *Upaniṣad* is well-informed by looking into the world and examining his or her own experience in the light of each revelation that is given in the *Upaniṣadic Kāṇḍas*. The chain of arguments given in each leads a person from an already accepted position to a more clear certitude which becomes even more acceptable as one grows in one's spiritual understanding. Thus this fundamental question of Pravāhaṇa is to be looked at from a fresh angle to make it relevant to our own times.

Mantra 3

athainam vasatyopamantrayāñcakre; anādṛtya vasatim kumāraḥ pradudrāva; sa ājagāma pitaram; tam hovāca, iti vāv kila no bhavānpurānuśiṣṭānavoca iti; katham sumedha iti; pañca mā praśnān rājanyabandhuraprākṣīta, tato naikañcana vedeti; katame ta iti; ima iti ha pratīkān-yudājahāra.

Word Meanings

atha - then; *upamantrayāñcakre* - (the king) invited; *enam* - him; *vasatyā* - to stay; *kumāraḥ* - the boy; *anādṛtya* - disregarding; *vasatim* - (the invitation) to stay; *pradudrāva* - hurried away; *saḥ* - he; *ājagāma* - went; *pitaram* - to (his) father; *uvāca* - (and) said; *tam* - to him; *bhavān iti* - did you; *avocaḥ iti* - tell; *naḥ* - me; *purā* - before; *anuśiṣṭān* - had instructed (me); *vāva kila* - fully; *katham iti* - what then; *sumedhaḥ* - (my) intelligent child; *rājanya bandhuḥ* - (that) apology for a *kṣatriya*; *aprākṣīt* - asked; *mā* - me; *pañca* - five; *praśnān* - questions; *veda iti* - (I) know; *na* - not; *ekañcana* - even one; *tataḥ* - of them; *katame* - what; *te iti* - (were) they; *ime iti* - these; *udājahāra ha* - (and he) quoted; *pratikāni* - their first words

Then the king invited him to stay. The boy, disregarding the invitation to stay, hurried away. He went to his father and said to him, "Did you not tell me before that you had fully instructed me?" "What then, my intelligent child?" "That apology for a *kṣatriya* asked me five questions, and I did not know one of them." "What were they?" "These," and he quoted their first words.

In mantra three we get a picture of Śvetaketu's pride in his erudition and his sharp reaction to the king who had defeated him. Pravāhaṇa had no ill will towards Śvetaketu. He knew the potential worth of the young boy. He only wanted to correct his pride so that he could become a benevolent and noble teacher like his father Āruṇi Uddālaka. Even though Śvetaketu did not seek wisdom from the king, the king was forgiving and invited him to stay so that he could be taught. The following mantras are a narrative of what transpired after this incident. As these mantras are self-evident of their purport, there is no need for us to make any comment on them. But in deference to the first commentator Śankarācārya, we reproduce here in brief his remarks.

Śankara's Rendition:

> After he had removed his pride of learning, the king invited Śvetaketu to stay, saying, "Please stay here. Let water be brought for washing your feet, and the customary offering to respected guests be made." The boy Śvetaketu, disregarding the invitation to stay, hurried away to his father. He came to his father and said to him, "Well, did you not tell me before, at the time of my finishing the study, that you had instructed me in every branch of learning?" Hearing the reproachful words of his son, the father said, "How did you get hurt, i.e., come by your grief, my sagacious child?" He said, "Listen what happened to me. That wretch of a *kṣatriya* asked me five questions, and I knew not one of them." "Which are they – those questions asked by the king?" – inquired the father. To which the son replied, "These," and he quoted the first words of those questions.

Mantra 4

sa hovāca, tathā nastvam tāta jānīthā yathā yadaham kiñca veda sarvamaham tattubhyamavocam; prehi tu tatra pratītya brahmacaryam vatsyāva iti; bhavāneva gacchatviti; sa ājagāma gautamo yatra pravāhaṇasya jaivaleräsa; tasmā āsanamāhṛtyodakamāhārayāñcakāra, atha hāsmā ardhyam cakāra; tam hovāca, varam bhagavate gautamāya dadma iti.

Word Meanings

saḥ - he (the father); *uvāca ha* - said; *tvam tāta* - (my) child; *naḥ jānīthāḥ* - believe me; *yat kiṁ ca* - whatever; *veda* - know; *tat* - that; *aham* - I; *avocam* - taught; *tubhyam* - you; *sarvam* - all; *yathā tathā* - that; *tu* - but; *prehi* - come; *pratītya* - (let us) go; *tatra* - there; *vatsyāvaḥ iti* - (we both) shall live; *brahmacaryam* - as students; *bhavān* - you; *gacchatu iti* - please go; *eva* - alone; *saḥ gautamaḥ* - then (Āruṇi, descended from) Gautama; *ājagāma* - came; *yatra* - to where; *pravāhaṇasya jaivaleḥ* - King Pravāhaṇa, the son of Jīvala; *asa* - was (giving audience); *āhṛtya* - (the King) offered; *tasmai* - him; *āsanam* - a seat; *āhārayāñcakāra* - had brought; *udakam* - water; *cakāra* - made; *asmai* - to him; *ardhyam* - reverential offering; *atha ha* - then; *uvāca ha* - (he) said; *dadmaḥ iti* - (we) offer; *tam bhagavate gautamāya* - venerable Gautama; *varam* - a boon

The father said, "My child, believe me, whatever I know I taught you all that. But come, let us go there and live as students." "You go alone, please." Then Gautama came to where King Pravāhaṇa, the son of Jīvala, was giving audience. The king offered him a seat, had water brought for him, and made him the reverential offering. Then he said, "We offer venerable Gautama a boon."

Śankara's Rendition:

The father, to soothe his angry child said, "My child, believe me, whatever of meditations I knew, I told you every bit of it. Who is dearer to me than you, for whom I would withhold anything? I too do not know what the king asked about. Therefore come, let us go there and live as students with the king to learn it." The boy said, "You go alone, please, I do not care to see his face." At this, Gautama came to where King Pravāhaṇa, the son of

Jīvala, was holding a sitting, or giving audience. The king gave him a respectable seat, had water brought for him, his guest Gautama, through servants, and made him the reverential offering *(ardhya)* through his priest, as also the *madhuparka* with sacred texts uttered. Having thus worshipped him, he said to him, "We will give to revered Gautama a boon," consisting of cows, horses, etc.

Mantra 5

sa hovāca, pratijñāto mā eṣa varaḥ; yām tu kumārasyānte vācamabhāṣathāstām me brūhīti.

Word Meanings

saḥ - he (Āruṇi); *uvāca ha* - said; *pratijñātaḥ* - you have promised; *me* - to me; *eṣaḥ* - this; *varaḥ* - boon; *brūhi iti* - (please) explain; *me* - to me; *tam yam* - that which; *abhāṣathāḥ* - (you) spoke; *tu* - about; *kumārasya ante* - to (my) boy

Āruṇi said, "You have promised me this boon. Please explain to me that which you spoke about to my boy."

Śankara's Rendition:

Gautama said, "You have promised me this boon. Make yourself firm in this promise. Please tell me what you spoke to my boy, or son, about - those questions. This is my boon."

Mantra 6

sa hovāca, daiveṣu vai gautama tadvareṣu, mānuṣāṇām brūhīti.

Word Meanings

saḥ - he (the king); *uvāca ha* - said; *tat* - that; *vai* - is a; *daiveṣu* - divine; *vareṣu* - boon; *gautama* - Gautama; *brūhi iti* - ask; *mānuṣāṇām* - a human boon

The king said, "That is a divine boon, Gautama. Please ask a human boon."

Śankara's Rendition:

The king said, "This what you ask, comes under heavenly boons, Gautama. Please ask some human boon."

Mantra 7

sa hovāca, vijñāyate hāsti hiraṇyasyāpāttam goaśvānām dāsīnām pravārāṇām paridhānasya, mā no bhavān-bahoranantasyāparyantasyābhyavadānyo bhūditi; sa vai gautama tīrthenecchāsā iti; upaimyaham bhavantamiti; vācā ha smaiva pūrva upayanti, sa hopāyanakīrtyovāsa.

Word Meanings

saḥ - he (Āruṇi); *uvāca ha* - said; *vijñāyate ha* - you know; *asti apāttam* - I have; *hiraṇyasya* - gold; *goaśvānām* - cattle and horses; *dāsīnām* - maid-servants; *pravārāṇām* - retinue; *paridhānasya* - (and) apparel; *bhavān mā* - (please do) not; *bhūta iti* - be; *avadānyaḥ* - ungenerous; *naḥ abhi* - towards me (alone); *vittasya* - regarding this wealth; *bahoḥ* - plentiful; *anantasya* - inexhaustible; *aparyantasya* - infinite; *saḥ* - (then) you; *icchāsau iti* - must seek it; *vai tīrthena* - according to form; *gautama* - Gautama; *aham* - I; *upaimi iti* - approach; *bhavantam* - you (as a disciple); *pūrve* - the ancients; *upayanti* - used to approach (a teacher); *ha eva* - simply; *vaca* - through declaration; *saḥ* - he; *uvāsa ha* - lived (with the king as a student); *upāyan kīrtyā* - by merely announcing (that he was at his service)

Āruṇi said, "You know that I have gold, cattle and horses, maid-servants, retinue, and apparel. Please do not be ungenerous towards me alone regarding this plentiful, infinite and inexhaustible (wealth)." "Then you must seek it according to form, Gautama." "I approach you (as a disciple)." The ancients used to approach a teacher simply through declaration. He lived with the king as a student by merely announcing that he was at his service.

Śankara's Rendition:

Gautama said, "You too know that I have them. So the human boon that you propose to give me will do me no good. Because I too already have plenty of gold, cattle and horses, maid-servants, retinue and dress." The word *apāttam asti* (there is attainment) should be connected with all the terms. "And what I already have, neither I should ask of you, nor you should give me. You have promised me a boon. You alone know what is proper under the circumstances – that you should keep your promise. I have also another thing in my mind: Having been generous everywhere, be not ungenerous, stingy, towards me alone regarding this wealth – plentiful, infinite, i.e., producing such results, and inexhaustible, i.e., reaching down to one's sons and grandsons. You should not deny such wealth to me alone. You will not deny it to anybody else." Thus addressed, the king said, "Then you must seek to have this learning according to form, that prescribed by the scriptures." At this Gautama said, "I approach you as a student." The ancients – *brāhmaṇas* seeking instructions from *kṣatriyas* or *vaiśyas*, or *kṣatriyas* seeking it from *vaiśyas*, as a matter of necessity – used to approach a teacher simply through declaration, not by actually approaching his feet or serving him. Hence Gautama lived as a student by merely announcing that he was at his service, without actually approaching the king's feet.

Mantra 8

sa hovāca, tathā nastvam gautama māparādhāstava ca pitāmahā yathā, iyam vidyetaḥ pūrvam na kasmiṃścana brāhmaṇa uvāsa; tām tvaham tubhyam vakṣyāmi, ko hi tvaivam bruvantamarhati pratyākhyātumiti.

Word Meanings

saḥ - he (the king) *uvāca ha* - said; *ma* - (please do) not; *aparādhāḥ* - take offense; *naḥ* - with us; *tvam gautama* - Gautama; *yathā tathā* - as; *tava* - your; *pitāmahāḥ* - paternal grandfathers (did not with ours); *itaḥ pūrvam* - before this; *iyam* - this; *vidyā* - knowledge; *na* - never; *uvāsa* - rested; *kasmiṃścana brāhmaṇe* - with any *brāhmaṇa; tu* - but; *aham* - I; *vakṣyāmi* - shall impart; *tam* - it; *tubhyam* - to you; *hi* - for; *kaḥ* - who; *arhati iti* - can; *pratyākhyātum* - refuse; *tvā* - you; *bruvantam* - (when) speak; *evam* - like this

The king said: "Please do not take offense with us, Gautama, as your paternal grandfathers did not with ours. Before this, this knowledge never rested with a *brāhmaṇa*. But I shall teach it to you; for who can refuse you when you speak like this?"

Śankara's Rendition:

When Gautama thus declared his preference for this unavoidable humiliation to ignorance, the king, thinking that he was hurt, said begging his pardon: "Please do not take offense with us, Gautama, as your paternal grandfathers did not with ours. That is to say, you should observe that attitude of your grandfathers towards us. Know that before this transmission to you, this learning that you have asked for never rested with a *brāhmaṇa*. It has all along come down through a line of *kṣatriya* teachers. I too should, if possible, maintain that tradition. Hence I said, 'This comes under heavenly boons, Gautama.

Please ask some human boon' (VI.2.6). But it cannot be maintained any more, for your boon cannot be withheld. I shall teach even this learning to you; for who else even can refuse you when you speak like this? Then why should I not teach it to you?"

As an introduction to the dialogue between Pravāhaṇa and Śvetaketu, Śankara gave certain hints to understand the context of the dialogue and the meaning of the words spoken by the king. In the first question which Pravāhaṇa asked, the reference is to people who start out walking in the same path. At some stage deviation comes, and some people walk in one direction while others go in another direction. Whatever the culture, education or beliefs they had originally, when they enter into divergent paths, great changes come over them. By taking divergent routes they do not arrive at the same goal. The king was asking why people who are alike in many things have a destiny which takes them in different directions. It is important to know how one attains realization while another takes the path of repeated births and deaths. The second question was in reference to the reincarnation of people: "How do people who have taken the path of return come back, after a certain period, to live in another body?" The third question was that if people continuously die and go to another world, that world should have a burst of population. But there is no evidence that such a thing happens. The king asked "Why?" The next question refers to the propitiations made at the time of sacrifice. When the libations are offered, after how many does the offered water conduct the spoken word of the *adhvarya?* It is believed that the person who chants the mantra and gives the libation along with it become identical.

Next was a reference to the mantra the king had heard, that some go to the path of shining ones (*devayāṇa*) and some ito the path of the departed ones. (*pitṛyāṇa*) The *karma* that is done by the individuated person determines the path one goes in. The king asked if Śvetaketu knew what discipline one should practice to be qualified to enter the world of shining ones. The mantra described the *karmas* related to the path of no return as different from the *karmas* that bring the departed back again. The king wanted Śvetaketu to give the pertinent mantra if he knew it.

Further the king said that the whole world has been subjected to the law which sends a few on one path and most on the other.

He says both paths lie between heaven (the father) and earth (the mother). Between these two worlds is a relativistic world where disciplines are necessary to go from the world of mortality to the world of immortality.

Śvetaketu was unable to answer any of the king's questions so the king generously requested that he remain as a guest. He was willing to initiate Śvetaketu into these secrets. But being haughty by temperament, Śvetaketu was angry with his father who he thought had taught him all there was to know. Śvetaketu had come to the conclusion that, under the tutelage of his father, Uddālaka, he had learned everything and that there was nothing more to be taught.

Uddālaka was the son of Āruṇi and Āruṇi was the son of Gautama. Thus he had a great spiritual heritage. So when he went to see Pravāhaṇa, the king received him with great honor. In those days it was customary for rishis to visit kings and the kings always honored them by giving them many presents. When Pravāhaṇa was about to honor Uddālaka, he said he did not come in search of gifts, but wanted to know the answers to the questions asked to his son. But the king said the answers to those questions pertained to the divine and asked him to make a request on the human level. Then Gautama politely said that the king himself knew that he was not in need of worldly gifts. He had plenty and had come as a disciple wanting to be bestowed with the gift of wisdom.

On hearing this, the king said that the imparting of wisdom from a *guru* to a disciple should be in conformity with tradition. Although it was not normal for a *brāhmaṇa* to learn wisdom from a *kṣatriya*, Uddālaka pointed out that even in previous days there had been occasions for *brāhmaṇas* to learn wisdom from *kṣatriyas* or *vaiśyas*. They were not expected to give special services to a *guru*, but needed only to say "Accept me as a disciple." Uddālaka was willing to openly recognize King Pravāhaṇa as his *guru* and wanted to be accepted as his disciple.

In response to this request of a *brāhmaṇa* of great repute, descending from a family of wisdom teachers, the king politely said: "Please do not consider that I have done any willful disgrace to you. Your father and grandfathers never considered our predecessors as intending to do any wrong to them. We have only incidentally come to this situation." The king again made it clear that the wisdom which he had had never been known by any *brāhmaṇa.* He had been preserving the traditional wisdom given to him by his predecessors and it was his duty to preserve it as a treasure. He repeated that the blessings Uddālaka was seeking belonged to the gods. But the king was very moved by the earnestness of Uddālaka as a seeker. So he said that when he made such a request, he could not refuse. The teaching which we are going to learn in the next several mantras is very rare.

Mantra 9

> *asau vai loko'gnirgautama; tasyāditya eva samit, raśmayo dhūmaḥ, aharārciḥ, diśo'ṅgārāḥ, avāntaradiśo visphuliṅgāḥ, tasminnetasminnagnau devāḥ śraddhām juhvati; tasyā āhutyai somo rājā sambhavati.*

Word Meanings

asau lokaḥ - that world (heaven); *gautama* - O Gautama; *vai* - verily; *agniḥ* - (is) fire; *ādityaḥ eva* - the sun (is); *tasya* - its; *samit* - fuel; *raśmayaḥ* - (the) rays; *dhūmaḥ* - (its) smoke; *ahaḥ* - the day; *arciḥ* - (its) flame; *diśaḥ* - the four directions; *aṅgārāḥ* - (its) cinders; *avāntaradiśaḥ* - the intermediate directions; *visphuliṅgāḥ* - (its) sparks; *tasmin etasmin* - in this; *agnau* - fire; *devāḥ* - the gods; *juhvati* - offer; *śraddhām* - faith; *tasyāḥ āhutyai* - out of that offering; *rājā* - King; *somaḥ* - Soma; *sambhavati* - is born

That world (heaven), O Gautama, verily is fire, the sun its fuel, the rays its smoke, the day its flame, the four directions its cinders, and the intermediate directions its sparks. In this fire the gods offer faith. Out of that offering King Soma is born.

To solve a problem in modern science, first a postulation is made. The verity of the postulation is proved by experimentation. Experiments are in-depth observations. The corresponding method used in the *Upaniṣads* is analogy (*upamāna*). The valid testimony behind analogy is the infallible truth of the *śruti*. The *śruti* is an *a priori* book of wisdom in which a person is given a formula which can be taken for deep pondering. To aid the pondering, examples are given. The votary of the *Upaniṣad* places his or her trust in the infallibility of the *śruti*. At the same time he or she is given full freedom to investigate its truth, not as a disbeliever or as an agnostic, but as one who is willing to go into all the details of the formula given.

Even if the inquiry does not give immediate results or conviction of the truth of what is said, the disciplined aspirant (*sādhaka*), is not in any haste to arrive at negative conclusions. Rather, if one does not arrive at a conclusive proof immediately, one makes oneself a fully restrained seeker without any break. This persistence is the *tapas* of the disciplined inquirer. *Tapas* is intensifying one's deep probe, anticipating all the while that at least certain positive signals will come to encourage one on one's path. Thus *svādhyāya* and *tapas* go hand in hand. *Svādhyāya* is self-study; *tapas* is intensifying one's search.

An illustration is only an indication and not a statement of facts. So it is advised that no allegory is to be pressed too far. In every descriptive illustration there will be only a few relevant points of correlation. When one comes to the tether end of a specific search, the student is advised to suspend judgment and further purify himself or herself so that no taint of ego will cast its shadow on the path of his or her search. This mantra presents a frame of reference which guides the student to look for a one-to-one correspondence between the details of a burnt sacrifice and a cosmic ensemble. It is mainly given to take the mind of the aspirant out of narrow parochial and relativistic contexts which cannot yield higher wisdom.

It begins with the revelation that the sky above (heaven) is fire. It is inevitable in a sacrifice to have fire in which to put the offerings. The fire is the main allegoric representation of purification and transformation of the earthly into the heavenly. Earth is considered as the chosen field in which to do sacrifice. The sacrificial fire leaps toward the heaven above taking along with it the smoke carrying the fragrance of whatever has been offered in the fire.

Our commentary on the horse (*aśva*) and horse sacrifice (*aśvamedha*) at the beginning of this *Upaniṣad* shows how it brought about an astounding revolution in Vedic culture by substituting the unclean and murderous forms of sacrifice with meditation and contemplation. In the earliest forms of sacrifice described in the *Śatapatha Brāhmaṇa* the victim was Viśvarūpa the Tvaṣṭra, a member of the demonic class. In the *Taittirīya Samhita* II.5.I.1, Viśvarūpa the Tvaṣṭra is said to have been a sister's son of the *asuras*, and house priest to the *devas*. He was killed by Indra because he had secretly contrived to let the oblations go to the *asuras* instead of to the *devas*. The habitation of both the *deva* and the *asura* are in the body/mind/spirit of a person. As austerities (*tapas*) and mortifications are mainly for the expiation of the sins of the body, the sacrificed animal is none other than the physical body of the sacrificer.

But it seems that from the very beginning of the Vedic cult, this essential key of symbolism was lost. Naturally one does not like to kill oneself, so in ancient days they killed another as an equal. This very unclean, diabolic, murderous ritual of killing a fellow human and roasting him in the altar got into the Vedic practices. If instead of self-immolation, burning another person alive was tolerated, then for the same reason burning of domestic animals instead of humans became a still more admissible practice. But in the eye of the rishi of the *Bṛhadāraṇyaka Upaniṣad* that was abominable, cruel and unclean. That is why he took it as a symbol and began with the description of the sacrificial horse as *viśvarūpa* (I.1.1):

> *AUM*. The head of the sacrificial horse is verily the dawn, the eye of the sacrificial horse is the sun, its vital force is the air, the open mouth the fire named *vaiśvānaraḥ*, the trunk the year, the back the heaven, the belly the sky, the hoof the earth, the flanks the four directions, the ribs the intermediate directions, the limbs the seasons, the joints the months and fortnights, the feet the days and nights, the bones the stars and the flesh the clouds, the half-digested food (in the stomach) is the sand, the blood-vessels are the rivers, the liver and spleen the mountains, the hairs the herbs and trees, the forepart the ascending sun, the hind part the setting sun. Its yawn is lightning, its shaking the body is thunder, its making water is rain, and its neighing is indeed speech. [55]

From all the items mentioned here we get a complete picture of the sacrificial horse described in the form of the universe (*viśvarūpa*). Obviously, nobody can strangle, kill or roast the universe. Hence this is not a sacrifice as conceived in the *Vedas*. It befits the spirit of *Vedānta* in which love and compassion are considered the highest qualities which enhance the dignity of humankind. Now at the close of the *Upaniṣad* the rishi is referring back to what was mentioned in the first *adhyāya* to emphasize that *Veda* and *Vedānta* are not to be taken literally, but poetically, allegorically, metaphorically and symbolically. Similarly when Narayana Guru saw the horrid practice of sacrificing goats in a temple, he denounced it and asked the priest to cut a cucumber if he could not complete his *pūja* without using his hatchet.

Although human beings give a lot of praise to restraint, compassion and a self-sacrificing attitude to save the world, we can see in all religions an admission of cruelty in the form of slaughter coming at the beginning stages. From this, religions derived the principle of the deluder as opposed to divinity. That comes in Genesis as the serpent, in Hindu theories as *avidyā*, in Islamic texts as Iblis, in Buddhist texts as Māra. Although the Buddhist and Christian senses of piety afterwards became a normative notion of the good, Hindus in Vedic *brahminism* thought it was illogical to conceive the whole or total without negativity. They saw good and evil as part and parcel of the whole. For example their concept of the female deity has four aspects. To begin with, the extreme negative female deity is called Mahākāli. From that a more evolutionary picture is given, that of the animal mother who is protective of her offspring; she is called Durga the Defender. *Durg* means a citadel. When the mother hen spreads her wings and keeps all her little ones under them to protect them from hawks, she is acting as Durga, making a fortress around her chicks with her own wings. The next is a more humanized deity, the ambitious Lakṣmi who represents both human and divine wealth. Finally we come to the sublime Mahāsarasvati, the patron goddess of music and wisdom.

We human beings have in us both the divine and the demonic. The fire in us has also all these gradations. Both males and females of living beings are struck by the lightning of erotic passions. The second fire in us is the fire of the digestive system into which gross food is offered, purified and transferred as vital energy to all the organs of the body. The third fire is in the heart as burning love or its counterpart hatred. A more noble aspect of fire is in the word we speak which can burn away false notions and uphold truth. The fire of the mind is more representative of all the fires on earth. It is accompanied by the five sense organs, the cognitive power and the volitional faculties. Hence the seven fires in a person are compared to the seven tongues of fire. The same fire is also seen in the fire of the hearth, the fire in earth as volcanoes, the fire in the cloud as lightning, the fire in the leaves of vegetation that cook the food and ultimately the fire in the sun. When we understand this the *Upaniṣadic* mantra makes sense. Fire is everywhere.

In his commentary, Śankara indicates one of the greatest secrets of *Upaniṣadic* diction: a term makes correct sense only when it is read as solely belonging to the given frame of reference on each occasion because the context gives the right meaning. Shifting the reference from one place to another carries with it an altogether different conceptual context and operational dynamics. We have already given the local fixation of fire in different situations. When the fire is at the tip of the spine, it is to be known as the dynamic of channeling vital or nerve energy to all parts of the body. Yogis meditate on that center as *muladhara*, visualizing in their meditation the golden fire from which the entire functional capability of the body arises. When the same fire is shifted to the *svādiṣṭhāna* at the base of the genital, its role is to perpetuate the proliferation of nature by rousing the libidinal erotics. All the latent urges of sexual passion are radiated from that center. When the same fire is located in the *maṇipura*, its function is to maintain the metabolism of the whole body and separate the nutrition of the food from what is being digested. It has the role of building up the psychophysical energy and also dealing with its correct distribution to each organ or faculty as is needed from moment to moment. The same fire occurring in the heart merges the bodily function into the mental. The heart has to cater both to the demonic urges of the body and the sublime demands of the Self, touching both the aesthetic needs as well as intellectual definitives. In the vocal faculty, the flame of fire has innumerable qualities such as of regularizing its sonal features and giving effect to the semiosis of transforming ideas into words.

Although the tongue is very involved in the expression of speech, the same tongue is literally fired by the appreciation of the taste buds which are in league with the nose to blend taste and odor. The fires in the tactual, visual and audio faculties are of a complementary nature in fixing the configurations of perception. This orderly way of shifting the energy dynamics from location to location causes variation in the psychophysical function of the chemistry of the body as well as the semiosis of our thought processes. In the present series of mantras, we see not only the shifting of the location of fire, but also the transformation that happens as we move from primary cause to secondary effect, each in turn becoming a succeeding causal factor.

First we read of the cosmic fire. The entire universe with all its innumerable galactical systems is operating on a thermodynamic basis. Hence, the main symbol of fire which is seen in the heavenly sky above us is the sun. Another methodologic excellence of the *Bṛhadāraṇyaka Upaniṣad* is that the ground always precedes the figure and the figure arises out of the ground. In this case what Pravāhaṇa calls "that world" is the ground and the figure located in it is the sun. Then that sun is explained as the fuel that is burnt. Here the fuel precedes the brilliancy and the radiance of the sun. Another beautiful implication is that when we move from the ground to the figure, the figure dominates the entire field. Hence it is said that when the sun burns, the heavens are illuminated. However bright and inestimable are the rays coming from the sun, the rays are the effect. The kindling of the sun comes first. When fire burns, for instance in a forest, what is seen in the distance is the smoke rising up. Similarly, in spite of the luminosity of the sunlight, its rays are termed by the rishi as smoke. If pure light is invisible and transparent, smoke has the effect of translucency because it combines within it the ability to highlight and produce simultaneously the shadow of the object on which it falls. Hence it is most appropriate to call the rays of the sun its smoke.

In burning fire we see the fuel changing into leaping flames, the leaping flames tapering and becoming invisible in the smoke that rises. In the center there is great brightness. The brightness of the sun illuminates the globe (earth) in alternations of day and night. Day is identified with the bright light in the center. So far as we are concerned, our orientation comes from witnessing the rising sun. After locating the East, we conceive of the West, South and North. Even after the sun has set, we carry in our minds the memories of the directions. Similarly, after the burning of a fire, we can still see the leftover cinders. Hence it is said the four directions are its cinders. Even though the day is a continuous illumination, it specifically highlights innumerable finite objects in all four directions. This finitude of the sunlight is called the sparks.

The gods dwell in us as our sense organs which can identify with the higher values of life. Our senses of hearing, touch, sight, taste and odor can all turn towards the highest. Hence it is said that in this fire the gods offer faith. In the opening *adhyāya* of the *Upaniṣad,* when the first *prajāpati* came out of the basic elements, it worshipped itself and water came from it. There was no other water for libation (*arcana*), hence it was called *arka. Arka* implies within it both the sun and water. Here faith is identified with liquid oblations. Out of that offering King Soma is born. In the actual sacrificial ritual a juice is crushed out of the *soma* creeper which has the quality of alcoholic spirits. In the *Śatapatha Brāhmaṇa* we hear that the sacrificial fire is pleased when the priests giving their service in sacrifice partake of the burnt leftover of the sacrifice and drink the wine. *Soma* is also the moon and the lord of the heart. We know that when a man consumes wine, his brain is doused and his heart is overjoyed. Hence the *soma* that is spoken of here is not to be mistaken for the moon in the sky, but real spirits that are drunk by the sacrificer. The symbolism given here helps us to go back and forth between the first *adhyāya* and the last *adhyāya* like a weaver with warp and woof. Considering all the technicalities brought in such subtle ways through poetic symbolism, the ingenuity shown by the rishi is to be admired as most praiseworthy. In literature we rarely read anything like these insightful intuitional correlatives that are so beautifully tied up. It gives us a model of relating one aspect of life to another.

In the Indian scriptures we find that all arguments oscillate between the macrocosm and the microcosm. Sun is the light of the macrocosm. In the microcosm the *ātman* is the sun which manifests in the sense organs. The world is a wide arena of life. Innumerable are the persons in this world who are all said to be individuations of the *ātman* or the Self. Every sense organ is like a sacrificial fire. Hearing, touching, seeing, tasting, and smelling are like flames licking whatever is sacrificed in the fire of perception. The energies that are pooled, separated, controlled and specifically directed are like the smoke produced when the fuel is in a process of burning. What is heard, touched, seen, tasted and smelled are all gathered into the mind to assess their meaning and value. When the smoke of fire clears, the flame alone is seen in the center; after the confusion of sensory apprehension there arises to each person a process of cognition. Cognition is made by the same faculty in everyone but people in this world are born under different circumstances, nourished differently and culturally variant, so the significance of each one's perceptions can diverge. In all living beings, we can see comparative variations in their growth patterns and qualitative variations as we go from one offspring to the next. All these are to be attributed to the activities and nourishment we get day after day ruled by the sun.

The sun aids our cognitive process, but we also have an emotional life with aesthetic variation and a spectrum of value dynamics which we do not live by the tenets of cold logic alone. Every experience we have evolves in us a certain like or dislike which adds to the preferential structuring of our lives. These are complementary to the search for value vision (*ānanda*) in the individual. Here we are told that a person is very much under the sway of *soma*, the invisible dynamics of the spirit.

The *Upaniṣads* maintain the validity of reincarnation in accordance with the *karma* of each person, how a person conducted himself or herself in the world, day and night, intellectually as well as emotionally. The question arises as to why there is incarnation at all. Microscopic forms of life like bacteria are made immortal with a scheme of duplication and replication. The life span of a bacteria is only for a short period during which it multiplies. Even if it is exposed to antibodies, it develops a power to resist their effect. In the scheme of things all forms of life have to be equipped with the ability to overcome time and death. The evolutionary process extended to human beings is to acquire the know-how of living through a number of trials and errors. One life-time is not enough to become fully adapted. Life in the day time under the sun is controlled by natural laws. But one's emotional life is in the throes of fluctuations all the time.

Earlier we spoke of the divine, demonic and human aspects dwelling in a person. In the *Śatapatha Brāhmaṇa* we read how the law of life reclaims the shining ones to return to this world, along with the dead person's spirit. The demonic aspects which are not resolved in one life are to be cleansed, probably by exposing that person again to a series of action situations in which several corrections can be made by him or her. The return is conceived as a descent back into earth. Of course, this is a highly speculative field and we have no scientific clues to get at the truth of what is concluded. There are several versions of the Book of the Dead, such as of the Egyptians, the Tibetans, the Hindus, the Christians, etc. On the whole, humanity everywhere assumes that death is not the final end, although the theories regarding what happens after death differ widely. Bearing this in mind, the mantra will give us more and more suggestions which are relevant to the theories of eschatology and reincarnation.

Mantra 10

parjanyo vā agnigautama; tasya samvatsara eva samit, abhrāṇi dhūmaḥ, vidyudarciḥ, aśanirangārāḥ, hrādunayo visphuliṅgāḥ, tasminnetasminnagnau devaḥ somam rājānam juhvati; tasya āhutyai vṛṣṭiḥ sambhavati.

Word Meanings

parjanyaḥ - Parjanya (the god of rain); *gautama* - O Gautama; *agniḥ* - (is) fire; *samvatsaraḥ* - the year; *tasya* - its; *samit* - fuel; *abhrāṇi* - clouds; *dhūmaḥ* - (its) smoke; *vidyut* - lightning; *arciḥ* - (its) flame; *aśaniḥ* - the thunderbolt; *aṅgārāḥ* - (its) cinders; *hrādunayaḥ* - the rumblings; *visphuliṅgāḥ* - (its) sparks; *tasmin etasmin* - in this; *agnau* - fire; *devaḥ* - the gods; *juhvati* - offer; *somam rājānam* - King Soma; *tasyaḥ āhutyai* - out of that offering; *vṛṣṭiḥ* - rain; *sambhavati* - is born

Parjanya (the god of rain), O Gautama, is fire, the year its fuel, the clouds its smoke, lightning its flame, the thunderbolt its cinders, and the rumblings its sparks. In this fire the gods offer King Soma. Out of that offering rain is produced.

In this mantra fire is identified with the god of rain and its fuel is the year. When the advent of *prajāpati* was first mentioned, there was a reference to the first form of life lying in wait in an egg for one year, *samvatsara*. Here time is not to be understood as the conventional time shown by the calendar. It is a measure of a process from its beginning to a peak of growth or maturation and finally reaching its terminus. From the beginning to the end is a unit of time, because time is eventuality. Bergson says that where there is no event, there is no time. Time is conditional and relative to becoming. Most people on earth have no idea what happens when an organism comes to the cessation of its biologic integrity. All that we know is that the functional dynamics of the organism are annulled.

As people have been seeing a versatile inner monitor in the living body, they cannot come to the sudden conclusion that the monitor no longer exists. So they think of it as a mysterious ghost or spirit that has secretly left the body and gone elsewhere. People describe the departure of the ghost from the dead body as a return to God or as a return to a hypothetical world of the dead. In the mind of most people, the location to which life has departed is "elsewhere." To conceive such an idea all that one needs is an ability to imagine. But that leads to Pravāhaṇa's next question to Śvetaketu: "How does that which has departed from a well-structured and functioning body into oblivion come back to claim another body and live in it?" Although this is a theme for speculation, one cannot easily give a convincing answer to the question.

When a sacrifice is made, the fire leaps into the sky. The spiraling smoke goes very high and looks as if it cannot be distinguished from a cloud that floats in the sky. The clouds vanish and, sometimes after days or months, gather again in the horizon and move in different directions until the sky is overcast. There are many varieties of clouds. Van Nostrand's *The Encyclopedia of Science* says that a full discussion of all varieties of clouds and supplementary features would be very elaborate. It mentions at least ten forms of clouds including cirrus (a high-altitude crystal cloud in the form of delicate white filaments), cirrocumulus (another high altitude cloud composed of supercooled water droplets), and altocumulus (a middle altitude water cloud). Clouds are mentioned in this mantra as a symbol of the Indian theory of the return of the departed. In a cloud formation, many particles in the atmosphere give themselves to become the nucleus of droplets which are forming. Rain contains innumerable such droplets which continuously change shape as they move.

Indians believe that after the maturation of the post-mortem existence of a departed person, when its unfinished *karma* weighs it down, it has to find appropriate parents. Just as it is said that marriages are made in heaven, in the coupling of male and female, a mysterious hand is supposed to bring together a male and female with polarized psyches which are complementary. This complementarity can also mean having reciprocity as well as contradiction. In any case, the formation of a droplet of rain is very much like the formation of a fruit in which a seed of programmed evolution is enclosed. The water droplets formed at high altitudes are like hungry parasites which eat various kinds of dust particles.

It is speculated that a departed soul lands in one such droplet and, with other droplets in a rain cloud, traverses through the atmosphere. By some mysterious destiny, an attraction between earth and the clouds happens which can be compared to a radar-operated aircraft being signaled to land at a particular spot by the ground engineer of an air station. One cannot say in which field or mountain or farm or watery area the rain will fall. If perchance that particular seeded droplet falls in the water and a fish gulps it, the theory goes that the incumbent *jīva* to be individuated in a person will lie in secret in the fish, waiting to be eaten by a prospective parent. Or it may go into a flower as honey where it remains for a prospective taster of the honey. Or, it becomes a seed along with the natural seeds of a plant. There are innumerable possible inlets for the revisiting soul to get hold of the right parents. In their mating, three factors become united: the essence of a previous person, the genetic code of the father and the genetic code of the mother. By reshuffling and restructuring, it is as if the visiting soul arranges the home where it will be nurtured to get a body that has all the instrumentation required for the continuity of its *karma*.

Every returning soul is said to be an unfinished gestalt. The new life begins with the loose ends of the *karma* of a previous life. It takes about a year (*saṁvatsara*) for it to be structured into the body of a male or a female. Thus, for the return of a departed soul, these things are necessary: rain and cloud with the backdrop of the sun or thermal energy representing the fire. A distinct difference between the theory of evolution and the Indian theory of rebirth is that of choice. The theory of evolution relies on the chance factor to explain the manifestation of mutation. But Indian eschatologists think that the individual to be born has a choice of parents. If for some reason a mistake is made in the choice, the embryo gives up the ghost, causing a miscarriage.

A question can be asked here: When there are forty-six chromosomes between father and mother, out of which twenty-three pairs are to be chosen, how does the incumbent life (*jīva*), choose from the father and mother the right kind of psychophysical elements to continue its *karma*? The answer is that the choice is made on the basis of the quality of the *karma* which is brought over by the subtle body which itself is carried to a new life by *sūtrātma*. If a magnet is placed under a paper on which iron filings are put, they suddenly move from their original position to the shape of the magnetic forces of the magnet kept underneath. Similarly, there is an attraction and repulsion operating in the selection of chromosomes in what is becoming an embryo. These are some of the subtleties hinted at by this mantra.

Mantra 11

ayam vai loko'gnirgautama; tasya pṛthivyeva samit, agnirdhūmaḥ, rātrirarciḥ, candramā aṅgārāḥ, nakṣatrāṇi visphuliṅgāḥ; tasminnetasminnagnau devā vṛṣṭim juhvati; tasyā āhutyā annam sambhavati.

Word Meanings

ayam - this; *lokaḥ* - world; *gautama* - O Gautama; *agniḥ* - (is) fire; *pṛthivī* - the earth; *tasya* - its; *samit* - fuel; *agni* - fire; *dhūmaḥ* - (its) smoke; *rātriḥ* - the night; *arciḥ* - (its) flame; *candramāḥ* - the moon; *aṅgārāḥ* - (its) cinders; *nakṣatrāṇi* - the stars; *visphuliṅgāḥ* - (its) sparks; *tasmin etasmin* - in this; *agnau* - fire; *devaḥ* - the gods; *juhvati* - offer; *vṛṣṭim* - rain; *tasyaḥ āhutyai* - out of that offering; *annam* - food; *sambhavati* - is born

This world, O Gautama, is fire, the earth is its fuel, fire its smoke, the night its flame, the moon its cinders, and the stars its sparks. In this fire the gods offer rain. Out of that offering food is produced.

In India it is a popular belief that only a poet can be a true seer. In the *Īśāvāsya Upaniṣad* this world is equated to the poetic creation of the Supreme. What is intuitively visualized and sung by the poet is spread out in time and space as this variegated world of immaculate beauty. There is nothing unnecessary in the fantasy of the creator. Good and bad, bright and dull, gold and mud, wise and idiotic, sane and insane, life and death - all are equally necessary to make our world. This mantra could have come only from a great genius, the best among poets.

Although this mantra was given fifteen hundred years before Jesus Christ, it is relevant for the particular time in which we live. It eulogizes the supreme excellence of earth. In our own time we have destroyed earth's supreme beauty and emptied out its crust in our greed for rare metals. We have poisoned the soil in the process of converting the simple livelihood of farming into agro-industry which reaps commercial dividends. The earth is dying every hour in agony and pain. From the deserts we are sucking out the last drops of oil. The sickly minds of belligerent leaders have set fire to billions of gallons of petrol which have polluted the earth, the water and the atmosphere. The poisons that are being spit out by innumerable industrial complexes around the world have destroyed the fragile ozone layer which protects the earth from harmful ultraviolet rays. Considering this, a comet hitting Jupiter is only a minor tragedy. It is about this earth the rishi is speaking to us so fondly. Today every reasonable person living anywhere in the world is agonized by the pathetic conditions of human enmity so blatantly shown to all the continents of the world.

When people stand at the foot of a Himalayan deodar or California sequoia, they are humiliated, feeling like small crickets lost in the shade of the trees. Ancient people were in love with these mammoth trees. Even now, in oriental countries we can see simple peasants offering flowers at the roots of a great tree, waving fires of camphor before it, and hugging it, seeking its blessings. In the ancient myths we read of trees like the holy fig (*asvatha*) in India, under which Buddha received his enlightenment. In the Old Testament we read of the Tree of Knowledge which opened the eyes of Adam and Eve. In the Scandinavian myths we read of the world tree of Yggdrasil. No Christmas festival is considered complete without a decorated Christmas tree.

When we read, "the earth is its fuel and fire is its smoke," what is the smoke referred to here? When fire burns, the smoke goes skyward. If the earth is the sacrificial fire, what issues out of it is not flame, but the sprouts of seeds. A seed which is smaller than a mustard seed can grow to great heights. It can cover a large area with its outspread branches. Some trees have such beautiful red blossoms that they can be mistaken for flames of the forest. The poetic allegory of seeing the vegetation of the earth as the earth's aspiration rising to kiss the sun is more true than a literary word of ornamentation. The fuel which people know is dry wood. If not interfered with by man, trees live for thousands of years. The Grand Duke of California is the pride of the North American nation. Many people go as pilgrims to show their reverence to this tree in the Sequoia forest which is nearly 4000 years old. In India, one of the most ancient temples at Kāncipuram near Madras is named after a mango tree. The self-born Śiva is worshipped in that temple as *ekāmbreśvara*. The mighty trunk of the tree is ancient, but every year the branches bring forth new sprouts, new flowers, and fresh mangoes. Scientists have decided that the tree is more than 4300 years old. It is almost a symbol of eternity.

When a tree is used as fuel, it changes into smoke. Even when it is standing firm, it makes its own food. It uses its leaves to receive the solar rays. The wind rejoices and comes to tickle leaves to give their eternal songs. Rain pours its oblation on the tree. The roots of the tree sense the water that is penetrating to the depths. The small capillaries of the roots are like the small hands of a baby. They suck the generous mother earth. What falls under the tree decays and becomes good earth again. It is diluted by the chemicals of earth and the watery sap goes from the root to every leaf and the tree continues to be healthy, strong and beautiful. This recycling of the parts of the tree is a conspiracy that is going on between mother earth and the tree. The great biologist and philosopher Guy Murchie speaks of the wonder that is seen as a tree on earth. He writes:

> What on earth could fill such a bill better than a tree. And the beauty of its being develops apparently by random chance, while every root and branch makes its

> seemingly independent search for water and light, the whole tending to a highly efficient radial symmetry about the central bole, from which the foliage, according to actual mathematical analysis, literally disposes itself so the largest number of leaves receives the greatest amount of sunshine for the longest possible period. The fast upward flow of sap (more than 99% water) is through tube-like cells in the solid interior wood of the tree, while the much slower downward flow of syrupy gruel (only about 95% water) is through smaller cells in the outer layer, known as bast, just under the bark. The two systems normally move in opposite directions, but are partially interconnected and in the growing season may go locally in the same direction for a while, particularly where the new shoots are being supplied by both systems at once. [56]

In every tree this magical supply of energy is going on. When we walk on earth, plow it and make burrows in it, we are apt to think that it is just dead matter. But if we have eyes to see the microscopic beings which abound, even in an area of a square centimeter, we will be baffled to see that the earth has a scheme more sensitive and alive than ours. Our earth is one of the most responsible heavenly bodies which cares for every living being on its surface. It rotates so that the energy from the sun is equally distributed to all forms of life. Just as we have the five senses of hearing, touching, seeing, tasting and smelling, our good earth is well-equipped to listen with the countless billions of ears living on earth, not only on humans, but birds, cats, dogs, etc.

It is astounding that when a tree has no need of its fruits, except to preserve a seed, there is an award given to the distributors of the seed by making the fruit big, hygienically packed, fascinating in color, with fragrance that is seductive. The meat of every fruit has its own special flavor: not too sweet, not too sour; sufficient salt; maintaining its acid/alkaline balance as if there is a chemist or pharmacist monitoring the growth of the fruit. Even before it comes on a tree, the earth has used various devices to attract butterflies, bees and hummingbirds to impregnate flowers.

That is something we have not fully understood about our good earth. Like us, it has mental states also, such as intuition, aesthetics, psychic capacity, hypnotic power, and even sleep.

There is a wonderful book, *Gaia*, written by James Lovelock, which gives us a very fascinating study of the earth's dynamics. A study of it will convince us how much the earth is holding herself responsible. In the *Seven Mysteries of Life*, Guy Murchie puts this question, "Why the world?" He quotes Edgar Mitchell, one of the space travelers who was impressed by the earth from a vantage point of his spaceship in outer space:

> The first thing that came to mind as I looked at...planet earth floating in the vastness of space...was its incredible beauty...a blue and white jewel suspended against a velvet-black sky. The presence of divinity became almost palpable and I knew that life in the universe was not just an accident based on random processes. This knowledge came to me directly – noetically...an experiential cognition. [57]

Our earth is one of the finest musicians among the spheres of the heavens. Almost all her creatures sing for themselves, sing for each other and sing for the good earth. Probably we all know how the English blackbird sings songs in German speaking countries and how the song of one such bird caught the musical ear of Beethoven a few years before he went deaf. He kept the memory of that bird song in his musical soul for over twenty years to present it to the world in his famous *Pastoral Symphony*. Is the earth not our fuel too? In the Spring season we sow seed underground in her crust. She provides all that is required for the seeds to grow. For the bees and butterflies there is honey, for birds and hummingbirds and rodents there are fruits, for caterpillars there are tender leaves, and for termites there is the fallen tree. Thus the earth has been converting herself into fuel for billions of years. Life on earth is like smoke coming from the fuel of earth.

The most wonderful metaphor given in this mantra is that the night is its flame. Even though there are millions of people living around us, hardly anyone has seen a couple copulating. They wait for the darkness of the night. Then they are roused and the fire of erotics bursts out in the dead of night. After some time the woman discovers that she is pregnant. Even if it is day for us, for lower animals it is night when they mate. This can be easily seen by sending a bitch in heat to a dog or a cow in heat to a bull. The dog does not want to have a good look at the beautiful face of the bitch. His interest is in her behind. When a bull mates with a cow he does not lick her; he does not fondle her; he straightway gets into the business; and he looks skyward. It looks as if he is mating with a heavenly cow, rather than the cow under his body.

By 'night' the rishi means that the earth shades off the sun for the convenience of life on earth. The stars are described as sparks and rain is the libation poured on the earth in the sacrificial rite. The fruit of the sacrifice (*karmaphala*) is the corn, wheat, barley and rice that grow manifold in farms around the world. Eating them, human beings multiply. Sacrifice cannot be described in more beautiful terms than given in this mantra.

Mantra 12

puruṣo vā agnirgautama; tasyā vyāttameva samit, prāṇo dhūmaḥ, vāgarciḥ, cakṣuraṅgārāḥ, śrotraṁ visphuliṅgāḥ; tasminnetasminnagnau devā annam juhvati; tasyā āhutyai retaḥ sambhavati.

Word Meanings

puruṣaḥ - man; *gautama* - O Gautama; *agniḥ* - (is) fire; *vyāttam* - the open mouth; *tasya* - its; *samit* - fuel; *prāṇaḥ* - the vital breath; *dhūmaḥ* - (its) smoke; *vāk* - speech (the word); *arciḥ* - (its) flame; *cakṣuḥ* - the eye; *aṅgārāḥ* - (its) cinders; *śrotraṁ* - the ear; *visphuliṅgāḥ* - (its) sparks; *tasmin etasmin* - in this; *agnau* - fire; *devaḥ* - the gods; *juhvati* - offer; *annam* - food; *tasyaḥ āhutyai* - out of that offering; *retaḥ* - the seed; *sambhavati* - is born

Man, O Gautama, is fire, the open mouth is its fuel, the vital breath its smoke, speech its flame, the eye its cinders and the ear its sparks. In this fire the gods offer food. Out of that offering the seed is produced.

In this mantra, man himself is taken as a sacrificial model. When a human child is born, the first organ that opens is the mouth. The mouth is the most representative organ of perception as well as action. We have seen that life is first generated in water. After coming to this world, the new-born requires liquid to open the passage from the lip to the gullet and from the gullet to the stomach. As its nose is likely to be clogged, its first breathing may be through the mouth. Thirdly, the mouth conceals in it the organ of speech. Thus three major needs of a person – the vital energy to breathe, the food for nourishment and the imperative need to communicate with the outer world – are all initiated by opening the mouth. Hence we read in this mantra that the open mouth is the fuel of the fire called man.

The mouth is certainly like a furnace. The first preparation of any nourishment happens in the mouth. The first interpersonal relationship comes in the form of the nourisher mother providing a supply of food to her hungry child through its mouth. The first cry is also inadvertently aimed at the mother who readily responds to it. The mouth and the nose are a twin arrangement. The nose is the main organ to breathe; the mouth is its secondary aid. The mouth is the main organ for the intake of food. But the incoming food is taken to the gullet with the aid of breath. The mouth is the main organ of speech. In Sanskrit and other Indian languages, every fifth sound of the alphabet is pronounced nasally. Thus the coupling of the nose and the mouth is purposefully structured for three of the major functions in a person. The processing of nourishment takes place in the mouth. Voice culture is also initiated in the mouth. It is admirable that an ancient rishi noticed the ingenuity implied in the structuring of the mouth in relation to both the head and the body. It is like a gateway to the world of somatic evolution and also to the world of psychic evolution.

Then we are told that it is from this fuel of the mouth the vital breath is spewing. Hence it is called the smoke. Where there is fire there is also smoke. Smoke will be followed by the flames of fire. We can light a lamp and do a hundred things in the serene glow of its light. Similarly, the fire that is generated in the mouth can affect both bodily functions as well as psycho-sociological functions. There is a very special kind of dialectical polarity involved in the articulation of thoughts. There is a coming together of the noem and the noetic. The noem comes from the cognitive faculty; the noetic is how it is accepted by the total personality centered in the heart. The two converge into the expression of an idea as thought. The carrier of the energy for speech comes from breath.

Without regard to the physiologic organ of respiration, the Indian people conceived a parameter of energy ascent and descent from the *mūlādhāra*, the synergic center at the base foundation of the spine, to the *sahasrāra*, the synergic center at the crown of the head. Between the two eyes is located the stream of consciousness with a wakeful awareness. This synergic center between the two brows is called *ājña*, where the will to live is concentrated. It is the faculty of volition and the main monitoring center for giving commands to the motor system. Indian mystics think of the heart as the true heaven of humanity. There is a graphic description of the world of the spirit expressing its psychic flourish within the heart. It is called the space of consciousness (*cidākāśa*).

All the psychophysical, moral and spiritual needs of the total person are to be gathered from all parts of the body and conveyed to the *ājña*. The processing of an idea into a word happens between the poles of the synergic center between the eyebrows (*ājña cakra*) and the synergic center in the heart (*anāhata*). That manifests in the synergic center which is mid-way between them at the throat (*viśuddhi*). It is significant that the *viśuddhi* from where the word is expressed is called the seat of purity. In the purposive life of a person it is expected that the facilities of the body are to be properly utilized and the thoughts and words which are invariably followed by actions are to be basically good. The flame of speech is a cleanser of thoughts and words. What is clean is the rhythm of truth which is conceived, imagined and expressed. Nobody can speak falsehood with the same ease with which he or she speaks truth. When untruth is about to be expressed in words, one looses one beat of one's heart. Only after a pause can one tell a lie. Thus the fire of the *ātman*, which is in the heart, restrains the faculty of speech from being polluted.

According to Hindu mythology, the fire that burns in us is the *āhavanīya agni*, the sacrificial fire which is ever-witnessing our memories, imagination, concepts, word formation and expression. Hence the fire is called the eternal witness. In ancient mythologies we can read that when a demon or a human falsifies truth, the gods always ask the sacrificial fire to testify to the truth of the spoken word. Even now it is considered most necessary in the courts of all countries to summon a person who is floundering to testify in front of a judge and jury. All this justifies saying that speech is its flame.

The eye can only see and it does not speak. It is a passive witness. Immediately after perception, the recording of the eye is transferred to the registry of memory and it is no longer in the eye. Hence it is said the eye is its cinders. The speech that comes sparks off as separate sounds. The ear gathers the sparks and the ear of the ear puts together the correlatives of the sound to make meaning. Hence hearsay has a secondary validity compared to the witnessing of the eye. In the mantra "the gods which offer food" means the volitional intelligence which judges what is appropriate to replenish the energy of an ever-functioning psychosomatic organism. This offering has two purposes: one is for the sacrificial fire to be kept alive and the other is for that sacrificial fire to bring forth the fruits of action. Human beings are not different from the other living creatures on earth, including bacteria. The world will continue to flourish only by the dying being replaced by the living. Only if food is offered as fuel in the mouth of a man is he able to formulate sperm in his testes which can be used by mother nature to make more individuals.

The previous mantra and the present one together answer another of Pravāhaṇa's questions: "How does the departed return, and, with all the deaths happening here, why does the world of the departed not have a population burst?" This mantra indicates that those who go and those who are called back from the world of the departed are more or less balanced. There is no unreasonable logic in it. If we simply make a census of men and women born in all countries, if only men were born for 100 years the species would not have continued at all. Thus in the mysterious scheme of things there is adequate arrangement for the dead as well as the living. This model of sacrifice adopts the same poetic method used as a literary device in the other mantras.

Mantra 13

> *yoṣā vā agnirgautama; tasyā upastha eva samit, lomāni dhūmaḥ, yonirarciḥ, yadantaḥ karoti te'ṅgārāḥ, abhinandā visphuliṅgāḥ; tasminnetasminnagnau devā reto juhvati; tasyā āhutyai puruṣaḥ sambhavati; sa jīvati yāvajjīvati, atha yadā mriyate.*

Word Meanings

> *yoṣā* - woman; *gautama* - O Gautama; *agniḥ* - (is) fire; *tasmin etasmin* - in this; *agnau* - fire; *devaḥ* - the gods; *juhvati* - offer; *retaḥ* - the seed; *tasyaḥ āhutyai* - out of that offering; *puruṣaḥ* - a person; *sambhavati* - is born; *saḥ* - one; *jīvati* - lives; *yāvat* - as long as; *jīvati* - (one) is to live; *atha* - then; *yadā* - when; *mriyate* - (one) dies

> Woman, O Gautama is fire. In this fire the gods offer the seed. Out of that offering a person is born. One lives as long as one is destined to live. Then, when one dies –

In the ninth mantra, the world is shown as the fire and the sun its fuel; in mantra ten the god of rain is given as fire and its fuel is the year; in mantra eleven this world is given as fire and the earth is spoken of as its fuel; in mantra twelve, man is given as fire and his mouth is described as the fuel. Thus so far we have spoken of four kinds of fire. Woman is the fifth fire. These fires are called *pañca agni*. The oblation was first of faith, then *soma*, then rain, then food. In the woman the oblation is the sperm. When a woman gives birth, the child speaks. Thus Pravāhaṇa's question, "Do you know after how many oblations are offered, water rises up possessed of a human voice?" is answered here.

The woman's genital has two fireplaces. Her vagina is the gate of entry for the man to offer his seed. It is taken afterwards to the womb which is a greater fire within the woman. There her heat of incubation goes on for eight to nine months. In that heat a child is cooked up. Considering the woman as a sacrificial spot, her whole personality is considered as the sacrificial altar. Although the sperm goes from the male, it is here described as the oblation made by the gods. This is only to show that there has to be a divine favor also for pregnancy to happen. A child is not conceived in the womb of a woman every time a man mates with her.

The first sacrifice spoken of in mantra nine is a perennial sacrifice. The world is exposed to the fire of the sun day after day. When the sun is setting in one spot, it is rising in another. All twenty-four hours, throughout the year, some part of the earth is exposed to the fire of the sun. As the movement of the sun is seen from East to West, and the poles are equidistant from the equator, the effect of the sunlight on earth is graded from the equator to the North Pole and the equator to the South Pole. The four directions are specifically mentioned. This eternal fire burning all year round over an unknown period of time is said to be intended by the divine to make the earth a well-cared for habitation of living beings from the protozoa to the human. The oblation in the first fire is the intentionality of the divine.

If the earth is the material cause of life, the solar rays come in the position of the efficient cause. The accidental cause which is close to the efficient cause is given in mantra ten as the rain god, and the oblation in this sacrifice is to make the earth a nursery of life. The choice of *soma* as oblation is to account for the spirit-matter conjunction. *Soma* represents the spirit and the earth warmed up by the sun is the material to be transformed into life. In mantra eleven we see how the universal system itself is like a fire which is transforming the earth into life forms using thermodynamics as processing. The oblation is rain.

In the twelfth mantra, man is given as a model of sacrifice. The constituents of a fully equipped psycho-somatic organism are presented, and the oblation is nourishment, out of which semen can be formed. In mantra thirteen, woman is the fire and her generative organ is the sacrificial pit, into which the sperm is offered. With five models of sacrifice, we come to the progeny which initiates the cycle of birth and death. And the fourteenth mantra will present the phenomenon of death to us. Thus the whole story of life evolving up to the human race is given.

Mantra 14

> *athainamagnaye haranti; tasyāgnirevāgnirbhavati, samit-samit, dhūmo dhūmaḥ, arcirarciḥ, aṅgārā aṅgārāḥ, vis-phuliṅgā visphuliṅgāḥ; tasminnetasminnagnau devāḥ puruṣam juhvati; tasyā āhutyai puruṣo bhāsvaravarṇaḥ sambhavati.*

Word Meanings

atha - then; *haranti* - they carry; *enam* - one; *agnaye* - to the (funeral) fire; *agniḥ* - the fire; *bhavati* - becomes; *tasya* - one's; *agniḥ* - fire; *samit* - the fuel; *tasya* - one's; *samit* - fuel; *dhūmaḥ* - the smoke; *tasya* - one's; *dhūmaḥ* - smoke; *arciḥ* - the flame; *tasya* - one's; *arciḥ* - flame; *aṅgārāḥ* - the cinders; *tasya* - one's; *aṅgārāḥ* - cinders; *visphuliṅgāḥ* - the sparks; *tasya* - one's; *visphuliṅgāḥ* - sparks; *tasmin etasmin* - in this; *agnau* - fire; *devāḥ* - the gods; *juhvati* - offer; *puruṣam eva* - the person; *tasyāḥ āhutyai* - out of that offering; *puruṣam* - the person; *sambhavati* - emerges; *bhāsvaravarṇaḥ* - radiant

– then they carry one to the funeral fire. The fire becomes one's fire, the fuel one's fuel, the smoke one's smoke, the flame one's flame, the cinders one's cinders, and the sparks one's sparks. In this fire the gods offer the person. Out of that offering the person emerges radiant.

For the first time in this *brāhmaṇa* the symbolism of sacrificial description is substituted with empirical perception. A dead person is taken by the ritualistic priests to the cremation ground where the body is placed on firewood. The cremation fire is actual fire, not a symbolic fire. The corpse of the dead person is placed on it with the intention of burning away the physical remains. The flames that burn the dead body are the flames of empirical fire. As the corpse has within it fat and watery substances, bones and hair, when the cremation takes place, the fire crackles and the body burns with various kinds of sounds, making sparks go in all directions. The agent of cremation is described here as the gods (*devas*). When a person is burnt in the fire, it burns high and it is described here as of golden hue, *bhāsvaravarṇaḥ*.

Mantra 15

te ya evametadviduḥ, ye cāmī araṇye śraddhām satyam-upāsate, te'rcirabhisambhavanti, arciṣo'haḥ, ahna āpūryamāṇapakṣam, āpūryamāṇapakṣādyānṣaṇmāsān-udaṅṅāditya eti; māsebhyo devalokam, devalokād-ādityam, ādityam ādityādvaidyutam; tānvaidyutān-

puruṣo mānasa etya brahmalokān gamayati; te teṣu brahmalokeṣu parāḥ parāvato vasanti; teṣām na punarāvṛttiḥ.

Word Meanings

te - those; *ye* - who; *veda* - know; *etat* - this; *evam* - as described; *ca* - and; *te* - those; *amī* - others; *ye* - who; *araṇye* - (living) in the forest; *upāsate* - meditate; *śraddhām* - with faith; *satyam* - upon the *satya brahman*; *abhisambhavanti* - reach; *arciḥ* - (the deity identified with) the flame; *arciṣaḥ* - from the flame; *ahaḥ* - (the deity of) the day; *ahnaḥ* - from the day; *āpūryamāṇapakṣam* - (the deity of) the fortnight of the waxing moon; *āpūryamāṇapakṣāt* - from (the deity of) the fortnight of the waxing moon; *ṣaṭ māsān* - (the band of deities of) the six months; *yān* - during which; *ādityaḥ* - the sun; *eti* - travels; *udaṅ* - northward; *māsebhyaḥ* - from (the deities of) the (above six) months; *devalokam* - to (the deity identified with) the world of the gods; *devalokāt* - from (the deity identified with) the world of the gods; *ādityam* - to the sun; *ādityāt* - from the sun; *vaidyutam* - the deity of lightning; *vaidyutān tan* - those that have reached (the deities of) lightning; *puruṣaḥ* - (then) a being; *mānasaḥ* - created from the mind of (*hiraṇyagarbha*); *etya* - comes; *gamyati* - (and) conducts; *te* - them; *brahmalokān* - to the worlds of *brahman*; *parāḥ* - become perfect; *vasanti* - dwell; *teṣu brahmalokeṣu* - in those worlds of *brahman*; *parāvataḥ* - for many superlative years; *teṣām* - for them; *na* - no; *punarāvṛttiḥ* - (there is) further return

Those who know this as described, and those others who, living in the forest, meditate with faith upon the *satya brahman*, reach the deity identified with the flame, from the flame the deity of the day, from the day the deity of the fortnight of the waxing moon, from the fortnight of the waxing moon the deities of the six months in which the sun travels northward, from those months the deity identified with the world of the gods, from the world of the gods the sun, and from the sun the deity of lightning. Then a being created from the mind of *hiraṇyagarbha* comes and conducts them to the worlds of *brahman*. They become perfect and dwell in those worlds of *brahman* for a great many superlative years. For them there is no further return to this world.

This passage also refers to the first question of Pravāhaṇa: "Do you know how people take different paths after death?" The subject here for meditation is the five fires described in the previous mantras. In the ancient world of Vedic culture, everything in this world was considered to have been created through a series of sacrifices which bring perfection to every created being. This mantra refers to a being that is created from the mind of *hiraṇyagarbha*. Human beings continue to live from day to day, strengthened, inspired and attending to their chores, because of the hope engendered in all beings that there is progress in life. *Hiraṇyagarbha* symbolizes that hope which nourishes and encourages.

At the very beginning of the *Upaniṣad*, it graphically portrayed the polarization between imminent danger on one hand and the possibility of escaping death on the other. *Vaiśvānara* is the imminent danger of death and *hiraṇyagarbha* is the hope of the future. What was originally pregnant in the golden egg, so to say, came out as the first model of life (*prajāpati*). In pregnancy, the state of being is potentiality. It is the potential that becomes actual. Sacrifice is also a model of pregnant possibility. Fire is like the eternal consumer. When the *vaiśvānara* and the life that is pregnant as *hiraṇyagarbha* are exposed to the consuming fire, the first thing that arises is smoke which is a declaration that the fuel is transforming into a golden flame. The flame of life that is kindled in the womb produces a burning cinder like the coal that is burning in a furnace. It is accompanied by the sparks of many subsidiary potentialities which are expressive of the dynamics of life.

The intentionality of the creator is offered into this sacrificial mode of the dynamic of transformation. Oblation symbolizes the faith of the creator by whose behest the creature comes to its perfection. In the preceding mantras we have seen that each time the oblation was offered in a sacrifice, a futuristic blessing came to the sacrificer. When the world was considered as fire and the sun its fuel, the gods declared their faith by pouring oblations into it. Out of it came the boon of *soma*. *Soma* is a drink which has the quality of fire-like alcohol. Those who partook of it felt transformed because of its invigorating quality. In the next model of sacrifice, Parjanya, the god of rain, was considered as fire; a period of time was considered as the fuel that was to bring the results. Into this fire *soma* was poured as oblation. Out of that came the boon of rain which was the special cause for cooling down the earth from its original mass of flames until it came to the present state which is conducive to bringing forth living beings in abundance.

The third model was of this world itself as fire into which was fed the earth. The oblation given into that earth which was being transformed was rain. The rain made earth a potential field for all kinds of life forms to emerge. The next model considered a man as the fire and his power of consumption was considered the fuel. The food offered to him was transformed into a seed, a promise of future life and the generative process of birth and death. The fifth fire is modeled as a woman. The fire is seen in her regenerative organ. So the fruition of the five fire-sacrifices comes in the form of a progeny. After these five symbolic fires, we were led to the actual fire used in rituals as the *āhavanīya* in which the person who is offered into it literally burns. In the present mantra we are told that the person who began first from the mind of *hiraṇyagarbha* is called back to the same *hiraṇyagarbha*, making a complete circle.

The *Bhṛgu Vālli* of the *Taittirīya Upaniṣad* says *brahman* is that from which a being is born, that which sustains it, that to which all beings finally return. The concept of *brahman* or the Absolute includes several variations. The ultimate is called *parabrahman*. *Brahman* as the cause of the world is called *kāraṇa brahman*; *brahman* as this world is called *kārya brahman*. In the present context, *brahman* is called *satya brahman*. This term was explained in V.5.1 which pointed out that *satya* consists of three syllables: *sa*, *ta* and *ya*. The first and last syllables, *sa* and *ya*, are truth; the middle one, *ta*, stands for untruth. The untruth is the created world or the world as an effect concealing the unknowable Absolute. The eternal immortal truth appears to be having birth and death and that is the untruth about it. One is shown to be many - that is untruth. There was another reference to *satya* in V.5.2 which talks about the sun, the orb of brilliance with which the world is illuminated. It only marks half of the truth of this world. The other half is in the eye that sees the illumination of the sun. It is our spiritual eye or third eye. When phenomenality closes that eye for us, we see a world of name and form with our two eyes.

This also comes in the *Īśāvāsya Upaniṣad* where a very intriguing appellation is given to the individuated person: *satya dharman*. When *brahman* becomes manifested it is presented as an integrated whole with many potentials. Each potential is a *dharma* in a person who is meant to be the perceiver of truth. *Satya* is handicapped by the division coming from being perceived through the functions of various faculties. Instead of having a comprehensive unitive vision of the Absolute, we perceive it as sounds, voices, words to be heard. When the voice transforms into a word and the word is heard in its delimitation, it becomes a noem and the noetic function of the ear superimposes a meaning on it. Every word becomes separated, each with a different implication or emphasis (*sphoṭa*). Similarly, the *brahman* that should please us with what we call the touch of the Absolute *(brahmasparśa)* comes to us as the fondling of the mother, the kissing of the lover, the tickling of a baby, which are all on the positive side, and painful diseases on the other. When the same comes as the joy of partaking, it is *ruci*, the flavor in the taste-buds which is further multiplied into several shades from sweetness to bitterness. The same can be said also of smell. Thus our world is made into a phenomenal world of pain and pleasure. This is how truth is falsified by the *dharma* of each faculty.

Hence, in the *Īśāvāsya Upaniṣad*, the dying person who is approaching the fire introduces himself as *satya dharman* and reminds the sun that however bright the sun in the outer sky is, its illumination is complemented by the eyes that see. The right eye is here substituted for *indha*, the all-knowing fire, otherwise called *indra*. The left eye is marked off as the empirical eyes with which a world of name and form and individual bodies are seen. The sun is shining so bright that the *satya dharman* cannot distinguish between its causal properties and its subsequent effect. So the *satya dharman* says, "Be mellow, gather your radiant beams so that I may see both aspects of my being: *satya* as well as *dharma*."

A person who has come to this world and passed through many generations may, after having perfected his life on earth, return to the Absolute (*satya brahman*). The function of the *satya brahman* is compared to a contrivance for drawing water from a well in which a series of bowls are fixed to an endless chain. In other words, in the cyclic function of life and death, there is always a filling in and always an emptying. A distinction is made here between time in the phenomenal which is marked by eventualities, and pure duration in which there is neither *dharma* nor *karma*. Hence in the *Bhagavad Gītā* we read (XVIII:66): "Renouncing all *dharmas* take refuge in Me, the Absolute, in which there is no duality." Such are some of the indications given in this mantra for us to meditate on.

Mantra 16

atha ye yajñena dānena tapasā lokāñjayanti te dhūmamabhisambhavanti, dhumādrātrim, rātrerapakṣīyamāṇapakṣam, apakṣīyamāṇapakṣādyānṣaṇmāsāndakṣiṇāditya eti, māsebhyaḥ pitṛlokam, pitṛlokāccandram; te candram prāpyānnam bhavanti, tāmstatra devā yathā somam rājānamāpyāyasvāpakṣīyasveti, evamenāmstatra bhakṣayanti; teṣām yadā tatparyavaityathemamevākāśamabhiniṣpadyante, ākāśādvayum; vāyorvṛṣṭim; vṛṣṭeḥ pṛthivīm te pṛthivīm prāpyānnam bhavanti, te punaḥ puruṣāgnau hūyante, tato yoṣāgnau jāyante lokānpratyutthāyinaḥ; ta evamevānuparivartante; atha ya etau panthānau na viduste kīṭāḥ pataṅgā yadidaṁ dandāśūkam.

Word Meanings

atha - while; *te* - those; *ye* - who; *jayanti* - conquer; *lokān* - the worlds; *yajñena* - through sacrifice; *dānena* - charity; *tapasā* - (and) austerity; *abhisambhavanti* - reach; *dhūmam* - (the deity of) smoke; *dhūmaḥ* - from smoke; *rātrim* - (the deity of) the night; *rātreḥ* - from the night; *apakṣīyamāṇapakṣam* - (the deity of) the fortnight in which the moon wanes; *apakṣīyamāṇapakṣāt* - from the decreasing half of the moon; *sat māsān* - (the band of deities of) the six months; *yān* - in which; *ādityaḥ* - the sun; *eti* - travels; *dakṣiṇā* - southward; *māsebhyaḥ* - from these months; *pitṛlokam* - (the deity of) the world of the departed ones; *pitṛlokāt* - (from) the world of the departed ones; *candram* - the moon; *prāpya* - reaching; *candram* - the moon; *te* - they; *bhavanti* - become; *annam* - food; *tatra* - there; *devāḥ* - the gods; *bhakṣayanti* - enjoy; *tān enān* - them; *yathā* - just as (priests drink); *rājānam* - the shining; *somam* - *soma* juice; *iti* - (saying) as it were; *āpyāyasva* - increase; *apakṣīyasva* - decrease; *yadā* - (and) when; *teṣām* - their; *tat* - that (past work); *paryavaiti* - is exhausted; *atha* - then; *abhiniṣpadyante* - (they) reach; *imam eva* - this; *ākāśam* - *ākāśa*; *ākāśāt* - from the *ākāśa*; *vāyum* - the air; *vāyoḥ* - from the air; *vṛṣṭim* - rain; *vṛṣṭeḥ* - from rain; *pṛthivīm* - the earth; *prāpya* - reaching; *pṛthivīm* - the earth; *te* - they; *bhavanti* - become; *annam* - food; *te* - (then) they; *hūyante* - are offered; *punaḥ* - again; *puruṣāgnau* - in the fire of a man; *tataḥ* - then; *yoṣāgnau* - in the fire of woman; *te* - (whence) they; *jāyante* - are born (and perform rites); *utthāyinaḥ* - with a view to going; *prati* - to; *lokān* - (other) worlds; *evam eva* - thus; *anuparivartante* - do they rotate; *atha te* - those however; *ye* - who; *na* - not; *viduḥ* - know (become); *etau* - these; *panthānau* - two ways; *kīṭāḥ* - insects, worms; *pataṅgāḥ* - moths; *yat* - (and); *idam* - these; *dandāśūkam* - frequently biting creatures (gnats and mosquitoes)

While those who conquer the worlds through sacrifice, charity and austerity reach the deity of smoke, from smoke the deity of the night, from night the deity of the fortnight in which the moon wanes, from the decreasing half of the moon the deities of the six months in which the sun travels southward, from these months the deity of the world of the departed ones, and from the world of the departed ones the moon. Reaching the moon they become food. There the gods enjoy them just as the priests drink the shining *soma* juice saying, as it were, "Increase, decrease." And when their past work is exhausted, they reach this *ākāśa*, from the *ākāśa* they reach the air, from the air rain, and from rain the earth. Reaching the earth they become food. Then they are again offered in the fire of a man, thence in the fire of a woman, whence they are born and perform rites with a view to going to other worlds. Thus do they rotate. Those, however, who do not know these two ways become insects and moths, and those frequently biting creatures (gnats and mosquitoes).

In mantra fifteen we were given a picture of a dead person who, after cremation, departs from this world through the northern route (*uttarāyaṇa*). This path is for those who have attained realization of the Self. Hence it is said that by going in the northward path the departed person goes to the sun and thence to the world of *brahma*. For such a person there is no return. In the present mantra we hear of people who walked in the path of relativistic worldly life, observing various religious rites. Instead of going into the northern way, the departed go the southern way (*dakṣiṇāyaṇa*), where the sun travels for six months in the southward direction. The deities of the world of the departed ones use the departed as victims for sacrifice. That is why we read in the first *brāhmaṇa* that when a person is being cremated, his friends and relatives implore the cremation fire not to darken the body too much so that it will be a proper offering to the deities.

In one sense, eating food and digesting it is the first model of the sustenance of life. It also continues to the very last. When the food we eat is treated as a sacrifice, the essence of it helps us to recoup our energy. Here it is said: "Reaching the moon these souls of the departed become food. There the gods enjoy them as the priests drink the *soma* juice, saying, 'Increase, decrease." The mantra goes on to describe the route that brings some people back to be born of a man and woman and others who are destined to become lower beings including insects.

Thus in the second *brāhmaṇa* we are given an amazing theory of every being, whether a gnat or mosquito or person, coming as the end product of a series of universal sacrifices in which the sun, moon, fire, water, earth, man and woman are all given their appropriate assignments to create the entire world. Guy Murchie and almost all biologists who have studied the interrelatedness of creatures are convinced that all have only one life to share. The cosmic agents who contribute to life on earth show equal attention to every form of life however important or insignificant they are to human beings. This is a subject which can help one to see one's Self in all and all in one's Self. Of all the forms of life which are now counted as species, even the mosquito and cockroach are much more ancient than human beings. The biologists consider our position precarious because we are only a single species among millions of species, most of which have been around in this universe for long periods. According to great geneticists from J. B. S. Haldane to Theodosius Dobzhansky to Sir Julian Huxley, all believe that the ancestry of all the species that we know now can be traced to one simple form of life. We recommend our readers to read Chapter 13 of *The Seven Mysteries of Life*, by Guy Murchie, which gives a very exhaustive account of the unity of life on earth. In this chapter he gives several interesting charts which give us an idea of human unity in a single glance.

The whole idea of sacrifice loses its religious significance once you know that the transformation of matter, from basic elements to a philosopher, always involves the same processes of burning to ashes, dissolving everything into a solution, restructuring and recycling. These are all symbolized by sacrifice. Once this was a religious way of understanding but now we see it in an elaborate sense in all the modern laboratories of the world. People in India are so conditioned by their religious terms that they cannot easily leave the shells of religious conditioning to accept truth in all its concreteness and abstraction. Both the archetypal books and the modern interdisciplinary studies of science present a quest for knowledge. Certain certitudes which were evolved in the age of religion still hold good in the world of science. The world of science has to trace its forgotten roots in religion. Such is the amalgam to which the *Bṛhadāraṇyaka Upaniṣad* brings us.

Brāhmaṇas 3 and 4

When the diction and style of the mantras of *brāhmaṇas* three and four are compared with that of the mantras we have studied so far, they seem to be an interpolation of material into the *Bṛhadāraṇyaka Upaniṣad* by those who were seeking justification for elaborate rituals. They go against all the noble teachings of the

Upaniṣads. Conventional practices which were derided by Yājñavalkya in the third, fourth and fifth *adhyāyas* appear in these two *brāhmaṇas*, quite contrary to the expectation of any reasonable person. Those who wanted to support the ritualistic *karma* of priests made an entry through the back door, so to say, by inserting ideas which can never be accepted as the normal aspirations of anyone who has any reverence for the teachings of the *Upaniṣads.*

In the third *brāhmaṇa*, the goals spoken of are of a person who wants to become famous in the social context so that he can amass enough wealth to pay the priests to conduct rituals on his behalf. What was given earlier as the greatest *udgītha*, the *gāyatrī*, is mockingly given the allure of a ritual which obscures the inspiring meaning attributed to it in the preceding *adhyāyas.* Great teachers of the *Upaniṣads* such as Uddālaka, Yājñavalkya, Cūla, Jānaka and Satyakāma are ridiculed by the instructions attributed to them in *brāhmaṇa* three. And in *brāhmaṇa* four, some of the interpolated mantras could even inspire misguided people to indulge in crime and rape.

Similarly, when we look at the established institutions in India begun by great teachers of peerless wisdom, we can see how the stability and dignity of those institutions has been undermined by so-called followers. Śankara, who is known for his uncompromising adherence to the wisdom texts of *brahmavidyā*, outright denies the validity of the third and fourth *brāhmaṇas.* As our interest is in the *śruti* which expound *brahmavidyā*, we see no reason to include this interpolated text as part of the highly venerated *Bṛhadāraṇyaka Upaniṣad.* We do not want to be a party to such indecent and obviously evil lessons being put into the sacred texts. So we have omitted the third and fourth *brāhmaṇas* altogether.

Brāhmaṇa 5

Mantra 1

atha vaṁśaḥ; pautimāsīputraḥ kātyāyanīputrāt, katyā-

yanīputro gautamīputrāt, gautamīputro bhāradvājī-putrāt, bharādvājīputraḥ pārāśarīputrāt, pārāśariputra aupasvastīputrāt aupasvastīputraḥ pārāśarīputrāt, pārāśarīputraḥ kātyāyanīputrāt, kātyāyanīputraḥ kauśikīputrāt, kauśikīputra alambīputrāc ca vaiyāghrapadīputrāc ca, vaiyaghrapadīputraḥ kāṇvī-putrāc ca kāpīputrāc ca, kāpīputraḥ

Word Meanings

atha - now; *vamśaḥ* - the line (of teachers). (Rest as in the translation.)

Now the line of teachers: the son of Pautimāṣī (received it) from the son of Kātyāyanī, he from the son of Gautamī, the son of Gautamī from the son of Bhāradvāji, he from the son of Pārāśarī, the son of Pārāśarī from the son of Aupasvatī, he from the son of another Pārāśarī, he from the son of Kātyāyanī, the son of Kātyāyanī from the son of Kauśikī, the son of Kauśikī from the son of Ālambī and the son of Vaiyāghrapadī, the son of Vaiyāghrapadī from the son of Kāṇvī and the son of Kapi, the son of Kapi –

Mantra 2

ātreyī putrāt, ātreyī putro gautamīputrāt, gautamīputro bhāradvājīputrāt, bharādvājīputraḥ pārāśarīputrāt, pārāśarī putro vātsīputrāt, vātsīputraḥ pārāśarīputrāt, pārāśarīputro vārkāruṇiputrāt, vārkāruṇiputro vārkāruṇīputrāt, vārkāruṇīputra ārtabhāgīputrāt, ārtabhāgīputraḥ śauṅgīputrāt, śauṅgīputraḥ, sāṅkṛtīputrāt, sāṅkṛtīputra ālambāyanīputrāt, ālambāyanīputra ālambīputrāt, ālambī putro jāyantīputrāt, jāyantīputro māṇḍūkāyanī-putrāt, māṇḍūkāyanīputro māṇḍūkīputrāt, māṇḍūkī-putraḥ śāṇḍilīputrāt, śāṇḍilīputro rāthītarīputrāt, rāthītarīputro bhālukīputrāt, bhālukīputraḥ krauñcikī-putrābhyam, krauñcikīputrau vaidabhṛtīputrāt, vaidabhṛtiputraḥ kārśakeyīputrāt, kārśakeyīputraḥ prācīnayogī putrāt, prācīnayogīputraḥ sāñjīvīputrāt, sāñjīvīputraḥ prāśnīputrād āsurivāsinaḥ, prāśnīputra āsurāyaṇāt, āsurāyaṇa āsureḥ, āsuriḥ

Word Meanings

(See the translation.)

From the son of Ātreyī, the son of Ātreyī from the son of Gautamī. the son of Gautamī from the son of Bhāradvājī, he from the son of Pārāśarī, the son of Pārāśarī from the son of Vātsī, the son of Vātsī from the son of another Pārāśarī, the son of Pārāśarī from the son of Vārkāruṇi, he from the son of another Vārkāruṇi, he from the son of Ārtabhāgī, he from the son of Śauṅgī, the son of Śauṅgī from the son of Sāṅkṛti, he from the son of Ālambāyanī, he from the son of Ālambī, the son of Ālambī from the son of Jāyantī, he from the son of Māṇḍūkāyanī, he from the son of Māṇḍūkī, the son of Māṇḍūkī from the son of Śāṇḍili, the son of Śāṇḍili from the son of Rāthītarī, he from the son of Bhālukī, the son of Bhālukī from the two sons of Karuñciki, they from the son of Vaidabhṛtī, he from the son of Kārśakeyī, he from the son of Prācīnayogī, he from the son of Sāñjīvī, the son of Sāñjīvī from Āsurivāsin, the son of Prāśnī, the son of Prāśnī from Āsurāyaṇa, he from Āsuri, Āsuri –

Mantra 3

yājñavalkyāt, yājñavalkya, uddālakāt uddālako'ruṇāt, aruṇa upaveśeḥ, upaveśiḥ kuśreḥ, kuśrir vājaśravasaḥ, vājaśravā jihvāvato bādhyogāt, jihvāvān badhyogo'sitād vārṣagaṇāt, asito vārṣagaṇo haritāt kaśyapāt, haritaḥ kaśyapaḥ śilpāt kaśyapāt, silpaḥ kaśyapaḥ kaśyapān naidhruveḥ, kaśyapo naidhruvir vācaḥ, vāg ambhiṇyāḥ, ambhiṇyādityāt, ādityānīmāni śuklāni yajūṁṣi vājasaneyena yājñavalkyenākhyāyante.

Word Meanings

imāni - these; *ādityāni* - (received) from the sun; *śuklāni* - pure, white; *yajūṁṣi* - Yajuses; *yājñavalkyena vājasaneyena* - by Yājñavalkya Vājasaneya; *ākhyāyante* - are explained; (Rest as in the translation.)

From Yājñavalkya, Yājñavalkya from Uddālaka, Uddālaka from Aruṇa, Aruṇa from Upaveśi, Upaveśi from Kuśri, Kuśri from Vājaśravas, he from Jihvāvat, the son of Badhyoga, he from Asita, the son of Varṣagaṇa, he from Harita Kaśyapa, he from Śilpa Kaśyapa, this one from Kaśyapa, the son of Nidhruva, he from Vāc, she from Ambhiṇī, she from the sun. These pure Yajuses received from the sun are explained by Yājñavalkya Vājasaneya.

Mantra 4

samānam ā sāñjīvīputrāt, sāñjīvīputro māṇḍūkāyaneḥ māṇḍūkāyanir māṇḍavyāt, māṇḍavyaḥ kautsāt, kautso māhittheḥ, māhitthir vāmakakṣāyaṇāt, vāmakakṣayaṇaḥ vacasaḥ rājastambāyanāt, yajñavaca rājastambāyanaḥ turāt kāvaṣeyāt, turaḥ kāvaṣeyaḥ prajāpateḥ, prajāpatir brahmaṇaḥ, brahma svayambhu; brahmaṇe namaḥ.

Word Meanings

(See the translation.)

The same up to the son of Sāñjīvī, the son of Sāñjīvī from Māṇḍūkāyanī, Māṇḍūkāyanī from Māṇḍavya, Māṇḍavya from Kautsa, Kautsa from Māhitthi, he from Vāmakakṣāyaṇa, he from Śāṇḍilya, Śāṇḍilya from Vātsya, Vātsya from Kuśri, Kuśri from Yājñavacas, the son of Rājastamba, he from Tura, the son of Kavaṣa, he from *prajāpati*, *prajāpati* from *brahman*. *Brahman* is self-born. Salutations to *brahman*.

We endorse as valid for *Muni Kāṇḍa* and *Khila Kāṇḍa* our commentary of the hierarchy of wisdom teachers given in the *Madhu Kāṇḍa*. Thus we come to the end of our commentary on the *Bṛhadāraṇyaka Upaniṣad*. In gratitude to the rishis who have expounded the *Madhu, Muni* and *Khila Kāṇḍas* we are adding to our commentary an Appendix of appreciation. We thank the wisdom teachers of all lands and all ages. We hold all of them as the one spirit which dwells in our hearts as the Self of all, which is obviously the one reason that guides the destiny of all to each one's supreme fulfillment of life.

APPENDIX I: Madhu Kāṇḍa

Adhyāya I

In his study of the *Upaniṣads* Sri Aurobindo gives a very thought-provoking epitomization of the *Bṛhadāraṇyaka Upaniṣad* which can serve as a key to the philosophy and mystical insight of this masterpiece of the *Upaniṣadic* rishis:

> The *Bṛhadāraṇyaka*, at once the most obscure and the profoundest of the *Upaniṣads*, offers peculiar difficulties to the modern mind...The time is fast coming when the human intellect will be aware of the mighty complexity of the universe, more ready to learn and less prone to dispute and dictate; we shall be willing then to read ancient documents of knowledge for what they contain instead of attempting to force into them our own truth or get them to serve our philosophic or scholastic purposes. To enter passively into the thoughts of the old rishis, allow their words to sink into our souls, mould them and create their own reverberations in a sympathetic and responsive material submissiveness, in short, to the *śruti* - was the theory the ancient themselves had of the method of Vedic knowledge – *girām upaśrutim cara, stomān abhi svara, abhi gṛṇīhi a ruva.* To listen in soul to the old voices and allow the *śruti* in the soul to respond, to vibrate, first obscurely, in answer to the Vedantic hymn of knowledge, to give the response, the echo and last to let that response gain in clarity, intensity and fullness – this is the principle of interpretation I have followed – mystical perhaps, but not necessarily more unsound than the insistences and equally personal standards of the logician and the scholar. [58]

Then Sri Aurobindo calls our attention to certain symbols which are basic to this grand *Upaniṣad*. Referring to the opening verse of the first *adhyāya* he remarks:

> The *Upaniṣad* begins with a grandiose abruptness in an impetuous figure of the Horse of the *aśvamedha*. . . . This passage full of gigantic imagery, sets the key to the *Upaniṣad* and only by entering into the meaning of its symbolism can we command the gates of this many-mansioned city of Vedantic thought. There is never anything merely poetic or ornamental in the language of the *Upaniṣads*. Even in this passage which would at first sight seem to be sheer imagery, there is a choice, a selecting eye, and intention in the images. . . . But there is a danger that etymological fancies may mislead us. It is necessary, therefore, to test our provisional conclusions from philology by a careful examination of the images of this parable. Yet before we proceed to this enquiry, it is well to note that in the very opening of his second *brāhmaṇa*, the rishi passes on immediately from *aśva* the Horse to *aśaṇaya mṛtyuḥ*, Hunger is death, and assigns this hunger that is death as the characteristic, indeed the very nature of the Force that has arranged and developed,– evolved, as the moderns would say, –the material world.
>
> The sun is the eye of this great Force, the wind is its life breath or vital energy, Fire is its open mouth. . . . We are here in the company of very familiar symbols. . . . Side by side with this spatial image is that of the seasons reminding us immediately and intuitionally of the connection of Time and Space. The seasons, determined for us by the movements of the sun and stars, are the flanks of the horse and he stands upon the months and the fortnights - the lunar divisions. Space, then, is the flesh constituting materially this body of Time which the sage attributes to his Horse of the Worlds. . . . He is *haya* to the gods, *arvan* to the *asura*, *vājin* to the *gandharvas*, *aśva* to men. *Ye yathā māṁ prapadyante*. . . . In reality they are made in His image, not He is theirs, and though He seems to obey them and follow their needs and impulses, though they have the whip, ply the spur and tug the reins, it is He who bears them on in the course of *yugas* that are

> marked out for Him by His hidden Self; He is free and exulting in the swiftness of His galloping.
>
> But what are these names, *haya, vājin, arvan, aśva?* Certainly, they must suggest qualities which fit the Horse in each case to the peculiar type of its rider; but the meaning depends on associations and on etymology which in modern Sanskrit have gone below the surface and are no longer easily seizable. [59]

Here Sri Aurobindo points out a lacuna which is glaring in the modern scholar's study of ancient wisdom. In the course of the historical changes that came to India over a period of three thousand years we have lost many essential keys which alone can restore the missing link between our ratiocination and our ancient forefather's intuitional comprehension.

Paul Deussen in his *The Philosophy of the Upaniṣads*, presents his understanding of the meaning of the word *"upaniṣad"*:

> The Indian writers were practically justified in explaining the term *upaniṣad* by *rahasyam*, "secret." Less easy it is at first sight to understand how the word *upaniṣad* has come to signify "secret meaning, secret instruction, a secret." For *upaniṣad* derived as a substantive from the root *sad*, to sit, can only denote a "sitting"; and as the preposition *upa* (near by) indicates, in contrast to *pariṣad, samsad* (assembly), a "confidential secret sitting," we must assume, even if actual proof is wanting, that this name for "secret-sitting" was used also in course of time to denote the purpose of this sitting, i.e. "secret instruction." [60]

Deussen is intrigued that the rishis of the *Upaniṣads* were not in favor of treating *brahman* or *ātman* as an altar piece to be worshipped. To provide us with proof he quotes *Kena Upaniṣad* 1.4:

> That shouldest thou know as *brahman*, not that which is there worshipped *(na idam yad idam upāsate)*. . . . The proposition is laid down that not the gods, but the *ātman* alone should be worshipped, by this is to be understood merely a polemic against the worship of the gods,

not a demand to worship. [61]

Deussen wants us to know that the reference to secret is to be understood as: secret word, secret text, secret import. He explains the last as follows:

> Certain mysterious words, expressions, and formulas, which are only intelligible to the initiated, are described as *Upaniṣad.* These contain either a secret rule for action and behavior....or secret information on the nature of *brahman.* When, then, the latter is described as *satyasya satyam (Bṛhad. Up.* 2.1.20; 2.3.6), or *tad vanam* (the final goal of aspiration) *(Kena Up.* 4.6), there is added, "thou hast been taught the *Upaniṣad.*" Of a similar nature are secret words like *tajjalān (Chānd. Up.* 3.14.1), "in him (all beings) are born, perish, and breathe," or *neti neti (Bṛhad. Up.* 2.3.6, and often). And when the worship of *brahman* under such formulas is enjoined, it is not implied that *upaniṣad* signifies "worship," but only, as already pointed out, that meditation on *brahman* under these mysterious terms must take the place of worship of the gods. [62]

In an age when all over the world people were seeking gods to worship, it was most unusual for the rishis of India to turn to truth as the adorable and they did not bring in any god to have sway over human destiny. Now Deussen is speaking about the secret texts:

> The extant texts themselves, as well as the older texts underlying them, are called Upanishads. Accordingly in the Taittirīyaka school especially a section often ends with the words, – *iti upaniṣad.* . . . Very frequently it is not a word or a text, but the secret allegorical meaning of some ritual conception or practice, which is described as *upaniṣad; e.g.* In Chānd. 1.1.10,- "for that which is executed with knowledge, with faith , with the upaniṣad (knowledge of the secret meaning of Udgītha as *Om),* that is more effective. . . . "Which of these three significations is the original?" We might decide for the third, and suppose that an allegorical interpretation was assigned to the ritual,

and the Upanishad doctrine developed thence. [63]

We are very happy that the methodology we have used in the present commentary of the *Bṛhadāraṇyaka Upaniṣad* was essentially based on the allegorical interpretation, because in the *Bṛhadāraṇyaka* it is the bard who speaks, and he reasons dialectically. So we have adopted a methodology which gives us the certitude of mathematical logic as well as poetical intuition.

The Symbol of the Sacrificial Horse for Intimate Meditation

In the first *brāhmaṇa* there are only two mantras, and they are devoted to familiarizing us with the symbol of the horse and with the ensemble of the preliminary arrangements for an actual horse sacrifice. In our commentary we have already made it clear that there is no reference to an actual molesting of a horse or the carrying out of a blood-shedding and carcass-burning sacrifice. The *aśvamedha brāhmaṇa* is thus a very provocative allegory to go from the actual to the ideal.

In considering the symbolic presence of the sacrificial horse we follow the advice of the great commentator Śankarācārya to look upon this presentation as a subtle meditation on the significance of the symbol. An intense meditation on a Vedic ritual can serve the Vedāntic purpose of knowing how the Supreme implied in the specific can be visualized in order to closely establish oneself in an intimacy with the Self (*ātma upāsana*). That is the same as entering into a deep *dhyāna*, that can make the meditator inseparable from the deity or object of meditation. This way of understanding the teaching of the *Upaniṣad* is sure to purify one's individuated self. To such a purified self the vision of non-dual *brahman* is easily accessible. Śankara is categorical in holding his decided view that the knowledge of the real alone secures liberation from the bondage of the phenomenal.

The sacrifice of a horse done by a King in order to become Emperor is an example taken from the world of social conventions. In the present case the individuated human being who belongs to the world of society has to be sacrificed to attain immortality, not by being killed but by purifying the mind conditioned with worldly values. The main prayer in the *Bṛhadāraṇyaka Upaniṣad* is to be lead from the unreal to the real, from darkness to light and from the mortal to the immortal. It is for this purpose the sacrifice itself is conceived as an *udgītha*, a prayer of propitiation to raise one's lower self to the higher Self. For several reasons, an aspirant who is ambitious to become immortal is at the level of an ordinary animal. Among the ordinary animals one of the most beautiful, efficient beings of great worth is the horse. Hence the sacrificer identifies with a horse which spends all its life doing service to humanity. A sacrifice means burning a thing with name, form, mass, structure and functions into a nameless, formless, bodiless, actionless, reality which can be one with the eternal. This transformation is brought through the power of fire that can purify and transform. Time for us begins with our waking up into the day; that is dawn. To think of dawn can also make us think of the experiences of the beginning of many things: beginning the day, beginning the world of perception, beginning the interpretation of the significance of perception, programming for the rest of the day, etc. Thus the more we think about it, the head of the horse vanishes, the horse vanishes, the world vanishes, and even the dawn vanishes.

Sri Aurobindo says:

> The *aśvamedha* or Horse-Sacrifice is, as we shall see, taken as the symbol of a great spiritual advance, an evolutionary movement, almost, from out of the dominion of apparently material forces into a higher spiritual freedom. The Horse of the *aśvamedha* is, to the author, a physical figure representing, like some algebraical symbol, an unknown quantity of force and speed. From the imagery it is evident that this force, this speed is something world-wide, something universal; it fills the regions with its being, it occupies Time, it gallops through Space, it bears on in its speed men and Gods and the Titans.
>
> "Dawn," says the Rishi, "is the head of the Horse Sacrificial." Now, the head is the front, the part of us that faces and looks out upon our world, – and Dawn is that part to the Horse of the worlds. This goddess must therefore be the opening out of the world to the eye of Being – for as day is the symbol of a time of activity, night of a time of inactivity, so dawn images the imperfect but pregnant beginnings of regular cosmic action; it is the Being's movement forward, thus its impulse to look out

at the universe in which it finds itself and waking to yearn towards it, to desire to enter upon its possession of a world which looks so bright because of the brightness of the gaze that is turned upon it. The word *uṣas* means etymologically coming into manifested being; and it could mean also desire or yearning. *Uṣas* or Dawn, to the early thinker, was the impulse towards manifest existence, no longer a vague movement in the depths of the Unmanifest, but already emerging and on the brink of its satisfaction. . . . (Time), a mental circumstance, is the body of this force of the material universe whose eye is the sun and his breath the wind. . . . [B]y movement in Space its periods are shaped and determined. Therefore we return always to the full idea of the Horse – not as an image of matter, not as a symbol of the unknown supra-material Power in its supra-material reality, but of that Power expressing itself in matter, materially, we might almost say, pervading and constituting the universe. Time is its body, – yes, but *samvatsara* not *kāla*. Time in its periods determined by movement in Space, not Time in its essentiality.

Moreover, it is that Power imaging itself in Cosmos, it is the Horse of the Worlds. For, we read, "Heaven is its back, the mid-region is its belly, earth is its footing" – *pājasyam*, the four feet upon which it stands. We must be careful not to confuse the ancient Seer's conception of the universe with our modern conception. To us nothing exists except the system of gross material world – *annamayam jagat* – this earth, this moon, this sun and its planets, these myriad suns and their systems. But to the Vedāntic thinkers, the universe, the manifest *brahman*, was a harmony of worlds within worlds; they beheld a space within our space but linked with it, they were aware of a time connected with our time but different from it. . . . Heaven is the back of the Horse, because it is on the mind that we rest, mind that bears up the Gods and Gandharvas, Titans and men; the mid-region is the belly, because vital energy is that which hungers and devours, moves restlessly everywhere seizing everything and turning it into food; earth is the footing, because matter, outward form, is the fundamental condition for the manifestation of life, mind and all higher forces. On Matter we rest and have our firm stand; out of Matter we rise to our fulfillment in Spirit. . . . "When he stretches himself, then it lightnings, when he shakes himself, then it thunders; when he urines, then it rains." *Vijṛmbhate* – extends himself in intensity, makes the most of his physical bulk and force; *vidhūnute* – throws himself out in energy, converts his whole body into a motion and force; these two words are of a great impetuosity and vehemence and, taken in conjunction with the image, extremely significant. The Yogin will at once recognize the reference to the electrical manifestation, visible, or felt, which accompany so often the increase of concentration, thought and inner activity in the waking condition, – electricity, *Vidyūtas*, the material symbol, medium and basis of all activities of knowledge *sarvāni vijñāna-vijṛmbhitāni*. He will recognize also the *meghadhvani*, one of the characteristic sounds heard in the concentration of Yoga, symbolical of *kṣatratejas* and physically indicative of force gathering itself for action. The first image is therefore an image of knowledge expressing itself in matter, the second is an image of power expressing itself in matter. The third, the image of rain, suggests that it is from the mere waste matter of his body that this great Power is able to fertilize the world and produce sustenance for the myriad nations of his creatures. "Speech verily is the voice of him." *Vāgevāsya vāk*. Speech, with its burden of definite thought, is the neighing of this mighty Horse of sacrifice; by that this great Power in matter expresses materially the uprush of his thought and yearning and emotion, the visible sparks of the secret universal fire that is in him – *guhahitam*. [64]

The horse and horse-sacrifice are like a preface to the *Bṛhadāraṇyaka Upaniṣad*. We enter into the most secret symbol of death as well as life in the next *brāhmaṇa*.

Prajāpati

The *Bṛhadāraṇyaka Upaniṣad* is an exhaustive commentary

on the science of the Absolute (*brahmavidyā*). It commences with salutations to *AUM* which symbolically represents *brahman*. In the invocation mantra what is suggested as *AUM* offers us three great consolations. One is that our origin before manifestation is the all-filling *brahman*, which is *pūrṇam*. *Pūrṇam* is to be taken here in the sense of having the potentiality to fill to the brim. When we look at the world, there is a multifarious implication of filling. The sun is continuously radiating in all directions and filling the entire sky. It goes from the source, it fills all of space. In that process it reveals myriads of forms and also puts energy into everything. This is one picture of filling. The minutest water particles collecting into water molecules and then droplets to fill the seven oceans with water, rivers streaming from all directions into these oceans, the same water droplets being reclaimed by sunlight and transported into clouds which are carried in all directions by winds to rain on mountain tops, valleys, farmlands, lakes, rivers and reservoirs. It reaches the tendrils of the roots of vegetation to green the whole world. Such a continuous cycle is another picture of filling. These are all perennial formations and manifestations. Similarly, the thermal force emerging from the sun, lightning, clouds, water, air and fire makes the biosphere for the earth, giving it a climate, an ecosystem.

Such is the potential of manifestation in *brahman*. It is like a golden hue of the Absolute which gives us hope to grow, to change, to transform, to multiply. In all these systems we see there is an overlordship which is instrumental to the manifestation. There is continuous structuring, coupling, opposites acting on each other, balancing, steadying, creating cataclysms and reshuffling in which every manifested aspect of the Absolute has a necessary position, relationship and functional dynamics. That is how the projection from the latent into the actual is taken care of from the minutest formation of the subtle to the macromanifestation of the unbounded universe. It is called *prajāpati*, *brahman*, *hiraṇyagarbha* and *virāj*. Different names are given only for distinguishing one function from another.

All these suggestions come from the first line of the invocation with which the book commences: *AUM pūrṇam adaḥ*. The potential we are experiencing in our here and now is in continuation of what was yesterday and out there. The movement of manifestation from what was to what is happens meticulously according to the continuous fulfillment of a law which can be called a supreme law. When the microcosm and macrocosm are integrally understood, there is no division in the continuing dynamics of structural and functional verity. With that holistic vision of the first cause and the continuous effects, one has to understand what is stated here as *pūrṇam idam*. Although there is no separation from the first cause and final cause, when the individuation is an empirical fact in the individuated person, it is necessary to think of time and space, motion and mass. Hence it is said, *pūrṇāt pūrṇam udacyate*. Out of the *pūrṇam* the *pūrṇam* is being projected. To postulate the beginning of the beginning, from a point which is not physically manifested we need to conceive of *sṛj*. *Sṛj* is an irresistible, irrefutable impulse that becomes a model for action. That is how we account for the emergence of *prajāpati*. *Praja* is that which has within it the law of being, the law of fecundity, the law of propagation, the law of proliferation. So *prajāpati* is to be understood as an eternal cause, continuously projecting innumerable possibilities of which some become immediate probabilities, and a selected few probabilities become actualized.

Prajāpati is the most philosophically intriguing and potent possibility. It causes and it is also the effect; it is birthless and yet it is giving birth to many; it is deathless and its death, through an act of sacrifice, fills space and time with many duplications, replications and variegated manifestations through an apparent evolution. It is the one hope that becomes multitudinous beacons of hope which automatically become springboards of minds. The *prajāpati* is mortal because it is through its death it immortalizes both life and death. Hence the *Bṛhadāraṇyaka Upaniṣad* begins with the mention of death, but a death which is a great promise of life. In order to die, the dying being has to live; it is dying so that the essence can return a million-fold as new actualization and promises of life. In the *Bible* Jesus Christ says that the grain that tries to preserve itself will perish, but the grain that allows itself to perish will return a hundred-fold. As there are countless attributes of *prajāpati*, the *Upaniṣad* describes millions of forms, selected from trillions of possibilities and millions of action propensities. Such is the magic being called *prajāpati*. Finally we are told the great secret that the filling (*pūrṇam*) detaches, liberates itself from the manifested fulfillment to go back to its source. It is a magic snake which swallows its own tail. That is given here as *pūrṇasya pūrṇam ādāya, pūrṇam eva avaśiṣyate*. Such is the initial presentation of the *prajāpati* flanked on either side by life and death and the death of life.

A student uninitiated into the secret of the Upaniṣadic language may find it difficult to conceive of a dual principle being presented in the concept of *brahman*. The cosmic hunger, the fire of the cosmic person *(virāj)*, is counterbalanced by the hope of fulfillment, *hiraṇyagarbha*. If *virāj* is the thesis, its antithesis is *hiraṇyagarbha* and the synthesis is *prajāpati*. Between hunger and the fuel fed into it, projections arise. In the *Śatapatha Brāhmaṇa* we read that one who sacrifices to the Self is better than one who sacrifices to the gods. Our first exposure to *prajāpati* is as the exemplifier of such a sacrifice. In that context *prajāpati* is the first emergence into a physical state from *hiraṇyagarbha* and *hiraṇyagarbha* is recognized as the being identified with the sum total of all minds.

To understand *prajāpati* we have to understand both *vaiśvānara* and *hiraṇyagarbha*. To understand *vaiśvānara* we have to understand what *virāj* is; to understand *hiraṇyagarbha*, we have to understand the whole theme of projection, of becoming arising out of being, passing through long periods of evolution and ultimately returning to *brahman*. For this we are given the discipline of drawing out of transcendence the whole cosmos of immanence and then dissolving the entire immanence back into transcendence.

In *Adhyāya* I, *brāhmaṇa* 2, *vaiśvānara* appears for the first time as the fire of death. Previous commentators identify *hiraṇyagarbha* with death. This is not quite appropriate as here death comes as hunger – cosmic hunger. So instead of *hiraṇyagarbha*, it should be presented as *vaiśvānara*. It is hunger which aspired to have a mind. There was no difference between body, mind, intellect and the Self. It was as if the Self emerged from the non-Self, just as there is a latent potential in death to generate life. The mind is mentioned as the first move, which is one of the marks of *ātman*. Another mark of the *ātman* is in *mṛtyu* itself as hunger, one who desires to eat. The first mind-like being is said to have worshipped itself and in the strain of thinking water sprang up (as sweat). The birth of *prajāpati* and *hiraṇyagarbha* is to be taken as a simultaneous manifestation. Although *hiraṇyagarbha* and *prajāpati* are complementary aspects, there cannot be two progenitors. Therefore *prajāpati* is considered to be the efficient cause which generates the golden germ, *hiraṇyagarbha*.

Hiraṇyagarbha in turn gave a design and structural embodiment to the *prajāpati*. This is close to the genetic concept of the ovum and the sperm diffusing into each other and growing into a fetus in the womb. For the modern mind it is difficult to understand how, without a manipulator, the self-born is both the nature and naturing as Spinoza puts it. Spinoza talks of both: nature-naturing and nature-natured. In spite of our expectation to find the origin of both *hiraṇyagarbha* and *prajāpati* in the *Ṛg Veda*, there is no clear reference until the tenth *maṇḍala*, the last in the *Ṛg Veda Samhita*. The sixth *ṛk* of *sūkta* 121 of the *Ṛg Veda*, says *avasa-tasta-bhāne*, "for the sake of protecting the world." The establishment of the sun as the energizing agent of the world is covertly termed as *prajāpati* by the commentators in the *Ṛg Veda Bhāṣya*. In *ṛk* 8 of *sūkta* 14 of the tenth *maṇḍala* is the word *dakṣam* which is given the meaning of *prajāpati*. With this reference, the Vedic civilization is slowly moving to the one among the many. It is called *dakṣam* in the *Veda* and *prajāpati* in the commentary. The word *prajāpati* appears for the first time in *ṛk* 10 of *sūkta* 121. There it is described as the all-pervading, the wielder and controller of everything.

Raimundo Pannikar's *Mantra Mañjari* is a thorough-going study of the *Vedas* and the *Upaniṣads*. From his very exhaustive indexes, we can see that he has gone though every *ṛk* of every *sūkta* of all the ten *maṇḍalas*. He agrees that both *prajāpati* and *hiraṇyagarbha* are abundantly referred to in the *Atharva Veda* whereas they appear in only one mantra or *ṛk* in the tenth *maṇḍala* of *Ṛg Veda*.

There is a very beautiful presentation of the birth of *hiraṇyagarbha* given in the *Mantra Mañjari*:

> Three leading themes concerning the mystery of existence emerge like melodies in a concerto, now sounding together in harmony and counterpoint, now repeated singly or with clashing effect. These three closely connected melodies are all expressed in the first stanza: (a) the origin of reality ("In the beginning arose the Golden Germ"); (b) the Lordship of God ("He was as soon as born the Lord of Being"); (c) the human adventure of returning to the primeval state ("What God shall we adore with our oblation?"). . . . We cannot call this first step a creation: God is not created. Nor can we call it evolution in the

usual sense of the word, nor a becoming, as if God first were not and later came to be. [65]

The *ṛk* we introduced here as the only one which speaks of *hiraṇyagarbha* and *prajāpati* is also pointed out by Pannikar. We get a clear picture of *hiraṇyagarbha:*

1. In the beginning arose the Golden Germ:
he was, as soon as born, the Lord of Being,
sustainer of the Earth and of this Heaven.
What God shall we adore with our oblation?

2. He who bestows life-force and hardy vigor,
whose ordinances even the Gods obey,
whose shadow is immortal life– and death–
What God shall we adore with our oblation?

3. Who by his grandeur has emerged sole sovereign
of every living thing that breathes and slumbers,
he who is Lord of man and four-legged creatures–
What God shall we adore with our oblation?

4. To him of right belong, by his own power,
the snow-clad mountains, the world-stream, and the sea.
His arms are the four quarters of the sky.
What God shall we adore with our oblation?

5. Who held secure the mighty Heavens and Earth,
who established light and sky's vast vault above,
who measured out the ether in mid-spheres–
What God shall we adore with our oblation?

6. Toward him, trembling, the embattled forces,
riveted by his glory, direct their gaze.
Through him the risen sun sheds forth its light.
What God shall we adore with our oblation?

7. When came the mighty Waters, bringing with them
the universal Germ, whence sprang the Fire,
thence leapt the God's One Spirit into being.
What God shall we adore with our oblation?

8. This One who in his might surveyed the Waters
pregnant with vital forces, producing sacrifice,
he is the God of Gods and none beside him.
What God shall we adore with our oblation?

9. O Father of the Earth, by fixed laws ruling,
O Father of the Heavens, pray protect us,
O Father of the great and shining Waters!
What God shall we adore with our oblation?

10. O Lord of creatures, Father of all beings,
you alone pervade all that has come to birth.
Grant us our heart's desire for which we pray.
May we become the lords of many treasures! [66]

Then we come to the reference to the Cosmic Person, *puruṣa*, in the *Puruṣa Sūkta* of the *Ṛg Veda*. The eleventh and twelfth *ṛks* of the *Puruṣa Sūkta* are probably interpolations put into it later to give sanctity to the four-fold *varṇas* which have made Hinduism a horrid sham for perpetuating and perpetrating impossible barriers of caste restrictions. *Ṛg Veda* was once considered the preeminent scriptural revelation. Then the *Śatapatha Brāhmaṇa* and the *Taittirīya Brāhmaṇa* rose to eminence. The *Bṛhadāraṇyaka* itself is a part of *Śatapatha Brāhmaṇa*.

In the search for a unitive philosophy Yājñavalkya moved towards the *Atharva Veda*. Some of the finest attitudes of life and the most noble contemplative thoughts which later became the main stream of Indian life come from the *Atharva Veda*. Even today at the end of religious functions there is often a group singing of the invocation of peace (*śāntiḥ*), given in the *Atharva Veda* 19.9:

1. Peaceful be heaven, peaceful the earth,
peaceful the broad space between.
peaceful for us be the running waters,
peaceful the plants and herbs!

2. Peaceful for us be the signs of the future,
peaceful what is done and undone,
peaceful to us be what is and what will be.

May all to us be gracious!

3. This supreme Goddess, Word, inspired by Brahman,
by which the awe-inspiring is created,
through her to us be peace!

4. This supreme Spirit, inspired by Brahman,
by which the awe-inspiring is created,
through them to us be peace!

5. These five sense organs, with the mind as the sixth,
within my heart, inspired Brahman,
by which the awe-inspiring is created,
through them to us be peace!

14. Peace be to earth and to airy spaces!
Peace be to heaven, peace to the waters,
peace to the plants and peace to the trees!
May all the Gods grant to me peace!
By this invocation of peace may peace be diffused!
By this invocation of peace may peace bring peace!
With this peace the dreadful I now appease,
with this peace the cruel I now appease,
with this peace all evil I now appease,
so that peace may prevail, happiness prevail!
May everything for us be peaceful! [67]

In the *Vedas* and *Upaniṣads*, just as in all world religions, the three strands of cosmology, psychology, and theology are intertwined and each one infuses its spirit in the other. Indians are not ashamed of their anthropomorphism. We have seen that at the very outset the archetypal mind was used to formulate the first of beings, *prajāpati*, and *prajāpati* was given as an answer to the great hunger of *vaiśvānara*. Hence the concept of *ātman* as the eater of the food itself is derived from *anna*, the food. The concept of food is also a model for sacrifice. Sacrifice is also considered to be what nourishes the gods.

We find the same equation in the Last Supper of Jesus where he held out a loaf of bread and said that it was his flesh and a bowl of wine and said that it was his blood. He was giving himself as a sacrifice to redeem others of their sins. We see the origin of that belief in the *soma* spirituality and theology given in the *Śatapatha Brāhmaṇa*. The *Śatapatha Brāhmaṇa* recalls the primordial sacrifice of *prajāpati* and addresses *agni*, the first born of the mouth of *prajāpati*, as a consumer of food. It relates how *prajāpati* had to reproduce himself because there was no other food than himself. Later it is accepted in the *Bhagavad Gītā* also that sacrifice is the means to sustenance. Thus the *Bṛhadāraṇyaka Upaniṣad* presents a scheme of sustaining life through sacrifice. Here two things go together: a ritualistic sacrifice of what is most dear to strengthen everyone else accompanied by the most lofty prayer called *udgītha*.

Udgītha

The ancient forms of sacrifice in all religions are revalued in the *Udgītha Brāhmaṇa* into a compassionate appeal to the human sense of dignity. Thus the *Bṛhadāraṇyaka Upanisad* sets a model not only for Indian religious people, but also for all religions of the world. The Indian religions can be classified as five-fold: the Śaiva, the Jain, Vaiśnava, Vedic and Śāktya. A lofty sense of peace, (*śānti*) and a universal sense of uniting all in the embrace of love is expressed in the contemplative serenity of the original votaries of Indian religions. In the history of India's Śiva religion, the first evidence came from the excavations of Mohanjadaro and Harappa which have given us the seals of Paśupati Śiva whose image was embossed in bricks which are as ancient as 7000 years before Christ. Paśupati is shown as a yogi seated in a lotus posture. Śiva was called *paśupati*, the Lord of Beings. The later Vedic term *prajāpati* was a close imitation of the term *paśupati*. There are also references in the *Āgamas* to Śiva as *prajāpati*.

In the seal of Paśupati Śiva, what is most beautiful are the various figures shown around the main figure, such as the birds of the sky, fish on either side, forest animals like leopard or tiger, closely guarding him, and domestic animals lying at his feet. All beings were originally called *paśu*. Thus the first contemplative picture of Śiva was a symbol of uniting the animal world through his peaceful and loving relationship with all. Much later, in Śankara's time, this great contemplative *guru* is described as *dakṣiṇamūrti*, making the wisdom gesture with his right hand. Thus the first emblem of the primary exemplar of yoga spells peace to the world. The term *śiva* itself means peace.

Historically, people think of Jainism as contemporary to Buddhism. This is not true. The last Jain sage, Mahāvīra Tīrthankara, was the twenty fourth in the hierarchy of teachers. If we trace back the times of the previous *tīrthankaras* to the first one, Ṛṣabhadeva, he would have been contemporary with the mythology connected with Paśupati Śiva. Further, the main teaching of the Jain religion is very close to the unifying and contemplative love ideals of Śiva. Jainism has a great affinity to the simple natural living exemplified by Śiva. We do not see Śiva depicted anywhere with gorgeous crowns, jewelry, or stylish clothes. Dancing in the charnel fields, wrapped in an elephant skin, with his matted hair and his body smeared with ashes, he is a picture of abandon, which afterwards became a model for *sannyāsa* as well as *yoga*. The image of Gomateśvara, a Jain Guru revered in India, stands stark naked completely oblivious of the external world. Creepers entwine around his legs and hands. He represents one ideal of the superconsciousness of a yogi going into transcendence. There is a great affinity between contemplative Śiva and the Jain *tīrthankaras*.

In the world of symbolism, Viṣṇu and Śiva are like two contrasting counterparts in Indian mythology. Viṣṇu sustains everything and Śiva dissolves everything. In Indian mythology Śiva is seated in a yogic posture at the summit of mount Kailāsa, completely drawn inward. Jungle snakes fondly crawl all over him; his vehicle is considered to be a mountain bull. He holds a trident symbolizing the triple aspects of Śaivism: *paśu*, *pati* and *pāsam*. He is always established in an all-knowing transcendence which is not deep sleep, not the dream sleep and which is not the waking state.

Viṣṇu is shown as lying in a state of dream; the phenomenal universe is considered to be the dream of Viṣṇu. His bed is the great snake Vāsuki and he is placed in the milk ocean. Thus everything pleasing, amorous, and belonging to the world of memory is associated with Viṣṇu. His vehicle is Garuḍa, the seabird. The Vaiṣṇavite people call him *samasta kalyāṇa guṇi*, adorned with attributes, whereas Śiva is *guṇātita*, one who transcends all attributes. From the navel of Viṣṇu comes the creator, Brahma, who became identified as *prajāpati*. Thus it became common to accept Brahma, the creator, Viṣṇu, the sustainer, and Śiva, the annihilator, as the three male concepts of God. Each of the three has a female counterpart: Śakti for Śiva, Lakṣmi for Viṣṇu and Saraśvati for Brahma.

In the course of time, the mythology around these divinities snowballed. As human beings were drawn more and more to the necessities of life, their symbols of divinity also became darkened by the world of necessity. Necessity makes people callous, hateful, jealous, competitive, amorous and blood-thirsty. Thus what began in peace, joy and love became burdened with all human vices. This tendency of the profound to transform into the profane continues. We can see a parallel in the Semitic religion which begins with the beautiful presentation of Genesis in the *Torah* and the *Old Testament*. As we pass from Genesis, especially after the sons of Adam and Eve got into competition for God's favor, the religious texts of the Semitic religions go through several winding paths of cruelty with parallel streaks of great charity. Until we come to the story of Jesus Christ, Jewish history is very much like the Indian history of spirituality with illustrations of the most adorable as well as the most abominable.

Towards the end of the *Ṛg Veda*, the Vedic people came to have the notion that truth is only one. In the Semitic religions the unity of God was emphasized by Moses. Thereafter the same oneness of God was affirmed by both Jesus Christ and the Prophet as it was revealed to him through the *Holy Qur'an*.

When we consider the modern world ensuing from these ancient non-historical or pre-historical speculations, ponderings, and poetic imaginations, we come across religions in the mid-Asian countries, ranging from Jerusalem to the Pacific, which have gathered around them a culture which is very similar. Indian thought and spiritual outlook influenced China and Japan. The Buddhist upheaval came like the aspirations of several generations of suppressed people – Lord Buddha spoke for the spirit of the human love for liberation. An amalgam of religions evolved, theistic as well as natural. While these dramas were being played in the Asian hemisphere, Mediterranean countries from Egypt to Greece contributed a new outlook based more on mathematics and a veneration for objective truth. Two stalwarts in that field were Plato and Aristotle. As an offshoot of the Greek flair for reason, a critical acumen came in the mind of people to investigate the origin of the world. Starting with philosophers like Thales, Anaximander, Anaximenes, Leucippus and Lucretius, it has continued to our own century, resulting in the theory that the world came out of the big bang of some unknown entity.

In spite of trying to formulate a theory of Genesis without a God, modern scientists have had to accept all the attributes of God, one by one. Just as the Indian people envisioned the role of mother as Śakti to counterbalance Śiva, modern science conceived matter and energy. A little confusion comes from saying that matter and energy are like Śiva and Śakti, because, to the Indian people, Śakti is energy and the source of energy is in Śiva. In the Western world, matter became equivalent to mother (*mater* is the Latin term for mother). There is no general conclusion because mythology, organized religion, history, legends, accurate documentation, and the proofs of modern science are all still in the melting pot. With clarity we have to discern the strands of truth and untruth which intertwine in the general civilization of human beings. This is partly what we want to do with this study of the *Upaniṣad.* Our ambition is to clean the stable and to admit whatever is conducive to human dignity and reject whatever brings distress and depression to human beings.

The world relates to all living beings. It is like a ground for all. However insignificant a living being may seem to be, the world supports all life forms with absolute care. Except for humans and domestic animals, the world providentially sustains living beings without the need for any contract. Because of the close association between humans and domestic animals like horses, cattle, sheep, goats, cats, dogs, chickens and love-birds caged in private homes, the animals look upon their keepers like people who expect God to provide for them. They have come to have a sort of humanized mind and expectations by being considered as part of a home.

Biologically, all homo sapiens are a single species. Due to evolution there are several peripheral distinctions among human beings which have resulted from three inevitable conditions to which all humans are exposed. First is the habitat, including the ecosystem in which they are placed, which influences the anthropologic peculiarities of social groups. Second are the geologic factors which include climate and what the good earth in each area of human habitat provides as staple foods such as wheat, rice, maize, corn, barley and various kinds of tubers, fruits, and nuts. Third is the time that percolates into the culture of societies. Although the time shown by the clock is the same, except for the changes made for convenience, people do not live at the same time. Current social behavior patterns, languages, culture and technology are often delayed and sometimes denied to some members of society living in the same home or community with others. Each society has its span of time which can become like a stagnant pool in the experiences of some people.

In spite of all such differences, it is inevitable for an individual to have a subject/object relationship with this world. To each person "this world" means everything outside the person, including parents, brothers and sisters, friends and neighbors. An individual has to act with an objective relationship to all these persons also. The main relationship between a person and their world is conducted with the word. The word that is uttered comes from the deepest core of an individual. He or she cannot trace the exact source from where ideas pop up and get clothed in words. Words come from an unknown depth and are spoken out. They may be directed to an individual person, like father, mother, brother or sister, or to a group of intimate people. This is only a small part of our speech. Throughout one's wakeful hours and dream hours, a person is speaking to himself or herself using words. At the same time, the person is also experiencing various non-verbal emotional moods such as love, fear, anxiety, wonder, pathos.

Just as we experience an inner depth, we also postulate a height where we conceive of the presence of a greater Self or Providence which is something like the totality of all to which we can supplicate. This is the spiritual counterpart of one's being. Each one of us has physical counterparts, social counterparts, and a spiritual counterpart, whether we are Eskimo, Cuban, Swahili, Italian, Chinese or Indian. We all need to speak to the external world, the internal world, and to that which is considered to be intimate with each individual with a moral sense of loving care, justice and truth. Religious people in various countries have made caricatures of what is postulated as a superior being in an adorable form, which they address with a certain name, even though they are not very sure whether the higher being has any name, form or describable dimensions.

A person is most aware of his or her own pain, pleasure or indifference. Pain can be slight, acute, unbearable; pleasure can also be gentle, exciting or overwhelming. Indifference can be something sheerly oblivious or it can be of different degrees of boredom or disgust. Both pain and pleasure make it imperative for a person to tell someone what he or she wants. In the *Bṛhadāraṇyaka Upaniṣad* this acute need to attend to one's own security is portrayed as inevitable. Therefore speaking out is not only shown to be the main source of life, but also a measure of behavior to be immediately implemented. In the Christian context, this is divided into piety and works. The Hindus call it *ukta* and *yajña*. *Ukta* means to speak out; *yajña* means to perform. When they are philosophically understood, *ukta* has a simple origin in the cognitive factor which brings information to the knower. What comes as in-formation necessitates the transformation of one's energy into out-formation. That means one conveys oneself to another with the aid of words which have a sonal form and an inner context of meaning. In Sanskrit these are called *śabda* and *artha*. Every person in the world is familiar with his or her sounds and the meaning of the word that is automatically expressed by one's own breath and the organ of speech.

When one unites oneself with the need to speak (*ukti*), an element of reasoning evolves. This is called *yukti*. When you reason it is an argument. An argument is to convince the listener that you have an earnest appeal to make. It can be a prayer, request or praise. It can be the assignment of value. In the course of evolution humanity made a super image of its own personal notion, and eulogized that as God Supreme, the Oversoul. Human beings conceived that the Supreme Being must have the same necessity to speak out and that the world came to be from the speaking of the Supreme. This is very well exemplified in the Genesis of the *Old Testament* and *Torah* where God is presented as a spirit living on the surface of the waters surrounded by darkness. God was pictured as having the necessity to speak out: "Let there be light." Consequently light came. In the *Bṛhadāraṇyaka Upaniṣad*, the first concept was not of God but of the dire necessity of hunger to be appeased. Hence it is said that hunger came to the tether end of its wits and like God saying, "Let there be light," hunger said, "I need a mind to face the problem of death." Consequently, mind manifested.

Thus in both Semitic and Indian cultures, the concept of the Supreme came from the psychological needs of human beings. We begin to live by expressing our needs, so we think God must also have been like that. Our theological notions are a direct outcome of our psychological needs. Naturally we brought our psychological notions to bear upon everything we experience as outside factors. We can even see this in our use of language. We say the wind blows, the sun shines, the cloud rains. Even where there is no personal actor, we attribute action to everything in the perceptual world. There is no religious, political, social, familial, interpersonal or even intrapersonal life without speech.

When we analyze speech, we see that we begin in a state of confusion in which our personal consciousness is fused into the indiscernible matrix of sensations. Our first struggle is to stand apart and push the source of sensations to an object out there. This automatically brings a cleavage between the knower and the known. Once a thing is even partially known, it is added to the individual consciousness as an extension of consciousness through an act of mimicking. That is memory. If the earth is our ground, memory is the ground on which mind grows into multifarious dimensions. Day by day, the field of memory becomes more and more enormous. To answer the problems of confusion, the mind relies on itself. The cognitive factor takes for granted that whatever was obscure, mimicked, and made part of memory is a valid documentation. This belief is a time/space body image which gives asylum to personal consciousness to live always in memory. Then we transpose our memories into each other.

Like the individual mind, a social mind is also manufactured. The first community consciousness we come across in the *Bṛhadāraṇyaka Upaniṣad* is the community of the sense organs, abstracted also into the central memory in which hearing, touching, seeing, tasting and smelling are all given their rightful positions as part of an ensemble of consciousness. The first prayer in the *Bṛhadāraṇyaka Upaniṣad* is made by the breath which is solely responsible for keeping an organism alive. The breath makes a supplication to speech to give a prayer for the protection of the community. But a part can never be the whole. Mind itself first came from the word which is expressed through the breath in the mouth. The main content of the speech was perceiving a defect and seeking a redemption from it. Three such defects were located: untruth, ignorance and fear of death. Just as the Semitic God said, "Let there be light" and there was light, the *Upaniṣad* says, "Let us be redeemed from untruth to truth; let us be redeemed from the darkness of ignorance to the light of wisdom; let us be redeemed from the fear of death to immortality." This supplication is not only of the Hindus, but of all groups of people all over the world. Only the format of the prayer is different.

Humans are not the only beings who make supplications: when the cow is hungry and thirsty, she makes her supplication with the sound, "moo." The cat mews, the dog barks. When the crossroads of life is even more acute such as when one does not know where providence is, the call is for light to lead a person from non-knowledge to knowledge. The calamity can be more tragic when death glares in your eyes. Then you have no time to waste, you have to cry out for life - "SOS!" It is then we have to say, "Please deliver us from death to immortality." This is the main gist of the *udgītha*, which comes as a song of the soul. An effort is necessary to speak out and relate oneself with providence. That effort is the fountain source of sacrifice. The present is sacrificing for the future. Even a blade of grass makes supplication. In the scorching sun, it withholds the chlorophyll from the periphery of the leaf and takes it into the stems, then withdraws it from the stems to the root where it is preserved until the hot days are over. It undergoes a kind of self-immolation in order to be re-born in the rainy season. Sacrifice (*yajña*) is another way of speaking or giving supplication (*ukti*).

If *ukti* belongs to knowledge, its application belongs to action. The *Bṛhadāraṇyaka Upaniṣad* elaborates these two fundamentals in human life in six *adhyāyas*, falling into three *kāṇḍas*: *Madhu Kāṇḍa*, *Muni Kāṇḍa*, and *Khila Kāṇḍa*. It is like the two hands coming together. Speech and action have to go hand in hand, first to perish wantonly, willingly, then to re-emerge with more perfection, vigor and persistence. That is behind every prayer. When the prayer becomes less and less vociferous, it is a meditation; when it becomes an argument with well-structured words spoken out with emphasis, it becomes rhetoric or narration.

The *Bṛhadāraṇyaka Upaniṣad* first presents the theme of the great search called *brahmavidyā* with the horse and horse sacrifice. Both the philosophies of Yoga and *Vedānta* have a tradition of the invocation of the spirit which is more or less like preparing one's mind for a life-long commitment. When this is ritualistically done, it is *upāsana*. When it is contemplatively performed it is *dhyāna*. In the Buddhist tradition it is recommended that one should make a wish which is equivalent to a prayer: the search for the highest can be done just like a simple man expressing his desire to be enlightened in the form of a prayer. Thus *udgītha* is universally recognized in India.

In the *Bṛhadāraṇyaka*, the *udgītha* is first identified with the *upāsana* of the horse sacrifice. The *Upaniṣad* makes a big break from what was known in India up to that time as a ritual locally conducted according to traditions to please a chief of a community of people. From such a puerile and make-believe worship, the *Upaniṣad* carries its votaries to a vast scenario where the panorama includes the sun and moon, the starry heavens and the ocean which girdles the globe. For the sacrificial fire, the sun that shines bright in the firmament and the eye that sees it from earth are brought into a single configuration. The rishi leads us into that haven of freedom on the horse of our aspiration. We read in I.1.2 the following mantra,

> Verily the day arose for the horse as the sacrificial vessel which stands before. Its place is the eastern sea. Verily the night arose as the sacrificial vessel which stands behind. Its place is the western sea. Verily these two arose on both ends of the horse as the two sacrificial vessels. Becoming a steed he carried the gods, a stallion, the *gandharvas*, a courser, the demons, a horse, humans. The sea indeed is his relative, the sea is his place. [68]

The gods, the *gandharvas*, the *asuras* and the *manuṣyas* are all goal-oriented beings who ride on their respective horses to their goal. The ultimate aim as well as the starting point are both the self - the self aspiring to rise to the higher Self. This is the *udgītha* mentioned first. Then the theme changes. When the symbols are enumerated, the horse's eye is identified with the sun, its vital force *(prāṇa)* with air, and its open mouth with the fire of hunger. The world opens up to us only when the sun illuminates it. But from our side we should have breath to turn our eyes to that world. The breath needs the nourishment of food. Thus the first *udgītha* shown to us is of a practical nature of empirical validity. The allegory gives us a handle to hold something so vast in our imagination. Further it is said that this cosmological phenomenon rests on a psychological function of the life energy moving into the stream of time. Instead of a fragmentary time notion like a second or a minute, time is referred to here as *samvatsara* – a whole year which includes four seasons, twelve months, twenty-four fortnights, and several days and nights.

The air as a material for breath substantially changes into the vital energy which transforms basic elements. Through its alchechemy, quantities of things are merged into a unitive quality. A fire element in the air gives air the dynamic to move things. Like *yin* and *yang*, when heat and cold make blasts and counterblasts, the alchemy of creation happens. This transfers *udgītha* from a chanting at the altar to a transformation of values, causing a person to be both intellectually and emotionally destructured in order to be restructured again. In the model of a *yajña*, every structured element is cast into burning flame. Air, fire and vitality are combined into the restructuring of a new spirit with a new vision. The passive aspect of the chanting of a mantra is transformed into a personal reconstruction. That is the next phase of the *udgītha brāhmaṇa*.

In *brāhmaṇa* 4 we go from the horse sacrifice to the sacrifice of the *prajāpati*. In the first mantra, *prajāpati* is identified with the cosmic person *(virāj)*:

> In the beginning, this universe was verily the Self (*virāj*), in the form of a person. He pondered and beheld nothing else but himself. He first said, "I am he." Therefore he got the name "I." Hence even now when anyone is accosted, one first says, "It is I," and then tells the other name that one has. Because he was the first (among the aspirants to the status of *prajāpati*), and (before) this whole group consumed all evils, therefore he is called *puruṣa*. One who knows thus verily consumes anyone who wishes to be (*prajāpati*) ahead of one. [69]

The *udgītha* given in this context is: "From evil lead me to good; from darkness lead me to light; from death lead me to immortality. In all three mantras of the *udgītha*, each one explains the previous one. When one makes the prayer, "May I be delivered from the non-Self to the Self, from evil to the good," a question arises, "What is evil? What is non-Self?" The answer comes from the next line, "From darkness to light," or "From ignorance to wisdom." So ignorance is evil and wisdom is good. Ignorance is where one is confronted with mortality. Therefore the good is where the self-same truth is established on itself as the immortal. *Prajāpati*, who had not a second, decided to sacrifice its unified personality. *Prajāpati* sought greater glory by bringing out of itself the world of manifold names and forms. The elaboration of *prāṇa* in a single-celled body cannot be taken any further unless it is broken into many. Thus cell multiplication itself is seen as the *prāṇa upāsana.* The *prāṇa upāsana* becomes the *udgītha upāsana.*

Although in an actual act of worship many persons associate and each one contributes the merit of his or her *prāṇa* to give the various chants, when there is only one being there cannot be any literal sacrifice in the conventional manner. Hence the community is to be formed with the organ of perception and the organ of action, presided over by the mind. Thus it becomes imperative to treat the one Self with many divisions. Just as Jesus says, "I have many chambers in my father's mansion," these chambers are here the endorsement of instruments carrying out a more elaborate form of life. Out of *prāṇa* comes the power to hear, to touch, to see, to taste, to smell, and the power to sort all the others out and to assign separate duties to each. When the *prāṇa* is monitoring the functions of the various senses it is called *mātariśvān.* Within a body many new areas of function begin to operate, and on the same principle the one is made into the manifold. This is the first sacrifice of the *prajāpati* described in the *Puruṣavidha Brāhmaṇa.* When the *puruṣa* as Manu split into *pati* (Manu) and *patni* (Śatarūpa), between them all forms of life came to be. Thus in this *udgītha* we arrive at a gradation of reality from single-celled beings to the human.

Now if we reverse the order of the *udgītha* given in the first *adhyāya* we can see that death can be avoided only by knowing how the Self is the substantial. To know the Self to be substantial one should know the distinction between mortality and immortality. If immortality is recognized as a characteristic of *brahman,* and if *brahman* is identified with *ātman,* and if true knowledge is identified with the knowledge of the Self, then *Udgītha Brāhmaṇa* is prompting a person to meditate on his Self. On one side is the body which is perishable, on the other side there is *brahman* which is imperishable and bodiless. The *Udgītha Brāhmaṇa* in its truest sense is continuously moving away from the perishable to the imperishable. In *Vedānta* this is recognized as *nitya anitya vastu viveka.* Hence *Udgītha Brāhmaṇa* initiates us into the very first discipline of what Śankara calls *sādhana catuṣtaya,* the four-fold discipline for realization: to be consistent in one's judgment to stand by the eternal *(nitya)* and never to err into the shadow world of transience *(anitya).* This now prepares us to move further because the ability to distinguish between the real and unreal makes a seeker qualified.

A historical tracing of the origin of life in the evidence of geological surveys and the avenues of astrophysics can easily convince us that the earth is an inert solid mass with no trace of life in it. By the speculation of modern science we presume that the heavenly universes originated from the dust flying in air which assumed thermal energy. Dust is suggestive of earth; air is suggestive of pure motion in space, fire comes to us as a byproduct of earth and air, and excessive heat tends to become shifted into its opposite. Thus the gaseous aspect implied in fire produces water.

If we do not go in for an anthropomorphic symbolization of the beginning of the universe we arrive at the most kinetic gaseous form and the inertial earth as the two poles of bipolar relationship which produce between them first the fire and then the water. For this reason, Śureśvarācārya comes to the conclusion that nature is demonic. The original powers of nature such as terrific motion move towards morbidity or inertia. Thus the basis of manifestation is the inertial towards which the kinetic moves. That can be allegorically called the night of the chaotic beginning of the universe. For this reason, when Sri Aurobindo gives the symbol of dawn in his epic poem *Sāvitri*, he commences the origin without any god, order or purpose. In this beautiful allegory we read:

> It was the hour before the Gods awake.
> Across the path of the divine Event
> The huge foreboding mind of Night, alone
> In her unlit temple of eternity,
> Lay stretched immobile upon Silence' marge.
> Almost one felt, opaque, impenetrable,
> In the somber symbol of her eyeless muse
> The abysm of the unbodied Infinite;
> A fathomless zero occupied the world.
> A power of fallen boundless self awake
> Between the first and the last Nothingness,
> Recalling the tenebrous womb from which it came,
> Turned from the insoluble mystery of birth
> And the tardy process of mortality
> And longed to reach its end in vacant Nought.
> As in a dark beginning of all things,
> A mute featureless semblance of the Unknown

Repeating for ever the unconscious act,
Prolonging for ever the unseeing will,
Cradled the cosmic drowse of ignorant Force
Whose moved creative slumber kindles the suns
And carries our lives in its somnambulist whirl.
Athwart the vain enormous trance of Space,
It formless stupor without mind or life,
A shadow spinning through a soulless Void,
Thrown back once more into unthinking dreams,
Earth wheeled abandoned in the hollow gulfs
Forgetful of her spirit and her fate. [70]

The narration of the *Bṛhadāraṇyaka Upaniṣad* is more a poetic version of science than religion. As the first cause of everything, including the nebula which stretches into the magnitude of the galaxy or several galactic systems, it is only appropriate that the rishi wanted to explore the dynamics of wind. We are closer to no other element than the air that we breathe in and breathe out. When breathing commences we call it birth; when breathing is silenced we call it death. The wind, which is called *prāṇa* in the *Upaniṣad,* begins with the throb much before we come into the open and breathe through our nostrils. It is the pulsation in the primordial cell. We have to understand the world by understanding ourselves; we have to conceive of God by looking at our own structural and functional reality. Just as Jesus said, "As above so below," we have to say, "As we are, so the universe." Our consciousness has emerged from our unconscious states. Our functional behavior slowly rises to an appreciable event from the motionless stagnation of a pool of chemicals. As the main springboard of creation commences with electrolysis, there is an apparently unknown source from which all events commence. So naturally when the functions cease, we have to see how we return to the source.

The details of the first structured being describe a model which helps to understand the beginning as well as the end. When we trace the beginning we see that there are a series of beginnings coming to a terminal point and making a quantum jump to another beginning. Similarly, the end is a merger with a momentum to return with the added force of remergence. Thus birth and death do not have any exaggerated meaning beyond being the two ends of a segment. The proliferation of nature adds innumerable segments to one which has already expressed itself. Hence the postulation that all forms of life begin with the mode of a demon (*asura*). *Asura* only means brute force unlit by reason. In the *Īśāvāsya Upaniṣad* the world of demons is described as a sunless world. The primary forms of life in nature are the most ancient beginning of life. We still maintain that inheritance in us. This is being appreciated by modern science which considers all beings as belonging to one biological reality. However, that theory has been over-extrapolated to such an extent that they think that what is good for a mouse is also good for a human.

Scientists see the whole world as an ever-proliferating colony of bacteria and viruses, compared to whose numbers and powers humanity is just an accident. The *Upaniṣad* rishi thinks in a similar manner. To begin with were the *asuras* who were innumerable. From brute action a rationale of functions evolved. The appreciation of the functional correlatives evolved as intelligence in the advancement of this self-projected universe. So it is proper to think that we are all embedded in the dark inertial morass of nescience, and it is from nescience we are to be transported to science. Hence the first prayer of the *Udgītha Brāhmaṇa, asato mā sat gamaya*, has within it an innate verity of the evolution of reason itself.

There is a close identification between the inertial and the unknown. The unknown becomes known only when the unconscious becomes conscious. That is a further step in the evolution of life – the emergence of conscient beings. The scheme of life to begin with is to vivify, to proliferate. Death is essential to generate a new mode of life which has more resistance, more prowess, and more adaptability. Adaptability is the meeting ground in which the unconscious evolves into the conscious and the conscious waits for the favor of the unconscious. For the Vedāntin there is no glory in being the causal factor. Cause and effect represent the gamut of transforming the real into the unreal. Hence when the prayer says *tamaso mā jyotirgamaya*, "Let us be delivered from ignorance to knowledge," the petition is actually to go beyond cause as well as effect. Transcendence becomes the final refuge because all experiences are within the falsifying of the transcendent by the elaboration of cause and effect relationships.

The *udgītha* is the first experimental theme recognized by life forms by which they recognize that they are in the plight of having the real in them mutilated again and again in the process of the adaptation of the organized matter of the physical body in which life is imprisoned. All prayers are primarily meted out to one's own agonized self. The one who gives the prayer is also the one who listens to it and struggles to find a way out. The eternal game is the natural evolution of mute nature and a counter evolution that comes from the light of reason which is ignited in the problem-solving individuation. However cruel it looks, every form of life is left to itself to make its own multiplication of cells and self-delivery from the mesh of nature. If you watch how a mosquito comes out of its larvae or a colorful butterfly emerges out of its pupa, you can see how hard it is to transform oneself and take to a new life, spreading one's wings in freedom.

To the *Upaniṣadic* rishi, these incidents reveal how the world is a self-expression with a plethora of laws which converge like a telescope into one unitary law. The idea of a god comes much later. The *Udgītha Brāhmaṇa* conceives that our ability to fashion the word out of *prāṇa* is primarily to educate ourselves and secondarily to call for the help of fellow creatures. It assumes the sophistication of a prayer when one's consciousness slowly evolves into an extravagance of poetic imagination. Thus the unaccountable, unexplainable source which is called *brahman* has almost nothing to do with the theistic concept of a god. It is only a speculative monomark such as in mathematics – a supposition which can explain a number of things when the monomark is treated like an equation.

These are some of the implications of the *udgītha*, which is contrasted with *japa*. If *japa* is the harping on a symbol in an unexpressed way to prepare one's mind, the *udgītha* is a process of self-education and self-inducement to extricate oneself from the crude scaffolding of nature and to emerge into freedom. The *udgītha upāsana* is mainly described as *abhyārohana japa*. *Ārohana* is the same as going upward. What goes upward? The *prāṇa*. So *udgītha brāhmaṇa* becomes *prāṇa upāsana*. In the *prāṇa upāsana*, *prāṇa* mainly brings the word of propitiation to the hearing level of the person who chants the *udgītha*. Therefore *prāṇa* becomes instrumental in coining words of propitiation as well as bringing them to the cognizance of the Supreme. Thus *prāṇa upāsana* itself becomes an exercise to make the propitiating person a lord of the word. The word invokes the triple aspects of the person who chants the invocation. The person who chants is also the person who hears. Therefore the word represents the witnessing of the need of the individuated person to the higher Self. But the higher Self is not above or below. It is both the cause (*kāraṇa*) for transforming the psychosomatic system of the individual as well as the employment of the instrumentality of the faculty of speech. And hence the word becomes part of the causal factor, the inner organ which is prompting the organ of speech to sing aloud. The word participates both as a causal agent and as instrumental efficiency. The prompting of the invocation comes from the indweller (*antaryāmī*), which we have studied as both the controller as well as the seer of all faculties. When the word becomes the efficient cause in the propitiation, knowledge and ritualistic action come together without the edge of one hurting the other. In such a case there is a unification of the intention, means, and goal in the performance of the chanting. The chanting becomes a means to meditate on what is being chanted. It is happening in the here and now, but its excellence is not fixed in locality or time.

As the body is the immediately available instrument with which to aspire for the highest, three forces are put together in the performance of chanting. The energy that arises in the body through food (*anna*) processed by vital breath (*prāṇa*) is strength (*bala*). It is the first to be counted. The second is the organ of hearing, listening to the sound of what is being chanted by the organ of speech. When this happens, the inner organ of the mind channels the stimulation of hearing to the purview of the intellect. The intellect, which is trained to distinguish the essential from the non-essential, the permanent from the transitory, and the eternal from the transient, elevates consciousness. Thus the intense aspiration of the person reaches forward to the supreme meaning of the word which is chanted. In such a state the aspirant becomes a master of words, *vācaśpati*.

The kind of word referred to here is used to shed all shades of distinct ideas as well as ratiocinative logical encumbrances. The pure intellect goes from the mere word to the meaning and value content of "That" or *brahman*, and hence the *vācaśpati* becomes *brāhmaṇaśpati*. What is being performed in a ritualistic sacrifice is the burning away of all conditional symbols which are considered inadequate. The consequent result is to arrive at a state of consciousness which was not known before. The truth of the Absolute is not dependent on anything, while all other things are dependent on the Absolute. Hence there is no need to establish *brahman.* All the means suggested here are to raise the contaminated consciousness from conjunction with conditions (*upādhi samparka*) so that there will not be any hindrance to the individual consciousness feeling identified with the supreme state.

In the *Bhagavad Gītā* this attitude by which one raises oneself is recognized as *bhakti bhāvana.* Verse 6, Chapter 8 describes it as *sadā tat bhāva bhāvitaḥ.* There is a twist in this example: When a man is driving a car, he looks into the mirror fixed in front of him to see what is behind the car. He seems to be looking forward, but he is observing what is behind. We are guided by the instrument of our inner organ in which the pure light (*jyotis*) of the Self is reflected. Hence it is like looking into a mirror which shows the right as the left and the left as the right. What is in front suggests what is behind. This individuated state is called *ābhāśa caitanya.* And from the image reflected in it (*bhāṣya*), we are not trying to know what it is reflecting, but with what light the reflection is making an image.

The context of the above-quoted verse of the *Bhagavad Gītā* is the time of death when a person is concentrating on one's own Self as the Absolute. Curiously, although the body is dying at that time and the person is in a mortal situation, what fills his or her consciousness is immortality. This is what is described in the *Gītā* as raising oneself with the Self. There are two different meanings of the "Self" implied. One is the self lost in the conditional body context. It is raised by and to the unconditional Self where body, senses, mind and the function of the inner organ itself are irrelevant.

All these implications are inherent in the *Udgītha Brāhmaṇa* which contains sufficient instruction for us to learn how to discipline ourselves to transcend all the relative and conditional references of our individuation. The scheme of *udgītha* is *abhyārohana,* which means the correct raising of one's being from the physical to the psychological, and from the psychological to the spiritual. The formula given for that is the invocation of three mantras: *AUM bhuḥ bhuvaḥ svaḥ. AUM bhuḥ* pertains to the terra firma on which we are established. There is a homogeneous principle shared by the earth and our being. The existentiality of our body is made up of gross physical stuff which can be easily identified with earth. When we exist only physically we are earth-earthy.

From the beginning of the first *adhyāya* up to the third *brāhmaṇa* the *Bṛhadāraṇyaka Upaniṣads* familiarizes us with manifestation at three levels: cosmological, psychological and spiritual. There is no theological reference. Till we come to the middle of the first *adhyāya*, the manifestation of the world is presented just as we can observe it. We can reasonably put together the cause that goes into the effects. The scheme is very much of a self-originating, self-growing and self-evolving entity. So there was no need for a creator or a protector to begin with.

When we turn to *AUM bhuvaḥ* we enter into the world of atmosphere where water, fire, and air are distributed in a harmonious manner. Our own body structure and function incorporates a device by which we can be in the here and now of physical existence and can also reach forward by inventing the word (*vāk*). At the physical level manifestation comes through the respiration of the vital breath. Now the power to express is posited into the vital breath. A spoken word carries its impact to the faculty of hearing and then the sound waves die out. But the impression of the word does not leave us. It reverberates, giving us a long-lasting impression of that word as we discover its meaning in the course of time. The word itself has the triple constituents of vibratory motions bursting into meaning and generating an image which is different from the sound symbol. Every word has a sonal impact which initiates us into an interest connected with the meaning of the word and then generates more relevant mental images which can take us to the farther reaches of the word.

The impact of a word has three other qualities. One is presenting a notion or an awareness which is delimited with a frame of reference (*prakhya*). This induces an action program in the listener. One reacts to the significance of the word heard. This is called *pravṛtti*, carrying out an action. The interpretor of the word, *vācaśpati*, interacts with the cosmos. Beyond our atmosphere is the sun that shines in the firmament and several other luminaries. The interest to act upon the cosmos is presented to us through the word. The wielder of the word uses the same word to enter into a dialogue with cosmic forces. All five senses and the organs of action, especially the tongue, are used to establish an intimate link between the physical, psychic and cosmic aspects of the world. That is why the mantra *svaḥ* is put after *bhuvaḥ*. It represents the third step of raising a person from a mundane and psychic existence to spiritual sublimity. The word gives freedom to the soul to rise from the ground into the atmosphere and beyond the atmosphere to infinitude. When the *vācaśpati* uses devices by which an all-round relationship can be established with the cosmic elements such as the sky, the sun, the wind, the ocean, and the earth, he becomes a *brāhmaṇaśpati*.

The most beautiful thing about the *Bṛhadāraṇyaka Upaniṣad* is that from the beginning the self-originated being itself finds ways and means to promote its higher interests. To activate the word potential a ritual is conceived which is like offering the past into the present and bringing out of it the future. Time is sacrificed in time to renew and restructure it. This entire scheme is given just in these three mantras: *AUM bhuḥ, bhuvaḥ, svaḥ*. This whole scheme is presented in the revised sacrificial ritual (*yajña*). There is a sacrificer, there is a sacrificial fire into which the best of the sacrificer is offered and the burnt victim of sacrifice is transformed into a more perfected being.

After having presented such a scheme the *Upaniṣad* tells us how, from the origin of life, the first being which was only solving the problem of necessity (hunger) becomes more and more proficient in guiding the mind with the powers of the word. Thus a ritual is to be accompanied by thought-provoking words and the sacrificer has to go deep into the significance of the word uttered. At every level, *agni* or fire is solicited to bring forth the transformation. After identifying the onward progress as getting more and more insight into *prāṇa*, it is as if the very word roused by the vital breath itself is giving birth, or rather proliferating, in more and more efficient words. Thus we see a whole liturgy issuing forth which is different from mere verbosity. In the newly generated words there is the fire of spirit which brings the undying flames of inspiration. When the word is sung with one's full mind, soul and strength, it is as if one is igniting the sensibility of one's own words to mean something higher, as if the true song of the soul is coming out.

From there on consciousness is free to go beyond the limits of the body. Then we gain a vision which can be turned in all directions. It is said that when the sun shines, to the extent the sunbeams go, to that extent the sun also shines. Corresponding to that, we have an ability to go in all directions of the beyond with the expanded meaning of the words we wield. All that we know is the quality of our awareness. When the first person, the primeval *prajāpati*, expanded into all aspects of time and space, it could not see anything but itself. So it said, "Everything is 'I am'." Instead of a 'me' held in a body, the transcendental consciousness identified that knowledge with all and said, *aham asmi* (I am all this).

We come across this in the first mantra of the fourth *brāhmaṇa* of the first *adhyāya*. From there on, step by step, the development of the first being is given. The *Upaniṣad* began with reference to the primeval fear which enveloped everything. But at that time there was no mind and hence the fear was only a potential in death. When mind came, the awareness that "everything is myself" also brought the idea that "there is no one besides myself". That brought fear. Although the first being knew there was not anything besides its being, it desired to have another for company. If there is another, there can be interaction. To interact is to enrich your words through dialogue and enrich your action through the supplementation and complementation.

One of the earliest inventions of the being was looking instead of just seeing. Looking is monitoring; there is desire behind it which is object-oriented. When *prajāpati* looked it saw that its own being which is none other than this world is the burning spirit (*soma*), the fuel (*anna*) and the burner (*annada*). Out of these a subject/object relationship came. *Soma* as the *anna* and fire as the *annada*, the eater of food. *Prajāpati* created out of its own being an ideational reality and the facts of the morbid world. These are symbolized by the words *deva* and *asura*. They represent the idea of freedom and the idea of necessity. Necessity is bound to the inevitable; freedom is the ability to transcend all the bonds of necessity. Thus out of the mortal the immortal came to be. Hence in mantra six of *brāhmaṇa* four of the first *adhyāya*, it is said:

> This is a surpassing creation of *brahman* (*virāj*), because he created the gods, who are even better than he. In as much as, being himself mortal, he created the immortals, therefore this is a surpassing creation. [71]

A further discovery was how the one can become many, and each identification can be of a different form, meaning and value. In mantra seven of the same *brāhmaṇa* we read:

> When it only performs breathing etc., it is called the vital force; when it speaks, the vocal organ (i.e. the speaker); when it thinks, the mind (thinker). [72]

In this plurality of beings he could also see the unity. The unitive is recognized as the Self. Hence the most important injunction of the *Bṛhadāraṇyaka Upaniṣad* comes in the seventh mantra of the fourth *brahman* of the first *adhyāya*, which says:

> One should meditate upon it only as the Supreme Self, because in it all these become one. Of all these, this entity called the Self alone is to be known, because one knows all these through it just as one can find (a missing animal) through its footprints. One who knows thus attains knowledge of unity and liberation. [73]

The unity of the Self is held firm with happiness or the value dynamics. It begins with the existential *(sat)*, is elaborated by the subsistential *(cit)* and becomes evanescent in the value dynamic *(ānanda)*. The being has knowledge and the knowledge is blissful. But how to proliferate the individuation of beings, the individuation of subsistence, and how to make every being happy? Something was missing. *Prajāpati* was alone. In the place of the aloneness came the power to act. The transparency of pure being was supplemented with a colored mind. *Sattva* transformed into *rajas*. This is the fragmentation of the original into *brāhmaṇa* and *kṣatriya*. The pure transparent *sattva* and the colored psyche gave rise to apprehension. From anxiety, calculative desires emerged *(vaiśya)*. As the Indian people are obsessed with their caste system, prior commentators have identified these references as being to caste gradations. However, they should properly be understood as colorations of the psyche. The ultimate happiness was still missing. Hence in mantra thirteen there comes the unusual statement: the earth itself changed into the all-nourishing *śūdra* and took responsibility to care for all the beings that proliferate from the *prajāpati*. But there was still some defect in the manifestation. Taking responsibility for all makes one obsessed with necessity. It is up to the mediating mind whether one should be free to go into transcendence or to accept necessity in all its shades.

There is an innate freedom by which one can fashion one's destiny. For that there came to be the self-sustaining law of integrity called *dharma*. *Dharma* is the ground for any configuration to be established. It evolves from one's own understanding, knowledge and insight. Two aspects of *dharma* are identifying oneself with truth and living with the truth that one represents. All modalities arise out of the desire to accomplish or to achieve which it is considered to be the basis of nescience. Where there is pure-clear wisdom, there is no action propensity. Hence, where wisdom is, there is freedom.

Where manipulation is, there is bondage. The lure of nescience is such that the relativistic world is established in the conditional states of mind. Hence, those who cannot absolve themselves from the call of necessity have the life-style of the householder. For the householder, action is more primary than knowledge or wisdom. The householder is the source of sustenance for the shining ones through the conducting of sacrifices. Through the householder's sustaining power, the world of institutions survives. Even the smallest of beings like an ant gains sustenance from the *karma* of the householder. At the same time, there are the released. The bound person thinks he should have a companion, so he takes a wife. Then he desires to be born in his wife as his own child. There is no end to such desires. If he runs a family he needs wealth. Thus he is bound by many obligations. But the wise person thinks, "My companion is my own mind, and that mind is none other than my Self. My wife is my word; my breath is my child; my eye is my wealth, and my ear is my divine wealth. My body is my action."

This brings us to the fifth *brāhmaṇa* of the first *adhyāya* where we are given a description of the individual expanding into a society. As the original life model, the *prajāpati* is the root cause of all this. So, in the fifth *brāhmaṇa, prajāpati* is promoted to the role of the father of all. The evolutes from the first seed of being to the world of innumerable species and levels of living can be seen as an elaboration of evolution. In the subsequent *brāhmaṇas* we are given a detailed explanation of how the love for freedom and obedience to the stringent laws of necessity alternatively impact the minds of all. Every need is like a hunger and every satisfaction is like a food.

Here there is a promotion of the individual to a cosmic person. There is a person living within us as part and parcel of who we are. We share with that cosmic person our days and nights, our wakeful hours and dream hours, our deep sleep and transcendence. In turn, we can forget our small being and identify with the cosmic aspect. Over time, the symbol of sacrifice became more elaborate. As we proceed further, we are taught how through meditation (*jñāna*) and ritual (*karma*), we can always be on the forward march of the progress of the spirit, always approximating perfection.

Adhyāya II

The second *adhyāya* of the *Bṛhadāraṇyaka Upaniṣad* initiates a major revision in the Vedic tradition in India. Before the advent of *Vedānta*, i.e., the *Upaniṣads* which were appended to the last portion of the *Samhitas* and *Brāhmaṇas*, there was a belief in India that the *Vedas* were infallible, *a priori* texts of wisdom which should not be questioned. In the *Bṛhadāraṇyaka Upaniṣad* there is a crossing over from the three traditionally maintained *Vedas*, *Ṛg*, *Yajur* and *Sāma* to *Atharva Veda* which is derogatorily referred to by the adherents of the other three *Vedas*. There is a hidden clue which is given in the *guruparampara* at the end of each *Kāṇḍa*. Instead of beginning the *parampara* from the first *guru*, the enumeration is from the last *guru* backward. The rhetoric of this section which appears thrice in the *Upaniṣad* creates a smoke screen. The meaningless repetition of names will make anyone tired by the time the list is half read. We dare to say this is a trick played on the general public.

In the *Khila Kāṇḍa* we are given a mandate to be as critical as possible so that all the uncharted areas of the Vedic tradition can be clearly understood and restated. The *guruparampara* of the *Madhu Kāṇḍa* comes in the sixth *brāhmaṇa* of the second *adhyāya*. In the presentation, the hierarchy of *gurus* is divided into three. The first *guru* is the last named: *brahmaṇe namaḥ*. What issues from *brahma? Brahma svayambhu*. *Brahman* is taught in the *Upaniṣad* itself as *neti neti*, "not this, not this" and *satyasya satyam* "the truth of truth". No personification is made. *Brahman* is not created by anyone. It is a self-contained truth, or, rather, the only self-contained truth.

From that is derived Paramesthin. Paramesthin is a reference like *AUM gurur brahma* in which *brahma* is not a person. It is the *'A'* of *AUM* which stands for the principle of creation, projection, or creativity. Just as the *aumkara* has *akara (A)*, *ukara (U)* and *makara (M)*, the creative function always has origin, a state of being and dissolution. Next in the listing come the terms Sanaka, Sanatana and Sanaru. Only those who know descending dialectics can tackle the secret in it. The phrase, *AUM gurur brahmā, gurur viśṇur, gurur devomaheśvara* covers the triple aspects of projection, phenomenal existence and dissolution. Then there is a pause. After the pause, the mantra says, *gurur sākśāt param brahma* by which the three godheads of phenomenality are virtually annulled. *Brahman* is once again described as the incomparable. It is incomparable because it is defined as *neti neti.* The hierarchy is one of descending dialectics. Up to Sanāru the reference is to the generic entity and not any specific entity.

Then when we hear that Vyaṣṭi came from Sanāru, Vyaṣṭi means the individual. Again it is not an actual individual, but the principle of individuality. After this three backward steps are given. The principle of individuation is applied to Vipracitti, that is, a state of mind which can comprehend the Absolute. The resultant of Vipracitti is Ekarṣi. Ekarṣi is described as that which brings a canceling out, Prādhvaṁsa. Prādhvaṁsa, i.e., demolition or destructuring, is identified with Mṛtyu, death. From death alone, or from the principle of death, we come to the divine, Atharva. Atharva is none other than Śiva. The first reference to a divinity is to Śiva.

From Śiva or Atharvaṇa comes Dadhyac. From Dadhyac *brahmavidyā* was passed on to the Aśvini Devas. From the details given in the *Śatapatha Brāhmaṇa* we can see how the *Ṛg Vedic* god Indra was a jealous god who did not allow the Aśvini Devas to enter into the hall where the elixir of immortality was shared. Again we see in the text of the *Bṛhadāraṇyaka* how Indra tried to stop Dadhyac from imparting *brahmavidyā* to the Aśvini Devas. This is part of the dirty politics in the Vedic lore. For the first time we are opening it for all people to see that the highly venerated Vedic text has in it a malicious intention. After the reference to Dadhyac, metaphorical symbols are used for the in-between Gurus who are actually only functions in the structural creation of life, such as Viśvarūpa, Ābhūti, Ayāsya and Āṅgiras.

These kinds of literary devices were mainly intended to cover up the schism that led to two recensions of the *Śatapatha Brāhmaṇa,* such as the *Mādhyandina* tradition and the *Kāṇva* tradition. We presume that Śankara favored the *Kāṇva* tradition because of his revolutionary views. Śankara was bold enough to open *brahmavidyā* to all, irrespective of their Vedic learning. Of course, in Śankara's own *Bhāṣya* there are later interpolations introduced by his disciples who had certain vested interests. Śankara closely followed the mode of revaluation presented by Yājñavalkya who even included a woman, Gārgī, as a collaborator in his formulation of the *Śukla Yajur Veda* in opposition to the *Kṛṣṇa Yajur Veda* championed by Vaiśampāyana. Even a general glance at the *Taittirīya Brāhmaṇa* will convince anyone why Yājñavalkya could not agree with Vaiśampāyana, who took advantage of *Yajur Veda* to heap rituals over rituals.

The *brāhmaṇic* pride of the Vedic followers is taken up as an issue to be smashed by Yājñavalkya in the second *adhyāya* where the *brāhmaṇa* Gārgya encounters King Ajātaśatru. Up to that time it was believed that in the area of wisdom, a *brāhmaṇa* was to teach and a *kṣatriya* was only to be an obedient follower. But Ajātaśatru, the king of Kāśi, was instrumental in turning the tables. Gārgya the Proud presented *brahmavidyā* to Ajātaśatru, a patient listener, from mantra two to fourteen of the first *brāhmaṇa*. Ajātaśatru, well established in his knowledge of the Absolute, rebutted every presentation until Gārgya's self-esteem was undermined. Gārgya was, however, a lover of truth, so he approached the *kṣatriya* king with the attitude of a disciple. This is the first break in tradition in the Vedic lore.

We cannot consider this a mere accident because in the very last section of the *Upaniṣad*, Śvetaketu, son of Uddālaka, the most famous among the erudite scholars of Vedic India, encountered another *kṣatriya*, King Pravāhaṇa. Śvetaketu, who came with the pride that he knew *brahmatattva* absolutely, was soon thrown out of gear. Pravāhaṇa asked him five questions which Śvetaketu could not answer. Although the king offered hospitality and was willing to teach him, Śvetaketu was a haughty young man, full of pride. He went to report to his father the inadequacy of the *brahmavidyā* he had taught him. On hearing this, the most venerated Uddālaka Aruṇi himself came to the court of Pravāhaṇa seeking discipleship. When something is repeated twice in a scripture it has a doctrinal importance. Thus at the beginning of the *Upaniṣad* a *kṣatriya* defeats a *brāhmin* and becomes his *guru*, and at the end of the *Upaniṣad* a *kṣatriya* defeats the most honored *brāhmin* and makes him a disciple. This is a big blow to the *brāhmaṇic* pride of ancient India. Even Śankara admits the need for such a correction. That is why he wrote the *Manīṣa Pañcakam* in which he was bold enough to say that even a *caṇḍāla* (outcaste) can be revered as a *guru* if he is an exemplar of wisdom. We have to keep this in mind to get to the heart of the *Madhu Kāṇḍa* and the *Muni Kāṇḍa*.

All sentient beings live in their respective bodies, with special arrangements to use external devices for observation and internal devices for interpreting the significance of what is observed. For instance, the ears of a person are poised to catch any sound that comes from any direction. If the human head is considered the functional center of a person, all other physical bodies in the world are around the head that listens and thinks. This is not only true of all the sides of the head, but also what is above and what is below. The human head is created somewhat in the model of heavenly luminaries. The earth is a sphere around which the planets and their moons rotate. The axis of the planet earth is a central device around which the earth revolves.

The head of a family is like a force of energy around which all the activities of the members of the family take place. All environmental factors are assessed by the five sense organs which are established in the head of a person. From there, orders are given to all the organs of action to deal with the objects noticed by the ear, the skin, the eye, the taste buds and smell. All these belong to what is called the field. The field is gross, and the constituents of the field are also gross. A gross body is such that you cannot interpenetrate another body into it.

In the same head we experience awareness. There is no limit to the contents of awareness. It neither overflows, nor does it burst its container. So there is a paradox: does the brain contain awareness, or does awareness contain the brain? It is here that one of the greatest miracles of the world happens. The sound that we hear is only a vibratory function in space communicated to the ear by the vibrations in air which come like waves. A tactual sensation is a stimulation given to the receiving end of our receptors which is then conveyed through an electrical function to the brain. Recent studies prove that, apart from the conduction of electrical impulses from the receptor to the cognitive center of the brain, there are also transmitters which are not operated by the conduction of the nervous system. When light falls on an object and is reflected from it, then falls on the retina of the eye, the photons that stimulate the rods and cones of the retina are so disciplined that many irrelevant sensations of light are screened off and what is of most interest becomes the focus of attention.

The same can be said of other sensations also.

What is important to know is that there is a physical element in the body which establishes a bridge with everything physical in the external world. But once the contact is made between the external world and the periphery of the senses, no other advancement of the specific energy received in the receptors is allowed. The vibration that impacts the tympanum of the ear drum ceases to be sound. From that point on it becomes an electrical impulse that can stimulate cells of the auditory area of the brain to make a suggestion to the consciousness of the individual. A certain significant relationship is seen between the inner spectator and the energy which makes a breakthrough into the receptor. Consequently a gross material thing is transformed into an ideational entity called hearing. Just as every form has a unique mark, every sound also has a unique mark of generating a conceptual presentation of the experience. What is happening to the ear is also true of what is happening in the eye. There are audio-visual signals which manifest at first as simple electrical impulses, but turn out to be elaborate images of vast dimensions. The inner interpreter is the real seer. The sight seen by the eye is an indiscernible admittance of light into the visual front gate.

Everything outside is called the field of knowledge or perception (*kṣetra*), and the inner core, the perceiver of the field (*kṣetrajña*). The external structural arrangement with cells and tissues molded out of biochemicals is only a framework. However, it is necessary for the functional verity of the Self. The magic is that a gross thing changes into a subtle idea which has behind it the purposiveness of the universe called the cause or *kāraṇa*.

The *Bṛhadāraṇyaka Upaniṣad* wants to call our attention to the gross to have an understanding of the subtle which in its turn can take us to the deeper core of our Self. Three examples are given in the *Upaniṣad* to illustrate how this happens. They also refer to the three aspects of spiritual discipline: listening to the word (*manana*), pondering on its significance (*śravaṇa*) and living the outcome of it (*nididhyāsana*). The three examples given are of a drum, a conch shell, and a *vīṇa* or lute.

We come across many such objects in the world. However minutely you look at those objects, looking alone will not reveal their functional quality. When we take a drumstick and beat the sides of a drum for the first time, a sound comes out of it which we never expected. The more we familiarize ourselves with the qualities of the drum, the more we become familiar with rhythm. That rhythm can introduce us to the musical quality of the sound. The mere thumping on a flat piece of leather can produce varieties of sounds which enthrall the listener.

This is a way of saying that the field where we live with its innumerable qualities remains voiceless until its true voice is elicited. Only then will we be able to decipher its secrets. By merely living in the world we do not live its essence. It is to be sought by going near it. Just looking at a drum does not produce any sound. You have to take it in your hand and strike it. This takes us to what we call *manana*. Listening *(śravana)* is the first thing; that is familiarization. Familiarization is followed by interpretation. Even when only one man is playing on a percussion instrument, hundreds of people can be listening to it and experiencing their body/minds becoming attuned to the particular mode of percussion. That means there is a dialectical possibility of the seer who sits in the middle of the field bringing to every listener a uniform value which is homogeneous in its makeup.

The next object presented is a conch shell. A conch is a sea animal with a lot of flesh inside it. After the death of that animal, when the flesh rots away, the shell becomes clean with nothing in it except a specially structured inside into which you can blow. It produces a very exciting sound which is musical. It reverberates in the atmosphere. The conch shell is different from the drum. It leads us to different kinds of activities. On the drum we are striking or thumping, while we have to blow through the conch shell.

Next is the *vīṇa*, a string instrument. An expert who knows how to play the *vīṇa* tunes its wires and plucks it, alternately putting pressure on the strings and then releasing them. According to the frequency created by the tension and release of the wire, we hear musical sounds of the most captivating kind. This tells us that the gross world, however big it looks, becomes meaningful only when every bit of it is interpreted for us by an indwelling witness.

Names and forms are varied. Functions are also variegated. Yet through everything runs a golden thread of joy-evolving dynamics. This is compared by the *Upaniṣad* to what even very small insects can understand. Bees can fly guided by some message which comes from blooming flowers. In a garden there may be a hundred varieties of flowers produced by plants, trees, or herbs of varying pharmacological properties. Instead of sipping honey from one flower and being satisfied, the bee hovers over hundreds of flowers and takes a little honey from each one. Then it is stored in the honey comb. When the honey from a honey comb is gathered into a bowl, we cannot say which molecule of honey has come from which flower. There is a unity in the liquid form of honey which does not reveal to us its many sources. The human soul is also like that. We live in millions of bodies. But the essence of life is one, like the honey gathered from many flowers. The *Upaniṣad* uses the example of honey to teach us that our own essence represents the essence of all. It is as if there is a homogeneity of the joyous core (*ānanda*) not only of human beings, but of all those who partake of the values of the phenomenal world.

Just as the earth can be honey to all living beings, all living beings can also be honey to the earth. This how the *Upaniṣad* rishi brings us to the essential teaching of *Vedānta:* the *ānanda* that ensues from the function of a living being can unite us with the entire world. Hence this section is called *Madhu Kāṇḍa. Madhu* is sweet and joyous, and everybody is in love with it. In our experience of the existential verity *(sat)* of the gross world, individual items look different. But all those entities, however different their forms, are all part of our awareness *(cit)*. When that awareness is further processed, we come to know the essence of a thing more that its external details. There we come into touch with its joy-giving dynamics *(ānanda)*.

In the three levels of *sat, cit, ānanda,* we move progressively from plurality to unitiveness. This is a subject which the *Bṛhadāraṇyaka Upaniṣad* presents to us in the *Madhu Brāhmaṇa.* The honey section of the *Madhu Kāṇḍa* commences with II.5.1:

> This earth is honey to all beings and all beings are honey to this earth. This shining immortal person who is in this earth is honey to all beings and all beings are honey to this person. This shining and immortal person who dwells as spirit in the body is honey to all beings and all beings are honey to this person. The Self is none other than this. This is the immortal. This is *brahman.* This is all. [74]

Here we see various projections which constitute the earth and what contributes to the life propensity on earth. The Self is integral to the scheme of correlation. The first item to be seen is that the earth is honey to all beings; the second is that all beings are honey to this earth; the third is that the shining immortal person is seen in the body. The honey suggests the *ānanda*. There is an indiscernible principle of existence in everything that can at best be referred to as this (*tyam*) or that (*ayam*). Out of the confrontation with *tyam* or *ayam* the question comes, "What is this?" or "What is that?" Only then do we come to know that in the experiencing of the Self in its manifested nature there are two factors to be reckoned with. One is that which rouses the question "What?" in our cognitive consciousness. The other is that which presents itself to be looked into or probed into.

In the next mantra water is honey to all beings and all beings are honey to water. The four-fold aspects are given here also. After sweat came to the *prajāpati* as tepid water, the water cooled and the fire left the water. Two elements came out of the same liquid - fire and water. Therefore in the third mantra we read, "This fire is honey to all beings and all beings are honey to fire." Then comes air (*vāyu*). In the following mantras, the sun, quarters, moon, lightening, cloud, space, *dharma*, truth, human and the Self are all described as honey to all beings and all beings as honey to them. Finally in the fifteenth mantra we read that the Self already mentioned is the inner controller and governing principle of all beings. Just as all the spokes of a chariot wheel are fixed to the hub and to the rim, so are all the elements, all the shining principles, all worlds of interests, and all individual selves directed and ruled by this Self. The uniting of the outer rim and inner hub into a wheel is analogous to the relationship between the experiencing mind and the illuminating consciousness of the Absolute. The particular style of the honey section has a mystical flavor. The language also has musical intonations which make it a very enjoyable piece of rhapsody.

In the bipolar relationship between earth and the beings who are using the earth, both poles are supportive of each other. The first mantra is commented upon by Śureśvarācārya in his *Vārtika* as follows:

> All beings created the earth by their own doings for the enjoyment of the fruits of their various activity. Hence the earth is for them Madhu.
>
> The earth also has created all the beings for its own enjoyment. Thus, being the product of the earth, they

also are Madhu.

Since the bodies of embodied beings are made of (the stuff of) the earth, therefore, they are (to be taken as created by the earth; we see in them the continued existence of the earth.

Thus, owing to the reason that the earth and the beings have a mutual relationship of (cause and) effect, therefore there is established a mutual relationship of the enjoyer and the enjoyable. [75]

Maitreyī Brāhmaṇa

In the *Bṛhadāraṇyaka Upaniṣad* the *Madhu Brāhmaṇa* comes after the *Maitreyī Brāhmaṇa*. We are here presenting *Maitreyī Brāhmaṇa* after *Madhu Brāhmaṇa* for the simple reason that the problem implied in the *Maitreyī Brāhmaṇa* can be better understood and appreciated when we are familiar with the *Madhu Brāhmaṇa*. The *Maitreyī Brāhmaṇa* could have been totally avoided if the *Upaniṣad* wanted us only to know about *ātman*. In *Maitreyī Brāhmaṇa* we are given a very realistic situation in which human beings are brought together by *ātman*. Yet phenomenal attractions and repulsions naturally arise which can make life very complicated. Even for wise people it is difficult to know why there are compulsions in life. One cannot foresee the winding paths of *karma*. However difficult it is to relate with the Self one hundred percent, the wise see the Self clearly. Yet, as the same wise persons possess bodies, senses, inner organs and individuation, there are many contingent issues that can be presented only if we take a classical example from factual incidents that weave themselves into a fabric of life which is at once phenomenal, psychological, social and historical in its set-up.

In the culture of a country where a certain attitude and philosophical vision has come to stay, there is a togetherness in the philosophical vision arrived at by the mind and the urges and compulsions of nature which are in the makeup of every cell of the body. Only a highly disciplined seer can see the matrices in which the truth of life runs like threads of linen with both horizontal and vertical arrangements. The warp and woof of life make a matrix. The abstractions of philosophy are mostly made without considering the ontological facts of everyday life. But Yājñavalkya was a clear thinker and envisioner of both pure wisdom (*jñāna*) and applied wisdom (*vijñāna*). He did not want to avoid any situation that was likely to bring problems that would be difficult to solve. We can understand the full implication of the Maitreyī-Yājñavalkya episode only by clearly studying *jñāna yoga, karma yoga, karma sannyāsa yoga*, and *sannyāsa yoga*.

In the *Gītā* it is said that in human life what is difficult to decipher is the subtleties of *karma*. It also states that even most wise men may find it difficult to know where *karma* could lead one under special circumstances. We should bear this in mind when we look at the relationship between Maitreyī and Yājñavalkya. Maitreyī was the daughter of the sister of Gārgī who was an equal to any seer of her time in applying dialectical reasoning in a most excellent manner. In a community of people with identical status, if one succeeds in self-liberation, another one will come under the influence of the liberated person and will also want to have a similar kind of liberation. As Gārgī participated in the conferences in which Yājñavalkya was the main exponent of *Vedānta*, Maitreyī had many occasions to listen to the penetrating vision of Yājñavalkya.

Most people have a prejudiced view that a woman is emotional by nature and she will be attracted to a man only on sexual grounds. The example of Maitreyī is astounding since she proved that she was an aspirant for truth who could love wisdom for wisdom's sake and did not seek any other benefit that might come from a male support from Yājñavalkya. Even when Yājñavalkya's wife Kātyāyanī advised Maitreyī to be her co-wife, Maitreyī never wanted to have any physical or even emotional relationship with Yājñavalkya. She was only keen on getting to a clear envisioning of the Self. The story of Maitreyī presented twice in this *Upaniṣad* shows that women also have merit and virtue to be fully conversant with the mystical and philosophical subtleties implied in the search for truth.

Yājñavalkya taught Maitreyī: *ātma vā re dṛṣṭavya* – hearing of *ātman* is an *a priori* discipline; seeing the *ātman* is *a posteriori*. Seeing *ātman* is not like seeing an object - it is seeing through objects. Only a mind that is disciplined to extricate itself from the perceptual contingencies and to spread itself into a universal empathy can have imperiential identity with *ātman*. Maitreyī wanted to learn from Yājñavalkya how there can be a union of the perceiver and the perceived with regard to the Self. This is explicitly given to us in the *Yoga Darśana* of Narayana Guru in his *Darśana Mālā*. In the opening verse of *Yoga Darśana*, Guru says,

> That which always unites
> and also gets united with *cidātma*,
> which is in the form of restraining mind,
> that is praised as *yoga*. [76]

When Yājñavalkya speaks of the perceptibility of the Self, Narayana Guru makes it more clear in verse seven of *Yoga Darśana:*

> What is seen has not the perceived reality,
> because what is seen is the seer itself.
> Who is thus united in the seer,
> he is the best among *yoga*-knowers. [77]

These are the subtle lessons we have to learn from the aspirations of Maitreyī. In between there was the incidental social tie of Maitreyi's marriage with the rishi. She never took advantage of that situation even for one day or night. Her mind was only engaged with the arguments of the wise seer.

Actually Yājñavalkya had the greater problem because he was socially recognized. Hence he had to convince people that he fairly settled the claims of his two wives to his property before he retired from the position of householder. Yājñavalkya did not want to bolt away from the situation. He wanted to set an example to the people of his country how the social contract of a publicly recognized marriage has to be resolved in terms of social justice. One issue involving the discipline of a wisdom seeker and another involving the discipline of a married couple were both to be resolved with satisfaction. The episode of Yājñavalkya and Maitreyī gives us a clear example for our analysis and assessment.

Incidentally, the property settlement which Yājñavalkya made with Maitreyī and Kātyātanī is still in the annals of Indian history. It is mentioned at the beginning of the Indian Hindu Law's narratives of doing legal justice to a married woman at the time of the resolution of her marriage. Settlement of properties between two wives of a husband who undergoes civic death is important to the world of social norms (*samsāra*). Maitreyī's value vision that any extraneous arrangement affecting her lifestyle which would hamper her natural right to become spiritually liberated is an issue very important to human rights from a spiritual angle which is also to be protected.

Ātman, the Self, is one, indivisible and homogeneous. Nature (*prakṛti*), on the other hand, is multifarious. It has innumerable parts. There are crisscross relationships between the various structural parts and the many projections that continuously arise from nature. In human beings we see the mark of the Self and the functional variegations of nature. Consequently, wise people have developed a scheme of correlation as well as a frame of reference to accommodate the one ever-changing reality. In the Western world, modern psychologists like C.G. Jung have given a four-fold division of the human types, such as the extrovert and the introvert, and among the extroverts the extrovert-extrovert and extrovert introvert; and among the introvert the introvert-introvert and introvert-extrovert. All textbooks of wisdom have this kind of schematic reference to human types. The introvert is essentially poised towards the search for the Self; the extrovert is of a pleasure-hunting type who is very busy apprehending the objects of the senses. The extrovert mainly depends on the data of specific objects presented to the senses while the introvert discards the instrumentation of the sense organs and instead sympathetically meets the non-empirical and intuitive facts of life.

In the context of the *Maitreyī Brāhmaṇa*, two types of females are given. Yājñavalkya speaks of his two wives Kātyāyanī and Maitreyī. Kātyāyanī was a *dharmacāriṇī* who cared for her home, her husband, her children, her relationship with people in the community and incidentally also for physical wealth such as the estates and cows which her husband was leaving for her care. She was in the category of extrovert-introvert. To understand her husband and his teaching she became an introvert; to care for the family she became a sophisticated extrovert-introvert. Among the males we have Yājñavalkya and Janaka, the King of Videha, Bālāki the proud, and Ajātaśatru. If Bālāki was an extrovert-extrovert, Ajātaśatru was an introvert-extrovert who had a certain normalization in his relationship between the inner world and outer world. Yājñavalkya opted for *sannyāsa*, while Janaka exemplified the ideals of the *Īśā Upaniṣad* such as living for a hundred years, carrying out all his duties without regret or remorse and, at the same time, working out the realization of the Self with meticulous care from moment to moment.

In India there have always been these two examples of the recluse living away from human community, mostly alone, and of a person fully oriented to the empirical world and the diverse facts of life. In the subsequent *adhyāyas* we come across many ritualistically minded brahmins who, in spite of their erudition of Vedic scholarship, have not quelled their desires and who are in a competitive mood. In this very book we get a chance to compare several types and see how one can best orient one's life and educate oneself. This dialogue between Yājñavalkya and Maitreyī gives us many opportunities to consider serious doubts that can confront young seekers of wisdom.

We have already seen how the traditional form of worship is revalued to be performed more as a meditation than as a mundane action. The interchangability between ideas presented in pure consciousness and action that is done in a mystical fervor are taken for comparison. All through the *Bṛhadāraṇyaka Upaniṣad, jñāna* and *karma* are held in a integrated unitive discipline rather than making one oppose the other. Yājñavalkya is careful not to vote entirely on the side of either social duties or of the pure discipline of wisdom.

Maitreyī is a woman who is very unusual. For future generations, she wants to establish that a woman can be on par with a man in her spiritual search and realization. The Yājñavalkya-Maitreyī episode is not a story for entertainment. It is to be taken to several depths in the cultural heritage of India and properly analyzed and presented so that those who are seeking wisdom will not stand bewildered by the several possibilities. The wise person should not only have a theory of wisdom but also a well-defined and disciplined program of action which is perfectly in tune with the highest wisdom. In the *Bhagavad Gītā*, Chapter Five a serious doubt is put forward by Arjuna to Kṛṣṇa:

> You recommend the effective transcending of action, O Kṛṣṇa, and again *yoga* also. Tell me duly determined, which one of these two is spiritually better.

This has been a common confusion among the people of India for ages. A kind of thick line is drawn between spiritual life and worldly life. Actually life is only one. The spirit as well as the body are held together in each individual. Hence, no one is completely shorn of his or her spirit and no one lives without a body. Many propositions can be placed to discuss the merit of both. In the next *adhyāya* we will see that Janaka, who lived all his life as a man of authority and responsibility, never shirking from any *dharma*, also reaches the ultimate without giving up the duties that naturally came to him. The unification of action in wisdom and wisdom in action is a theme which is very dear to the wise teachers of India.

In the *Maitreyī Brāhmaṇa* what is usually termed in social life as love is reviewed by Yājñavalkya. The individuated self in a popular sense is only the ego that is steeped in very many passions both of desires to possess and also compulsions aggravated by the ignorance of the body sense. Yājñavalkya narrates to Maitreyī that in a final analysis there is only one love, that is the Self's identity with the Self. Hence love is to be understood as one without a second. In the social context, the second is either husband or wife, child or parent, or the possession of wealth and the possessor, the desiring person and the desired. In all such dualities, the culprit is the ego steeped in passions. If there is no other, there is only the Self which is founded on *ānanda*. It is for the sake of *ānanda* that both the existential aspect of the world and its elaboration in subsistence are considered.

Before the close of the *brāhmaṇa*, Yājñavalkya gives a teaching which will occur again at the close of the fourth *adhyāya*. As we are born into this phenomenal world with our sense organs poised outward, we are very impressed by the data our senses bring to our minds. From this data we generalize three main factors: the origin of things, the existence of things, and the final dissolution of things. The world outside is a macro-image of the world inside us. Within us, there is a pre-existing state of the unconscious. When the physical organism wakes up to function, all the sense organs are commissioned to relate with their respective objects of perception. Several images come to our minds. We relate to each object, identifying it with a name, a form and a function. Even when no name is given, we can watch a form. After knowing a form and learning its name, even when the form disappears, we can still recall it to our mind just by remembering the name. These two factors are given to us through an act of perception.

When we watch the qualities of the body/mind complex, we get an insight into not only its formal or nominal reality, but also its functional reality. When name, form and function become a confection, an impression is laid on our conscious mind and the mind itself is processed to identify with the subjective counterpart of the objective-body and name presented to us. It becomes a memory stacked in the depth of our consciousness which can be recalled any time when we see the form or hear the name associated with the object/subject memorization of a phenomenal entity. Then it is called a concept.

Between the occurrence of percept and the processing of memory, many modifications are brought to our study of the percept. To begin with, experiences are of specific objects. From their individual presentation we slowly move to their class character. A percept is individualized, while a concept oscillates between the specific and the general. When the time-space occasion of a percept and its connected concept are replaced by another object of interest and subject of observation, what was entertaining up to that point in our conscious mind disappears. The mind is something like a teacher's blackboard. What is of immediate interest is shown on it. When the interest lapses, it is erased and the same space is given to another subject. But our memory system is such that there is no need to erase it. It retains the potential of being recalled whenever an appropriate occasion arises. Thus in our minds there is a presentation, a state of being held existentially valid, and a disappearance as well as the potential of being recalled. Outside also we see objects being presented, remaining for a period of time and being removed.

A central question arises – "What is the source from which the external world comes to its objectified state? What holds it for some time and into what does it dwindle away?" "From where is a mental image presented? What maintains the mental image and into what oblivion does it disappear?" In other words, there is a point of origin, a state of existence, and a point of vanishing. But vanishing does not erase the possibility of its existence for ever. Behind all the temporary phases, we see a permanent existence. This leads people to conceive of a governing principle which relates to the specific and which is always maintaining the general. According to their training, intellectual ability, visualizing power and logical judgment, different people call it different names such as truth, Self, God, the creator, the sustainer, the dissolver. Each of these is a word with meaning ascribed to it, according to the situation in which the phenomena is presented.

The appearing and disappearing phenomena can be seen as a magical entity. The holding together of something without actual cohesive structural control looks amazing. When that which has been daily presenting, relating, communicating with us, is suddenly not seen anywhere, its origin, state of being and disappearance all look magical. People have conceived of one truth behind everything, beyond the comprehension of logic. It maintains facts of life, so we make wild guesses about a manipulator of the world sitting hidden somewhere. With awe and fear, people may call upon such an entity as their creator, or lord of sustenance, and may make prayers and worship. In that area religions thrive.

We exist in a biological system with the physical constituents of a body which are elemental governed by biophysical and biochemical laws in which language and logic are two aids for observation, critical judgement and value assessment. We make our concepts as infallible as possible, either by basing them on the requirements of mathematical logic or by postulating the validity of poetic analogies. There is a dialectical polarity between the eternal and the transient, the unmanifested and the manifested. In the manifested we have individuated forms of values to which we relate, such as in the relationship between a wife and a husband, a parent and a child, or wealth which can arise as profit and diminish as loss. Yājñavalkya wants to make it very clear to Maitreyī that there is a general confusion about the entire gamut of value systems and individual relationships with them. To illustrate this he tells Maitreyī (II.4.5):

> Verily the husband is dear (to the wife) not for the sake of the husband, my dear, but it is for the sake of the Self that the husband is dear. Verily the wife is dear (to the husband) not for the sake of the wife, my dear, but it is for the sake of the Self that she is dear. Verily children are dear (to parents) not for the sake of the children, my dear, but it is for the sake of the Self children are dear. Verily wealth is dear not for the sake of wealth, my dear, but it is for the sake of the Self that it is dear. Verily the *brāhmaṇa* is dear not for the sake of the *brāhmaṇa*, my dear, but for the sake of the Self the *brāhmaṇa* is dear. Verily the *kṣatriya* is dear not for the sake of the *kṣatriya*, my dear, but it is for the sake of the Self that the *kṣatriya* is dear. Verily worlds are dear not for the sake of worlds, my dear, but it is for the sake of the Self that they are

dear. Verily the *devas* are dear not for the sake of the *devas*, my dear, but it is for the sake of the Self that they are dear. Verily *bhūta* (beings) are dear not for the sake of the beings, my dear, but it is for the sake of the Self that they are dear. Verily all is dear not for the sake of all, my dear, but for the sake of the Self all is dear. The Self (*ātman*), my dear, Maitreyī, should verily be realized: should be heard of, reflected on and meditated upon. *Ātman* is that which is heard, reflected on and meditated upon. [78]

The rishi wants Maitreyī to notice that the one becomes many. Then he wants her to know how the many can again return to one. So he gives another example (II.4.11-12):

As the sea is the one merging place of all sorts of water, as the skin is the one merging place of all kinds of touch, as the nostrils are the one merging place of all odors, as the tongue is the one merging place of all savors, as the eye is the one merging place of all forms, as the ear is the one merging place of all sounds, as the mind is the one merging place of all deliberations, as the intellect is the one merging place of all kinds of knowledge, as the hands are the one merging place of all actions, as the organ of generation is the one merging place of all pleasures, as the anus is the one merging place of all excretions, as the feet are the one merging place of all kinds of walking, as the organ of speech is the one merging place of all *Vedas*.

As a lump of salt thrown into water only dissolves into the water, and none can at all pick it up, but from whichever part one takes the water, it has only a saline taste, even so my dear, this great, endless, infinite reality is only homogeneous intelligence. On account of these elements, (the Self) stands out (separately), and as soon as these are destroyed, (its separate existence) is also destroyed. After attaining (isolation) it has no (particular) consciousness. This is what I say, my dear. [79]

APPENDIX II: Muni Kāṇḍa

Adhyāya III

The *Muni Kāṇḍa* has a dramatic opening scene. The venue is a sacrificial site in the court of Emperor Janaka. The Emperor offered an unusual program to establish certain truths for his own personal purpose as the emperor of the country and also for the public. He called to his court all the erudite scholars who claimed to have knowledge of the science of the Absolute, *brahmavidyā*. He ordered a thousand cows to be brought there with their horns decked with gold ornaments. When all his courtiers and advisors, and the best of the rishis and scholars were gathered in his court, he called their attention to his program of gift offering, called *bahudakṣiṇa*. He did not plan a burnt sacrifice, but to give away the cows and gold to the best knower of the Absolute. Naturally, a large crowd of scholars came from neighboring countries thinking that everyone would be honored and would get some present from the king. But to the utter amazement of all, he said that there was only one gift to be given – all the cows decorated with gold would go to one person. Anyone in the assembly could get up and say, "I am the best among the knowers of *brahman*." If no one challenged him, he could receive all the cows from the king. As everybody desired to have some gift from the king, they were all disappointed. They thought it was not in good taste for anyone to say "I am the best!"

There was a silence for some time. Nobody dared to get up and claim the cows. Then Yājñavalkya, a very young rishi, not even thirty years old at the time, got up and said, "I shall receive the cows." Turning to his disciple he said, "Somaśravas, my dear disciple, lead all these cows to our ashram." The young boy did this. Seeing this, all the brāhmins present became infuriated. Aśvala, the high priest of the emperor, was in the assembly. He never thought that his claim to supreme wisdom would be neglected by his own Emperor. He could not accept the impudent behavior of Yājñavalkya. He was not only the high priest but also a scholar of great repute. So, he got up and challenged Yājñavalkya. In his great anger he could not even address Yājñavalkya politely. He simply asked, "Yājñavalkya, are you indeed the best Vedic scholar among us?" All those who were present thought there would be a big confrontation between Yājñavalkya and Aśvala. But Yājñavalkya politely bowed and said, "I give my salutations to all the best knowers of wisdom. I love cows; that is all I have said."

There is a secret here. King Janaka knew that there was no one equal to Yājñavalkya in the knowledge of the Absolute. But he did not want to declare it to the public. He wanted the public to be convinced of it by listening to his wisdom. He knew that if he disregarded his own high priest Aśvala, and gave a chance to Yājñavalkya to take away the cows, Aśvala would certainly question Yājñavalkya's claim. There were also others who were of great merit in the assembly, who were likely to challenge Yājñavalkya. Janaka felt that after they were given a chance to fence words with Yājñavalkya, people would be convinced that he had no equal.

Four countries or principalities were taking part in this contest. Apart from Janaka, the King of Videha, there were also the kings of Kāśi and scholars from the countries of the Kurus and Pañcālas. It was a very formidable assembly of scholars. No one understood the secrets implied in the king's offering. His single gift had two aspects: the cows, living beings, and gold, a dead metal. Yājñavalkya only cared for the cows. But for the ordinary scholars, the gold was far more tempting than the cows. There was so much gold on the horns of the thousand cows that it naturally aroused a devastating greed on the part of the brāhmins.

In the old legends of India, there are references to cows like Kāmadhenu, Surabhi, and Nandini. These cows were all protected with great zeal by lovers of cows. Hoarding gold is one thing, while taking care of a dumb being like a cow requires a lot of compassion on the part of the keeper. The cow's many needs are to be attended to. It should not be allowed to go hungry or thirsty. It should not be exposed to the extremes of the weather. It is to be mated at the right time for calving. When the calves come they are to be protected like human children. Thus a lot of responsibility is called for. In the present case there was not just one cow, but one thousand cows. So it was not just receiving a gift, but undertaking a great responsibility to sentient beings. Only someone with a valiant spirit like Yājñavalkya could accept it. Of course, Yājñavalkya also knew that he would be questioned by the other scholars. After paying his obeisance to all the knowers of wisdom, he said that if anybody doubted that it was just for him to receive the cows, they could question him. No sooner did he say so, than Aśvala came out with his unusual questions which were difficult to answer (III.1.3): "Yājñavalkya, since everything here is overtaken by death and overcome by death, by what means does the sacrificer free himself from the reach of death?" [80]

Yājñavalkya accepted the question as a fair initiation of a dialogue. His answer was pithy, relevant, and even generous. He said, "The redeemer is the speech." Then he qualified the speech as the fire of truth. Then he identified fire with the *hotṛ* priest. We should know that in this context Aśvala was the *hotṛ* of Janaka, and Janaka is the sacrificer who would be saved. Further Yājñavalkya said, "The *hotṛ* is the voice or speech of the sacrificer." Thus he showed how Aśvala had a binding responsibility to liberate his master Janaka with the fire of his speech. This answer made everyone go into silence. Yājñavalkya was not angry with Aśvala. Instead he was placing an encomium on the *hotṛ* Aśvala as the liberator of the sacrificer, King Janaka.

A better mood came to prevail between Aśvala and Yājñavalkya. Inwardly Aśvala felt pleased that his rival was not taking away his glory. But he did not want Yājñavalkya to escape with such an answer. So he asked (III.1.4): "Yājñavalkya, since everything here is overtaken by day and night, and influenced by the bright and the dark, by what means does the sacrificer free himself from the bondage of day and night?" [81] This question was not too hard for Yājñavalkya. He answered that the *adhvaryu* was the eye of the sacrificer, which was identical with the sun. He equated the sun in the firmament and the priest at the sacrificial site.

Once again Aśvala was flattered. But he was not an ordinary person to accept defeat. So he aimed a third question at Yājñavalkya (III.1.5): "Yājñavalkya, since everything here is overtaken by the bright and dark fortnights, and overcome by the bright and dark fortnights, by what means does the sacrificer free himself from the influence of the bright and dark fortnights?" [82]

Yājñavalkya accepted the question with delight and equated the vital force, *prāṇa*, and the *udgatṛ*, saying that *prāṇa* is liberation. Aśvala found that the ball had come back to him not to shame him, but to honor him as the high priest of Janaka, since it was his duty to sing the *udgatṛ* properly and bring liberation to the king. On seeing that Yājñavalkya was resourceful about his knowledge of ritualistic worship *(upāsana)*, Aśvala changed his question slightly and asked (III.1.6): "Yājñavalkya, since the sky is, as it were, without a support, by means of what support does the sacrificer attain heaven?" Yājñavalkya was ready with his answer: "(Through) the *brahmā* priest and the mind looked upon as the moon. The sacrificer's mind is the *brahmā*. The mind is the moon; this moon is the *brahmā*. This is (the means to) liberation. So far about the ways of complete liberation; now about the meditation based on resemblance." [83]

The priest referred to here by Yājñavalkya was the master of ceremonies. As Aśvala was the chief among the priests, this had direct reference to him. Even at this point, Aśvala was not ready to let Yājñavalkya off the hook. So he asked him several more questions about sacrifice, the role of the priests, and the hymns to be sung. When Yājñavalkya was able to explain the symbolic meaning of all the parts of the ritual, Aśvala was silenced. Usually Vedāntins are not well-versed in the ritualistic part of the Veda. But in this encounter Yājñavalkya was successful in showing everyone that he was as much an adept in *Veda* as in *Vedānta*.

After Aśvala, the next aspirant to the title of the best among the knowers of the Absolute who questioned Yājñavalkya was Ārtabhāga of the line of Jaratkāru. The questions by Ārtabhāga and the answers given to him by Yājñavalkya refer to one of the major problems of individuated life. Hence, this *brāhmaṇa* is of topical importance. Ārtabhāga asks Yājñavalkya how many *grahas* (organs) and how many *atigrahas* (objects) there are. To this Yājñavalkya answers that there are eight *grahas* and eight *atigrahas*.

In all major religions of the world there is a postulation that humans are basically bound by the very nature of their embodied state. Therefore each person is in dire need of liberating himself or herself from the shackles of bondage. In the Semitic religions, bondage is considered to be born of a divine scheme. Each person is expected to work out his or her liberation by spiritually disciplining his or her life through an intense act of loyalty to God. Each of the three major Semitic religions, Judaism, Christianity and Islam, has a unique conceptualization of God. Still, they have common features. One is that God is the creator of the world, the source of the many. Another common factor is that God is One and he is One without a second. The masculinity of God is not questioned in Semitic religions. In all three, man is considered to be created by God in his own image.

One of the specialties of the Jewish concept is that God as a transcendent being is unknowable. Yet God accomplishes his designs through Logos. It is this Logos that is referred to in the Gospel according to St. John as the Word. For historical reasons, the *Talmud* suffered several catastrophes. One was that several Hellenized Jews became absorbed into Christian communities; another was the onslaught of the Romans on the Jewish temple. Consequently, the original Jewish religion branched off into different sources that claim authority over Jewish belief. But to this day, the Jewish concept, which is mainly presented in the Ten Commandments of Moses, portrays God as the only Creator and the only authority before whom man has to bow and pray for his redemption.

A great shift in Jewish theological and cosmological speculations stemmed from the Platonic concept of the transcendent which trickled into Jewish philosophy through Philo Judaeus, who lived between 20 BC and 40 AD. It is a hard job now to discern the original Jewish belief about God free from the Platonic notion of the intelligible world (*kosmos noetos*). All the references in that concept pertain more to what may be called the thought of God rather than of God as such. One source for the Jewish concept of God is the *Midrashim* which belongs to the Talmudic literature.

The early Christian writings on God are mainly a presentation of anecdotes connected with the life of Christ. They did not begin with a metaphysical or theological system to present the idea of God. Jesus himself was a Jew and was naturally familiar with the Jewish concept of God and God's relationship with man. He spoke mainly of the reality of God. The followers of Jesus began speaking of God in a three-fold manner as Father, Son and Holy Spirit. From that they also derived the divine creation of the universe, human sinfulness, the incarnation of God in the person of Jesus the Christ, his founding of the Christian church and continuing operation of his spirit in it, the eventual end of human history and fulfillment of God's plan for his creation. In Christianity, the faith in human sinfulness is universal and categorical. It is considered an observable fact; one can easily see how men and women are persistently self-centered and even their highest moral achievements are quickly corrupted by selfishness. This necessitates the need for the redeemer. The role Jesus played was that of the reconciler of man to God. The Biblical story of the fall of man depicts this situation by means of the myth that man was originally created perfect but fell by his own fault into his present state in which he is divided from his own self, from his fellows, and from God. His liberation from this chronic state of bondage has to come from justification by his faith.

The followers of Islam, like the original Jewish believers, proclaim the uniqueness and oneness of God, a status of supreme importance which He does not share with anyone. At the same time, even in the *Fātiḥa*, the prayer with which the *Holy Qur'an* begins, a dichotomy is made between those favored by the grace of Allah and those on whom the wrath of Allah falls:

> Show us the straight way.
> The way of those on whom
> Thou hast bestowed the Grace,
> Those whose (portion)
> Is not wrath
> And who go not astray. [84]

Although from the beginning to the end of the *Qur'an*, Allah is described as the most gracious and the most merciful, in most of the chapters we can read about the anger that Allah holds out to nonbelievers and hypocrites. The one condition that is given throughout the *Qur'an* for man's redemption is his honesty in belief.

In all three Semitic religions, God has his supreme rival, the deluder of the human mind: the Devil in the Jewish literature, Satan in Christianity and Iblis in Islam. These are not metaphysical concepts. There is an anthropomorphic personalization of the agent who deludes man into sin as well as the one who redeems man from the evil to which he is lead by the negative relativistic deluder.

In absolute contrast to such an anthropomorphic concept of bondage, the *Upaniṣad* presents the natural duality that exists between conditional knowledge and unconditional knowledge. According to the *Upaniṣadic* concept, individuation comes along with the corporeal organization which is at the alpha point of the circumlimitation of a mirrored aspect of the spirit. Hence the entire concept of bondage and redemption is figured out in the phenomenal frame of reference. Individuation is considered to be the borrowing of the physical instrumentation by the spirit to experience the unlimited possibilities which can occur as a result of the graded co-mingling of knowledge and ignorance comparable to the several shades with which light and darkness can proportionately relate with each other.

Ārtabhāga's question is about *graha*. The word *graha* itself means that which grasps and consequently gets into a compromising relation with whatever it grasps. Yājñavalkya gives eight classical examples of the spirit getting into conditional states. The two counterparts here are the spirit that is lured into bondage and the coloring or conditional quality of that which is being grasped. The eight *grahas* enumerated by Yājñavalkya are: the organ of smell (*prāṇa*); speech (*vāk*); the organ of taste (*rasena*); the eye (*cakṣuṣ*); the ear (*śrotra*); the mind (*manas*); the hands (*hastau*); and the organ of touch (*tvak*). Ārtabhāga sees each one of these *grahas* as a fit food for death. We don't have to go into any involved philosophy to see how these eight causal factors of necessity bring the inevitable compulsions which cause a living organism to tire itself out to the very end of its life, seeking fulfillment of the desires which they evoke.

Ārtabhāga follows up his questions about the eight *grahas* and *atigrahas* with a more relevant question: "Since all this is the food of death, who is that god to whom death is the food?" That focuses us more on the idea of death. Normally when we think of death we think of coming to a terminal point. The *Upaniṣad* is interested in establishing the natural curiosity of people to know if there is anything beyond death. Hence Ārtabhāga asks Yājñavalkya: "When such a person dies, what is it that does not leave him?" The answer given to this is "The name." An individuated organism has a perishable aspect and an imperishable aspect. The perishable aspect is the form and the deed. The imperishable aspect is the name and the essential meaning of the deed that is carried over to a further perpetuation of the spirit in bondage. The discussion of that continues until the end of the second *brāhmaṇa*.

As there is an unexplainable mystery that lurks between death and afterlife, a literary device is employed by the *Upaniṣad* rishi. He says that ultimately Ārtabhāga and Yājñavalkya retire to a secret chamber to discuss the problem. Their discussion is not revealed in the text for any discursive reasoning.

In *brāhmaṇas* three and seven an unusual literary device is resorted to in order to open an enquiry into the mysteries lying buried in the world of myth. Science and its rational pursuits keep us engaged in the world of the visible, which to some extent can lead us to the metaphysical frontiers of the intelligible. Religious people, on the other hand, forsake the merits of rational thinking and are preoccupied by mystical speculation in which esoteric language and symbolism thrive. It is to such a world Bhujyu calls the attention of Yājñavalkya. He narrates an anecdote involving a strange phenomena he happened to come across in his wanderings. He went to a family which was steeped in ancestral traditions. There he saw a young woman, the daughter of his host, who was possessed by a spirit. Most people do not know what a spirit is or whether anything corresponding to that word exists. Yet, when a person shows disorderly behavior, that person speaks and acts as if he or she is being encountered by a force which is unfamiliar to rational-minded people for whom valid testimony is perception. When a person is subjected to an emotional or behavioral disorder, it looks as if an unknown entity belonging to a mysterious dimension other than time and space is causing a baffling kind of correlation and coordination in the neuro-muscular system.

The modern world, which has lost or is fast losing the sense of wonder and mystery, may think it is a waste of time to probe into such a phenomena. But in every field of knowledge we come to the frontiers of normalcy. Beyond the horizon of the rational, human interests go to unaccountable expansions. Thus chemistry has alchemy; physics has metaphysics; and poetry elaborates itself into songs, sagas and eulogies to the unknown called the *mysterium tremendum*. As *brahmavidyā* accepts everything into its ambit, the bright as well as the dark, the hilarious as well as the tragically distressing are to be accounted for. No field is extraneous to the interest of the *Upaniṣad*. The two references to a person becoming possessed by a spirit open up a different channel to go into the cultural grass roots of Indian people where their unconscious is identified with the symbols of myth. Mythical symbols lie buried in the formation of semantics and philology. We do not have any facts and figures to check and compare notes with when the mind is directed to an unknown field. However, it is fascinating even when nothing is known of it.

In the incident narrated by Bhujyu, certain perennial interests which lie buried in the collective unconscious are presented to us. C.G. Jung alludes to them as archetypal notions of belief. We have archetypes pertaining to nouns as well as verbs or rather to the proto-language of beliefs which are preserved for their mysterious ability to feed certain thought streams into us. A word can make secret suggestions because of its tonal or even rhythmic impact on the human psyche. We see people going into certain emotional effusions such as when a musician improvises on a mode of singing which is, language-wise, riveted to certain notions which are governed by the grammar, logic and rhetorical necessities to which the author or the composer maintains a loyalty. At the same time, within the field of improvisation, the musician can create nuances which evoke responses in the listener. It is like the artist and listener get into a collusion which is outside the scheme or the mode yet is universally appreciated by the inexpressible aspect of the aesthetic ability to which all works of art give haven.

The highly cryptic structures of the fundamental rituals of religion are sometimes epitomized into a simple incident such as a burnt sacrifice. But the priest, like the musician or the artist, can make a ritual very elaborate. Throwing a perishable entity into a flaming fire is the essential suggestion. The priest can throw a *tulasī* leaf or single flower into the fire of a sacrificial pit. Its place can be taken by graded varieties of items that please our senses, nourish our bodies or fill our minds with exaggerations of sensibilities. The highest libation that can be offered into the fire is one's own corporeal being; that may resemble a suicidal act. Those who do not go that far may sacrifice a fellow human. Sophistication in human culture delimited sacrifice to molesting a dear animal such as a horse.

The reference in *adhyāya* three, *brāhmaṇa* three, mantra one is to *aśvamedha*. This symbol includes named objects and actions in the form of creative art. We tend to make two errors in such a field. One is failing to recognize the trees that stand huddled to make the mass of a forest. We say, "By seeing the forest, the tree is not noticed." The other error is caused by fixing one's interest on a single tree and missing the magnificence of the forest. In a ritualistic context some people are lost in the chanting of liturgy and others are lost in the sensory infatuation roused by roasted meat and the spirits they gulp.

Unfortunately, most students of the *Upaniṣads* and the *Vedas* are at a complete loss to understand the significance of the appearance of a spirit classified as *gandharva*. The backdrop of these mantras is in the text itself. Unless one uses one's penetrative skill to decipher the literary device of the *Upaniṣad* rishi, these secrets elude our attention. The spirit which affected the daughter of Patañcala confessed that he was Sudhanvan, a *gandharva*. *Gandharva* is a term that suggests a quality of earth (*gandha*) and an ability to fly in the sky. It is a phenomena that has a kind of magical dimension with a spectrum of interest from the down-to-earth world to the most celestial apparition. The name Sudhanvan indicates he is not a crude spirit of black force but one of high erudition with a contemplative ability to understand the divine scheme of cosmic and psychic interest.

In *brāhmaṇa* seven, Uddālaka narrates a parallel incident in which the wife of Patañcala is possessed by a *gandharva* called Kabandha. Kabandha is a very important character in the *Bṛhadāraṇyaka Upaniṣad*, being none other than Dadhyac, whose head was cut off by Indra and fitted with the head of a horse by the Aśvinis so that he could teach them *brahmavidyā*. This connection has been treated as being of no significance by prior commentators. Sometimes such ciphers are not deciphered because they are so deeply involved. This is not true in the present case because the identity of Kabandha as Dadhyac stands out even to people who cursorily read the *Upaniṣad*. The omission of this reference is a clear indication that some vested interest on the part of orthodoxy is being kept up because of the strange unpopularity of acknowledging that a wisdom teacher could arise from the Śiva context.

In mantras one and two of *brāhmaṇa* three, some of the basic concepts of *brahmavidyā*, the science of the Absolute, are discussed. An insight into these concepts will hold good in understanding *Vedānta* correctly. One is the concept of the transcendent principle of the Absolute (*brahman*) and its immanent manifestation as the physical universe unitively governed and controlled by causal consciousness. Its cosmological unity can be seen in what is termed the imperishable (*akṣara*), the indweller (*antaryāmī*) and the overlordship of an all-embracing principle with dual emphases such as the manifold purposiveness in relating spirit and matter (*hiraṇyagarbha*) and the basis for relationship between the generic and the specific individual (*prajāpati*). What comes within the frame of reference of the specific is the individuated consciousness, which is equivalent to a supervising and operational spirit in the corporeal body (*jīvātma*) and the psycho-physical contents that go into the manifestation of an individuated organism.

This is very different from the theological concepts of Semitic religions. Although they are pronouncedly opposed to idolatry, in the actual experiencing of Semitic religions, these principles are anthropomorphically conceived as a personal God. That God shares the rational and emotional characteristics of the individuals who are said to be created and controlled by him, whether he is popularly called Jehovah, Father, Son and Holy Spirit, or Allah, the benevolent and compassionate. We do not want to go into the merits and demerits of the Semitic concepts. We only want to stress that the Vedāntic concept given in this chapter has no similarity to them.

Another fundamental aspect of *Vedānta* deals with the world of imagination. The term "imagination" is derived from the word "image" in the sense of an artificial representation of an object, a likeness or a mental representation. In the Vedāntic context, forms recognized by names are classified as gross (*sthūla*), subtle (*sūkṣma*) and causal (*kāraṇa*). The causal aspect is always first referred to as the principle of immanence which in turn is oblivi-ated by transcendence. Thus the causal aspect of an image is like a scheme. The principle of immanence allows several shades of existence. For instance, a pot is basically clay which is gross. In the transformation of a lump of clay into an accomplished pot, accompanying properties are being graded through the insertion of imagery which is purely mental. The causal aspect mainly belongs to the will to make in the potter. To fashion the gross clay into another gross state, there has to be a destructuring and a restructuring, both of which are governed by the purpose of creation. Hence, the Vedāntin considers it inevitable that there is a technology of transformation which can be significant in the material as well as in the process of changing shapes. These mantras represent a deep analysis of the possibility of the gross being diluted into the subtle by a causal principle and recreated to become gross again.

A hinterland is imagined between the transcendental and the immanent which in the *Upaniṣad* is called *avyākṛta ākāśa*, the potential space out of which imagery has to guide all the constituent factors to be reshuffled and recreated. A host of suppositions are made about this imaginary world, which is mainly governed by a proto-language of signs and symbols. Because of the poetic flair of Indian scholars, many stories are made out of personified images. This makes Indian philosophy very difficult to be clearly understood unless the student is always careful to decipher signs, symbols and poetic exaggerations. The sounds and expressions in language give us semantic, noematic and philological clues to decipher each image in the context of the rich source of literature traditionally passed down as legends, epics, fiction, fairy tales and stories which have been purposefully created for precipitating and perpetuating ethical values.

The term "being possessed" is considered to be a disorder in the faculty of memory called *apasmara*. The world of memory is called *smarana* which has a reference to Smara, the symbolized demi-urge of erotics. Smara is personalized as a male god of love who is supposed to be inducing love in human hearts. His female counterpart is Rati, the manifesting aspect of infatuation. Infatuation is the main cause of relating the faculty of memory and recall. According to legends, Īśvara, the supreme governing principle, is opposed to sporadic love affairs. Love as *bhakti* is the main dynamic for the achievement of the highest value actualization. When it deviates from *dharma*, it is considered an evil. According to legends, Śiva burned Smara, the god of love, to ashes. He was revived to life without any visible physical body. A misplaced memory is here referred to as the spirit that possesses.

The interlinking principle, called *yoga*, can be seen in all kinds of unifications. What is important in it is the ability to further any relationship which comes into being. As the senses and mind are susceptible to the pleasure principle, one can easily slip away from *yoga* to *bhoga* (pleasure-seeking). Or, if a pathologic infection comes to the body or mind, there is an implied dynamic which perpetuates the same condition, like the running of a river. The Sanskrit term *ro* means 'to cry'. Hence a pathological state is called *roga*. When such a thing happens, an opposing dynamic should be used to bring a patient back to health. This is called *yoga*.

There are many modes of reasoning. The most popular is that of deducing a conclusion from the popular hearsay of the public. An improvement on this is made by logically correlating every effect to its causal source, then continuing the chain of reasoning as an unbroken chain of cause and effect relationship. This is mostly so in linear thinking. Reasoning by alluding to illustrations or anecdotes cannot be easily ingested by those who are used to listening to arguments. A far deeper mode of reasoning is to take extreme possibilities and reduce their variegations by advancing from the two poles of a situation to a central possibility where one comes to a neutral zero. This is exemplified by Socratic reasoning which is described by Plato as dialectic, the touch stone of wisdom. This brings us to the inseparable dual aspects of the same truth. In the *Upaniṣad* we very often come across a situation in which the Absolute is presented as the treasure house of many relativistic factors, each of which draws its essence from a contributory factor of the Absolute.

The one example we want to consider here is the concept of the *prajāpati*, the archetypal model of the self-creating and the natural origin of the proliferating aspects of creation. The *prajā* represents a process which ranges from an alpha point of zero to an omega point of final cessation. The *prajāpati* is born and causes many to be born. Thus, in the chain of reasoning, when we trace the origin of the many, we come to the ultimate cause. If it is pressed further, the ultimate is obliviated by transcendence. Thus *prajāpati* is an archetypal model for all life forms.

Each individuated life form has to have the coming together of constituent elements for it to be initiated. A period of growth, development and structuring takes place. When it is mature, all inward-bound details are reduced once again to a prime cause. The reference can be to the emergence of a bacteria, the chrysalis of a mosquito or the inception in a human mother's womb of an idiot or a genius unparalleled in history. In the process there can be occurrences of subnormalcy, normalcy and abnormalcy. The collective forces which operate in the matrix of cause-effect transformation are of a varying nature controlled by variegated forces, so the end result cannot be predicted for the same reason that Heisenberg held out his theory of uncertainty. In the present context, we should understand *prajāpati* to be both the archetypal model of emanation and the countless millions of emanated end results. It is enigmatically both the cause of causes and the effect of effects.

In all these studies we are led to consider the continuity of being through a categorical determination of relationship. In the

Bhagavad Gītā, the phenomenon of the relationship of all life forms and all manifestations of values is allegorically described as a string on which many beads are strung. For obvious reasons, this is a highly simplified picture. Instead of a single string, we have to imagine a cosmic matrix of entangled strings within the time-space continuum presenting varying relationships which can throw light on value-structuring. Essentially this concept places before us the invisible numinous fact of existence, the phenomenal fiction of name, form and temporally experienced phenomenal importance. The thread is presented in this chapter as *sūtrātma*, the all-binding consciousness in which the cause and effect cannot be separately established or accounted for.

Another archetypal allegory is of the egg. The entire cosmos is called *brahmāṇḍa*, the cosmic egg. The individuated organism ranging from a single cell to multicelled organisms is also presented as an egg that matures in time to produce a unique individuated being. Such specific references point towards bodies with dimensions, three dimensional or n-dimensional. When an embodied being is located as an inception within a gamete, it is called *piṇḍāṇḍa*. *Piṇḍa* means a material mass, *aṇḍa* is an egg. The whole universe is said to be hatched out of the egg of *hiraṇyagarbha*. With reference to its process of maturing, what was in the pregnancy of the golden promise is called *brahmāṇḍa*. The same model is validated to explain the origin of finite beings. Thus the similarity of *brahmāṇḍa* and *piṇḍāṇḍa* is held valid in the *Upaniṣad* to explain the relationship between the cosmic being and microcosmic being.

In *brāhmaṇas* four and five, Yājñavalkya is questioned by Uṣasta and Kahola respectively. The most important subject presented in these *brāhmaṇas* is the explication of the concept of the Self as the indwelling reality. After Kahola's questioning, Gārgī asks about the support of everything and its warp and woof.

Gārgī's questions are followed by those of Uddālaka in *brāhmaṇa* seven. A secret scheme of creation, governorship and control is given in mantras thirteen through twenty-three. The first pair of principles mentioned in mantras thirteen and fourteen respectively are darkness and light. It is significant that darkness is followed by light. In mantra fifteen we come to the presentation of the elements (*bhūtas*). Then references are given which identify the body with the nose, the organ of speech, the eye, the ear, the mind, the skin, the intellect and the semen that contains the seed.

By immersing ourselves in a deep contemplation of these eleven mantras we can get a clue to the structural engineering of the spirit, psyche, mind and biological functions.

It is common in references to the beginnings of things to have the secrecy of darkness laid out as a primary factor from which potentials emerge into the light of actuality. The potentials are basically covered up such as in a seed or a sperm. But the functional ability of a thing is implied in the design of the structures from which functions are to emerge. Darkness and light are to be taken as the greatest mystery of everything. The miracle of the mystery is darkness hiding the potential and light revealing whatever is hidden. We can see this in the *Genesis* given in the *Pentateuch.* Transformation of the unknown into the known is presented in all religions as an act of revelation. For this reason, the ultimate testimony of truth always comes as a revelation. In *Vedānta,* immediate perception, inference, analogy, contradiction and the improbability are all accepted as testimonies in phenomenal experiences. Knowledge of the numenon or the Absolute is confined to the testimony of the word of revelation (*śabda*). The role of darkness in concealing the possible, probable and actual makes us think of the causal factor having within it a deliberation to first invest the unknown with possibility, then selectively promote the potential to become probable and ultimately actualize only the fully structured.

After the dichotomy of darkness and light, the physical body is presented as being animated by the joint effort of the breath and the word. Word cannot be uttered without the energy endorsement of *prāṇa* (air). All the same, the teleological meaning of creation has to come from the word that is articulated by *prāṇa.* In the Upaniṣadic context, there is a conspicuous absence of an anthropomorphic God using the word to create. Once manifestation arises, what is revealed first is a mode that can be distinguished from another by its form. Hence we are asked to think of the body as eye (III.7.18). After the presentation of a physical body, it is invested with the faculty of hearing, the faculty of mind and the overall equipment of tactual sensation by the enclosure of the body in skin.

The mind is a generic term which covers all four aspects of the inner organ with which the organism initiates mentation: doubting and questioning, recalling and remembering, cognizing and judging and, finally, registering the affectivity of pain and pleasure. Useful practical knowledge (*vijñāna*) is separated out of the generic mind as an instrument to guide the specific role of each embodied being. We do not want to elaborate on this any further but the student is expected to sit with each of these mantras and go into a deep contemplative search to find out the exact structural details arising from each mantra. The engineering design put into these mantras can guide each individual person to a well-coordinated and well ordained functional ability which takes each instance of embodiment from the seed to the seed, or primary cause to ultimate cause, or, as Aristotle would put it, from the material cause to the final cause.

In *brāhmaṇa* eight, mantras one to twelve, we get a dialogue between Gārgī and Yājñavalkya which serves to tie up all the loose ends. Then in *brāhmaṇa* nine, Yājñavalkya gets one more chance to explain all the secrets connected with the concept of the shining ones (*devās*). This arises from a dialogue between Śakalya called Vidagdha and Yājñavalkya. This being the last *brāhmaṇa* of the third *adhyāya*, many conclusive teachings of the *Upaniṣad* occur in this discourse. It also brings a drastic dismissal of theories not supported by direct experience as well as by imperiential identification with the Absolute. In the commentary, we have given all necessary suggestions for the aspiring student to conduct himself or herself through searching questions. On the whole, the path chalked out in the third chapter may look very involved, like a labyrinth, but there is no easy way to come to grips with the most treasured truth presented by the *Upaniṣad*. The best way is the right way.

Adhyāya IV

In the first *brāhmaṇa*, the dialogue is between Yājñavalkya and Janaka. Janaka reports to Yājñavalkya the instructions about *brahman* which he received from several different teachers. The first *guru* he mentions is Jitvan who instructed him that the word is *brahman*. On questioning Janaka, Yājñavalkya finds that the wisdom Janaka gained from Jitvan was one-footed because his *guru* did not give him instruction on the abode and foundation of the word. Also, he was not told how *brahman* was to be meditated upon as word.

Realizing that the instruction he has received is fragmentary, Janaka turns to Yājñavalkya for a complete instruction. Yājñavalkya agrees that Jitvan was right to mention the word but he adds that the word has the organ of speech for its abode and *ākāśa* for its foundation. It is to be meditated upon as pure consciousness. We have given a detailed commentary on the word, the organ of speech and how the hidden consciousness relates itself with the outer consciousness through the organ of speech.

The next *guru* mentioned by Janaka is Udaṅka who instructed him that the vital breath (*prāṇa*) is *brahman*. That too is dismissed after Yājñavalkya questions Janaka because Janaka does not know its abode or foundation. Yājñavalkya teaches Janaka about the source from where all dynamics of force come. Motion does not merely mean an operational force. Each thing also has its characteristics. Anything that can be referred to as a thing is derived from the meaning of the word with which it is indicated, *padārtham* (*padam* means 'word', *artham* means 'meaning').

There can be many words which come under different classifications. For instance, substance is basic to things. Thingness refers to substance which gives the possibility for something to be. Substances are such that they can be analyzed and synthesized. They can transform with certain particles of another substance in one case and other substances in other cases. This flexibility of substance resembles the viscosity of water. Hence it is called *dravyam*, that which allows composition and transformation. But the motion that generates a particular composition of substance can be different from another, quantitatively and qualitatively. Hence *dravya*, substance, always goes along with its qualitative characteristics, *guṇa*, i.e. the property that differentiates one compounded substance from another. In our individual body/mind complex, there are several categories of substance such as our skin, flesh, nervous system, the blood that circulates, gaseous things and hard substances like bones. From an almost microscopically finite mode, all these substances are produced and differently channeled by the vital breath. Hence, the vital breath is to be considered as the dynamics of all motion.

Even before a word is to be articulated, the conceptual possibility is to be sought in certain tonal modes which can give the desired meaning. In the study of this, one goes to the primary electrical impulse which comes as a throb. This throb decides what is to be formulated. It is the formless origin of the form (*virūpa pariṇāma*). From that, the entire world of forms has to evolve. The formation from a single cell to the entire universe is called cosmic evolution (*viśva pariṇāma*). In cosmic evolution thermodynamics is understood in terms of entropy in dialectical polarity with negentropy. This study branches off into several special considerations such as of many species becoming concomitant within a genus and the species deriving characteristics from the common characteristics of individuation. In Indian systems of philosophy, the species and the genus are called *vyaṣṭi* and *samaṣṭi*. That also gives rise to the kind (*jati*) and the class (*samanya*). In these mantras, the term used for the abode or body is *āyatana*, that in which a certain thing stays. In the case of vital breath (*prāṇa*), that itself is *āyatana*. It is to be meditated upon as *priya*, that which induces desire.

In mantra four Barku is the teacher mentioned. He taught Janaka that the faculty of vision is *brahman*. Yājñavalkya objects to this, asking how a person would relate with *brahman* if he were blind. Here also, the faculty of vision is the *āyatana* (home) of itself. It is established in the *ākāśa* and is to be meditated upon as truth (*satya*). In India, a blind person is called *prajña cakṣuṣ*, one whose faculty of vision is not considered to be in the external eyeball but in the seat of consciousness of the soul. Truth is to be discerned by first determining what is untruth. The determination of untruth is called *asatya niścaya* or *abhava niścaya*, the power to see through phenomenality, knowing that the real is different from appearance. A person with eyes perceives many forms, real and unreal, generic and specific. The main role of the eye as the organ of perception is to distinguish the eternal from the transient. Hence one should meditate on truth to see how the faculty of vision is intrinsically established in *brahman*.

The next in order is the teacher Gardabhīvipīta. He taught Janaka that the faculty of hearing is *brahman*. This also Yājñavalkya dismisses as a fragmentary teaching. Yājñavalkya identifies the faculty of hearing with directions. Infinite is the dimension to which all directions belong. One has to meditate on this as the unlimited (*anantam*). In fact for the definition of the Absolute (*brahman*) we come across the Upaniṣadic dictum *sat cit anantam brahma*. Although we quite often give *sat cit ānanda* as a definition of *brahman*, the word *ānanda* is not in the *Upaniṣads* in that context. Only *ananta* is there.

In the sixth mantra, the teacher mentioned by Janaka is Satyakāma Jabālā. He taught Janaka that mind (*manas*) is *brahman*. Yājñavalkya corrects the notion of Janaka and says mind is the *āyatana* or abode of mental activity. It is established in the *ākāśa* and to be meditated upon as *ānanda*. In the understanding of *brahman* different considerations are to be taken. Realization of the Self did not come to Satyakāma Jabālā from a human teacher's instruction. He first received instruction from a bull about the four directions, East, West, South and North. Satyakāma was taught how these directions are to be meditated upon as four limbs of brightness. His second teacher was also not a person. It was the fire he lit to give himself and his cows warmth one night. The fire taught him another four aspects of infinitude. They were the earth, atmosphere, sky and ocean. He was taught how to meditate on these four limbs of the infinite as the unbounded. The third teacher of Satyakāma was a swan who taught him four other aspects of the Absolute: fire, sun, moon and electrical energy. He was asked to meditate on these as the shining principle. The fourth teacher of Satyakāma was a diver bird. It taught him four other limbs of the Absolute: the vital breath, faculty of seeing, faculty of hearing and faculty of mentation. He was told that they were to be meditated upon as the home of all.

In mantra seven, the teacher who is said to have instructed Janaka is Vidagdha, the son of Śākala, also called Śakalya. According to him, the heart is *brahman*. Yājñavalkya adds that the heart is the home of everything. It is also the foundation and establishment of all other things. It is to be known as the Absolute (*brahman*). In this mantra, the highest realization of *brah man* known as *aparokṣa brahma nirupāna* comes to an end.

Brāhmaṇa two of *adhyāya* four gives an intimate intimation to every individual who wants to know one's exact position and assignment in this world. Yājñavalkya asks Janaka if he knows where he will go after leaving the body. Janaka does not know and wants to learn it from Yājñavalkya. Gaining a little insight into one's life retrospectively and prospectively as well as into one's immediate programs will easily convince one that each comes alone, lives alone and also leaves alone. Mind is a repository of memories. Memories are colored. From the brightest of the bright to the darkest of the dark, impressions are there, not only of one person but of everyone with whom one comes into intimacy. Nothing is more contagious or infectious than what one mind does to another. Consequently, just like environmental contamination affects a person through the air they breathe and the incoming stimulation of the senses, the fears, hopes, woes and glad tidings of one person impact others. Mind is like a magnet. In fact, there is no mind except an electromagnetism of high-power attraction that sits concealed in every atom of the body, monad-like. Hence, life enters into the vast field of unaccountable pains, disturbances and distraction from the moment of the inception of an individuated life.

We have many technologically conceived devices to enhance the correct functioning of our faculties of knowledge, locomotion and extension. When these function mechanically, wear and tear causes us to discard the old and get improved devices without much remorse. Similarly a thoughtful person does not grieve or feel remorse or regret about leaving one psycho-somatic system provided by nature and getting another. Just as birth is a well-designed way to come into the world-scene, death is an equally ingenious method of getting out of it. The life-giving and life-preserving laws of the organism also function meticulously to squeeze life out of a living body.

The appropriate questions about death are: "Is it a bodily function or is it an abstraction? Does it refer to the end of life or the beginning of another life? Does it bring our three-dimensional life into a single dimension or does death shatter the dead into a million destructurings? Is death the relief of a long period of disease called life or is it a prison cell for the splendor of the Self? Is it a mirror that gives us a chance to look into the secret of life or is it a window that can be closed against the seeming duality of the Self? Is it relativistic or can it be called the Absolute? Will we ever resolve these puzzles?"

Many thinkers have made their best searches to answer these questions. One great book that gives several useful hints is the *Bhagavad Gītā*. One can profitably refer to II:26-27, IX:9, X:34 and XII:6-7. In X:34 the relationship between death and the all-governing divine principle is referred to. The cyclic aspect of death is referred to in IX:3.

The stamp of divinity was scraped away from the organism of a living body when doctors proved that they could take a part of a dead body to repair the defect of a living body. To raise the screen of mystery, in *brāhmaṇa* two, mantra two, Yājñavalkya introduces the bicameral mind. In it pure vision and conditioned and colored visions are neatly synchronized so that one uses a universal mind as the supreme device to perceive. It is complemented with a million colorations and conditionings of a permanent nature until the body is dropped. The triple states of consciousness further enhance the relativistic division of consciousness while, like a light looking on, the common foundation of all life provides for a backdrop in every individuated being. Uniqueness and universality function without separation and with efficiency. Pure consciousness is the basis, while the sensory and motor systems of the body are the receiving and responding devices which meet all the contingencies of life from moment to moment.

To know most of the details we can profitably use the descriptions given in modern medical physiology which deals with the organization of the nervous system and basic functions of the synapses. A good resource is *The Textbook of Medical Physiology*, Arthur Guyton, International Edition, 1981, W.B. Saunders Co. A more recent study of this phenomena is given in the book *The Brain Has a Mind of Its Own*, Richard Restak, Harmony Books, New York, 1991.

In mantras five, six and seven, the Self is properly defined and described. Then, in mantra eight, Yājñavalkya establishes that, as soon as it occurs, life correllates itself with tendencies which are detailed by religions as sin. With death, that tendency is overcome. This categorical recognition of sin as a phenomenon only pertaining to one life term dismisses a possible day of ultimate judgment and relegation of the individuated Self to hell or heaven. This is the greatest contribution of *Vedānta* to humanity. We read "That very person, on being born or assuming a body, is conjoined with evils and on dying or leaving the body, discards these evils." Even people outside the Semitic religions entertain the thought that sin is a phenomena which is vicariously continued through generation after generation. It is this belief that the above mantra rules out. Where there is no body, there are no sense organs. Where there is no sensation or sense data, there is no mind also. *Anna* (food), *prāṇa* (vital breath) and *manas* (mind) all belong to nature and are governed and controlled by nature modalities. Extrapolating the mind into a non-physical, non-sensory world of abstraction is only a product of imagination. From wrong premises, most religions build up an imaginary world and threaten believers about the consequences of their actions as if they are deeply painted on the soul of a person. In Judaism, Christianity and Islam, the belief in the Day of Judgment is a cardinal article of faith. The votaries of these religions think that only such a belief will deter a person from indulging in evil. This is like adults trying to discipline innocent children by telling them stories of imaginary ghosts and goblins to tame them and make their minds submissive to the dictates of their elders. The havoc such a wrong faith does to a person, in principle, as well as in practice, inflicts a deep mental injury on individuals which makes their bruised minds bleed with anxiety and pain all their lives.

An alternative way of making life upright is developing one's attention and knowing the intrinsic nature of the laws by which living organisms are exposed to environmental factors. Within the ambit of contradiction and agreement, there is the law of contraries. Contraries are seemingly contradictory to non-contemplative minds. Those who contemplate can easily see that everything in this world has a dialectical counterpart. These counterparts are to be related in the intrinsic terms of universal laws. Complementarity is the first law to look into. In honor of this law wise people say that no man is an island in this world. Parents are complemented with their progeny. A husband is complemented with his wife. Height is complemented with depth, bright with dark, right with left, above with below, master with a follower, government with the governed and so on and so forth. A more active principle of complementarity is reciprocity. With reciprocity, what is lacking in one is present in its counterpart. The husband impregnates, the wife bears the child and brings it forth. We find this principle functioning as the warp and woof of all aspects of creativity. One has to remember and recognize who or what are one's complementary counterparts and how to relate with them attentively. In most of our functions we are meant to collaborate with our counterparts. In complementarity the stress is on understanding, while in reciprocity it is on attentively carrying out action with efficiency in one's response.

To think that two and two make three or five is not a sin to be confessed or absolved from. It is an error to be recognized and corrected. After carrying out one's correction there is absolutely no need to brood over a corrected mistake or for a third person to mete out justice. The error itself is the punishment and one does not have to wait for the error to be corrected by another. Of course an intelligent and attentive person is always benefited by learning right and wrong from those who know. There are inevitable contradictions in life. One should not run away from them. Contradictories cancel out each other with a natural rhythm. After oscillating between the extremes of contradiction, those who are patiently attentive for homeostasis to be established are sure to come to a neutral zero which is like Max Planck's constant 'h'.

Here one is not scared of destiny, nor conceiving of an angry or jealous God to correct and control one's life. Intensifying one's attention (*śraddha*) to the law of life brings a graded understanding to move along. The life in a body (*jīva*) is totally identified with its structural anatomy and functional dynamics. That warrants giving one's attention to every constituent factor in the body and its reciprocal or complementary counterparts in the environment. One should not underrate or evade the purpose for which the body is structured. This is adherence to the physical law of life. Physical laws are complementary to the biologic purposes of each organism. The dictum "Know Thyself" does not mean that one should discard the periphery to know the imagined innermost Self. The Self is the whole universe and, in the whole scheme, even the flimsiest hair, properly structured and fitted into the body as an antenna of sensation, is as important as major faculties like the heart that circulates blood or the respiratory system that fills the body with energy. In the sensory system, there is the alternating function of the synapses which respond to inhibitions as well as obsessions. Any mistake anywhere has its consequence then and there. It is this natural law of reciprocity, appropriate reaction and responsive carrying out of one's task which is enjoined by *Vedānta* on its votaries who seek a smooth fulfillment of life.

A question can arise that if everything is to be maintained smoothly, why does the *Upaniṣad* also refer to sin (*pāpa*)? The world itself is an instrumentation to carry out the purposiveness of cosmic function. A little contemplative insight into the cosmic anatomy will easily convince us that if the sun were not there, our eyes would be useless. If there were no oceans and waters, we would not have a biologic life-preserving principle. However, no relative factor can be absolutely flawless. And one flaw can contribute to another. Hence, in spite of human attention, incorrect visions can tamper with the harmonious functioning of any organism. So the *Upaniṣad* recognizes sin as a possible error.

Two kinds of error are admitted, generic and specific. All human beings with healthy optical devices are bound to see the sky as blue even though there is no blue there. This is a generic error. One person mistaking a rope for a snake is a specific error. Contemplative programs are necessary to discipline us to transcend the incidence of both kinds of error. In Judaism, Christianity and Islam, this possible failure is given maximum attention. In principle, the admission of sin in religion is not a wrong thing. However, to take advantage of people's inability to see clearly because of the weakness of their faculties is a greater sin than individuals stumbling on their mistakes. In established religions the punishment of sin is threatened with horrifying pictures of hell. The followers are treated like little lambs formulated into flocks which are to be led by God's intervention or the protective care of a savior or the adherence to the laws of a church or masjid.

From the study of the natural flow of biologic function, we are again led to the inevitable compulsions to which all living beings are exposed such as the changing modes of consciousness: wakeful, dream and deep sleep. Here again, it is the cosmic structure that is responsible for all living organisms being alternately exposed to day and night and to various solar, lunar and other astral energies that control life. The passing of consciousness from the wakeful to the dream and the dream to a period of suspension in deep sleep is examined. We are advised not to cry over spilt milk and to bear with integrity the inevitabilities of life. The dream aspect is studied in detail in mantras thirteen and fourteen. Deep sleep is described as a natural overhauling and regenerating device of the stream of life. The votaries of the *Upaniṣad* are assured that God has nothing to do with a person's virtues or vices.

In mantras twenty to thirty-eight, we come across several studies of valid testimonies that can help us to avoid errors as much as possible. In any case, the individual is made directly responsible for winning one's freedom and becoming free of mental distresses.

Brāhmaṇa four commences with the closing scene of the death of the organism. The zest for life becomes anemic. Nothing is distinct any longer to the cognitive faculty; its presence in the senses diminishes to a zero point. Like the leaves of a tree withering; becoming pale and dry and the nourishing sap of the tree leaving one branch after another, life stands staring at the flickering flame of the Self. The eye is no longer seeking the sun that illuminates the world. The world of songs, lyrics and sweet voices gives way to utter silence. The outgoing breath causes an exit through which death can go into the vastness of the desert.

We read in the *Aitareya Upaniṣad* that in the beginning, only the Self *(ātman)* was here – no other winking thing whatsoever. Everything came from that unwinking numenon. The first spark of life is that which is walking everywhere before. That pioneer is called *puruṣa-pura agragamane*, meaning "the cause of all causes that walks toward its destiny." Nature is that which structures itself in manifold. The same dynamic by which everything proliferates also systematically de-structures all that has been accomplished. In the Semitic religions, the first person who emerged as the will of the Divine was Adam, *adau* in Hebrew, meaning "the first." What follows is Eve, like eve following the dawn. The second and third mantras of *Aitareya* indicate a graded ordering of the vaporous waters. First the mirage arrived like magic when light rays penetrated vapor. Then came morbidity (*mara*) and, finally, that which dissolves all forms. In mantra four of the *Aitareya* we get the whole picture of the emergence of faculty after faculty. A cosmic counterpart of each psychosomatic principle is placed outside, such as the breath inside and wind outside, the sight inside and the luminous sun in the sky, the hearing inside and the quarters of heaven spread out over 360 degrees, the sensitive skin and hair on the body and plants and trees to green the good earth, the mind inside to ruminate and the moon in the sky to come as a sheen that bewitches the mind to dream.

At the end of life, it is as if everything is withdrawn back into the unwinking numenon from which it emerged. The entire scheme is an unfolding and a refolding; the unfolding of a seed which can be finally epitomized into another seed for tomorrow. From the moment of inception and the kindling of the unconscious to flare up into consciousness, it is the sole player. Both knowledge and action are elaborated until everything specifically known is merged into the general, every act of manipulation is finally given up and the great sport is terminated. What comes between the moment of inception and the termination of life is the incubation of the meaning of life. In Sanskrit it is called *tapas*. In the formation of a baby bird, incubation spells the introduction of the being into life. Then the whole process of becoming unfolds. After the bursting of the shell, the bird has to take upon its slender beak the responsibility of feeding itself. With beaks and claws, it gathers the stamina of life to spread its wings and fly into freedom. When it is tired, it goes to roost. This kind of cyclic repetition is seen in all forms of life.

The programming of life is a meticulous scheme, alternating between effortful action and restful rejuvenation. The sun witnesses countless efforts of the day, and the moon presides over all entertaining dreams, sweet and bitter, and also gives a taste of the final return to naught, night after night. With its initial throb, the heart rouses the respiration for a whole lifetime. The being that is swished around in time and space creates a magnificent world of excitement and sorrow, generating a million designs of fabulous geometric and algebraic values. And it is ready to fold again with the last throb of the heart. The return to the heart is indicated in mantra two of *brāhmaṇa* four of the fourth chapter:

> The eye becomes united with the subtle body; then people say one does not see. The nose becomes united with the subtle body; then people say one does not smell. The tongue becomes united with the subtle body; then people say one does not taste. The vocal organ becomes united with the subtle body; then people say one does not speak. The ear becomes united with the subtle body; then people say one does not hear. The mind becomes united with the subtle body; then people say one does not think. The skin becomes united with the subtle body; then people say one does not touch. The intellect becomes united with the subtle body; then people say one does not know. Like that, the upper end of the heart lights up and by that light, the self departs, either through the eye or through the head or through other parts of the body. When it goes out, the vital breath follows; and when the vital breath goes out, all the organs follow. The self becomes endowed with particular consciousness and passes on to the body brought light by that consciousness. Knowledge, work and previous impressions follow it. [85]

In the *Madhu Kāṇḍa*, we were introduced to the secret of the honey-like Self. A tree with its manifold branches, trunk as well as roots, has no storage of sweetness in it, but from the whole tree, the essence percolates the sweetness of life through all its sap to the calyx of each flower and it is made even more substantial in the fruit. This is nature's allegory which demonstrates the desirable fruitfulness of a whole life. In every mantra, in every concept that lurks in the sound of the expressed words, there resides a wonder that is fresh, new and unique. Only if one receives its fragrance, taste, warmth and embrace will one expand into one's cosmic totality to be in resonance with the All.

In mantra eight, *brāhmaṇa* four, Yājñavalkya calls the attention of Janaka to an ancient song of the bards so that Janaka may know that the greatest secret is hiding in the uncharted heart of truth:

> The subtle, ancient path stretching far away has been touched by me; I have realized it myself. By this path the wise, the knowers of *brahman*, having been freed, reach the realm of liberation after release from this body. [86]

One of the greatest secrets in the creation and dissolution of this magnificent universe is the brevity that is put into the design of each faculty in an organism and the manifoldness of each faculty's variegated functional ability along with the extensive achievements that can arise from the simple anatomical engineering of a structure. The faculty of vision is one, but what it visualizes from the day of birth to the final day cannot be accounted for by any branch of science even if all studies are put together. Light and darkness are the two shades with which everything is painted, so neatly, so marvelously. The paradox of life itself is a commingling of the light and the dark, the known and the unknown, and truth triumphs over the duality of both.

In the fourth chapter of the *Muni Kāṇḍa* we move to clear and precise knowledge about the various aspects of knowledge itself. Even microbes which live as parasites in other living bodies have an instinctive urge which prompts their actions and makes every moment an onward movement for the actualization of the implied purpose of their lives. Particles move in accordance with irresistible laws. There are not separate physical laws for minerals, chemicals and biologic entities or, for that matter, even what we consider psychic phenomena. In that great stream of occurrences which can be termed physical, which generates biochemical and biological functions, we come to the story of humanity. All of us who are presently living at the fag end of the twentieth century, making preparations to seek our fortunes in the twenty-first century, are chronological contemporaries. But substantially we are not contemporaries. Some of us belong to a value vision and behavioral pattern which can be justly called modern, while there are those among us who still live like primitives.

Because of these disparities in anthropological evolution and socio-cultural refinement, hardly any two of us have the same purpose of life. The various forms of difference between us are considered in mantra fourteen of *brāhmaṇa* four which moots a very important question: Why do some of us stand in the forefront of human society with the most up-to-date knowledge gained from scientific and technological research? Why are a few among us even superior to the best of scientists, able to foresee the future and program themselves to possess a futuristic insight into life? What is that quality of knowledge that makes a few people absolutely superior to the rest? The positive progress we see in the human race also should burden us with the question of why countless millions of people live a hand-to-mouth existence completely weighed down by socio-economic necessities, destined to plan each of their actions to meet with the requirements of their social dictators.

In spite of all the socio-political and religio-spiritual entanglements of large masses that make up a modern country, how is it that there are a few who live in absolute freedom without being tied down to any time/space sense or obligations that cannot be transcended? Humanity has before it certain exemplaries whose visions have been valid for over a thousand years. They are like beacon-lights to humanity. Their visions, words, behaviors and the examples of the paths they have trod are a legacy which has enabled several thousands to feel that they have also found meaning in life. If this meaning had never been discovered, life for most people would have been a profitless pursuit. Hence the rishi puts this question: How can one imperientially and experientially identify oneself with the transcendent truth which is at once universal and immanent? The advice given by the rishi is that the Absolute is to be identified with as Self (*ātman*). Like lighthouses of wisdom, in the path of humanity we see, even from very early times, there have been certain exemplaries whose words have been continuously inspiring people. A great change comes in the lives of those who have understood that they have a goal to reach, a path to tread and a light they can trust illuminating their path. They have a contentment as if they have found the fulfillment of their lives. When one sits back with the solidarity of a mountain and feels for sure that what one knows is of eternal value, one breathes in peace and looks at all with a compassion born of a sense of equality.

The seeker and the seer are on the same path. All the same they are not the same kind of beneficiaries of wisdom. The seer has solved age-old riddles in his or her heart. The seeker again and again gets lost on the slippery pathway to certitude. The quality of life is decided by how happy you are, how consistently you are happy and how you are established in that happiness. Those who lack this excellence are always haunted by the questions: "What next? Where should I turn? Whom can I approach? How can it be accomplished? How can I know that what I seek is truly what I need or what I want?" From the examples of those who have gone before us, we discover that, in most cases, those who have succeeded had someone to guide them, someone to hold their hand with compassion. The successful have been led to the sanctuary of satisfaction where there is no longer any remorse or sense of inadequacy. The masters who lead the seekers are called preceptors of wisdom.

The seers are different from the seekers because they definitely know what is naught. Untruth can make the most astounding impact on the mind of a seeker. A consistent discovery of untruth is needed to lead the seeker to the limelight of certitude. Hence, in the Indian schools of thought a few are considered to have crossed across the ocean of phenomenality and their grace is sought after to bring redemption. The knowledge of such authority or assurance is not looked upon as an office or a social achievement. The absolute knowledge and the revealer of knowledge are not considered as separate from each other.

To begin with, there is the sharing of public truth. Public truth is the foundation of language. Every language which has been helping millions of people to traverse the path of search has coined words that suggest concepts with common features. They are able to instill into the heart of history certain landmarks of truth which are used irrespective of time and clime to aid in discerning empirical truth. Empirical truth has both an objectivity of perceptual perspective and a conceptual verity which is communicable in a world of common interest and common trust. It helps us to push away from our path the looming illusions which come to us from physical inadequacies, physiological malfunctions or dysfunctions and the enormity of biochemical confusion. There is a large field of opposition to marching towards truth. To find his or her way from the path of empiricism to the normative notion of the Absolute, the seeker has to acquire a discipline in the art of philosophical and mystical discrimination. He or she has to persevere with great vigilance and even a superior kind of cunning. This is a grey area of human search where various kinds of psychic and psychotic disturbances can hold us back in our onward march.

What comes at this juncture is two exaggerations of the mind, one pertaining to old memories and the other belonging to wishful thinking prompted by conditioned urges. The impact of crystallized memories on the makeup of a personality is a die-hard phenomena which has a morbid crust supported by social ratifications and religious beliefs. The Vedāntins call it *vikalpa*. Such memories are not only of a single person. Religious books like the *Vedas* and the *purāṇas* and, in the Semitic context, the imaginary speculative chronicles of the Jews, Christians and Muslims, act like fetters that imprison most of their believers in an uncompromising bulwark of insistence which they cannot easily shake off. Socio-biologic urges which necessitate the abandoning of certain old beliefs in favor of the new are victimized by the appeal of fantasizing dreams.

We are warned in this *brāhmaṇa* to cross that terrible area of confusion. We are given three touchstones of wisdom with which to investigate each assignment that comes our way. First is to decide the existential verity of a thing in the past, the irrefutability of it in the present and the continuity of the same into the future. Any decision taken on this basis opens the secret doors of eternal existence as the foundation of perennial truth. The second assignment is to decide the finality of the cause by looking at the ensuing effects with anticipatory aspiration which alone decides the value content of whatever we seek. The last is a far more difficult assignment. That is to relate the existential with the assurance of a value which has always been there, which is in the here and now, and which will be forever. To interpolate the existential and its crowning value with a methodological knowledge of subsistence brings the recognition of *sat, cit* and *ānanda*.

Once this hurdle is overcome, then there is something beyond the personal endeavor to be considered – how favorable is the length of your lifetime to mastering this wisdom-scheme for realization? The period granted to one is called *ayus*, the life term. In the world of cause and effect, in the essence of one fully organized, structured and functioning individuated being, another is projected which accounts for every separate embodied being from the virus to the human. All are designed to be self-propelling, self-maintaining and self-repairing until the purpose for which they manifest biologically is fulfilled. In almost all lower forms of life, this purposiveness is carried out without fail. When the program is over, the organism is depleted, defused and de-arranged.

Human beings are the one great exception to the above-given model of life. The three natural programs for each day, as it were, come in the form of finding food, partaking of it and nourishing oneself, expelling the excess from the body as various kinds of excretions, and filling the day with joyous preoccupations by resorting to playful sports or companionship. On the side of physiological, psychological and sociological personal expression, these three compulsions are felt by human beings. In and through the altering phases of consciousness, the wakeful, dream and deep sleep, there is also an implied fourth (*turīya*) which always remains as their sustaining foundation of spirit. Hence, those who have cultivated a higher sensibility to seek perfection can go beyond the claims of nature to the vertical axis which always remains as a parameter between the origin and ultimate unity of all. This is the spiritual search for which individuated life seems to have all provisions, equipment and motivating drives.

In the Vedāntic scheme, the first quarter of life is reserved for familiarizing oneself with the supporting foundation of one's uniqueness as an individual and working on it with diligence so that one's uniqueness can be kept in resonance with universality. This is the term in life called walking in the path of truth (*brahmacārya*). *Brahmacārya* is, so to say, the perfected conveyor for the *jīva* to traverse through the other phases of life: the householder, the philosopher who weans oneself away from the obligatory compulsions of society, and the ultimate stage of the recluse whose sole intent is to realize the Self. Spiritual search, growth and final perfection are the true purpose of a person. All other aspects of life are only to help in that pursuit.

If people are to live dignified lives with self respect and self-reliance, and if they are bent on reaching out into the resplendent light of wisdom that can come to them by right, they are given all that they require. Yet, except for a small percentage of humans, the rest are tied down by their own ignorance to live a life of slavery. The innate nature of the individuated constitution combines in it the physical and physiological on the one hand and, on the other, the *elan vital* that prompts a person to transcend the claims of nature. Victor Hugo depicts the plight of the man who seeks freedom from his own nature in the great novel, *Toilers of the Sea.*

In the preface to the *Toilers of the Sea*, Matthew Josephson writes:

> After having sought to console and purify Misery (in *Les Miserables*) the author here attempts the glorification of Toil. What greater theme than human toil! Civilization is naught but man's toil capitalized. Human effort against the elements is the most august effort of man. He struggles with the Angel; he struggles with God. . . . The author has set man face-to-face with immensity. Progress, an indefinable force, at grips with Nature and her infinite power. [87]

Another kind of slavery comes from the social set-up to which a person intrinsically belongs. Unlike other animals, human beings are destined to live their lives in proper alignment with the lives of all their fellow beings who have formed their past, enabling them to live in the present and motivating them to go into the future. This is the theme of Victor Hugo's *magnum opus*, *Les Miserables*. In *Les Miserables*, Hugo records the urgency of looking into the bondage of the social man:

> Permit me to ask you to adhere to the utmost fidelity in your task. My book is written to clear up and combat prejudices in France, England, and the whole world. [88]

In the search for one's higher Self, somewhere in some manner, each person owes his or her loyalty to the Unknown, mostly represented by the religion to which one voluntarily gives oneself or the spiritual dictates of the individual's own conviction. The shackles of religion are more weird and painful than a person's psycho-somatic needs or the fulfilling of social demands. This Hugo vividly portrays in *The Hunchback of Notre Dame.* To work out their deliverance, those who are smitten by their religious conscience have to live a full life of what the Vedāntins would stress as *dharma, artha, kāma* and *mokṣa. Mokṣa* is deliverance from the three-fold bondage of the individual's own nature, society and one's deeper convictions.

In the *Bhagavad Gītā* we read, in verse three of chapter seven:

> Among thousands of men, one perchance strives for perfection. Even among the striving who have attained, one perchance knows Me according to proper principles.

The inevitable kinds of bondage that wait in ambush to victimize any passer-by in the road of life are poignantly put in mantras eleven and twelve, *brāhmaṇa* four:

> There are those worlds known as cheerless covered by blinding darkness. To them after death go those who are ignorant and devoid of Self-knowledge.

> If a person knows the Self as 'I am this', then desiring what and for whose sake will one suffer in the wake of the body? [89]

As a reply to these questions, we should also consider mantras thirteen and fourteen:

> Whoever has realized and intimately known the Self, which has entered the perilous and perplexing place (the body), is the maker of the universe, for he is the maker of all. All is his Self and he again is the very Self of all.

> Dwelling in this very body, we have somehow realized That; otherwise we would have remained ignorant and great destruction would have overtaken us. Those who know That become immortal, while others only suffer misery. [90]

This naturally brings us to the attempt to discern what provisions of life we should have for our onward march. Mantra twenty-four turns our attention to hunger and the food which appeases it. The Self (*ātma*) is the indwelling immortal principle of everything. The word *ātma* itself is derived from the word *atti* meaning one who consumes food. Nourishing food is connected with the faculty of cognition, memory and recall. It also enables an embodied being to be motivated to carry out actions. Thus food is very basic to knowing, to doing, to willing and realizing through a series of actualizations. As the same Self is differently present in different parts of a living organism, its needs are varied. The modes of nourishment will also vary. Two of the five elements of the world cannot leave any space unoccupied. These two elements are *ākāśa* (space) and air. *Ākāśa* has the quality of the vibratory function of sound which uses space as a medium. Although for convenience we speak of *ākāśa* as the fifth element, in the biosphere of earth, wherever there is *ākāśa*, there is also air.

Air turns into *prāṇa* as soon as it enters a living body. No-one has yet found out how a simple seepage of air into the body through the nostrils or other openings changes into life-sustaining *prāṇa*. A living body which is deprived of *prāṇa* gasps and struggles. As we breathe freely and are always filled with the energy of *prāṇa*, the most natural need or hunger of the life in a body is automatically filled by air from outside. This vacuum in a body is a hunger. Filling a gap within a living body by air transforming into *prāṇa* is like feeding fuel into a furnace. The air that we breathe, on becoming *prāṇa*, transforms itself into all the functioning faculties of a living body. The energy in the body is maintained with the dual principles of electrical and magnetic function. When sound waves are transmitted in the area where there is a living body, by a force of attraction, the sound reverberates in the body, rhythmically setting each part of the organism to various modes of balance.

Prāṇa is divided into many subsidiary functional elements. The main function is to breathe. Then comes speaking out one's needs by using words. Where there is the hunger to communicate, word is the food. A person is not a machine. The body is constituted of several millions of cells. Even though each cell is a separate entity autonomically functioning, the colony of cells incorporated in the body also function corporately. The many act according to the requirement of the one life that presides over everything. That which brings coordination between every part of the body, and maintains the interior atmosphere is not always at the gross level. Very subtle functions such as metabolism and the autonomous functioning of the sensory and motor systems are all to be grouped and aligned in terms of the purpose of life. *Prāṇa* is remodified and reorganized so that it can be used by different processes in different parts of the body. The circulation of blood, air, hormones, enzymes and various glandular secretions is accomplished through the complementarity and reciprocity between the thermodynamic and electromagnetic principles which govern the cardio-vascular system.

Each sense organ has a divisional management. At the same time, every part of the body is related to every other part, directly or indirectly, or through the channels of circulating energy. Here we come to a network of cause and effect where causes can turn into effects and effects can remodulate into another cause. There is nothing which is free from the hunger of getting related with another, whether subatomic particles or cosmic bodies.

What is most surprising in the world of things is how two opposite kinds of forces are always paired. What is good now in one context is not good in another moment when the context changes. Consequently, demand and supply, hunger and fuel are to be seen as the very theme of life. In our commentary on mantra twenty-four, we have given a detailed study of the inner composition of the body and the mind and how they complement each other. What we term as food or fuel need not necessarily be entities. For example, dream is a great hunger in which the *taijasic* energy that resides in a single individual is a food. Many memories secreted by bodily and mental functions are reassembled so they can all first be absorbed into a deep silence and then restored to each area of the body for the mind to recreate again and again, centrally relating them all to one's ego-identity. Here ego is not used as in the Freudian context, but only as a central point necessary to give orientation from moment to moment.

In the context of needs and supplies, various hungers and appeasements, we have also to see the spiritual need of a recluse and the wisdom need of a seeker. That is discussed in the fifth *brāhmaṇa* which reconsiders Maitreyī's request for renunciation. In the *Madhu Kāṇḍa* when Yājñavalkya decided upon *sannyāsa* and informed his wives that he was settling the property rights of his first wife, Kātyāyanī, and second wife, Maitreyī, he thought his settlement was fair. He decided to give them each half of his landed properties, cows, gold and such riches. Kātyāyanī did not raise any objection. Maitreyī, however, not only disagreed with Yājñavalkya but also insisted that he reconsider what his true wealth was so that he could make the right decision and give her what was of highest value. Maitreyī's relationship with Yājñavalkya was not truly of a wife but of a wisdom student. What she valued in Yājñavalkya was his wealth of wisdom. Maitreyī was attracted to Yājñavalkya only because of his knowledge, she didn't want anything from him other than his wisdom.

Sureśvarācārya knew from his own experience the tragedy of a female being disqualified on account of her gender. He decided to make a plea in his *Bhāṣya* on the *Bṛhadāraṇyaka Upaniṣad* that real justice should be shown to Maitreyī who was hurt by the inconsiderate rejection of her teacher and husband, Yājñavalkya. Once Śankara came to the abode of Mandanamiśra (Sureśvara) to challenge him to prove the excellence of *Mīmāmsā* over *Vedānta*. Mandanamiśra was one of the highest authorities in *Mīmāmsā*. They agreed that if Mandanamiśra failed to convince Śankara of the merit of *Mīmāmsā* over *Vedānta* he was to renounce his wife and follow Śankara as a mendicant. On the other hand, if Śankara failed, he was to marry and lead a householder's life. After several days of argument Mandanamiśra failed. The umpire between Śankara and Mandanamiśra was Bharitī, Mandanamiśra's own wife, who was probably the wisest among Vedic women. When Mandanamiśra failed, he was obliged to leave his dear wife, who was not accepted by Śankara as his disciple. Naturally he must have been very grieved, even though Śankara accepted him and gave him the name Sureśvara.

Śankara also exacted a promise from him that he would not write a criticism of Śankara's *Vedānta Sūtra Bhāṣya*. Sureśvara kept that promise. But, in India, tradition allows a disciple to complement the writings of his *guru* by supplementing the *guru's* writing with what the *guru* should have said but did not say. Secondly, the disciple has the permission of tradition to rephrase the argument of his *guru* if the latter's words do not properly serve to establish and arrive at the conclusion intended by the *guru*.

The *Vārtika* written by Sureśvara goes into all details of the arguments in the mind of Maitreyī and fights to establish that justice should be done to her; she should not be denied the right to be taught just because she was a woman. Even if a student concentrates on the scriptural text and comes to the conclusion that what was verbally heard was the ultimate, that will not bring realization. The same is to be heard from the *guru* with whom the disciple has an absolute bipolar relationship. Three statements are before the seeker which cannot be easily analyzed and explicated by metaphysical pondering. The first one is the statement: *neti neti*, "not this, not this." The second is the statement *satyasyasatyam*, "the truth of truth," and that truth is one. The third is that with the discrimination of the eternal and non-eternal, untruth is to be discarded and truth should be identified with the Self, bringing the conviction that the truth is the full and the one that is to be known.

Methodological problems arise from these statements. The opening mantra of the *Īśāvāsya Upaniṣad* says *yat kiñca jagatyām jagate*: "Whatever is here, even the least, pertaining to the phenomenal world, that too is *brahman*." After categorically denying "this is not, this is not" in the *Bṛhadāraṇyaka*, how can one validate the dictum of the *Īśāvāsya* that "Whatever there is in the phenomenal world, that is the Absolute"? To begin with, what is in the phenomenal is names and forms. Names and forms are conditional relativistic projections. It is these projections that are denied as unreal when the *rishi* says "this is not, this is not." Mere verbal teaching by a *guru* alone will not establish the irrefutable facts of life. Even now in the spiritual center which was Śankara's seat of absolute wisdom, ritualistic worship is given to idols, many liturgies are chanted and there are modes of worship based on the belief that desires can be fulfilled by performing rituals. There should be an absolutist way of proving to oneself that the scriptural injunctions are the last and final, to be accepted without compromise. That is why the statement: the truth of truth is the name of truth, *brahman*. Unless it is imperientially established in oneself, all other pursuits are nothing more than comic make-believe.

Coming to the close quarters of search, we pointedly put the question, "What is the relationship between *brahman* and *puruṣa*?" The identification of *brahman* with *puruṣa* is like the existential identity of the sun's radiant effulgence with the sun itself. If taken like that, except in the sound formation of the words, *brahman* and *puruṣa*, there is nothing to be held distinct. It is the first truth that is again known as the second truth. Aristotle also knew this when he spoke of the *prius* and *nous*. But there is a distinction between the numenon and the phenomenon. If numenon is self-effulgent light, the phenomenon is the shadow cast by the light. Therefore, Śankara was quite right in saying *brahman* is truth and *jagat* is untruth. If everything in this world other than *brahman* is untruth, how can a great philosopher like Yājñavalkya disqualify Maitreyī on the grounds that she is a female? If the whole world (*jagat*) is unreal, is there anything remaining in the phenomenal world which is not untrue? Then why is Maitreyī's womanhood true? It should equally be untrue.

Yājñavalkya was a young man, physically, intellectually and morally bold. He was fearless with a certitude that was impeccable. Maitreyī was young, beautiful and perfect in conducting the affairs of her life. Her personal qualities were incomparable – peaceful, compassionate, forbearing. When such is the case, what justice was there on the part of her husband in saying "I will renounce you?" If it was for realizing truth that Yājñavalkya had to renounce Maitreyī, does it not arise from such a statement that "Maitreyī is untruth and she causes distraction from truth?" After her husband proving she is untrue, if she meditates on her own truth, what truth remains with her after all to be realized? This is the most unjust hurt of all that a teacher can give to his disciple. If there is only one absolute self foundation, one absolute knowledge of one's foundation and only one blissful state, what decides that it is in the man and not in the woman? Maitreyī wants to know if such are the conjectures to be made, into which course should she turn to know this traditional dichotomy made between the male and the female? If this was Yājñavalkya's finding about Maitreyī, when she first requested him to teach her what he considered most dear to him, why did he say, "Oh Maitreyī, you were always dear to me, and now you are saying what is most dear to me. I shall teach you"? At least for sometime Yājñavalkya did not consider her as unqualified to be taught and he promised to teach her. Here Sureśvara takes up the cause of Maitreyī, wanting to analyze threadbare the problem of disqualification cunningly projected on the womanhood which comes to a person incidentally.

Instead of making a clear-cut dichotomy between knowledge (*jñāna*) and action (*karma*), we should properly understand the implications of these concepts, both in the person of wisdom and in the person of action. The correct perspective will give us an insight into what is called unitive action and the wisdom way of life in which action is an expression of correct procedures and compassion of the highest quality. Right knowledge is not to be relegated to bound volumes. It also should be applied in all its meticulous details.

For people in the world who have lived all their lives in the sentiments of erotic passion, it is difficult to understand why Yājñavalkya wants to walk alone, while being generous to give Maitreyī all the secrets implied in the contemplative discipline of *Vedānta*. To express compassion without being sentimental or getting into spurious attachments, is a correct attitude recommended by *Vedānta*. Whether man or woman, disciple or wife, each person has to live his or her own life and conduct it carefully and wisely to reach one's own perfection. One cannot give realization to another. When Yājñavalkya says he is obliged to go alone for his own perfection, that is equally the way in which Maitreyī also has to find perfection through her own wisdom. If Yājñavalkya refuses to instruct her, that is quite a different attitude which can only be interpreted in terms of aversion or aggrandizement. Just as Yājñavalkya declares that he has to be on his own, Maitreyī also has a normal and expected request to make to Yājñavalkya, as she came to live with him for the single purpose of being instructed. He had willingly accepted her and their personal relationship was entirely of a *guru* and disciple. She was making steady progress in understanding the instructions of Yājñavalkya in all their subtleties. She needed time to go further to where she could go on her own. Therefore, she says to Yājñavalkya, "What you consider essential for you to attain, what is good for your Self, that only I request you to inform me." She is not insisting that she should be allowed to live with him forever. It is only a matter of experiencing.

When we look at this dialogue between Yājñavalkya and Maitreyī, we should also know the backdrop of historical India with its several conceited social prejudices and the thick veil of ignorance which was hiding spiritual truth from the worldly-minded. If Maitreyī wanted only wisdom from Yājñavalkya, why was she obliged to marry him? We have clearly explicated this in our appendix on the Yājñavalkya-Maitreyī dialogue given in the *Madhu Kāṇḍa*, first volume of the *Bṛhadāraṇyaka Upaniṣad*. In the ancient world of social prudery, a young and beautiful woman living with a person who was not her father or husband was an anathema. Cruel jealousy invaded people's minds when they were exposed to such situations.

Some tragic historical events can be remembered to know how explosive such situations are. The one classical example that stands out is the relationship between St. Abelard and his student Heloise. When they were teacher and taught, Abelard was not a saint; he was only a friar. The church felt deceived on discovering that the young friar was teaching theological secrets to Heloise as a part of his intense love for her and her passionate devotion to him. The entire world around him considered his behavior blasphemous, a violence against the dictum of chastity maintained by the Catholic Church. Consequently, Abelard was physically captured and mutilated. Neither the objection of the church or the mutilation of Abelard and his early death caused Heloise to give up her devotion. She proved herself to be an equal in the wisdom-teaching of Abelard. She carried on with her mission to convey the teaching of her lover-teacher Abelard.

In spite of all the theoretical excellence of Yājñavalkya in discerning the numenal from the phenomenal, as a member of society very exposed to public reference, Yājñavalkya had a lurking blindness preventing him from seeing clearly that Maitreyī's natural demand came purely from her quest for realization and not from any wish for personal intimacy. This brought him to a situation where he was obliged to talk more like an irritated or angry person than as a compassionate and wise *guru*. Although Yājñavalkya made a public announcement that he was cutting himself off from family bonds, the fact that he did finally condescend to give Maitreyī the final teaching of liberation absolves him from any momentary semblance of social friction that was seen in him for a little while. Maitreyī refused compromise with the wrong judgment that she could not receive the highest and final teaching from her *guru*.

In mantras IV.5.12-13 Yājñavalkya makes an earnest effort to teach Maitreyī the highest secret which he had been holding till that time. He said:

> As the sea is the one merging place of all water, as the skin is the one merging place of all touches, as the nostrils are the one merging place of all odors, as the tongue is the one merging place of all savors, as the eye is the one merging place of all sounds, as the the mind is the one merging place of all deliberations, as the intellect is the one merging place of all knowledge, as the hands are the

> one merging place of all action, as the organ of generation is the one merging place of all pleasures, as the anus is the one merging place of all excretions, as the feet are the one merging place of all walking, as the organ of speech is the one merging place of all *Vedas*.
>
> As a lump of salt has neither inside nor outside and is altogether a homogeneous mass of taste, even so my dear, this Self has neither inside nor outside and is altogether a homogeneous mass of consciousness throughout. On account of these elements, the Self stands out separately, and as soon as these are destroyed, its separate existence is also destroyed. After attaining isolation it has no particular consciousness. [91]

At this point Maitreyī tells Yājñavalkya that she is confused. "Just here, venerable sir, you have thrown me into the midst of confusion. I do not at all understand it." It is this objection from the side of Maitreyī which prompts Yājñavalkya to think she is making a ploy to hang on to him with the pretext of wanting to learn more from him. Sureśvaracārya did not want to leave Maitreyī in the lurch so he reconstructed the dialogue between Yājñavalkya and Maitreyī. He reproduced the seven irrefutable questions of Maitreyī. On seeing that Yājñavalkya is about to leave her, Maitreyī asks the categorical question: "Even if this earth with all its riches is possessed by a person, will that bring immortality to that person, or, by not having any riches will that person not get immortality?" She wants an answer from Yājñavalkya himself.

What she had asked for was immortality and Yājñavalkya is giving her an inheritance of landed properties, gold and cows. That is why she asks if it will give her immortality. She also wants to know if she renounces what he is offering her, if it will stop her from becoming realized. With these questions, she wants Yājñavalkya to make his intention clear. Yājñavalkya answers, "With all the wealth in the world one will not get immortality." Then she asks "O great one, you have taken a decision which is much against my spiritual progress. Maybe it is by some fault of mine which only you see. As I do not know what that fault is, I should know what is wrong in my request. To whom else can I ask this except you? That is why I am asking you." Without waiting for a reply, she goes on to the next question: "Is offering your inheritance to me an act of compassion when the example you are showing me right before my eyes is that you are renouncing all your wealth for your spiritual progress? How can your example be unbecoming to me? If you are renouncing the riches because they will stop you from attaining perfection, how on earth can you impose such wealth on me, fully knowing it will increase my distress and bondage in *samsāra*?"

Her next question is "If you think by accepting your heritage of worldly wealth, I will have spiritual progress, why do you hold such hatred for wealth and want to release yourself from it? If you are purposely putting yourself into a path which is bound to increase my ignorance and bind me to distress, have you any sound reason for showing such cruelty to me? If you claim that your attitude and behavior are born of your compassion to me, why don't you decide to give me your wealth of knowledge which will not diminish by being shared with another person for that person's spiritual benefit? If you are in search of the Absolute and it is a wealth which is beginningless, endless, having no middle and will never be expended, why don't you make me also eligible to have such wealth? That being the case, why do you prompt me to accept the transient in lieu of the never-diminishing?"

When Maitreyī shows that she is resolute in her decision to get the secret from Yājñavalkya, he repeats the same mantra he gave her in II.4.5. Although she heard it once before it was only a verbal expression to her then. Now it is coming as a hard-earned answer for her undaunted attention. Anyone might happen to hear the verbal expressions of the highest concepts of the Absolute, if perchance they listen to great masters. But such listening does not enlighten them. People are mainly idolatrous. Idols can be of all mediums. Icons made out of earth, stone, wood, metal – these are all articles of little worth. But an even worse kind of idolatry can come by making an idea an icon. The world at large is suffering more from the icons of the mind than from those of the visible world. Love and hatred are generated by merely hearing words which refer to what one does or doesn't like. One can make an idol of one's own being. Then it is certainly not one's real Self, but only a mental icon made out of fanciful thinking. In the path of spirituality there are several such concepts on which people stumble. The word that is spoken by a person only stimulates another person to conceptualize it and generate a conceptual cliché. The *Upaniṣad* wants us to go beyond such kinds of imaginations. After making this clear to Maitreyī, Yājñavalkya bids farewell to her, released from all sense of obligation. With this, the fifth *brāhmaṇa* comes to a close.

We have provided this recapitulation of *Madhu Kāṇḍa* and *Muni Kāṇḍa* so that the reader would have a ready reference at hand to compare notes. The purpose of this book is not to present to the world another tome of academic interest. This brings us to the last stage of our pilgrimage to the Self and adventure in spirit. We take this opportunity to express our deepest gratitude to the unceasing inspiration given to us by the rishis who are of the past, the present and the future.

The sense of being filled enables us now to repeat the *śanti mantra* with which we began the *Bṛhadāraṇyaka Upaniṣad.*

AUM pūrṇamadaḥ pūrṇamidam
pūrṇatpūrṇamudacyate
pūrṇasya pūrnamādāya
pūrṇamevāvaśiṣyate

AUM śantiḥ śantiḥ śantiḥ.

NOTES

1. Robert Hume, *The Thirteen Principal Upanishads*, Oxford University Press, London, 1971, p. 177-178.
2. This and all succeeding English translations from Sanskrit and Malayalam not otherwise attributed are by the author.
3. Hume, *Thirteen Principal Upanishads*, 1971, p. 339.
4. Ibid., p. 340.
5. Ibid., p. 349.
6. Swami Vimalananda, *Māhanarayanopaniṣad*, Sri Ramakrishna Math, Madras, 1979, p. 350-351.
7. This and all succeeding quotes from the *Bhagavad Gītā* are from Nataraja Guru's translation, published by Narayana Gurukula Publishing House, Varkala, 1989.
8. Hume, *Thirteen Principal Upanishads*, 1971, p. 392.
9. Ibid., p. 392.
10. Guy Murchie, *The Seven Mysteries of Life*, Houghton Mifflin, Boston, 1978, p. 378.
11. William F. Ganong, *Review of Medical Physiology*, Prentice-Hall International, Inc., New Jersey, 1989, p. 517.
12. These references can be easily looked into in G. A. Jacobs, *A Concordance to the Principle Upaniṣads and the Bhagavad Gīta*, Published by Motilal Banarasidass, New Delhi, India.
13. Adapted from *Chāndogya Upaniṣad*, translated by Swami Swahananda; Sri Ramakrishna Math, Madras, 1956, p. 458-459.
14. Raimundo Pannikar, *The Vedic Experience, Mantramañjarī*, All India Books, Pondicherry, 1977, p. 829.
15. Ibid., p. 839.
16. *The Complete Poems of Emily Dickinson*, Ed. Thomas H. Johnson, Little, Brown and Company, Boston, 1960, p. 3.
17. Bruce Alberts, et. al., *Molecular Biology of the Cell*, Garland Publishing Inc., New York and London, 1983, p. 67.
18. Ibid., p. 67.
19. Nataraja Guru, *Life and Teachings of Narayana Guru*,

East-West University, Fernhill, 1990, p. 542-547.
20. Ibid., p. 548-551
21. Panikkar, *The Vedic Experience*, p. 38-43.
22. Vihari Lala Mitra, *The Yoga-Vāsiṣṭha Mahārāmāyaṇa of Valmiki*, Bharatiya Publishing House, Delhi, 1978, p. 85.
23. Sri Aurobindo, *The Secret of the Veda*, Sri Aurobindo Birth Centenary Library, Sri Aurobindo Ashram Trust, Pondicherry, 1971, p. 524-528.
24. Ibid., p. 272-273.
25. Rabindranath Tagore, *Collected Poems and Plays*, Macmillan, London, Ltd., Hong Kong, 1982, p. 14.
26. Nitya Chaitanya Yati, *The Bṛhadāraṇyaka Upaniṣad, Volume I: Madhu Kāṇḍa*, D.K. Printworld, New Delhi, 1994, p. 252.
27. Lao Tsu, *Tao Te Ching*, translated by Gia-Fu Feng and Jane English, Random House, New York, 1972, p. 13.
28. Hume, *The Thirteen Principal Upanishads*, p. 289.
29. Swami Swahānanda, *The Chāndogya Upaniṣad*, Madras, Sri Ramakrishna Math, p. 20-22.
30. Ibid., p. 617.
31. Murchie, *The Seven Mysteries of Life*, p. 1-2.
32. Ibid., p. 15.
33. Swami Mādhavānanda (trans.), *The Bṛhadāraṇyaka Upaniṣad*, Advaita Ashrama, Calcutta, 1988, p. 601-602.
34. R.G.H. Siu, *The Tao of Science*, MIT Press, Cambridge, 1976, p .72.
35. Swami Madhavananda, *The Bṛhadāraṇyaka Upaniṣad*, Advaita Ashrama, Calcutta, 1988, p. 615-616.
36. G. A. Gaskell, *Dictionary of All Scriptures and Myths*, New York, Avenel Books, 1981, p. 254-255.
37. Ibid., p. 254-255.
38. Ibid., p. 255.
39. Ibid., p. 255.
40. Thomas Gilby, (trans.), *St. Thomas Aquinas Philosophical Texts*, New York, Oxford University Press, 1962, p. 309.
41. Ibid., p. 309.
42. Ibid., p. 309-310.
43. Ibid., p. 310.
44. Gaskell, *Dictionary of All Scriptures and Myths*. p. 643.
45. Ibid., p. 643-644.
46. Ibid., p. 644.
47. Ibid., p. 644.

48. Ibid., p. 644.
49. Ibid., p. 644.
50. Ibid., p. 645.
51. Ibid., p. 646.
52. Ibid., p. 646.
53. Geoffrey Zubay, *Genetics*, The Benjamin/Cummings Publishing Company, Inc., Boston, 1987, p. 830-31.
54. Alberts, Bruce, *Molecular Biology of The Cell*, p. 778-779.
55. Yati, *Volume I: Madhu Kāṇḍa*, p. 10.
56. Murchie, *The Seven Mysteries of Life*, p. 44.
57. Ibid., p. 618.
58. Sri Aurobindo, *The Upaniṣads*, Sri Aurobindo Birth Centenary Library, p. 397-398.
59. Ibid., p. 399-407.
60. Paul Deussen, *The Philosophy of the Upaniṣads*, Rev. Geden, trans., Dover Publications, New York, 1966, p. 12-13.
61. Ibid., p. 14.
62. Ibid., p. 16.
63. Ibid., p. 16-17.
64. Sri Aurobindo, *The Upaniṣads*, p. 400-405.
65. Raimundo Pannikar, *The Vedic Experience*, p. 67-68.
66. Ibid., p. 71.
67. Ibid., p. 305-306.
68. Yati, *Volume I: Madhu Kāṇḍa*, p. 20-21.
69. Ibid., p. 153-154.
70. Sri Aurobindo, *Savitri*, Sri Aurobindo Ashram Trust, Pondicherry, 1950, p. 1.
71. Yati, *Volume I: Madhu Kāṇḍa*, p. 166.
72. Ibid., p. 170.
73. Ibid., p. 170.
74. Ibid., p. 509.
75. Sureśvara, *Vārtika on Madhu Brāhmaṇa*, Motilal Banarsidass, New Delhi, 1988, p. 9.
76. Nitya Chaitanya Yati, *The Psychology of Darśanamālā*, Gurukula Publishing House, Fernhill, 1987, p. 37.
77. Ibid., p. 37.
78. Yati, *Volume I: Madhu Kāṇḍa*, p. 476-477.
79. Ibid., p. 493-497.
80. Nitya Chaitanya Yati, *Bṛhadāraṇyaka Upaniṣad, Volume II: Muni Kāṇḍa*, D.K. Printworld, New Delhi, 1995, p. 19.
81. Ibid., p. 24-25.

82. Ibid., p. 28.
83. Ibid., p. 33.
84. *The Holy Qur'an*, Abdullah Yusuf Ali, trans., The Islamic Center, Lahore, 1978, p. 15.
85. Yati, *Volume II: Muni Kāṇḍa*, p. 529.
86. Ibid., p. 562.
87. Victor Hugo, *Toilers of the Sea*, Heritage Press, New York, 1961, p. XVIII.
88. Victor Hugo, *Les Miserables*, Heritage Press, New York, 1938, Translator's Preface.
89. Yati, *Volume II: Muni Kāṇḍa*, p. 572.
90. Ibid., p. 573-574.
91. Ibid., p. 631-632.

SANSKRIT INDEX

GENERAL INDEX